Ethics and Existence

Ethics and Existence

The Legacy of Derek Parfit

Edited by
JEFF McMAHAN
TIM CAMPBELL
JAMES GOODRICH,
and
KETAN RAMAKRISHNAN

UNIVERSITY PRESS

OXFORD
UNIVERSITY PRESS

Great Clarendon Street, Oxford, OX2 6DP,
United Kingdom

Oxford University Press is a department of the University of Oxford.
It furthers the University's objective of excellence in research, scholarship,
and education by publishing worldwide. Oxford is a registered trade mark of
Oxford University Press in the UK and in certain other countries

© Oxford University Press 2022

The moral rights of the authors have been asserted

First Edition published in 2022

Impression: 1

All rights reserved. No part of this publication may be reproduced, stored in
a retrieval system, or transmitted, in any form or by any means, without the
prior permission in writing of Oxford University Press, or as expressly permitted
by law, by licence or under terms agreed with the appropriate reprographics
rights organization. Enquiries concerning reproduction outside the scope of the
above should be sent to the Rights Department, Oxford University Press, at the
address above

You must not circulate this work in any other form
and you must impose this same condition on any acquirer

Published in the United States of America by Oxford University Press
198 Madison Avenue, New York, NY 10016, United States of America

British Library Cataloguing in Publication Data
Data available

Library of Congress Control Number: 2021945520

ISBN 978-0-19-289425-0

DOI: 10.1093/oso/9780192894250.001.0001

Printed and bound by
CPI Group (UK) Ltd, Croydon, CR0 4YY

Links to third party websites are provided by Oxford in good faith and
for information only. Oxford disclaims any responsibility for the materials
contained in any third party website referenced in this work.

Contents

List of Figures	vii
Contributors	ix
Introduction *Jeff McMahan*	1

PART I. CAUSING PEOPLE TO EXIST AND THE NON-IDENTITY PROBLEM

1. The Asymmetry *Ralf M. Bader*	15
2. The Value and Probabilities of Existence *M. A. Roberts*	38
3. Comparing Existence and Non-Existence *Hilary Greaves and John Cusbert*	61
4. The Impure Non-Identity Problem *Patrick Tomlin*	93
5. Abortion and the Non-Identity Problem *Elizabeth Harman*	112
6. A Partial Solution to the Non-Identity Problem: Regretting One Was Born and Having a Life Not Subjectively Worth Living *Andrew McGee and Julian Savulescu*	130

PART II. THE REPUGNANT CONCLUSION, FUTURE GENERATIONS, AND EXTINCTION

7. Population Ethics Forty Years On: Some Lessons Learned from "Box Ethics" *Larry Temkin*	159
8. Totalism without Repugnance *Jacob M. Nebel*	200
9. Context-Dependent Betterness and the Mere Addition Paradox *Johann Frick*	232

10. Saving Posterity from a Worse Fate 264
    Niko Kolodny

11. Against Large Number Scepticism 311
    Andreas L. Mogensen

12. Are We Living at the Hinge of History? 331
    William MacAskill

13. On Theory X and What Matters Most 358
    S. J. Beard and Patrick Kaczmarek

PART III. EVALUATIVE IMPRECISION, INCOMMENSURABILITY, AND VAGUENESS IN VALUE

14. How to Avoid the Repugnant Conclusion 389
    Ruth Chang

15. Can Parfit's Appeal to Incommensurabilities in Value Block the Continuum Argument for the Repugnant Conclusion? 430
    Wlodek Rabinowicz

16. Population Ethics and Conflict-of-Value Imprecision 461
    Gustaf Arrhenius

17. On Evaluative Imprecision 478
    Teruji Thomas

18. Sorites on What Matters 498
    Theron Pummer

PART IV. PRIORITARIANISM IN POPULATION ETHICS

19. Prioritarianism, Population Ethics, and Competing Claims 527
    Michael Otsuka

20. Quarantining Prioritarianism 552
    Shlomi Segall

Index 577

List of Figures

1.1.	Lives No Longer Worth Living	27
2.1.	Miserable Child Case	42
2.2.	Three Outcome Case	44
2.3.	Better Chance Case	49
2.4.	Bad Lives Case	55
2.5.	Medication Case	58
4.1.	Double Overdetermination Cases	109
7.1.	Diagram One	160
7.2.	Diagram Two	163
7.3.	Diagram Three	164
7.4.	Diagram Four	178
7.5.	Diagram Five	188
9.1.	The Spectrum Argument for the Repugnant Conclusion	234
9.2.	The Mere Addition Paradox	235
9.3.	Decomposing the move from A to B	236
9.4.	Comparing A and A+	237
9.5.	The Up-Down Case	238
9.6.	A Mere Addition Case with different individuals in A+ and B	259
9.7.	A Mere Addition Case with different extra people in A+ and B	260
10.1.	Reasonable Trade-Off	269
10.2.	Reasonable Trade-Off (Negative)	270
10.3.	Repugnant Choice	279
10.4.	Ignoring the Best Off	280
10.5.	Mere Addition	284
10.6.	Sadistic Choice: Critical Level	287
10.7.	Sadistic Choice: Average Utilitarianism	287
10.8.	Constructing a Sadistic Choice: Step 1	288
10.9.	Constructing a Sadistic Choice: Step 2	288
10.10.	Reasonable Trade-Off	294
10.11.	Mere Addition	295
10.12.	Cycling	298
10.13.	Ignoring the Unaffected: Equality	301
10.14.	Ignoring the Unaffected: Average	302
10.15.	Ignoring the Unaffected: Sadistic Choice	302
12.1.	The value lock-in view	341
12.2.	How influentialness may vary over time	342
13.1.	Mere Addition Paradox	369
13.2.	Another Version of the Mere Addition Paradox	374
14.1.	Parfit's continuum	393

14.2. The Zone	396
14.3. Against incomparability	399
14.4. Parfit's Imprecise Lexicality Solution	408
14.5. The Parity Solution	412
16.1. Figure 16.1	462
16.2. The Quantity Sequence	467
16.3. The Sequential Dominance Addition Paradox	470
16.4. Figure 16.4	474
19.1. Prioritarian moral value of a person's well-being	529
19.2. Utilitarian moral value of a person's well-being	530
19.3. Case 1	540
19.4. Case 1*	540
19.5. Case 1'	547
19.6. Case 2	549
19.7. Case 2*	549
20.1. The Repugnant Conclusion	554
20.2. The Sadistic Conclusion	558
20.3. Critical Level Prioritarianism	559
20.4. Welfare dispersal (fixed numbers)	560
20.5. Welfare dispersal (non-fixed population)	561
20.6. The Negative Repugnant Conclusion	563

Contributors

Gustaf Arrhenius, Institute for Futures Studies and Stockholm University

Ralf Bader, Université de Fribourg

S.J. Beard, University of Cambridge

Ruth Chang, University of Oxford

John Cusbert, independent scholar

Johann Frick, University of California, Berkeley

Hilary Greaves, University of Oxford

Elizabeth Harman, Princeton University

Patrick Kaczmarek, University of Cambridge

Niko Kolodny, University of California, Berkeley

William MacAskill, University of Oxford

Andrew McGee, Queensland University of Technology

Andreas Mogensen, University of Oxford

Jacob Nebel, University of Southern California

Michael Otsuka, Rutgers University

Theron Pummer, University of St. Andrews

Wlodek Rabinowicz, Lund University

Melinda Roberts, College of New Jersey

Julian Savulescu, University of Oxford

Shlomi Segall, Hebrew University of Jerusalem

Larry Temkin, Rutgers University

Teruji Thomas, University of Oxford

Patrick Tomlin, University of Warwick

Introduction

Jeff McMahan

This book is the second in a series of three volumes of essays written in honour of the philosopher Derek Parfit. The first volume, *Principles and Persons: The Legacy of Derek Parfit*, was published early in 2021. It contains essays on personal identity and the basis of rational egoistic concern, as well as on a variety of topics in normative ethics, such as the nature of reasons, convergence among moral theories, aggregation and overdetermination in ethics, equality and priority, and supererogation. The third volume will consist of essays in intellectual biography and memoir.

Ethics and Existence and *Principles and Persons* are companion volumes, as is indicated by their shared subtitle. Both are composed of essays on philosophical issues that Parfit believed really matter and both had their origin in a pair of jointly coordinated conferences, one at Rutgers and the other at Oxford, held in remembrance of Parfit during the eighteen months following his death in 2017. Many of the chapters in both volumes developed from papers presented at one or the other of these conferences.

As I explained in the Introduction to *Principles and Persons*, most of the chapters in that book addressed issues that Parfit had discussed in his first book, *Reasons and Persons* (1984), rather than issues that were the primary topics of his subsequent trilogy, *On What Matters* (2011 and 2017). The same is true of the essays in *Ethics and Existence*, all of which are in the area of ethics known as *population ethics*.

Population ethics is concerned with moral issues raised by causing people to exist. Until about fifty years ago, there had been almost no discussion of these issues in the entire history of philosophy. But in the late 1960s, as philosophers began to think more carefully about the practical implications of utilitarianism and other moral theories, it occurred to some that it might be an implication of utilitarianism that there are quite stringent duties of procreation. For there are two ways of increasing total happiness: increasing the happiness of existing people and bringing happy people into existence. Yet it is counterintuitive to suppose that there is a duty to have a child that, because fulfilling it would result in the net happiness in an entire life, is generally stronger than the duty to save a person's life, fulfillment of which would result in the net happiness in only a part of a life.

Reflection on such matters prompted a few philosophers to think more deeply about the morality, in general, of causing people to exist. The philosopher who thought most deeply, by far, was Derek Parfit. He began to think about these matters in the early 1970s, producing a series of drafts, initially called 'Overpopulation', later to become 'Overpopulation, Part I' and 'Overpopulation, Part II', in which he gradually developed the ideas that would eventually be published in Part Four of *Reasons and Persons*. In this early work, Parfit almost single-handedly discovered the many deep and intractable problems and paradoxes in which population ethics abounds, thereby effectively establishing the field itself. Part Four of *Reasons and Persons* is thus the *locus classicus* of population ethics. Although a great deal of brilliant work has subsequently been done by others, I think most of those who have done that work would concede that Parfit's original work is still, almost forty years after its publication, the most original, perceptive, imaginative, and rigorous work in the field. It remains unsurpassed.

The following are among the many foundational questions in population ethics. Can individuals be harmed or benefited by being caused to exist? Is there a moral reason not to cause individuals to exist if their lives would be miserable, or not worth living? Most of us believe there clearly is. But, if there is, is there also a moral reason to cause individuals to exist just because their lives would be worth living, or well worth living? If, as most people seem to believe, there is no moral reason to cause a well-off individual to exist when the alternative is simply not to cause any new individual to exist, is there nevertheless a reason to cause a well-off individual to exist when the alternative is that a different, less well-off individual will come into existence instead? That is, does it make a difference to whether there is a moral reason to cause a well-off individual to exist that the alternative is that a less well-off individual will come into existence rather than that no new individual will come into existence? If there is, contrary to common sense intuition, a reason to cause a well-off individual to exist rather than not to cause any individual to exist, can an increase in the number of lives worth living always morally offset a decrease in the overall quality of life? And if, again, there is such a reason, how strong is it in comparison with the strength of the reason to produce an equivalent amount of well-being in the lives of existing individuals—for example, by saving individuals' lives? Can an act be wrong if it would be worse for no one, would violate no one's rights, and would indeed be good for all those affected by it? If so, would an act be wrong to an even greater degree if it would bring about an outcome that was relevantly the same except that the individuals affected *would* be affected for the worse, or would have rights that *would* be violated? This difference is possible when the individuals affected by the first act would not have existed had the act not been done, whereas those affected by the second act would have existed even if it had not been done.

Parfit probed these and many other questions obsessively, and in doing so exposed pervasive confusions, inconsistencies, absurdities, and limitations of scope not only in foundational assumptions of common sense moral thought but also in all of the major moral theories. The problems that he revealed have continued to challenge the ingenuity of many of the best moral philosophers, so that the literature on population ethics is now enormous and continues to burgeon.

Most of the questions I cited are about reasons. But much of Parfit's work, and perhaps even more of the subsequent literature, addresses questions about the values of outcomes, or states of the world, and in particular seeks to establish rankings of possible outcomes in order of their 'betterness'. The area of population ethics that is concerned with such evaluative rankings is known as 'population axiology'. Both types of question—those concerned with what we have reason to do and those concerned with the evaluation of outcomes—are well represented in the chapters that follow.

All of the questions enumerated above are dauntingly difficult, but moral philosophers are becoming increasingly aware that finding the best answers to them is necessary for understanding a large range of issues in practical ethics. In some instances, the relevance of population ethics is obvious—for example, to the evaluation of governmental policies intended either to stimulate or limit population growth, as well as to issues such as climate change that raise questions about our duties concerning future generations. But the range of other issues in practical ethics that cannot be adequately understood until fundamental questions in population ethics are resolved is surprisingly large and heterogeneous. These issues include abortion, prenatal injury, preconception or prenatal screening for disability, genetic enhancement and eugenics generally, causing animals to exist in order to eat them, factory farming, the suffering of animals in the wild, reparations for historical injustice, the threat of human extinction, and even proportionality in war. While some of these issues are broached in certain of the following chapters, the essays in this book are concerned primarily with the more theoretical issues in population ethics that Parfit pursued in his own work.

Although these essays are in general devoted not so much to the discussion of Parfit's ideas but to the resolution of problems he uncovered, his work has nevertheless set the agenda for all the essays in the book. I think I speak for all the contributors in saying that our aim in producing this book has been to make progress in thinking about issues that Parfit rightly believed matter morally, and to the resolution of which he devoted his prodigious philosophical powers for many years, with only very partial success. His monomaniacal devotion to philosophy had, however, almost no tincture of egoistic motivation. He was always excessively generous in attributing ideas and arguments that may have emerged in discussions with his students or colleagues to them rather than to himself. Although he would no doubt have preferred to be the one to solve some intractable problem in moral philosophy, what mattered most to him was that it be satisfactorily solved. While the contributors to this book make no pretence of having finally solved any of the deepest problems of population ethics, it is, I believe, undeniable that they have advanced our understanding of issues with which Parfit was engaged. And to have done that is perhaps the most fitting tribute they can offer him.[1]

Chapter Abstracts

Ralf Bader: 'The Asymmetry'

This chapter provides an account of the asymmetry in population ethics. The first half of the asymmetry is explicated by means of a person-affecting view, whereas the second half is established by means of a structural consistency constraint. This account can be integrated into a general theory that can handle (i) cases where there are externalities in that members of the original distribution are positively or negatively affected by bringing the miserable life into existence, (ii) cases in which one is concerned not only with bringing individual persons into existence but also groups of people, and (iii) situations in which it is uncertain whether an action will result in the addition of lives that are worth not living.

M. A. Roberts: 'The Value and Probabilities of Existence'

The purpose of this chapter is to explore the Better Chance Puzzle and, with that puzzle, a question not entirely resolved by Derek Parfit in *Reasons and Persons* or in his later work: whether, other things being equal, an additional worth-having existence makes things better. The Better Chance Puzzle commences with the surely correct claim—the *Better Chance Claim*—that the fact that a given choice creates a *better chance* of a future person's coming into existence often makes an otherwise wrong choice permissible. A fertility pill might, for example, come with side effects that burden a future child. But if taking the pill is necessary for that child to have any significance chance of ever existing at all, and the existence itself is worth having, the choice to take the pill is, we think, permissible. The Better Chance Claim is (however quietly) used in the construction of many of the most powerful versions of the nonidentity problem, including Parfit's own risky policy and depletion examples. At the same time, Parfit introduces us to what he calls the Person Affecting *Intuition*, the idea that, other things being equal, the addition of the worth-having existence *doesn't* make things better. Though Parfit himself considered the intuition problematic, we may nonetheless continue to find it compelling. And thus the puzzle: how can the better *chance* of existence, in some sense, make things morally better when the actual *fact* of the additional existence is capable of no such thing?

Hilary Greaves and John Cusbert: 'Comparing Existence and Non-Existence'

Existence comparativism holds that it can sometimes be better or worse, for a given person, that that person exist rather than not. The dominant argument in

---

[1] I am deeply grateful to Kida Lin for preparing the index.

the literature on this issue is the Metaphysical Argument, which purports to show that existence comparativism is metaphysically incoherent. The argument of this chapter is that the Metaphysical Argument fails. Even if existence cannot be personally better than non-existence, the Metaphysical Argument cannot be the reason for this, since the argument proves too much. Denying its first premise means holding that personal betterness comparisons between a fixed pair of possible worlds are contingent; some recent work has taken this course. Denying the second premise means holding that A can be better for S than B even when S does not exist. This chapter presents the case for denying the second premise. Contrary to something of a consensus in the literature, this is not absurd in general metaphysical terms. And there is a particular analysis of personal betterness comparisons that explains in more detail how one outcome can be better than another for an individual who does not exist. The chapter therefore concludes that existence comparativism, whether true or false, is metaphysically coherent.

Patrick Tomlin: 'The Impure Non-Identity Problem'

Some of Derek Parfit's most significant work concerns the non-identity problem. Briefly put, this is the problem of how, morally speaking, we should understand cases in which we can act in one way, and produce persons with sub-optimal lives, or act in another way, and produce different persons with better lives. Discussions of the non-identity problem tend to assume that it is a single problem, raising a single set of moral issues. This chapter seeks to complicate this picture. It introduces 'Impure Non-Identity Cases'. These are cases in which a policy, or group of acts, is a non-identity case, and so nobody is harmed, or made worse off, by the policy, or group of acts, but some (and maybe even all) of the individual acts within the policy or group are *not* non-identity cases, and are harmful. The chapter investigates the moral implications of such cases, and the problems and questions they raise, aside from those raised by 'Pure Non-Identity Cases'.

Elizabeth Harman: 'Abortion and the Non-identity Problem'

How is the ethics of abortion related to the non-identity problem? Some cases of deciding whether to abort turn out to raise the non-identity problem: for the same reasons that it is morally required to wait to conceive in some temporary condition non-identity cases, it is also morally required to abort some pregnancies. This implies that the following surprising claim is true: sometimes it is morally required to kill a being for its own sake, although continuing to live would be better for it. The chapter defends this surprising claim. The chapter also argues that we should understand non-identity phenomena more broadly, to encompass cases of affecting what *the moral status facts* are. This includes affecting who exists, affecting whether beings have moral status, and affecting what level of moral status beings have (if there are levels of moral status).

Andrew McGee and Julian Savulescu: 'A Partial Solution to the Non-Identity Problem: Regretting One Was Born and Having a Life Not Subjectively Worth Living'

This chapter takes a fresh look at the non-identity problem and presents a partial solution that is different from those that have so far been attempted. Its solution focuses on Parfit's remark that, if a person born from a 'different people choice' has a life worth living, and so does not regret existing, the decision wrongs no one. But some 'different people choices' can produce people who regret being born even though they are glad to be alive and have lives worth living. These cases have so far not been discussed in the literature on the non-identity problem, and seem to escape the paradoxical conclusions that Parfit draws in other 'different people choices'. This chapter argues that the chance of future regret provides a reason not to select a given embryo or possible person.

Larry Temkin: 'Population Ethics Forty Years On: Some Lessons Learned from "Box Ethics"'

This chapter explores some lessons learned from Parfit's seminal work on population ethics, and some unresolved problems it leaves us with. It illustrates how the Repugnant Conclusion, Hell Three, and other examples generate important insights about axiology. It shows how the Standard Model of Utility and the Standard Model for Combining Ideals jointly entail the Repugnant Conclusion. It offers an alternative approach for assessing outcome goodness, the Capped Model of Ideals, which avoids the Repugnant Conclusion, but notes that it is limited in scope, and faces various worries. It considers whether we should be neutral both within and between different possible locations of the good—persons, spaces, and times; and whether, setting aside cases involving special relations, we should treat people, spaces, and times the same. It argues that in certain cases we should give preference to people over spaces and times, and times over spaces, but that, surprisingly, in other cases we should give preference to times over people. It considers four approaches to a Capped Model of Ideals, noting both advantages and disadvantages of each. It argues that Parfit's Absurd Conclusion may not be absurd after all. It concludes by noting that while much progress has been made in population ethics, many of Parfit's deepest problems and paradoxes remain unresolved.

Jacob M. Nebel: 'Totalism without Repugnance'

Totalism is the view that one distribution of well-being is better than another just in case the one contains a greater sum of well-being than the other. Many philosophers, following Parfit, reject totalism on the grounds that it entails the repugnant conclusion that, for any number of excellent lives, there is some number of lives that are barely worth living whose existence would be better. This chapter develops a theory of welfare aggregation—the lexical-threshold view—that allows totalism to avoid the repugnant conclusion, as well as its analogues involving suffering populations and the lengths of individual lives. The theory is grounded in some independently plausible views about the structure of well-being, identifies a new source of incommensurability in population ethics, and avoids some of the implausibly extreme consequences of other lexical views, without violating the intuitive separability of lives.

Johann Frick: 'Context-Dependent Betterness and the Mere Addition Paradox'

This chapter proposes a new solution to Derek Parfit's Mere Addition Paradox. It argues that the paradox trades on an ambiguity about the context of choice. There is a sense in which *all three* intuitive judgments about Parfit's case are true, namely as pairwise comparisons in a *two-possible* case, i.e. in a choice situation where the option set contains only *these two* outcomes. The air of paradox arises from the assumption that these pairwise judgments carry over to a *three-possible* case, in which all three outcomes are possible. But this, the chapter argues, is not the case. If sound, this argument shows how we can make sense of each of our pairwise intuitions in the Mere Addition Paradox, without incurring the cost of intransitivity *within an option set*. This solves the Mere Addition Paradox and blocks the argument toward the Repugnant Conclusion. Parfit's case also holds a general lesson about the nature of value, but one that is less revisionary than some had thought. Correctly understood, Parfit's Mere Addition Case challenges not the transitivity of the "better than" relation, as Larry Temkin has argued, but instead a different, and less sacrosanct, idea, namely the so-called Independence of Irrelevant Alternatives principle. What Parfit's puzzle teaches us is that betterness is sometimes *context-dependent*: the relative goodness of two outcomes can depend on whether or not a third outcome could have instead been chosen.

Niko Kolodny: 'Saving Posterity from a Worse Fate'

Suppose we must choose among different outcomes, in which people fare better or worse. Suppose different people, or different numbers of people, will ever exist in such outcomes. That is, suppose our choice affects the growth of the population, or the identities of future people. Which outcomes, if any, are wrong for us to choose? There are two ways of approaching such questions. The more familiar way might be called "Benefit Thinking." We should make the choice that benefits people more. The less familiar way might be called "Worse-Fate Thinking." We should make the choice that leaves fewer people to a worse fate. It is surprisingly hard to come up with non-question-begging grounds to favor Benefit Thinking over

Worse-Fate Thinking: to view Benefit Thinking as the more natural extension of our concern for how people fare, as reflected in "ordinary" moral choices, which don't affect who or how many come to exist. This chapter suggests that Worse-Fate Thinking, or a combination of Worse-Fate and Benefit Thinking, gives more intuitive answers than does Benefit Thinking to many of the questions of population ethics.

Andreas L. Mogensen: 'Against Large Number Scepticism'

According to large number scepticism, intuitions about the Repugnant Conclusion and related problems in normative ethics shouldn't be trusted because we can't adequately grasp the very large numbers involved. This chapter argues that the case for large number scepticism is unconvincing. I respond to arguments for large number scepticism offered by John Broome and Michael Huemer, as well as more empirically grounded arguments due to Joshua Greene and Adam Cureton. I consider what we can learn from evidence of scope insensitivity in contingent valuation, people's diminishing sensitivity to increasing numbers of lives lost or saved, well-established limitations of the mind/brain's core number systems, and evidence that people are more moved by single victims than by groups. In each case, I argue that the case for large number scepticism should not convince us.

William MacAskill: 'Are We Living at the Hinge of History?'

In the final pages of *On What Matters*, Volume II, Derek Parfit comments: "We live during the hinge of history...If we act wisely in the next few centuries, humanity will survive its most dangerous and decisive period...What now matters most is that we avoid ending human history." This passage echoes Parfit's comment, in *Reasons and Persons*, that "the next few centuries will be the most important in human history". But is the claim that we live at the hinge of history true? The argument of this chapter is that it is not. The chapter first suggests a way of making the hinge of history claim precise and action-relevant in the context of the question of whether altruists should try to do good now, or invest their resources in order to have more of an impact later on. It then canvasses arguments for and against the hinge of history claim, and suggests that, though we certainly live at an unusual time, we don't have sufficient evidence to think that the present is the most influential time ever.

S. J. Beard and Patrick Kaczmarek: 'On Theory X and What Matters Most'

One of Derek Parfit's greatest legacies was the search for Theory X, a theory of population ethics that avoided all the implausible conclusions and paradoxes that have dogged the field since its inception: the Absurd Conclusion, the Repugnant Conclusion, the Non-Identity Problem, and the Mere Addition Paradox. In recent years, it has been argued that this search is doomed to failure and no satisfactory population axiology is possible. This chapter reviews Parfit's life's work in the field and argues that he provided all the necessary components for a Theory X. It then shows how these components can be combined and applied to the global challenges Parfit argued matter most: preventing human extinction, managing catastrophic risks, and eradicating global poverty and suffering. Finally, it identifies a number of challenges facing his theory and suggests how these may be overcome.

Ruth Chang: 'How to Avoid the Repugnant Conclusion'

Derek Parfit thought that his continuum argument in population ethics leading to the Repugnant Conclusion—viz., that a world with a vast number of people leading lives barely worth living is better than a world with many people enjoying excellent lives—raised a puzzle that must be solved before we can hope to arrive at a correct theory of morality, what he called 'Theory X'. This chapter critically examines four possible 'structural' solutions to continua arguments like Parfit's—solutions according to which the structure of continua is not as continua arguments suppose. It is argued that incommensurability, incomparability, indeterminacy, and indeed Parfit's own preferred solution, 'lexical imprecision', fail to provide the break in structure needed to defuse continua arguments. An alternative structural solution is then proposed according to which, somewhere along the continuum, items are on a par with their immediate predecessors. Being on a par is a *sui generis* fourth basic way two items can be compared beyond being better or worse than one another or equally good. The parity solution is shown to have two significant advantages over the other structural proposals. First, only the parity solution allows us to maintain the very plausible thought at the heart of continua arguments, viz., that as we proceed along the continuum, a small diminution in quality of value can be compensated for by a large increase in quantity of value. Second, by appealing to a tetrachotomous, rather than a trichotomous, view of value—a view of value that includes parity—we can vindicate first-blush, untutored, intuitive reactions as to what goes wrong in continua arguments. Thinking about what some may have too readily dismissed as a 'mere puzzle' opens up new ways of thinking about the very structure of normativity and the shape of Theory X.

Wlodek Rabinowicz: 'Can Parfit's Appeal to Incommensurabilities in Value Block the Continuum Argument for the Repugnant Conclusion?'

Parfit proposed blocking the Continuum Argument for the Repugnant Conclusion by letting incommensurabilities ("imprecise equalities" in his terminology) intervene at some points in the argument's population sequence. It is an attractive option. But the relevant incommensurabilities need to be very thoroughgoing if the argument is to be blocked: they must persist even if the next population in the sequence is improved by making it arbitrarily larger. While such persistency might well seem problematic (not just in this case but also when it comes to blockings other spectrum arguments), this chapter suggests how it can be explained and defended if incommensurability is interpreted on the lines of the fitting-attitudes analysis of value relations. On that analysis, two items are incommensurable if divergent preferential attitudes towards them are permissible (i.e., not unfitting); for example, if it is permissible to prefer one item to the other but also permissible to have the opposite preference. It is shown how to provide a modeling of this kind for persistent incommensurability and how to account for this persistency. However, even if Parfit's main suggestion can in this way be defended, one of his substantive value assumptions—the Simple View regarding the marginal value of added lives—should be given up,to avoid implausible implications.

Gustaf Arrhenius: 'Population Ethics and Conflict-of-Value Imprecision'

In an article published in 2016, Parfit suggested a new way of avoiding the paradoxes and impossibility theorems in population ethics by revising our beliefs about fundamental axiological concepts such as "equally good" and "better than". More specifically, Parfit suggests that "We might claim that...given the conflict between...values, [w]orlds are only imprecisely comparable, and would be imprecisely equally good." From this it follows that many of the comparisons of different future populations will involve imprecise comparisons and hence that transitivity of "better than" might fail. Parfit suggests that this move in combination with an appeal to lexically superior values will open up a way of avoiding the Repugnant Conclusion without implying other counterintuitive conclusions, and thus solve one of the major challenges in ethics. This chapter tries to clarify Parfit's proposal and evaluate whether it, or a possible development of it, will help us with the impossibility theorems in population ethics.

Teruji Thomas: 'On Evaluative Imprecision'

This chapter presents several arguments related to Parfit's notion of evaluative imprecision and his imprecisionist lexical view of population ethics. After sketching Parfit's view, it argues that, contrary to Parfit, imprecision and lexicality are both compatible with thinking about goodness in terms of positions on a scale of value. Then, by examining the role that imprecision is meant to play in defusing spectrum arguments, it suggests that imprecision should be identified with vagueness. Next, it argues that there is space for robust moral realists to think of evaluative vagueness as a semantic phenomenon, illustrating this view with a version of conceptual role semantics on which the precisifications of betterness are correctness conditions for the precisifications of preference. Finally, it gives a probability-based argument against the imprecisionist lexical view.

Theron Pummer: 'Sorites on What Matters'

Ethics in the tradition of Derek Parfit's *Reasons and Persons* is riddled with sorites-like arguments, which lead us by what seem innocent steps to seemingly false conclusions. Take, for example, spectrum arguments for the Repugnant Conclusion that appeal to slight differences in quality of life. Several authors have taken the view that, since spectrum arguments are structurally analogous to sorites arguments, the correct response to spectrum arguments is structurally analogous to the correct response to sorites arguments. This *sorites analogy* is here argued against. There are potential structural disanalogies between spectrum arguments and sorites arguments. But even if these arguments are relevantly structurally analogous, they differ in their content in ways that show the sorites analogy to be implausible. Two content-based disanalogies are here explored—one is inspired by Parfit's work on reductionism, and the other involves hypersensitivity. The chapter concludes with a methodological lesson.

Michael Otsuka: 'Prioritarianism, Population Ethics, and Competing Claims'

In his restriction of prioritarianism to cases in which the same people would exist in all the possible outcomes, Parfit stakes out an unstable position, both for himself and more generally. There is no plausible rationale for a prioritarianism that is so restricted, which is consistent with the key features of Parfit's elaboration and defence of this view and his other commitments. The principles that might be appealed to, in an attempt to justify such a restriction, give rise to a different view—one that is sensitive to the presence or absence of the competing claims of different individuals, where both the existence and the magnitude of these claims are determined by gains and losses to individuals in a manner that is not fully captured by Parfit's prioritarian weighting.

Shlomi Segall: 'Quarantining Prioritarianism'

While utilitarianism is vulnerable to a Repugnant Conclusion with regard to populations of variable sizes, prioritarianism, it has been observed, does even worse. Because it gives greater weight to utility at lower absolute levels, prioritarianism encounters a Super Repugnant Conclusion. It is not surprising, then, that in his last published paper on prioritarianism, Derek Parfit argued that the priority view ought not to apply to cases involving 'different people'. Prioritarianism, in other words, ought to be 'quarantined', and restricted to 'same people' cases. This chapter advances four related claims with respect to quarantined prioritarianism. First, contra Parfit, it shows that it is far from obvious that prioritarianism ought to be quarantined in the first place, and that doing so entails a certain cost, namely sacrificing its alleged 'completeness'. Second, it shows that if prioritarianism is, for some reason, to be quarantined, then that should hold, contra Michael Otsuka, with respect to Different Numbers Choices and never with respect to Same Number Choices. Third, this 'narrow' quarantining approach is in fact consistent with other tenets of Parfit's axiology that we have good reason to endorse (such as his 'No Difference View' and his views on the Value of Existence). And fourth, it is shown that future generations do, after all, present a certain difficulty to standard formulations of prioritarianism (e.g. Nils Holtug's), and that a minor yet important revision to how we understand the priority view is called for.

PART I
CAUSING PEOPLE TO EXIST AND THE NON-IDENTITY PROBLEM

1
The Asymmetry

Ralf M. Bader

1.1 The Basic Account

The asymmetry in population ethics:

- The fact that a life would be worth living does not, by itself, generate reasons to bring it into existence.
- The fact that a life would be worth not living does, by itself, generate reasons to not bring it into existence.[1,2]

Accounting for this intuition is one of the key desiderata of any satisfactory theory of population ethics. The asymmetry, however, is difficult to explicate. Attempts at making sense of it run into a dilemma. On the one hand, a person-affecting view can account for the first half, on the basis that it is not better for the happy person to exist than not to exist. Yet it struggles with the second half. Given that a miserable life is not worse than non-existence, a person-affecting view has difficulty in explaining what could speak against bringing such a life into existence. On the other hand, an impersonalist view can deal with the second half. Miserable lives should not be brought into existence because their existence is taken to be impersonally bad, i.e. bad from the point of view of the universe rather than that of any individual. However, it is unable to explain the first half, given that the impersonal goodness of lives that are worth living likewise generates reasons. As a result, the asymmetry is difficult to sustain.

We have two unpalatable symmetrical options that either over-generate or under-generate reasons. Either existence and non-existence are comparable with respect to some value, in which case one has reason not to create miserable lives but then also has reason to create happy lives, leaving one with an impersonalist axiology that violates the neutrality intuition; or they are non-comparable, in which case one does not have reason to create happy lives but then ends up not

---

[1] The qualification 'by itself' implies that we set aside effects on others in evaluating reasons for adding / not adding lives.
[2] Terminological note: lives that are worth living are also referred to as 'happy lives' and lives that are worth not living as 'miserable lives'.

Ralf M. Bader, *The Asymmetry* In: *Ethics and Existence: The Legacy of Derek Parfit*. Edited by: Jeff McMahan, Tim Campbell, James Goodrich, and Ketan Ramakrishnan, Oxford University Press. © Oxford University Press 2022.
DOI: 10.1093/oso/9780192894250.003.0002

having reasons not to create miserable lives, leaving one with a radical person-affecting view (such as that espoused by Heyd: 1992) that has counter-intuitive commitments (cf. McMahan: 2009).

	IMPERSONAL	PERSON-AFFECTING	ASYMMETRY
worth living	$R(\text{add})$	$\neg R(\text{add})$	$\neg R(\text{add})$
worth not living	$R(\neg \text{add})$	$\neg R(\neg \text{add})$	$R(\neg \text{add})$

Impersonalist theories consider the existence of happy lives to make things better, in the same way that the existence of miserable lives makes things worse. Yet, if adding happy lives makes the world a better place, then one has reason to add such lives. This means that in order to underwrite the first half of the asymmetry, impersonalist approaches would have to find a way of making these reasons disappear.[3] They would have to explain why the value of happy lives does not provide reasons, whereas the disvalue of miserable lives does provide reasons. Making value count only in the one case but not in the other is difficult and conflicts with plausible bridge-principles connecting values and reasons.

Person-affecting approaches, by contrast, do not have to make any reasons disappear. The problem that they have to address is to explain why there are reasons not to add miserable lives, even though there are no axiologically based reasons that speak against adding miserable lives. This is much less problematic, since one can bring in additional resources that supplement axiologically based reasons in order to explain the asymmetry. Person-affecting theories thus have a crucial advantage over impersonalist theories when it comes to underwriting the asymmetry, since one can explain why there are reasons against ϕ-ing in a situation in which there are no axiologically based reasons against ϕ-ing, by appealing to supplementary non-axiologically based reasons, whereas one cannot explain why there are no reasons in favour of ϕ-ing in a situation in which there are axiologically based reasons in favour of ϕ-ing.

1.1.1 The First Half

The first half of the asymmetry follows from the intuition of neutrality. According to this intuition, adding a person neither makes a distribution any better nor any worse but is instead axiologically neutral.[4]

---

[3] The first half of the asymmetry states not merely that it is permissible not to add such lives (which could be explained in terms of prerogatives), but that there is no reason, not even a *pro tanto* reason, to add them.

[4] Adding a person can have positive or negative effects on other people, yet such effects are set aside when examining whether the existence of the person makes things better or worse by itself.

This intuition can be explained by means of an account of conditional goodness, according to which the goodness and reason-giving force of a person's well-being is conditional on the existence of the person. We can compare the goodness of existing lives and order them in terms of how good they are. Yet, we cannot compare existence with non-existence. We cannot compare something that has goodness with something that lacks goodness. Given that goodness is conditional on existence, we should be neutral about existence. Existence is not better than non-existence. Nor is non-existence better than existence. Yet, existence and non-existence are not equally good either. Instead, existence and non-existence are not comparable. No betterness relations hold between existence and non-existence. Existence is not better than non-existence and there is hence no reason to bring a happy life into existence. Instead of having reason to bring lives into existence, one only has reason to improve lives that exist.[5] 'We are in favor of making people happy, but neutral about making happy people' (Narveson: 1973, p. 80).

The idea of conditional goodness and the attendant commitment to the non-comparability of situations in which the condition is satisfied with those in which it fails to be satisfied applies straightforwardly to considerations of personal good. According to non-comparativism, it is not possible to compare existence with non-existence from the point of view of personal good. Any attempt to make a comparison to the effect that it is better for a person to exist than not to exist is confused and misguided. The personal betterness relation only holds between situations in which the person in question exists. One situation can be better for x than another situation only if x exists in both situations. Accordingly, existence is not better for x than non-existence. These scenarios are not comparable with respect to x's good.[6]

If x exists, then it is better for x to be happy than not to be happy. Yet, it is not better for x to exist and be happy than for x not to exist. That x's life goes well is not better for x than that it is not lived at all. Non-existence is neither better nor worse for x than either a happy or a miserable existence. The difference between happiness and misery makes no difference when these states are compared with non-existence, since both of them fail to be comparable with non-existence. If the condition is not satisfied, then goodness is not applicable. The value of a non-existent life is undefined. It lacks value rather than having zero value. The field of

---

[5] The notion of existence is not to be understood in a temporal manner, i.e. that we have reason to improve a life after it has come into existence. Instead, it is to be construed atemporally. We have reason to improve lives if their existence is given and not contingent on our actions (i.e. every member of the set of alternatives is such that it contains the lives in question).

[6] The personal betterness relation is a dyadic relation that has lives as its *relata*. In particular, the 'better for x'-relation is a dyadic relation that compares x's lives. When comparing existence with non-existence, one of the two *relata* is missing, which ensures that the relation cannot apply. Moreover, there is a lack of good-making features in the case of non-existence. Non-comparativism thus follows from the fact that there cannot be a betterness relation without *relata* and from the fact that there cannot be goodness without good-making features. Cf. 'The neutrality of existence' (Bader: manuscript).

the personal betterness relation is, accordingly, not complete but restricted to existence cases. Situations falling within the field are not comparable to ones falling outside it. The normative significance of happiness/misery, i.e. the ability of these features to make a difference, is thus conditional on existence.

The rejection of comparability in terms of personal good leaves open whether one can compare existence with non-existence from some other point of view, such as the point of view of general good or impersonal good. If one were to adopt an impersonal approach, for instance, then one could hold that, even though it does not make sense to ask whether x's existence is better for x than x's non-existence, it is intelligible to inquire as to whether x's existence is impersonally better than x's non-existence. Although the state of affairs in which x exists is not comparable in terms of personal good, it may well be comparable in terms of general or impersonal good. A person-affecting approach, however, forecloses this possibility. If a person-affecting view is adopted, then non-comparativism regarding the personal betterness relation leads to unrestricted non-comparativism.

A person-affecting approach requires all betterness claims to ultimately be reducible to claims about how persons are affected. Distributions are to be evaluated in terms of how they affect various people and the goodness of distributions is reducible to the goodness for the members of the distributions.[7] The reducibility requirement is stronger than a mere supervenience or functional dependence requirement. The fact that D_1 is better than D_2 has to consist in facts about personal betterness. Put differently, the betterness relation between distributions has to consist in nothing other than the obtaining of personal betterness relations amongst the members of the distributions. Facts about general good have to be reducible to facts about personal good, such that facts about general good just are plural facts about personal good. The general betterness relation is then to be construed as a plural comparative.[8]

Two key commitments follow from this reducibility requirement, namely (i) that considerations of general good are countenanced only as long as they are reducible to considerations of personal good, and (ii) that considerations of impersonal good are rejected altogether on the grounds of being irreducible. All claims of goodness are then either directly about the personal goodness of individual lives or reducible to such claims. Non-comparativism about personal

---

[7] What is known as the 'person-affecting restriction', namely that a distribution D_1 cannot be better than another distribution D_2 unless there is someone for whom D_1 is better than D_2, is a necessary condition on betterness orderings that is both too strong and too weak. It is too strong, since it mistakenly builds in a rejection of impartiality. It is too weak, since it can be satisfied by impersonal theories that merely assign ethical relevance but not ethical significance to personal good. The positive commitment of a person-affecting view, as it is understood in this chapter, is the commitment to the reducibility of general good and the rejection of impersonal good.

[8] For a detailed development and defence of this person-affecting approach, cf. 'Person-affecting population ethics' (Bader: manuscript). A crucial upshot of this approach is that distributions are only comparable when they are equinumerous.

good together with the reducibility of general good implies non-comparativism with respect to general good. Together with the rejection of an impersonal standpoint, this implies that one ends up with there not being any point of view from which existence can be compared with non-existence. In short, existence cannot at all be compared with non-existence because (i) non-comparativism about personal good ensures that such a comparison is not possible from the personal point of view, (ii) the reducibility of general good rules out such comparisons from the general point of view, and (iii) the rejection of impersonal good excludes the possibility of a comparison from the impersonal point of view.

Adopting a person-affecting approach thus ensures that one ends up with unrestricted non-comparativism. Conditional goodness, consequently, applies both to personal good and to general good. According to both the personal and the general betterness relation, it is better that a person who exists is happy rather than not happy. Given that someone does exist, that person's happiness matters from the point of view of personal good as well as from the point of view of general good. Yet, it is not better according to either of these betterness relations that a happy person exists than that such a person does not exist.

This commitment to conditional goodness explains the first half of the asymmetry.[9] Since the goodness of a person's happiness is conditional upon the existence of the person, it follows that the addition of a happy person does not make things better. Instead, it has a neutral impact, where neutrality is to be understood in terms of non-comparability, given that we cannot compare a situation in which the condition is satisfied with one in which it fails to be satisfied. The fact that a life would be worth living, consequently, does not by itself generate reasons for bringing it into existence.

1.1.2 The Second Half

Accounting for the second half of the asymmetry is not so straightforward. The commitment to neutrality is unrestricted. The addition of a life is axiologically neutral in the case of all possible lives and not only in the case of lives falling within a certain range. Existence is non-comparable with non-existence, no matter how good or bad the life in question is. In the same way that it is not better that a happy life is lived, it is not worse that a miserable life is lived. As a result, there seems to be nothing that speaks against bringing miserable lives into existence.

---

[9] In addition, one has to argue that non-comparative considerations do not generate reasons to bring happy lives into existence, e.g. that people can be non-comparatively benefited by being brought into existence since, even though a life that is worth living is not better than non-existence, it is nevertheless good for the person (cf. Parfit: 1984, appendix G; McMahan: 2013). For an argument that non-comparative considerations cannot speak in favour of bringing happy lives into existence, cf. 'The neutrality of existence' (Bader: manuscript).

To avoid this unpalatable situation, one has to appeal to non-axiological resources.[10] This section explains why we have reasons not to bring miserable lives into existence in terms of a structural consistency constraint that actions have to satisfy. This allows us to combine a symmetrical account at the axiological level with an asymmetry at the level of reasons, without undermining standard bridge-principles connecting values and reasons and without having to bring in independent considerations, such as justice-, fairness-, or rights-based considerations.[11]

To begin with, we need to consider what it is for a life to be worth not living.[12] Given non-comparativism, one cannot explicate this notion in terms of a life being worse than non-existence. One cannot simply compare a life with non-existence and evaluate whether it is better for the life to be lived than not to be lived, i.e. whether it is better for the person to exist than to not exist, such that a life is worth living if it is better than non-existence, neutral if it is equally as good as non-existence, and worth not living if it is worse than non-existence. Instead of a life worth not living being one that is worse than non-existence, it is one that is equally as good as some member of the following set:

$$\{L: \forall t \exists t'[t'<t \wedge V(L_{0-t'})>V(L_{0-t})]\}$$

Every life in this set is such that for any point in time t in that life the value of the life up to that point, i.e. $V(L_{0-t})$, is smaller than the value of the life up to some earlier point t'. We cannot say of these lives that it would have been better if they had never been lived, but only that it would have been better had they ended sooner rather than later: the shorter they are, the better they are.

If we partition all lives into equivalence classes under the relation of being equally as good as and use the betterness relation to impose an ordering on these equivalence classes, then the class of neutral lives is the least upper bound of the set of classes that have the members of the aforementioned set as members, whilst those lives that are better than neutral lives are lives that are worth living.

[10] Bringing in non-axiological resources is unproblematic since the asymmetry concerns the level of reasons, not the level of values.

[11] Substantive non-axiological considerations are problematic. First, they do not straightforwardly apply to non-existent entities. For instance, it is dubious to hold that there can be a right against being brought into existence since there cannot be a rights-bearer that can have this right: as long as the person does not exist there is no rights-bearer and hence no right, yet once the person does exist, that person cannot have a right not to be brought into existence, since it is impossible to make it the case that something that already exists never comes into existence. Second, they are likely to yield reasons against creating miserable lives that are too strong and that cannot be adequately integrated into a general theory. One needs to be able to weigh up the reasons not to add miserable lives against other reasons in order to deal with (i) cases involving externalities whereby other people are positively or negatively affected by the addition of the life, (ii) cases in which groups of people are added, some of whose lives are worth living whilst others are worth not living, and (iii) cases in which there is uncertainty as to whether a particular action will result in the addition of lives that are worth not living (cf. sections 1.2.2–1.2.4).

[12] The notion of a life worth living is an axiological notion based on the notion of well-being. It is concerned with what is good/bad for the person and is to be distinguished from the notion of a meaningful life. That a life is not worth living does not imply that it is meaningless.

In this way, it is possible to explain what it is for a life to be worth not living in terms of the internal structure of the life, in particular in terms of the axiological ordering of various initial segments of the life. This account does not compare existence with non-existence but only compares different shortenings of the life. One compares shortenings of the life with other shortenings, without having to appeal to the non-sensical idea that it is worse for the life to be lived than for the life not to have been lived at all.[13]

A paradigm case of a miserable life is one that is constantly getting worse, in the sense that lifetime well-being is constantly decreasing. For every point in this life, the value of the life up to that point is smaller than the value of the life up to each earlier point. Consider such a life L that occupies a temporal region that is topologically open on the left. Every shortening of such a miserable life is likewise a miserable life. Moreover, for every shortening s, there exists a prior shortening s^* such that $s^* > s$. When we start with a distribution D_1 and consider adding L, then, although the original distribution D_1 is not comparable with the extended distribution $D_2 = D_1 \cup L$ since they are not equinumerous, D_2 is comparable with distributions $D_{2'}, D_{2''} \ldots$ that contain various shortenings of L, e.g. $D_{2'} = D_1 \cup s'$. These extensions of D_1 form an open-ended series of distributions that has the original distribution as its limit.

For instance, if we consider a sequence of shortenings in which each member of the sequence is half as long as the previous member, i.e. the length of the nth shortening is given by $\frac{1}{2^n}$ times the length of the added life, then the limit of this sequence is:

$$\lim_{n \to \infty} \frac{1}{2^n} = 0.$$

As n tends to infinity, the life being added gets shorter and shorter, until in the limit it no longer exists. The original distribution is not a member of this sequence of ever shorter extensions and is not better than any member of this sequence. Instead, it is the limit of the sequence. The sequence of shortenings is such that, in the limit, the length of the added life is zero, i.e. $\frac{L}{\omega} = 0$, which means that no life is

---

[13] This account does not have atomistic presuppositions and does not make assumptions about separability across time, but is instead compatible with a holistic understanding of the value of a life. The underlying idea is that the goodness of a life depends on what happens in the life in such a way that the shorter the life is the less room there is for value in this life. This means that though there can be holistic goods, such as pattern goods, these goods have to depend on the length of the life in such a way that they matter less the shorter the life is. In short, every good and bad (whether atomistic or holistic) has to diminish with duration, such that an infinitesimal life can only contain an infinitesimal amount of value. Accordingly, there can be no duration-invariant holistic goods, i.e. holistic goods that are equally good no matter how long the life lasts and hence do not diminish or disappear as the life gets shorter and shorter. Such goods would not show up under shortening and would not generate reasons against shortening.

(If separability were accepted, one could identify a neutral time-slice as one that is such that the life with this time-slice is equally as good as the life without it. A neutral life can then be understood as one that is equally as good as a life that only consists of neutral time-slices.)

added and that D_{2^ω} is identical to D_1. In the limit, the life is not lived at all and the distribution is not extended. In other words, the original distribution is the limit of the sequence of extensions resulting from adding ever shorter shortenings of L.[14]

Such a paradigmatically miserable life is worse than all its shortenings. Moreover, each shortening is worse than all prior shortenings. The life gets better and better the shorter it is. Correspondingly, the extended distribution gets better and better the shorter the life is that is being added. This means that someone who can choose, not only to either add or not add this life, but also has the option to add various shortenings of the life, will choose the option of not adding the life. If one enriches the set of alternatives by including all the possible shortenings into the set of alternatives, i.e. $X = \{L, \frac{L}{2}, \frac{L}{4}, \ldots, \neg \text{ add}\}$, then the only admissible option is to not add the miserable life, i.e. $C(X) = \{\neg \text{ add}\}$. This holds not only for lives that are constantly getting worse but applies to all lives that are such that for every shortening s, there exists a prior shortening s^* such that $s^* > s$. In all these cases the life is made better and better by being made shorter and shorter, such that, in the limit, it is not lived at all.

An idealized agent who has the ability to shorten the life at any moment in time, i.e. can stop the effects of the action from unfolding, and who is ideally responsive to moral reasons cannot add a miserable life.[15] The commitment to shorten the life whenever doing so makes it better subsumes an infinite sequence consisting of ω-many actions that jointly prevent the life from coming into existence.

If t is the boundary on the left of the temporal region of the life, then a commitment to shorten the life whenever doing so makes it better implies that the life neither exists at t nor at any time after t. On the one hand, time t is the boundary of the life and is not part of the temporal region occupied by the life. On the other, if the life were to exist at $t + \frac{1}{2^n}$, then there would already have been a prior member of the sequence of shortenings, say number $n + 1$, which would have cut the life short at $t + \frac{1}{2^{n+1}}$. Put differently, were the life to exist at any time t'' after t, there would have been an earlier time t' (where $t < t' < t''$) at which the life would already have been cut short, contradicting the claim that the life exists at the later time t''. Since every time after t is such that there is a prior time at which the life would already have been cut short, it follows that the life cannot exist at any time after t. Given that adding the life implies that it exists at some time after t, and given that the life cannot exist at any such time, it follows that adding a

---

[14] The closeness measure is a temporal rather than an evaluative measure. Closeness is understood in terms of the length of the life, not the value of the life. We are dealing with a sequence of initial segments that has as its temporal limit the non-existence of the life, such that the corresponding sequence of actions, namely the sequence of earlier and earlier shortenings, likewise has as its causal limit the non-existence of the life.

[15] In the rest of this section miserable lives will be understood as lives that are never worth living. Lives that, though worth not living overall, nevertheless start out being worth living will be considered in section 1.2.1.

miserable life is logically precluded by the commitment (joined with the ability) to shorten it whenever one has reason to do so.[16]

There is thus a contradiction between (1) a miserable life is added and hence exists at some time after t, (2) for any time t'' in the life there is an earlier time t' such that it is better for the life to be shortened at t' than to continue until t'', and (3) for every time t' if it is better to shorten the life at t' than to let it continue, then it is shortened at that time. Adding a miserable life is, accordingly, incompatible with an effective commitment to performing at every point in time all those shortenings that would make the life better and that one would hence have reason to perform, i.e. $\forall t\ [R(\text{shorten at } t) \rightarrow \text{shorten at } t]$. This general commitment subsumes ω-many conditional commitments (shorten at t_1 if the life exists at t_1, shorten at t_2 if the life exists at $t_2 \ldots$). Adding a life is admissible only if these commitments do not preclude the possibility of adding the life, i.e. add $\in C(X)$ only if $\Diamond$ (add $\wedge\ \forall t\ [R(\text{shorten at } t) \rightarrow \text{shorten at } t]$).

The phenomenon that we are interested in differs importantly from cases in which the choice-set is empty when using a maximizing or optimizing function due to there not being any maximal element in the betterness ordering.[17] If there were an open-ended sequence on the positive side, for instance if there were an infinite number of possible extensions of a happy life, then there would not be any maximal element in the sequence of extensions. Yet no incompatibility would be generated.

---

[16] If the temporal region occupied by the life were topologically closed on the left (rather than open), then the sequence of shortenings would prevent the life from existing at any time after t but would not prevent it from existing at t. Instead of being prevented from coming into existence, there would instead be either a point-sized life occupying an extensionless temporal region, or a temporally extended life that occupies a temporal region corresponding to the minimum extent of a life and hence is such that none of its initial segments would classify as lives. For the argument to work, lives have to occupy regions that are topologically open on the left, since the sequence of shortenings would otherwise be closed. This happens naturally if time (or space-time) is not pointy but gunky, in which case every region has sub-regions, making it the case that there are no temporal points but only nested sequences of ever smaller extended temporal regions. Additionally, this can happen if lives cannot be instantaneous but must have positive extent without there being any minimum extent. If there is no minimal unit having axiological significance, then this implies that every axiologically significant unit is temporally extended and has temporally extended axiologically significant units as parts, i.e. the structure of axiologically significant units will be gunky if these conditions are satisfied, which can be the case even if time (or space-time) should fail to be gunky. (Furthermore, one can argue that even if there could be point-sized lives or lives that occupy a temporal region that is closed on the right and that are such that none of their initial segments classify as lives, these lives could not be miserable lives on the grounds that misery has to be temporally extended, without there being any minimal extent. This would still be sufficient for establishing the fine-grained asymmetry discussed in section 1.2.1.)

[17] It also differs from cases in which performing all the actions in a sequence of ω-many actions leads to sub-optimal outcomes, despite the fact that each action in the series is such that one has reason to perform that action (cf. Arntzenius & McCarthy: 1997, pp. 49–50 and Barrett & Arntzenius: 1999), requiring one to adopt a satisficing rather than maximizing or optimizing strategy. As Scott and Scott: 2005 have shown, such infinite exchange problems arise only given certain conditions involving the individuation and tracking of the units that are exchanged, none of which apply in the context that we are presently considering.

The key difference between the two scenarios is that in the former case the limit of the betterness ordering coincides with the limit of the temporal/causal sequence, since always extending amounts to adding either an infinitely long life or a life of finite duration (if the sequence asymptotically approaches a limit). In the latter case, by contrast, the evaluative limit comes apart from the limit of the temporal/causal sequence. The limit of the betterness ordering consists in a neutral life. The limit of the temporal/causal sequence, however, is not a neutral life. In fact, it is not a life at all. In the limit, no life is added and the distribution is not extended, since always shortening amounts to not adding the miserable life at all. Put differently, whilst $L \times \omega$ is simply a long life, $\frac{L}{\omega}$ is no life at all and is accordingly equivalent to $\neg\text{add}$. The problem is thus not that there is no maximal element, in that for every shortening there is a yet better shortening, but that the shortenings collectively preclude there being a life at all.

This difference can be brought out clearly if the idealized agent can perform supertasks, such that the set of alternatives includes $L \times \omega$ in the former situation and $\frac{L}{\omega}$, which equals $\neg\text{add}$, in the latter situation. Hence, the choice set will be $C(X) = \{\neg\text{add}, L \times \omega\}$ when dealing with a happy life that can always be further extended and thereby be made better and better, but only $C(X) = \{\neg\text{add}\}$ when dealing with a miserable life, thereby rendering the addition of the miserable life inadmissible. Whereas always extending a life is compatible with there being a life, namely one that is infinitely long or that asymptotically approaches a limit, always shortening a life is incompatible with the existence of a life since, in the limit, no life is lived, thereby rendering only the latter but not the former incompatible with the addition of a life.

When we evaluate actions from an axiological perspective, we usually evaluate their effects and compare the outcome of one action with that of another. We can, however, also evaluate the differences between outcomes, instead of evaluating the outcomes separately. The differences that ϕ-ing makes vis-à-vis ψ-ing can be evaluated and compared with various shortenings of those effects, where a shortening is a partial evaluation, i.e. one only evaluates the effects up to some time t. In the case of adding a life, the alternative is not to add the life. The difference that the action makes is thus the existence of the life and the various shortenings of the effects of the action are nothing other than shortenings of the life. One then evaluates not only the whole life but also various initial segments of the life. Importantly, the shortenings of the differences that ϕ-ing makes vis-à-vis ψ-ing can be comparable, even when the outcomes of ϕ-ing and ψ-ing fail to be comparable.

An action ϕ is inadmissible if it violates the shortening consistency constraint. This constraint is violated if there is some alternative ψ such that the difference that ϕ-ing makes vis-à-vis ψ-ing is such that there is a sequence of shortenings of these effects that starts with the degenerate shortening (which consists in the complete eventuation of the effects that result from ϕ-ing rather than ψ-ing) and that has the complete non-occurrence of these effects as its limit, i.e. the outcome of ψ-ing is the limit of the sequence of shortenings of the effects of ϕ-ing, whereby for every shortening s there exists a prior shortening s^* that is better than s.

The underlying idea is that one should not perform an action that is such that one should prevent its effects from eventuating (if one were able to do so). Whilst ϕ-ing is compatible with preventing some of its effects from unfolding, it is incompatible with preventing all of its effects from unfolding. In the case at hand, adding a life is compatible with cutting it short at some later point, yet adding a life is incompatible with cutting it short at every point (of a sequence that has the non-occurrence of the action as its limit). If an action is such that its effects should be completely precluded from unfolding, then this action should not be initiated.[18]

Adding a miserable life violates the shortening consistency constraint. There is a sequence of shortenings, each of which makes the life better than the subsequent shortenings, that has the non-existence of the life as its limit. The different shortenings jointly preclude the possibility of adding a miserable life. The shortening consistency constraint, accordingly, requires one to refrain from adding such a life, even though doing so is not worse than the alternative of not adding the life. This means that the reason against adding miserable lives is explained in terms of the very feature that makes them worth not living, namely that they are better the sooner they end. It is the internal axiological structure of a life that both explains why the life is worth not living and that leads to the violation of the consistency constraint and thereby makes it inadmissible to add such a life.

By contrast, no analogous reasoning can be used in the case of lives that are worth living to show that one has reason to bring them into existence. If we add lives that are worth living, then all that can happen is that it is better for such lives to continue rather than be cut short. Yet the fact that one should prevent such lives from being shortened does not generate a reason to bring them into existence in the first place. Accordingly, if the life is worth living, then it is both admissible to not extend the distribution and admissible to add the happy life. Both actions are admissible. They do not violate any consistency constraints and there are no alternative actions that are better than them. Given their non-comparability, one should be neutral between these options. The choice whether or not to extend the distribution by adding the happy life is then an existential choice.

---

[18] If the outcomes of ϕ and ψ are comparable, then the shortening consistency constraint rules out ϕ-ing whenever its outcome is dominated by that of ψ-ing (given the coarse-grained approach of section 1.2.1). The consistency constraint thus rules out all dominated alternatives. This means that the shortening consistency constraint is not an ad hoc principle that is brought in specifically to deal with the asymmetry, but is a general constraint that generates a choice function that selects all maximal elements that conform to the asymmetry. Every theory needs a choice function that gets us from the level of values/reasons to oughts. The shortening consistency constraint constitutes precisely such a criterion: it generates a same-number maximization requirement together with the asymmetry in one fell swoop.

Whereas the fact that adding a miserable life violates the shortening consistency constraint renders that action inadmissible and gives us reason not to perform it, the fact that adding a happy life satisfies this consistency constraint does not give us any reason to perform that action, but merely makes it the case that it is an admissible action. This is what explains the asymmetry.

1.2 Extending the Account

1.2.1 Lives that Are Initially Worth Living

The basic account applies to any miserable life that is such that for every point in that life t, there exists a prior point t' that is such that the life up to t' is better than the life up to t. Such lives only constitute a sub-class of all the lives worth not living, namely those that are never worth living (though they may be worth continuing at various points). Those lives that, considered as a whole, are worth not living even though they are worth living or neutral up to some point do not fall within the scope of the argument. In order to end up with an unrestricted asymmetry, the account needs to be extended to apply, not only to those lives that are such that every point in the life is such that it would have been better had the life been shorter, but also to lives that are worth living up to some point yet worth not living on the whole.

A life is no longer worth living at time t if $\exists t'(t' \leq t \wedge \forall t'' [t' < t'' \rightarrow V(L_{0-t'}) > V(L_{0-t''})])$.[19] The point after which a life is no longer worth living is the first point that is such that the life up to that point is better than the life up to all later points, i.e. the point at which it reaches its peak in terms of lifetime well-being (see Figure 1.1).[20] A life that is worth living up to some point yet that is worth not living considered as a whole is thus a miserable life that has the property of not being such as to be no longer worth living at all points in time. This means that there are points in time at which it is still worth living, yet such that the (net) goodness of any initial segment is not sufficiently large to outweigh the (net) badness accruing to the life during later segments when it is no longer worth living.

---

[19] A life, considered as a whole, can be worth living even though it reaches a point at which it is no longer worth living. The badness to be found in the life after that point simply has to be sufficiently insignificant as to not outweigh the goodness that has accrued up to that point.

[20] If the life has multiple peaks or a flat peak, then it is the final point at which it peaks that is such that after this point the life is no longer worth living, since only this final point is such that the life is better up to that point than up to all later points, whereas prior peaks fail to satisfy this condition due to there being later peaks that are equally good.

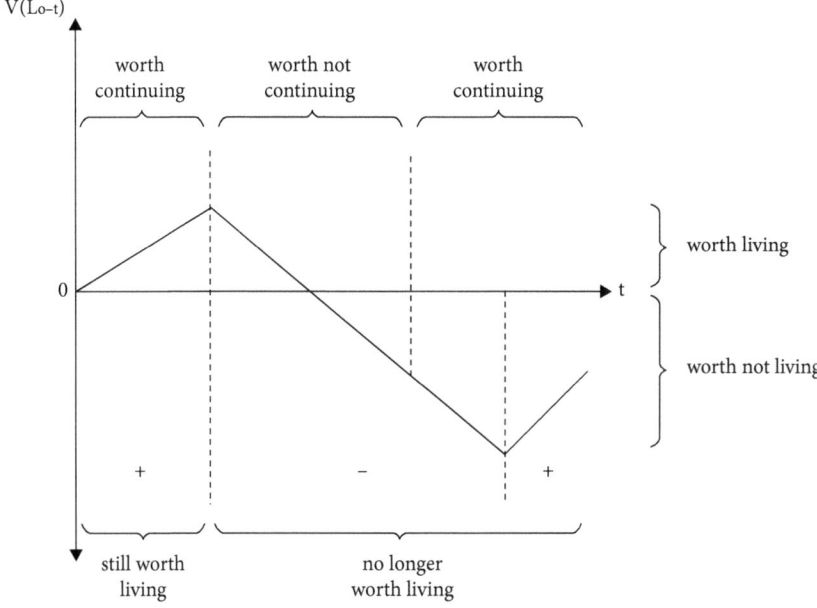

Figure 1.1 Lives No Longer Worth Living

1.2.1.1 Coarse-Grained Options

Given that a life that is worth not living is such that any goodness that accrues whilst it is still worth living will be outweighed by the badness accruing later on, it follows that there exists a sequence of shortenings of the life that has as its limit a situation in which the life is not lived at all, where each of the shortenings is one that makes the life better than the life would be if it were to continue to the end. Each shortening is such that the life lived up to that time is better than the life lived until the end.

The shortening consistency constraint thus only needs to be slightly weakened to preclude the addition of any miserable life (and not only of a restricted range of miserable lives). Rather than assessing whether there is a sequence of shortenings such that for every shortening s there exists a prior shortening s^* that is better than s, one assesses whether every shortening s is better than ϕ, such that there is reason to shorten the life rather than let it continue to the end. Since ψ-ing rather than ϕ-ing amounts to preventing the differences that ϕ-ing makes vis-à-vis ψ-ing from eventuating, one should ψ rather than ϕ, when the differences that ϕ-ing makes are to be cut short at every point of a sequence that has the complete non-occurrence of these effects as its limit rather than be allowed to fully eventuate. Accordingly, one should not add rather than add miserable lives, even when these lives are initially worth living.

Adding a miserable life implies that it exists at some time after t (where t is the boundary on the left of the temporal region of the life). However, for every time t'' after t, there exists a prior time t' (where $t<t'<t''$), at which the life would already have been cut short, since the life up to t' is better than the life lived to the end, thereby ensuring that it cannot exist at t''. Since it is precluded from existing at any time t'' after t, the addition of the life is precluded. Appealing to coarse-grained options, where one can either shorten the life or let it continue until the end but where one cannot decide to let the life continue until some later time at which it stops being worth living, allows one to extend the asymmetry to miserable lives that are worth living up to some point. If we compare a sequence of choices involving coarse-grained options, in which one does not compare different shortenings with each other, but rather compares the different shortenings with the option of letting the life continue to the end, then each choice-situation in the sequence will be such that it will be better to shorten the life than to let it run to the end.[21] Adding a miserable life thus violates the weakened shortening consistency constraint, since one will be required to shorten the life rather than let it continue to the end in each choice-situation, which in the limit amounts to not adding the life.

The weakened consistency constraint ensures that the asymmetry applies to all miserable lives, including those that are worth living up to some point. All miserable lives are such that there is a sequence of shortenings that has the original distribution as its limit and that is such that it is always better to shorten the life than to let it continue to the end. By contrast, any such sequence in the case of happy lives would have as its limit the point after which the life first becomes better than the life lived to the end and hence does not violate the shortening consistency constraint. Accordingly, no miserable lives are to be added, whereas one is to be neutral about adding happy lives.

1.2.1.2 Fine-Grained Asymmetry

Alternatively, one can adopt a fine-grained construal of the asymmetry, according to which the fact that a life is worth not living only provides us with reasons not to extend it beyond the point after which it is no longer worth living but not reasons to not add the life. One should be neutral about adding such lives, but not about extending them beyond the point after which they are no longer worth living. The fact that a life would be miserable does not suffice to speak against adding it, since a miserable life can be worth living up to some point. It is only miserable lives that are never worth living that one has reason not to add at all, since in the case of those lives every point is such that the life is worth not living.

---

[21] Since these different choice situations cannot be faced successively by one agent, they have to be construed counterfactually.

On this construal the asymmetry is not really about miserable lives but about lives that fail to be worth continuing after some point. The limit of the relevant sequence of shortenings will be the point t in the life after which it is no longer worth living. Every point t'' after that point will be such that there is a prior point t' (where $t<t'<t''$) that is such that the life up to t' is better than the life up to t''. What matters for the argument is that there is a point after which things go badly (in the sense that any continuation of the life after that point will have a negative net impact), independently of whether the misery accruing after this point is sufficient to outweigh the initial happiness and thereby make the life miserable on the whole, or whether it merely detracts from the value of the life without making it the case that the life is worth not living. In other words, the issue will be whether the life is still worth living, not whether the life is worth living on the whole. The difference between happy and miserable lives only becomes pronounced in the case of those miserable lives that are never worth living since such lives are not to be added at all, whereas this can never happen when it comes to happy lives since all such lives are such that one should be neutral about adding them (though not about extending them beyond the point after which they are no longer worth living).

1.2.2 Externalities

Discussions of the asymmetry usually hold everything fixed except for the addition of a miserable life. Correspondingly, the principles meant to explain the asymmetry are generally qualified by *ceteris paribus* conditions. Yet, it is not clear how these principles are to be extended to situations in which other things are not equal, for instance situations in which members of the original distribution are positively or negatively affected.

Dealing with these more complicated situations is difficult for theories that bring in deontological resources. They have to treat these deontic considerations as being commensurable with the relevant axiological considerations, so that they can be combined to yield an overall verdict. Appealing to substantive non-axiological resources thus generates problems and complicates the task of integrating the asymmetry into an overall normative theory. The shortening consistency account, by contrast, can be integrated into an overall theory that deals with situations in which *ceteris* is not *paribus*.

Prima facie, the proposed account might seem to consider the reason not to add miserable lives as being absolute, given that this reason is established, not on the basis of the disvalue of the resulting state of affairs, but on the basis of a violation of a consistency constraint. As such, it would seem to classify as a constraint rather than as a *pro tanto* consideration that could be outweighed. Since the reason not to create miserable lives is established by appealing to a consistency constraint, it is unclear what determines the strength of this reason and how it can vary with the degree of miserableness. It is hence unclear how one is to integrate the considerations deriving from the asymmetry with other considerations to end up with an overall verdict that specifies whether one has reason not to add the miserable life.

While the degree of miserableness is not required to establish the asymmetry (since the reasoning equally applies to lives that are only slightly miserable as it does to lives that are extremely miserable), the extent of the miserableness of the lives to be added matters when considering the effects that adding these lives has on other people. In particular, one can consider whether the reason for shortening is sufficiently strong to outweigh any positive externalities that might result from the addition of the miserable life. The question then is whether the good that is done by shortening the miserable life is sufficient for outweighing the positive effects that accrue to others, i.e. whether the amount of suffering prevented by shortening the life is greater than the benefits that accrue to others. The miserableness of the created life thus plays a role in determining how much happiness accruing to others can be outweighed to ensure that shortening is not only better as far as the miserable life is concerned but better all-things-considered.[22,23] When considering not only how much the shortenings improve the miserable life but also taking externalities into consideration, it becomes possible for the reason in favour of shortening to be outweighed. If the benefits are sufficiently significant, then there will not be a violation of the shortening consistency constraint from the perspective of an all-things-considered evaluation. In this way, the reason against adding miserable lives turns out not to be absolute.

If adding a miserable life brings about sufficient benefits to others, then it can turn out that we do not have reason against bringing it into existence. Accordingly, we should be neutral about adding miserable lives with sufficiently large positive externalities. Correspondingly, if adding a happy life brings about sufficient suffering to others, then it can turn out that we do have reason not to bring such a life into existence. This means that we should not be neutral about adding happy lives with large negative externalities. We should not create happy people if the negative effects on others are sufficiently significant.[24] However, it will never be the case that we have reason to extend a distribution because of the additional happiness that results for members of the original distribution. Such happiness only provides reasons when considered from the point of view of those

---

[22] In this context it is important to distinguish between axiologically generated reasons and deontic considerations regarding compensation.

[23] The added happiness to others does not have to result directly from extending the distribution but can be an indirect result or be due to a common cause. (It can even be entirely disconnected, though in such cases it is natural to suppose that the agent faces a further alternative in which this additional disconnected happiness is to be found but which does not include any added lives.)

[24] Given that effects on other people are taken into consideration, this claim conflicts neither with the asymmetry nor with the intuition of neutrality, since they are both restricted claims that abstract from effects on others and consider the added life in isolation.

who are benefitted, but not from the moral point of view that takes everyone into consideration.

1.2.3 Adding Groups

When considering adding groups of people, one needs to find a way for the happiness of happy lives to weigh against the misery of miserable lives. Otherwise, one miserable life would be sufficient for making the addition of any group of people morally problematic, no matter how many happy lives this group should contain. The happiness of those whose lives will be worth living must be able to neutralize the reason not to add the group deriving from the miserable life (cf. Sikora: 1978, p. 137).

The shortening consistency account can achieve this result by assessing whether it would be better if the miserable life were shortened, even if there were to be a corresponding shortening of the other lives being added. If there is a sequence of combined shortenings of the different lives that has the original distribution as its limit and that is such that each shortening makes the lives considered collectively better, as happens for instance when one is faced with the option of adding twins one of whom will be highly miserable while the other will only be moderately happy, then the shortening consistency condition implies that one should not bring this group into existence.[25] By contrast, if the happy lives being added contain sufficient happiness to outweigh the misery to be found in the miserable lives, then there will not be such a sequence of shortenings.

1.2.4 Probabilistic Cases

In the context of certainty, a unique outcome is associated with each alternative. When dealing with uncertainty, a number of possible outcomes can result from a particular action. The question then is what happens when there is a likelihood that ϕ-ing will result in the addition of a life that is worth not living. Under what conditions are there reasons against performing actions that have a chance of bringing about miserable lives? What is needed, in particular, is an account that can explain how the possibility of a life being happy can cancel out or weigh against the possibility of a life being miserable, in order to avoid the unpalatable commitment that any non-zero probability of a life being miserable would be sufficient to generate (overall) reasons against bringing it into existence.

---

[25] If the combined shortenings are defined in relative terms, e.g. where shortening s_n involves each of the added lives $L_1, L_2 \ldots$ being shortened to $\frac{L_i}{2^n}$, then all the comparisons amongst the members of the sequence of shortenings will be same-number (in fact same-people) comparisons.

Whilst cases of uncertainty pose difficulties for deontic asymmetries invoking rights- or justice-based considerations, given that we lack a clear account of the conditions under which the imposition of a risk amounts to a rights-violation, the shortening consistency account does not run into difficulties. The explanation of the asymmetry applies equally when working with expected value.

When acting under uncertainty, the question is whether shortening the life is expected to make things better such that one has reason to commit to shorten the life. This can be established by comparing the expected outcome with shortening to the expected outcome without shortening.[26] One has to evaluate whether for every time t, there is a prior time t', such that the expected value of the life up to t' is greater than the expected value up to t, i.e. whether $EV(L_{0-t'}) > EV(L_{0-t})$. In this way, one can apply the consistency principle to the expected value of shortenings of the life. In the case of uncertainty, the consistency constraint has to be understood, not in terms of shortenings that will make the life better, but instead in terms of shortenings that are expected to make the life better (and to which an agent who is fully responsive to reasons would make an *ex ante* commitment). Rather than assessing the shortenings that would make the life better, one assesses the shortenings that one has reason to commit oneself to performing to see whether they jointly preclude the addition of the life.

There are two ways of aggregating probabilistically discounted evaluations of the different possibilities to determine the expected value of shortenings of a life.

1.2.4.1 Time-Slice Aggregation

First one aggregates across states of nature and then across time. One determines the expected temporal well-being at different times and then aggregates these to arrive at the expected lifetime well-being (up to time t).

$$EV(L_{0-t}) = \sum_{0<j\leq t} EV(L_j) = \sum_{0<j\leq t} \sum_{i\in N} p_i \times V(L_j^i)$$

Time-slice aggregation runs into difficulties.

1. This way of aggregating presupposes the separability of times and hence precludes holistic evaluations of the value of lives.

   It might be suggested that one can apply a holistic value function to the expected time-slice profile, such that $EV(L_{0-t})$ is not determined by simply summing the expected time-slice values between 0 and t, but instead is determined by $f[EV(L_i)$ for all $i \in 0<i\leq t]$, where f is some non-separable holistic aggregation function. This, however, generates wrong results since

---

[26] The different shortenings can be characterized either in terms of absolute units, i.e. shorten after n units, or in terms of proportions relative to the longest life, i.e. shorten at $\frac{L}{n}$.

the holistic function is to be applied to the well-being profiles in particular states of nature. It is not the expected shape of the life that matters but the various possible shapes that the life can have in the various states of nature. For instance, if evenness matters, then (other things being equal) one should prefer a lottery over even distributions to a lottery over distributions that are uneven but that are such that the unevenness is cancelled out in the process of aggregation so that the expected shape of the life is even. This happens for instance in the case of a lottery with a 50% chance of a constantly increasing life and a 50% chance of a mirror-reversed constantly decreasing life. In this kind of case, one knows that the latter lottery will result in an uneven distribution and that one will consequently not get evenness, despite the expected time-slice profile being even.

2. This account cannot handle lives of different lengths. It leads to non-comparability since L_j will not be defined if L does not exist at time j. This, in turn, precludes aggregation, insofar as $\sum p_i \times V(L_j^i)$ will not be defined if not all of the states of nature contain a life that exists at j.

1.2.4.2 Initial-Segment Aggregation

One aggregates first across time and then across states of nature. One determines lifetime well-being (up to t) in the various states of nature and then aggregates their probabilistically discounted values.

$$EV(L_{0-t}) = \sum_{i \in N} p_i \times V(L_{0-t}^i)$$

The expected value of the life up to t is given by the aggregate of the probabilistically discounted values of the life in the various states of nature.[27] This account does not presuppose the separability of times. The value function applied to initial segments of the life can fail to be separable across times. Nor does it run into difficulties when the lives of the added person are of different lengths in different states of nature. Lifetime well-being up to t, i.e. L_{0-t}, is defined even if the life ceases to exist at some prior time $t'<t$. Accordingly, we need to aggregate probabilistically discounted lifetime well-being, rather than aggregate expected time-slice well-being.

1.2.4.3 Different-Number Cases

The account can straightforwardly deal with same-number cases, where one is adding a life (or a set of lives) such that it is a matter of chance whether it (or they)

---

[27] This account assumes that states-of-nature are separable. Whilst the independence axiom is plausible, one can build in a non-separable aggregation function over states of nature, i.e. $EV(L_{0-t}) = f[p_1 V(L_{0-t}^1), \ldots, p_n V(L_{0-t}^n)]$.

will be worth not living.[28] Difficulties arise in different-number cases, when it is a matter of chance how many (if any) people will come into existence whose lives will be worth not living, i.e. the different possibilities associated with a particular action involve different numbers of people.

Probabilistic cases involving different numbers seem to require aggregating non-equinumerous distributions. This, however, cannot be done by means of balancing (the aggregative procedure compatible with person-affecting views) since there will not be a bijective mapping with respect to which gains and losses are defined. Accordingly, the expected value of the distribution under various shortenings will not be defined for different-number cases and one cannot assess whether shortening is expected to make things better.

Although we cannot aggregate all the possible distributions associated with a particular risky action, we can supervaluate over them. If every possible distribution resulting from an action is such that it should not be brought about, then the action should not be performed. Moreover, we can partition the possible distributions into equivalence classes and then aggregate probabilistically discounted equinumerous distributions. If every equivalence class of possible distributions resulting from an action is such that it should not be brought about, then the action should not be performed.

Mixed cases, where some classes are neutral and others generate reasons against extending the distribution, are more difficult. The question then is whether some equivalence class being such that there is reason against it being brought about is sufficient for ruling out that action. Neither possibility is satisfactory. Either there being some equivalence class suffices for ruling out the action, in which case any non-zero chance of there being miserable lives that are non-comparable with the other possible outcomes will render an action impermissible, thereby over-generating reasons against extending the distribution. Or it does not suffice and instead all equivalence classes have to satisfy this condition, in which case any chance, no matter how small, of there being a number of happy lives that is non-comparable with the other possible outcomes will render an action permissible, thereby under-generating reasons against extending the distribution.

The question that needs to be addressed is whether one has reason to commit to shorten at *t* if there is a chance that it will make things better and a chance that it will make things worse, whereby the distributions with respect to which these betterness judgements are made cannot be aggregated. To answer this question one has to determine how strong the reason is to shorten, i.e. by how much shortening is expected to make things better in the states of nature in which a

---

[28] Given a commitment to impartiality, all that matters is the number of lives that are being added and not their identities. This means that the account can deal with cases, in which it is certain that one person will be brought into existence as a result of a particular action, but where it is uncertain whether it will be x or y that will be added, since one can abstract from the identity of the person.

distribution of size m will result, and how strong the reason is not to shorten, i.e. by how much shortening is expected to make things worse in the states of nature resulting in a distribution of size n. Whether one should commit to shorten depends on the comparative strength of these reasons.

For instance, an idealized agent would make an *ex ante* commitment to shorten at t' in a mixed case involving both m-sized distributions where shortening is expected to make things better and n-sized distributions where it is expected to make things worse if $EV(D_{0-t'}^m) - EV(D_{0-t}^m) > |EV(D_{0-t'}^n) - EV(D_{0-t}^n)|$. This comparison only involves value-differences. Even though m-sized distributions are not comparable to n-sized distributions, differences between m-sized distributions can be compared to differences between n-sized distributions. Such comparisons do not require different-number comparability. Even though it does not make sense to ask in mixed cases whether the distribution is expected to be better as a result of shortening, one can ask whether the *ex ante* reasons in favour of shortening are stronger than those against.

1.2.5 Absolute Harm

The degree of miserableness also matters when evaluating the extent to which the miserable person has been harmed by having been brought into existence. The notion of harm here is that of absolute rather than comparative harm. This means that the baseline with respect to which harm is determined is specified in terms of an absolute parameter, namely that of a neutral life, and not relative to other possibilities, such as the counterfactual scenario that would have obtained otherwise. The baseline is a normative baseline since it is specified in terms of what the agent has reason to do, in particular what actions the agent has reason to abstain from performing, i.e. what kind of life (namely a miserable life) the agent should not bring into existence. The distance from the normative baseline, and hence the degree of harm, is determined by the strength of the reason the agent had for not bringing about the relevant state of affairs. In other words, the person whose life is miserable has been harmed by having been brought into existence, not insofar as that person has been made worse off relative to non-existence (or relative to some other alternative), but insofar as that person has been put into a state that the agent had reason to not bring into existence (where the strength of the reason corresponds to the degree of miserableness).[29]

---

[29] This notion of absolute harm can be used to make sense of compensation, such that compensating someone for having been brought into existence with a miserable life does not amount to bringing about the status quo *ex ante* where the person did not exist, but instead amounts to undoing the absolute harm that was imposed on them.

This account makes room for non-comparative harms, without there being any non-comparative benefits. The normative baseline is one-sided due to the asymmetry. One is harmed by being brought into existence if one ends up below the baseline, whereas one is not benefitted by being brought into existence if one ends up above the baseline. The baseline is one-sided because there is a level, namely that of a neutral life, that is such that no one should be below that level, i.e. bringing someone into existence who is below that level amounts to acting in a way that is contrary to what one has reason to do. This ensures that anyone whose life is miserable (and hence below the level of a neutral life) is harmed by being brought into existence.[30] Yet, there is no level such that everyone (speaking with a possibilist quantifier) should be at or above that level, which implies that no one can be benefitted by being brought into existence. Bringing someone into existence who has a happy life does not constitute a case of doing something that one has reason to do, but merely classifies as a case of not doing something one has reason not to do.[31,32]

1.3 Conclusion

In the context of a person-affecting approach, the non-comparability of existence with non-existence implies that the fact that a life would be worth living does not give us reasons to bring it into existence. Instead, there are only reasons to improve a life on condition that its existence is given. Since paradigmatically miserable lives are such that they are better the shorter they are, there will be an ordering of shortenings of these lives that is such that, in the limit, they are not lived at all. Bringing these lives into existence, accordingly, violates the shortening consistency constraint. As a result, we have reason not to do so. By contrast, no

---

[30] In probabilistic cases in which it is uncertain whether the life will be lived, i.e. where the life is only to be found in some but not all states of nature, the evaluation of the extent of harm has to be restricted to those states of nature in which the life in question exists, given that the notion of harming is a strong person-affecting notion. This implies that the reason that the agent has to not bring x into existence is a function of the states of nature in which x exists and corresponds to the expected value of x's life.

[31] It might be objected that there cannot be absolute harms without absolute benefits, since not harming someone amounts to benefitting that person. However, failing to subject someone to this type of absolute harm amounts to either failing to create a miserable life by not bringing that person into existence, in which case no one is benefitted since there is no one who can be benefitted (i.e. the subject is missing), or to creating a happy life in which case no one is benefitted in absolute terms since the baseline is one-sided.

[32] If the life that is brought into existence features in several (but not all) alternatives, then the notion of comparative benefit/harm will also be applicable. In such cases, it makes sense to say that x was comparatively benefitted/harmed by being brought into existence in one way rather than another. Here, it is not the absolute level of well-being (whether the life is a happy life or a miserable life) that matters, but the comparative facts. If an agent can either add a life such that the life is slightly miserable or such that it is highly miserable, then bringing about the former possibility classifies as a comparative benefit relative to the latter possibility, but as neither a comparative benefit nor comparative harm relative to the possibility of not bringing the life into existence at all.

violation of this constraint is involved in adding happy lives, which means that there is no reason not to do so. The asymmetry is thus explained on the basis that the fact that an action violates a consistency constraint renders that action inadmissible and gives us reason not to perform it, whereas the fact that an action satisfies a consistency constraint does not give us any reason to perform that action, but merely makes it the case that it is an admissible action.[33]

References

Arntzenius, F., and McCarthy, D. The two envelope paradox and infinite expectations. *Analysis* 57, 1 (1997), 42–50.

Barrett, J., and Arntzenius, F. An infinite decision puzzle. *Theory and Decision* 46 (1999), 101–3.

Heyd, D. *Genethics—Moral Issues in the Creation of People*. University of California Press, 1992.

McMahan, J. Asymmetries in the morality of causing people to exist. In *Harming Future Persons*, M. Roberts and D. Wasserman, Eds. Springer, 2009, pp. 49–68.

McMahan, J. Causing people to exist and saving people's lives. *Journal of Ethics* 17 (2013), 5–35.

Narveson, J. Moral problems of population. *The Monist* 57, 1 (1973), 62–86.

Parfit, D. *Reasons and Persons*. Oxford University Press, 1984.

Scott, M., and Scott, A. Infinite exchange problems. *Theory and Decision* 57 (2005), 397–406.

Sikora, R. I. Is it wrong to prevent the existence of future generations? In *Obligations to Future Generations*, R. I. Sikora and B. Barry, Eds. Temple University Press, 1978, pp. 112–66.

---

[33] For helpful comments I would like to thank Dan Halliday, Johan Gustafsson, Kacper Kowalczyk, Theron Pummer, Johann Frick, and especially Tim Campbell as well as audiences at the Conference in Honour of Derek Parfit at the University of Oxford, the Merton Workshop on Applied Formal Ethics, the New Scholarship in Population Ethics conference at Duke University, as well as at Stockholm University and the University of York.

2
The Value and Probabilities of Existence

M. A. Roberts

2.1 Introduction

Is there value, *moral* value, in the existence of the additional happy person? Does the existence of the additional happy person make things *morally* better?

In asking the question, we assume that other things are equal—that we are in a case where neither the happiness nor the existence of anyone else is at stake. And we stipulate that to say a person is *happy* at a given world, outcome, or (I will say) *future* is shorthand for saying that that person at that future has a positive *wellbeing* level, leaving open, for purposes here, whether *wellbeing* itself is a positive, felt emotion (pleasure or happiness) or a capability to achieve certain functionings or something else entirely.[1]

The question is one of the great, unsettled questions of population ethics. But it's fair to say that many people find the idea that, other things being equal, there *isn't* any moral value in the existence of the additional happy person—the idea that the additional existence *doesn't*, on its own, make things morally better—compelling. They very much *want* to accept—though may feel, in the end, constrained *not* to accept—that *Existence Is Not a Moral Plus* (ENMP).

> Existence Not a Moral Plus (ENMP): Other things being equal, the addition of an existence worth having doesn't make a future better or convert an otherwise wrong choice into a permissible choice or an otherwise merely permissible choice into an obligatory choice.

Many people, that is, agree with Narveson: while moral law pushes us to *make people happy*, it's completely "neutral about *making happy people.*"[2]

Is ENMP a matter of *intuition*? Or does it just reflect the realization, thanks to Derek Parfit, that we get into a lot of trouble[3] when we take the position that, even

---

[1] By "wellbeing," I mean *raw* wellbeing, *unadjusted* for such values as justice, equality, priority, or fairness, or for any *existential* values that we may happen share. The *existential* values I have in mind include those laid out in the few paragraphs following this note.

[2] Narveson 1976, 73 (emphasis added).

[3] Even the more modest position—that the additional worth-having existence, other things being equal, doesn't make things worse—generates substantial difficulties. Here, I am thinking of the Repugnant Conclusion and the Mere Addition Paradox. Parfit 1987, 381–90 and 419–41.

when other things are equal, the additional happy existence *does* make things morally better?

It's not clear. In any case, ENMP itself is widely considered to be rooted in what Parfit called the *Person Affecting* or (I will say) *Person Based Intuition (PBI)*. We shall start off here with an incomplete, elliptical version of that principle since only later in the discussion will we find any clear direction as to how the ellipsis itself needs to be completed.[4]

> *Person Based Intuition (PBI) (elliptical version):* Where x and y are possible futures and y is accessible relative to x, x is *morally worse* than y, and a choice made at x *morally wrong, only if* x is *worse for* a person who *does or will exist* in x than _____ .

A future that makes things worse for a person—reduces, that is, a person's well-being level—*by way of* leaving that person out of existence altogether isn't, on those grounds alone, made worse than any other future. Thus ENMP.

The obvious plus of PBI—and ENMP—is that it tells us that there is no moral advantage to be gained in chasing around trying to bring additional happy people into existence when people who already exist, or people who will in the future exist, sorely need our help. Nor can we make up for the misery we have imposed on a person down the street or on the other side of the planet by simply bringing a new happy person into existence.

For purposes here, I take it for granted that PBI and ENMP themselves represent strongly held, widely shared intuitions.[5] But, as noted earlier, many philosophers who share those intuitions nonetheless have felt constrained for one reason or another to reject PBI. Parfit's close examination of PBI—which has left us not just with nonidentity problems of various sorts but also with problems relating to money pumps and the procreative asymmetry—has been critical here.[6]

---

[4] The elliptical version of the PBI that I introduce here is my own take on one of Parfit's most well-known statements of the intuition, that is, "what is bad must be bad for someone." Parfit 1987, 363 (emphasis deleted). See also Parfit 2017, 118–19. My version is *explicitly* elliptical; we'll need to say *just which alternate accessible future* is to go in the blank. (Just to note: it seems likely that Parfit himself believed that how the ellipsis is to be filled in was obvious and thus felt no pressure to spell things out.)
 The *accessibility* relation, critical to any credible formulation of PBI, is introduced in section 2.2.
 I have argued elsewhere that there is no reason to think that PBI commits us to *moral actualism*, a view that, in both its forms, seems clearly false. Roberts 2007, 2009, 2011a, and 2011b; see Hare 2007. Thus, PBI does not imply, and should not be understood to imply, that *only* people who do or will exist in the *actual* future, or *only* people who do or will exist *under the choice under scrutiny*, have moral status.

[5] My own view is that PBI, when properly formulated, in fact *does* represent a strongly held, widely shared intuition. But I also think that PBI is often *not* formulated with an eye to avoiding pitfalls that at this point are well-known. See sections 2.3.1 and 2.3.2.

[6] Parfit 2011, 217–31. Problems relating to money pumps arise under formulations of PBI that generate a betterness relation between possible futures that fails to conform with the demands of transitivity. The problem of "the asymmetry," first articulated by McMahan 1981 (see also McMahan 2009), arises by implication from still other formulations of PBI.

My own view has been that what are often thought of as *problems* requiring us to *reject* PBI can be reconstructed as *puzzles* susceptible to *solutions*—puzzles that we can *actually solve*; solve, that is, *without* discarding any of the puzzle pieces—that go into the construction of those puzzles.[7]

It may seem, however, that there's little room for optimism. For the moment we think we have gained the sort of clarity in connection with the *existential values* that ENMP and PBI reflect—the sort of clarity that enables us tidily to solve one puzzle or another—we almost immediately come to understand that still other puzzles, other problems, other obstacles, loom before us. We almost immediately come to understand that our existential values are, at best, far more interestingly complex than we may have thought.

And thus the dual goals of this chapter: to add one more obstacle to the long list of obstacles PBI has been asked to surmount—one that I shall (optimistically) articulate as a *puzzle*, the *Better Chance Puzzle*—which puzzle I shall then attempt to solve.

The puzzle commences with PBI and ENMP, which tell us that the existence of the additional happy person doesn't, other things being equal, make things morally better. However, as the cases will show, we are also compelled to accept what I will call the *Better Chance Claim*: the highly intuitive idea that a better *chance* of existence in some cases *incontrovertibly* makes things, in some sense, morally better. And that's, in short, the puzzle: we have now said that the better *chance* of existence can make things morally better *and* that the actual *fact* of existence is capable of no such thing. But if the better *chance* of existence can make things morally better, then how can the actual *fact* of existence *not*, and even more clearly, make things morally better as well? To *actually solve* the puzzle—to solve the puzzle *without* simply discarding any of the puzzle pieces—is to come to understand just how both strongly held, widely shared intuitions can be true.

2.2 Notes on Figures, Assumptions, Vocabulary

In what follows, the figures I will make reference to display (i) all available choices (c1, c2, etc.), (ii) all possible worlds, outcomes or (I will say) *futures* (f1, f2, etc.) that *accessibly* might arise out of each of those choices, and (iii) the probability (calculated just prior to choice on the basis of information available to agents at that time) that a future will arise under a given choice. Here, *accessibility* is a matter of what the agents, consistent with the laws of nature, logic, and so on, have the ability, power, or resources to bring about.[8] The future in which agents open

---

[7] For a brief discussion of the most challenging form of the non-identity problem, see section 2.6. See also Roberts 2007, 2009, 2011a, 2011b, 2020, 2022a, 2022b; Roberts and Wasserman 2017.

[8] To make certain that we for purposes here set aside still another set of challenging problems, specifically, problems relating to *collective action*, we should understand that the fact that agents *together* (whether they coordinate or collaborate with each other or not) having the ability, power, and resources to bring a given future about is sufficient to determine that that future is *accessible*.

the combination lock even without advance knowledge of what that combination happens to be is perfectly *accessible* (if improbable) while the future in which agents open the combination lock that has previously been welded shut and rendered impenetrable to human hands alone is plausibly not.

The figures also show people who do or will exist in a given future (those people's names are shown in bold) and people who will never exist in a given future (their names are shown in italics with an asterisk) as well as the wellbeing levels for each such person. To say that one future is *worse for* a person than another is to say that that person has *less wellbeing* in the one future than in the other. For purposes here, I assume *Nonexistence Comparability*, that is, that futures in which a person does or will exist can be better for—or, in other cases, worse for—that person than futures in which that person never exists at all.[9] The figures needn't be understood to show *each* person who does or will exist in each future. They just show those people who stand to be affected—*including* by way of coming into existence—by how the choice under scrutiny is made.

I use the term *person* to include many but not all human beings as well as many nonhuman animals.[10] Consciousness, or at least sentience, would be key here. The organism that may one day develop into a conscious being is not, on this view, itself a *person*. Live human body notwithstanding, the *person* that may eventually be properly associated with that body does not itself exist until consciousness emerges.[11]

One last point. This chapter is concerned both with the comparison, or ranking, of distinct futures in terms of their overall moral betterness and with the evaluation of the choices that give rise to those futures, with it generally being understood that the *telic* project and the *deontic* project are connected in some interesting and significant way—though not (as we shall see) *perfectly*. Thus my unqualified references to *betterness* between futures should be understood throughout as references to *moral* betterness: the sort of betterness between futures that at least has some potential for helping us figure out whether a given choice is permissible, obligatory, or wrong.

2.3 Commitments

Before turning to the Better Chance Puzzle itself, it is critical to clarify the commitments that ENMP and PBI require of us. We can't be expected to solve

---

[9] This assumption is somewhat controversial. See Bader, this volume (arguing that "[o]ne situation can be better for [a person] than another situation only if [that person] exists in both situations, and that, when "comparing existence with nonexistence, one of the two relata is missing, which ensures that the relation cannot apply"). I have elsewhere argued that the relevant comparative claims are both cogent and meaningful. See, e.g., Roberts 2011a, 2011b, 2022b (the fact that the person does or will exist in one of the two futures is sufficient to secure reference; we can say that *that* person is such that the future in which *that* person never exists holds no value at all, the equivalent of zero value, for that person; if the concern is that speakers within the future in which the person never exists can't properly *name* that person, those speakers can surely find other ways to talk about that person should the need arise).

[10] Singer 2011, 48–70.   [11] Roberts 2010.

the puzzle if we don't have a clear picture of the puzzle pieces themselves. Here, the great debt is owed to Parfit who, along with a handful of other philosophers,[12] has worked to identify the pitfalls any attempt to articulate a PBI-inspired array of existential values will need to avoid.

2.3.1 The Miserable Child Case: Why PBI Must Be *Very Narrowly Formulated*

The first thing to note is what ENMP and PBI *don't* instruct. They *don't* tell us that existence can't make things *worse*. They tell us *only* that existence can't make things *better*.

In that connection, we need to recognize two ways in which existence can make things morally worse. First, agents, other things being equal, make things worse when they bring a child into existence whose life is *less* than worth having—when they, that is, bring the thoroughly miserable child into existence (Figure 2.1). It's hard to fathom how that claim can plausibly be denied.[13]

In this case (Figure 2.1), Ann has no wellbeing at all in f1—she sustains no burdens, accrues no benefits—where she never exists and has a negative wellbeing level—a miserable life—in f2 where she does exist. The probability that f1 will arise given c1 is exactly 1, ditto for f2 given c2.[14]

	choice c1	choice c2
probability of future, given choice	1	1
	future f1	future f2
+0	*Ann**	
. . .		
-10		**Ann**

Figure 2.1 Miserable Child Case

[12] Other than Parfit's own work, the work of John Broome, Jeff McMahan, Peter Singer, and Larry Temkin has been especially critical here. I discuss the points regarding formulation made in this Section 2.3 in more detail in Roberts 2015.

[13] But see David Heyd, who argues that the combination of a person based approach and the position that a world in which a given person never exists (as a conceptual or logical matter) cannot be better (or worse) for that person compels us to accept that it doesn't make things worse, and indeed is permissible, to bring the miserable person into existence. Heyd 1992, 2009. But see note 9 above.

[14] That the probability is exactly one that any single future—where a future is just a world in all its detail going forward out of a particular history—isn't very realistic but it's a stipulation of the case.

To *both* say what we clearly need to say about this case—that f2 is morally worse than f1 and that c2 is wrong—*and* at the same time retain PBI, we must keep in mind that the principle requires, as a necessary condition on when a future is worse, that that future makes things worse for a person who does or will exist in that future. We must keep in mind, in other words, that PBI itself is *very narrowly drawn*. (The quite natural, if elliptical, version of PBI provided in section 2.2 above gets that much right.) Now, we'll also be able to articulate various person based necessary conditions on a future's being made *better*. Consider, for example, the following:[15]

> Where x and y are possible futures and x is accessible relative to y, x is *morally better* than y *only if* _____ is better for a person who *does or will exist* in y than y.

But notably that person based condition on *betterness* doesn't *mechanically* track our earlier person based condition on *worseness*. And indeed it *can't, if we want to retain the force of the original intuition*—retain, that is, the idea that it doesn't make things worse, and is permissible, to leave a person out of existence altogether. Why is that? Let's go back to the Miserable Child Case. The principle that *mechanically* tracks our earlier necessary condition on worseness would, I take it, look like this: one future is better than a second, only if that one future makes things better for a person who does or will exist in that one future than _____ does. Since Ann *never exists* in f1, such a principle would imply that f1 *isn't* better than f2. But that result seems clearly false; it seems *clearly* the case that f1 is better than f2. And there is no reason for us to adopt a principle, as a person based necessary condition on betterness, that would say otherwise. We have no reason to think we must *mechanically track* our earlier necessary condition on *worseness* when we turn to articulate a necessary condition on *betterness*; we have no reason to "read into" the person based view a principle that would generate clearly false results in that most basic of cases.[16]

2.3.2 The Three Outcome Case

A more contentious case is the *Three Outcome Case* (Figure 2.2).[17]

---

[15] This principle follows from the person based necessary condition on worseness just stated by virtue of the conceptual truth that, for any futures x and y, to say that y is morally *worse* than x is to say that x is morally *better* than y.

[16] My own understanding of the intuition itself is thus very different from that of many other philosophers who have simply taken it for granted that Parfit's "a bad act [one that makes things worse] must be bad for [make things worse for] someone [who does or will exist]" can be extended to "a good act [one that makes things better] must be good for [make things better for] someone [who does or will exist]."

[17] This case is John Broome's. See Broome 2004, 146–9.

	choice c1	choice c2	choice c3
probability of future, given choice	1	1	1
	future f1	future f2	future f3
+10			**Ben**
+5		**Ben**	
+0	Ben*		

Figure 2.2 Three Outcome Case

Here, Ben never exists in f1 under c1, exists and is pretty well off in f2 under c2, and exists and is better off still in f3 under c3.[18]

The Three Outcome Case helps us to see that any plausible person based theory will need to accept that the existence of the additional *happy* person—just like the existence of the additional *miserable* person—can, on some occasions, make things morally *worse*. Thus we retain ENMP: the worth-having existence, other things being equal, doesn't make things *better*. But we also accept that the worth-having existence, even when other things *are* equal, can make things *worse*—that is, that *Existence Can Be a Moral Minus* (*ECMM*).

Why is that? Why is it that, if we want to say that Ben's worth-having existence in f2 *doesn't* make things *better*, we must also say that Ben's worth-having existence in f2 *does* make things *worse*—not just worse than they are in *f3* (that much is obvious) but also worse than they are in *f1*. I credit the logic that answers that question to John Broome, though I am now redirecting that logic to show that—in the context of the particular case, the Three Outcome Case—f2 is worse than f1.[19] We will assume for *reductio* (in line (1) below) that f2 is at least as good as f1. Familiar and hard to deny conceptual principles[20] combined with that assumption, PBI, and a highly restricted Pareto principle (what we will call the

---

[18] Ben has, in other words, an unambiguously positive wellbeing level in f2, a wellbeing level clearly above any threshold or minimal acceptable wellbeing level, and has a higher wellbeing still in f3. Per Nonexistence Comparability, Ben has no wellbeing at all in f1—the functional equivalent of a *zero* wellbeing level in f1—where he never exists at all. That makes each of f2 and f3 better for Ben than f1.

[19] Here I refer to Broome's argument against what he calls the *neutrality intuition*. Broome 2004, 143–9.

[20] The conceptual principles put to work in this chapter include the following: for any futures x, y, and z, if x is morally at least as good as y and y is morally at least as good as x, then x is morally exactly as good as y; if x is morally exactly as good as y, then y is morally exactly as good as x; if x isn't worse than y, then y is at least as good as x; and if x is morally exactly as good as y and y is morally exactly as good as z, then x is morally exactly as good as z. Temkin has argued that at least some of these principles, translated to apply to *all things considered* betterness (which, arguably, may not be the same relation as *moral* betterness), produce controversial results in some cases, e.g., the spectrum cases and the mere addition paradox. Temkin 2012, 162–231. The cases of concern in this present chapter,

Same People Pareto Principle, applicable only when the futures to be compared contain exactly the same people[21]) generate an inconsistency (between lines (7) and (8)). And we conclude (in line (9)) that our assumption (in line (1)) was false. Thus:

1. f2 is at least as good as f1.   Assume for *reductio*
2. f1 at least as good as f2.   ENMP, from PBI
3. f1 is exactly as good as f2.   1, 2, conceptual principles
4. f3 is at least as good as f1.   PBI[22]
5. f1 is at least as good as f3.   ENMP, from PBI
6. f1 is exactly as good as f3.   4, 5, conceptual principles
7. f2 is exactly as good as f3.   3, 6, conceptual principles
8. But f3 is better than f2.   Same People Pareto Principle
9. f2 is worse than f1.   *Reductio*, 1, 7, 8

Now, at first glance, (9) might seem startling. It might seem that, when the only distinction between one future and a second is the addition of an existence that is itself worth having, that addition—that *mere* addition—can't make the second future *worse* than the first.[23]

---

however, do not seem to press us to deny any of the conceptual principles just noted—or force us to exchange a tripartite betterness relation of the sort described here for a relation that includes the options of *rough comparability* or *parity*.

[21] The uncontroversial Same People Pareto Principle, assumed for purposes here, states that, where two futures contain exactly the same people, and the second future makes things better for one person, and worse for no one, than the first future, then the second future is better than the first future. If we assume that the telic and deontic projects are *perfectly* connected, we would also say that it would be wrong to make the choice that gives rise to the first future. In many cases, including the case at hand, that inference will hold. But in cases involving probabilities—as we shall see—it may fail. See section 2.7.3.

[22] PBI implies both that f1 is at least as good as f3 (since no one who does or will exist in f1 is made worse off) and that f3 is at least as good as f1 (since each person who does or will exist in f3 is such that there exists no further future that makes any such person any better off). PBI thus includes a certain "*anti*-anti-natalist" component.

[23] This is a formulation of the widely accepted *Mere Addition Principle*. Parfit RP, 419–41. If (9) is true, then the Mere Addition Principle must be false. James Goodrich points out that one might think that, the Mere Addition Principle itself being clearly *true*, we can reverse the *reductio* to show that the PBI is false. Indeed we could. For purposes here, however, I won't try to battle intuition. I will just note that the Mere Addition Principle is a far stronger claim than it seems on its face to be. Thus if we do reverse the *reductio*, all we will have shown is that to say that mere addition *doesn't* make things *worse* is also to say that that same mere addition *does* make things *better* (is also to say, that is, that PBI is false). That, in itself, means the Mere Addition Principle in effect begs the question against PBI. Moreover, the idea that mere addition can—*can*, in some cases—make things worse on closer inspection *does* comport nicely with at least some of our intuitions. If we think our ranking of futures in terms of their overall betterness is itself foundational for purposes of determining what we ought to do (if we think the telic and deontic projects, that is, are closely connected), then a ranking that makes f1 exactly as good as f3 and f2 worse than both would mean that the choices that lead, respectively, to f1 and f3 are themselves perfectly permissible while the choice that leads to f2 is wrong. In other words: we aren't, other things being equal, obligated to bring new people into existence, but if we do bring them into existence, it would be wrong for us, other things being equal, to make things worse rather than better for them when we can. That seems an intuitive point—and is indeed reflected in PBI.

My view, however, is that the result that the additional worth-having existence *can*, even when, as here, other things are equal, make things worse should not, on further scrutiny, seem implausible or unwelcome at all, in view of the profound obstacles that we set for ourselves when we uncritically accept the deceptively modest, simple idea that *mere addition* can't make things *worse*. The better view is that it can, at least on some occasions, make things morally worse. When we bring a new person into a worth-having existence, what we've done doesn't *automatically* make things morally worse and is not *automatically* morally wrong. However, in any future in which we bring such a new person into a worth-having existence *and* make things worse for that person when we accessibly could have made things better for that person at no cost to anyone else at all, bringing that new person into existence *does* make things morally worse and *is* morally wrong.

2.3.3 Objection: Why PBI Must Be Understood as *Expansive*

It might be objected that the above argument takes as an *assumption* (for purposes of *reductio*) what is in effect an *implication* of PBI. The idea here would be that, there existing no one in f2 such that f2 is worse for that person *than f1 is*, PBI itself implies that f2 isn't worse than f1—that f2 is instead (as line (1) asserts) at least as good as f1. To put the point another way: it might be objected that, while we avoid one inconsistency by accepting that f2 *is* worse than f1—by accepting, that is, the conclusion (9)—we are then but a step or two away from still another inconsistency since PBI itself instructs that f2 *isn't* worse than f1. And that inconsistency is one that we can in the end avoid only by rejecting PBI itself.

But that objection takes for granted a certain formulation of PBI that we need to examine closely. It takes for granted that the ellipsis in our original statement of PBI is to be completed in a certain way: in a *blindered* way that leaves us with a principle that allows us, for purposes of comparing f1 against f2, to consider *only* the options available to Ben in f1 and f2 and thus immediately instructs that f2 isn't worse than f1.

But on close examination that's not the right way to complete the ellipsis. We should instead take the blinders off and opt for a more *expansive* approach. We should say that f2 is worse than f1, not in virtue of the fact that f2 is worse for Ben than *f1* is (it isn't), but in virtue of the fact that f2 is worse for Ben than *f3* is. The thought here is this. What makes f2 worse than f1 is that it's *avoidably* worse for a person who does or will exist in f2. And whether things are made *avoidably* worse for a given person in a given future can obviously not be determined by a simple pairwise comparison of that future against any *one* other alternate future. The determination of when a future is *avoidably* worse for a given person requires a more *expansive* inquiry. To determine whether a future x is avoidably worse for a given person than a future y, one must take into account what is going on with that person, not just at y, but also at each and every further future z that exists as an *accessible* future relative to x.[24]

Once we understand PBI to require that unblindered, more expansive inquiry before it generates any result at all, we see that the inference from PBI to the result that f2 is at least as good as f1 is blocked. And once that inference is blocked, the door is open for the result that f2 is worse than f1, not in virtue of the fact that f2 is worse for Ben than *f1* is, but rather in virtue of the fact that f2 is worse for Ben than *f3* is.

This construction of PBI might itself be considered problematic. It might be thought (i) that any legitimate betterness comparison of one future x against another future y, including a person based comparison, must conform to a certain rule for such comparisons—a rule that dictates that the comparison of x against y must proceed on the basis of what Temkin calls the *internal aspects* of x and y alone—and (ii) that the expansive construction of PBI that I have just proposed fails to conform to that rule.[25]

If the *internal aspects* of f1 and f2 *exclude* the fact that f2 is worse for Ben than f3, then it's true that the expansive construction of PBI fails to conform to that rule. Moreover, if the *internal aspects* of f1 and f2 are *restricted* to facts regarding the distribution of wellbeing across a given population, it's unclear why we should expect the person based approach to comply with that rule.[26]

But perhaps the internal aspects of f1 and f2 *aren't* so heavily restricted. Perhaps, e.g., it's counted as an *internal aspect* of f2 that agents in f2 have the

---

[24] The inquiry thus won't be *so* expansive as to cover the entire domain of *all* possible futures but rather the domain of all *accessible* futures. The future in which I at noon today clap my hands and cure cancer is a *possible* future—there's no *logical* inconsistency in the laws of nature undergoing a tidal shift that would rule out that scenario. The laws of nature, however, along with the current history of the world, being as they are, the future in which I at noon clap my hands and cure cancer *isn't* an *accessible* future. For additional detail on the concept of *accessibility* at play here, see section 2.2 above.

[25] Examples of approaches that accept such a rule on what determines betterness between futures include conventional formulations of *total utilitarianism* and *average utilitarianism*. Both those views commence their comparisons between two futures x and y by simply adding up the individual wellbeing levels of each person who ever exists in x and then doing the same for y. If the summation of individual wellbeing levels in x is greater than that in y, then on the total view x is better than y. If the summation of individual wellbeing levels in x divided by the number of people who ever exist in x is greater than the same calculation for y, then on the average view x is better than y.

The motivating idea behind both views is rooted in the intuitively attractive notion that each additional unit of wellbeing enjoyed (or had) by any person who ever exists itself is itself of intrinsic value, making it seem a necessary truth that, other things being equal, additional wellbeing in one future as compared against another will mean that the one future that has more intrinsic value than—is, that is, morally better than—the other. The thought, however, of this chapter, put in terms of intrinsic value, would be that additional *intrinsic value* and additional *wellbeing* are *not* one and the same thing—that additional wellbeing does not automatically produce additional intrinsic value—and that to figure out how much intrinsic value is added when additional wellbeing is added requires a different sort of inquiry, one that puts to work *both* our maximizing values (captured in, e.g., the Same People Pareto Principle) *and* our existential values (captured in, e.g., PBI and ENMP). For additional discussion, see Roberts 2022b.

[26] While the total and average views can easily accept that version of the rule, to insist that the person based approach accept it as well would beg the question against that approach.

ability, power, and resources to make things better for Ben—which is just another way of saying that f3 is *accessible* relative to f1 and f2—and that agents in f2 have instead made things worse for Ben. In that case, the proposed construction for PBI nicely complies with the rule. We need not, that is, look beyond f1 and f2 to determine that f2 is worse than f1, for f2 itself contains the seeds of its own slippage on the betterness scale. True, it would be a *modal* fact about f2 that makes f2 worse than f1 when it would otherwise be at least as good as f1— it's a fact about what agents at f2 *accessibly could* have accomplished. It's nonetheless a fact about f2.[27]

2.4 Formal Statement of PBI

The preceding discussion suggests that the construction of the person based intuition that we should want to defend should be *expansive* in one respect—it implies nothing until the requisite *expansive* inquiry has been completed—and *very narrow* in another respect—it provides only a necessary condition, not a sufficient condition, on worseness, and only a condition on worseness, not on betterness. We should, that is, want to defend, not just any old formulation of PBI, but rather *EVNPBI*.

Expansive Very Narrow Person Based Intuition (EVNPBI).

Where x and y are possible futures and y is accessible relative to x, x is morally worse than y, and choice c at x is morally wrong, *only if* there is a person p and an alternate choice c′ at an alternate accessible future z such that

(i) p does or will exist in x *and*

(ii) x is worse than z for p (where z may, but need not, be identical to y).

---

[27] A parallel defense of an expansive PBI can be made against an objection based on the Independence of Irrelevant Alternatives—and ultimately against an objection based on inconsistency. Consider a Two Outcome Case, one just like the Three Outcome Case but such that f3 isn't included as an accessible alternative. For the Two Outcome Case, even an expansively formulated PBI would imply that f1 is exactly as good as f2. Isn't that inconsistent with the result we've already insisted on for the Three Outcome Case? No. What we are comparing are possible *futures*—possible *worlds*—with possible worlds themselves being universally understood to have all their features *necessarily*. Contemplating the slightest "change" in any detail of any one possible future means that one is actually contemplating a *distinct* possible future. One detail is that in the one case the future in which Ben languishes at +5 agents have the ability, power, and resources to bring about f3. In the other case the future in which Ben languishes at +5 agents don't. That means that we cannot be talking about the same future in each of the two distinct cases: the "f2" in the Three Outcome Case just isn't the "f2" in the Two Outcome Case. For further discussion of Independence, consistency, and what we can call the *Accessibility Axiom*, see Roberts 2022b.

Having done the work of formulating PBI as EVNPBI—of constructing the intuition so that we now have something that's worth defending—we can turn to the Better Chance Puzzle.[28]

2.5 The Better Chance Puzzle

The Better Chance Puzzle is illustrated by the *Better Chance Case* (Figure 2.3). There, the agents—the would-be parents—seek to combat a medically diagnosed case of infertility. To that end, they must choose between c1, taking a fertility pill, and c2, basically doing nothing (let's say taking an aspirin). They are more likely to conceive a child under c1 than under c2. But any child they do conceive under c1 will predictably suffer a mild, wellbeing-reducing side effect.

Specifically, according to Figure 2.3, the choice c1 creates a certain probability—0.1—that Harry will be conceived and born and at +8 will be pretty well off. c1, that is, creates a certain substantial probability—0.1—that f1 will materialize in place of f2. In contrast, c2 creates a considerably lower probability—only 0.0001—that Harry will be conceived and born—that f3 will materialize in place of f4. But c2 also offers the possibility of a better existence for Harry: Harry at +10 would be significantly better off in f3 than he is in f1 at +8.

How does a person based approach compare the alternate futures in this case and evaluate the two choices? On the telic side, EVNPBI, in combination with certain conceptual principles, implies f2 is exactly as good as f3 and f3 is exactly as

	choice c1: take fertility pill		choice c2: take aspirin	
probability of future, given choice	0.1	0.9	0.0001	0.9999
	future f1	future f2	future f3	future f4
+10			Harry	
+8	Harry			
+0		Harry*		Harry*

Figure 2.3 Better Chance Case

---

[28] I thus propose EVNPBI as a defensible articulation of PBI, the intuition that Parfit captures (and ultimately rejects) in the words "what is bad must be bad for someone" (Parfit 1987, 363; emphasis deleted). It might seem that I have missed a decade or so since, however carefully articulated, PBI surely faces serious objections, including objections based on the nonidentity problem. But see notes 7 and 8 above (recognizing that objection and still others, but noting that those objections, arguably, can be countered); see also section 2.6.

good as f4.[29] The Same People Pareto Principle tells us that f3 is better than f1. Further conceptual principles would then add that f2 and f4 are each better than f1.[30] EVNPBI, in addition, has something to say on the deontic side, instructing there that c1 at f2, c2 at f3, and c2 at f4 are each permissible.

Those results together might suggest to us that c1 at f1 itself must be wrong. EVNPBI, of course, as a mere *necessary* condition on wrongdoing, implies nothing of the kind. But for purposes here we have taken for granted that EVNPBI is to be situated within a framework that considers our comparisons of futures in terms of their moral betterness and our evaluation of the choices that give rise to those futures to be connected in some interesting and significant way. If so, it may seem at least plausible that the bare fact that f2 is worse than each other accessible future *must* mean that c1 at f1 is wrong.

For other reasons as well, we may seem pressed to accept that a more complete person based approach—one that includes, among other things, not just necessary but also sufficient conditions on wrongdoing—will instruct that c1 at f1 is wrong. After all, the agents who choose c1 are taking a profound moral risk in a case where they have the option of choosing something, c2, that, according to EVNPBI, involves no moral risk at all. Moral risk would seem to be an inherently bad thing. And here the moral risk is itself clearly person based: the moral risk agents impose on Harry in choosing c1 is one that they might on his behalf avoid completely by choosing c2 instead. By hypothesis, no one else is affected however the choice is made. It may thus seem that in the end the more complete person based theory, the theory that includes but extends beyond EVNPBI, will surely direct that c1 at f1 is wrong.

Thus the first half of the Better Chance Puzzle. The second half of the puzzle is that that's not what we think at all. Person based theorists or not, we regard c1 at f1 as *perfectly permissible* notwithstanding the fact that the existing Harry in f1 under c1 is less well off than he might have been. We recognize, in other words, that the *better chance* of existence Harry has under c1 in some way *makes up for* Harry's *lesser* existence under c1 at f1. We recognize that Harry *might* end up better off under c2 than under c1. But we also recognize that it's far more probable under c2 than under c1 that Harry will never exist at all. We don't, in short, think there is a moral rule that states that we may never impose a moral risk. The upshot for us is that c1 at f1 is permissible.

The second half of the puzzle can be collected in the form of the *Better Chance Claim*.

Better Chance Claim. In some cases, the better *chance* of existence converts what we would otherwise consider a wrong choice into a perfectly permissible choice;

---

[29] See note 20 above (conceptual principles).   [30] See note 20 above (conceptual principles).

the better chance of existence *makes up for* the lesser existence; the better chance of existence, in at least that sense, makes things *morally better*.

And we can now provide a more succinct statement of the Better Chance Puzzle. We accept the Better Chance Claim even as we also insist on retaining EVNPBI. But how can the better *chance* of existence make things morally better when the actual *fact* of existence under EVNPBI does no such thing at all?

2.6 The Better Chance Case versus the Nonidentity Problem

It's worth taking just a moment to contrast the Better Chance Case with a certain type of nonidentity problem, the type where we think the choice is clearly wrong but at the same time acknowledge that there is some chance the apparent victim will exist and be better off under an alternate, clearly permissible choice. Variations on the nonidentity problem that are of this type include Parfit's depletion and risky policy problems, Kavka's slave child and pleasure pill cases, cases involving historical injustices and environmental cases (including climate change).

The cases that give rise to those particular versions of the nonidentity problem are structurally similar.[31] But they are all very different from the Better Chance Case. In each of the nonidentity cases, there is no basis for the thought that the clearly wrong choice confers on the future people (or at least on some of the future people) an elevated chance of coming into existence. The *sotto voce* assumption that the choice under scrutiny somehow *does* confer such a chance is just a mistake, an instance, perhaps, of *post hoc ergo propter hoc*. The better view is that in each of the nonidentity cases the individuals who *appear* to be victims—the child who is turned over into slavery at birth pursuant to the terms of a preconception slave child contract; the future population struggling under the effects of depletion or a risky policy—*really are* victims. They are people agents really have made worse off when those same agents accessibly could have made at least some of those same people better off. Of course, no particular victim of, e.g., depletion will accrue a probability of 1 of existence under depletion. But nor is any particular victim of depletion any *more* likely to exist under depletion than that same person is to exist under conservation, where probability must now be measured, in connection with both choices, as of that moment just prior to choice. (Just as, just prior to choice, there exist a vast number of ways in which *conservation* might be implemented and, correspondingly, a vast number of futures that might materialize under conservation, so too, just prior to choice, are there a vast

---

[31] Roberts 2007, 2009.

number of ways in which *depletion* might be implemented and, correspondingly, a vast number of futures that might materialize under depletion. Any *particular* victim's chances of existence, calculated just prior to choice, are thus extremely minute, and equally so, whether conservation *or* depletion is chosen.)

If Kavka's *pleasure* pill really were a *fertility* pill, we wouldn't think that the parent's choice to take the pleasure pill was wrong. We would analyze it just as the Better Chance Claim analyzes the Better Chance Case. We might be told that the people who exist under depletion *would* never have existed at all under conservation. (Indeed in some versions of the depletion case such a counterfactual is included as a stipulation.) But that stipulated counterfactual in fact has no relevance to the moral analysis at all. Rather, it's our realization that at least some of the people who exist and suffer under depletion *accessibly could* have existed under conservation and that they'd have been at least as likely—though still not very likely at all—to have existed under conservation as under depletion that, underneath all the chatter, supports our intuition that the choice of depletion is wrong.

2.7 Solving the Better Chance Puzzle

To solve the Better Chance Puzzle is to answer the following question about the Better Chance Case:

> If Harry's *better* chance of existence makes c1 morally better—converts the choice we would otherwise consider morally wrong into a choice we consider morally permissible—in the Better Chance Case, why doesn't the *lesser* chance of Harry's existence make c2 *worse*—convert the choice we would otherwise consider permissible into a choice we consider morally *wrong*? If Harry's better *chance* of existence makes c1 at f1 morally better, why doesn't the *actual fact* of Harry's existence make f1 better than f2—and f3 better than f4?

To solve the Better Chance Puzzle is to provide a *PBI-consistent account*—an account consistent, at the very least, with the core values of the person based approach and with EVNPBI—of how Harry's better chance of existence under c1 makes c1 permissible.

For purposes of the remainder of this chapter, I will mainly focus on the deontic question—the question of what makes c1 permissible in the Better Chance Case. For it's not clear that the parallel puzzle emerges on the telic side—or that we, in the end, will want *so* perfectly to connect the telic and the deontic projects that we are *compelled* to say that whatever it is that makes c1 permissible in that case *also* makes f1 at least as good as f3. We thus leave open the option of saying instead that the choice that gives rise to f1 *isn't* wrong *even though* f1 is worse than f3 and in fact deploy that option in section 2.7 below.

2.7.1 Two Proposed Solutions Based on the Concept of *Expected Value*

It isn't far-fetched to suppose that what makes c1 at f1 permissible in the Better Chance Case has something to do with the *expected value* (*EV*) c1 at f1 clearly generates on behalf of Harry. (Under an expected value approach, probabilities are, as before, calculated as of the moment just prior to choice and on the basis of information available to agents at that moment.)

We have multiple options for implementing such an approach. For purposes here, we examine two such options.

2.7.1.1 Unadulterated Expected Value Approach

Under an *unadulterated* expected value approach, we adopt an other-things-equal principle that provides both necessary and sufficient conditions on the permissibility of a given choice at a given future based on whether the apparent victim's expected value is *maximized* by that choice. Thus:

Unadulterated expected value principle (deontic). Where no one other than p is affected by whether a given choice c at a given future x is made, c at x is permissible *if and only if* there exists no alternate choice c′ and alternate accessible future y such that EV of c′ at y for p > EV of c at x for p.[32]

This principle tells us, correctly, that c1 is permissible. The difficulty is that it also tells us that c2 is wrong. It's thus not PBI-consistent. Indeed, it's flatly at odds with EVNPBI, according to which c2 is permissible. The unadulterated principle thus doesn't solve the puzzle but instead simply throws out one of the puzzle pieces.

2.7.1.2 Combination Approach: EVNPBI+EV

A better option might seem to include the less-than-maximized expected value level only as a *necessary* condition on wrongdoing while retaining the other conditions that EVNPBI proposes. Thus:

EVNPBI+EV (deontic). c performed at x is wrong *only if* there is a person p and an alternate choice c′ performed at an alternate accessible future z such that:

(i) p does or will exist in x *and*
(ii) x is worse for p than z *and*
(iii) EV of c′ (at z) for p > EV of c (at x) for p.

---

[32] For purposes of fixing the expected value of a given choice, I take it that we have no need to relativize that choice to a particular future. The qualifications "at y" and "at x" toward the end of the stated principles are thus unnecessary (but seem to me to aid in seeing how the principle itself would apply in any given case).

EVNPBI+EV generates the plausible results that c1 and c2 are both permissible in the Better Chance Case. (Thus c1 at f1 is permissible in virtue of the fact that condition (iii) is failed, and c2 at f3 is permissible in virtue of the fact that condition (ii) is failed. c1 at f2 and c2 and f4 are permissible in virtue of the fact that in both cases condition (i) is failed.) Notably, EVNPBI+EV also avoids an unfortunate result when applied to the type of nonidentity problem discussed in section 2.6. It, for example, avoids the result that the choice of depletion is permissible. (Since EV generated by depletion for each of the apparent victims of depletion is less than EV generated by conservation, condition (iii) is satisfied. Conditions (i) and (ii) are also satisfied. The door is thus left conveniently open for the result, under still other person based principles, that the choice of depletion is wrong.)

A problem, however, for EVNPBI+EV comes in the form of the *Bad Lives Case* (Figure 2.4).[33]

In that case, agents choose between (just) c1 and c2. c1 is the choice to take a progeny-affecting longevity pill immediately post-conception, a pill that is highly iatrogenic but such that, if its upside eventuates, will increase the term of the ordinary good life of +10 by factor of 2000; and c2 is the choice to take aspirin immediately post-conception.

Agents have the choice, in other words, to take a pill that *might* greatly extend longevity for any person they conceive but that is *far* more likely to end in a life that is *less* than a life worth living or in effect to do nothing—to let, that is, nature take its course. Consider, then, c1 and assume that it's f2 that in fact unfolds under c1—exactly as the probabilities themselves predict. EVNPBI+EV implies that c1 at f2 is permissible. But that result seems clearly false.

This seems not to be the problem we are accustomed to facing in connection with calculations based on expected value. We might easily accept that a 100% shot at $100 is exactly as good for us as 50% chance at $200 and nonetheless balk at the claim that c1 at f2 is permissible.[34] We think the agents ought to have chosen c2 instead. At least: we think that c1 at f2 is wrong.

The Bad Lives Case demonstrates that we need to take a closer look at our cases—that we haven't yet identified, for the Better Chance Case itself, the probability-related, good-making feature of c1 at f1 that makes c1 permissible when c1 would otherwise be wrong or, for the Bad Lives Case, the probability-

---

[33] The development of the Bad Lives Case owes much to discussions with Dean Spears. In previous work, I proposed a principle very like EVNPBI+EV in connection with discussions of various types of nonidentity problem. See e.g. Roberts 2009, 2010. The suggestion of this present chapter (see also Roberts 2022a) is that, while a proper accounting of the probabilities is essential for purposes of solving the nonidentity problem, we must find an alternate approach to how those probabilities are to be taken into account.

[34] The idea that it's false that c1 at f2 is permissible is thus *not* a reflection of intolerance to risk (or risk aversion) but rather of rationality. We can, in other words, reject the claim that c1 at f2 is permissible and remain neutral with respect to risk.

	choice c1: take longevity pill			choice c2: take aspirin	
probability of future, given choice	0.009	0.99	0.001	0.1	0.9
	future f1	future f2	future f3	future f4	future f5
+20,000			Jill		
+10					Jill
+0	Jill*			Jill*	
−10		Jill			

Figure 2.4 Bad Lives Case

related, bad-making feature of c1 at f2 that should block the inference to c1's permissibility under any plausible person based approach. If the reference to expected value in condition (iii) isn't helpful, then what *is* helpful?

2.7.2 Probable Value Approach

A morally significant distinction between the two cases would seem to be that c1 at f2 in the Bad Lives Cases, though it maximizes *expected* value for Jill, also reduces that we can call the *probable* value of c1 at f2 for Jill. In the Bad Lives Case, the choice c1 made in the context of f2, in other words, represents a high probability that Jill will end up with—as she does in f2—the extremely low wellbeing f2 in fact assigns to Jill—a wellbeing level that makes her existence *less* than one worth having. In contrast, in the Better Chance Case, the choice c1 made in the context of f1 represents a relatively high probability that Harry will end up with a relatively high wellbeing level—a wellbeing level that makes his existence *well* worth having. That distinction reflects the fact that the one case involves a tradeoff we consider morally permissible—there is *something in it for Harry* that c1 at f1 is how things end up, namely, a better chance of a worth-having existence—and the other case involves no such tradeoff at all—there is *nothing in it for Jill* that c1 at f2 is how things end up.

More generally:

> Where a choice c made at a future x creates a probability n that p will have a wellbeing level of w at x, we can say that the *probable value (PV)* for p under c at x is n(w).

And we can then reformulate EVNPBI as follows:

> *Expansive Very Narrow Person Based Intuition + Probable Value (EVNPBI+PV) (deontic).* c at x is wrong *only if* there is a person p and an alternate choice c' at an alternate accessible future z such that:

(i) p does or will exist in x *and*
(ii) x is worse for p than z *and*
(iii) the PV for p under c′ at z > the PV for p under c at x.[35]

In the Better Chance Case, the necessary condition (iii) on c1 at f1 being wrong is failed, with the result that c1 at f1 is permissible. In the Bad Lives Case, the necessary condition (iii) on c1 at f2 being wrong is satisfied as is each other condition—and we accordingly avoid the result that c1 at f2 is permissible.

EVNPBI+PV (deontic) does a similarly good job in the context of the nonidentity problem. For at least some of the people who eventually exist in a given future under, e.g., the choice of depletion, the probable value of that future for that individual under that choice will be less than the same calculation for that individual for the choice of conservation. With condition (iii) failed, we avoid the result that the choice of depletion is permissible.

2.7.3 Summing Up the Solution; Implications for Connection

EVNPBI+PV recognizes multiple routes to permissibility. Thus, according to EVNPBI+PV, it is the *probabilities* that are at stake in the Better Chance Case that make the choice of c1 permissible. It's Harry's better *chance* of ever existing at all under c1 that makes c1 at f1 *permissible* when c1 would otherwise be deemed *wrong*. But it doesn't follow that c1 at f1, or c2 at f3 or at f4, is wrong. Though on very different grounds, EVNPBI+PV deems all those choices permissible as well.

Now, EVNPBI+PV itself takes up only the deontic project. But EVNPBI+PV is perfectly consistent with EVNPBI itself, which takes up *both* the deontic and the telic projects. Thus we can accept the telic components of EVNPBI for their help in determining how futures compare in respect of their moral betterness and how the choices that give rise to those futures are to be evaluated and *also* accept EVNPBI+PV for its *further* help in completing that latter task. EVNPBI thus implies that f2 is exactly as good as f4 and that f3 is exactly as good as each of f2 and f4 while at the same time leaving the door open for the result—under the Same People Pareto Principle—that f1 is worse than f3.

Which is just to say that Harry's better chance of existence does, in some sense, make things morally better—it converts a choice that would otherwise be wrong into a choice that is perfectly permissible—even though the *actual fact* of Harry's existence in f1 or f3 doesn't make those futures any better than f2 or f4.

---

[35] The definition of *probable value* proposed here is designed to address a difficulty in a still earlier attempt to articulate the concept pointed out to me by Tomi Francis. Nonidentity Workshop, Institute for Future Studies, Stockholm (Feb. 8–9, 2020).

Now, we get into trouble here if we insist, further, that the connection between the telic and the deontic projects isn't just interesting and significant but instead is *perfect*: that c1 at f1 being permissible *entails* that f1 is at least as good as f3. But I see no reason for us to insist on that point. We can agree that the connection between the telic and the deontic projects is interesting and significant *without* accepting that it's *perfect*.[36]

2.8 Avoiding the Nonidentity Fallacy

This chapter does not exhaust the alternate possible explanations for why c1 is permissible in the Better Chance Case. But we should note that at least some of those alternate possible explanations—including some that may seem attractive at first glance—clearly fail.

Thus it might seem that the reason c1 at f1 is permissible in the Better Chance Case is that the value f1 in fact assigns to Harry under c1—let's call that the *actual value (AV)* of f1 for Harry under c1[37]—is at least as great as (indeed it's far greater than) the EV of f3 for Harry under c2.

Putting that idea to work, we would reformulate condition (iii) of EVNPBI+PV to read:

EV of c′ at z for p > AV of c at x for p

Such a principle—call it *EVNPBI+AV/EV*—immediately generates a plausible result in the Better Chance Case—that c1 at f1 is permissible. But it's a mistake—indeed a *fallacy*, which I have elsewhere called the *nonidentity fallacy* since it's a mistake that so regularly appears in discussion of the nonidentity problem[38]—to think that it's the *actual* value level Harry has in f1 (+8) that is doing the work here. Rather, what's doing the work here is more plausibly related to the probabilities that we think we need to take into account in comparing one choice against the other—*probable* value, under my proposal, rather than *expected* value, but in any case the probabilities we think we need to take into account—*across the board*, not, that is, just for the *one* choice at *one* future but also for *any* alternate choice at *any* alternate accessible future.

The Medication Case (Figure 2.5) makes this point.

---

[36] To retain a *perfect* connection between the telic and deontic projects, we would need to say that facts about probabilities, themselves embedded in the futures to be ranked, on their own are enough to make one future worse than another. For reasons noted in section 2.7.1.1, however, that is not a position we want to accept—or *can* accept, consistent with *actually solving* the puzzle rather than simply throwing out some of the puzzle pieces.
[37] There is no implication here that f1 is (in a particular case) the *actual* future.
[38] See notes 7 and 8 above and section 2.6.

	choice c1: prescribe pill 1		choice c2: prescribe pill 2	
probability of future, given choice	0.0001	0.9999	0.0001	0.9999
	future f1	future f2	future f3	future f4
+10			Lavinia	
+3	Lavinia			
+2				Lavinia
+1		Lavinia		

Figure 2.5 Medication Case

AV of f1 under c1 for Lavinia is +3. EV of c2 for Lavinia is 2.0008 (0.0001 × 10 + 0.9999 × 2). EVNPBI+AV/EV implies that c1 at f1 is permissible. But c1 seems clearly wrong. So EVNPBI+AV/EV seems clearly false.

It might be objected that any plausibly formulated PBI will be *compelled* to accept that c1 at f1 is permissible. The basis for that objection would be as follows: PBI connects wrongdoing to an existing or future person's being made worse off; and Lavinia arguably *isn't* worse off under c1 *in the case where f1 in fact eventuates* than she is under c2 where we *just don't know* what would have happened to her under c2 but *do* know that the odds are *against* things turning out *well* for her.

But I see no reason to think that any plausibly formulated PBI will imply that Lavinia *isn't* worse off under c1 at f1. c1 at f1 is worse for Lavinia, in terms of AV, than an alternate accessible future is. It's worse for Lavinia, in terms of EV, than an alternate choice is. It's worse for Lavinia, in terms of PV, than c2 at f3 is or than c2 at f4 is. There really are no grounds at all except for a confused understanding of when a given person has been made worse off—an understanding that, mistakenly, tries to root that result in a comparison of AV against EV—for the claim that PBI implies that c1 at f1 is permissible.

For the case at hand, we should *concede* that we *just don't know* how things would have turned out for Lavinia under c2. But the critical point for the purpose of a moral analysis that *isn't* confused is *not* that we lack that knowledge but *rather* that *prior to choice* the same holds for c1—we *just don't know* how things will in fact turn out for Lavinia under c1, either—*and* that things (by far) *look* to be better for Lavinia under c2 than under c1. If the "we just don't know" in advance of choice point is a moral minus for c2, it's a moral minus for c1 as well.

The Medication Case thus gives the person based theorist a sound basis for rejecting EVNPBI+AV/EV. EVNPBI+PV, in contrast, performs just as well in the Medication Case—it, that is, avoids the result that c1 at f1 is permissible and is perfectly consistent with the result that c1 at f1 is wrong—as it does in each of the other cases examined here.

2.9 Conclusion

Derek Parfit, far more clearly than any other philosopher, both dangles the person based intuition—PBI—before us, tantalizing us with the thought that there is a clear, morally significant distinction to be made between making people worse off by never bringing them into existence to begin with and making people worse off by making the existences they do or will have less than they easily could have been, and then, so very persuasively, leads us step by step in another direction entirely. Yet in his very last paper—the last paper, at least, that he shared with me, just a few weeks before his death—he continued to play with that same intuition, twisting it this way and that, examining it with ever-fresh eyes. Perhaps it's acceptable then that this present chapter continues in that vein. To his warm and kind thanks for my comments on his paper, I'm grateful that I had the time to tell him that it had been a great pleasure and honor for me to have prepared those comments. I only wish I had found the time, and he had had the time, for us both to say a great deal more.[39]

References

Bader, Ralf M (this collection).

Broome, John 2004. *Weighing Lives*. Oxford University Press.

Hare, Caspar 2007. "Voices from Another World: Must We Respect the Interests of People Who Do Not, and Will Never, Exist?" *Ethics* 117: 498–523.

Heyd, David 1992. *Genethics: Moral Issues in the Creation of People*. University of California Press.

Heyd, David 2009. "The Intractability of the Nonidentity Problem," in M. Roberts and D. Wasserman (eds.), *Harming Future Persons*. Springer.

McMahan, Jeff 1981. "Problems of Population Choice." *Ethics* 92(1): 96–127.

McMahan, Jeff 2009. "Asymmetries in the Morality of Causing People to Exist." In *Harming Future Persons*, edited by M.A. Roberts and D.T. Wasserman, pp. 49–68. Dordrecht: Springer.

---

[39] The final version of this chapter owes an enormous debt to the careful, insightful comments of James Goodrich on an earlier draft of this chapter as well as to comments of the participants at the Oxford Parfit Conference (Jeff McMahan, organizer, Oxford University, May 18–20, 2018) when I presented a still earlier draft of this chapter.

Narveson, Jan 1976. "Moral Problems of Population," in Michael D. Bayles (ed.), *Ethics and Population*. Schenkman.

Parfit, Derek 1987. *Reasons and Persons*. Oxford University Press (originally published 1984).

Parfit, Derek 2011. *On What Matters: Volume Two*. Oxford University Press.

Parfit, Derek 2017. "Future People, the Non-Identity Problem, and Person-Affecting Principles," *Philosophy & Public Affairs* 45/2: 118–57.

Roberts, M.A. 1998. *Child versus Childmaker: Future Persons and Present Duties in Ethics and the Law*. Rowman & Littlefield.

Roberts, M.A. 2007. "The Nonidentity Fallacy: Harm, Probability and Another Look at Parfit's Depletion Example," *Utilitas* 19: 267–311.

Roberts, M.A. 2009. "The Nonidentity Problem and the Two Envelope Problem," in M.A. Roberts and D. Wasserman (eds.), *Harming Future Persons*. Springer, pp. 201–28.

Roberts, M. A. 2010. *Abortion and the Moral Significance of Merely Possible Persons: Finding Middle Ground in Hard Cases*. Springer.

Roberts, M.A. 2011a. "The Asymmetry: A Solution," *Theoria* 77: 333–67.

Roberts, M.A. 2011b. "An Asymmetry in the Ethics of Procreation," *Philosophy Compass* 6/11: 765–76.

Roberts, M.A. 2015. "Population Axiology," in Iwao Hirose and Jonas Olson (eds.), *Oxford Handbook of Value Theory*. Oxford University Press, pp. 299–323.

Roberts, M.A. 2020. "Parfit, Population Ethics and Pareto Plus," in A. Sauchelli (ed.), *Derek Parfit's Reasons and Persons: An Introduction and Critical Inquiry*. Routledge.

Roberts, M.A. 2022a (forthcoming). "The Person-Based Intuition and the Better Chance Puzzle," in G. Arrhenius, K. Bykvist and T. Campbell (eds.), *The Oxford Handbook of Population Ethics*. Oxford University Press.

Roberts, M.A. 2022b (manuscript). *The Existence Puzzles*.

Roberts, M.A. and David T. Wasserman 2017. "Dividing and Conquering the Nonidentity Problem," in Matthew Liao and Collin O'Neil (eds.), *Current Controversies in Bioethics*. Routledge, pp. 81–98.

Singer, Peter 2011. *Practical Ethics* (3rd ed.). Cambridge University Press.

Temkin, Larry 2012. *Rethinking the Good: Moral Ideals and the Nature of Practical Reasoning*. Oxford University Press.

3
Comparing Existence and Non-Existence

Hilary Greaves and John Cusbert

3.1 Introduction and Motivations

Many ethical theories require us to make comparisons of overall betterness among possible worlds. Such comparisons are plausibly constrained by which worlds are better than which *for various persons*. For example, if A and B are exactly alike except that *A* is better than *B* for Jones, this suggests that A is better than B overall. It is therefore important to determine as much as we can about the extensions of the personal betterness comparisons themselves.

This essay is concerned with whether or not it can be better (or worse), for a given person, that that person exist rather than not. *Existence comparativism* (henceforth simply 'comparativism') holds that it can. On the *full comparativist* view, if a person S exists in *A* but not in *B*, then *A* is better (resp. worse) for S than B iff S has positive (resp. negative) well-being in *A*; if S has zero well-being in *A* and does not exist in *B*, then *A* and *B* are equally good for S (Roberts 1998; Holtug 2001; Roberts 2003; Adler 2009; Fleurbaey and Voorhoeve 2015). *Full anti-comparativism* holds that unless S exists both in *A* and in *B*, *A* and *B* are incomparable for S (Narveson 1967; Heyd 1988, 1992; Dasgupta 1995; Broome 1999, 2004; Buchanan et al. 2001; Bykvist 2007). Both views agree that if S exists in both *A* and *B*, and has higher well-being in *A* than in *B*, then *A* is better for S than *B*. These two positions are not jointly exhaustive, but they are the most popular positions in this debate. (We discuss some additional possibilities in section 3.3.)

There are three reasons why the dispute between comparativism and anti-comparativism is important. The first concerns the following principle:[1]

Person-Affecting Principle (PAP): If *A* is better than *B*, then there is some possible person for whom *A* is better than *B*.

---

[1] Outside the context of population ethics, statements of the person-affecting principle usually simply say 'person' rather than 'possible person'. Once one moves to population ethics, however, interpreting the principle in the way stated here, to include all *possible* persons, is near-obligatory. We defend this claim in section 3.3.

Our statements of this and other principles are to be understood schematically.

PAP is intuitively compelling, and often serves as a good guide in *fixed*-population ethics. Consider, for example, the question of whether one can improve things by 'levelling down': that is, by reducing the welfare of some person who initially has higher welfare than the average in her population, without increasing the welfare of anyone else. Such levelling down might decrease inequality. Thus egalitarians may be committed to the (perhaps problematic) conclusion that levelling down makes things better at least in some respect. It seems clear, however, that levelling down cannot make things better *overall*. And PAP seems to provide the correct explanation of why this is so: levelling down cannot make things better, because it does not make things better *for* anyone (Parfit 1991, 17; Temkin 1993, chap. 9, 2003a, 2003b, 2012, chap. 3).[2]

As is well known, however, if anti-comparativism is true, then PAP leads to counterintuitive results in certain nonidentity cases (Parfit 1984, chap. 16). For example, let C be a world in which everyone has extremely high well-being, and let D be a world in which the same number of people have lives barely worth living; let the populations of C and D be entirely disjoint. If anti-comparativism is true, then it is not the case that C is better than D for any of the C-people (and clearly C is not better than D either for any of the D-people or for anyone else), so PAP implies that C is not better than D. But this seems absurd. Therefore, if anti-comparativism is true, the apparently compelling PAP is inconsistent with sensible verdicts in nonidentity cases.

Many have concluded from this variable-population case that PAP is false, with potentially significant ramifications even for fixed-population ethics. But if comparativism is true, then this rejection of PAP is unmotivated: according to comparativism, C is better for the C-people than D, so, we can maintain that C is better than D but still accept PAP. The truth of comparativism would thus allow us to avoid the nonidentity problem within a person-affecting framework, and would render inappropriate the designation of population axiologies like (say) totalism as 'impersonal'.

Second: if one accepts comparativism, it becomes much harder to deny the Repugnant Conclusion. As is also well known, the Mere Addition Principle and Non-Anti-Egalitarianism (together with some plausible structural conditions) entail the apparently unacceptable Repugnant Conclusion:[3]

---

[2] A second example of the significance of 'person-affecting' ideas in fixed-population ethics concerns the choice between utilitarianism on the one hand, and any non-utilitarian approach to aggregation on the other. It has been argued that only on a utilitarian account is the *degree* to which one state of affairs is better than another overall proportional to the *degree* to which the first is better than the second for people, and that any non-utilitarian account is therefore objectionably 'impersonal' (Persson 2001).

[3] This is one version of the 'Mere Addition Paradox' (Parfit 1984, chap. 19; Carlson 1998). Other versions of the argument use 'at least as good as' or 'not worse than' in place of 'better than'; these distinctions are largely unimportant for present purposes.

The structural conditions in question are that 'better than' is transitive, that the well-being scale has the Archimedean property, and a domain richness assumption.

Mere Addition: If everyone who exists in A also exists and has the same well-being level in B, but B also contains a positive number of additional people all with positive well-being (and no-one else), then B is better than A.

Non-Anti-Egalitarianism: If Z has the same size population as B, Z has higher average well-being than B, and there is perfect equality of well-being in Z, then Z is better than B.

Repugnant Conclusion: For any world A, there exists a world Z in which no-one has a life that is more than barely worth living, such that Z is better than A.

Virtually no-one is willing to deny Non-Anti-Egalitarianism. Thus those who reject the Repugnant Conclusion almost always deny Mere Addition. But if comparativism is true, then the Mere Addition Principle follows from a standard Pareto principle:[4]

Pareto Principle: If A is at least as good as B for every possible person, and there is some possible person for whom A is better than B, then A is better than B.

The Pareto principle is very hard to deny: it is one of the very few just-about-uncontroversial principles of distributive ethics. Therefore, if comparativism is true, it is hard to deny Mere Addition, and correspondingly hard to deny the Repugnant Conclusion.

A third and complementary point is that if comparativism is true, then the Repugnant Conclusion is in any case far less repugnant. If A is even slightly worse than Z for sufficiently enormous numbers of people (viz., those who in Z have lives that are worth living and in A do not exist), then person-affecting reasoning (together with a reasonable approach to aggregation over persons) seems to weigh against A and in favour of Z. This point can of course be taken either way: as a further reason to doubt comparativism, or as a further reason to doubt one's anti-repugnance intuitions (or the required aggregative assumptions). Either way, the central point for our purposes is that comparativism is an important thesis: much else of importance to population ethics may hang on it.

Intuitions regarding the truth and falsity of comparativism go both ways. Some find comparativism intuitively compelling: if Peggy has a good life, they think, then Peggy is lucky to have been born, which makes sense provided the actual world is better for Peggy than a world in which Peggy doesn't exist. To others, the intuitive position is instead that while the actual world is better for Peggy than a

---

[4] Here and throughout, the Pareto principle we discuss is one half of what is normally called the Strong Pareto principle. We omit consideration of other Pareto principles for conciseness.
We formulate the principle in terms of goodness, as opposed to preferences. Broome (2004) calls the goodness version of the Strong Pareto principle the 'Principle of personal good'.
As in the case of the person-affecting principle, we write 'possible person' in our statement of this principle, in place of 'person' as is normally done outside the context of population ethics.

world in which Peggy exists with fewer goods (less pleasure, health, knowledge, and so on), a world in which Peggy doesn't exist is a different matter, since non-existence entails not only that Peggy doesn't possess such goods, but also that she isn't there to lack them.

The Metaphysical Argument, as we will call it, purports to establish that anti-comparativism follows from basic matters of metaphysics, so that there is no work for such substantive evaluative intuitions to do here. The purpose of this essay is to argue against this position. We will argue that the Metaphysical Argument should not sway us either way on the question of existence comparativism.

The structure of the essay is as follows. Section 3.2 sets out the Metaphysical Argument, identifying principles that we will call *Limited Invariance* and *Ontological Commitment* as its premises. Many have taken this argument to establish anti-comparativism. We show that this line of reasoning is not cogent: the key premise of *Ontological Commitment* is in fact inconsistent with full anti-comparativism (as well as with full comparativism). Further, the argument proves too much: accepting both premises of the argument leads naturally to conclusions that are near-uncontroversially absurd.

We turn then to the possibility of denying *Ontological Commitment*. This is the route we will eventually take. But we must proceed with care: *Ontological Commitment* seems at first sight a natural expression of the idea that only actuals, not mere possibilia, have ontological status. To date, this line of thought has not received an adequate reply.

The main aim of this essay is to supply the needed reply. Before taking up this task, section 3.3 clarifies the coherent alternative. Since *Ontological Commitment* and an Invariance premise jointly prove too much, if one is not to deny *Ontological Commitment* then one must deny the Invariance premise. This is the route taken by variantism. A variantist view might be either comparativist or anti-comparativist: the basic strategy is to agree with the full comparativist (resp. the full anti-comparativist) whenever doing so would not violate *Ontological Commitment*, but to defer to the latter whenever that imposes any restriction on personal betterness comparisons. Variantism suffers from no terrible internal flaws, but is unmotivated if (as we will argue) *Ontological Commitment* is unmotivated.

The remainder of the essay explores how *Ontological Commitment* might fail, and the implications for the debate over existence comparativism. Section 3.4 explores several principles that might seem natural applications of the idea that 'only actuals have ontological status' to the present case, and concludes that none succeeds in establishing *Ontological Commitment*. In several of the cases, however, plausibly *Ontological Commitment* can fail only if the grammatical and semantic structure of sentences of the form '*A* is better for *S* than *B*' come apart, in ways that have particular features.

Section 3.5 develops in more detail one example of an analysis according to which the required features are indeed present. We call this the *Lives Account*. According to the Lives Account, sentences of the form 'A is better for S than B' more fundamentally express not a three-place relation with S as one relatum, but instead a two-place relation holding between two 'ways' (or 'lives'): the way things would go for S if A obtained, and the way things would go for S if B obtained. We argue that such an analysis is independently motivated, and that on the account in question, nothing in the general metaphysics presents any obstacle to full comparativism (or to full anticomparativism). Section 3.6 replies, on behalf of a Lives Account, to an argument that Krister Bykvist has offered in favour of the usual practice of interpreting 'A is better for S than B' simply as a three-place relation with S among its relata.

Section 3.7 considers a different analysis: one that reduces personal betterness *comparisons* to prior ascriptions of monadic personal goodness *amounts*. This suggests a different argument against existence comparativism, which we will call the Well-being Argument. The Well-being Argument also invokes a premise that is somewhat in the spirit of *Ontological Commitment*, but avoids the pitfall of thereby proving too much that plagues *Ontological Commitment* itself. We argue here, though, that the Well-being Argument begs the question against existence comparativism.

Section 3.8 summarizes. We do not conclude that existence comparativism is true, but we do conclude that there is no reason *of general metaphysics or semantics* why it cannot be true.

3.2 The Metaphysical Argument against Existence Comparativism

3.2.1 The Argument

The Metaphysical Argument is succinctly stated by Broome:

> [I]t cannot ever be true that it is better for a person that she lives than that she should never have lived at all. If it were better for a person that she lives than that she should never have lived at all, then if she had never lived at all, that would have been worse for her than if she had lived. But if she had never lived at all, there would have been no her for it to be worse for, so it could not have been worse for her. (Broome 1999, 168)

Here is our official formulation of the argument:[5]

---

[5] Our formulation of the argument deals with 'better for' statements, rather than also discussing 'worse for' and 'equally good for' statements, only by way of abbreviation. Everything in our discussion would equally apply, *mutatis mutandis*, to sentences of these other forms.

Limited Invariance: If it is possible that A is better for S than B, then A would be better than B both if A obtained and if B obtained.

Ontological Commitment: Necessarily, if A is better for S than B, then S exists.

Therefore,

Betterness Requires Double Existence: If it is possible that A is better for S than B, then S exists both in A and in B.

This is not precisely Broome's formulation, but we take it that our reconstruction is faithful to the intended spirit of the argument (and that it is the argument that many other discussants have at least sometimes had in mind; we take these to include, for instance, Holtug 2001, sec. 4; Bykvist 2007; Arrhenius and Rabinowicz 2015; and Fleurbaey and Voorhoeve 2015). A different argument, which might (with somewhat more effort) be read into Broome's paragraph, is the Well-being Argument that we discuss in section 3.7 below.

3.2.2 Accepting Anti-comparativism

The conclusion of the Metaphysical Argument—*Betterness Requires Double Existence*—implies anti-comparativism, and seems inconsistent with comparativism.[6] Many authors accept anti-comparativism, and do so apparently on the basis of the Metaphysical Argument.

A little closer inspection, however, shows that this line of reasoning is not cogent. For *Ontological Commitment*, by itself, rules out both comparativism *and anti-comparativism*, as those theses are normally understood (and as we stated them above).[7] To bring out this point, consider:

Example 1. Connie exists both in A and in B, though not in the actual world @. She is better off in A than in B:

	@	A	B
Connie	-	20	10

In Example 1, full comparativists and full anti-comparativists alike hold that A is better for Connie than B. But Connie does not actually exist. So it follows from *Ontological Commitment* that A is not (actually) better for Connie than B.

---

[6] Why only 'seems'? The point is that if persons exist necessarily, then the consequent of *Betterness Requires Double Existence* is trivially true—as are both full comparativism and full anti-comparativism, as stated above. Cf. footnote 9.

[7] Thanks to Teru Thomas for pressing this central point.

Although inconsistent with both full comparativism and full anti-comparativism, perhaps *this* conclusion is acceptable; section 3.3 discusses views that accept it. However, things are otherwise when *Ontological Commitment* is combined with the thought that the truth-values of personal betterness comparisons should not vary from one world to another.

This brings us on to our second point. The Metaphysical Argument, as we have formulated it, assumes a premise of *limited* invariance: propositions of the form '*A* is better for *S* than *B*' must be true at both *A* and *B*, if true anywhere.[8] But there seems no reason to believe this without also believing a stronger condition of *full* invariance, according to which the truth-values of propositions of this form are invariant across *all* possible worlds. In Example 1, all parties to the present discussion want to agree at the very least that *if A or B had obtained*, *A* would have been better for Connie than *B*. But (as we noted above) *Ontological Commitment* prevents the proposition that *A* is better for Connie than *B* from being true at any world in which Connie does not exist; if so, a principle of full invariance would then prevent it from being true at *A* or at *B* either. That is, we are driven to the conclusion that it is impossible that any world is better than any other for any contingent being. Assuming (as we will) that persons exist merely contingently, that is absurd.[9]

We conclude that on pain of either motivational incoherence or absurdity, one must anyway reject at least one of the premises of the Metaphysical Argument, whatever one's views on existence comparativism. There is plenty of territory to explore here, in that both of the premises of the Metaphysical Argument are at least *prima facie* very natural. But the open question can only be *in precisely what way* one or both of the premises fails, and whether that more detailed account turns out to support or to undermine existence comparativism—or, as we will argue, neither.

---

[8] True *at* both *A* and *B*, not *in* *A* and *B*. The notion of truth *in* a world raises additional complications that are irrelevant for our purposes; cf. footnote 16.

[9] This assumption is widespread, but not universal. According to necessitism, *everything* exists necessarily (if at all); this includes persons alongside, for instance, atoms, rocks, institutions, and shapes. A necessitist will still, of course, recognize that *some* line can be drawn roughly where we normally say the line between existence and mere possibility lies. According to Williamson (2002, 2013), it is the divide between the concrete and the non-concrete. A modal realist position in the spirit of David Lewis' (1986) might also be necessitist; the divide in that case is between the actual and the non-actual, understood indexically.

It is natural to think that if necessitism is granted, then all the obstacles to full comparativism and full anti-comparativism discussed in this paper simply evaporate. (Something like this suggestion is made by Williamson himself regarding the comparativism/anti-comparativism debate (2013, sec. 1.8), though the argument that he has in mind is closer to the Well-Being Argument that we discuss in section 3.7.) We are skeptical of this, but we lack the space to explore that here.

In any case, for the remainder of the paper, we will largely set aside the possibility of necessitism.

3.2.3 Denying *Ontological Commitment*

Might one deny *Ontological Commitment*?

The intuitive reason for thinking not, we take it, is that *Ontological Commitment* seems to follow from the metaphysical actualist idea that only actuals, not mere possibilia, have ontological status. Mere possibilia do not exist, and so—surely?—are not there to have any properties at all, the property of *A* being better for oneself than *B* being just a special case of this.

A very few contributors to the debate over existence comparativism have resisted this line of thought. An example is Fleurbaey and Voorhoeve, who deny the following principle:

> *No Properties of the Never-Existent*: An individual who never exists cannot have any properties, not even the relational property of something being better or worse for her. (Fleurbaey and Voorhoeve 2015, 98)

This principle seems to have struck most discussants, however, as non-negotiable. And this is understandable. For, at least at first sight, denying it would seem (for example) to undermine too much of our usual account of how we can read ontological commitments off from data about which sentences are held true. The reason why the sentence 'Tom sees Mary' cannot be true unless Tom exists, for instance, seems to be that this sentence is asserting that a certain two-place relation holds between Tom and Mary, and that relations cannot hold unless their relata exist.[10]

We agree with Fleurbaey and Voorhoeve on this: the principle they call 'No properties of the never-existent', if interpreted so that it entails *Ontological Commitment*, is false (as is *Ontological Commitment* itself). But more needs to be said if we are to dispel the sense that these claims are absurd. The main purpose of the essay is to execute this task.

3.3 Variantism

Let us first clarify the coherent alternative. What we call the 'variantist' response accepts *Ontological Commitment*, but resists the Metaphysical Argument by denying *Limited Invariance*.

Consider again Example 1 from the previous section. If *Ontological Commitment* holds, then '*A* is better for Connie than *B*' cannot be *actually* true:

---

[10] It is incumbent on a necessitist to further explain why 'Tom sees Mary' cannot be true unless Tom is *concrete*; cf. footnote 9.

Connie does not actually exist. If we deny full invariance, however, this does not prevent the proposition in question from being true at worlds at which Connie *does* exist, including A and B. According to the variantist, this possibility is realized: *If A or B had obtained, then A would have been better for Connie than B.*

The positions we are interested in go further, and also deny the weaker principle of *Limited Invariance*. The resulting variantist positions might be either comparativist or anti-comparativist in inclination. To see the difference, consider an example of the type that takes centre stage in the dispute between comparativists and anti-comparativists:

Example 2. Peggy exists and is happy in @, but does not exist in B.

	@	B
Peggy	10	-

A variantist, of course, will insist (as per *Ontological Commitment*) that if B had obtained, then @ would not have been better for Peggy than B. But on the question of whether @ is *actually* better for Peggy than B, both comparativist and anti-comparativist options are open. The position that we will call *comparativist variantism* (resp. *anti-comparativist variantism*) reproduces the verdicts of full comparativism (resp. those of full anti-comparativism) whenever these are consistent with *Ontological Commitment*, and defers to *Ontological Commitment* otherwise. So, for example, the comparativist variantist holds that @ is (actually) better for Peggy than B, although it would not have been if B had obtained.[11]

We will also have occasion to consider a 'mirror-image' of Example 2:

Example 3. Jenny exists and is happy in B, but does not exist in @.

	@	B
Jenny	-	10

On either variantist position, of course, B is not better for Jenny than @ (though the comparativist variantist holds that it would have been, if Jenny had existed).

Whether anything of importance hangs on the dispute between a variantist position and the corresponding invariantist one depends on precisely what are the associated principles linking personal to overall betterness (hereafter, 'link principles'). As in the discussion in section 3.1, the key link principles are the Pareto

---

[11] Comparativist variantism is defended by Arrhenius and Rabinowicz (2015). Remarks in the same spirit are also made by Nagel (1970, 78) and by Holtug (2001, sec. 5). We are not aware of any literature defending (or indeed discussing) anti-comparativist variantism.

and Person-Affecting principles. Suppose first that these principles consider only actual people and actual personal betterness relations:

Actualist Indicative Pareto Principle: If A is at least as good as B for every actual person, and there is some actual person for whom A is better than B, then A is better than B.

Actualist Indicative Person-Affecting Principle: If A is better than B, then there is some actual person for whom A is better than B.

The actualist indicative link principles lead to unacceptable conclusions even aside from an insistence on *Ontological Commitment*. For instance, consider again Example 1, and let us take it that no-one except Connie exists in either A or B. Then there is no actual person for whom A is better than B: the only otherwise plausible candidate is Connie, and she is not actual. So the above Pareto principle fails to imply that A is better than B; the above Person-Affecting-Principle goes further, and implies that A is not better than B. While this conclusion might be rationalized by appeal to the 'moral actualist' idea that only the interests of actual persons matter morally, they are otherwise highly counterintuitive. We will take it for the purposes of this essay that such strong moral actualism is unacceptable.[12]

If so, the actualist indicative link principles must be wrong. Note again that this line of reasoning does not make use of any premises concerning the extension of the personal betterness comparisons. In particular, therefore, it is independent of whether or not one accepts *Ontological Commitment*, and so independent of variantism.

The culprit in the above example, clearly, is the restriction to actual persons. This suggests the following possibilist link principles (as in section 3.1):

Possibilist Indicative Pareto Principle: If A is at least as good as B for every possible person, and there is some possible person for whom A is better than B, then A is better than B.

---

[12] Moral actualism is not to be conflated with the *metaphysical* actualism that motivates much of the discussion of the present essay. For discussion of moral actualism in the context of population ethics, see (Hare 2007; Greaves 2017, sec. 5.3; Arrhenius ms, chap. 9).

Let us anticipate a possible objection. It might be argued that the conclusion that A is not better than B in Example 1 is after all acceptable, on grounds that no moral-actualist *normative* implications need follow from it. Why think the latter? Well, since it is essential to the verdict that neither A nor B is actual, there seems little danger that the variantist position will imply that someone did no wrong in choosing B over A — *ex hypothesi*, nobody chose B (or A). However, this is not sufficient to block normative implications. An agent might make a choice that commits her to B conditional on some event E, rather than to A conditional on E. Absent some further factor to justify the choice, this choice seems wrong *even if, as things turn out, E does not occur*. So objectionable normative implications can easily follow from the claim that A is not better than B; it is indeed important to have link principles that avoid this axiological conclusion.

Possibilist Indicative Person-Affecting Principle: If A is better than B, then there is some possible person for whom A is better than B.

If (as full comparativism and full anti-comparativism agree) A is better for Connie than B, then the Possibilist Indicative Person-Affecting Principle (correctly) refrains from ruling out that A is better than B. If A and B are equally good for possible persons who exist in neither of these states of affairs, then the Possibilist Indicative Pareto Principle goes further, and (again, correctly) implies that A is better than B.[13]

If *Ontological Commitment* is accepted, however, then 'going possibilist' with one's link principles is not enough to avoid the unwanted moral-actualist conclusions regarding overall betterness. For, again, on any view that accepts *Ontological Commitment*, A isn't (actually) better for Connie than B. Rather, on a variantist view, it is only that *if A or B had obtained*, then *A would have been* better for Connie than B. So, to get the desired implications (and absences of implications) to follow from a variantist view, we need versions of the principles that are not only possibilist, but also subjunctive:

Possibilist Subjunctive Pareto Principle: If for every possible person S, A could have been at least as good for S as B, and there is some possible person for whom A could have been better than B, then A is better than B.

Possibilist Subjunctive Person-Affecting Principle: If A is better than B, then there is some possible person for whom A could have been better than B.

Even on a variantist view, this Person-Affecting Principle refrains from implying that A is not better than B, and (modulo the issue discussed in footnote 13) this Pareto principle implies that A is better than B— as desired.

To sum up: on pain of moral actualism, any population ethicist must allow link principles to quantify over merely possible persons, and the variantist must (in addition) opt for subjunctive versions of the link principles. Since the subjunctive principles are themselves reasonably elegant, and have a clear motivation in terms of the denial of invariance, however, this is perhaps no significant cost of the variantist view.[14]

---

[13] If instead A and B are incomparable for possible persons who exist in neither A nor B— a position that seems coherent, and somewhat in the spirit of anti-comparativism—then the Possibilist Indicative Pareto Principle as stated is silent on Example 1. We could get stronger implications by replacing the first clause of this principle with the weaker condition 'if there is no possible person for whom B is better than A', though the resulting principle might be less compelling in the presence of widespread incomparability.

[14] Up to largely aesthetic differences in the statements of the link principles, the moves above are essentially the ones made by Arrhenius and Rabinowicz (2015), though they do not consider cases like Example 1, or the possibility of anti-comparativist variantism.

To say that variantism does not suggest any (new) unacceptable conclusions regarding overall betterness, however, is not to say that variantism is correct. In fact, we will argue, the motivation for variantism—the sense, that is, that *Ontological Commitment* is unassailable, or even probable—springs from a misapplication of the relevant metaphysical ideas.

3.4 Metaphysical Actualism

The issues posed by Example 2 on the one hand, and Examples 1 and 3 on the other, are importantly different. In Example 2, *Ontological Commitment* requires that *if Peggy had not existed*, then @ *would not have been* better than B for Peggy— but actually, Peggy does exist. In Example 1 (resp. Example 3), *Ontological Commitment* requires that A (resp. @) *is* not better than B for Connie (resp. Jenny), on the grounds that Connie (resp. Jenny) *actually* does not exist. Let us set out these two principles explicitly:

OC1: If S does not exist, then A is not better for S than B.
OC2: If S does not exist in A, then if A had obtained, A would not have been better than B for S.

OC2 is just a reformulation of *Ontological Commitment* itself; OC1 is a weakening. Ultimately, we will argue that both of these principles should be rejected. But the metaphysical issues raised by the strengthening from OC1 to OC2 are somewhat distinct from those that are already raised by the weaker principle OC1, so we will treat them separately.

In both cases, the rejection of the principle at least arguably presupposes the availability of a suitable reanalysis of the sentences of interest, so that at a deeper level, the truth-conditions of these sentences do not involve a relation obtaining with the person S as relatum. We will further indicate our own proposal for an (independently motivated) reanalysis that has these features; that is the task of section 3.5. But clarity is served by also understanding the workings of the language we normally speak, not only the 'deeper level'. The present section focuses on that task.

3.4.1 Property Actualism

We have so far worked fairly directly with the actualist slogan that 'only actuals, not mere possibilia, have ontological status'. But there are several more precise theses that this slogan might suggest. One is:

Property actualism: For any object x and property P, it is not possible that x should have had P but not existed:

$$\forall x \forall P \,\Box\, (Px \to Ex).$$

The restriction to properties rather than relations more generally is inessential: one might equally postulate:[15]

Relations actualism: For any objects $x_1, \ldots, x_n$ and any relation R, it is not possible that the x_i should have stood in R to one another but not all existed:

$$\forall x_1 \ldots \forall x_n \forall R \,\Box\, (Rx_1 \ldots x_n \to Ex_1 \wedge \ldots \wedge Ex_n).$$

These theses, if true, would ground both OC1 and OC2. However, as is well recognized in the literature on metaphysical actualism, *property (and relations) actualism is false*, unless the notion of 'property' is carefully restricted (see e.g. Fine 1985). To see why, consider the property of not existing. According to property actualism, it is not possible that Socrates should have had the property of not existing but not existed. Yet this seems just a convoluted way of saying that it is not possible that Socrates should have not existed—that is, that Socrates exists necessarily. But this seems absurd. (Furthermore, if the 'absurd' conclusion is true—if, that is, necessitism is true—then property actualism, while true, loses its bite.)

One might insist that non-existence, and other features that do not presuppose existence in the way insisted by relations actualism, is not a genuine *property*; perhaps it is instead a mere 'condition' (Plantinga 1983). This insistence could be related to the distinction between grammatical and semantic structure. Grammatical structure is relevant for the purpose of assessing a sentence as grammatically correct or incorrect; semantic structure is relevant for determining ontological commitments; the two can come apart. One who says 'the average woman has 2.3 children' is not ontologically committing to the existence of an average woman, for all that the term in question is grammatically a noun phrase. Rather, significant reanalysis is required to identify the semantic structure of, and thence the ontological commitments of, this sentence.

The thought, then, is that the semantic structure of 'Socrates does not exist' is (something like) $\neg Es$. And the term 'property' is (on this account) to be reserved for items that occupy the corresponding position in the sentence's *semantic* (not grammatical) structure. So (on this account) this sentence is not attributing a

---

[15] Henceforth, we will usually write of property actualism for simplicity of exposition, but everything we say will apply equally to relations actualism more generally.
 We take the term 'property actualism' from Fine (1985). Plantinga (1983) calls the same view 'serious actualism'; Williamson (2013, sec. 4.1) calls it 'the being constraint'.

property to Socrates; rather, it is *denying* that x has a particular property, and 'x does not exist' is a mere *condition* of x.

There is of course nothing objectionable about choosing to use one's technical language in that way. But if one makes this move, one must then not be too quick to move from the observation that some condition of x can be expressed in ordinary language to the conclusion that the condition in question is a genuine property. Here, we will contrast 'positive' (existence-requiring) and 'negative' (not existence-requiring) properties, rather than 'properties' and 'mere conditions', but nothing of substance hangs on this choice of terminology.

The point, then, is that while perhaps (for all we have said so far) it is not possible that there be any x that possesses some property but does not exist— $\Box \forall x \forall P(Px \rightarrow Ex)$ — this relatively innocuous thesis is crucially distinct from property actualism. For property actualism rules out even that (actual) individuals can possess any properties *at other possible worlds* in which they don't exist, and that is what created the trouble about Socrates.[16]

Non-existence is the canonical example of a negative property, but it is far from the only one. We noted above that 'Tom sees Mary' cannot be true unless Tom exists; *seeing Mary* is a positive property. But *not seeing Mary* is a negative property: if Tom had not existed, he would not have seen Mary. Similarly for *being such that Ameena's house is free of oneself*: if Tom had not existed, Ameena's house would have been free of Tom. One should not be convinced by an argument that 'If Tom had not existed then there would have been no him for Ameena's house to be free of, so Ameena's house could not have been free of him'.[17]

Similarly, many explicitly modal properties, e.g. the property of possibly seeing Mary, are such that individuals can possess those properties even at worlds in which the individual does not exist. If Tom hadn't existed, it would still have been *possible* that Tom sees Mary, since Tom's existence would still have been possible.[18]

So there are at least some negative properties. We must therefore countenance the possibility that 'A is better for S than B' expresses a relation that is negative with respect to S. If it is, then actualist scruples perhaps still underwrite OC1,

---

[16] Let A be a world in which Socrates does not exist. A distraction in the present discussion is that the proposition that Socrates does not exist arguably itself does not exist in A (since, arguably, Socrates is a constituent of that proposition; see section 3.4.2). This generates one sense in which the proposition that Socrates does not exist would not have been true if A had been actual: if the proposition hadn't existed, *a fortiori* it wouldn't have been true either. But, clearly, there is also another sense in which it would have been true: the proposition actually exists, and what it says accurately describes one aspect of A. We might say that the proposition is true *at A*, though it is not true *in A*: by stipulation, truth in A, but not truth at A, requires that the proposition in question exists according to A. Our discussion concerns truth-at, not truth-in. (Fine (1985, 192) discusses the same distinction in terms of 'inner' and 'outer' truth.)

[17] Thanks to Jeff Russell for this latter example.

[18] A similar example is considered in the context of the present debate by Fleurbaey and Voorhoeve (2015, 98).

which we have so far said nothing against (and which seems to follow from the more innocuous principle $\Box \forall x \forall P(Px \to Ex)$). But the modal contexts involved in OC2 are a different matter. Consider again, in Example 2: 'If Peggy had not existed, that would have been worse for her than the actual state of affairs'. According to OC2, this statement is false (or even 'absurd' (Arrhenius and Rabinowicz 2015)). But if we are dealing with a negative relation, it could be true. Peggy (by hypothesis) actually exists, and the statement says something about how things would have been with respect to her if she had not existed—just, perhaps, as 'If Tom had not existed, Ameena's house would have been free of Tom' says something about how things would have been with respect to Tom if he had not existed.

We must countenance this possibility, but we cannot simply *postulate* that it is realized. Of the reasonably uncontroversial examples of negative properties that we have seen, most have contained either an explicit negation ('Tom doesn't see Mary', 'Socrates does not exist') or explicitly modal terminology ('Tom might see Mary'). The only example not containing either of these instead contained the locution 'free of her', which itself is naturally analysed in terms that involve negation. This suggests that property (and relations) actualism might yet be true *of a fundamental language* (a language, that is, in which grammatical and semantic structure coincide), and that perhaps they are false of ordinary English only insofar as grammatical and semantic structure there come apart. If so, any suggestion that some property is negative is hostage to the existence of a nontrivial reanalysis explaining how that comes to be.[19]

We will argue in section 3.5 that indeed such a reanalysis of '*A* is better for *S* than *B*' is readily available. By way of high-level preview, our claim there will be that '*A* is better for *S* than *B*', like 'Tom possibly sees Mary', is an implicitly modal locution; furthermore, that its semantic structure is such that *S* herself does not figure as a relatum in the truth-conditions. But first, let us consider OC1.

3.4.2 Singular Propositions

The above way of denying property actualism does nothing to impugn OC1, and therefore does not occasion any change from the variantist's position on statements of the form '*A* is better for *S* than *B*' (with no modal prefix), *where S is a merely possible person*. Thus denying property actualism is still not enough to open the door to either full comparativism or full anti-comparativism. We still

---

[19] Williamson (2013, sec. 4.1) argues that even contingentists, and not only adherents of the necessitist view that he himself favours, should subscribe to property and relations actualism. But Williamson's discussion concerns semantic structure, not the grammatical structure of a natural language; the point that these theses are false *of ordinary language* remains secure.

apparently cannot have, for instance, that *A* is better for Connie than *B*, in Example 1. There is not, actually, any such person as Connie to possess even a *negative* property.

This suggests the following position. In Example 2, it might (or might not) be that if *B* had obtained, @ would (still) have been better for Peggy than *B*—because Peggy is actual, and so can serve to render this modal assertion true by standing in a negative relation, even though the assertion concerns a counterfactual circumstance in which Peggy does not exist. But in Example 3, analogously to Example 1, it cannot be that @ is worse for Jenny than *B*, because there is no Jenny to stand in even a negative relation.

In a certain metaphysical frame of mind, this position might seem natural. But on reflection, it is odd. Consider again the relatively uncontroversial examples of negative properties that we considered above. One was '*x* is not rich'. We understand how it could be true that *if Tom hadn't existed* then Tom would not have been rich. But if this is so, it also seems highly plausible that my merely possible sister is not rich. Similarly for (e.g.) the plight of Ameena's house. Further, given the course that our discussion of negative properties has taken, this should not seem paradoxical. For (recall) we conceded that some reanalysis is necessary if we are to explain how '*x* is not rich' and 'Ameena's house is free of *x*' come to express negative properties, and we suggested that the key would be postulating a semantic structure according to which, at the deeper level of semantic structure, what is being expressed is not of the form '*x* has property ϕ' at all. But then it seems that whatever the further details of the reanalysis, the same reanalysis is likely to explain how locutions of the form 'S is not rich' and 'Ameena's house is free of S' can be true of a merely possible person. And, if so, similarly for '*A* is better for S than *B*'.

In section 3.5, we will argue (in the context of suggesting a particular reanalysis) that this scenario is indeed realized. First, though, we address a concern to the effect that it couldn't possibly be realized.

A *singular proposition* is a proposition that is 'directly about' a particular individual, in the sense of having that individual as a constituent. The proposition that Plato was wise, for example, plausibly has Plato as a constituent. This is to be contrasted with propositions such as that the teacher of Aristotle was wise. The latter is also 'about' Plato in an indirect sense, in that the description 'the teacher of Aristotle' picks out Plato; but the proposition contains Aristotle and the teacher-of relation as constituents, rather than Plato himself. Plausibly, propositions cannot exist unless their constituents all exist, just as sets cannot exist unless their members do. So the proposition that Plato was wise would not exist if Plato did not; the proposition that the teacher of Aristotle was wise, in contrast, could exist without Plato (though of course in some such situations it would not be true).

Perhaps, then, the relevant actualist thought is:

Singularity: Statements of the form 'A is better for S than B' express propositions that are singular with respect to S.

It follows from *Singularity*, together with the auxiliary claim that propositions ontologically presuppose their constituents, that neither 'B is better for Jenny than @' in Example 3 nor 'A is better for Connie than B' in Example 1 is true (because neither of them succeeds in expressing a proposition; the intended propositions fail to exist). That is, *Singularity* seems to underwrite an insistence on OC1 (though not OC2).

If *this* is the explanation of why 'A is better for S than B' requires the existence of S, however, there seems no reason not to extend the thesis to cover modal contexts, thus:

Extended Singularity: Statements of the form 'If C had obtained, A would have been better for S than B' express propositions that are singular with respect to S.

But *Extended Singularity* leads to trouble. *Perhaps* it is acceptable for 'A is better for Connie than B' (in Example 1) to fail to be true, given that (once we impose subjunctive link principles) nothing untoward follows from this at the level of overall betterness. But *Extended Singularity* further implies that even the counterfactual statements 'if A [or B] had obtained, A would have been better for Connie than B' fail to be true. Given this verdict, in the case of Example 1, for instance, it follows even from the subjunctive link principles that A is not better than B. As noted in section 3.3, this conclusion is unacceptable.[20]

What has gone wrong? Well, on reflection, it is perfectly obvious that in our discussion, 'Connie' (for instance) is functioning as an abbreviation for a description (whatever is the correct account of the semantics of ordinary names for *actual* people). Recall how we introduced 'Connie'. We outlined some non-actual possible worlds, and we introduced the 'Connie' as a name for the merely possible person occupying such-and-such qualitative place in the worlds thus described. And of course, nothing in this account is specific to Connie: this *has* to be the way the apparent names are functioning, whenever we use apparent names for merely possible persons (as we often do, in particular, in the context of population ethics).

The upshot is that both *Singularity* and *Extended Singularity* are false whenever they would place any restriction on the truth-values of the statements of interest.

---

[20] There is a further problem for the fan of *Extended Singularity* (compared to the discussion of the otherwise similar point in section 3.3). Even to get the conclusion that *if A had obtained then A would have been better than B*, we will need somehow to bring in Connie (else there is no *explanation* of A's counterfactual superiority over B). It is unclear how this can be done without similarly opening the door to the possibility that if A had obtained then A would have been better *for Connie* than B, and thereby abandoning the core of the 'singular propositions' idea.

Metaphysical-actualist restrictions on personal betterness comparisons cannot be motivated via considerations of singular propositions.[21]

3.4.3 Metaphysical Actualism Revisited

If not property actualism (because that is either false or toothless), and not a view about singular propositions (because that is false of the fragments of language we are interested in), what is the correct expression of the basic metaphysical-actualist idea that 'only actuals have ontological status'?

In the hands of Kit Fine (1977, 1985), actualism is a commitment to a fundamental language in which the *quantifiers* are all actualist. In that case, it seems at first sight that one cannot say things like 'Connie is a merely possible person': for, taken at face value, this statement quantifies over possible persons, and not only over actual persons. This form of actualism also underwrites the above thought that the more innocuous principle $\Box \forall x \forall P(Px \to Ex)$ is non-negotiable: if the quantifier $\forall x$ is actualist (that is, it quantifies only over actual objects, and not over mere possibilia), then the principle is indeed trivially true, simply because of the more basic truth that is then expressed by $\Box \forall x Ex$.

Crucially, there is no suggestion here of rejecting talk of mere possibilia across the board. Use of non-fundamental languages is not a crime, and indeed such languages are often the most perspicuous for the task at hand. And in the present case, as Fine himself is at pains to emphasize, 'talk of possible worlds and possible individuals appears to make perfectly good sense' (1985, 177). So, if actualism is true, there had better be some partial translation from the non-fundamental possibilist language to the more fundamental actualist language, preserving the coherence of at least the more obviously innocuous possibilist assertions.

There is no guarantee, though, that *everything* that is expressible in a possibilist language will also be expressible in the actualist language. So there is in principle a question of whether locutions of the form 'A is better for S than B', with S a merely possible person, are among those that survive the translation to the actualist language. It seems clear to us that they are, though we omit consideration of the details of possible translations for reasons of space.[22]

---

[21] Absent some other wise teacher, of course, not only the proposition that Plato was wise but also the proposition that the teacher of Aristotle was wise would not have been true if Plato had not existed. That is, even propositions that are *indirectly* about some object often require that the object in question exist in order for the proposition to be true, as (apparently) per the general principle that if x does not exist then x has no properties. But this thought just returns us to the demand for reanalysis that we have already recognized, and that we will address in section 3.5.

[22] The most popular type of actualist reduction of possibilist discourse is proxy reduction, in which one finds some suitable surrogate, from among actual entities, for the otherwise problematic possibilist entities. For instance, one might represent possible worlds by propositions, and possible individuals by properties (see Lewis 1986, sec. 3 for an overview of these ersatzist approaches). A different approach is outlined by Fine (1977, 1985).

3.5 The Lives Account

In section 3.4, we considered various theses of a metaphysical-actualist flavour, and we concluded that none presents a convincing argument either for *Ontological Commitment* itself, or for its weakening OC1. But at several points in that discussion, we were forced to leave a hanging thread. In all the relatively uncontroversial examples of locutions that seem to involve negative properties, or that seem to predicate something of a mere possibilium in such a way as to result in truth, we could see how grammatical and semantic structure plausibly come apart, and (crucially) it was this coming-apart that explained the otherwise puzzling feature in question. So our suggestion that '*A* is better for *S* than *B*' could exhibit similar behaviour is hostage to the availability of a suitable explanatory reanalysis.

But such a reanalysis is near at hand, and independently motivated. Suppose, by way of warm-up, that Inaaya has never eaten beans, and in fact never will. Her father urges her to commence: beans, he says, are good for her! Quite plausibly, Inaaya's father speaks truly; but how can beans do any good for anyone who never goes near them? The appearance of a puzzle here dissolves when we recognize that the content of the father's assertion is (roughly) that *if Inaaya ate beans*, her health would improve. It is, that is, an implicitly modal assertion.

Similarly, the content of '*A* is better for *S* than *B*' is at least roughly that *if A obtained*, things would be better for *S* than they would be *if B obtained*. Developing this thought leads to a reanalysis on which it is unmysterious how '*A* is better for *S* than *B*' (and related assertions) can be true in cases in which, in any of several senses, *S* does not exist.

3.5.1 Comparing Possible Lives

At a superficial level, '*A* is better for *S* than *B*' expresses a three-place personal betterness relation holding between the states of affairs (or possible worlds) *A* and *B*, and the possible person *S*. That, of course, is what gave rise to the worries surrounding *Ontological Commitment*. But perhaps at a deeper level, what is being expressed is no relation of *S* at all.

This type of explanation is indeed suggested by the idea that what is being said is more fundamentally that *if A obtained, things would be better for S than they would be if B obtained*. Rephrasing slightly: *the way things would go for S if A obtained is personally better than the way things would go for S if B obtained*. Suppose we reify these 'ways things might go for a given possible person'. Then what is being asserted, when we say that *A* is better for *S* than *B*, is more fundamentally that a *two*-place personal betterness relation holds between two of these 'ways'. At this more fundamental level *S* herself is not among the relata, and thereby *Ontological Commitment* can fail. Thus the absurd implications of combining *Ontological Commitment* with *Full Invariance* are easily avoided on this account. This might make the account appealing to comparativists and anti-comparativists alike.

For convenience of terminology (only), let us refer to 'ways things might go for S' as possible *lives* that S might have had. It is natural to identify these lives with *properties*. At a maximally fine-grained level, the property corresponding to the way things would go for S if A obtained includes a complete description of the corresponding possible world (the property, that is, of being such that A obtains), as well as properties that distinguish between different individuals (for example, the property of eating mushrooms every Friday). For many purposes, this extreme degree of fine-graining will not be necessary, and we could take the lives in question to be significantly coarser-grained objects. The degree of fine- or coarse-graining will be largely irrelevant for our purposes. Our only constraint is that the account must be sufficiently fine-grained to distinguish between lives that are different in respects relevant to well-being. (Which respects those are, of course, is a matter of substantive theory of well-being: hedonists, preference-satisfaction theorists, and objective list theorists will disagree here.)

Here is an example, to fix ideas. In the actual world, let us suppose, Abdullah has the properties of breaking his arm by falling out of a tree aged 6, completing a degree in clinical psychology aged 23, smelling cow parsley for the first time aged 33, and many more besides. Like all of us, he also has the degenerate properties of being such that Comet Neowise passes within 65 million miles of Earth in July 2020, and being such that $2+2=4$. Let $l^@_{Abdullah}$ be the compound property corresponding to the conjunction of *all* the properties that Abdullah actually has and that are relevant to the individuation of his life, whichever those are. We then identify $l^@_{Abdullah}$ with Abdullah's (actual) life.

The Lives Account, then, postulates that the relevant deeper structure involves:

- A set L of possible lives.
- A two-place personal betterness relation $\succ (j, k)$, where $j, k \in L$.[23]

If we say 'A is better for S than B', we are comparing S's life in A (l^A_S) with S's life in B (l^B_S), and asserting that the former is personally better than the latter

---

[23] Within the Lives Account, we refer to $\succ$ as a 'personal' betterness relation simply to distinguish the intended sense of betterness from *contributive* betterness, i.e. from the question of which lives are such that adding them to a given state of affairs improves the state of affairs by more. This choice of terminology should not mislead us into exaggerating the extent to which the instantiation of $\succ$ in the Lives Account requires the existence of persons; we discuss below (sections 3.5.2–3.5.3) the question of whether or not it does.

Strictly speaking, the account should postulate a two-place personal 'at least as good as' relation, $\succeq$, and define the strict betterness relation $\succ$ from $\succeq$ in the usual way. We formulate the account here directly in terms of $\succ$ for ease of exposition.

$(l_S^A \succ l_S^B)$.[24] Thus, in the (strained) sentence 'The actual world is better for Deepti than the world that would have been actualized if she had stayed at home last night', the comparison being made is between the life Deepti actually has, and a different possible life (perhaps only slightly different) that she would have had if she had stayed at home last night. Many other forms of sentence, more natural-sounding in ordinary language, have truth-conditions that are best explicated by first finding a corresponding sentence of the above form, and then applying the above principles. For instance, the (natural) sentence 'Tonya would have been better off if she had jumped' corresponds to the (strained) sentence 'The actual world is worse for Tonya than the one that would have obtained if she had jumped'.[25]

Like the question of how finely lives must be individuated, the *extension* of the dyadic personal betterness relation $\succ$ is of course determined by substantive first-order evaluative theory: hedonists will disagree with preference-satisfaction theorists, and so on.

On a Lives Account, *Ontological Commitment* is false. The condition $l_S^A \succ l_S^B$ requires only that the lives l_S^A and l_S^B exist; S herself is not among the relata. Since lives are properties, their existence is (we take it) uncontroversial for present purposes.[26] The account provides, meanwhile, no reason to doubt *Limited Invariance*: If life l_1 is better than life l_2, then necessarily l_1 is better than l_2. If the Lives Account is correct, variantism is unmotivated.

3.5.2 Existence Comparativism and Null Lives

Variantism is unmotivated, but this leaves open both invariantist possibilities: full comparativism, and full anti-comparativism. How should we choose between those?

Within the Lives Account, making sense of existence comparativism requires postulating that the set L includes at least one *null life*, corresponding to never being born. This notion of a null life might seem obviously problematic: a 'null

---

[24] Since we are postulating a reanalysis of the sentences of interest in terms of a quite different deeper structure, rather than offering a semantic value directly for the term 'S' as it appears in the original sentence, we do not hereby commit the Lives Account to the view that persons are lives.

Krister Bykvist and Wlodek Rabinowicz have both pressed us on the issue of whether a Lives Account can give an adequate treatment of compound sentences of the form 'Peggy decides to stay at home, even though going out would be better for her', without taking on something like this commitment. We hold out hope that it can, though we lack the space to explore this here.

[25] In both cases, ultimately we will want a more sophisticated account—for instance, to deal with unit comparisons of well-being, rather than mere level comparisons. But the required moves in the direction of greater sophistication are, as far as we are aware, orthogonal to the features of the Lives Account that are important for the purposes of this essay.

[26] That is, for present purposes we can set aside any nominalist scruples. One does not usually object that '*A* is better for *S* than *B*' cannot be true on the grounds that the states of affairs *A* and *B*, being putative abstract objects, do not exist. It is incumbent on the nominalist to explain how to make do without our apparent commitment to the existence of abstract objects in general.

life', one might think, is not really a life at all (it is more like the *absence* of life). But nothing should hang on our choice of technical vocabulary. Given the theoretical role of the notion of a life in this framework, postulating null lives in fact seems unavoidable. For, again, the notion of a life is supposed to represent a way things might have gone for a given person. Clearly, not having been born is one way that things might have gone for each of us—or more than one way, if other details of the worlds in which we do not exist (besides the fact of our non-existence) are relevant to how things go for us in those worlds.

Since L includes null lives, nothing *in the structure of the general framework* prevents existence comparativism from being true. We postulated above that 'A is better for S than B' is true iff $l_S^A \succ l_S^B$. If S does not exist in A (resp. in B), l_S^A (resp. l_S^B) is a null life. *If in addition* these null lives stand in relations of personal betterness to non-null lives, it follows that sentences of the form 'A is better for S than B' can be true even when S does not exist in one of the worlds in question. The natural way of filling in the detail is then to hold that any null life is personally worse than (resp. personally better than, personally equally as good as) all non-null lives that have positive (resp. negative, zero) well-being. In that case, for example, '@ is better for Peggy than A' is true iff Peggy's life in @ is worth living—as per existence comparativism.[27]

The crucial question for evaluating existence comparativism, in this framework, is whether or not null lives stand in the $\succ$ relation to any other lives. This is a substantive evaluative question, about which ethicists might disagree. But it cannot be settled by appeal to anything like a general principle of metaphysics or semantics.

3.5.3 Objections

Let us dispose of some objections. First, one might worry that it makes no sense to say that a person has a null life in a world in which that person does not exist, just as one might worry that it makes no sense to say that A is better for Connie than B in a world in which Connie does not exist. 'How can a person have any properties, including that of having a null life, without existing?' But, as we pointed out in section 3.4, this line of thought implicitly assumes that the properties in question are positive rather than negative ones. And since the property of having a (particular) null life is just the property of not existing (and perhaps also being such that some further conditions obtain), it is quite clear that to have a null life is

---

[27] Indeed, it is natural, if existence comparativism is granted, to take this to be *definitional* of the zero level of well-being, and thereby of the notion of a life being 'worth living' or 'worth not living'. See Arrhenius (ms, chap. 2) for a survey of other possible definitions.

to possess a negative property. This is, in fact, the canonical example that we used to introduce the notion of negative properties in the first place.[28]

A second objection is closely related. We have identified possible lives with properties—in principle, maximally specific properties. This makes them sound very much like centred worlds, as indeed they are. But we are accustomed to thinking of a centred world as a pair (A, i), where A is a world and i is a possible person *who exists in A*. Again, if lives were constrained to be this sort of object, then there could not be any null lives.

What this observation brings out is that although the 'lives' in our account are very much *like* centred worlds, there is a crucial difference. By construction of the usual notion of centred worlds, it is necessary that a person exist in w in order for there to be any centred worlds in which she is the centre and w is the corresponding uncentred world. But it is not necessary that a possible person exist in w in order for her to have a life that includes *being such that* w *obtains*. Again, this freedom is required if lives are to represent ways things could have gone for persons. Therefore lives cannot be identified with centred worlds as the latter are normally understood. We must stick to the more fundamental notion in terms of properties.[29]

Third, and again relatedly, one will be led astray if one thinks of the 'lives' in our framework as things that can possibly be *lived* by persons. This criterion is met for non-null lives, but plausibly, one cannot *live* a null life: the notion of living is such that one cannot live anything if one does not exist. But this shows only that not all possible lives (in our sense) are things that can be lived. There is no comparable obstacle to *having* a null life—having, that is, a certain negative property—in a world in which one does not exist.

A different possible objection is that that since, on the Lives Account, persons (as opposed to their lives) do not ultimately appear as semantic values, the account implies that when we say (for instance) '*A* is better for Connie than *B*', we are not strictly speaking *talking about Connie*; and perhaps this seems odd. But this objection is merely an echo of the thought that '*A* is better for Connie than *B*' must express a proposition that is singular with respect to Connie. We saw above (section 3.4.2) that this insistence is misguided, at least in the case of merely possible persons. In the case of actual persons, it would be possible to flesh out the account in such a way that Peggy herself is a constituent of the proposition being expressed (via a description that is used to pick out the life in question as the ones

---

[28] Indeed, it has the unusual feature of being (furthermore) what we might call a *strictly negative* property: a possible person can possess this property *only* in worlds in which she does not exist.
[29] If the details of w can matter for how well things would go for x if w obtained, where w is a world in which x does not exist, then existence comparativists would need to revise their usual account. It could not then be the case that the zero point of well-being corresponds to *the* point at which existence is equally as personally good as non-existence, since there would not then be any unique such point. While this would complicate the overall theory, it does not raise any problems of deep principle for the comparativist.

that *Peggy* has in the worlds in question), provided one does not mind having a dual account that treats merely possible persons differently. But in the case of merely possible persons, this is obviously impossible, and we should be used to living with that. It does not follow that we cannot 'talk about' merely possible persons, in a less strict (but still perfectly respectable) sense of that phrase.

3.5.4 Other Applications of the Lives Account

We have proposed the Lives Account, in the first instance, as an explanation of how sentences of the form '*A* is better for *S* than *B*' might be true even if *S* does not exist. But the account is independently highly plausible, and it has other uses besides this one. We will highlight two.

First, the Lives Account facilitates a more elegant treatment of interpersonal well-being comparisons. To theorize about well-being in an approach that takes personal betterness comparisons to be fundamentally matters of ternary relations with persons among their relata, one starts from a collection of individual betterness orderings of worlds, one for each possible person *taken separately* (all the betterness-for-S facts *for some fixed S*). These orderings directly concern *intra*personal well-being comparisons between states of affairs; one then has to perform an additional manoeuvre in order to 'bolt on' facts about *inter*personal well-being comparisons.[30] In contrast, in the Lives Account, one starts from a single betterness-for-the-individual ordering of all possible lives (i.e. regardless of 'who lives' which lives in which possible worlds), so that interpersonal well-being comparisons are present from the start, as soon as we have any information about well-being at all. This is more elegant.[31]

Second, moral theories that subscribe to a principle of *anonymity* find a special affinity with the Lives Account. According to anonymity, if two states of affairs agree on the assignment of well-being levels to persons up to a bijection from the one set of persons to another—if, that is, the two states of affairs agree on *how many* persons live at each well-being level, and disagree only over *who* lives at each level—then the two states of affairs in question are equally good. This might affect how one chooses to describe states of affairs in the first place. In the literature on population ethics, for instance, it is common to take 'populations'—the objects that are meant to capture everything about possible worlds that is relevant to population axiology—to be assignments of well-being levels to possible persons.

---

[30] We here assume that there are positive interpersonal well-being comparisons. This is almost universally agreed among moral philosophers, though some economists disagree. For discussion, see e.g. (Fleurbaey and Voorhoeve 2016, sec. 3).

[31] Something like this point is made by Broome (2004, 97), who also suggests that theorizing in terms of lives is more straightforward, and says that he has stated his account of interpersonal well-being comparisons in terms of persons only because the latter framework is 'more familiar'.

But if anonymity obtains, given the theoretical apparatus of the Lives Account, one might instead identify populations with multisets of possible lives (or non-null lives). Populations in that latter sense arguably contain less information, since they do not specify *who lives* each of the lives in question. But if anonymity holds, then that omitted information is evaluatively irrelevant, in which case considerations of elegance favour omitting it. Thus, if anonymity holds, it is an additional nice feature of the Lives Account that it then facilitates a more elegant setup of overall moral theory. Theories that violate anonymity, however, can still be stated: we *can* talk the language of the Lives Account and nonetheless still specify who has each of the lives in question.

3.6 Bykvist's Argument

The account we offered in section 3.5 explains how it might come about that *Ontological Commitment* fails. It is an essential feature of this account that at some deeper level, the truth-conditions for '*A* is better for *S* than *B*' do not involve any relation holding with *S* as relatum. This goes against an assumption that the literature against existence comparativism usually makes tacitly. Witness, for example, Arrhenius and Rabinowicz:

> [I]f we took a person's life to be better or worse for her than nonexistence, then we would have to conclude that it would have been worse or better for her if she did not exist... Clearly, this is unacceptable. Nothing would have been worse or better for a person if she had not existed... *A triadic relation consisting in one state... being better for a person p than another state... cannot hold unless its three relata exist.* (Arrhenius and Rabinowicz 2015, 427–8; emphasis added)

Krister Bykvist, to our knowledge uniquely in the existing literature, explicitly states and suggests an argument for the assumption in question:[32]

> I take the value-for relations *good for*, *bad for* and *neutral for* at face value, that is, as genuine relations holding between states of affairs and (actual) persons— *mutates mutandi* for the comparative counterparts *better for*, *worse for*, and *equally as good as for*. This gives us a neat explanation of why the following inferences are valid:
>
> Exercise is good for me. So, there is someone for whom exercise is good.

---

[32] This is not to suggest that Bykvist himself would insist the assumption is inviolable. In the passage we quote, he is merely making explicit the presuppositions of his own discussion (whose concern is with related but different matters), a move that we applaud.

Everything that is good for me is bad for you. Exercise is good for me. So, exercise is bad for you.

Exercise is better for me than binge drinking. So, there is something that is better for me than binge drinking.   (Bykvist 2007, 339–40)

We agree that a satisfactory account of 'A is better for S than B' must explain the validity of obviously valid inferences. So let us consider: can the Lives Account similarly explain the data that Bykvist adduces?

Bykvist considers three value-theoretic locutions: 'good for', 'bad for', 'better for'. Since our primary interest is in comparative statements, we will consider his argument-sketch as applied to 'better for'. There are two quite different cases to consider. First:[33]

(I1): Exercise is better for Krister than binge drinking. So, there is something that is better for Krister than binge drinking.

Since the Lives Account does not take better-for statements as genuine relations holding between states of affairs and actual persons, Bykvist's 'neat explanation' of the validity of this inference is unavailable on the Lives Account. But an alternative explanation is forthcoming. Recall that we suggested identifying lives with properties (viz., compounds of whichever properties that are relevant to individuation of lives). Presumably, the property E of doing exercise and the property D of engaging in binge drinking are among the properties that are relevant. Let us write $\vDash$ for the entailment relation among properties. The Lives Account suggests understanding 'exercise is better for Krister than binge drinking' as (roughly): in all sufficiently nearby and sufficiently mutually close possible worlds A, B, if $l^A_{Krister} \vDash E$, $l^B_{Krister} \vDash D$, $l^A_{Krister} \vDash \neg D$ and $l^B_{Krister} \vDash \neg E$, then $l^A_{Krister} \succ l^B_{Krister}$. Similarly, it suggests understanding 'there is something that is better for Krister than binge drinking' as (roughly): there exists a property p such that in all sufficiently nearby and sufficiently mutually close possible worlds A, B, if $l^A_{Krister} \vDash p$, $l^B_{Krister} \vDash D$, $l^A_{Krister} \vDash \neg D$, and $l^B_{Krister} \vDash \neg p$, then $l^A_{Krister} \succ l^B_{Krister}$. But the latter straightforwardly follows from the former. So the Lives Account, no less than the 'face value' reading, is able to explain the validity of (I1).

We might also consider an inference that involves existential quantification over persons, as opposed to over activities:[34]

---

[33] We replace the pronoun 'me' with the proper name 'Krister' because complications arising from indexicals are orthogonal to the present discussion.

[34] Inferences of precisely this form are not on Bykvist's list, though they are analogous to his first example involving absolute goodness ascriptions ('Exercise is good for me. So, there is someone for whom exercise is good').

(I2): Exercise is better for Krister than binge drinking. So, there is someone for whom exercise is better than binge drinking.

If it were also a datum that *this* inference is valid, then this might be a datum that the Lives Account, as we have considered developing the latter, is unable to capture. But this is no datum (unless the 'someone' quantifies over merely possible persons). For 'exercise is better for Krister than binge drinking', unless given a special reading that distinguishes it from the general locution '*A* is better for *S* than *B*', seems similar in all relevant respects to 'exercise is better for Connie than binge drinking', where Connie is again some particular, but merely possible, person. And we argued in sections 3.4–3.5 that this can be true despite the non-existence of Connie.[35] So (I2) is invalid, on the reading that understands the locutions in question as being the ones with which the Lives Account deals.

We conclude that Bykvist's argument does not impugn the Lives Account.

3.7 The Well-being Argument

Let us now set the Lives Account aside. The task of the present section is to briefly consider a different possible reanalysis of sentences of the form '*A* is better for Peggy than *B*'. The basic ideas of this analysis are consistent with, but do not presuppose, the Lives Account.

The key thought for this second reanalysis is that personal betterness *comparisons* are reducible to more fundamental ascriptions of monadic personal goodness *amounts* (that is, well-being levels). This thought suggests a quite different argument against existence comparativism. We will call this the Well-being Argument:[36]

WB1: *A* is better for *S* than *B* iff *S* has a higher well-being level in *A* than in *B*. *(Premise)*

WB2: If *A* is better for *S* than *B*, then there is some well-being level that *S* has in *A*, and there is some well-being level that *S* has in *B*. *(From WB1)*

WB3: A person cannot have a well-being level in a world in which she does not exist. *(Premise)*

---

[35] We concede that 'exercise is better for Connie than binge drinking' sounds a little odd if Connie is merely possible, but that is for reasons of conversational context that do not undermine the essential point. Consider instead: 'A world in which Connie enjoys a preserved climate and abundant resources is better for Connie than a world in which she suffers the effects of extreme global warming'.

[36] For the purposes of this discussion, we assume a condition of full invariance (cf. section 3.2). This means that the truth-values of sentences of the form '*A* is better for Peggy than *B*' do not need to be relativized to worlds. The possibility of variation of truth-values across worlds is orthogonal to the concerns of the Well-being Argument, and would only complicate the exposition.

WB4: If A is better for S than B, then S exists both in A and in B. *(From WB2 and WB3)*

WB5: Comparativism is false. *(From WB4)*

Like the Metaphysical Argument, one of the thoughts underlying the Well-being Argument also invokes the idea that an object must exist in order to possess a property. But there is a crucial difference. The Well-being Argument does not insist that property-bearers exist *in the world of evaluation* in order for propositions ascribing properties to them to be true: only that the bearer exists *in the world that the proposition describes*. Thus, for all this argument says, there is no obstacle to 'Connie has well-being level w in A' being true even at a world in which Connie does not exist, provided she exists in A.[37] This means that unlike the Metaphysical Argument, the Well-being Argument does not prove too much: it stops precisely where the advocate of anti-comparativism wishes to stop. This may well be the argument that many anti-comparativists intend to make.

A detailed discussion of the Well-being Argument lies beyond the scope of this essay. We note, though, that for reasons related to our above discussion of the Metaphysical Argument, the Well-being Argument is in danger of begging the question against existence comparativism. Again, we already know (cf. section 3.4) that some properties are negative: not existence-requiring. And we already know that the existence comparativist's position is that either 'has well-being level zero' is one of them (so that WB3 is false), or that WB1 is not true in full generality (with cases of non-existence constituting the exceptions). Furthermore, much more so than in the case of 'A is better for Connie than B' absent any reanalysis, denying WB3 in this case seems far from ad hoc: the notion of zero well-being quite plausibly has enough 'negativity' about it make this a reasonable move.[38] A complementary point is that it is far from clear that monadic ascriptions of well-being levels are in any relevant sense 'prior' to personal betterness comparisons; if instead the order of priority is the reverse, and existence comparativism is true as a feature of how those comparisons behave, then the failure of WB1 and/or WB3 follows naturally. Nothing in this argument as outlined above, or (as far as we are

---

[37] Of course, the proposition in question is not true *in* the world in which Connie does not exist, but that is beside our point; cf. fn. 16.

[38] Roberts quite explicitly denies WB3, on the grounds that a non-existent person 'has no properties at all', and that therefore these properties 'add up to a zero level of well-being' (2003, 178). While there is scope to say more here, Roberts' remarks should not seem paradoxical if one is armed with a positive/negative property distinction.

Arrhenius and Rabinowicz write in reply that '[h]aving a zero degree of well-being is arguably the kind of property the instantiation of which requires the existence of property bearers' (2015, 429), but they do not supply the suggested argument.

Holtug (2001) can be read as arguing that the property of having zero well-being is a negative property, on the basis of considering various substantive theories of well-being.

aware) in the existing discussion of these ideas in the literature, hints at why these positions are untenable.

3.8 Summary and Conclusions

Existence comparativism is a controversial and important thesis in population ethics. A common view in the population ethics literature is that existence comparativism is false, and furthermore that the reason for this is given by the Metaphysical Argument. In this essay, we have argued against the second component of this view.

First, the Metaphysical Argument anyway proves too much. There is no reason to believe its premise of *Limited Invariance* that isn't equally a reason to believe the stronger thesis of *Full Invariance*. Meanwhile (modulo issues of necessary existence) *Full Invariance* and the other premise of the Metaphysical Argument (viz., *Ontological Commitment*) jointly imply the absurd conclusion that no world is ever better than any other for any contingent person. So even those who are sympathetic to the argument's intended anti-comparativist conclusion must reject one of its premises.

Ontological Commitment might initially seem non-negotiable, and seems to have struck many contributors to the debate this way. If so, the only coherent option is to deny *Limited Invariance*. This leaves open both a 'comparativist variantist' position in the spirit of existence comparativism, and an 'anti-comparativist variantist' position in the spirit of anti-comparativism. A choice between these positions would have to be settled on grounds that have nothing to do with the Metaphysical Argument.

Ontological Commitment, however, is in fact highly dubious. It follows from property actualism, and this seems to explain its initial appeal. Property actualism does indeed initially seem appealing, but we have noted (following existing work in metaphysics) that property actualism is not true in general. *Ontological Commitment* would also follow if the property of S that is expressed by 'A is better for S than B' happened to be one of those ('positive') properties for which property actualism does hold; but we have seen that there is also strong independent reason to doubt that. Nor does any other plausible precisification of the idea that 'only actuals have ontological status' provide any good argument for *Ontological Commitment*. So the Metaphysical Argument is unsound, and variantism is also insufficiently motivated.

What we called the Lives Account develops the thought that sentences of the form 'A is better for S than B' express that the way things would have gone for S if A had obtained is personally better than the way things would have gone for S if B obtained. It is clear how, on this account, either full comparativism or full anti-comparativism could come about. In particular, it is clear that 'A is better for S than B' expresses a negative property of S.

Finally, we considered the possibility that 'betterness for S' comparisons are reducible to more fundamental matters of monadic well-being ascriptions. This is part of the line of thought behind a different argument against existence comparativism: the Well-Being Argument. We conjecture that besides the Metaphysical Argument, something like this argument is the source of much of the existing resistance to existence comparativism. The Well-Being Argument is in one sense an improvement on the Metaphysical Argument, since it does at least stop with the anti-comparativist conclusion, without going on to prove too much. Until and unless more is said, however, the Well-being Argument simply begs the question against existence comparativism, for some of the same reasons that we discussed in connection with the Metaphysical Argument. For instance, the argument assumes that possession of the zero level of well-being is a positive property, but again, there is significant independent reason to doubt that, and no argument has been provided in favour of the assumption.

We have not attempted here to *settle* the debate as to whether or not existence comparativism is true, or whether its important upshots otherwise hold (and the authors of this essay incline towards different views on these matters). Our point is only that existing arguments against it are inadequate.

Acknowledgements

For valuable discussions, we are grateful to Gustaf Arrhenius, Krister Bykvist, Tim Campbell, Toby Ord, Theron Pummer, Wlodek Rabinowicz, and to audiences where earlier versions of this work were presented at the Australian National University, Sydney University, and the Institute for Futures Studies. Special thanks are due to Jeff Russell, Ted Sider, and Teru Thomas.

References

Adler, Matthew. 2009. 'Future Generations: A Prioritarian View'. *George Washington Law Review* 77 (5/6): 1478–520.

Arrhenius, Gustaf. ms. *Population Ethics: The Challenge of Future Generations*. Unpublished manuscript.

Arrhenius, Gustaf, and Wlodek Rabinowicz. 2015. 'The Value of Existence'. In *The Oxford Handbook of Value Theory*, edited by Iwao Hirose and Jonas Olson, 424–44. Oxford Handbooks in Philosophy. New York: Oxford University Press.

Broome, John. 1999. *Ethics out of Economics*. Cambridge: Cambridge University Press.

Broome, John. 2004. *Weighing Lives*. Oxford: Oxford University Press.

Buchanan, Allen, Dan W. Brock, Norman Daniels, and Daniel Wikler. 2001. *From Chance to Choice: Genetics and Justice*. Cambridge: Cambridge University Press.

Bykvist, Krister. 2007. 'The Benefits of Coming into Existence'. *Philosophical Studies* 135 (3): 335–62.

Carlson, Erik. 1998. 'Mere Addition and Two Trilemmas of Population Ethics'. *Economics and Philosophy* 14: 283–306.

Clayton, Matthew, and Andrew Williams. 2000. *The Ideal of Equality*. London: Macmillan; New York: St. Martin's Press.

Dasgupta, Partha. 1995. *An Inquiry into Well-Being and Destitution*. New York: Oxford University Press.

Fine, Kit. 1977. 'Postscript: Prior on the Construction of Possible Worlds and Instants'. In *Worlds, Times and Selves*, edited by Kit Fine and Arthur Prior. University of Massachusetts Press. Reprinted as Chapter 4 of Fine (2005).

Fine, Kit. 1985. 'Plantinga on the Reduction of Possibilist Discourse'. In *Alvin Plantinga*, edited by James E. Tomberlin and Peter Van Inwagen, 145–86. Dordrecht: Reidel. Reprinted as Chapter 5 of Fine (2005). Page numbers in citations refer to the reprint.

Fine, Kit. 2005. *Modality and Tense: Philosophical Papers*. Oxford: Clarendon Press.

Fleurbaey, Marc, and Alex Voorhoeve. 2015. 'On the Social and Personal Value of Existence'. In *Weighing and Reasoning: Themes from the Philosophy of John Broome*, edited by Iwao Hirose and Andrew Reisner, 95–109. Oxford: Oxford University Press.

Fleurbaey, Marc, and Alex Voorhoeve. 2016. 'Priority or Equality for Possible People?' *Ethics* 126 (4): 929–54.

Greaves, Hilary. 2017. 'Population Axiology'. *Philosophy Compass* 12 (11).

Hare, Caspar. 2007. 'Voices from Another World: Must We Respect the Interests of People Who Do Not, and Will Never, Exist?' *Ethics* 117 (3): 498–523.

Heyd, David. 1988. 'Procreation and Value: Can Ethics Deal with Futurity Problems?' *Philosophia* 18 (2–3): 151–70.

Heyd, David. 1992. *Genethics: Moral Issues in the Creation of People*. Berkeley, CA: University of California Press.

Holtug, Nils. 2001. 'On the Value of Coming into Existence'. *The Journal of Ethics* 5 (4): 361–84.

Lewis, David. 1986. *On the Plurality of Worlds*. Oxford: Blackwell.

Nagel, Thomas. 1970. 'Death'. *Noûs* 4 (1): 73–80. Reprinted as Chapter 1 of Nagel (1979).

Nagel, Thomas. 1979. *Mortal Questions*. Cambridge: Cambridge University Press.

Narveson, Jan. 1967. 'Utilitarianism and New Generations'. *Mind* 76 (301): 62–72.

Parfit, Derek. 1984. *Reasons and Persons*. Oxford: Clarendon Press.

Parfit, Derek. 1991. 'Equality or Priority?' Department of Philosophy, University of Kansas. The Lindley Lecture, University of Kansas, November 21, 1991. Reprinted as Chapter 5 of Clayton and Williams (2000).

Persson, Ingmar. 2001. 'Equality, Priority and Person-Affecting Value'. *Ethical Theory and Moral Practice* 4 (1): 23–39.

Plantinga, Alvin. 1983. 'On Existentialism'. *Philosophical Studies* 44: 1–20.

Roberts, Melinda A. 1998. *Child versus Childmaker: Future Persons and Present Duties in Ethics and the Law*. Studies in Social, Political, and Legal Philosophy. Oxford: Rowman & Littlefield.

Roberts, Melinda A. 2003. 'Can It Ever Be Better Never to Have Existed At All? Person-Based Consequentialism and a New Repugnant Conclusion'. *Journal of Applied Philosophy* 20 (2): 159–85.

Temkin, Larry S. 1993. *Inequality*. New York: Oxford University Press.

Temkin, Larry S. 2003a. 'Egalitarianism Defended'. *Ethics* 113 (4): 764–82.

Temkin, Larry S. 2003b. 'Equality, Priority or What?' *Economics & Philosophy* 19 (1): 61–87.

Temkin, Larry S. 2012. *Rethinking the Good: Moral Ideals and the Nature of Practical Reasoning*. New York: Oxford University Press.

Williamson, Timothy. 2002. 'Necessary Existents'. In *Logic, Thought and Language*, edited by Anthony O'Hear. Cambridge: Cambridge University Press.

Williamson, Timothy. 2013. *Modal Logic as Metaphysics*. Oxford: Oxford University Press.

4
The Impure Non-Identity Problem

Patrick Tomlin

4.1 Introduction

The aims of this chapter are to convince you of the following claims and their importance, and to explore their implications for moral theory. First:

The Impure Non-Identity Claim: a set of acts can affect who comes into existence and be neither harmful to nor worse for any particular individual, even though each act in the set does harm, in the sense of being worse for, some individual or individuals. These are Impure Non-Identity Cases.

Given this, I will argue for this second claim:

Two Non-Identity Problems: Impure Non-Identity Cases pose important moral questions which Pure Non-Identity Cases do not. Therefore, there are two importantly different non-identity problems.

Before presenting my arguments for these claims, and discussing the moral issues they raise, I will, by way of background, describe two issues with which the chapter engages. The philosophical problems I investigate in this chapter sit at the intersection of these two issues, both of which Derek Parfit illuminated in more-than-seminal ways.

The first is the non-identity problem, which I will discuss in more depth in the main body of the chapter. One of my arguments here is that it is really two problems, or that there are two sub-problems: there are Pure Non-Identity Cases, which raise a set of issues, and Impure Non-Identity Cases, which raise additional issues.

Here is a Pure Non-Identity Case: A couple planning to have children find out that, due to a virus one of them currently has, if they conceive within the next month, the baby will have some serious health issue that will negatively affect its

---

I am grateful for discussion with the attendees of the conference held in Derek Parfit's memory at Oxford in April 2018, especially Mike Otsuka and Jonathan Dancy. I am grateful to Jeff McMahan and Victor Tadros for discussion, extensive written feedback, and conflicting advice.

quality of life. Its life will nonetheless be worth living. If the couple wait, however, their baby will not have this serious health issue. On the one hand, it seems the couple ought to wait because of the way the health issue will affect the child's wellbeing. On the other, if they wait, they will have a different child. Having the child earlier, with the attending health problem, is not *worse for* that child—the only other option is that the child would never exist.

The non-identity problem is the problem of whether we can defend and explain the intuition that the couple who don't wait act wrongly. If they do act wrongly, this seems to be a major challenge for person-affecting or complaint-based theories of morality. One of Parfit's many towering achievements was to introduce us to this problem, and, perhaps more importantly, to show us how far it reaches in its challenges to all moral theories, and what its implications are for both public policy and private decisions. It is a foundational element of perhaps the most revolutionary part of the most revolutionary book in twentieth century moral philosophy.[1]

The second issue with which this chapter engages is what Parfit called 'moral mathematics': puzzles that arise when we collect acts together into courses of action, either as groups or as individuals. Parfit made great strides in exposing these puzzles, and investigating them, in his 'Five Mistakes in Moral Mathematics'.[2] One such puzzle involves overdetermined harm—groups of acts in which we appear to collectively harm somebody, but in which no individual act appears to harm. Consider a course of action in which five individuals simultaneously stab a person, for example the murder of Julius Caesar. Collectively, they kill Caesar. But had each of them not acted as he did, Caesar would still have died—one stab is sufficient to kill him. Had one individual, Brutus, not stabbed him, Caesar would still have been killed. And so Brutus does not appear to kill Caesar. The same applies to all the other individuals. Collectively they kill Caesar, but no individual kills him. If harming is making people worse off than if you had not acted, no individual harms Caesar.

The cases I want to consider here are, in some senses, the opposite of cases of overdetermined harm: in my cases, each individual act makes someone worse off, but the collection of acts does not make anyone worse off.

4.2 Two Non-Identity Cases

The non-identity problem arises when an agent faces a choice of whether to bring into existence a person who will be well off, or to bring into existence a different person who will be less well off. On the one hand, it seems intuitive there's at least some moral reason to bring into existence the well off person. On the other, since

---

[1] Parfit, *Reasons and Persons*, Part IV. [2] Ibid., ch. 3.

one is choosing which of two people (or groups of people) to bring into existence, neither choice is *worse for* or *better for* any particular person (assuming all will have lives worth living). Since nobody is made worse off, arguably, nobody has any complaint about the choice.

For the sake of clarity and precision, it will help to introduce some terminology:

Harm: someone is made worse off than they otherwise would have been.[3]

Impersonal Loss: someone is caused to exist who will have lower wellbeing than some other person who otherwise would have existed.[4]

Negative Wellbeing Effect: an umbrella term encapsulating both harm and impersonal loss—where wellbeing is lower than it otherwise would have been, regardless of whether the same person, or some different person, would have otherwise existed (keeping numbers of people constant).

Identity-Fixing Act: The act of selecting an option which determines who will exist.

Non-identity cases are, therefore, those in which an option which will have a negative wellbeing effect will also be an identity-fixing act. Since both of these features are present, this means that the negative wellbeing effect is one of impersonal loss rather than harm.

Here are two famous cases that Parfit uses to illustrate the non-identity problem. They demonstrate its reach by showing how it applies to both personal and political decisions:

The 14-Year-Old Girl: This girl chooses to have a child. Because she is so young, she gives her child a bad start in life. Though this will have bad effects throughout this child's life, his life will, predictably, be worth living. If this girl had waited for several years, she would have had a different child, to whom she would have given a better start in life.[5]

Depletion: As a community, we must choose whether to deplete or conserve certain kinds of resources. If we choose Depletion, the quality of life over the next three centuries would be slightly higher than it would have been if we had chosen

---

[3] There are, of course, all sorts of objections to counterfactual views of harm, especially simple counterfactual views. These stem from overdetermination and pre-emption cases in particular. But this definition of harm nevertheless seems to capture what is at stake in non-identity cases. In cases in which identity is not affected, someone has a complaint because they have been made worse off. In non-identity cases, someone is badly off but they have not been made worse off.

[4] In Parfit's later work on the non-identity problem, he affirmed a wide person-affecting view to underpin his No Difference View. Under the wide person-affecting view, impersonal loss would be better defined as a lower level of existential benefit. I do not think that this difference is important for the issues and arguments presented here. For the wide person-affecting view, see: Parfit, 'Future people, the non-identity problem, and person-affecting principles.'

[5] Parfit, *Reasons and Persons*, p. 358.

Conservation. But it would later, for many centuries, be much lower than it would have been if we had chosen Conservation. It is not true that, whichever policy we choose, the same particular people will exist in the further future. Since the choice between our two policies would affect the timing of later conceptions, some of the people who are later born would owe their existence to our choice of one of the two policies.[6]

Parfit appears to see these two cases as posing the same problem, and the vast literature that has followed in his wake has tended to agree.[7] But they're importantly different, as *Depletion* potentially poses moral problems that *14-Year-Old Girl* does not.

This is because, in my terminology, *14-Year-Old Girl* is a Pure Non-Identity Case while *Depletion* is potentially an Impure Non-Identity Case. Pure Non-Identity Cases are those in which each identity-fixing act also causes impersonal loss. There is, in other words, no way that the resulting person or persons could have existed at a higher level of wellbeing. Impure Non-Identity Cases, in contrast, are those in which a course or collection of acts is both identity-fixing and causes impersonal loss, but different acts within the course or collection have the identity-fixing and negative wellbeing impacts for given individuals. This means that, without some of the acts, the individual could have existed at a higher level of wellbeing. As a result, the collection of acts cause impersonal loss, but the individual acts are harmful.

In order for a case to be an Impure Non-Identity Case, it must be a course or collection of acts. But this is not sufficient. Cases involving a plurality of acts can still be Pure Non-Identity Cases. Consider this case:

One Thousand Acts: Government is considering funding an education policy that will convince teenagers to delay parenthood. If they fund the policy, one thousand teenagers who would otherwise have conceived will choose to delay parenthood.[8]

This is a policy-level decision, which involves affecting the choices and actions of many others. But it is still a Pure Non-Identity Case—it is simply *14-Year-Old Girl* writ large. Either the teenagers have children, and one thousand children will exist, with less good lives, or they wait and some other one thousand children will exist,

---

[6] Ibid., pp. 361–2. All the words in the case are Parfit's from across these two pages, though I have reordered some passages.

[7] See, for example, the way that they are initially introduced and discussed in Roberts, 'The nonidentity problem'. However, both John Broome and Michael Otsuka describe climate change policy as an area where the policy decisions are non-identity cases but individual emissions decisions are not. Otsuka, 'How it makes a moral difference'; Broome, *Climate Matters*, p. 64.

[8] This case is structurally similar to one of the policies that Parfit introduces in his *Two Medical Programmes* case, in order to argue for his No Difference View. Parfit, *Reasons and Persons*, p. 367; Parfit, *On What Matters: Volume Two*, p. 221.

and will have better lives than the teenagers' children would have had. If the government don't fund the policy, the children of the teenagers will have no complaint, for if the government had funded the policy they simply wouldn't have existed. The negative wellbeing effect is one of impersonal loss.

In sum, Pure Non-Identity Cases are those in which the resulting person or persons can have no complaint about, and have not been harmed by, *either* any individual act, *nor* the policy or collection of acts.

In contrast, Impure Non-Identity Cases are those in which, because it is identity-fixing, the collection of acts harms no one, but at least some of the individual acts do harm someone, and perhaps *all of them* do. I will focus on this latter kind of case, in which each and every individual act harms someone, even though the collection of acts harms no one.

4.3 Impure Non-Identity: Circle Cases

It will be easiest to understand how Impure Non-Identity Cases work by looking at some of them. There are at least two kinds of Impure Non-Identity Case. In this section, we will examine the general structure of one of these. In order to do so, I need to introduce a further bit of terminology. Imagine that my parents could either have had me or waited a month and had some other child. That other child—let's call her Patricia—and I are, obviously, different individuals. But let's say my parents would only ever have had one of us. Therefore, Patricia and I share a *placeholder*. There is some space in the world for my parents' child—that is the placeholder—and it could have been filled by either Patricia or me. In the following, let Child A, etc., stand for the placeholder, and Child A1, Child A2, etc., stand for the different individuals who might have filled that placeholder.

> *Circle*
>
> Act 1 causes Child A1 to exist instead of Child A2, and has a negative wellbeing effect on Child B.
>
> Act 2 causes Child B1 to exist instead of Child B2, and has a negative wellbeing effect on Child C.
>
> Act 3 causes Child C1 to exist instead of Child C2, and has a negative wellbeing effect on Child D ...
>
> Act N causes Child X1 to exist instead of Child X2, and has a negative wellbeing effect on Child A.

Each act harms someone. For example, consider Act 2. If Act 2 does not occur, then there will be no negative wellbeing effect on the Child C placeholder. Let's say that Act 3 goes ahead regardless of whether Act 2 does. Then C1 will exist, and there will be no negative wellbeing effect on C1. So, Act 2 makes a difference to whether Child C has a better or worse life. But since C1 exists regardless of whether Act 2 goes ahead or not (it is Act 3 that is identity-fixing for Child C), Act 2 *harms* C1.

However, this *course* of action does not harm anybody. C1 is harmed by Act 2. But without the course of action, C1 would not have existed. Therefore, provided C1 has a life worth living, they are not harmed by the course of action.

Let's call these *Circle Cases*.[9] There are some sub-types of Circle Cases. They differ from one another in two respects. The first concerns whether a single person or a group of people carry out the individual acts. The second concerns the relationship between the group of acts and how coordinated they are. One especially interesting kind of case is where a group or individual (a policy-maker, for example) makes a decision (or an order) that they foresee will cause others to act in certain ways.

Here's a case in which a group of agents carries out the acts, prompted by the decision of a policy-maker:

Pollution Regulation: A government official must decide whether to relax pollution restrictions on factories. At present, factories are required to employ pollution monitors. Companies will be free to fire these monitors if pollution restrictions are relaxed. If the restrictions are relaxed, the official foresees the following chain of acts will occur:

Act 1: Company A will fire Monitor A. Monitor A will get a better job, and she and her partner will move to live by Lake B. They will have child A1, instead of Child A2. Increased pollution in Lake A caused by Company A will negatively affect any child who grows up next to Lake A.

Act 2: Company B will fire Monitor B. Monitor B will get a better job, and he and his partner will move to live by Lake A. They will have child B1, instead of Child B2. Increased pollution in Lake B caused by Company B will negatively affect any child who grows up next to Lake B.

First let's examine the acts of the two companies. In firing their pollution monitor, and increasing pollution in Lake B, Company B have a negative wellbeing effect on any child who grows up in next to Lake B. Due to Act 1, this is Child A1. However, since Company B's decision has no effect on whether Child A is Child A1 or A2, they harm Child A1 through their decision. Company A's act has a negative wellbeing effect on any child who grows up next to Lake A. Due to Act 2, this is Child B1. But since Company A's acts have no impact on Child B's identity, this is a harm to Child B1. Act 1 and Act 2 are therefore harmful acts.

---

[9] I call them this because Act N ends up having a negative wellbeing effect on Child A, and so the chain loops back round. We can also imagine chain cases without this looping.

Now let's examine the policy-maker's act. The policy-maker's act—namely instituting the policy—will harm nobody. If they do not act, A2 and B2 will exist. If they do act, there will be a negative wellbeing effect, but it will be an impersonal loss, as A1 and B1 will exist, and will have lives worth living.

In making her decision about whether or not to relax pollution controls, the policy-maker thus finds both of these statements to be true:

Statement 1: If I relax pollution controls, two children will be harmed by polluters.

Statement 2: If I relax pollution controls, I will cause impersonal loss, but I will not cause any harm.

In *Pollution Regulation* a policy-maker makes a decision, and then independent agents implement, or react to, that decision with their own decisions. However, imagine a modified version of the case in which a single company owns two factories, A and B. The head of the company must decide whether to pursue a policy of firing pollution monitors or not. If she does fire the monitors, she foresees the effects will be the same as those in *Pollution Regulation*. In considering whether or not to fire the monitors, she finds both the following statements to be true:

Statement 1: If I decide to relax pollution controls, I will harm two children.

Statement 2: If I decide to relax pollution controls, I will harm nobody.

Statement 1 is true of individual acts she will undertake if she decides to implement the policy. Statement 2 is true of the collection of acts she will undertake if she decides to implement the policy.

In Pure Non-Identity Cases, individual acts have a negative wellbeing effect on, and are identity-fixing for, the *same* individuals. Therefore, the individual acts each produce impersonal loss, but no harm. In these Circle Cases, all the acts are both identity-fixing *and* produce negative wellbeing effects, but different acts within the group of acts have the negative wellbeing effect, and are identity-fixing for, given individuals. Therefore, there was a chance (where the acts are sufficiently independent) that the individual could have existed but without the negative wellbeing effect. So the negative wellbeing effect of the act is a harm. But the collection of acts, as it has both a negative wellbeing effect *and* is identity-fixing, is a case of impersonal loss.

4.4 Impure Non-Identity: Overdetermination of Identity

In this section, I want to discuss a different set of Impure Non-Identity Cases. These are courses of action that have negative wellbeing effects *and* are identity-fixing, but in which no individual act from the set determines identities, since the identities are overdetermined within the set of acts. Here's an attempt at formulating the general structure of such a case.

> *Overdetermination of Identity:* If N or more acts are performed, Group A will exist. If fewer than N acts are performed, Group B will exist. A set of acts, each of which later negatively affects an individual, is performed. There are more than N acts.

Here's a more concrete example.

> *Landmines:* The commanding officer in a war orders 2000 soldiers lay one landmine each. They all foresee that these will have the intended effect of deterring the enemy. They also foresee, however, that many years later, each of these mines will be stepped on by a child, so that 2000 children will be seriously wounded. If, as in fact happens, 1000 or more landmines are laid, families will vacate the area, and Set A of 2000 children will be born. If fewer than 1000 landmines had been laid, the families would have stayed, and Set B of 2000 children would have been born. Later the 2000 children of Set A are seriously injured.

The commander's act of ordering the laying of the mines is non-identity case. The children who are injured, Set A, would not have existed if the course of action ordered by the commander had not taken place. No one, therefore, is harmed by the commander's action, even though no children would have been injured had he not ordered the laying of the mines. The loss is impersonal. But the act of each individual soldier—each laying of a landmine—is *not* a non-identity case. Each soldier's act, therefore, *harms* a child.

Consider the contrasting ways in which the commanding officer and an individual soldier might assess their acts. The commanding officer might think, of his act of ordering that the landmines be laid, 'it was ordering the laying of these landmines that caused Set A of children to exist. If I hadn't ordered the laying of the landmines, Set B would have existed instead. And so, even though many children were injured, none of them were harmed by my order.' Let's now take a specific soldier, Soldier 1173, and his act of laying a landmine. Soldier 1173's landmine injured Child A1173. But this child would have existed whether Soldier 1173 had laid his landmine or not. While the *course of action* determined the identity of the children who were later injured by the landmines, no *individual act* of laying them did. If Soldier 1173 hadn't laid his landmine, there would still have been more than 1000 landmines laid, and so Set A would still have existed. So, if Soldier 1173 hadn't laid his landmine Child A1173 would have existed, but not have been injured. Therefore, Soldier 1173 harmed Child A1173. The same reasoning applies to each of the 2000 soldiers and the child injured by the landmine they laid.

Imagine that many years later the commanding officer is reflecting on his war experience, and he thinks about this command in particular. He finds both the following statements to be true:

Statement 1:   I ordered 2000 soldiers to perform acts which, foreseeably, seriously harmed 2000 children.

Statement 2:   My order did not harm any children.

4.5 Moral Implications

We have seen that Pure Non-Identity Cases are non-identity cases all the way down. Either they consist of one act (as in *14-Year-Old Girl*), or a series of acts in which each individual act is a non-identity case of its own (as in *One Thousand Acts*). There is unquestionably no harm in such cases (insofar as we understand harm as being made worse off). By contrast, Impure Non-Identity Cases are harmful when viewed as individual acts, but not when viewed as a collection of acts.

The literature on the non-identity problem, and its moral significance, is vast, and I cannot rehearse, or do justice to, all of it here. But, broadly speaking, there are two groups of responses to the problem. The first, endorsed by Parfit,[10] is the No Difference View:

No Difference View: It makes no moral difference whether a negative wellbeing effect is an impersonal loss or a harm.

The second group of responses to such cases (which is a varied group) is what I will call the Difference View. The Difference View, in essence, is any view which rejects the No Difference View, and claims that harm is morally significant:

Difference View: It makes a moral difference whether a negative wellbeing effect is an impersonal loss or a harm. Either impersonal losses cannot make actions wrong, or harms are, all else equal, harder to justify than impersonal losses.

As I have stressed, dividing the terrain into these two camps seriously simplifies a complex literature. But doing so is helpful for our purposes here.

---

[10] Parfit, *Reasons and Persons*, p. 369; *On What Matters: Volume Two*, pp. 219–21; 'Future people, the non-identity problem, and person-affecting principles'. Parfit explored two different rationales for accepting the No Difference View—impersonal principles and wide person-affecting principles.

Here are two interesting sets of moral questions raised by Impure Non-Identity Cases. The first concerns the general question of how to respond to the non-identity problem—the question of whether we should accept some version of the Difference View, or some version of the No Difference View. I will argue that consideration of Impure Non-Identity Cases should be considered here, and could push us toward the No Difference View.

The other interesting set of questions raised by Impure Non-Identity Cases concern how those who endorse the Difference View ought to morally assess both the policy-maker's acts and the individual acts in such cases. Since, for those who hold the No Difference View, whether a case is a non-identity case or not makes no moral difference, the Impure Non-Identity Cases do not pose particularly difficult questions. But if we hold some variant of the Difference View, I will argue, difficult moral questions arise in such cases.

4.5.1 Impure Non-Identity Cases and the No Difference View

That there are Impure Non-Identity Cases may affect how plausible we find the No Difference View. In my view, it might push us toward that view.

If we are attracted to the Difference View, we must place a lot of moral weight on the question of whether harm has occurred or not. In Pure Non-Identity Cases whether harm has occurred is clear cut—the negative wellbeing effect is clearly not harm. Therefore, we see a bright line that is capable of bearing the moral weight that the Difference View places on it. But we now see that in these Impure Non-Identity Cases, matters are more complex, for the parties are harmed by individual acts, but not by the collection of acts, or policy. Therefore, whether a person has been harmed is not clear cut—it depends upon whether we are asking the question of the individual acts or of the policy. And whether this harm matters morally will depend upon which we ought to ask the question of. For example, if we should only ask the question of the policy, it might be true that the individual acts harm, but morally this does not matter.

Take *Landmines* as an example. If Child A1173's moral standing to make a complaint relies on whether or not she would have existed *without* the landmines that injured her being laid, then whether or not she has a complaint appears to depend upon whether the she is addressing the complaint to the commanding officer or Solider 1173. This may well make us sceptical of putting too much weight on the distinction between harm and impersonal loss—for the same injury can be *both*, depending on whether we are looking at individual acts or collections of acts.

A second way in which Impure Non-Identity Cases might push us toward the No Difference View is that whether or not something is a Pure Non-Identity Case can hang on what seem to be morally inconsequential details. For example, compare *Landmines* with a case in which the commanding officer simply presses a button and 2000 landmines are released (call this case *Automated Landmines*). This is a single act, and a Pure Non-Identity Case—the same act makes it the case that Set A of children will exist, and that they are later injured, and so nobody is harmed. We might question whether the commander pressing a button versus ordering the soldiers can make a big moral difference, when the same people are created and injured either way. Indeed, imagine the commanding officer faces a choice between ordering the soldiers or pressing the button. Would he have moral reason to press the button, since there will then be no harm? What if pressing the button injures an additional child, compared with ordering the soldiers? Would the moral gravity of one child being harmed plus the impersonal loss of 2000 children having less good lives still be the lesser evil compared to 2000 children being harmed, even though the 2000 are the very same children in both cases? That would seem a hard sell to the additional child who is injured.

Some philosophers with whom I have discussed these issues feel that they seriously undermine the Difference View. Others have found their confidence in the Difference View unshaken—after all, they say, we know that collections of acts throw up all kinds of morally knotty problems, as Parfit's moral mathematics showed us. Why should we expect population ethics to be any different? The challenge for the Difference View is to address these problems, not to fold in the face of them. How the Difference View might go about addressing these issues is something I address in the next section.

At the least, however, it does seem that consideration of Impure Non-Identity Cases should be part of the debate. The debate has been constructed around Pure Non-Identity Cases. That there are these more complex Non-Identity Cases should affect the way we address the issues, and test the views. In particular, once we have figured out how the Difference View can best handle such cases, that will in turn affect our assessment of that view.

4.5.2 Impure Non-Identity Cases and the Difference View

What should proponents of the Difference View say about Impure Non-Identity Cases? This is an important question for two reasons. First, many accept some version of the Difference View, and, as I hope to show, the Impure Non-Identity Cases offer difficult questions for the view. Second, how (and how satisfactorily) the Difference View handles such cases will help us choose between it and the No Difference View.

We should ask two moral questions of Impure Non-Identity Cases: What should we say, morally speaking, of bringing about the course of conduct (e.g., the policy-maker's, or the commanding officer's act)? And what should we say, morally speaking, about the individual acts within the course of conduct?

For simplicity, let's say we're committed to a view in which harms are twice as hard to justify as impersonal losses of the same magnitude. Harms are given a 2W moral weighting, while impersonal losses are given a W moral weighting.

So far as I can tell, there are, broadly speaking, four options as to how we should treat Impure Non-Identity Cases:

1. The policy-maker's act should be viewed as causing impersonal loss (W), while the individual actors' acts should be viewed as causing harm (2W).
2. Both policy-maker and individual actors' acts should be viewed as causing impersonal loss (W). In other words, the acts of all involved should be treated in the same way as if this were a Pure Non-Identity Case.
3. Both policy-maker and individual actors' acts should be viewed as causing harm (2W). In other words, the acts of all involved should be treated in the same way as if this were not a non-identity case at all.
4. All actors' acts should be treated as neither like ordinarily harmful actions or as Pure Non-Identity Cases. Impure Non-Identity Cases, and the moral assessment of them, lie somewhere in between.

The idea in Option 1 is that we recognize that the policy-maker does no harm, while the individual actors do. So when we assess the policy-maker's act, we assess it as we would a non-identity case, and when we assess the individual actor's acts, we assess them as harmful actions.

This view has two major problems. The first is that, in cases such as the modified version of *Pollution Regulation*, where the same person makes the decision to initiate the course of conduct, and carries out the individual acts, the person is left with no guidance, or conflicting guidance, as to how to assess their behaviour. Qua policy-maker, they are told to treat this as a non-identity case, and the ensuing negative wellbeing effects as impersonal losses, whilst qua individual actor, they are told to weight the negative wellbeing effects as harms. But if, according to the Difference View, whether or not the course of conduct is permissible depends on whether the negative wellbeing effects are impersonal losses or harms, then the person is told that the course of conduct is permissible but none of the individual acts are.

The second problem with Option 1 is that it seems to lead to odd situations in cases such as *Landmines*. In *Landmines*, according to Option 1, the commanding officer's act of ordering the laying of the landmines ought to be weighted as causing impersonal loss, while the soldiers' acts of laying them ought to be weighted as causing harm. Imagine that the country the soldiers fight for is under threat. In order for their acts of war to be just, they must be proportionate. Imagine that, under the Difference View, the goodness of defending the country will render the impersonal loss of 2000 injuries proportionate, but will not render

2000 harms of the same magnitude proportionate.[11] If this is the case, under Option 1, the commander's orders are proportionate, and he is permitted to the issue them, but the soldiers' acts are disproportionate, and they are not permitted to carry them out.

Options 2 and 3 both insist that the policy-maker's and the individual agents' acts must be assessed in the same way—either as non-identity cases, causing impersonal loss, or as causing harm. In other words, according to Option 2, individual agents can either appeal to the wider course of action of which they are part to claim that they are not *harming* those affected by their acts (or at least, morally speaking, that their acts should not be weighted as harmful acts), or the policy-maker must accept that they are causing harm.

It is tempting to think that *either* Option 2 or Option 3 must be the correct one. But this is not necessarily the case.[12] It is possible that sometimes Option 2 is appropriate and sometimes Option 3 is. We should also consider that policy-makers and the acts that are caused by their policies have a variety of differing relationships, and these may affect whether it is appropriate to apply Option 2 or Option 3. In particular, if it is the case that either Option 2 or Option 3 is appropriate, we should consider the nature of the relationship between the policy-maker and the individual actors, and the nature of the relationship between the policy and the individual acts. By way of example, let's compare *Pollution Regulation* and *Landmines*.

In *Pollution Regulation* the relationship between the principal actors is a regulatory one between the government official and companies who trade within that jurisdiction. In *Landmines* the relationship between the actors is one of between commanding officer and his troops. Both of these are relationships of authority, though perhaps importantly different ones. Regulators set terms within which companies or individuals choose how to act. Commanding officers direct those under their command.

In terms of the relationship between the policy and the individual acts, the commanding officer *commands* his troops to lay the landmines, in the expectation that they will do so. That is the desired outcome. In *Pollution Regulation*, meanwhile, the regulator removes a barrier which the companies take advantage of. The government official does not tell them to, or encourage them to, or hope that they will, fire their pollution monitors. She simply foresees that they will do so.

This discussion is possibly driving us toward the vexed issue of group agency—something I cannot tackle here. What I will say is that the more authority the policy-maker has, and the extent to which the acts that cause the negative

---

[11] I explore this case, and its consequences, in greater detail in Tomlin, 'Proportionality in war: Revising revisionism'.

[12] I am grateful to Mike Otsuka for useful discussion here.

wellbeing effects are not merely foreseen but intentionally brought about by the policy-maker, the more plausible it is that we should see these acts not merely as a collection of independent acts, but as a cohesive group of acts. And then it is more plausible that the policy-maker should see the acts of the individual actors as her 'own', and that the individual agents can appeal to the wider context in assessing their acts as causing impersonal loss rather than harm.

So far we have examined two different factors that may be relevant to whether or not a policy ought to assessed as causing harm or impersonal loss. Here is a third: is the policy designed to produce individual acts, or a collective of acts? Is it that each individual act makes sense, in terms of the aims of the policy-maker, on its own terms, or does it only make sense as part of a collective. Imagine, for example, that a policy-maker creates a policy which aims to incentivize ten actors to each do Act A. Every time Act A is performed, it creates 20 units of good. Now imagine a policy-maker creates a policy which aims to incentivize ten actors to each do Act B. If all ten perform the action, 200 units of good will be created. But if fewer than ten actors perform Act B, no good will be created. Both policies are Impure Non-Identity Cases.

Morally speaking, should we treat the negative wellbeing effects as impersonal losses (as per Option 2), or as harms (as per Option 3)? My claim here is that it seems more plausible to treat the case in which Act B is encouraged as impersonal loss. This is because the whole course of action, if it were to be justified, must be justified together—it can only be justified if there is sufficient prospect of all ten performing Act B, for if fewer than ten perform Act B no good will be done. So because the policy's putative justification is as a collection of acts, its costs can also be viewed as a collection of acts. Meanwhile, the policy which seeks to encourage Act A does not need to be justified as a whole. Each Act A is independently producing good (as well as negative wellbeing effects). In seeing whether the goods outweigh the bads, we ought to look at each act independently, which would involve weighing the bads as harms (2W).

I have thus far examined Option 2 and Option 3. I have suggested that we do not need to make a single choice between them, but rather look at several factors—relationship between policy-maker and actors, relationship between policy and the acts it causes, and the justification of the policy—as to whether Option 2 or Option 3 applies. However, these considerations may instead push us toward Option 4. Option 4, like Options 2 and 3, suggests that we cannot view the policy-maker's act as one thing and the individual acts as something else. However, it denies that Impure Non-Identity Cases must be treated *either* like Pure Non-Identity Cases or as Pure Harming Cases (i.e., that negative wellbeing effects must be given a W or 2W weighting). Rather, Option 4 invites us to see these cases as somewhere in between—harder to justify than Pure Non-Identity Cases, but easier to justify than cases of straightforward harm. We could see how hard some negative wellbeing effect is to justify as a scale—with pure harms at one end, and pure impersonal losses at the other. And the considerations I canvassed above might help us place Impure Non-Identity Cases somewhere along this scale.

In closing this section, I would like to make clear an interesting entailment of accepting either Option 4 or a view under which we sometimes accept Option 2 and sometimes Option 3. This entailment concerns intervening agency. In these cases, intervening agency has the *opposite* significance from that which it usually has. Ordinarily, intervening agency, if it has any moral effect, makes harm *easier* to justify than if one brings it about oneself. It isn't as bad to sell a gun to someone one knows might use it to unjustifiably harm someone as it is to directly risk unjustifiably harming someone. Here the intervening agency makes things *harder to justify*. And the stronger, more independent, that intervening agency is, the harder the act becomes to justify. If I merely foresee that my act may cause unrelated others to act in a certain way, I should view the negative wellbeing effects I cause as harms, or as closer to harms in terms of justification. But if I order my subordinates to bring about negative wellbeing effects, or press a button bringing those about, I should view these as more like my own acts, and so I should treat them as impersonal losses, or more like impersonal losses in terms of justification.

4.6 Double Overdetermination Cases

In the introduction, I briefly mentioned overdetermination of harm cases, such as the assassination of Julius Caesar. In introducing Impure Non-Identity Cases I have also mentioned cases in which identity is overdetermined. In considering overdetermined harm cases, we kept identity constant. And in considering overdetermination of identity cases, we kept the individual negative wellbeing effects independent. But what if we put the two forms of overdetermination cases together?

That will give us cases such as this:

Double Overdetermination: If fewer than x acts of Type T occur, Person 1 (or Group 1) will exist. If x or more acts of Type T occur, Person 2 (or Group 2) will exist. If fewer than y acts of Type T occur, the person (or group) will have a higher level of wellbeing. If y or more acts of Type T occur, the person (or group) will have a lower level of wellbeing.

This sort of case has two important thresholds—a point which is an identity threshold, and a point which is a negative wellbeing effect threshold.

Here is a concrete example:

Emitters: Country X has a choice—it can either radically reduce its emissions, or not. If it does not radically reduce its emissions, two consequences are foreseeable. First, at some point, the level of emissions will cause the country's main source of income, a certain plant, will die out, and life will become less good (threshold A). Second, at some point, the level of emissions will cause flooding, which will cause a major migration, which will have a major effect on who exists in the next generation (threshold B). Each individual act of emitting contributes toward Country A reaching both of these thresholds.

Double Overdetermination Cases (cases in which both thresholds are passed by at least one act) are not Impure Non-Identity Cases as I have defined them thus far. In Impure Non-Identity Cases, the course of action is a non-identity case, and thus not harmful, but the individual acts are harmful. In Double Overdetermination Cases, neither the course of action nor the individual acts are harmful.

Imagine, for example, that Country A does not reduce its emissions. The next generation, left badly off, seeks to complain to the older generation about their plight. Policy-makers can note that since, taken collectively, this is a non-identity case, the future generation has not been left any worse off. Individual emitters can note that, since the negative wellbeing effect was overdetermined, their acts were also not harmful—take any individual act of emitting away, and the same still would have occurred.

This is troubling. The response we'd ordinarily make, and that Parfit suggests we make, to one of the emitters in an overdetermined harm case would be to point out that it doesn't only matter what I have done, it matters what I have done *in conjunction with others*. Were Brutus to claim that he had not harmed Caesar, we would rightly reply that while that is true of his act *taken alone*, it is not true of the collection of acts of which his act was part. But this reply is unavailable to us in Double Overdetermination Cases. Had the *collection* of acts not taken place, the complainant wouldn't have existed.

Should Double Overdetermination Cases be treated in the same way as Pure Non-Identity Cases then? Do those caused to exist in a Double Overdetermination scenario lack any standing to complain? In what follows, I try to construct an argument for those left badly off having complaints in at least some Double Overdetermination Cases.

Consider Figure 4.1. The y axis represents the wellbeing of the group. The x axis represents the number of acts of Type T. While it is easy to think of the x axis as representing a temporally ordered series of acts, so that it in essence represents time, these acts could be simultaneous, or some of them might happen simultaneously.

At point A on the graph, we reach threshold A—the negative wellbeing effect threshold. Enough acts of Type T have been performed at that point that there is an irreversible decline in wellbeing. The identity tipping point, threshold B, could occur either before or after the negative effect tipping point, or exactly at the same point. It could occur at point B1, so that to the left of point B1, Group 1 will exist,

THE IMPURE NON-IDENTITY PROBLEM   109

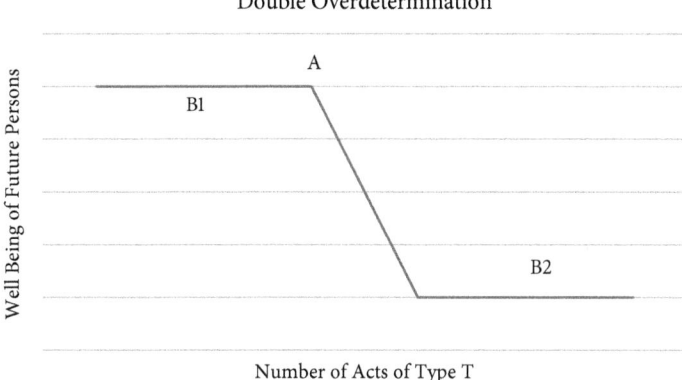

Figure 4.1 Double Overdetermination Cases

and to the right of point B1, a different set of people, Group 2, will exist. Or it could occur at point B2, so that to the left of point B2, Group 1 will exist, and to the right of point B2, Group 2 will exist.

As we have seen, neither the individual acts nor the collection of acts harm in Double Overdetermination Cases. But perhaps there is nevertheless some room for complaints in these cases. Consider, first, the *ex post* situation in the case in which the identity tipping point, threshold B, is at point B1. In this case, Group 2 may not have been harmed by any individual action or by the whole group of actions, but there was a possibility that they could have lived at the higher level. If there were enough Type T acts to get them past point B1, so that they existed, but not enough to get to threshold A, they would have had very good lives.

In cases in which agents are uncoordinated, Group 2 possibly has a complaint against each individual actor since each act raised the probability that they would exist but also raised the probability that they would live at the lower level, and not the higher level. Where agents are at least informed about each other's decisions, particularly weighty complaints might be pressed against those who acted after it became clear that the point B1 threshold (the identity threshold) had been reached but not yet clear that the threshold A (the negative wellbeing effect threshold) would be reached. If the group acted collaboratively, a complaint could be pressed against the group, as there is a sub-set of acts (those beyond point B1) that collectively harm the Group 2. The group could have stopped before they reached point A.

Consider, in contrast, the *ex post* situation in the case in which the identity tipping point is at point B2. In this case, there is no scope for complaint. This is more like a Pure Non-Identity Case, since, although what determines identity and what determines wellbeing are independent, the person or group who is now living at the lower level could not have existed at the higher level. This is why it matters whether the identity threshold or the negative wellbeing effect threshold comes first.

Consider now the *ex ante* perspective. In the case where the identity tipping point is at point B2, then there is a risk of harming Group 1—as things stand, they will exist, but there is a risk that by performing acts of Type T we will reach point A, but not point B2. There is a risk that Group 1 will exist *with a complaint*.

Here is an interesting question. Imagine we are at the point where we have passed the negative effect tipping point (point A) but have not yet reached point B2. Would we now have reason to perform more Type T acts so as to ensure that Group 2 exists? On the one hand, this looks like a straight choice between two groups who will live at the same level of wellbeing—there is nothing to choose between them. On the other, if Group 1 exists they will exist *possessing a complaint*, whereas Group 2 will not have a complaint. This raises an interesting question for those of us attracted to the Difference View—is it better to ensure that people exist with no complaint than that people exist with a complaint, even though they will be equally well off? I find the idea that we ought to push on with Type T acts, so as to ensure Group 2 exists, counter-intuitive. It seems that Group 1 is being (further) punished for being wronged, or at least potentially wronged.

4.7 Concluding Remarks and Practical Applications

This is a work of abstract philosophy. I make no apologies for that. Even if the issues had no practical relevance, they are theoretically fascinating and important. But we shouldn't be led by the abstract nature of the work, and the stylized examples, into thinking that these issues are of little or no practical importance. The topic we have here concerns courses of action that, together, are non-identity cases, but individually are not. I have focused here on cases in which *each and every individual act* is harmful, but the collection of acts is not. But Impure Non-Identity Cases need not be so, well, pure. The important point is that some individual might owe their existence to a collection of acts, but not to each individual action within that collection. Here are two real world examples where the Impure Non-Identity Problem seems like it has relevance. The first is war. An individual act of war will have comparatively few identity-determining effects. Wars, on the other hand, clearly have far-ranging identity-determining effects. Wars can also make life very bad (or very good) for future generations.

The second is climate change. Both Michael Otsuka and John Broome describe climate change policy as an Impure Non-Identity Case (though they do not use that language). Otsuka notes that (as in *Depletion*) if we choose to reduce greenhouse gas emissions in the present, this will affect who later comes to exist. He writes:

If, therefore, we *collectively refrain* from taking the requisite greenhouse-gas-reducing measures, distant future people will not have any complaints of the stronger form that [according to the Difference View] only those whose existence is choice-independent can press.

The effects of the carbon footprint of a *single individual* might, however, give rise to such stronger complaints from those whose existence is independent of that individual's choices...[John] Broome maintains that it is 'extraordinarily unlikely' that a typical individual's [lifetime] net emission of 800 tons of carbon dioxide will make *nobody* worse off than he would have been.[13]

Identifying Impure Non-Identity Cases, and discussing how our moral theories can and should handle them, is of both theoretical and practical importance. I have tried to show here that Impure Non-Identity Cases exist, their structure, and the moral questions they pose.

References

Broome, J., *Climate Matters: Ethics in a Warming World* (W.W. Norton, 2012).

Otsuka, M., 'How it makes a moral difference that one is worse off than one could have been', in *Politics, Philosophy & Economics* 17 (2018): 192–215.

Parfit, D., *Reasons and Persons* (Clarendon Press, 1984).

Parfit, D., *On What Matters: Volume Two* (Oxford University Press, 2011).

Parfit, D. 'Future people, the non-identity problem, and person-affecting principles', in *Philosophy & Public Affairs* 45 (2017): 118–57.

Roberts, M.A., 'The nonidentity problem,' in E.N. Zalta ed., *The Stanford Encyclopedia of Philosophy* (Winter 2015 Edition): <https://plato.stanford.edu/archives/win2015/entries/nonidentity-problem/>.

Tomlin, P., 'Proportionality in war: Revising revisionism', in *Ethics* 131 (2020): 34–61.

---

[13] Otsuka, 'How it makes a moral difference', pp. 209–10. Italics in original. Otsuka is drawing on Broome, *Climate Matters*, p. 64.

5
Abortion and the Non-Identity Problem

Elizabeth Harman

5.1 Introduction

In this chapter, I will investigate the relationship between two different topics in procreative ethics: the ethics of abortion and the non-identity problem.[1] There are a number of questions that we might ask about the relationship between these two topics. I will develop answers to the following questions.

- Does the choice whether to abort sometimes raise the non-identity problem?
- On which views of the moral status of fetuses does the choice whether to abort sometimes raise the non-identity problem?[2]
- What can we learn about the ethics of abortion by considering the choice to sometimes raise the non-identity problem?
- What can we learn about the non-identity problem by investigating its relationship with the ethics of abortion?

I will argue that the choice whether to abort does sometimes raise the non-identity problem.

In section 5.2, I explain the non-identity problem and the solution I advocate. My solution vindicates the apparent truth that the actions in non-identity problem cases are morally wrong because they harm the relevant future persons. In section 5.3, I discuss two views of the moral status of early fetuses, the No Moral

---

[1] I'm honored to be contributing a chapter to this series of volumes in memory of Derek Parfit. No other philosopher's writings have had a greater impact on me. Derek taught my first philosophy course, at Harvard in fall of 1993. Although the course had teaching assistants, he felt it was his duty to provide written comments to all students. This strong sense of duty was evident again years later when Derek and I co-taught at NYU and he insisted that he do no less work than he would have if teaching alone; since I was junior faculty, he was happy to lighten my load, and to put me in the role of discussant ("heckler," I thought of it) as he led most class sessions. While my conscious memories of Derek begin in 1993, that is not when we first met—Derek knew me "when I was in my cot," as he mentioned just seconds before he examined me on my undergraduate senior thesis. The thesis was about abortion, and toward the end of his several-pages-long written comments, he urged me to square some of my claims with issues raised by the non-identity problem. Twenty-three years later, Derek, I'm still working on that.

[2] I will also give a partial answer to this question: On which views of the non-identity problem does the choice whether to abort sometimes raise the non-identity problem? See the final paragraph of section 5.3.

Status View and my own view, the Ever Conscious View; both of these views imply that nothing morally bad happens in an early abortion, and that there are no moral reasons against early abortion. I argue that if either of these views is correct, then in some cases the choice whether to abort does raise the non-identity problem. This means that in some cases, abortion is not just morally permissible but is actually morally required.

In section 5.4, I briefly discuss the view that early fetuses have the full moral status of persons, and I point out that if this view is true, then the choice whether to abort never raises the non-identity problem.

In section 5.5, I turn to discussion of a common view, the Low Moral Status View, according to which early fetuses have a low level of moral status, and their level of moral status increases over time as the pregnancy progresses. I argue that there is a compelling line of thought that would commit a proponent of the Low Moral Status View to seeing some abortions as morally required—even though the early fetuses in question have some moral status.

In considering objections to lines of thought discussed in sections 5.3 and 5.5, I discuss the claim that it cannot be morally required to kill a being *for its own sake* when continuing to live is better for it. I distinguish three different versions of this claim. I argue that we should reject the strongest version of the claim, embracing a second, weaker version of the claim instead. And I argue that a proponent of the Low Moral Status View should reject the second version as well, embracing a third, even weaker version of the claim.

In section 5.6, I argue for a new understanding of what makes something a non-identity case; on this new understanding, the abortion cases I discuss are genuinely non-identity cases in their own right (assuming certain views of the moral status of early fetuses).

5.2 The Non-identity Problem and Its Solution

The non-identity problem arises because there are certain cases in which an action seems to be morally wrong, and this seems to be because it harms someone, yet that person would not have been better off if the action had not been performed, because they would not have existed at all. There is an argument that such actions cannot harm the affected people. A solution to the problem would explain why these actions are indeed wrong in virtue of harming the affected people. Here is a case that gives rise to the problem:

> Temporary Condition: Amy has a temporary condition that will cause any child she conceives now to have a painful chronic condition, though the child will be able to have a life well worth living. If she waits three months, she can conceive

a child who would not have the painful chronic condition. If she does not conceive now, she will conceive later.

It would be morally wrong for Amy to conceive now. And it seems that her action would be wrong because it would *harm* the created child. However, the following claim is intuitively plausible:

> Worse Off: An action harms someone only if it makes them worse off than they would otherwise have been.

If Worse Off is true, then Amy's conceiving now would not harm anyone. Her created child would not have been better off if she had conceived later; rather, she would have had a different child instead.[3]

There are four main views of cases like Temporary Condition. The first three views hold that Worse Off is true. Conceiving now does not harm anyone in these cases. Here are the views:

- Amy's conceiving now would not be wrong, because the only way her action could be wrong is if it harmed someone, and it does not.[4]
- Amy's conceiving now would be wrong, but would not harm or wrong the created child. Rather, her action would be wrong because the action would have worse consequences than the alternative.
- Amy's conceiving now would not harm the created child, but would *wrong* the created child by violating his rights. So her action is morally wrong.

The first view is false because Amy's conceiving now would be morally wrong. The second view is false because it is not in general true that we are morally required to do whatever would have the best consequences. Furthermore, even if we have moral reasons to do whatever would have the best consequences, we have stronger and more stringent duties to avoid harming others; and Amy has this kind of strong reason not to conceive now. The third view accommodates the thought that Amy does something wrong *to the created child* but it posits wrongful rights

---

[3] Let me clarify how Worse Off should be read. It is a claim about whether a person is worse off, overall, given that an action is performed; that is, it is about whether they have a worse life, overall. An action that kills someone who would have otherwise had a good future makes that person worse off, in that it makes their life worse than it otherwise would have been. (We should not read the Worse Off claim as holding that an action harms someone only if it puts them into a particular state that is worse than an alternative state they could have been in. A state that someone is in at a particular moment doesn't tell us whether, overall, an action is worse for them, which is what the Worse Off claim is about. But this reading would also handle killing incorrectly: people who are killed are not in any state at all, thus they are not in worse states than they otherwise would have been in. Thanks to Jeff McMahan for raising this issue.)

[4] Someone who takes this view need not hold that the only thing that *ever* makes an action wrong is harming; the view is simply that in these cases the actions are wrong only if they harm.

violations that are somewhat unmotivated; there is a worry that the view is ad hoc.[5]

The three views above do not *solve* the non-identity problem; rather, they concede that the problem is unsolvable. The fourth view of the non-identity problem is that Amy's conceiving now is *morally wrong*, and that this is so *because she harms the child she creates*. These are the claims that seem initially obvious about the Temporary Condition case. A genuine solution vindicates these claims. My own view is in this fourth camp. Here are the claims my view makes:

- Amy's conceiving now would be wrong because it would harm the created child.
- An action (or omission) harms someone if it *causes* her to suffer a harm. Having a painful chronic condition is suffering a harm.
- Worse Off is false. It is true that an action cannot *wrongfully* harm someone if it is necessary to prevent *worse harm* to her. But it is not true that an action cannot wrongfully harm someone if it also provides *greater benefits* to her, or if it affects whether she exists.
- It is hard to justify harming; the mere fact that a harming action also provides greater benefits does not justify the action.
- When one option would lead to someone's existence, both harming her in a particular way and benefiting her, but the alternative would bring someone else into existence who would not be harmed in that particular way but would be similarly benefited, then the benefits in question are *not eligible to justify* the particular harming.[6]

---

[5] Parfit (in *Reasons and Persons*) takes the second route, and Woodward (in "The Non-identity Problem") takes the third. I discuss their views in Harman, "Can We Harm and Benefit in Creating?"

[6] I argue for this view in Harman, "Harming as Causing Harm." A harm-based solution to the non-identity problem is also offered by Hanser, "Harming Future People"; I discuss his view in Harman, "Can We Harm and Benefit in Creating?" Shiffrin, in "Wrongful Life," argues compellingly that harming cannot be justified by the mere provision of accompanying benefits.

My view of the non-identity problem does not involve (and does not imply) the claim that life with a painful chronic condition is likely to be a *worse life* than the life of an ordinary person who is born without any chronic conditions. The second view of the non-identity problem listed above, which holds that Amy's conceiving would be morally wrong because it would have worse consequences, does require the claim that life with a painful chronic condition is likely to be worse. But that claim can be challenged, and it's good that my own account does not rely on it. One challenge arises from the idea that a painful chronic condition also tends to bring with it special benefits that outweigh and compensate for the condition; this is implausible as a general prediction. The challenge that I would advance arises from the idea that what really matters to the value of a life are experiences of loving connections with others and meaningful life experiences (such as having meaningful work, and appreciating art), while merely painful experiences, though bad, are relatively trivial and insignificant when we think about the overall value of a person's life. If this idea is right, then it's false that life with a painful chronic condition is likely to be worse overall.

Now that I've pointed out that my view does not involve the claim that a life with a painful chronic condition is a worse life overall, an objector might ask why nevertheless I believe that it would be morally wrong for Amy to conceive now. The answer is that, on my view, it is hard to justify harming someone—but the reason we have against harming does not stem from its being true that the harming

My solution to the non-identity problem proceeds as follows. If Amy conceives now, then her child will have a painful chronic condition. The child would not have had the condition if she had not conceived now, so her conceiving now *causes* the child to have the condition. Causing a painful chronic condition is harming. So, her conceiving harms the child. Is the harming somehow justified? Well, in conceiving, Amy also causes the child to have all the benefits in their life; does the fact that she benefits the child justify her harming them? On my view, it does not. On my view, when one would be harming someone in creating them, but would also be benefiting them, and one has an alternative in which one would create someone else who would be similarly benefited, the benefits are *ineligible* to justify the harming. (What makes them ineligible? The basic idea is that the fact that Amy would be benefiting someone does not tell *in favor of* conceiving now rather than later, since she would similarly benefit someone in the alternative.[7])

Temporary condition cases are *same-number* cases: the same number of people will exist regardless of how the agent acts now. Another aspect of the non-identity problem arises from consideration of *different-number* cases. One kind of different-number case involves choices, such as large-scale policy choices, that will affect who exists in the future but will also affect *how many people* exist in the future in ways we cannot predict. Let's set those cases aside.[8] Here is another kind of different number case:

> Permanent Condition: Betsy has a permanent condition that will cause any child she conceives to have a painful chronic condition, though the child will be able to have a life well worth living.

Cases like this add two elements to the non-identity problem. First, they add a further moral datum to be explained. If Betsy conceives, what she does is *not as bad* as what Amy does if she conceives; how can this be explained, since they do the exact same things to their created children? (Note that saying that what Betsy does is "*not as bad*" does not commit us to saying that what Betsy does is at all bad.) Second, these cases are *hard cases*. There is more disagreement about

---

makes the person's life worse overall. Just as, on my view, harming is not justified by the mere fact of accompanying benefits, harming is also not justified by the mere fact (if it is one) that this episode of harming is relatively trivial when it comes to the overall value of the person's life.

[7] Note that the principle is restricted to cases of harming and benefiting in creating. When it comes to people who exist independently, if we fail to benefit them then they still exist, and miss out on the benefit—on my view, this makes benefiting of independently existing people eligible (in principle) to justify harming. (Though, on my view, it's still difficult to justify harming.) See section 7.4 of Harman, "Harming as Causing Harm."

[8] In Harman, "Harming as Causing Harm," I argue that non-identity actions in such cases are morally wrong because, for all the agent knows, she is choosing between a greater population of people not harmed in a particular way and a smaller population of people harmed in that particular way. Harming in such a case is wrong for similar reasons to the reasons it is wrong to harm in same-number cases.

whether Betsy's conceiving would be permissible than there is disagreement regarding Amy's conceiving. This is one more thing to be explained: why are these hard cases?

In my view, if the painful chronic condition is painful enough, then it would be morally wrong for Betsy to conceive, but the explanation of the wrongness of her action is different from the explanation of the wrongness of Amy's action. In the case of Amy's action, the benefits that her child will receive are *ineligible to justify* the harming of the child, because Amy can bestow similar benefits on another child by waiting. But in Betsy's case, the benefits her child will receive are in principle available to justify the harms to the child. On my view, there are two moral thresholds that are relevant to this case. Some harms are so bad that we should not cause them in creating children, and no amount of benefit can justify causing them. The first threshold has to do with how bad the painful chronic condition is: if the painful chronic condition is painful enough, it will not be possible to justify causing it. For each harm that could in principle be justified, there will be a second threshold of how much benefit must come along with the harm to justify causing it. On my view, people disagree about these cases because they implicitly believe these thresholds fall in different places. Because they are simply thresholds, it is easy to be a bit wrong about where they fall.[9]

To further understand my solution to the non-identity problem, let's consider two further questions: What does my view say about the morality of ordinary procreation? And does my view imply that we are always morally required to create the least harmed children we could create?

On my view, ordinary procreation is permissible. In procreating, one massively harms the person one creates (in that one causes all the harms they will experience), but one also massively benefits them. These benefits are *eligible* in principle to justify the harming, because in the alternative (not procreating at all), one does not similarly benefit anyone. My view furthermore holds that the benefits of ordinary procreation do justify the harming that is part of ordinary procreating—they fall above the relevant threshold.

My view doesn't imply that we are always morally required to create the least harmed children we could create. While it's clear that Amy should not conceive now, we can consider a variant case in which our view would be different. Suppose that if a woman conceives now, her child will have a painful chronic condition but will also have an extraordinarily wonderful life. In the alternative, she would wait a few months and create a child without the painful chronic condition, who would have an ordinary good life. This case is very different from Amy's. It's not at all clear that this woman must wait to conceive later. My view accommodates this thought. In this case, the benefiting that the woman would be doing in conceiving

---

[9] See Harman, "Harming as Causing Harm," for expansion of these points.

now *is eligible* to justify the harming she would be doing, because her alternative does not involve similarly benefiting anyone (but rather involves providing less benefit). On my view, whether this woman may conceive now will depend on two questions: Is the painful condition sufficiently bad that harming in this way cannot be justified? And if not, are the accompanying benefits sufficiently good to justify it?

My primary focus in the discussion to follow will be on whether the choice between aborting and not aborting could raise the non-identity problem by bringing the same moral issues into play as are present in *temporary condition cases* like Amy's. (But it's also interesting to ask whether in any cases the choice whether to abort raises the non-identity problem by bringing the same moral issues into play as are present in *permanent condition cases* like Betsy's. See footnote 14.)

5.3 The No Moral Status View and the Ever Conscious View

Consider the following common view of the moral status of preconscious fetuses:

> The No Moral Status View: Fetuses that have never been conscious lack moral status.

Many people believe that early abortion is morally insignificant because the fetuses that die in early abortions lack moral status. The No Moral Status View would imply that view of early abortion.[10] But another view would also have that implication:

> The Ever Conscious View: A living being has moral status just in case it is ever conscious.

I argue for the Ever Conscious View in other work.[11] On this view, because early fetuses that die in early abortions are never conscious, they lack moral status—and thus, early abortion is morally insignificant. But those early fetuses that will become persons will be conscious in the future, so they have moral status. Thus, the Ever Conscious View holds that you and I had moral status back when we were pre-conscious early fetuses, though, had we been aborted, we would not have had moral status as early fetuses. The Ever Conscious View explains why some

---

[10] I assume throughout the chapter that fetal consciousness does not arise until some time after the first trimester of pregnancy.
[11] Harman, "The Ever Conscious View and the Contingency of Moral Status." In Harman, "Creation Ethics," I argue for a more narrow version of the Ever Conscious View, which I call "The Actual Future Principle."

early fetuses are the appropriate objects of love, and the view offers a better account of our reasons not to harm some early fetuses by smoking or drinking excessively during pregnancy than that offered by the No Moral Status View.[12]

Let's suppose that one of these views is true, and consider the following case:

> Early Pregnancy: Carla is pregnant and learns early in her pregnancy that her fetus will have a painful chronic condition, but will be able to live a life well worth living. If Carla aborts, then later she will conceive a child who will not have the painful chronic condition.

Does Carla's choice whether to abort raise the non-identity problem? That is: is this choice morally equivalent—or sufficiently morally similar—to the choice in a non-identity case, so that a moral account of the non-identity case would also apply to this abortion case?

I believe so. If early abortion is morally insignificant because early fetuses that die in early abortions lack moral status, then the choice whether to abort is, morally, the choice whether to *create* a morally significant being right now. If one continues the pregnancy, a new person is created. If one aborts the pregnancy, it turns out that no morally significant being was created.

If that is right, then the moral explanation of why it would be morally wrong for Amy to conceive now will also apply to Carla. If Carla continued her pregnancy, she would be *harming* her child by causing her child to have a harmful condition, and the benefits Carla would also be bestowing are not even eligible to justify the harming because she has another option that would provide similar benefits to someone but would not involve harming in this way at all: aborting now and conceiving later.

Here is the first important claim of my chapter:

> If the No Moral Status View or the Ever Conscious View is true, then in the Early Pregnancy Case, the choice whether to abort is (roughly) morally equivalent to a temporary condition non-identity choice, so that the moral account of temporary condition non-identity cases applies to the choice whether to abort.[13]

Relying on my view of temporary condition non-identity cases, I also make the following claim:

---

[12] See Harman "Creation Ethics."
[13] The two choices are only roughly morally equivalent because, for example, the burdens on a person of waiting to conceive are lighter than the burdens of undergoing an abortion.

If the No Moral Status View or the Ever Conscious View is true, then in the Early Pregnancy case, it is morally required to abort.[14]

Relying on the claim that either the Ever Conscious View or the No Moral Status View is true, I also make this claim:

In the Early Pregnancy case, it is morally required to abort.

Let's turn now to considering three objections.

> Objection: Sometimes one should kill someone to prevent their suffering a harm; sometimes one should engage in compassionate killing. But in such cases, death is better for them than continuing to live. By contrast, in the Early Pregnancy case, killing the fetus prevents it from having anything good in its life; but allowing it to live would enable it to have a life well worth living. It simply cannot be true that one should kill a being *for its own sake*—to prevent it from suffering a harm—when continuing to live is better for it than dying now would be.

The objector is right that, on my view, Carla should kill the fetus to prevent its suffering a harm, even though killing it is worse for it. But it is tricky to evaluate the claim that on my view, one should kill the fetus for its own sake. When Carla is faced with the choice whether to abort, she is in a weird situation. She is choosing between a possibility in which the fetus is something that never has moral status, on the one hand, and a possibility in which the fetus is something that does have moral status, on the other hand. (On my view, the Ever Conscious View, the fetus has moral status from the moment of conception in this second possibility; on the No Moral Status View, the fetus will develop moral status in the future in this second possibility.) My claim is that she should abort because failing to abort would involve impermissibly harming a being with moral status—the being that is now a fetus and that would have moral status if she failed to abort. By aborting, she would kill the fetus, making its life devoid of meaningful goods rather than full of them. But this is nothing to be said *against* aborting, because if she aborts, the fetus lacks moral status, and what is bad for the fetus does not matter morally.

I will grant to my objector the claim that my view is properly described as holding that Carla is morally required to kill the fetus *for its own sake*; it is at least

---

[14] We can also consider a variant case, Early Pregnancy—Permanent Condition, in which the pregnant woman has a permanent condition such that whenever she conceives a fetus, it will have a painful chronic condition. Via similar reasoning, we can conclude that the choice whether to abort in Early Pregnancy—Permanent Condition is roughly morally equivalent to the choice in a permanent condition non-identity case; thus, in some of these cases (but not in all of them), abortion is morally required.

true that on my view, Carla is morally required to kill the fetus in order to prevent the fetus's suffering a certain harm.

The objector is offering this claim:

> For Its Own Sake, Strong Version: It cannot be that one is morally required to kill a being *for its own sake* when killing it would be much worse for it than allowing it to live.

I do deny this claim. But the fact that I have to deny it is not a serious cost of my view, because I can endorse this closely related claim instead:

> For Its Own Sake, Weaker Version: For a being that has moral status independently of whether one kills it, it cannot be that one is morally required to kill it *for its own sake* when killing it would be much worse for it than allowing it to live.

My claims do not run afoul of this principle; I can endorse the Weaker Version of the claim. When we compare the Strong Version with the Weaker Version, we can see that the Strong Version would require us to take seriously what is better or worse for a being—such as a fetus that dies in an early abortion—that lacks moral status. But such considerations do not provide moral reasons. Once we allow that it's possible that moral status is contingent (once we allow the possibility of the No Moral Status View or the Ever Conscious View), we should reject the Strong Version in favor of the Weaker Version of the For Its Own Sake claim. (I will argue in section 5.5 that some people should reject even this Weaker Version as too strong, adopting an even weaker version of the claim instead.)

> Objection: Suppose that the proposed view of the non-identity problem is true. Nevertheless, it applies to actively conceiving a child. It holds that Amy would act wrongly by actively conceiving. But Carla would not be doing anything active. She would simply be allowing her pregnancy to continue. The moral reason against what Amy would be doing by conceiving is stronger because she would be *actively harming*. Carla would simply be *allowing* harm to occur. So the correct moral account of Amy's choice does not apply to Carla's choice.

I will respond to this worry in two ways. First, it is a tricky matter to say whether one is related to an outcome in the making-way versus in the allowing-way. One might perform an action and thereby *allow* something to happen, as when one removes an obstacle and allows a rock to roll down a hill, or removes life support and allows someone to die. One might omit to act in a particular way and thereby *make* something happen, as when a parent omits to feed her child and thereby kills her child, or as when one declines to raise one's hand for a vote, defeating the motion.[15] It is odd to say that by not aborting, a pregnant woman simply *allows* an early fetus to develop into a baby. Such a thought betrays an odd naivety about both the mechanics and the experience of pregnancy. By not aborting and carrying a pregnancy to term, a woman devotes her body to *nurturing* the fetus and *making it into* a baby.[16] Along these lines, Thomson (in "A Defense of Abortion") suggests that abortion is best thought of as the withdrawal of positive aid. So, my first response to this objection is that it may be a mistake to see Carla as merely *allowing* her child to develop if she does not abort; rather, she would be *making* her fetus into a baby.

Second, I want to comment that I think there are real worries about how to tell the correct moral story about the non-identity problem while taking seriously that we have stronger reasons against making someone suffer a harm than we have against allowing someone to suffer a harm. My own discussions of the non-identity problem to date have not tackled this challenge.[17]

> Objection: The right view of the non-identity problem will hold that it matters that we cannot *identify* the individuals who would exist in the options we are choosing between. By contrast, when a woman is pregnant, the individual who will exist if she does not abort *already exists* and thus is identifiable. This makes the choice whether to abort utterly morally different from a non-identity choice.

I do not think that the fact that we cannot identity who would exist in either scenario matters to the non-identity problem. Some people have thought the fact of unidentifiability makes it hard to hold that non-identity actions are wrong because of harming or that non-identity actions would wrong the people they would create. On my view, these thoughts are mistaken.

There is an interesting view of the non-identity problem that would also see non-identity choices and Carla's choice whether to abort as different for a reason that is related to identifiability. Melinda Roberts has argued that Amy's conceiving now is morally wrong for the following reasons.[18] Suppose Amy does conceive now. In that case, Roberts claims, her action of conceiving actually had only a very small chance of creating the particular person who is in fact created; and she had an alternative option of waiting and conceiving later which would also have given

---

[15] On making versus allowing, see McGrath "Causation and the Making/Allowing Distinction," and Woollard, "The Doctrine of Doing and Allowing."

[16] If a pregnant woman is not given the option of abortion, she is forced into this particular activity. (Failure to have the option of abortion does not make pregnancy any less active.)

[17] Thanks to Peter A. Graham for pointing out this worry, in a conversation about my paper "Can We Harm and Benefit in Creating?"

[18] Roberts, "The Nonidentity Fallacy."

the same small chance to the creation of that very child, but without the painful chronic condition. Thus, Amy should have waited because the prospects for every possibly created person are better if she waits. Roberts's solution only applies to some temporary condition cases. The moral explanation it offers is surprising and in my view ultimately incorrect. But it is interesting as an example of a view that holds that conceiving now in temporary condition cases would be wrong *because of how one treats the created child* and yet the view would not apply at all to choices whether to abort.[19]

5.4 The Full Moral Status view

Consider this view:

> The Full Moral Status View: Human fetuses have the full moral status of persons from the moment of conception. One has as strong moral reason not to kill an early human fetus whose life would be well worth living as one has not to kill a 10-year-old whose continued life would be well worth living.

On this view, Carla's choice whether to abort simply does not raise the non-identity problem. It is in some ways like the choice whether to kill one's already-born baby and then conceive a new baby. (But it is not exactly like that choice. As Thomson argues in "A Defense of Abortion," abortion is killing by withdrawing life-sustaining and burdensome aid. A pregnant woman who does not want to aid her fetus's development may permissibly abort, even if the fetus has the moral status of a person, Thomson argues. Still, whether or not Thomson is correct, if the Full Moral Status View is true, it is not true that Carla should abort to avoid the fetus's growing into a baby that suffers from the harm that Carla can now predict. Carla's choice is nothing like Amy's choice.)

---

[19] Let me briefly mention two more objections that might be raised; both objectors believe it is *morally wrong* to abort a pregnancy because the fetus has a serious medical condition. One objector says that we should not disturb the natural course of procreation; if we do so, then we will lack humility about our own gifts and benefits. (See Sandel, "Mastery and Gift.") This objection is easily dismissed by pointing out that we are often morally required to intervene in the natural course of human lives in a variety of ways, most obviously using medicine, but in plenty of other ways as well. Another objector says that abortion in such cases would be morally wrong because it is cruel and unfair to those people who will have the serious medical condition in question—not all cases will be found in utero and aborted, so there will be a population of people with the condition. But this population will be smaller, and thus less likely to garner public understanding and support (for example in the form of medical research aimed at the condition). Aborting in such cases makes things worse for those who do have the condition. To this objector, we should concede that aborting has this bad effect. But we should reply that it would be wrong to impose the condition on the fetus in question out of solidarity and in an effort to help the others who will have it—this is not an acceptable justification of harming.

5.5 The Low Moral Status View

Consider this view:

> The Low Moral Status View: Human fetuses have a very low level of moral status at the beginning of pregnancy and their level of moral status grows throughout pregnancy so that at 9 months, a fully developed fetus has the full moral status of a person. There is a moral reason not to abort a first-trimester fetus, but it does not have anything like the strength of our reasons not to kill persons; it is more like a moral reason against killing an animal, such as a rabbit.

A view like this is common among ordinary people. It relies on the idea that there are levels of moral status; I have argued elsewhere that we should deny that there are degrees or levels of moral status in this sense.[20] But let's consider what the Low Moral Status View would imply about the Early Pregnancy case. Carla's choice whether to abort would not be roughly morally equivalent to the choice in a temporary condition non-identity case. Instead, if the Low Moral Status View is true, there is a harm-based moral reason against Carla's aborting. Let's assume I'm right that harm-based reasons are weighty, and that harm is hard to justify. But on the Low Moral Status View, the reason against abortion is weakened by the low moral status of the fetus. So the Low Moral Status View implies that Carla has a weak harm-based moral reason against aborting.

There is a compelling line of thought that would commit a proponent of the Low Moral Status View to the claim that, in Early Pregnancy, Carla is morally obligated to abort the fetus to prevent it from suffering the particular harm she knows will befall it if it lives. I will call this line of thought "the Rabbit Argument."

Consider the following case:

> David's 5-year-old daughter will develop a painful chronic condition unless David kills a rabbit and uses its glands to make a special medicine for his daughter.

The first premise of the Rabbit Argument is that David is morally obligated to kill the rabbit to save his daughter from suffering a serious harm.

The second premise of the Rabbit Argument is that the Low Moral Status View is true. The third premise of the Rabbit Argument is that if the Low Moral Status View is true then we should see Carla's choice as roughly morally equivalent to David's choice regarding the rabbit. If Carla aborts, then she kills a being with a

---

[20] Harman, "The Potentiality Problem." In arguing against levels of moral status, I rely in part on an argument of Singer's (in "Equality for Animals?"), though he would not agree with my view that we have strong reasons to refrain from killing human babies. For a recent defense of levels of moral status, see Kagan, *How to Count Animals*.

low level of moral status; so does David, if he kills the rabbit. This is harming a morally significant being, and there is *some* moral reason against it. If Carla does not abort, then a person suffers a significant harm; similarly if David does not kill the rabbit. David should kill a being with low moral status to avoid a person's suffering this significant harm; similarly, the Rabbit Argument concludes, Carla should abort to avoid the fetus's developing into a person who would suffer a significant harm.

One might object to this moral account of Carla's choice by pointing out that the rabbit and David's daughter are different beings, and that David's daughter *gets to have a good life* if the rabbit is killed. By contrast, Carla's fetus is the same being as the one who will avoid future harm if the fetus is killed. And if the future harm is prevented, the person who would have been harmed does not get to have a good life or any life at all. This objection to the Rabbit Argument raises two distinct worries. The point that the daughter gets to live a good life while Carla's fetus does not should be set aside; consideration of non-identity cases shows that sometimes one should act to avoid harm to someone, even though one thereby prevents that person from existing. (The temporary condition cases show this, but we can also think of the choice whether to create someone who would have a brief life of pure misery; we should not create him, though by avoiding harm to him we do not thereby give him a good life.) The other point the objector makes is that David chooses to kill one being (the rabbit) for the sake of another (his daughter). Carla, much more bizarrely, would be choosing to kill a being, depriving it of a life well worth living, for the sake of sparing that very same being from a significant harm.

Thus, we might flesh out this objection by asserting this claim which we embraced earlier:

For Its Own Sake, Weaker Version: For a being that has moral status independently of whether one kills it, it cannot be that one is morally required to kill it *for its own sake* when killing it would be much worse for it than allowing it to live.

The objector holds that surely the Weaker Version of the For Its Own Sake claim is correct, and so the Rabbit Argument must be unsound. A proponent of the Rabbit Argument can respond by denying the Weaker Version of the claim and embracing instead:

For Its Own Sake, Even Weaker Version: For a being that has *an exact level of moral status* independently of whether one kills it, it cannot be that one is morally required to kill it *for its own sake* when killing it would be much worse for it than allowing it to live.

If there are levels of moral status, and if some beings start out with a low level of moral status and then grow to have a higher level of moral status, as the Low

Moral Status View holds, then the Weaker Version of the For Its Own Sake claim should be rejected in favor of the Even Weaker Version. Future harms that would impact a being that would then have a *high* level of moral status should matter more to us than a more severe harm now to a being that currently has a *low* level of moral status; but the Weaker View would not accommodate that. A proponent of the Rabbit Argument should say that once we allow that a being's level of moral status can grow over time, then we should see that only the Even Weaker Version of the For Its Own Sake claim is plausible.

Let me close this section by briefly explaining why I reject the existence of levels of moral status in the sense posited by the Low Moral Status View, and thus why I do not embrace the Rabbit Argument. It might seem obvious that there are levels of moral status. Suppose that you could save the life of a human baby or a rabbit; surely you should save the baby. What explains this? We might think the explanation is that the baby has a higher level of moral status. I think that is incorrect. Rather, we have a stronger reason to save the baby because much more is at stake for the baby. The baby stands to lose life as a person; the rabbit merely stands to lose life as a rabbit. This explanation of our stronger reasons to be careful of babies cannot ground the claim that early fetuses have a lower level of moral status: they, like babies, stand to lose lives as persons if they die. Human fetuses have just as much at stake, when their lives are imperiled, as human babies do.[21]

Because I do not hold the Low Moral Status View, I reject the Rabbit Argument, and I continue to embrace the Weaker Version of the For Its Own Sake Claim. Some readers may join me in thinking that the Weaker Version is clearly true, and that it should not be rejected in favor of the Even Weaker Version; consideration of the Rabbit Argument may give us additional reasons (beyond those I outlined in the last paragraph) to reject the Low Moral Status View.

5.6 A General Account of Non-Identity Cases

So far, I've discussed whether the Early Pregnancy case can be seen to be *roughly morally equivalent* to a non-identity temporary condition case. In this section, I will make a more radical claim: that, properly understood, the Early Pregnancy case is a non-identity case. We should broaden our understanding of what counts as a non-identity case.

Non-identity cases are typically seen as cases in which an agent's action affects who exists: the agent is choosing between two possibilities which differ in terms of *which beings exist*. Our discussion of the No Moral Status View and the Ever Conscious View illustrated that, if either of these views is right, then the Early

---

[21] Harman, "The Potentiality Problem."

Pregnancy case is crucially a case in which *whether a being has moral status* differs between the two possibilities available to the agent. Our discussion of the Low Moral Status View illustrated that, if that view is right, then the Early Pregnancy case is crucially a case in which *what level of moral status a being has* differs between the two possibilities available to the agent. All three phenomena can be captured as follows: these are cases in which *the moral status facts* are not identical between the two possibilities.

Here is a general characterization of non-identity cases:

Non-identity cases (original *and* new) are cases in which:

(a) An agent's choice affects *the moral status facts*: the moral status facts in the different options *are not identical*. The moral status facts include *which beings* exist, *whether* those beings have moral status, and (if there are levels of moral status) *what level of moral status* each being has.

(b) The agent has an option that would be morally wrong because it harms a being.

(c) Taking that option does not make that being worse off than they would otherwise be.

The final claim of my chapter is that we should see non-identity phenomena in this broader way.[22] The non-identity problem arises because there is a puzzle about how certain actions can be morally wrong. In all of these cases (original and new), the same basic puzzle arises: due to the way the actions affect the moral status facts, the actions wrongfully harm some beings without making them worse off.

5.7 Conclusion

I have argued that the ethics of abortion and the ethics of (the original) non-identity cases are tied together. If the No Moral Status View or the Ever Conscious View is correct, then some cases of deciding whether to abort raise the non-identity problem. Relying on either the No Moral Status View or the Ever Conscious View, we get this further conclusion:

---

[22] On my view, the Early Pregnancy case is a non-identity case, given a new, broader understanding of non-identity phenomena. But some people should count Early Pregnancy as a non-identity case even using the original, narrow conception of what a non-identity case is. McMahan holds that we were never early fetuses (in *The Ethics of Killing*; see p. 267). On his view, we are embodied minds who did not come into existence until those early fetuses became conscious. Thus, on his view, deciding whether to continue a pregnancy is literally deciding whether to create a person who doesn't yet exist.

If a harm that a created child would suffer is such that it would be morally wrong to procreate now in a temporary condition non-identity case, then it is also morally required to abort to prevent one's fetus from growing into a person who would suffer that harm (if one would go on to conceive a fetus that would not suffer that harm).

I've also laid out an argument that concludes that if the Low Moral Status View is true, then the above claim holds. (But I don't embrace a moral picture that allows for levels of moral status in that sense.)

Along the way, I've argued for the following:

Sometimes one is morally required to kill a being for its own sake, when killing it would be much worse for it than allowing it to live.

And I've argued that a proponent of the Low Moral Status View should think that this can be true even if killing the being would be killing something with moral status.

Finally, I have argued that non-identity phenomena occur more broadly than previously recognized. There is a more general moral category of which the classic non-identity cases are just a special case: cases in which *the moral status facts* are not identical across an agent's alternatives. This category encompasses cases in which *who exists* varies across the alternatives, cases in which *whether* some beings have moral status varies across the alternatives, and (if there are levels of moral status) cases in which *what level of moral status* some beings have varies across the alternatives.[23]

References

Hanser, M., "Harming Future People," *Philosophy and Public Affairs* 19/1 (1990): 47–70.

Harman, E., "Can We Harm and Benefit in Creating?" *Philosophical Perspectives* 18 (2004): 89–113.

Harman, E., "Creation Ethics: The Moral Status of Early Fetuses and the Ethics of Abortion," *Philosophy and Public Affairs* 28/4 (1999): 310–24.

---

[23] For helpful comments on earlier drafts of this paper, I thank Tyler Doggett, Laura Gillespie, Alex Guerrero, Jeff McMahan, and audiences at the Central APA Meeting, the Eastern APA Meeting, the National Institute of Health, the Rutgers University Conference in Memory of Derek Parfit, Princeton University's Center for Human Values, Stanford University, University of Sydney, University of Texas at Austin School of Law, and University of Vermont.

Harman, E., "The Ever Conscious View and the Contingency of Moral Status," in Clarke, S., Savulescu, J., and Zohny, H. (eds.), *Rethinking Moral Status* (Oxford University Press, 2021).

Harman, E., "Harming as Causing Harm," in Roberts, M. and Wasserman, D. (eds.), *Harming Future Persons* (Springer, 2009), 137–54.

Harman, E., "The Potentiality Problem," *Philosophical Studies* 114/1–2 (2003): 173–98.

Kagan, S., *How to Count Animals, more or less* (Oxford University Press, 2019).

McGrath, S., "Causation and the Making/Allowing Distinction," *Philosophical Studies* 114/1–2 (2003): 81–106.

McMahan, J. *The Ethics of Killing: Problems at the Margins of Life* (Oxford University Press, 2003).

Parfit, D., *Reasons and Persons* (Oxford University Press, 1984).

Roberts, M., "The Nonidentity Fallacy: Harm, Probability, and Another Look at Parfit's Depletion Example," *Utilitas* 19 (2007): 267–311.

Sandel, M., "Mastery and Gift," *The Case Against Perfection: Ethics in the Age of Genetic Engineering* (Harvard University Press, 2007), chapter 5.

Shiffrin, S., "Wrongful Life, Procreative Responsibility, and the Significance of Harm," *Legal Theory* 5/2 (1999): 117–48.

Singer, P., "Equality for Animals?" in *Practical Ethics*, Second Edition (Cambridge: Cambridge University Press, 1993).

Thomson, J. J., "A Defense of Abortion," *Philosophy and Public Affairs* 1/1 (1971): 47–66.

Woodward, J., "The Non-identity Problem," *Ethics* 96/4 (1986): 804–31.

Woollard, F., "The Doctrine of Doing and Allowing I," *Philosophy Compass* 7/7 (2012): 448–58.

6
A Partial Solution to the Non-Identity Problem

Regretting One Was Born and Having a Life Not Subjectively Worth Living

Andrew McGee and Julian Savulescu

6.1 Introduction

The non-identity problem is more than forty years old.[1,2] It has spawned a great deal of academic literature, with many articles appearing in the leading philosophy journals in the world.[3] Many others feature in the field of reproductive ethics where the implications of the non-identity problem are still widely and intensively debated.[4] While most of these articles suggest solutions to the problem, none has seemed compelling[5] and, in *On What Matters* and in a paper published posthumously in 2017, Derek Parfit presented the problem again and claimed that it was still 'often overlooked'.[6] In this chapter we take a fresh look at the non-identity problem and present a solution that is different from those that have so far been attempted.

Our solution focuses on Parfit's remarks that, if a person born from a 'different people choice'[7] has a life worth living, and so does not regret existing, the decision

---

[1] We are greatly indebted to the late Derek Parfit for remarks on an earlier draft of this chapter, and also to Guy Kahane for comments on an earlier version. Thanks also to Jimmy Goodrich for helpful comments.

[2] Its origins, at least, are traceable back to Adams (1972). See also Parfit (1976); Adams (1979); Kavka (1982); Parfit (1982, 1987). Derek Parfit is the author who coined the term 'non-identity problem', having originally called it 'the identity problem'.

[3] We will refer to some of these below but for a comprehensive overview, see Roberts (2020).

[4] For recent debates in medical ethics, see Hope and McMillan (2012) and commentaries; Smajdor (2014); Williams and Harris (2014); Lawlor (2015); Hope (2015). For well-known papers on or related to the non-identity problem in the bioethics and legal literature, see Brock (1995); Shiffrin (1998); Savulescu (2001); Archard (2004). An important collection of papers is Roberts and Wasserman (2009).

[5] Interesting recent attempts are Liberto (2014); Hurley and Weinberg (2015); and Bontly (2016). We take a different approach in this chapter.

[6] Parfit (2011: 218); Parfit (2017: 122).

[7] Parfit (1987: 356); we explain this and related terms in section 6.2.

is worse for no one. Some 'different people choices', we claim, can produce people who regret being born even though they are glad to be alive and have lives worth living. These cases have so far not been discussed in the literature on the non-identity problem, and seem to escape the paradoxical conclusions that Parfit draws in other 'different people choices'. These cases suggest that the life not worth living criterion—the criterion that Parfit adopts as the only way we can claim that different people choices can affect people for the worse—may not be the only possible criterion to adopt in explaining why such different people choices may be wrong in person-affecting terms. It may be enough if a person regrets existing to condemn these different people choices, notwithstanding that they have a life worth living. We call our solution 'partial' because we do not address cases where those who are born from different people choices do not regret being born. Nonetheless, we believe our discussion of all these cases can make progress towards addressing the non-identity problem since the chance of having a regrettable life is a reason against bringing that life into existence.

6.2 The Challenge of the Non-identity Problem

Parfit distinguishes between 'same people choices' and 'different people choices'.[8] Suppose Anna is pregnant and is experiencing nausea. She can be offered a drug which will cure her of the nausea, but will cause her child to develop a severe depressive disorder which will come and go throughout the child's life, and is not curable. During extended bouts of depression, the child will experience suicidal thoughts and attempt to take her own life many times. In this case, it is best for the mother not to take this drug. If she doesn't take it, her child will live a normal life and will not develop the depressive disorder. This is a 'same people choice' because, other things being equal, the same child can exist both in circumstances where she would develop the disorder and in circumstances where she would not.

Now suppose Zelda is a mother who wants to become pregnant. She has a temporary illness that, if she conceives now, will mean that the child she conceives will inherit a similar incurable depressive disorder, with similar consequences. However, if she waits for two months, the illness will have cleared and the child she conceives will not inherit the depressive disorder. This is a 'different people choice' because the same person cannot exist in the two respective outcomes of Zelda's choice. If Zelda waits, a different spermatozoon will fertilize a different egg, and so the resulting child in two months' time will be numerically different from the child she would conceive if she does not wait. Waiting is therefore not better for the child she conceives if she does *not* wait, for that child would not exist

---

[8] Parfit (1987: 356). He also distinguishes between same number and different number choices, but aside from remarks where relevant, we leave this distinction aside.

if she waits. Parfit claims that, in a different people choice, provided the child has a life worth living, such a child is not worse off for existing. And if we construe existence as a benefit, we might even say that the mother's decision *benefited* this child.[9] If we think it is wrong for the mother not to wait, how do we explain why not waiting is wrong?[10] This is the non-identity problem.

Parfit also claims that, if we have a life worth living, we will not *regret* being caused to exist.[11] In the context of a discussion about whether the non-identity problem can be solved by appealing to a child's rights, Parfit says: '[S]ince my life is worth living, I would not regret that my mother caused me to exist.'[12] He then states that 'where we cannot ask for someone's consent, we should ask instead whether this person would later regret what we are doing' (373). Applying this to the victims of a risky energy policy (which changes the identity of those who come to exist) who die at the age of 40 as a result of the release of radiation, he states: 'These people would regret the fact that they will die young. But, since their lives are worth living, they would not regret the fact that they were ever born. They would therefore not regret our choice of the Risky Policy' (373). It is on this basis that Parfit believes the rights solution fails. Since I would not regret existing (because my life is worth living), I would *waive* any right I held.[13] Suppose, for example, I am the child of Zelda and I have inherited the severe depressive disorder because she chose not to wait until her illness had cleared up. I now in my late teens discover, on hearing a *BBC Science* bulletin on Zelda's illness, that my mother could easily have waited two months for her condition to clear up. On

---

[9] Parfit (1987: 359).

[10] So called 'non-comparative' concepts of harm have been suggested, most notably by Shiffrin (1998); Harman (2004, 2009); Hanser (2008, 2011). These accounts resolve the problem by revising the concept of harm involved, thereby providing a stipulative solution to the problem. For example, they involve rejecting Parfit's all-things-considered notion of harm and insisting that you are nonetheless harmed if you exist in a state that has bad effects for you, such as the effects of your disability, even though you could not have existed in any other state and your life is worth living. However, it is worth noting that even Parfit's all-things-considered notion of harm—which can occur if different people choices result in a life not worth living—is also non-comparative, to the extent that Parfit acknowledges that, if we say that it is worse for this person that they exist, we do not imply that there would be a person who does not exist, for whom their not existing would be better. We are not, Parfit says, comparing existence with non-existence. Our solution is ultimately in a similar vein to Parfit's, but we believe that it does not require that life be so bad as to be not worth living, but does involve regret that one was born. It is bad if the child regrets being born, provided the regret is genuine and rational. We will argue that this regret is rational even if she has a life subjectively and/or objectively worth living.

[11] This criterion, as we shall see, applies to whether a life is *subjectively* worth living only. There are cases of severe mental impairment where the child might not be capable of any regret, and where the life is not worth living. This is a case where life is not *objectively* worth living. We discuss these distinctions below.

[12] Parfit (1987: 375). See also the following: 'Since they will not regret their existence, they will not regret our choice' (526).

[13] Parfit (1987: 375). It is not clear whether we would waive the original right, or whether we would waive any rights arising about of the breach of the original right. In breach of contract, for example, I don't waive the rights that were breached, but only the rights arising from the breach. If the latter, we might claim that my lack of regret only *excuses* the conduct, but does not make it *permissible*. But we set this possible approach aside.

hearing that bulletin, I complain to her. After listening to me, she replies, 'Are you glad to be alive?' If I am honest and reply that I am, she can say,

> If I had waited two months before becoming pregnant, you would never have existed. I would have produced another child from a different egg and a different sperm. Your life, even with your disorder, is worth living. You never had a chance of existing without the disorder. So I have not harmed you at all.[14]

This reply seems to be an adequate answer to my complaint. As soon as I try to articulate why I think I have been wronged[15] by my mother, it seems I must concede that, if I don't regret being alive, I have not been wronged.

But what if, instead, I am ambivalent in my reply? What if there are times when I really wish I had not been born, even if I have a life objectively worth living? Parfit is concerned with rational regret (360–1). He may well have responded that it is not rational to regret a life which is objectively worth living. We will question this claim in what follows. We will argue that one can have reason to regret a life which is objectively worth living.[16] One way of exploring this possibility is to look a little more closely at how the offspring resulting from these decisions could come to regret the mother's choice.

6.3 Preliminary: Some Basic Concepts

In order to discuss this possibility, we first need to distinguish between the following concepts which will all be used in the rest of this chapter:

1. The concept of regretting one's existence.[17]
2. The concept of a person's life being objectively or subjectively worth living or not worth living, where 'objectively' refers to the fact that no reasonable

---

[14] Singer (2011: 109), eloquently explaining the difficulty of accounting for the wrong of deliberately conceiving a child with a disorder. The word 'harm' means 'harmed in an all-things-considered way': Parfit (1976: 374); Parfit (1987: section 25).

[15] Some would object that I can be wronged, even though I have not been harmed. See Kumar (2005), and, for an earlier version of this view, Woodward (1986). We later advance a different version of this claim as a possible option in section 6.4.

[16] It is worth noting at this point that earlier in *Reasons and Persons*, Parfit says, speaking of the Pythagoreans' regret that the square root of two was not a rational number: 'We can regret truths even when it is logically impossible that these truths be false' (175). He makes this claim in rejecting the objection that I cannot logically regret not existing in the period prior to my birth. Parfit claims we can regret the fact that we did not exist earlier (176). Perhaps we can regret existing even if it is mathematically impossible for our life to be not worth living (because it contains more good, say, than bad).

[17] With a minor qualification we discuss later, we exclude cases where the subject's regret is *irrational* even though capacitous—an example is young love in which a heart-broken lover considers suicide.

person would regard the life as worth living (say, a life wracked with irreversible and unbearable pain, or a life of permanent unconsciousness[18]), as opposed to whether a person *in fact* genuinely does regard her life to be a life not worth living (this being the subjective sense of a life not worth living, about which people might reasonably take differing views);
3. The concept of subjective and objective rightness. It might be subjectively wrong to take the risk of regret, or of a life not subjectively worth living, if it is a reasonably foreseeable possibility. This is because, even if it does not always eventuate (so that, when it does not, the decision is not objectively wrong), it *might* have eventuated. As Parfit explains,

> [w]e must...distinguish between what is *objectively* and *subjectively* right or wrong...We often do not know what the effects of our acts would be. And we ought to be blamed for doing what is subjectively wrong. We ought to be blamed for such acts even if they are objectively right.[19]

For reasons we shall see, although it might seem that the notion of regret in 1 and the notion of a life not worth living subjectively in 2 should coincide, this is not *always* so. A person can have a life worth living subjectively (she values her life) yet still regret existing—she might be a product of a rape, for example, and so regrets existing, both for her own sake and for her mother's sake,[20] even though she is happy (we will defend this claim in section 6.4). Regret therefore need not coincide with whether a person thinks she has a life not worth living. This is why we treat these categories separately. But in many cases, of course, regret will take the form of subjectively disvaluing one's life.

An example of a life subjectively not worth living but perhaps objectively worth living may be Daniel James, the quadriplegic who ended his life at the Dignitas clinic in Switzerland in 2008. Because he was, prior to this disabling accident, a very active athlete, we can understand James' decision in the sense that it would at least arguably be too harsh to call it an irrational decision, even though many of us

---

[18] Sometimes the former is understood as a life worth *not* living, while the latter is a life not worth living. Nothing turns on this difference in this chapter. Also, where a life is not objectively worth living and the subject is aware (as when it is not worth living because of unbearable pain), then in many cases such a life is not worth living either objectively or subjectively. But as will be seen just below, Jeff McMahan has given an example of someone having a life not worth living objectively, but worth living subjectively. So it is important to keep these categories separate even though, where not objectively worth living, the subjective judgement will often coincide with the objective one.

[19] Parfit (1987: 25). Parfit has recently expressed this distinction differently, in terms of what he calls 'belief-relative' and 'fact-relative senses'. For ease of exposition, we stick with Parfit's original terms, which he does not expressly reject.

[20] The regret is also for her own sake, and not just the mother's, because (a) her knowledge of how she was conceived may mean that her own sense of self-worth is heavily compromised by feelings of guilt, shame, and unworthiness and (b) her concern for her mother is a self-interested concern. We give a concrete example in the next section.

would probably claim that, objectively speaking, the life of a quadriplegic might still be a life worth living (as many reports in the press claimed).[21] Although James does not think his *whole* life is not subjectively worth living, but only the part of his life from becoming a quadriplegic, we will later suggest that there can be cases where someone might take this view of their whole lives.

If a person does not have a life worth living subjectively, she would regret her existence and so a life not worth living subjectively in category 2 introduced above will coincide with regret in category 1. Once again, however, we are keeping these categories separate because of cases we shall present later where life is both subjectively and objectively worth living but the subject of the life regrets being born. It may help to put it this way: all cases of a life subjectively not worth living are cases where the person regrets her existence, but not all cases of regretting one exists need be a case where one's life is subjectively not worth living—one may regret existing even if one is happy (and so subjectively life is worth living) and if life is objectively worth living.[22] We can outline some of the relevant cases as follows:

(i) A life worth living objectively and subjectively (objectively, existing is better than not existing, and the person herself is happy to be alive).
(ii) A life worth living objectively and subjectively but the person nonetheless regrets existing (objectively, existing is better than not existing and the person herself is happy to be alive, but she wishes she hadn't been born for some reason—for example, because of the impact of her conception and birth on her mother and on herself).
(iii) A life worth living objectively but not subjectively (objectively, existing is better than not existing, but the person herself is not happy to be alive). Daniel James is perhaps an example. Regret coincides here with not being happy.
(iv) A life not worth living objectively and subjectively. Regret here again coincides with a life not subjectively worth living.[23]
(v) A life not worth living objectively, but worth living subjectively. Jeff McMahan gives the example of Hitler.[24] This life is not the kind of life that it is good for anyone to have, though the subject of the life himself is happy.

---

[21] This example may be less straightforward. It seems as though there can be reasonable debate about whether one would want to continue to exist if one became a quadriplegic. But there are many who do want to continue to exist, so doubts about that should be put in the subjective category.

[22] We don't think there is a case of someone regretting existing even if they are happy (so having a life subjectively worth living) but who does not have a life objectively worth living.

[23] In some cases, a life is not worth living objectively, while whether it is worth living subjectively doesn't apply (it might, e.g., be a life of permanent unconsciousness). Our solution does not apply to this case, and so we don't discuss this case in detail here.

[24] McMahan (1998). There may also be other ways of drawing this distinction. One is Shelly Kagan's distinction between someone's *personal* wellbeing, and whether their *lives* go well. Applying Kagan's view, we could say that while Hitler's personal wellbeing was high, his life went incredibly badly. See Kagan (1994). Thanks to Jim Goodrich for the pointer.

6.4 How the Notion of Regretting Being Born May Come Apart from the Notion of a Life Not Worth Living

In his discussion of another non-identity case (Depletion), Parfit had claimed that, 'If these people knew the facts, they would not regret that we acted as we did'.[25] And, in discussing *Jane's Choice*, which is relevantly similar to Zelda's case, Parfit says: 'since my life is worth living, I would not regret that my mother caused me to exist. And if I was told that it *was* wrong, because it caused me to exist with a right that cannot be fulfilled, I would *waive* this right'.[26] Our questions are: can a person regret our choice even though she has a life worth living? If so, does this mean that this person is still wronged? Further, can we really be sure that we *know* this person will have no such regrets?

There are two kinds of case. One is where, although having a life that is objectively worth living, the person in question does not have a life that is subjectively worth living. Another kind of case, however, is possible. This is where someone regrets being born even though (a) they are glad to be alive and (b) their lives are worth living, both subjectively and objectively. To the extent that this person regrets being born, it is possible that this person has been wronged by being born by Parfit's own lights, as noted above. This case has not so far been considered in this debate. Here is a real life example of this second kind of case.

In 2012, Lynn Beisner wrote an article in *The Guardian* claiming that she wished her mother had aborted her, even though she was glad to be alive. This article is instructive because Beisner's mother is effectively in the position of the 14-year-old girl, and Beisner herself is the child given a poor start in life. In that article, Beisner claims, 'I love my life but I wished my mother had aborted me.'[27]

Beisner is aware, of course, that this claim is, *prima facie* at least, paradoxical. But this is how she explains her position:

> I make even my most ardent pro-choice friends and colleagues very uncomfortable when I explain why my mother should have aborted me. Somehow they confuse the well-considered and rational: 'The best choice for both my mother and me would have been abortion' with the infamous expression of depression and angst: 'I wish I had never been born.' The two are really very different things, and we must draw that distinction clearly.[28]

Beisner claims that it is perfectly consistent to believe that the best choice for her, and her mother, would have been an abortion, while refraining from claiming that she wished 'she had never been born'. When she makes the claim that she does not wish she had never been born, she takes the latter claim to be an expression of

---

[25] Parfit (1987: 365). [26] Parfit (1987: 375). [27] Beisner (2012).
[28] Beisner (2012).

depression and angst—the kind of depression and angst we might suffer from if we think our lives are not worth living, or if we are totally fed up with life and, to use an older expression, we cursed the day we were born. Understood in that way, she does not wish she had never been born. However, to the extent that she wishes that her mother had had an abortion, she does of course wish she had not been born; she means only that, by having such a wish, she is not expressing any depression or angst about her life not being subjectively worth living. She regrets the act of conception but nonetheless subjectively values her current life.

She explains her claim, beginning with why an abortion would have been better for her mother, as follows:

> An abortion would have absolutely been better for my mother. An abortion would have made it more likely that she would finish high school and get a college education. At college in the late 1960s, it seems likely she would have found feminism or psychology or something that would have helped her overcome her childhood trauma and pick better partners. She would have been better prepared when she had children. If nothing else, getting an abortion would have saved her from plunging into poverty. She likely would have stayed in the same socioeconomic strata as her parents and grandparents who were professors. I wish she had aborted me because I love her and want what is best for her.[29]

So it is consistent for her to wish her mother had aborted her, while admitting that she loves her life, and that it is worth living, because she loves her mother and believes her mother would, quite simply, have had a much better life if she'd had an abortion. This suggests a different solution to the non-identity problem: the interests of others, who would have lived in either outcome. This is one solution that Parfit himself recognizes, but Parfit rightly claims that it does not provide a full solution. But what is different about this version of that point is that it is made *from the standpoint of the daughter*. Beisner can meaningfully wish she had been aborted out of her love for her mother and appreciation of the things her mother missed out on—but this can be an interest of Beisner's own, so that it would be artificial to say that Beisner is here considering the situation from the standpoint of her mother's interests only, and not from her own; she has self-interested reasons to be concerned for her mother's welfare and these reasons, if they are what Parfit calls object-based (rather than desire-based) reasons,[30] are not limited to interests she would have after birth. This means that we should not simplistically separate Beisner's interests and her mother's interests here. We could look at these in *relational* terms. In short, we could broaden the concept of regret here to include the mother's own interests within Beisner's interests, to do justice to the

[29] Beisner (2012). [30] Parfit (2011: vol 2).

fact that Beisner has *self-interested* reasons to care about her mother's interests, so that the concept of regret is less *exclusively* connected to the fact that Beisner is happy with her *own* life, where 'own life' refers to everything *other* than her relationship with her mother and the part played by her mother in her own life.

However, in making this claim, we do not mean to suggest that this is *enough* to answer the non-identity problem; we should still distinguish between different *objects* of her regret, and examine the claim as it applies to the impacts on Beisner's *own* life other than impacts on her life which are *also* impacts on her mother's life. Beisner also believes her mother should have aborted her, because of the impacts on her own life, where these are understood exclusively as affecting only her. She explains why she thinks an abortion would have been better for *her* in the following way:

> Abortion would have been a better option for me. If you believe what reproductive scientists tell us, that I was nothing more than a conglomeration of cells, then there was nothing lost. I could have experienced no consciousness or pain. But even if you discount science and believe I had consciousness and could experience pain at six gestational weeks, I would choose the brief pain or fear of an abortion over the decades of suffering I endured. An abortion would have been best for me because there is no way that my love-starved, trauma-saddled mother could have ever put me up for adoption. It was either abortion or raising me herself, and she was in no position to raise a child. She had suffered a traumatic brain injury, witnessed and experienced severe domestic violence, and while she was in grade school she was raped by a stranger and her mother committed suicide. She was severely depressed and suicidal, had an extremely poor support system, was experiencing an unplanned pregnancy that resulted from coercive sex, and she was so young that her brain was still undeveloped. With that constellation of factors, there was a very high statistical probability that my mother would be an abusive parent, that we would spend the rest of our lives in crushing poverty, and that we would both be highly vulnerable to predatory organisations and men. And that is exactly what happened. She abused me, beating me viciously and often. We lived in bone-crushing poverty, and our little family became a magnet for predatory men and organisations.[31]

It might be thought that Beisner's reference to abuse, and being beaten viciously and often, are contingent in the sense that they are wrongs that can be avoided if those who perpetrate them act differently. Would they really relate to the non-identity problem? The answer is yes.[32] Although these later wrongs could be avoided, if we can foresee at the time we conceive that they are likely to occur (hoping they don't being no more than wishful thinking), and that they are the

---

[31] Beisner (2012).   [32] See Parfit (1986) and below note 45.

types of wrong that might make someone wish they had not been born,[33] we can still ask whether the decision to conceive is good for the child. Since the alternative is her non-existence if we answer in the negative, the case is a non-identity case. It is on bases such as these that Parfit's 14-year-old girl case is a non-identity problem case (the possible neglect of some of the child's needs by the 14-year-old mother is contingent; the child could be immediately adopted out to alternative older parents of greater maturity, etc., but these possibilities do not prevent our viewing this as a non-identity case given that the child will likely still be brought up by the 14-year-old girl).

Since Beisner admits she loves life—she has a life worth living objectively and subjectively (she is happy)—can she consistently regret being brought into existence? Remember, Parfit has said that 'since my life is worth living, I would not regret that my mother caused me to exist'.[34] Beisner's remarks are relevant, and puzzling, to the extent that she both claims to love life, *and* wishes she had been aborted. Beisner's case is a case where life is worth living both objectively and subjectively, but where she nonetheless wishes she had not been born, and so her case raises the question of whether the 'not life worth living' criterion for judging whether a person is 'worse off' for existing is exhaustive of the question whether we can explain the wrong in 14-year-old girl cases (and our Zelda case) in person-affecting terms. If the life not worth living criterion is not exhaustive of person-affecting wrongs in different people choices, then this might be an example of person-affecting wrong that does not meet Parfit's own criterion for person-affecting wrong in such choices, because Beisner regrets existing despite having a life worth living. We believe that Beisner may coherently still regret being born even at the very moment she now acknowledges she has a life worth living. Her remarks can therefore be taken to challenge the view that having a life not worth living is the only rational basis on which one can judge, *in person-affecting terms*,[35] whether a wrong has been done in bringing somebody into existence. In such a case, regretting one was born comes apart from the notion of a life worth living (either objectively or subjectively understood).[36]

---

[33] Later we discuss whether this would apply to all of us, committing us to the well-known but implausible view that it is better for all of us not to have been born.

[34] Parfit (1987: 361).

[35] As Parfit himself notes, on some views, even if one has a life not worth living, one is not harmed because there is no alternative state under which I could exist and be better off. In Appendix G to *Reasons and Persons*, Parfit claims that this 'two-state' requirement (discussed in relation to benefits but applicable, *mutatis mutandis*, to harms) can be relaxed in the cases we are concerned with. But for those who continue to have doubts about the applicability of 'harm', Parfit suggests, following Jeff McMahan, that we can ask whether existence is *good* or *bad* for the person (489)—McMahan's notion of *existential* harm, which is non-comparative. Either way, we can talk of effects on the person that are person-affecting wrongs where life is not worth living. We also suggest in section 6.5 that, even if we do not understand this wrong in person-affecting terms, it is not reducible to an impersonal wrong.

[36] These remarks have implications for the criticisms levelled at the claim that conceiving in Beisner's mother's circumstances is a violation of the child's *rights*. The so-called rights solution to the non-identity problem has widely been taken to have foundered on the basis that, since the person

It might be objected that, if we allow that Beisner's claims are coherent and rational here, they would apply too broadly, for we could make this claim of *everyone's* life. There are, it might be claimed, at least *some* occasions on which we think our lives are not worth living or regret being born. We might, for example, feel this way when grieving over a lost loved one. It is certainly foreseeable, the objection might continue, that we will lose loved ones during our lives. But is this a reason for any of us not to be conceived? Surely this would be absurd. However, while there is some plausibility to this objection, we need not accept it. The kind of suffering that Beisner speaks of is *life-defining* suffering, in the sense that it defined both her childhood, and who she became as an adult. Further, those experiences continue to have effects on her through her adult life. This is a degree of suffering, at least as she describes it, that goes beyond the suffering we all experience in losing a lost loved one. It is otherwise if the loss of a loved one occurs in unusual or mysterious circumstances, such as where the loved one is murdered or has disappeared without trace. These cases might define the lives of those who are left behind; they may never be able to rest in peace or move on from what has happened until the mystery about their loved one is resolved. But these are cases that are *not* foreseeable at the time the people who will eventually endure this suffering are conceived.[37] We therefore believe that Beisner's claim could not be made by many of us.

Our claims also apply to the cases discussed earlier of severe depression, where, during the bouts, the person wants desperately to end their lives. These cases, too, do not apply to most of us. They are also clearly foreseeable effects (we have said that Zelda, for example, knows that her child is likely to develop the depressive disorder). Their foreseeability makes it meaningful to judge this different person choice to be wrong.

There are also other cases. These include people who regret being conceived after being donated as a leftover donor embryo such as Gracie Crane,[38] and people conceived from donor gametes. Some of these people have claimed they wish they had not been born[39] or 'hate my conception'[40] and have set up foundations

---

conceived has a life worth living and will not regret her mother's choice, she would waive any right not to be born in the circumstances causing the rights violation. Beisner's position, by contrast, shows that being glad to be alive is not consent or a waiver of any rights violation. Space prevents us from pursuing this possibility any further in this chapter. For defences of the rights view, see Woodward (1986), Smolkin (1999: 195–6); for criticisms, see Parfit (1986), McMahan (1998), Boonin (2014). Our claims here may respond to Parfit's criticisms.

[37] We admit the line we are drawing here is not precise. What if it is a *child* who loses a lost loved one, say, a parent? But we believe the distinctions we are drawing here are reasonable. We discuss the point again later in the chapter.

[38] Helen Carroll, 'Donor IVF baby who says "I wish I'd never been born"', *Daily Mail*, 26 June (2014). Carroll discusses the case of Gracie Crane.

[39] Carroll 2014.

[40] As told to the 'Them Before Us' blog site on 3 January 2018, <https://thembeforeus.com/author/thembeforeus/>; see also 'Testimony of Alana S Newman...to the California Assembly Committee on Health', 30 April 2013 <http://ccgaction.org/uploaded_files/Testimony%20of%20Alana%20S.%20Newman.pdf>.

opposing donor conception.⁴¹ They have claimed, perhaps not unreasonably, that they feel abandoned by their genetic parents, discarded as a leftover embryo or sold away to make some other would-be parent happy, and that this has had a profound effect on their sense of identity, which feels 'ripped away'.⁴²

Some of these stories might be described as cases where the subject's life was not a life *subjectively* worth living. However, this description seems less apposite to Beisner given her claim that she does 'love my life'. It is better to see each of these cases as regretting the decision to conceive, and therefore precisely in the terms that Beisner describes, as being a simple wish not to have been born, but one that does not express 'depression or angst'.⁴³

Although these people have lives worth living, they regret being born and, as Parfit admits, this fact provides some objection to these different people choices. We turn next to possible objections to this claim.

6.4.1 Two Possible Objections

Objection 1:   Beisner has effectively excused any wrong by admitting she is glad to be alive.

Parfit might reply that, if the notion of regret comes apart from the notion of a life subjectively not worth living, then Beisner cannot claim to have been wronged even though she wishes she hadn't been born; provided she is glad to be alive, the threshold condition for person-affecting harm in different people choices is not met. But this doesn't seem to us to be right, for it discounts the fact that she really does regret having been born. On what basis can we really ignore this regret if it is genuine?

Consider Parfit's comments about a 'different people choice' that causes a person to exist with rights that cannot be fulfilled.⁴⁴ Parfit says that this person would waive these rights. By analogy, he might argue that Beisner has excused any wrong by admitting she is glad to be alive, even though she says she wishes she hadn't been born.⁴⁵ But Beisner does not appear to us to be excusing this wrong,

---

⁴¹ 'Testimony of Alana S Newman…to the California Assembly Committee on Health', 30 April 2013 <http://ccgaction.org/uploaded_files/Testimony%20of%20Alana%20S.%20Newman.pdf>.
⁴² 'Them Before Us' blog.
⁴³ The case of Gracie Crane, who developed from a donated embryo left over from her genetic parents' IVF procedures, might be explained merely as teenage angst, as she makes her claim at only the age of 16. But some of the other donor cases cannot so easily be dismissed, as the regret is expressed when they are adults. Also, the case of Zelda's child, though dealing with a depressive disorder, is arguably distinct from the depression or angst that Beisner refers to in contrast with her own wish she had not been born, though it is of course impossible to know what she might have had in mind.
⁴⁴ Parfit (1987: 375).
⁴⁵ We say 'by analogy' because it is not clear that, in Beisner's case, there are any rights she has that are incapable of being fulfilled; as Parfit concedes in discussion with James Woodward (Parfit 1986: 860 n), the

even though she is glad to be alive. If you wish you weren't born—and consider your being conceived to have been wrong—that seems to mean that it is a wrong that is not now compensated for by your being glad to be alive. Only if Beisner were saying that she can see that it was wrong, but she's *glad the wrong was perpetrated* would we say that she excuses the wrong. But this is not what she is claiming. Instead, she is claiming that she wished the wrong was *not* perpetrated in spite of the fact that she is now glad to be alive. She points out, for example, that, had she been aborted, she would not have lost out because she was just a collection of cells. She would therefore have been spared the harm that she later suffered, and would have been spared this harm at a time when she could not have known what she would miss out on. We therefore think that this is a real case that escapes the non-identity problem.

> *Objection 2*: Beisner cannot rationally regret being born if she has a life worth living.

It might instead be objected that, even if the regret is genuine and any perceived wrong is not excused, or any rights violation is not waived, Beisner nevertheless has not been wronged because she has a life worth living (subjectively and objectively, or either). Beisner therefore cannot rationally wish that the wrong was not perpetrated, and so cannot rationally refuse to excuse any wrong, or waive any rights violation.

It is not clear exactly why the fact that she has a life worth living should mean that it is irrational for Beisner to regret the wrong was perpetrated. The objection would have to be that it is irrational for Beisner to believe any wrong was perpetrated at all. It is hard to believe, however, that Beisner—who was herself abused by her mother and by the men in her mother's life, who was often viciously beaten, and who is clearly driven by this suffering to wish she had not been born— is being irrational. It is not clear why having a life worth living would preclude Beisner from claiming the decision to be wrong. To see this more clearly, consider first a different case, taken from a UK legal judgement, the case of *CICA Insurance v Y*.[46] This is a case where a father repeatedly raped a daughter, who eventually gave birth to a child (the father's son and grandson), who inherited Huntington's disease. Leave aside, for the moment, the Huntington's disease. Being conceived of a rape goes to the very heart of one's sense of identity and can taint one's existence, one's life, one's sense of self-worth. This is all the more so of someone born of an incestuous rape. Add to this the foreseeable 50 per cent chance of passing on

---

wrongs done to her by her mother and the men in her mother's life are all avoidable harms, and so may be person-affecting in the straightforward sense; Beisner could have existed without these harms being perpetrated.

[46] [2017] EWCA Civ 139.

Huntington's disease, and let us ask: can anyone seriously claim that, if this child regrets being born,[47] both because of the impacts on himself and on his mother,[48] this is an irrational claim, or one that we should avoid endorsing? In asking this question, we do not claim that Y's life is worth *ending*. Our claim is only that Y should clearly not have been conceived. Returning to Beisner, her judgement of her own mother will not, of course, be as harsh as our judgement of Y's 'father'. But it is reasonable for Beisner to argue that, even though she is glad to be alive, this is not relevant to our assessment of the mother's choice. At one point in his discussion, Parfit distinguishes between cases where people making relevant choices know about the non-identity problem, and cases where they do not.[49] He claims that 'we can deserve blame for doing what we *believe* may be greatly against the interests of other people' and that 'this criticism stands even if our belief is false'.[50] Where the mother does not know about the problem, we ought to continue to assess the mother's choice on the basis that the choice to conceive is a same people choice. She cannot deserve any credit for thinking about how existence might compensate for the wrong of conceiving or proceeding to give birth, if this is not an issue she has turned her mind to. It would be *subjectively* wrong for her to make this choice, and it is against this notion of wrong that we should judge her choice—relative to what she knows. This, so far as we know, is the applicable claim about Beisner's mother. We can assume that she did not know about the non-identity problem. It seems that we can rationally condemn this mother's choice.

Let us now assume, however, a case where the mother knows about the non-identity problem. To remove doubts about how harshly we can judge a 14-year-old girl, let us return to Zelda's case, who knows that, if she conceives now, she is likely to conceive a child with a severe depressive disorder who will suffer from many bouts of depression during which her child will want to take her own life. We can imagine that Zelda is faced with the decision about whether to conceive now at the age of 28. Her options are to conceive now, while she has the illness that will likely cause the depressive disorder in her child, or she can wait for two months, after the illness is cleared up, and after which she will conceive a child who will not be affected by any illness. Assume now she knows about the non-identity problem and thinks to herself:

---

[47] Could we distinguish between the manner of conception, and the fact that I am alive, so that I could regret the former but not the latter? Only, e.g., if it would have been possible for me, the very same person, to have been conceived without being the product of an incestuous rape. This is not, however, true of the cases we are discussing.

[48] The treatment of the mother itself being, as we pointed out earlier, also an interest of his own.

[49] Parfit (1987: 372–3). Empirical surveys have now been undertaken to gauge the extent to which the general public is aware of the non-identity problem and the difference the general public believes the problem makes to judging the morality of same people choices and different people choices. See Doolabh et al. (2019). See also Doolabh et al. (2017).

[50] Parfit (1987: 372).

My child will have no rational grounds for complaint. Provided she has a life worth living, then, even if she thinks I act wrongly, she would be wrong to think this. The non-identity problem shows that, since she has a life worth living, I will not have harmed her. I may well have benefited her by conceiving now. Even if she rejects the view that existence is a benefit, I can at least say that she is not worse off for existing.

It is not clear to us that Zelda's reply to her child is a complete reply. Zelda's child could respond by claiming that there is something perverse about exploiting[51] a metaphysical point on the possible necessity of our origins in this way[52]—that it adds insult to 'injury' for Zelda to make these claims. Although we won't rest our argument on this point, it is at least arguably reasonable to claim that Zelda has shown no regard for one of the things most parents would surely consider in deciding whether to proceed: how will my child view this when she is an adult (even *if* she *does* have a life worth living)?

Returning once again to Beisner, she says that abortion would have been better for her. She claims that since she was just a conglomeration of cells, then nothing would have been lost; she would have experienced no consciousness or pain. She adds that, even if this were not so, she would 'choose the brief pain or fear of an abortion over the decades of suffering I endured' (Beisner 2012). It seems to us to be reasonable for Beisner to imagine looking ahead at some of that suffering—in particular, the abuse she was to suffer at the hands of the men in her mother's life—and wish she did not have to undergo it, even if the only way that could be achieved is not to be born. As she herself points out, she can wish she had not been born, without that entailing that she now wishes to die. Her stance is rational because it concerns harms that no reasonable person would wish to endure. She can rationally exercise her autonomy in such a way as to hold this view, even if the benefits outweigh the harms. It is true, of course, that she can only exercise this rationality later, and is not in a position to consent or refuse consent at the time

---

[51] For an interesting paper that explores the point implicit in this remark, see Liberto (2014).

[52] This possible response is supported by the empirical research in Doolabh et al. (2019), which suggests that the general public tend not to attribute any real moral significance to the non-identity problem. Of course we must be careful not to derive an ought from an is here, but Doolabh et al. note that these surveys can have significance where there is considerable philosophical disagreement about the moral relevance of an issue, but the disagreement is not shared by the general public. As Doolabh et al. note, the philosophical literature on the non-identity problem does indeed exhibit considerable philosophical disagreement about its moral relevance, a disagreement that is not replicated in the survey of the general public undertaken by Doolabh et al. The argument is that, in cases where policy-makers look for guidance but only find disagreement, the absence of disagreement in the results of public surveys may mean that we can legitimately treat those surveys as a tie-breaker. Here, that would mean not attributing any moral significance to the fact that the choice is a different people choice. This would in turn mean that the child's response to Zelda would be a reasonable response.

her mother makes her choice to conceive. But, as Parfit notes, '[w]hen we cannot ask for someone's consent, we should ask instead whether this person would later regret what we are doing'.[53] Since Beisner *does* later regret her mother's choice, we ought to respect her later reaction even if we disagree with it. Note also the distinction between whether we can *reasonably* disagree with Beisner's view, and whether her view is *irrational*. We can disagree with it, without dismissing it as irrational. We discuss this distinction again in the following sub-section.

There is a parallel here with our duties to respect the autonomous decisions of those who refuse life-saving medical treatment even when we think that these people are wrong on the basis that it's clearly in their interests to have this life-saving treatment. In these cases, because we can ask for their consent, we have a duty to respect their decision if they do not consent. We cannot do this in the case of decisions to conceive people. But when Parfit says that where we cannot ask for consent, we should ask instead whether this person would later regret what we are doing, we might appeal to the reasonable foreseeability of later regret. If that regret is foreseeable as a genuine possibility (thus distinguishing her case from that of everyone—see above) and is in fact expressed, we can claim that the mother's decision is wrong.[54]

A similar case is the famous Texas burn victim Dax Cowart. Dax experienced terrible burns, refused treatment, and attempted suicide several times during his treatment. However, he was treated against his will. He later recovered and became an attorney. Despite going on to live a life which was happy and worth living, he maintained that he should have been allowed to die.[55]

---

[53] Parfit (1987: 373).

[54] There remain important differences between the autonomous refusals of treatment cases, and our Beisner type cases. While in the law a competent person's refusal of treatment must be respected regardless of how irrational it is (and the foreseeability of the refusal would be irrelevant), the proviso we added in Beisner's case that the regret must be genuine and foreseeable as a possible reaction means that we must be able to understand why she might have the reaction that Beisner in fact has, so that it is sufficiently foreseeable. If the regret is so irrational as to make the regret unforeseeable, then we could not condemn the mother's decision on this ground. But someone born into 'bone-crushing poverty', and who is 'abused, viciously beaten, and often' does not fall within this latter category. A further difference is that, in emergency situations where a person is unconscious and so cannot consent to treatment we can be justified in treating that person even when we do not know what they would have wanted or whether they would consent (they are unconscious and there is no evidence of their wishes), since the danger of being wrong if we *don't* treat them seems weightier than the risk of treating them when this is not what they would have wanted. Where a patient subsequently regrets the doctor's choice, we may justifiably say that the doctor's choice is not wrong or, if it is, it is excused. (Note, though, that if there is evidence that the patient would not want to be treated, this prevails even if we think treatment is in the patient's best interests.) There is no equivalent danger, in the Beisner case, of being wrong in the sense that there is no existing entity whose interests we set back if we decide not to proceed with conception. Since this consideration does not apply in the Beisner case, we can legitimately claim that, should someone like Beisner come to regret the mother's choice, the mother has indeed acted wrongly. Further discussion of this analogy with treatment decisions is provided in section 6.5.

[55] <https://en.wikipedia.org/wiki/Dax_Cowart>.

6.4.2 How Many People Born in Beisner's Circumstances Are Likely to Share Her Reaction?

Will everyone conceived in Beisner's circumstances have Beisner's reaction? Clearly not everyone does. But we believe that someone in Beisner's circumstances, or those of Crane[56] or Y, may, when they turn their minds to the circumstances in which they are conceived, regret being born even though they may now be happy to be alive. They can regard the circumstances of their conception as something that taints their lives. Most of us will regret the Holocaust took place and the Second World War. Many of us will only exist because of that war. But when we turn our minds to it and reflect more about it, most of us would still condemn the attitudes and events that led to this war.[57] We are therefore claiming that the conditions for our existence were wrong, even though we are glad to be alive. Clearly it would be better if such events had not occurred. It is true that we would not consider *ourselves* to have been wronged by the events that led to the war. But this point does not apply to the Beisner cases, where Beisner condemns the effects of the action on her, and not just on her mother. If Beisner can, and does, rationally regret being born, she can claim that, while her life should not *now* be ended (just like Dax Cowart's life should not have been ended after he recovered), it should not have been started, and should have been ended while she was in the womb. She lives with the effects of having a life that should not have been started and was continued when it should have been ended; she sees her life as tainted by the circumstances of her conception and birth.

In addition to the Beisner category, there are also those who really do claim that their lives are not subjectively worth living (understood from an all-things-considered perspective), even though they are objectively worth living. Zelda's child might have depressive bouts that make even the anticipation of those bouts intolerable to her. This might mean that she has a life not subjectively worth living rather than merely regretting being born. Or, consider again a child of a rape victim who is conceived as a result of that rape. This person may not be glad to be alive at all, unlike Beisner. Their lives are objectively worth living, but they find their lives—living with the circumstances in which they were conceived—intolerable. These people have lives that are not subjectively worth living, and are therefore wronged in person-affecting terms. This is a case where the notion of regret does not come apart from a life not subjectively worth living, and so even

---

[56] See notes 38 and 43.

[57] Compare Levy (2002). Our analysis differs from Levy's in an important respect. Levy claims that condemning wrongs from the past is like condemning someone for having paid money to enter a lottery, even though they win the lottery. The chances of winning the lottery are so small, that paying for a ticket is a bad decision, and this remains so even if they win because the judgement about the badness of the decision is made before the result. However, Parfit can reply that Levy's lottery analogy does not work in the case of the non-identity problem, on the basis that we know in advance that a person is likely to have a life worth living, and so will have no regrets.

if the previous arguments about the Beisner case are wrong, that will not affect this case.

An objection to this latter point, however, is that it seems to imply that, provided she *believes* she has a bad life, then even if she has a good life, the belief that she has a bad life means that she *does* have a bad life—an implication that is clearly implausible. However, we have not made this claim. As noted above, Beisner has herself claimed that her life is good, not bad. This is what makes her case so interesting. She admits her life is good, but still wishes she had not been born. However, in the previous paragraph we were discussing those cases where a person *does* claim that their life is bad, at least subjectively. Is our claim about this case subject to the objection just raised? No it is not. We are dealing here with cases where it is at least reasonable or understandable that someone should take this view of their own lives, and so where there is some room for debate, and for reasonable disagreement. If this person happens to be one of those who reacts by subjectively disvaluing her life, believing it is not worth living, then she suffers to the extent that she holds this view, and that *is* a bad thing. We can make this judgement even if we believe that her life is good, and that she has a distorted perspective on her own life. In the case we are considering, the people in question are judging their lives not to be *subjectively* worth living. This judgement is one of the effects of the conception decision on their lives. That her life is worth living *objectively*, however, is not always a decisive reason for rejecting this *subjective* judgement. Consider again the example of Daniel James (the rugby player), and the recent case of the 104-year-old scientist, David Goodall, who ended his life in Switzerland in 2018 after claiming that his life was no longer worth living. As noted earlier, Daniel was a quadriplegic who ended his life at the Dignitas clinic in Switzerland in 2008. Because he had been a very active athlete before the accident, we can understand James's decision, even though many of us would probably claim that, objectively speaking, the life of a quadriplegic might still be a life worth living. Similarly with David Goodall, we can respect his abiding view that, at 104 years of age, 'my abilities have been declining over the past year or two and my eyesight over the past six years and I no longer want to continue to live'.[58] We might take the view that these lives are objectively worth living, but most of us can understand why these people wanted to end their lives. It would be a very harsh judgement of them indeed to think that, regardless of their suffering, they were making an *irrational* decision. We might reasonably *disagree* with their decision. But they, equally, can reasonably disagree with our judgement. Since there can be reasonable disagreement, these judgements should fall on the subjective side of the subjectively worth living versus objectively worth living distinction (those who

---

[58] *ABC News*, '104-year-old academic David Goodall says in his final hours he has "no hesitations whatsoever"' <http://www.abc.net.au/news/2018-05-09/dr-david-goodall-has-no-hesitations-about-dying-in-switzerland/9744610>.

disagree with these two examples need only substitute an example of their own, over which they would concede it to be reasonable for people to have different views). There is a distinction between cases that are clearly objectively not worth living (say, a wretched life full of unimaginable suffering from birth about which no one would reasonably claim it is a life worth living) and cases like that of Daniel James or David Goodall, about which reasonable people might take different views. Daniel's judgement about his own life is subjective in the sense that not everyone would agree that such a life is not worth living, but it is reasonable in the sense that people can rationally take different views. These cases, over which there can be different judgements and different reactions, are precisely the kinds of cases in which the person's own judgement of her life ought to prevail. Someone who can therefore reasonably take the view of their lives similar to that of Daniel James can therefore claim to have been harmed on a subjectively not worth living criterion.

6.5 Subjective Valuation as Expression of Autonomy

We have made several analogies to people who, though they have lives worth living, wish to end their lives. We have claimed that, while we might disagree with their decisions, we cannot always dismiss these decisions as irrational. We understand why some people may wish to end their lives. David Goodall said that he did not value his life any longer because he could no longer do the things he used to be able to do. There are many cases of this kind which have been debated in the end of life context. On one view, these people should be allowed to exercise their autonomous choice to die provided they are competent, they are informed of the relevant facts and thinking clearly about them, and their decision is not coerced. In Appendix G of *Reasons and Persons*, Parfit claimed that if someone can look at the rest of their lives ahead of them and prefer not to undergo it, they can look at their whole lives and prefer not to live that life (Parfit 1987: 487, 2017: 134). Adapting and applying this remark, we can claim that the expression of autonomous values at the end of life need not be restricted to the end of life. The expression of such values can apply also to *whole lives*. Such a person can take such a view retrospectively. As noted earlier, Parfit claims: 'Where we cannot ask for someone's consent, we should ask instead whether this person would later regret what we are doing' (1987: 373). When Parfit made these remarks about preferring not to have lived and about whether a person would later regret our choice (to conceive), he had in mind a life not worth living. He claimed that someone might decide that, had he known what lay ahead of him, 'these parts of his life were better or worse than nothing' (487) (a claim that can also apply to the whole of his life). But, as we have noted, there is the extra category of the case that we have discussed in this chapter, of someone who regrets their existence even if they admit that their lives *are* better than nothing. We believe that Parfit's remarks can also apply to this case. They could therefore apply to Beisner.

One way of explaining why Parfit may not have considered the cases we consider in this chapter is that he may have believed that autonomy forms part of wellbeing. However, we believe that autonomy is logically separate from wellbeing.[59] To illustrate this distinction, consider the decision about whether to have children. We can consider this decision from the point of view of the mother's wellbeing, and try to make the difficult calculation of whether having children will be worse or better for her life. It might be better for her not to choose to have children because she will have a much better career and be happier as a result. However, although these considerations are important, we do not usually take them to be decisive. We consider instead that it is rational for her to have children, provided that the mother is acquainted, so far as is reasonably practicable, with all the relevant facts when she decides. We recognize that, regardless of what other people may think, she is entitled to make her own autonomous decision to conceive in such a context. In this sense, autonomy is logically independent of considerations of wellbeing. R. M. Adams (1979) has argued, more generally, that we can rationally prefer our own actual lives if our lives are good, even though we might have lived a life that is even better, with different projects, friendships, and attachments to those we actually have.

We recognize this independence, too, in other contexts. In the law, for example, a person is entitled to make a decision that is against their best interests, such as refuse life-saving treatment that will not only save their lives but even cure them of the ailment from which they are dying. In privileging autonomy over wellbeing, the law states that one has the right to make a decision that is ill-advised, wrong, and even irrational. As Lord Donaldson expresses it:

> the patient's right of choice exists whether the reasons for making that choice are rational, irrational, unknown or even non-existent. That his choice is contrary to what is to be expected of the vast majority of adults is only relevant if there are other reasons for doubting his *capacity* to decide.[60]

Since it is possible to make decisions that go against one's wellbeing, autonomy should be seen as logically independent of the latter. This explains how it can be that, even if someone has a life worth living, we can do wrong by violating their autonomy. We can do this in several ways. In the case of a competent person refusing to consent to treatment in their best interests, we can wrong them by treating them against their will, committing a battery. In the case of someone like Beisner, we can wrong them both by bringing them into existence, and by refusing

---

[59] For detailed argument that this is so, see Persson (2017: chapter 1).
[60] *Re T (adult: refusal of medical treatment)* [1992] 4 All ER 649, at 653, 662.

to recognize the legitimacy of their regret at being brought into the world. Remember, as Parfit himself has claimed, if someone can wish they did not have to live *part* of their lives (e.g., at the end of their lives), such views 'can apply, I believe, to whole lives' (Parfit 1987, 487). In a note, he adds that such a person can 'wish . . . he had never been born' (531, n 17). We can claim that people such as Beisner, and others like Crane or those who object to their donor conception, have been wronged because it is wrong to bring people into the world who foreseeably wish never to have been born[61] just as, on Parfit's own view, we can wrong people by bringing them into the world with lives that are foreseeably not worth living. We also ought to avoid the reasonably foreseeable possibility[62] that they will exercise their autonomy by regretting they were born, or by subjectively disvaluing their lives. It is a further wrong to them to dismiss their own subjective valuation on the basis that they have lives worth living, thereby privileging wellbeing over autonomy. If it is objected that we cannot wrong these people if they would not have existed at all had we acted differently, we can adopt Parfit's reply to this very objection in his discussion of whether we can benefit people by creating them: we know, of any existing person who prefers not to have been born, *who it is* who holds this preference. We know that this person has been wronged because there is this person, now existing, who would prefer not to have existed (Parfit 1987: 488).

Of course, we cannot control how a person will feel about their own life and some degree of idiosyncratic regret or gratitude is possible, but, as we have argued in section 6.4, the cases we are considering in this chapter are different in kind from these, and are reasonably foreseeable possibilities. We are not claiming that we wrong those who irrationally wish they had not been born. So in this sense, there is no equivalent wrong, in the conception cases, to treating someone who competently refuses medical treatment against their wishes on wholly irrational, and hence unpredictable, grounds.[63] While we can lament the fact that someone irrationally regrets that they were born, we claim only that a mother or father who can *reasonably foresee* the possibility—a degree of foresight greater than that which would apply to *anyone*—that a Beisner might regret existing wrongs that person if the person does indeed regret existing. It is reasonably foreseeable that someone in Beisner's circumstances, or someone who is the product of a rape, can come to regret existing. Where we have a choice to conceive in these

---

[61] We accept that the donor conception case is more controversial than the rape or incest cases. Those not happy with the donor conception cases can ignore them.

[62] As discussed above, the possibility that they regret existing has to be reasonably foreseeable, so that we can meaningfully distinguish this category of people from the rest of us (for whom such a reaction is not reasonably foreseeable). It would be subjectively wrong to take the risk of this reasonably foreseeable possibility eventuating. See text below.

[63] As indicated earlier, if we accept there are degrees of irrationality, then *some* cases of irrationality might be foreseeable, but we do not base our arguments on this qualification.

circumstances, it may be better not to conceive in them; it is subjectively wrong to take the *risk* of this regret.[64]

It might be objected that we can only truly respect Beisner's autonomy by creating Beisner. To respect autonomy, we must respect her capacity to decide for herself whether she regrets being born or not. We cannot do this unless we create her; if we decide *not* to create her, we are deciding *for* her, and not letting her decide for herself. So creating her cannot itself be a violation of her autonomy. This objection would have force if only objective rightness applied. Although Beisner's actual reaction is foreseeable, it is possible, as we have noted, that she may have reacted differently. She may not have regretted being born. Her mother's decision would not then have been objectively wrong. But, given our argument that Beisner's reaction is clearly foreseeable, we have claimed that it is subjectively wrong for her mother (or father) to have taken the risk of that reaction. And, given her actual reaction, the decision turns out to have been objectively wrong. If we did not even acknowledge that this decision could be subjectively wrong, we could make no room for Beisner's actual reaction. And we would fail to respect her autonomous view that she regrets existing, overriding her view by refusing to regard her foreseeable reaction as a reason not to proceed. Since a failure to conceive does not violate anyone's autonomy (there being no one whose autonomy can be violated), but conception *can* violate a person's autonomy, we conclude that this objection fails.

Another objection to these claims is that what we are calling autonomy is just a different name for what a subject *thinks* is in her best interests, as opposed to what is *objectively* in her best interests. On some views, then, what we are referring to as autonomy is merely another name for *competing views* about wellbeing and best interests. We need not deny this. The very concept of autonomy is meant to record the idea that people are entitled to come to their own conclusions about what is in their own best interests, or about what best promotes their own welfare, or what they have most reason to do. However, provided that the distinction between what is *objectively* the case about their own welfare and best interests and what is *subjectively* the case about these is intact—even in cases where there is no right answer as to the former—we can limit the concept of wellbeing to its objective plane, and speak of the subject's own evaluation of these as part of her autonomy.

One consequence of the distinction we are drawing here between autonomy and wellbeing is that, on a narrow interpretation of 'person-affecting' which refers only to harming or setting back one's interests—making them worse off than they otherwise would have been—our solution may be *neither* person-affecting *nor*

---

[64] What about people conceived from donor embryos? Is it reasonably foreseeable that they could come to regret existing? Some cases—such as people born of an incestuous rape—may seem more obvious than others. But it would be useful to gather empirical evidence about how common such regret is in the population for these categories.

impersonal. Suppose that we do restrict person-affecting wrong in this way, to decreases in wellbeing which thereby make a person worse off than they otherwise would have been. We may then say that someone who autonomously wishes they had never been born, in spite of having levels of wellbeing well above the threshold of a life worth living, has been wronged, even if they have not been harmed, that is, made worse off than they otherwise would have been. The wrong we would be describing here would not be a person-affecting form of wrong.[65] But neither would it be an impersonal wrong, bringing about a worse state of affairs than another state of affairs that could have been brought about where the same number of people will live. This is because it would still be wrong in different number cases, which the impersonal account of wrongdoing has famously been unable to accommodate.[66] Rather it is an 'autonomy-infringing wrong'. Even if a decision to conceive Beisner, or to implant an anonymously donated embryo that will thus be genetically unrelated to the social parents, is a different number choice rather than a same number choice, it can be wrong on our account, on the basis that it is reasonably foreseeable that these people will autonomously disvalue their own lives. On a narrow construal of 'person-affecting wrong', then, we think it necessary to add a third category to impersonal versus person-affecting wrongs, the wrong of bringing into existence someone who will autonomously disvalue their existence: an autonomy-infringing wrong. On the other hand, if being wronged is person-affecting in the wider sense of wronging someone even if their wellbeing (or interests) has not been affected for the worse, then this form of wrong can remain a form of person-affecting wrongdoing in that broader sense. We have been using this broader sense of 'person-affecting' throughout this chapter. This is 'person-affecting' in the broader sense that, while not referring to wellbeing, it is an autonomously expressed regret that can be 'bad' for people in McMahan's (2013) and Parfit's (2017) existential sense, while yet not requiring that their lives not be worth living.

6.6 Conclusion

We have attempted here to draw attention to a category of case that has not been considered in the debate about the non-identity problem, and to draw distinctions that Parfit did not draw—between a notion of regret that comes apart from the

---

[65] As we will see shortly, however, it would be person-affecting in the broader sense that it would be a wrong to the person; it just wouldn't be a *harm* in the sense of setting back interests or making someone worse off than they otherwise would have been. It could be person-affecting in the sense that rights violations are still person-affecting even though they don't always make a person worse off (Woodward 1986).

[66] Parfit famously said we need 'Theory X' to accommodate them, but Parfit never found Theory X. He later (Parfit 2017) endorsed what he called the 'wide dual person-affecting principle' which he claimed could avoid the Repugnant Conclusion, removing the need for Theory X.

notion of a life not worth living, and also a more nuanced distinction between different senses of a life not worth living, the subjective and objective senses which Parfit does not delineate in his famous work on this problem. These categories of case seem to represent examples which escape the non-identity problem even though they are 'different people choices'. The pool of people who can be wronged by these choices is larger than Parfit may have realized. However, our solution is only a modest or partial[67] solution to the problem. It does not purport to account for the cases where there is no regret, either because the person conceived is born with a condition but does not regret existing (such as an incurably blind person), or has a sufficient degree of cognitive impairment to make her incapable either of regretting existing or of being glad to be alive. We would need a different solution for these cases, but it is not within the scope of the present chapter to address these other cases. We think it is of sufficient interest to introduce the extra category of cases that we have considered in this chapter: autonomy-infringing wrongs. It may be possible, however, to extend the considerations we have raised in this chapter to conditions that do impact on autonomy, which we have distinguished from wellbeing. This suggestion will be taken up elsewhere.

References

Adams, R. M. (1972) 'Must God create the best?', *The Philosophical Review*, LXXXI: 317–32.

Adams, R. M. (1979) 'Existence, self-interest, and the problem of evil', *Nous*, 13: 53–65.

Archard, D. (2004) 'Wrongful life', *Philosophy*, 79: 403–20.

Beisner, L. (2012) 'I wish my mother had aborted me', *The Guardian*, <https://www.theguardian.com/commentisfree/2012/aug/15/i-wish-my-mother-aborted-me> accessed 21 July 2020.

Bontly, T. D. (2016) 'Causes, contrasts, and the non-identity problem', *Philosophical Studies*, 173: 1233–51.

Boonin, D. (2014) *The Non-Identity Problem and The Ethics of Future People*. Oxford: Oxford University Press.

Brock, D. W. (1995) 'The non-identity problem and genetic harms—the case of wrongful handicaps', *Bioethics*, 9: 269–75.

Doolabh, K., Caviola, L., Savulescu, J., Selgelid, M., and Wilkinson, D. (2017) 'Zika, contraception and the non-identity problem', *Developing World Bioethics*, 17: 173–204.

---

[67] Boonin (2014) claims that a solution to the non-identity problem must be sufficiently robust in the sense that it accounts for all cases in which the problem can be raised. But this requirement may be too stringent in that it may lead us to ignore cases where the non-identity problem *can* be solved.

Doolabh, K., Caviola, L., Savulescu, J., Selgelid, M., and Wilkinson, D. (2019) 'Is the non-identity problem relevant to public health and policy? An online survey', *BMC Medical Ethics*, 20: 46.

Hanser, M. (2008) 'The metaphysics of harm', *Philosophy and Phenomenological Research*, 77/2: 421–50.

Hanser, M. (2011) 'Still more on the metaphysics of harm', *Philosophy and Phenomenological Research*, 82: 459–69.

Harman, E. (2004) 'Can we harm and benefit in creating?', *Philosophical Perspectives*, 18: 89–113.

Harman, E. (2009) 'Harming as causing harm', in M. Robert and D. Wasserman (eds), *Harming Future Persons: Ethics, Genetics and the Non-Identity Problem*, 137–54. New York: Springer.

Hope, T. (2015) 'Response to: "Questioning the significance of the non-identity problem in applied ethics" by Lawlor', *Journal of Medical Ethics*, 41/11: 897–98.

Hope, T. and McMillan, J. (2012) 'Physicians' duties and the non-identity problem', *American Journal of Bioethics*, 12/8: 21–9.

Hurley, P. and Weinberg, R. (2015) 'Whose problem is non-identity', *Journal of Moral Philosophy*, 12: 699–730.

Kagan, S. (1994) 'Me and my life', *Proceedings of the Aristotelian Society*, 94: 309–24.

Kavka, G. (1982) 'The paradox of future individuals', *Philosophy and Public Affairs*, 11/2: 93–112.

Kumar, R. (2005) 'Who can be wronged?', *Philosophy and Public Affairs*, 31/2: 99–118.

Lawlor, R. (2015) 'Questioning the Significance of the non-identity problem', *Journal of Medical Ethics*, 41/11: 893–6.

Levy, N. (2002) 'The apology paradox and the non-identity problem', *Philosophical Quarterly*, 52: 358–68.

Liberto, H. (2014) 'The exploitation solution to the non-identity problem', *Philosophical Studies*, 167: 73–88.

McMahan, J. (1998) 'Wrongful life: Paradoxes in the morality of causing people to exist', in J. Coleman and C. Morris (eds), *Rational Commitment and Social Justice: Essays for Gregory Kavka*, 208–47. Cambridge: Cambridge University Press.

McMahan, J. (2013) 'Causing people to exist and saving people's lives', *The Journal of Ethics*, 17: 5–35.

Parfit, D. (1976) 'Rights, interests and possible people', in S. Gorovitz (ed.), *Moral Problems in Medicine*, 369–75. New Jersey: Prentice Hall.

Parfit, D. (1982) 'Future generations: Further problems', *Philosophy and Public Affairs*, 11/2: 113–72.

Parfit, D. (1986) 'Comments', *Ethics*, 96, 832–72.

Parfit, D. (1987) *Reasons and Persons*. Oxford: Clarendon Press.

Parfit, D. (2011) *On What Matters*. Oxford: Oxford University Press.

Parfit, D. (2017) 'Future people, the non-identity problem, and person-affecting principles', *Philosophy and Public Affairs*, 45: 118–57.

Persson, I. (2017) *Inclusive Ethics*. Oxford: Oxford University Press.

Roberts, M. (2020) 'The nonidentity problem', in E. N. Zalta (ed.), *The Stanford Encyclopedia of Philosophy* (Winter 2020 Edition), <https://plato.stanford.edu/archives/win2020/entries/nonidentity-problem/>accessed 21 July 2021.

Roberts, M. and Wasserman, D (eds). (2009) *Harming Future Persons: Ethics, Genetics and the Non-Identity Problem*. Dordrecht: Springer.

Savulescu, J. (2001) 'Procreative beneficence: Why we should select the best children', *Bioethics*, 15: 413–26.

Shiffrin, S. (1998) 'Wrongful life, procreative responsibility, and the significance of harm', *Legal Theory*, 5: 117–48.

Singer, P. (2011) *Practical Ethics*, 3rd edn. Cambridge: Cambridge University Press.

Smajdor, A. (2014) 'How useful is the concept of the "harm threshold" in reproductive ethics and law?', *Theoretical Medicine and Bioethics*, 35: 321–36.

Smolkin, D. (1999) 'Toward a rights-based solution to the non-identity problem', *Journal of Social Philosophy*, 30: 194–208.

Williams, N. and Harris, J. (2014) 'What is the harm in harmful conception? On threshold harms in non-identity cases', *Theoretical Medicine and Bioethics*, 35: 337–51.

Woodward, J. (1986) 'The non-identity problem', *Ethics*, 96/4: 804–31.

PART II
THE REPUGNANT CONCLUSION, FUTURE GENERATIONS, AND EXTINCTION

7

Population Ethics Forty Years On

Some Lessons Learned from "Box Ethics"

Larry Temkin

7.1 Introduction

It is an honor, and privilege, to be contributing a chapter to this volume honoring Derek Parfit. Derek was, to my mind, the greatest moral philosopher since Kant. However, for me, Derek was so much more than just an extraordinarily brilliant philosopher. It is no exaggeration to say that I owe my philosophical career to Derek. Indeed, were it not for Derek's unflagging encouragement, it is quite likely that I would have left philosophy years ago. Derek was my teacher, mentor, inspiration, editor, and long-time colleague. I am immensely proud to have been the first graduate student for whom Derek served as the main dissertation advisor, and we remained in close contact throughout his life. When Derek passed away, on January 1, 2017, I lost my oldest, and dearest, friend in the profession. Suffice-it-to-say—a locution Derek used to love to tease me about for overusing it—this chapter is dedicated to Derek.

In 1977, I took a seminar with Parfit where he presented an early version of what eventually became Part Four of *Reasons and Persons*.[1] In that seminar, Parfit laid much of the foundation for what we now recognize as the field of population ethics. Parfit asked questions that had never been asked before. He introduced a new methodological approach (at least new to philosophy)—"box ethics," identified a host of new principles and considerations, and created entirely new terminology for addressing the questions he was raising. In pursuing his questions, Parfit brought a unique combination of argumentative rigor, penetrating insight, and extraordinary originality. Along the way, he also discovered a host of deep puzzles and paradoxes that we are still grappling with forty years later.

In this chapter, I aim to present some of the lessons that I have learned from thinking about population ethics. I shall also indicate areas where problems remain or questions remain open. Some issues I shall only briefly touch on with little or no argument. Others I will delve into more deeply. Some I shall simply

---

[1] Oxford: Oxford University Press, 1984.

ignore. Some of the topics I ignore, such as the *Non-Identity Problem*[2] and the *Mere Addition Paradox*,[3] are no less important than the ones I address. However, one cannot address every topic in a single chapter, and I hope, and trust, that other contributors to this volume will address those that I do not. Since my thinking about this topic has, from the very beginning, been deeply influenced and intertwined with Parfit's, some of the claims I make are straightforwardly owing to Parfit, others to me, and some to our collaborative efforts over many years.

This chapter has six sections. Section 7.2 addresses lessons that can be gleaned from the Repugnant Conclusion and some other "box" cases.[4] Section 7.3 discusses a *Capped Model of Ideals*. Section 7.4 addresses the relative status of people, places, and times from an impartial, neutral, perspective. Section 7.5 considers different views concerning the scope of a Capped Model of Ideals, and raises various problems and unanswered questions that a Capped Model faces. Section 7.6 summarizes the chapter's main claims.

7.2 The Repugnant Conclusion and Some Other "Box" Cases

In his early population ethics work, Parfit drew two simple figures, as presented in Figure 7.1.

Today, Figure 7.1 is familiar to most readers of this volume. However, when Parfit first began using such figures most readers had no clue how to interpret them. Parfit patiently explained that his figures represented groups or populations in different possible outcomes, with the height of the figures representing how well off the people in an outcome were, and the width the size of the population. In this

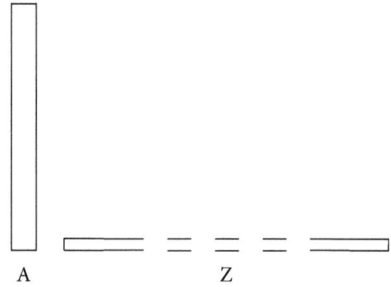

Figure 7.1 Diagram One

---

[2] See chapter 16 of *Reasons and Persons*.

[3] See chapter 19 of *Reasons and Persons*. Elsewhere, I have argued that the Mere Addition Paradox is Parfit's most interesting and important paradox, and that it has profound implications for our understanding of morality and practical reasoning. See my "Intransitivity and the Mere Addition Paradox," *Philosophy and Public Affairs* 16, 1987: 138–87, and my *Rethinking the Good: Moral Ideals and the Nature of Practical Reasoning*, New York: Oxford University Press, 2012.

[4] Parfit's Repugnant Conclusion is presented and discussed in chapter 17 of *Reasons and Persons*.

particular case, we were to imagine that A represented a very large population, say of ten billion people, all of whose members were exceedingly well off, and Z represented a *much* larger population, all of whose members had lives that were barely worth living. Considering such figures, Parfit asked us to consider, which, if either, of the two possible outcomes would be *better*, all things considered. Parfit was asking us a question about *axiology*—though at the time, nobody used that word; he was asking us how the two outcomes compared, all things considered, in terms of their *goodness*.

Many people, initially, were bewildered by such figures. They weren't sure what to make of them, or whether they could trust any intuitions that they had about such abstract, oversimplified figures involving populations of unimaginably large size. Indeed, in the early days of population ethics, a common reaction to Parfit's figures was: "what do *boxes* have to do with *ethics*?" But Parfit persevered, patiently explaining what, exactly, the "boxes" represented, and eventually many people came to recognize that, at least in Parfit's extraordinary hands, "boxes" could teach us a *lot* about ethics and, in particular, they could illuminate many of our deepest beliefs about the nature and structure of the good.

When I presented Figure 7.1, I asked my audience to imagine that in A, ten billion people existed, they were all equally well off, and each of them led lives that were better than those of any human who had ever lived. I asked my audience to imagine that their lives were *filled* with *whatever* makes a human life valuable—for example, long life, good health, great artistic and scientific achievements, deep friendships, enduring loves, gustatory delights, acquisition of vast amounts of important knowledge, profound appreciation of beauty, immensely satisfying sex, etc. Moreover, one was to imagine that the lives of those in A were free of pain, hunger, dissatisfaction, doubts, ennui, jealousy, or other negative elements.

In Z, on the other hand, one was to imagine a massive population, as large as one might like, all of whose members where equally well off, but whose overall balance of positive and negative elements in their lives left them with a life that was *barely* worth living. As I often liked to put it, although their lives were *in fact* worth living, if they had only stubbed their toes *one* more time over the course of their lives, then their lives would *not* have been worth living. Indeed, in that case, their lives would have been worth *not* living, and it would have been better for them if they had never been born! Alternatively, I would sometimes ask my audience to imagine that Z's vast numbers were comatose for virtually all of their lives, but that for *one* brief moment they rose to consciousness, during which time they felt an ever-so-slight positive experience—perhaps the equivalent of a brief, warm hug—after which they fell back into total unconsciousness and eventually died.

Faced with such alternatives, the *vast* majority of people agree that an outcome like A would be *much* better than an outcome like Z, and they believe this no matter *how many* people might exist in Z. To think otherwise is to accept:

> *The Repugnant Conclusion*: For any possible population of at least ten billion people, all with a very high quality of life, there must be some much larger imaginable population whose existence, if others things are equal, would be better, even though its members have lives that are barely worth living.[5]

Parfit thought that the *Repugnant Conclusion* was genuinely repugnant. He firmly believed that an outcome like A was much better than an outcome like Z. As indicated, the vast majority of people agree with Parfit.

"So what?" one might wonder. After all, it seems like an obvious, trivial truth that we should reject the Repugnant Conclusion. Still, that simple truth—assuming it *is* true, which I shall not defend here—generates many important insights, thanks to the penetrating exploration to which Parfit subjected it. More cautiously, when combined with other plausible assumptions, insights, and arguments, reflecting on the Repugnant Conclusion can lead to a host of important ethical conclusions. Let me turn now to an enumeration of some of these.

First, at the time Parfit was originally writing, much of normative ethical theorizing concerned whether one should accept some form of utilitarianism or some form of Kantianism. Leading utilitarian positions included total utilitarianism and average utilitarianism, where it was often debated as to whether these positions should be combined with a narrow hedonic theory of the good (pleasures and pains are all that matter), a broader mental state theory of the good (positive and negative conscious states are all that matter, but not all positive mental states are pleasures and not all negative mental states are pains), a preference satisfaction theory of the good (satisfying or frustrating preferences or desires are all that matter), an objective list theory of the good (some states are objectively good or bad *for* people beyond the extent to which they affect the quality of their mental states or involve the satisfaction or frustration of their preferences), or some combination of such positions.[6]

So, the first point to note is that rejecting the Repugnant Conclusion immediately requires one to reject, or drastically revise, any version of *classical total utilitarianism*, with its simple additive-aggregationist approach to assessing outcome goodness. A is a finite outcome. So, no matter *how* good each person's life is in A, on total utilitarianism there will be a *total* finite amount of good in A, say, X, determining how good A is all things considered. By hypothesis, for each person in Z, the overall balance of pleasure versus pain is positive, so even though each person's life is *barely* worth living, the net amount of utility she has is positive, say U. Now, no matter how small U is, as long as it is finite, there will be some number of people, N, such that $N(U) > X$.

---

[5] *Reasons and Persons*, p. 388.
[6] Other questions that people debated included whether one should be a direct or indirect utilitarian, or an act or rule (or some other form of two-tiered) utilitarian.

POPULATION ETHICS FORTY YEARS ON   163

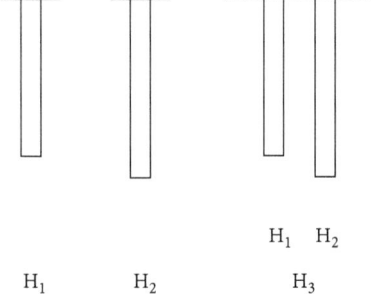

Figure 7.2 Diagram Two

It follows that on the simple additive-aggregationist approach of classical utilitarianism, if the population size of Z were N, the *sum total* of utility in Z would be greater than that in A, in which case, according to total utilitarianism, Z would be *better* than A. But this, of course, is the Repugnant Conclusion. Thus, the first lesson of the Repugnant Conclusion (assuming, as I will do in the remainder of the chapter, that we should, indeed, reject it) is that we must reject or substantially revise classical utilitarianism, with its simple additive-aggregationist approach to assessing outcome goodness.

The preceding considerations may be thought to lend support to *average utilitarianism*, the view that holds that the best outcome, all things considered, will be the one with the highest average level of utility of all its sentient members who ever live. After all, the average level of utility in A is much higher than the average utility in Z, so average utilitarianism can capture our views about the Repugnant Conclusion. However, Parfit offered a compelling objection to average utilitarianism by considering another example from population ethics, represented by (the boxes of) Figure 7.2.[7]

In Figure 7.2, H_1 represents a possible outcome, which we will call *Hell One*, in which ten billion people exist, and their lives are all unbelievably miserable. Each person is worse off than any human who has ever lived. Day after day they suffer unbelievable agony and, quite rationally, each day they wish they were dead and that they had never been born. H_2 represents a possible outcome, *Hell Two*, in which ten billion different people exist, and, incredibly, their lives are all even worse than those of Hell One, though not by a lot. H_3 represents a possible outcome, *Hell Three*, in which Hell One *and* Hell Two *both* exist.

Most people firmly believe, rightly I think, that Hell One is a horrible outcome, Hell Two is an even *worse* outcome, and Hell Three is *by far the worst* outcome of the three. After all, in Hell Three, *twenty* billion people suffer unrelenting agony, rather than the "merely" *ten* billion people who suffer unrelenting agony in Hell

---

[7] Parfit's version of this example, which he calls *Hell Three*, is presented on p. 422 of *Reasons and Persons*.

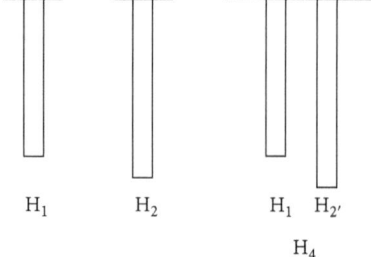

Figure 7.3 Diagram Three

One or Hell Two. However, as Parfit rightly observes, on average utilitarianism, Hell Three would be *better* than Hell Two, since the *average* level of utility is lower in Hell Three than it is in Hell Two. Parfit finds this impossible to believe. How could the *addition* of an outcome like Hell One, to an outcome like Hell Two, make the resulting outcome, Hell Three, *better* regarding utility, merely in virtue of the fact that it would increase the outcome's *average* level of utility, when such a move would do *nothing* to improve the agonizing lives of those in Hell Two, while bringing into existence ten billion people all of whom would be worse off than any human who had ever lived, and whose agonizing lives would be so bad that each day they would, quite rationally, wish they were dead?

Indeed, we can strengthen the argument against average utilitarianism by tweaking the example a little. Consider Figure 7.3.

In Figure 7.3, H_1 and H_2 represent the same horribly bad outcomes as they did in Figure 7.2. $H_{2'}$ involves the very same people as H_2, but they are even *worse* off in $H_{2'}$ than they are in H_2. H_4 involves both of the outcomes H_1 and $H_{2'}$, but the extent to which the people in $H_{2'}$ are worse off than they were in H_2, is not quite as bad as the extent to which the people in H_2 are worse off than the people in H_1, so that the average level of utility in H_4 is higher than the average level of utility in H_2. Surely, Parfit would contend, H_2 is better than H_4, since, in comparison with H_4, H_2 is *better* for *everyone* who exists in H_2 and spares an additional *ten billion people* agonizing lives.

Variations of Gustaf Arrhenius's *Sadistic Conclusion* support a similar conclusion.[8] Most people firmly believe that if, in fact, utility matters, it should always be better, *regarding utility*, to add people with lives that are *well worth living* to an outcome than to add people whose lives are *so miserable* that they are worth *not* living. Yet, one can easily see that if there were a large number of people already existing with supremely good lives, say, ten billion people at level 1,000,000, then adding many people with lives that were well worth living, say, ten billion people at level 500,000, could be *worse*, according to average utilitarianism, than adding a

---

[8] See, for example, Gustaf Arrhenius's "An Impossibility Theorem for Welfarist Axiology," *Economics and Philosophy* 16, 2000: 247–66.

large, but smaller number of people with utterly miserable lives, say, ten million people at level −1,000,000, since the former might lower the average utility of the world (from one million to 750,000) by more than the latter (from one million to ~ 998,000).

Similarly, if there were a large number of people already existing with extremely terrible lives, say, ten billion people at level −1,000,000, then adding many people with lives that were terrible, but not *as* terrible, say, ten billion people at level −500,000, could be *better*, according to average utilitarianism, than adding a large, but smaller number of people with really wonderful lives, say, ten million people at level 1,000,000, since the former might raise the average utility of the world (from −1,000,000 to −750,000) by more than the latter (from −1,000,000 to ~ −998,000).

We see, then, that thinking about issues in population ethics give rise to powerful worries about both total and average utilitarianism. Our views about the Repugnant Conclusion, illustrated by the "boxes" in Figure 7.1, cast doubt on total utilitarianism; while our intuitions about the various "Hell" outcomes, illustrated by the "boxes" in Figures 7.2 and 7.3, together with our views about variations of the Sadistic Conclusion cast doubt on average utilitarianism.

Return to the second version of the Repugnant Conclusion discussed above, where we imagine that each of many people lead most of their lives unconscious, but for one brief moment when they have a single conscious experience that is mildly positive; akin, perhaps, to the positive experience of a brief, warm hug. Some people have argued that it is actually *bad* for humans to live such lives. There are two versions of this claim. On one, these people grant that living such a life is not actually bad *for* the liver of the life—that such a life would, in fact, be *subjectively* worth living, even if only barely so; but they nonetheless insist that for a *human* to be living such a life would be an *objectively* bad feature of the outcome. On the second version, it is claimed that such a life *would be* bad *for* the liver of that life.

Both versions recognize that human beings are capable of *so* much more than mild positive experiences. They are capable of acquiring knowledge, appreciating beauty, attaining great achievements, being virtuous, acting morally, engaging in deep meaningful relationships, and so on. So, both versions see a human life that only contains a single, fleeting, mildly positive experience as *severely* lacking relative to what humans are capable of. More generally, both might recognize that there are forms of human existence, which are so lacking in what makes a human life valuable, lives below a certain level of human flourishing that Parfit called the *Restricted Level*, that we should regard it as bad for any human to be living at such a level.[9]

---

[9] The notion of a Restricted Level was first introduced in Gregory Kavka's path-breaking article "The Paradox of Future Individuals," *Philosophy and Public Affairs*, 1982: 93–112. Parfit discusses this notion, which he also refers to as the *Bad Level*, in *Reasons and Persons*, section 147, pp. 432–3.

However, as indicated, there are two importantly distinct interpretations of the locution "bad for" in this context. On one, it is *subjectively* bad for the person to be alive at that level; they have self-interested reason to regret being alive at that level.[10] On the other, it is not *subjectively* bad for the person to be alive at that level—from a purely self-interested standpoint, they have reason to be glad that they exist even if only at such a meager level—but nonetheless it is *objectively* bad for any human to exist at such a level—from an impersonal perspective, there is reason to regret any human being living at such a Restricted Level, not only in comparison with an alternative where such a person would live a life of *higher quality*, but in comparison with an alternative where such a person *never lived at all*.

In thinking about such cases, it is useful to contrast how we think about a *human* living such a life, with how we might think of a much "lower" animal or form of life living at such a level. Suppose, following Plato, that there was a form of oyster that existed that was psychologically capable of low levels of conscious contentment, equivalent to what humans experience with a brief, warm hug.[11] But suppose that such "contented oysters" were incapable of any of the higher forms of human experience—for them, there was no possibility of inter- or intra-sentient relationships of any kind, much less deep loves or friendships, no possibility of acting rightly or virtuously, appreciating beauty, acquiring knowledge, creativity or achievements, etc. Most people would continue to reject a version of the Repugnant Conclusion which held that an outcome containing a large enough number of contented oysters would be better than an outcome containing ten billion flourishing people, all of whom were better off than any humans who have ever lived. However, importantly, most people don't think that it would be subjectively *bad for* the contented oysters to exist with their low levels of psychological contentment, nor do they think that the mere existence of large numbers of such contented oysters would *itself* make an outcome *bad*, any more than they think that a large number of existing trees or grasses would itself be an objectively bad-making feature of an outcome.

If this is right, this suggests, to paraphrase Putnam, that "goodness ain't solely in the head."[12] More particularly, from the inside, it *could* be that there were no psychological differences in terms of pleasures and pains, or the phenomenal *quality* of their mental states more generally, or even between the content of any preferences and desires that might be had by the humans that felt and, we may

---

[10] The idea here is not merely that they have reason to regret being alive at that level, in comparison with some other higher level at which they might have lived, but that they have reason to regret being alive at that level because being alive at that level is, *in itself*, bad, in self-interested terms. This corresponds to Jeff McMahan's notion of a *non-comparative bad* (see section 4.4 of McMahan's *The Ethics of Killing: Problems at the Margins of Life*, New York: Oxford University Press, 2002).

[11] Plato introduces the notion of a contented oyster in his dialogue, *Philebus*.

[12] Putnam famously claimed that "meanings ain't in the head" in his landmark article "The Meaning of 'Meaning,'" *Minnesota Studies in the Philosophy of Science* 7, 1975: 131–93.

suppose, desired nothing but low level contentment equivalent to that of a brief, warm hug, and the contented oysters who felt and, we may also suppose, desired nothing but their equally low level of contentment. Nevertheless, for many, given the vast difference between the natures, capabilities, and potential of a normal human being, and that of a normal contented oyster, we might think that there was something terribly tragic, and bad, about a member of the human species being in such a state, and yet nothing tragic or bad about a member of the contented oyster species being in such a state.

There is much more to be said about all this than I can present here.[13] But together, such considerations may lead to a number of important conclusions. First, as seen, we may want to distinguish between *subjective* goodness—what is good or bad *for* sentient beings from the standpoint of individual self-interest, and *objective* goodness—what are the good- or bad-making features of an *outcome*. Second, there is reason to move beyond a narrow hedonic conception of the good, a broader mental state theory of the good, and even a desire satisfaction theory of the good. Ultimately, pleasures and pains *are* relevant to the good of individuals, as are the quality of non-hedonic mental states, and perhaps the satisfaction or frustration of preferences or desires are also relevant to the good of individuals, but if we believe that a life that might be worth living for an oyster might not be worth living for a human being, then we should probably adopt an objective list theory of the good for individuals as the best way to account for this. Moreover, if we believe that, subjectively, the human who experiences and desires nothing but brief warm hugs is just as well off in terms of welfare or wellbeing as the contented oyster with qualitatively indistinguishable experiences and desires, but that nonetheless an outcome filled with human beings in such a condition would be worse than an outcome filled with oysters in such a condition, then there is good reason to accept an objective list theory about the goodness of outcomes.

Relatedly, thinking about all the factors that might make an outcome like A much better than an outcome like Z in Figure 7.1, can lead one to recognize that in addition to *personal* ideals, whose values lie solely in the extent to which their realization promotes the welfare or wellbeing of sentient beings, there are also *impersonal* ideals, whose values lie, at least partly, in the extent to which their realization promotes the goodness of an outcome *independently* of the extent to which it promotes the individual welfare or wellbeing of the sentient beings in that outcome. Moreover, one may come to recognize that many of the ideals that humans value most—including equality, justice, perfectionism, acting morally or virtuously, respect for life in all its forms (including non-sentient forms),

---

[13] For more on these topics, see my "Harmful Goods, Harmless Bads," in *Value, Welfare, and Morality*, eds. Frey, R. G. and Morris, Christopher, pp. 290–324, Cambridge University Press, 1993; my "Equality, Priority, and the Levelling Down Objection," in *The Ideal of Equality*, eds. Clayton, Matthew and Williams, Andrew, pp. 126–61, Macmillan and St. Martin's Press, 2000; and *Rethinking the Good*.

ecological preservation, originality and creativity, and knowledge for its own sake—are impersonal. While the realization of such values often promotes the wellbeing of sentient individuals, their values are not solely determined by the extent to which this is so.

Classical utilitarianism combined the view that one should maximize the good, with a relatively narrow conception of the good tied to the wellbeing of sentient individuals. For classical utilitarianism, the goodness of an outcome was determined in a simple additive way as a function of the individual wellbeing of each of the sentient individuals in that outcome. Thinking hard about issues in population ethics forces one to recognize that even if one believes that there is reason to maximize the good, one needs a much broader conception of the good than wellbeing. Thus, insofar as one believes that one should maximize the good, one should be a *consequentialist*, rather than merely a *utilitarian*. The best outcome will require the realization of a host of impersonal ideals, *as well as* those personal ideals whose promotion contributes to the wellbeing of that outcome's sentient beings.

Return to the Repugnant Conclusion. If one agrees that one should reject the Repugnant Conclusion, then one believes that at some point merely adding more people (or contented oysters!) to an outcome will not make that outcome (significantly) *objectively* better, even if each extra life is worth living, and so *subjectively* valuable for the liver of that life. I shall say more about this shortly. But, for now, I note that many who accept this believe that this is true across a wide range of cases. That is, many people believe that it is *generally* true that merely adding more people to an outcome does not, itself, make the outcome better, whether the additional people would have lives that were only barely worth living or well worth living.

Jan Narveson held such a view. Narveson famously claimed that "Morality has to do with how we treat whatever people there are... [We] do not think that happiness is impersonally good. We are in favor of making people happy, but neutral about making happy people."[14] I believe that Narveson overstated his claim, and in a bit I'll mention four ways that we may wish to qualify or restrict his general claim. Still, many people accept Narveson's claims for a wide range of cases. They accept what John Broome has called:

The Neutrality Intuition: there is a neutral range, in terms of the quality of people's lives, such that merely bringing people into existence whose quality of lives would lie within that neutral range would not itself make the outcome better, but neither would it make the outcome worse.[15]

---

[14] Jan Narveson, "Moral Problems of Population," *The Monist* 57, 1973: 73, 80.
[15] *Weighing Lives*, Oxford: Oxford University Press, 2004, section 10.2, pp. 143–6. The qualifiers "merely" and "itself" reflect the fact that here, and below, I am not discussing any possible *indirect* effects on others from the addition of extra people that might make the outcome better or worse all things considered.

This view accords with the widely shared view that, in general, if a couple is deciding whether to have a child, or whether to have two children or four, the mere fact that the child or children would have lives that are worth living does not *itself* provide them with a reason to have the child, or four children rather than two. In sum, for a wide range of cases it seems plausible to believe that improving the lives of anyone already existing would make the outcome at least in one respect better, but merely bringing more people into the world with lives that would be worth living would not.

It is easy to see how the Neutrality Intuition fits well with most people's views about the Repugnant Conclusion. After all, it is clear that a world, A, of ten billion flourishing people would be much better than a world, S, with ten billion people whose lives were barely worth living. But then, if the Neutrality Intuition is true, merely adding many more people to S who also have lives that are barely worth living won't make the resulting outcome, Z, in any way *better*. So, Z, like S, will be much worse than A.

The judgment that A would be better than S accords with a view that Parfit finds plausible:

The Same Number Quality Claim, or Q: If, in either of two outcomes the same number of people would ever live, then, if everyone in one outcome would be better off (or have a higher quality of life) than everyone in the other outcome, then the former outcome would be better than the latter.[16]

Note, that combined with the Neutrality Intuition, Q supports the following position:

The Different Number or General Quality Claim, or GQ: If, in either of two outcomes a different number of people would ever live, then, if everyone in one of the outcomes is better off than everyone in the other (or has a higher quality of life), then the former outcome would be better than the latter.

As indicated, the Neutrality Intuition is plausible in a wide range of cases. Still, it is worth noting several points that it leaves open, and several ways in which it may need to be restricted in scope.

First, in an extremely small population, with only a few, or a few thousand, or perhaps even only a few million people, we may think that adding more people with lives (well) worth living *would* make that outcome better. Likewise, if the alternative were a universe entirely devoid of well off people, or one filled with well

---

[16] See *Reasons and Persons*, p. 360. I have formulated the view differently than Parfit does, but I think the way he formulates it is slightly confusing, and I believe that this accurately reflects the view he was intending to express.

off people, we may think the latter is much better than the former. Thus, we may think that Narveson's plausible sounding claim that "we are in favor of making people happy, but neutral about making happy people" is in fact *only* plausible when we are considering outcomes in which a large number of happy people *already exist*, and doesn't apply to outcomes in which no one exists, or only a relatively small number of people exist.

Second, given the concern for the quality of people's lives, reflected in principles like Q and GQ, one might think that merely adding more people to an already large population won't make that outcome better, *if* the additional people would be no better off than *large numbers of people who already exist*. On the other hand, if the additional people would be better off than those who were already existing, or there were only a small number of people in the existing outcome who were as well off as the additional people would be, one might think that in *such* cases adding more people *would* make the outcome better, even if the quality of their lives would lie within the so-called "neutral zone."

Third, note that, as stated, the Neutrality Intuition leaves open the possibility mentioned above, that there could be lives whose quality was sufficiently low, below the so-called Restricted Level, that adding more people at such levels would make the outcome *objectively* worse, even if such lives were *subjectively* worth living, and so not *bad for* the livers of those lives. Likewise, the Neutrality Intuition leaves open the possibility that there could be lives whose quality was sufficiently high—for example, above a *Wonderful Level*—that adding lives of *such* high quality to an outcome *would* always make an outcome better, no matter how many other beings already existed at, or above, that level. So, for example, one might think that an angel's life might be *so* good, that bringing more angels into existence *would* always make the outcome better.[17]

Finally, for many, there is an important asymmetry in their thinking about lives that would be worth living—those *above* the so-called *zero level*—and lives that would be worth not living—those *below* the zero level. Specifically, they believe that while adding lives that are worth living to an already large population of lives that are equally well or even better off would *not* make the outcome *better*, adding lives that are worth not living to an outcome *would* always make the outcome *worse*.

This asymmetry raises problems of its own, which I shall return to in the next section. But, if we accept the asymmetry in question, then we would have reason to reject the Different Number or General Quality Claim, GQ, for outcomes involving lives below the zero level, even if we continue to accept the Same Number Quality Claim, Q, for such cases. So, for example, we might agree, in accordance

---

[17] I owe the term "Wonderful Level" to early drafts of *Reasons and Persons*. For corresponding notions, see Parfit's discussion of the *Valueless Level* and the *Blissful Level* in sections 139, 140, and 145 of *Reasons and Persons*.

with Q, that an outcome like H_1 would be better than an outcome like H_2 in Figure 7.2, yet also believe that an outcome with a vastly larger population in which everyone was at the level of those in H_1 would be worse than an outcome like H_2, contrary to what GQ entails, as currently formulated.

Indeed, *if* we believe that the addition of lives below some Restricted Level is *objectively* bad, even if such lives are above the zero level, and so subjectively good for the people in question, then there would be reason to reject GC for any populations whose members were all below the Restricted Level, whether or not they were below the zero level.

7.3 The Capped Model of Ideals

Classical utilitarians were concerned to maximize the total amount of utility, where, roughly, this was determined by employing a simple additive function of the wellbeing of each individual sentient being. Importantly, those who find the Repugnant Conclusion genuinely repugnant, don't deny that there is much *more* utility, or total wellbeing, in Z than in A, in Figure 7.1. What they deny is that merely adding *more* utility to an outcome always makes it *better*. In carefully considering the differences between A and Z, in terms of what really matters, we note that, by assumption, A scores very highly with respect to *every* ideal that is relevant to the assessment of outcomes: justice, equality, autonomy, achievement, virtue, acting rightly, knowledge, beauty, creativity, utility, etc. Z, by contrast, scores highly regarding at most two ideals, equality and utility, and, by assumption, it scores *zero* with respect to every other ideal relevant to assessing the goodness of outcomes. Moreover, it is no better than A regarding equality. Given this, is it any wonder that most regard Z as much worse than A?

The simple thought is that however much we might care about the ideal of utility, we don't care about it, and *shouldn't* care about it, more than *virtually every other moral ideal combined*! Indeed, this is a general truth. No one ideal, no matter how important, is more important than virtually every other moral ideal combined. To be a really good outcome, *all things considered*, one must score highly along *many* morally relevant dimensions. It is not sufficient to score highly, even really highly, along just one or two dimensions.

This way of thinking is extremely plausible in a wide range of cases, and it manifests itself in a host of judgments that we make. For example, to be the best all-around female gymnast, it is not enough to be *really* good with respect to a single skill, say, the uneven parallel bars. One must *also* be good with respect to the balance beam, the vault, and the floor exercises. A gymnast who couldn't successfully do any vaults, who couldn't stay on the balance beam, and who couldn't complete even a rudimentary tumbling pass would never be judged amongst the best female gymnasts, *all things considered*, no matter *how* good she was on the uneven parallel bars. Likewise, no matter how courageous Attila the Hun might be, he would never be counted among the most virtuous of people, if he were lacking virtue along every other relevant dimension. To be a *really* virtuous person, *all things considered*, one must possess most, if not all, of the relevant virtues to a high degree—including, among others, the virtues of honesty, kindness, generosity, loyalty, trustworthiness, dependability, helpfulness, friendship, compassion, gratitude, *and* courage.

I believe that, in thinking about utility, many people implicitly accept six basic assumptions which I call:

The Standard Model for Utility:

1. Utility is non-instrumentally valuable—meaning that there is some value to utility over and above the extent to which it promotes other valuable ideals.

2. Utility is intrinsically valuable—meaning that each unit of utility contributes to the value of an outcome, and each unit contributes the same amount of value as every other, so that two units of utility add twice as much value to an outcome's goodness as one unit of utility.

3. The ideal of utility is strictly neutral with respect to sentient beings, places, and times—meaning that a given amount of utility will count just as much no matter who experiences it, where it is experienced, or when it is experienced.

4. The ideal of utility is strictly impartial—meaning that no sentient being should be given preference over any other when it comes to promoting utility.

5. Insofar as one cares about utility, one should care about total utility.

6. How good an outcome is regarding utility is a simple additive function of how much utility sentient beings have in that outcome.[18]

In addition, I believe that, in thinking about how to assess the goodness of outcomes, most people implicitly accept a position I call:

The Standard Model for Combining Ideals: How good an outcome is all things considered is an additive function of how good it is regarding each ideal, so that insofar as an outcome gets better regarding any particular ideal it will, to that extent, be getting better all things considered.[19]

Together, the Standard Model for Utility and the Standard Model for Combining Ideals straightforwardly entail the Repugnant Conclusion. Thus, if we reject the

---

[18] I introduce the Standard Model of Utility in *Rethinking the Good*, p. 315. Here, I have slightly shortened my characterization of the second assumption, and slightly rephrased my characterization of the fourth assumption.

[19] *Rethinking the Good*, p. 315.

Repugnant Conclusion, as most people do, we must revise or reject either the Standard Model for Combining Ideals or the Standard Model for Utility, or both.

Ultimately, there may be good reasons related to the issue of holism to reject the Standard Model for Combining Ideals. However, one can accept the Standard Model for Combining Ideals if one revises one's model of utility to make it compatible with a position which I call:

The Capped Model of Ideals:

1. For each ideal relevant to assessing outcomes, each outcome will merit a (rough) numerical "score" (or range of scores, henceforth, I'll drop this qualification, but assume it applies throughout) representing how good that outcome is regarding that ideal.

2. How good an outcome is all things considered will be an additive function of how good it is regarding each ideal.

3. There is an upper limit regarding how much better any individual ideal can make an outcome, all things considered, and hence an upper limit on the maximum score that can be given for any ideal, representing how good an outcome is regarding that ideal.

4. There is an upper limit on the total score that any given outcome can get, and hence an upper limit on how good an outcome can be, all things considered.[20]

The scoring system that was in place in women's gymnastics until 2005 reflects the thinking underlying the Capped Model. No matter how good one might be on any given event, there was an upper limit of 10 that one could receive for each of the four individual events and, as such, there was an upper limit of 40 on the total score that one could receive on all of the events combined. Accordingly, to be recognized as the best female gymnast, all things considered, it wasn't enough to be extraordinarily good, or even perfect, regarding a single event, say, the uneven parallel bars, but miserable in the other three events. After all, in theory, such a gymnast might receive a *perfect* score of 10 on the parallel bars, but scores of 0 for the vault, the balance beam, and the floor exercises, for a total overall score of only 10. In contrast, someone who was outstanding in all four events, might receive scores of 9 for each event, an overall score of 36, and be rightly judged as the much better female gymnast, all things considered.

Of course, one might think that depending on the comparisons in question, some factors are more important than others for ranking alternatives, and the Capped Model can reflect such judgments. Still, it should be clear how the Capped

---

[20] *Rethinking the Good*, pp. 329–30. For much more on the Capped Model, see chapter 10 of *Rethinking the Good*, especially sections 10.6–10.9.

Model could capture our attitudes regarding Attila the Hun and the Repugnant Conclusion.

Suppose, for example, for simplicity, that one thought that the ten factors listed previously were the only ones relevant for comparing outcomes in terms of their overall goodness: justice, equality, autonomy, achievement, virtue, acting rightly, knowledge, beauty, creativity, and utility. Suppose further, purely for the sake of argument, that one thought that utility was *the* single most important ideal, and that it was twice as important as justice, equality, virtue, and acting rightly, which in turn were each twice as important as achievement, knowledge, beauty, and creativity. On the Capped Model for Ideals, one might then arbitrarily assign a highest possible score of 100 to the factors of achievement, knowledge, beauty, and creativity, a score of 200 to the factors of justice, equality, autonomy, virtue, and acting rightly, and a score of 400 to the factor of utility, for a highest possible all things considered score of 1800.

In Figure 7.1, A represents a perfectly equal extraordinarily flourishing society which will be close to the cap along every dimension. So, for the sake of argument, let's suppose that perfectly equal A scores a 200 for equality, a 180 for each of justice, autonomy, virtue, and acting rightly, a 90 for each of achievement, knowledge, beauty, and creativity, and a 375 for utility. A's *all things considered* score would then be very high, as we intuitively think it should be: 1655 out of a possible 1800.

Z, in Figure 7.1, is also perfectly equal, and so will also receive a perfect score of 200 for equality. Moreover, let us assume (for now, we shall question this assumption shortly) that Z is nearly perfect regarding utility, and so receives, let us say, a score of 395 regarding utility. However, by assumption, Z will receive a zero regarding every other factor, so its total score will be 595 out of a possible 1800.

Thus, we see how a Capped Model of Ideals can capture most people's views regarding the Repugnant Conclusion. Moreover, it does so in a way that seems to accurately reflect *why* people find the Repugnant Conclusion so repugnant. Most people believe, rightly I think, that to be a great outcome *all things considered* an outcome must be great with respect to all, or at least most, of the factors that are relevant to assessing outcomes. It is *not* enough to be good—even stupendously good—with respect to only one or two factors, as no one or two factors are themselves important enough to outweigh substantial losses regarding *virtually every other factor combined*.

In sum, if, indeed, the Repugnant Conclusion should be rejected, then, for *certain* comparisons at least (and this qualification is *hugely* important), we need to replace the combination of the Standard Model for Utility and the Standard Model for Combining Ideals, with some other model for comparing outcomes in terms of their overall goodness. I have suggested one model, the Capped Moral for Ideals, that I believe is worth further development and exploration, as it seems to capture and reflect our thinking about the Repugnant Conclusion and other, similar, cases. But I have not claimed that the Capped Model is the only, or ultimately the best, approach for doing so.

There are a host of questions and problems raised by the Capped Model, most of which, unfortunately, I don't have time to delve into here.[21] However, let me briefly note just three important topics that a Capped Model must address.

First, should there be a single cap for each ideal, or might there be more than one cap for certain ideals? Intuitively, there will be a single cap—a maximum value—for how good an outcome can be regarding equality. However, intuitively, one might think that there could be different caps for utility, reflecting important differences of quality that utility might involve. Bentham's view, that if the quantity of pleasure provided is the same "push-pin is of equal value with... music and poetry" suggests that there should be a single cap for the ideal of utility; while Mill's doctrine of higher pleasures suggests that perhaps there should be different caps for the ideal of utility, for utilities of different quality.[22]

In considering the Repugnant Conclusion, some people might judge that if only there are *enough* people in Z, then Z would be better than A, *regarding utility*, even if Z would be worse than A, *all things considered*. However, many people would judge that A is better than Z *even in terms of utility itself*, and not merely all things considered. On their Millian-type view, we suppose that the *quality* of people's experiences or utility is so much higher in A than in Z that no amount of the lower quality of Z's utility can outweigh the significant amount of the higher quality of Z's utility. Such a view reflects an anti-additive-aggregationist approach to assessing the overall goodness of Z's utility which can be captured by a Capped Model of Ideals that places different upper limits on how good an outcome can be with respect to utility, depending on the quality of the utility involved.[23]

Similarly, one might think that there should be different caps for other ideals, such as the ideal of freedom. For example, one might think that some freedoms, such as the freedom of religion, are so much more important than other freedoms, such as the freedom to choose which chips to buy, that no number of infringements of the latter freedom would be worse than some number of infringements of the former. Again, this sort of anti-additive-aggregationist position could be captured by a nuanced Capped Model of Ideals, which recognized different upper limits concerning the goodness of achieving freedoms of different normative significance.

---

[21] For a partial list of complications and considerations to explore concerning a Capped Model, see sections 10.8 and 10.9 of *Rethinking the Good*.

[22] Mill's Doctrine of Higher Pleasures is presented in chapter II of *Utilitarianism*. Bentham's view is attributed to him by Mill, based on a passage from Bentham's 1830 book, *The Rationale of Reward* (reprinted by General Books in 2009) where Bentham wrote "Prejudice apart, the game of push-pin is of equal value with the arts and sciences of music and poetry."

[23] There is an extensive discussion of this point, and of anti-additive-aggregationist principles and reasoning in *Rethinking the Good*, see chapters 2, 3, 5, and, especially, 10.

Second, as noted previously, many people are attracted to the Neutrality Intuition. However, most people who accept such a view believe that it has a restricted scope. In particular, they believe that in a world filled with many flourishing people, merely bringing additional people into existence with similar quality lives (at least if those lives were below the Wonderful Level) wouldn't make the outcome *objectively* better, even if the lives in question would be *subjectively* good *for* the people living those lives, though neither would it make the outcome worse. However, most such people believe that in a world filled with many miserable people, whose lives were *below* the level at which life ceased to be worth living, bringing additional people into existence with similar quality lives would not only be *subjectively* bad *for* the people living those lives, it would also make the outcome *objectively* worse. Following Jeff McMahan, Parfit has called the difference in many people's attitudes to the objective value or disvalue of adding additional people to an outcome depending, in part, on whether their lives were above or below the zero level, *the Asymmetry*.[24]

Reflecting on the Asymmetry has led many people to conclude that a Capped Model of Ideals is plausible for *positive* ideals or values, but not for *negative* ideals or *dis*values. On such a view, there may be upper limits on how *good* an outcome can be, objectively, regarding freedom, equality, justice, pleasure, etc.; however, there are no lower limits on how *bad* an outcome can be, objectively, regarding suffering, subjugation, inequality, injustice, etc. Although many find the Asymmetry intuitively plausible, together with a Capped Model for positive ideals but a Non-Capped Model for negative ideals, there are a number of open questions concerning the combination of views in question, such as whether a principled, non-ad-hoc justification can be given for them, whether they are ultimately consistent, and whether they have unacceptable implications.[25]

Third, if one does accept a Capped Model, at least for positive ideals or values, what is the scope of the cap? Does it pertain, for example, to the whole of the universe or to subsections of it, and if the latter, do the caps apply to different regions of space, different regions of time, or both?[26] I shall return to these questions in section 7.5. However, before doing that, it will be helpful to consider first some important general questions about the normative relations between people, spaces, and times, to which I turn next.

---

[24] See *Reasons and Persons*, p. 391; and McMahan's "Problems of Population Theory," *Ethics* 92, 1981: 96–127.

[25] See chapter 18 of *Reasons and Persons*, where Parfit acknowledges the plausibility of the Asymmetry, but also suggests that it leads to the *Absurd Conclusion*, discussed later in section 7.5.

[26] The importance of addressing this question, and some considerations relevant to it, are presented in *Rethinking the Good*, chapter 10, and also in "Rationality with Respect to People, Places, and Times," *Canadian Journal of Philosophy* 45: 576–606, 2015; doi: 10.1080/00455091.2015.1122386.

7.4 Neutrality Intuitions, Dominance Principles, and the Relative Normative Significance of People, Spaces, and Times

Most people accept that, except when special relations are involved, we should be *neutral* with respect to people, spaces, and times. And surely there is something right about this. If we could help one stranger, or another, it seems we should treat them equally, and it doesn't seem to be relevant whether one of the strangers would be nearer to us in space or time. So, for example, from a moral perspective, if we could save one person from ten minutes of a mild headache, or another from ten hours of excruciating torture, it seems clear that, *other things being equal*, we should do the latter, and it wouldn't matter *at all* if we learned that one of them was 1000 miles from us, and the other 1,000,000 miles from us, or if we learned that one of them would be alive 10 years from now, and the other wouldn't be alive for another 1,000,000 years. Among two strangers, we should prevent the torture rather than the headache, wherever, and whenever, the two people might be located in space or time.

So, barring special relations (a very important qualification), *mere* differences in *who* is affected, or *where* or *when* something will occur, are, by themselves, morally irrelevant. This is a point about which there is, and I believe should be, widespread agreement. Still, this leaves open a host of questions that have been largely unexplored, but which considerations of population ethics open up. For example, what is the relation, if any, between people and spaces, or people and times, or spaces and times in terms of their relative normative significance?

To help focus this discussion, consider the view of a classical utilitarian who believes in the *impersonal* value of utility. On such a view, persons are not *themselves* valuable, rather, their value is *instrumental*—it lies solely in the fact that they are producers or containers of that which *is* valuable, such as, for example, pleasure or positive states of consciousness. On this view, if water molecules could contain pleasurable experiences, then one should be indifferent between a body of water containing a multitude of pleasurable experiences and a continent of people containing an equal number of qualitatively indistinguishable experiences. More generally, then, one might hold that people, spaces, and times are all different possible *locations* of the good, and that one's aim should be to maximize the total amount of good in the universe regardless of *whose* good it is (or if it is *anyone's* good at all, for that matter), *where* the good is, or *when* the good is.[27] On this view, then, one should, for the purposes of normative evaluation, treat people, spaces, and times the same, and be neutral not only between different people, between different spaces, and between different times, but *also*

---

[27] Here, I am following Broome's terminology regarding people, places, and times as being different possible "locations" of good. Cf. Broome's *Weighing Goods*, Oxford: Basil Blackwell, 1991; and also *Weighing Lives*.

between people and spaces, people and times, and spaces and times. Such a view *seems* perfectly coherent, and it even has some initial plausibility. The question is whether it is normatively correct. I have serious doubts as to whether it is.

Consider, for example, the following three dominance principles regarding utility:

> *Spatial Dominance Principle*: for any two alternative outcomes, A and B, if A and B involve the same region of space, S, which is made up of a set of non-empty sub-regions of space, $s_1, \ldots, s_n$, if A is better than B regarding utility in *every* sub-region of space, s_i, then A is better than B regarding utility.
>
> *Temporal Dominance Principle*: for any two alternative outcomes, A and B, if A and B involve the same period of time, T, which is made up of a set of non-empty sub-periods of time, $t_1, \ldots, t_n$, if A is better than B regarding utility in *every* sub-period of time, t_i, then A is better than B regarding utility.
>
> *Personal Dominance Principle*: for any two alternative outcomes, A and B, if A and B involve the same people, and A is better than B regarding utility for *every* person who will ever live, then A is better than B regarding utility.

Intuitively, many would find each of the preceding dominance principles plausible, and they might assume that if, for the purposes of practical reasoning, we should treat people, spaces, and times the same, and be neutral between each of them, then if one of them is true the others must also be true. But this assumption is clearly false. To see this, consider Figure 7.4.

O_1 is one possible outcome. In that outcome, there is one person, P_1, living in time period one (T_1), and spatial region one (S_1), who has a *good* life, well *above* the level at which life ceases to be worth living, but, unfortunately, there are *twice* as many other people, P_2 and P_3, who have *bad* lives, well *below* the level at which life ceases to be worth living. In time period two (T_2), P_1 through P_3 have moved to

T_1, S_1 P_1 Good Life (*GL*); P_2, P_3 Bad Life (*BL*) $\qquad$ T_1, S_1 P_1 Bad Life (*BL*); P_2, P_3 Good Life (*GL*)

T_2, S_2 P_{1-3} GL; P_{4-9} BL $\qquad$ T_2, S_2 P_{1-3} BL; P_{4-9} GL

T_3, S_3 P_{1-9} GL; P_{10-27} BL $\qquad$ T_3, S_3 P_{1-9} BL; P_{10-27} GL

T_4, S_4 P_{1-27} GL; P_{28-81} BL $\qquad$ T_4, S_4 P_{1-27} BL; P_{28-81} GL

$\vdots$ $\qquad\qquad\qquad\qquad\qquad$ $\vdots$

$\vdots$ $\qquad\qquad\qquad\qquad\qquad$ $\vdots$

$\vdots$ $\qquad\qquad\qquad\qquad\qquad$ $\vdots$

O_1 $\qquad\qquad\qquad\qquad\qquad$ O_2

Figure 7.4 Diagram Four

spatial region two (S_2), where they all enjoy good lives, but, unfortunately, in that time period, and at that location, twice as many other people, P_4 through P_9, have come into existence, and their lives are as bad as P_2 and P_3's lives were during T_1. In time period three (T_3), P_1 through P_9 have all moved to spatial region three (S_3), where they all enjoy good lives, but, unfortunately, in that time and location, twice as many other people, P_{10} through P_{27}, have come into existence, and their lives are as bad as P_2 and P_3's lives were during T_1. O_1 continues to unfold, in this ever expanding manner, forever, with each time period lasting for one day, and each person living for a hundred years in total, before dying. Here, and henceforth, we assume that the positive value of each good moment is the same, the negative value of each bad moment is the same, and that the two values sum to zero. Hence, by hypothesis, a life containing an equal number of moments of good and bad life will have a net value of zero, a life containing more moments of good life than bad will have a positive net value, and a life containing more moments of bad life than good will have a negative net value.

O_2 is a possible outcome that is analogous to, though the reverse of, O_1. In O_2, there is one person, P_1, living in time period one (T_1), and spatial region one (S_1), who has a *bad* life, well *below* the level at which life ceases to be worth living, but, fortunately, there are *twice* as many other people, P_2 and P_3, who have *good* lives, well *above* the level at which life ceases to be worth living. In time period two, P_1 through P_3 have moved to spatial region two, where they all suffer bad lives, but, fortunately, in that time period, and at that location, twice as many other people, P_4 through P_9, have come into existence, and their lives are as good as P_2 and P_3's lives were during T_1. In time period three, P_1 through P_9 have all moved to spatial region three, where they all suffer bad lives, but, once again, fortunately in that time and location, twice as many other people, P_{10} through P_{27}, have come into existence, and their lives are as good as P_2 and P_3's lives were during T_1. As before, O_2 continues to unfold, in this ever expanding manner, forever, with each time period lasting for one day, and each person living for a hundred years in total, before dying. Finally, we assume that P_1 is the very same person in both outcomes, and similarly for all the other members, P_k, of the two outcomes.[28]

We can now ask how O_1 and O_2 compare regarding utility. Comparing them spatial region by spatial region, or temporal region by temporal region, O_2 would

---

[28] The example I am giving here is a variation of one that I first heard from John Broome, in conversation, many years ago, which he called "Expanding Heaven and Expanding Hell." Broome credited his example to James Cain's "Infinite Utility," *Australasian Journal of Philosophy* 73, 1995: 401–4. Although my views about this topic were arrived at independently, other philosophers have developed similar arguments in order to make similar points. See, for example, Peter Vallentyne's "Utilitarianism and Infinite Utility," *Australasian Journal of Philosophy* 71, 1993: 212–17; Luc Lauwers's "Infinite Utility: Insisting on Strong Monotonicity," *Australasian Journal of Philosophy* 75, 1997: 222–33; Peter Vallentyne and Shelly Kagan's "Infinite Value and Finitely Additive Value Theory," *Journal of Philosophy* 94, 1997: 5–26," Theory and Decision 49, 2000: 291–5; Nick Bostrom's "Infinite Ethics," *Analysis and Metaphysics* 10, 2011: 9–59; and Tim Campbell's *Personal Ontology and Bioethics*, PhD diss., Rutgers University, 2015.

be clearly *better* than O_1, in accordance with the Spatial and Temporal Dominance Principles. This is because for *every* spatial sub-region, S_n, and *every* temporal sub-region, T_n, there will be twice as many people with good lives as with bad lives in O_2, while there will be twice as many people with bad lives as with good lives in O_1.

So, should we conclude that O_2 really *is* better than O_1 regarding utility? I think not. This is because O_1 is *better* than O_2 in accordance with the *Personal Dominance Principle* regarding utility. After all, by hypothesis, the *same* people exist in both outcomes, and they are all *clearly* better off in O_1, where they each suffer for only *one* bad *day* followed by *ninety-nine* good *years* and 364 good days, than they are in O_2, where they each do well for only *one* good *day*, followed by *ninety-nine* bad *years* and 364 bad days.

In this example, we can accept the dominance principle regarding *people*, *or* we can accept the dominance principles regarding *space* and *time*, but we *cannot* do both! Here we have a *proof* that we cannot accept *all three* dominance principles. More particularly, we see that in this case, at least, we *should* not, and *cannot*, treat space and time the same way as we treat people. In *this* case, at least, I give priority to people over space and time. Notwithstanding the fact that O_2 *is* better than O_1 at every sub-region in space and time, I judge O_1 as *better* than O_2, because it is better for every person who will ever live.

Before proceeding, let me add the following. As the literature cited in note 28 reveals, many people have recognized that Dominance Principles fail in infinite cases. Moreover, many people have expressed a general skepticism about appealing to infinite cases in thinking about normative issues. Given the difficulty of intuitively grasping the infinite, the latter attitude is understandable. Nevertheless, I think it is deeply mistaken. I believe that if one is careful, one can usefully consider infinite cases when doing normative philosophy, and that there can be great philosophical payoff from doing so. I also believe that since it is very possible that we live in an infinite universe, it would be deeply problematic if our moral principles were only plausible for, and applicable to, finite realms.

Unfortunately, the issues connected with this topic are too complex to pursue here. Still, I believe that the infinite examples canvassed in this chapter are appropriate for the purposes to which I put them, and that we can usefully gain insight into this chapter's topics by considering them. I might add that many people assume that even if the Dominance Principles fail in infinite cases, surely they succeed in finite cases. However, I believe that this intuitively plausible position is also mistaken, for reasons that I have given elsewhere and won't repeat here.[29]

---

[29] For reasons relevant to rejecting the Personal Dominance Principle, even in finite cases, see my *Inequality*, New York: Oxford University Press, 1993; "Equality, Priority, and the Levelling Down Objection," in *The Ideal of Equality*, eds. Clayton, Matthew and Williams, Andrew, London: Macmillan

One might suppose that even if we agree that we should give normative priority to people over places and times, it is clear that we should treat space and time the same for the purposes of practical reasoning. However, I have serious doubts about that, as well.

Many people believe that the goodness of a life depends on more than just the sum total of utility in a life; it also depends, they think, on how that utility is spread throughout the course of life. Relatedly, many believe that the *shape* of a life matters, so that, for example, a life that begins poorly but steadily improves and ends well, would be better than one that begins well, but steadily worsens and ends poorly.[30] So, supposing that 10 represented a poor quality life, and 100 a high quality life, an eighty-year life that was at level 10 for the first twenty years, level 40 for the second twenty years, level 70 for the next twenty years, and level 100 for the final twenty years would be judged, by many, as better than one that was at level 100 for the first twenty years, level 70 for the second twenty years, level 40 for the next twenty years, and level 10 for the final twenty years, even though the sum total of utility would be the same in the two lives. Here, the *temporal* order of events within the life of a person seems to have practical significance. However, nobody makes a similar claim about the *spatial* order of events within the life of a person. So, for example, a life that went from 10 in San Francisco, to 40 in Denver, to 70 in St. Louis, to 100 in Washington DC, would be no better or worse than one that went from 10 in Washington DC, to 40 in St. Louis, to 70 in Denver, to 100 in San Francisco.

Similarly, I am inclined to think that the shape or arc of life in the universe matters temporally, but not spatially, even if different civilizations that might exist in the universe lack the physical, psychological, or causal connections that lead us to speak of the narrative structure of an individual life. That is, imagine that there might be a hundred unconnected civilizations scattered throughout the universe, and that the average level (of quality of life) in civilization 1 was 100, the average level in civilization 2 was 200, the average level in civilization in 3 was 300, and so on, with the average level in civilization 100 being 10,000. Next imagine that level 100 is a very poor quality of life, and level 10,000 an exceptionally high quality of life, and that improvements in the quality of life are accompanied by similar sized improvements in scientific and artistic achievements, as well as social, political,

---

and St. Martin's Press: 126–61, 2000; "Egalitarianism Defended," *Ethics* 113: 764–82, 2003; "Personal versus Impersonal Principles: Reconsidering the Slogan," *Theoria* 69: 20–30, 2003; and *Rethinking the Good: Moral Ideals and the Nature of Practical Reasoning*, New York: Oxford University Press, 2012. For reasons relevant to rejecting the Spatial and Temporal Dominance Principles, even in finite cases, see *Rethinking the Good* and "Rationality with Respect to People, Places, and Times," *Canadian Journal of Philosophy* 45: 576–606, 2015.

[30] See, for example, David Velleman, "Well-Being and Time," in *The Possibility of Practical Reasoning*, Oxford: Oxford University Press, 2000, 56–84; Michael Slote, "Goods and Lives," in *Goods and Virtues*, Oxford: Oxford University Press, 1984, 9–37; Francis Kamm, "Rescuing Ivan Ilyich: How We Live and How We Die," *Ethics*, 113, 2003, 202–33; and my own *Rethinking the Good*, chapter 3.

and moral advances. Finally, imagine that each civilization persisted for a period of 50,000 years.

We can now imagine four different scenarios. In the first scenario, the hundred civilizations are arrayed throughout time. The first civilization arises and persists in a given galaxy for 50,000 years and then dies out. One billion years later, long after all remnants of the first civilization have disappeared, the second civilization arises and persists for 50,000 years in the same galaxy, and then dies out. One billion years later, long after all remnants of the second civilization have disappeared, the third civilization arises and persists for 50,000 years in the same galaxy and then dies out, and so on. So, in the first scenario, though the different civilizations are wholly unrelated to each other, causally or otherwise, the arc of life within the universe is steadily getting better and better with the passage of time, as each successive civilization is, by hypothesis, better along every significant dimension of value than its predecessor.

The second scenario is analogous to, thought the reverse of, the first. Once again the hundred civilizations are arrayed through time, but in this scenario it is civilization 100 that arises first, persists for 50,000 years, and then dies out, followed a billion years later by unconnected civilization 99, which also persists for 50,000 years, and then dies out, followed a billion years later by unconnected civilization 98, and so on. So, in the second scenario, though the different civilizations are wholly unrelated to each other, causally or otherwise, the arc of life within the universe is steadily getting worse and worse with the passage of time, as each successive civilization is, by hypothesis, worse in terms of every significant dimension of value than its predecessor.

In the third scenario, each of the hundred civilizations is contemporaneous with each other. They each arise at the same time, persist for 50,000 years, and then die out. However, they each exist in different galaxies, roughly one billion parsecs apart, that lie along a roughly linear path throughout the universe. Looking from a certain perspective, civilization 1 exists in a galaxy which we might arbitrarily call galaxy 1, civilization 2 exists in a galaxy to the "right" of galaxy 1, which we might arbitrarily call galaxy 2, the third civilization exists in a galaxy to the "right" of galaxy 2, which we might arbitrarily call galaxy 3, and so on, until, finally, located roughly 100 billion parsecs to the right of the first galaxy, civilization 100 exists in galaxy 100.

The fourth scenario is analogous to, though the reverse of, the third. All hundred civilizations exist simultaneously, but on this scenario it is civilization 100 that exists in galaxy 1, civilization 99 that exists in galaxy 2, civilization 98 that exists in galaxy 3, and so on, with civilization 1 existing in galaxy 100, roughly a hundred billion parsecs to the right of galaxy 1.

Reflecting on these four scenarios, my own view is that the first scenario, where there is steady improvement from civilization to civilization along every relevant value dimension, is better than the second scenario, where there is steady deterioration from civilization to civilization along every relevant value dimension. Moreover, I have this view even though, by hypothesis, the first and second scenarios are equally good in terms of utility and, importantly, the *same people* exist in both scenarios, and *there is no one who is better off in the first scenario than they are in the second*. As between the third and fourth scenarios, however, I am *completely indifferent*. I believe that each would be equally good.

Not everyone will accept my view regarding the difference between the first and second scenarios, but many will. And most will agree with me regarding scenarios three and four. If, in fact, I'm right about these scenarios, then we do not, and should not, treat time and space the same for the purposes of practical reasoning. In these cases, at least, relative locations in time seem to have a practical significance that relative locations in space do not. Moreover, relative location in time can have normative significance in its own right, independently of its effects on the quality of lives of the people living in an outcome.

Consider next the following thought experiment. Suppose I learn that our civilization will live in our galaxy another 10,000 years, and then die out. I also learn that in a distant galaxy another advanced civilization will exist for the same 10,000 years and then die out. I then learn that this is also the case in some third and fourth distant galaxies. I find this all quite interesting. It is somewhat *pleasing* to me to learn that there are, in fact, advanced civilizations living in galaxies far away.

Next, suppose I also learn that beyond the fourth galaxy there is nothing but cold, empty, space. This, too, I find interesting. However, I must confess that learning that fact doesn't bother me very much. Indeed, if events beyond the fourth galaxy were about to unfold which would make those distant reaches inhospitable to all life forms, I wouldn't think it *especially* important for us to make significant sacrifices, if we could, to prevent that from happening.

Suppose, on the other hand, I vary the story. As before, I learn that civilization in our galaxy will die out in 10,000 years, but I learn that after ours dies out another advanced civilization will arise and persist for 10,000 years in a second galaxy. I also learn that this will happen again, a third and fourth time. But after that, I learn, there will be *nothing* but cold, empty, space, *forever*. For some reason, *that* knowledge would bother me a *lot*. Indeed, if events were about to unfold which would make the universe uninhabitable for any life forms 40,000 years from now, unless we made significant sacrifices to prevent that from happening, I would feel quite *strongly* that we should do so, and I would feel that way even if I knew that *our* civilization was going to die out in 10,000 years, and that the distant future civilizations would do nothing to further *our* particular hopes or projects. Here, as above, I treat time and space differently for the purposes of practical reasoning. Roughly, I think it very important that vast *temporal* periods be filled with high quality life, but much less important that vast *spatial* regions be filled with high quality life.

Samuel Scheffler has argued that having descendants, who will help realize some of our deepest hopes, projects, or ideals, helps to give our lives value and meaning that they would otherwise lack.[31] Scheffler's views are entirely compatible with my own, and I am happy to accept them. But, they point to *other* reasons why one might be more concerned about the future than about what happens elsewhere in space than those I am trying to illuminate here. As my example makes plain, I believe that even if the future civilizations were wholly unrelated to our own, and would do *nothing* to further *our* particular hopes, projects, and ideals, I *still* believe that there would be strong reason to ensure that such civilizations would exist if they would have high quality lives. In addition, I believe that such reasons would be stronger than any we would have to ensure, were it possible, that such civilizations obtain elsewhere in space contemporaneous with our own.

Similarly, Jeff McMahan has suggested a variety of considerations that might lead us, in general, to give greater weight to there being high quality sentient lives existing in the future, than to there being high quality sentient lives existing elsewhere in space.[32] According to McMahan, these might include views we have about the importance of the preservation of value, views about the importance of progress, and views about the importance of greater diversity of experiences. My response to McMahan is threefold.

First, as with what I said about Scheffler's view, I don't regard my position as incompatible with McMahan's. Depending on the details of the case, there could be more than one reason for valuing the existence of *future* civilizations over the existence of contemporaneous civilizations elsewhere in *space*. But second, in certain of my examples, I wasn't, in fact, assuming that there was greater diversity of experiences over time than across space, nor was I assuming that there would be *progress* between our current civilization and the future, unrelated, civilizations. Thus, my views about such cases weren't, in fact, turning on such factors. Moreover, importantly, I note that the notions of *preservation* of value, and *progress*, have a temporal dimension built in to them, but not a spatial dimension. So, McMahan's suggestions regarding those factors would, if correct, not be a *rival* to my own, but rather a further elucidation of some of the *reasons* why we should treat space and time differently for the purposes of practical reasoning.

Let us consider, next, a related example to the previous one.[33] This example involves four scenarios in which a *vast* number of people—ten billion billion—are going to each live for a hundred years. Suppose that the very same people will exist in each scenario. Suppose, further, that in scenarios five and six, each person is going to suffer *miserably* for the duration of her life, while in scenarios seven and

---

[31] In *Death and the Afterlife*, New York: Oxford University Press, 2013.
[32] In personal communication, October 2, 2015.
[33] This example was suggested to me by Jeff McMahan, after a talk that I gave to Oxford's Moral Philosophy Seminar, Spring, 2016.

eight, each person is going to *flourish* for the duration of her life. In particular, suppose, that in scenarios five and six each person's life will be well *below* the level at which life ceases to be worth living, so that at each moment of her life she will wish that she had never been born, and will rationally want her life to end as soon as possible; while in scenarios seven and eight each person's life will be well *above* the level at which life ceases to be worth living, so that at each moment of her life she will be glad that she had been born, and will rationally want her life to continue as long as possible. Finally, suppose that in scenario five, all of the miserable people will live during the same hundred-year period, distributed across a billion different planets spread throughout space, before and after which the universe will be empty, while in scenario six, all of the miserable people will live on a single planet, but be distributed temporally, so that for hundred billion straight years, there will always be ten billion miserable people in existence. Likewise, suppose that in scenario seven, all of the flourishing people will live during the same hundred-year period, distributed across a billion different planets spread throughout space, before and after which the universe will be empty, while in scenario eight, all of the flourishing people will live on a single planet, but be distributed temporally, so that for a hundred billion straight years, there will always be ten billion flourishing people in existence.

Reflecting on these different scenarios, I believe that scenario five is better than scenario six, and that scenario eight is better than scenario seven. Moreover, I believe this even though, by hypothesis, all four scenarios involve the very same people, and even though there is no difference in the quality of lives of the people in scenarios five and six, and no difference in the quality of lives of the people in scenarios seven and eight. I realize that not everyone will share my view, but based on the reactions to these scenarios of many audiences in many different countries, it is clear that many do. Those of us who have these views are treating space and time differently. Furthermore, we believe that there can be normative significance to how the good is distributed temporally, *beyond* the impact that such distribution may have on the quality of people's lives. We think it important that different periods of time be filled with large numbers of high quality lives, and that different periods of time *not* be filled with large numbers of miserable lives. In addition, we think it is much less important that different regions of space be filled with large numbers of high quality lives, and that different regions of space not be filled with large numbers of miserable lives.

Here is a different example. Suppose that God has decided to populate an infinite number of planets with sentient beings whose lives would be *miserable*. In addition, She has decided to populate an infinite number of time periods, of one hundred years each, with sentient beings whose lives were *miserable*. Her plan is to have ten billion miserable beings living on planet one billion and one, during time period one billion and one, ten billion *different* miserable beings living on planet one billion and two, during time period one billion and two, ten billion *different* miserable beings living on planet one billion and three, during time period one billion and three, and so on, for all of eternity. Just before doing so, God decides that She will create the *very same* miserable beings as She was originally intending to, and that each of them will live during the *very same* time periods as She was originally intending for them, but that She will *shift* which particular *planets* they occupy, so that *each* person's *spatial location* would be different. Specifically, suppose that God decides to put the people who *would* have occupied planet one billion and one on planet one, instead; the people who *would* have occupied planet one billion and two on planet two, instead; the people who *would* have occupied planet one billion and three on planet three, instead, and so on. One might, if one likes, imagine that each of an infinite number of planets are spaced an equal distance apart, say k miles, along an infinite, straight, Euclidean line, so that God's choice involves placing each person on the planet She originally intended for them, or, instead, shifting each person k billion miles in the same direction along the line of planets to a different planet. To my mind, the difference between these two prospects has no moral significance. As between *these* options, in which everything would be the same except for *where* in *space* the infinite people would live, I would be utterly indifferent.

Suppose next, however, that God decides that She will create the *very same* miserable beings and place them on the *very same* planets as She was originally intending to, but that She will shift *when* they live. Specifically, suppose that God decides to put the people who *would* have occupied time period one billion and one in time period one, instead—on the assumption that time period one begins a hundred billion years *earlier* than time period one billion and one; that She decides to put the people who would have occupied time period one billion and two in time period two, instead; the people who would have occupied time period one billion and three in time period three, instead; and so on. I find the difference between *these* two prospects to be morally significant. Notwithstanding the so-called "fact" of infinity that tells us that, over the course of time, there will be just *as much* miserable existence in each of the two alternatives, and notwithstanding the fact that, by hypothesis, there will be no individual who is worse off in either of the two alternatives, I believe there is reason to favor God's original plan, over Her revised plan, in which miserable existence will begin a hundred billion years *earlier*, and then continue, unabated, afterwards. Here, too, I believe that the temporal distribution of goodness has practical significance beyond its impact on the quality of people's lives, and that it has a significance that spatial distribution of goodness either lacks entirely or possesses to a lesser degree.

The considerations presented here are hardly conclusive. However, they suggest several tentative conclusions.

First, although goodness can be "located" in persons, space, and time, there is reason to doubt the wholly impersonal perspective of certain classical utilitarians, which would require us to be completely neutral about *where* the good is located.

Moreover, this is unrelated to standard objections that have been raised against utilitarianism that appeal to distributive principles such as justice, equality, or priority, and also unrelated to standard deontological objections that have been raised against utilitarianism based on agent-relative duties, permissions, or prohibitions, or the special relations that different individuals bear to others.

Second, in some contexts, at least, it appears that we should give preference to how the good is distributed across people, rather than to how it is distributed across space and time. Also, in some contexts at least, it appears that we should give preference to how the good is distributed across time, rather than to how it is distributed across space.

Third, in general, it is important that large temporal regions contain high quality life, and seemingly less important that large spatial regions be filled with high quality life.

Fourth, in some contexts at least, rearranging or shifting the temporal location of goods may have practical significance, and this is so *independently* of there being anyone *for whom* such rearranging or shifting is good. This is another respect in which it appears that we should treat space and time differently for the purposes of practical reasoning, since it appears that merely rearranging or shifting the spatial location of goods lacks practical significance, *independently* of the extent to which such rearranging or shifting would be good *for* someone, or would be accompanied by a relevant shift in the temporal location of the good.

7.5 Some Open Questions Concerning a Capped Model of Ideals

In light of the foregoing considerations, let me next return to some of the questions broached at the end of section 7.3, concerning the scope of a Capped Model of Ideals. One question I asked is whether a Capped Model applies to the whole of the universe or to subsections of it, and if the latter, do the caps apply to different regions of space, different periods of time, or both? To help think about this question, consider Figure 7.5.

For the purposes of this discussion, I shall set aside the view that there may be no caps on lives above the Wonderful Level. If one holds that view, then one can imagine that in the cases I'm considering here, no lives are in fact above the Wonderful Level. The large blocks in Figure 7.5 represent outcomes that include vastly large numbers of people who are extraordinarily well off, living in civilizations that are extraordinarily advanced artistically, scientifically, socially, politically, and morally. Moreover, the outcomes represented by the large blocks extend across arbitrarily large expanses of space and time. Perhaps each is the size of a solar system, and persists for ten million years, but perhaps each is the size of a galaxy and persists for ten billion years. The small blocks in Figure 7.5 represent

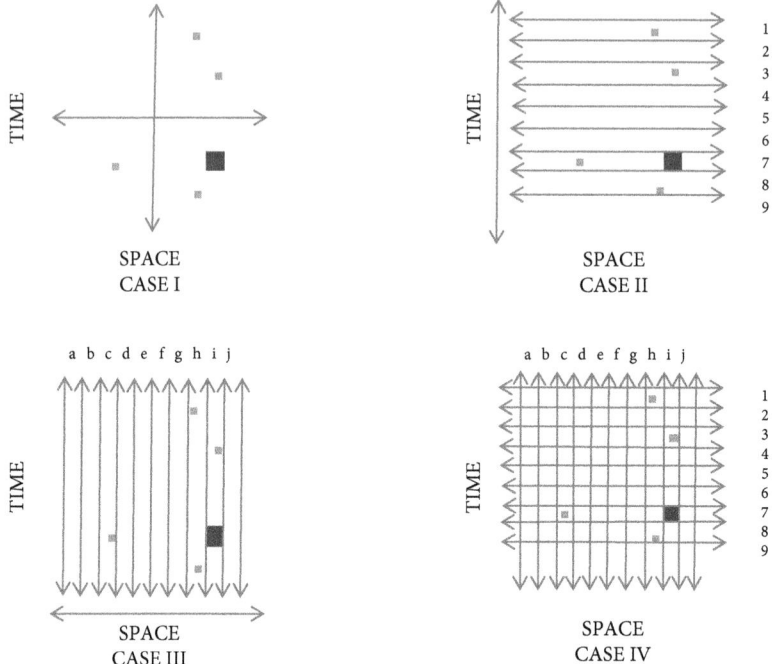

Figure 7.5 Diagram Five

outcomes that include large numbers of people who are very well off, but the people living in those outcomes are not as many, and not as well off, as those living in the outcomes represented by the large blocks. In addition, the outcomes represented by the small blocks extend across large expanses of space and time, but they are only a quarter the size and duration of the outcomes represented by the large blocks.

On the Capped Model of Ideals, there is an upper limit on how good any given outcome can be regarding each ideal, and also an upper limit on how good any given outcome can be all things considered. I shall assume that the outcomes represented by each large block in Figure 7.5 are *so* good regarding each relevant ideal that the upper limit has been reached by those outcomes, so that nothing could be done to make those outcomes better.[34] Cases I through IV represent four different ways of thinking about the scope of the Capped Model.

Case I represents the view that the caps of the Capped Model apply across *the entire universe*. So, on this view, if, in fact, the outcome represented by the large

---

[34] The presentation here involves a slight oversimplification. On some views of a Capped Model, one can approach, but never reach, the cap. Accordingly, one can always make an outcome *better*, but after a point nothing one can do can make the outcome *significantly* better, as it is already *so* close to the upper limit. I shall set aside this slight complication for ease of presentation.

block is already at the cap, then the universe is as good as it could be, and *nothing further* could be done to make the universe better. So, on this view, adding more people with high quality lives within the space and time period occupied by the large block would not improve the outcome, but neither would adding more people with high quality lives outside the space and time period occupied by the large block. That is, once the upper level had been reached by the outcome represented by the large block, there would be nothing *bad* if the entire rest of the spatial and temporal regions of the universe, no matter how vast, were entirely devoid of high quality life or advanced civilizations, and nothing objectively good about adding high quality lives and civilizations elsewhere in the universe. *A fortiori*, all the high quality lives of the people living in the outcomes represented by the four small blocks of Case I are otiose, from the standpoint of objective goodness. While the people living in the areas where there are small blocks have lives that are *subjectively* good *for them*, that these people exist, with lives worth living, does not make the outcome *objectively* better.

Case II represents the view that caps apply to different time periods of arbitrarily large length. On this view, having already reached the cap in time period seven, merely adding more people with high quality lives elsewhere in space during that same time period would not make the outcome objectively better. So, on this view, the high quality lives of the people living in the outcome represented by the small block in time period seven of Case II is otiose, from the standpoint of objective goodness. On the other hand, the existence of high quality lives represented by the small blocks in time periods one, three, and eight do make the universe better. Moreover, improving the lives of the people living in those outcomes (as opposed to improving the lives of the people living in the outcome represented by the small block in time period seven) would make the outcome objectively better, as well as subjectively better for the people whose lives we had improved. Furthermore, adding high quality lives and advanced civilizations in every other time period currently devoid of people (periods two, four, five, and six, as well as all of those time periods preceding time period one, and following time period nine) would make the universe objectively better.

Case III is analogous to Case II, but it represents the view that caps apply to different *spatial* areas, rather than temporal periods, of arbitrarily large size. On this view, having already reached the cap in spatial area i, merely adding more people with high quality lives elsewhere in time within the same spatial area would not make the outcome objectively better. So, on this view, the high quality lives of the people living in the outcome represented by the small block in spatial area i of Case III is otiose, from the standpoint of objective goodness. On the other hand, the existence of high quality lives represented by the small blocks in spatial areas c and h do make the universe better. Moreover, improving the lives of the people living in those outcomes (as opposed to improving the lives of the people living in the outcome represented by the small block in spatial area i) would make the outcome objectively better, as well as subjectively better for the people whose lives we had improved. Furthermore, adding high quality lives and advanced civilizations in every other spatial area currently devoid of people (areas a, b, d, e, f, g, and j, as well as all those spatial areas preceding spatial area a, and following spatial area j) would make the universe objectively better.

Case IV represents the view that caps apply to *both* spatial and temporal areas of arbitrarily large sizes. On this view, having already reached the cap in the spatial and temporal area (i, seven), merely adding more people with high quality in that particular spatial and temporal area would not make the outcome objectively better. However, the existence of high quality lives represented by the small blocks in the spatial and temporal areas (h, one), (i, three), (c, seven), and (h, eight) does make the universe objectively better. Moreover, one could improve the universe further by improving the lives and civilizations in those areas, adding more people with high quality lives and advanced civilizations to those same areas, or adding high quality lives and advanced civilizations to any spatial and temporal areas of the universe currently devoid of people.

My own view is that if we choose to accept a Capped Model, we should either go with a version reflected by Case II, or a version reflected by Case IV. Case II reflects the view that it is important that different temporal regions be filled with flourishing beings, but not important that different spatial regions be filled with flourishing beings. Case IV reflects the view that it is important that *both* temporal and spatial regions be filled with flourishing beings. Even if we accept the sort of view reflected by Case IV, we might do so in a way that attaches *more* weight to filling different temporal regions with high quality life than different spatial regions with high quality life. On such a view, all of the extra high quality lives represented by the small blocks in Case IV would add additional objective value to the outcome beyond that already contributed by the large block of spatial temporal region (i, seven); however, the small blocks present in the spatial temporal regions (h, one) and (h, eight) would add the most extra value to the outcome, in virtue of obtaining in both spatial and temporal regions that would otherwise be empty, the small block present in the spatial temporal region (i, three) would add the next most extra value, in virtue of obtaining in a temporal region, but not spatial region, that would otherwise be empty, and the small block present in the spatial temporal region (c, seven) would add the least extra value, in virtue of obtaining in a spatial region, but not temporal region, that would otherwise be empty.

Let us take stock of a few of our results. If one accepts a Capped Model of positive ideals, at least for certain comparisons, but still believes, as I do, that it is important for different time periods to be filled with advanced civilizations and high quality lives, then one will want a version of the Capped Model reflected by Cases II or IV of Figure 7.5. Similarly, if one accepts a Capped Model of positive ideals, at least for certain comparisons, and believes, as I do, that it would be better for vast numbers of high quality lives to be distributed throughout different time periods than for everyone to exist during a single time period distributed throughout space, then one will want a version of the Capped Model reflected by Case II of Figure 7.5, or a version reflected by Case IV of Figure 7.5, but one that implies that filling distinct time periods with high quality life counts for more than filling distinct spatial periods with high quality life. Of course, if one thinks that once a sufficient number of high quality lives obtain in a given time period there is *no* value in adding high quality lives elsewhere during that same time period, then one should favor a version of the Capped Model reflected by Case II of Figure 7.5, and reject a version reflected by Case IV of Figure 7.5. On the other hand, if one believes there is always *some* value in filling empty regions of space with high quality lives during any given time period, no matter how many high quality lives already exist in some other populated spatial regions during that same time period, then one should favor a version of the Capped Model reflected by Case IV over one reflected by Case II. And, of course, if one accepts a Capped Model for certain comparisons, but still believes that it is important, and equally so, to fill both empty spatial regions and empty temporal regions with high quality lives, then one should reject a version of the Capped Model reflected by Case II in favor of one reflected by Case IV that does not prioritize filling time with high quality lives over space with high quality lives, and, correspondingly, one should reject my previous suggestion that it would be better for vast numbers of high quality lives to be distributed throughout different time periods than for vast numbers of high quality lives to exist during a single time period distributed throughout space.

The preceding has direct implications for an argument that Parfit offers against a version of the Asymmetry according to which adding more people with lives worth living to an already existing population which involves many high quality lives does not make an outcome better, but adding more people with lives worth *not* living to an outcome always makes the outcome worse. Parfit's argument appeals to:

The Absurd Conclusion: In one possible outcome, there would exist during some future century both some population on the Earth that is like the Earth's present actual population, and an enormous number of other people, living on Earth-like planets that had become part of the Solar System. Nearly all of the people on these other planets would have a quality of life far above that enjoyed by most of the Earth's actual population. In each ten billion of these other people, there would be one unfortunate person, with a disease that makes him suffer, and have a life that is not worth living.

In a second possible outcome, there would be the same enormous number of extra future people, with the same high quality of life for all except the unfortunate one in each ten billion. But this enormous number of extra future people would not all live in one future century. Each ten billion of these people would live in each of very many future centuries.

On our view [the Asymmetry], the first outcome would be very bad, much worse than if there were none of these extra future people. The second outcome would be very good. The first would be very bad and the second very good even though, in both outcomes, there would be the very same number of extra future people, with the very same high quality of life for all except the unfortunate one in each ten billion.[35]

Of the Absurd Conclusion, Parfit writes,

The first outcome is exactly like the second, except that all of the extra future people live in the same rather than in different centuries. If the second outcome would be very good, and the first outcome differs only with respect to *when* people live, how can this difference in timing make the first outcome very bad?[36]

In challenging the Asymmetry, Parfit is expressing the neutralist perspective of the classical utilitarian that requires us to be *neutral* between different times, and to treat places and times the same from a practical perspective. Parfit's view may also draw plausibility from a *welfarist view*, according to which, ultimately, the goodness of an outcome depends *solely* on the extent to which that outcome is good or bad *for* the sentient members of that outcome. Thus, on the welfarist view, *if* the same people were to live in two outcomes, and be equally well off in each, then the two outcomes *must* be equally good.

Both the neutralist perspective and the welfarist view have great intuitive plausibility. However, as I have shown elsewhere, there are powerful reasons to reject the welfarist view,[37] and as our discussion here illustrates, there are also

---

[35] *Reasons and Persons*, pp. 410–11. See chapter 18 of *Reasons and Persons*, "The Absurd Conclusion," for Parfit's original and fascinating discussion of many of the issues that I am grappling with here. Unfortunately, though our understanding of the topics that Parfit launched has in many ways significantly advanced, many of the most fundamental problems that he discovered remain unresolved.

[36] *Reasons and Persons*, p. 411.

[37] See "Harmful Goods, Harmless Bads," "Equality, Priority, and the Levelling Down Objection," and "Personal versus Impersonal Principles: Reconsidering the Slogan," *Theoria* 69, 2003: 20–30. Although I believe the welfarist view is deeply mistaken, I readily acknowledge that it has great initial plausibility, and that it is widely accepted. The roots of the welfarist view lie in classical utilitarianism, and it is accepted, typically without argument, by most economists and other social scientists. The deep, unquestioned commitment to the Pareto Principle that most economists have is one reflection of this view (where, roughly, the Pareto Principle holds that, where the same people are involved, one outcome must be better than another if it is better for at least one person, and worse for no one). Among philosophers, Roger Crisp and Nils Holtug are two of the many proponents of welfarism. See Crisp's *Reasons and the Good*, Oxford: Oxford University Press, 2006; and Holtug's *Persons, Interests, and Justice*, Oxford: Oxford University Press, 2010.

reasons to reject the neutralist perspective. There may well be good reason to treat time and space differently for the purposes of practical reasoning. Moreover, while *mere* differences in spatial or temporal location may have no practical significance, such differences *can* have practical significance depending on the context in which those differences obtain.

For certain comparisons, at least, something like a Capped Model of positive values or ideals seems correct. And I have suggested that *one* plausible version of the Capped Model of positive values that one might accept is represented by Case II in Figure 7.5. If one accepts such a view, and combines it with an *Uncapped Model* of negative values or ideals, then the so-called Absurd Conclusion need no longer seem absurd. On such a combination of views, adding lots more people with lives worth living to an outcome that already contains a large number of people with lives worth living won't make the outcome better, if it occurs within the same temporal region, while adding lots more people with lives worth not living within the same temporal region will always make the outcome worse. This explains how it *could* be the case that adding *lots* of planets with ten billion well off people and one miserable person during the *same* time period that a lot of other people already exist with lives well worth living could, ultimately, make the outcome bad, all things considered. It also explains how it *could* be the case that adding *lots* of planets with ten billion well off people and one miserable person during *different* time periods that would otherwise be devoid of people could be very good, as the high quality lives in each such period would make the outcome better and outweigh the negative impact of the single miserable life within each period.

Of course, by adopting a version of the Capped Model of positive values reflected by Case IV in Figure 7.5, one could hold that while, in accordance with the Asymmetry, adding lots more people to a given spatio-temporal region that was already at the cap for positive values could make the outcome worse, even if the ratio between high quality and miserable lives added was ten billion to one; adding such lives to *different* spatial or temporal regions that would otherwise be devoid of sentient beings would make the outcome *better*. However, as we have seen, one could hold this and still hold that it would be *better* to populate different temporal regions with planets containing ten billion well off people and one miserable person, than different spatial regions with such planets.

We see, then, that even if one accepts the Asymmetry, one needs to come to terms with the proper scope of that view, along the lines we have been discussing. Moreover, on some plausible versions of doing that, the so-called Absurd Conclusion would *not* be absurd, and differences in *when* people lived could be practically relevant to an outcome's goodness.

Let me conclude this section with several observations and queries, many of which merit further consideration, but which I cannot pursue here.

First, elsewhere I have argued that many ideals are *impersonal* in nature, meaning that their realization has value *distinct* from the extent to which their realization is good or bad *for* anyone.[38] The value of filling different periods of time (and/or regions of space) with high quality lives or advanced civilizations would be impersonal in this sense. Accordingly, while in some cases, such as the one exemplified by Figure 7.4, we rightly give priority to people over time, in others, it might be appropriate to give priority to time over people. Thus, just as we don't merely care about *how much* utility obtains in a given outcome, but also care about how the *distribution* of that utility *affects* people for better or worse, so, we may also rightly care about how utility is distributed throughout different temporal periods (and perhaps spatial regions). These are two different legitimate normative concerns, and either may have greater normative weight than the other depending on the case in question.

Second, I have suggested that we may need to invoke something like a Capped Model to capture certain judgments that we make. However, I have not claimed, nor do I think it is true, that the Capped Model can plausibly capture all of our judgments about the goodness of outcomes. In fact, I believe that the Capped Model, or something like it, is relevant for making certain kinds of comparative judgments about the goodness of outcomes, but not others.

Third, I have not taken a stand on whether we should accept a Capped Model of Ideals for negative ideals or disvalue. Many find it hard to believe that there is a lower limit beyond which an outcome couldn't become (significantly) normatively worse regarding such factors as suffering, injustice, or inequality. However, it is not clear whether one can plausibly reconcile a Capped Model for positive ideals for certain comparisons with an Uncapped Model for negative ideals for all comparisons.

Fourth, any Capped Model will face charges of being arbitrary and ad hoc, and this is especially so for those whose scope is less than the entire universe. For example, what could possibly set the upper limit for how good an outcome could be regarding ideals like utility, perfection, or autonomy? Perhaps merely adding more people to an outcome that already has ten billion high quality lives in it wouldn't make the outcome better, regarding utility, but why think one will already have reached the upper limit with ten billion such lives, rather than a hundred billion such lives, or a hundred billion billion such lives? Likewise, if one believes that the Capped Model applies to different temporal or spatial regions, how could one possibly determine the relevant temporal and spatial boundaries in a non-arbitrary manner? Should we look at temporal regions of 50,000 years, or fifty million years, or fifty billion years, or what? And should we focus on planet-sized regions that may or may not vary with the size of the planet; or solar-system-

[38] Ibid.

sized regions that may or may not vary with the size of the solar system; or galaxy-sized regions that may or may not vary with the size of the galaxy; or what? There don't appear to be any principled answers to such questions; yet, as should be apparent, different answers will often generate very different answers regarding the relative goodness of different outcomes.

Fifth, relatedly, is it really plausible to believe that significantly improving the lives of people, or adding billions of additional high quality lives, might do *nothing* to (significantly) improve the overall objective goodness of an outcome if such changes took place on one side of a temporal or spatial boundary where the cap might already have been reached, and yet might have a significant positive impact on the overall objective goodness of the outcome if such changes took place just on the other side of such a boundary, perhaps only a few miles, or moments, away?[39]

Sixth, if one adopts a Capped Model whose scope is anything less than the entire universe, then one will seemingly face variations of the Repugnant Conclusion across different temporal and spatial regions. Suppose, for example, that one adopts a version of the Capped Model represented by Cases II or IV of Figure 7.5. Suppose further that the large block in those cases represents an outcome in which the upper limit has been reached for how good an outcome can be—it is filled with countless high quality lives and countless advanced civilizations spanning some significant temporal and spatial regions. Then just imagine a single oyster-like life being lived in *innumerable* other temporal regions. If the caps only apply within given temporal and spatial regions, then, if only there are *enough* of them, wouldn't the overall good of the oyster-like lives obtaining in the innumerable temporal periods be greater than the overall good obtaining in the temporal and spatial region that is filled with incredibly high quality lives and incredibly advanced civilizations? Does this suggest that if one of the main motivations of the Capped Model of Ideals was to help us avoid implications like the Repugnant Conclusion, then we need to adopt a version whose scope applies to the entire universe after all? Or could there be different caps—caps both within and between different spatial and temporal regions, that would enable us to capture most of what we want to say about these topics?

Addressing these many questions and concerns remains, in my judgment, one of the most important, and underexplored areas of population ethics and practical reasoning more generally.

---

[39] One is reminded here of Pascal's biting remark on humanmade "justice" and the "ethics" of war: "Why are you killing me for your own benefit, I am unarmed?" "Why, do you not live on the other side of the water? My friend, if you lived on this side, I should be a murderer, but since you live on the other side I am a brave man, and it is right" (Blaise Pascal, *Pensées*, translated by A.J. Krailsheimer, New York: Penquin Classics, 1966, p. 44 (fragment 293)). Note, one can slightly lessen the philosophical sting of the worry expressed in the text by invoking "thick" borders between regions with separate caps, or perhaps by invoking vagueness. However, lessening the sting of the worry is a far cry from removing it altogether.

7.6 Conclusion

Let me conclude this chapter with a summary of some of my main claims. In section 7.2, I noted how careful reflection on the "The Repugnant Conclusion and Some Other 'Box' Cases" in population ethics leads to a host of important normative insights and conclusions. These include the following.

- Rejecting both total and average utilitarianism.
- Distinguishing between personal and impersonal values.
- Distinguishing between subjective and objective goodness.
- Recognizing that "goodness ain't in the head" and that we might need both an objective list theory of the goodness of outcomes, and an objective list theory of the goodness for individuals, depending, for example, on whether we believe that a human life might be bad in a way that a contented oyster's life would not, even if the mental lives of the two were phenomenologically indistinguishable.
- Recognizing an important kernel of truth to the claim that we want to make people happy, but are neutral about making happy people.
- Recognizing that numerous important qualifications must be made to the claim that we are neutral about making happy people; some of which may involve distinguishing between a Wonderful Level, a Neutral Range, and a Restricted Level—so that, other things being equal, adding more people above the Wonderful Level would improve an outcome's goodness, adding people below the Restricted Level would be objectively bad, and so detract from an outcome's goodness, even if such people had lives that were subjectively worth living, and adding people within the Neutral Range (between the Wonderful and Restricted Levels) would, in a large set of cases, neither improve nor detract from an outcome's goodness.
- Noting that there are important asymmetries in our thinking regarding lives that are above the zero level and lives below the zero level.
- Recognizing that if there is no Restricted Level, then while both the Same Number Quality Claim, Q, and the Different Number or General Quality Claim, GQ, will be plausible for comparing large populations whose members all have lives that are above the zero level, only Q will be plausible for comparing populations whose members have lives that are below the zero level.
- Recognizing that if there is a Restricted Level, then while both Q and GQ will be plausible for comparing large populations whose members all have lives that are above the Restricted Level, only Q will be plausible for comparing populations whose members have lives that are below the Restricted Level.

In section 7.3, on "The Capped Model of Ideals," I suggested that many people implicitly accept two positions that I called the Standard Model of Utility and the Standard Model for Combining Ideals. I noted that while both positions are natural and may be plausible for certain contexts of comparison, together they entail the Repugnant Conclusion. Hence, if we want to avoid the Repugnant Conclusion, we must develop an alternative approach for assessing outcome goodness for comparing outcomes like A and Z. I proposed the Capped Model of Ideals as one possible approach for comparing such outcomes. On the Capped Model, there is an upper limit to how good any outcome can be with respect to any individual ideal, and also an upper limit on how good an outcome can be, all things considered.

I noted that the Capped Model has a fair amount of intuitive plausibility, reflecting the view that no matter how important any given ideal may be, no single ideal is more important than every other ideal *combined*. I noted that a Capped Model seems to underlie our thinking in a range of cases. For example, it helps explain the view that to be the best all-around gymnast, it is not enough to be extraordinarily great regarding any single gymnastic skill and, similarly, to be a highly virtuous person, it is not enough to possess any single virtue to an extraordinary degree. I then showed how a Capped Model of Ideals could plausibly capture and explain most people's views regarding the Repugnant Conclusion.

Although I find the Capped Model attractive for a wide range of cases, I acknowledged that it is not plausible for other cases, implying that it must be limited in scope. I also acknowledged that we might seek another model for explaining the judgments for which it seems plausible. In addition, I noted several further topics and worries that advocates of a Capped Model will need to address. First, there is the question of whether there should be a single cap for each ideal, or whether any given ideal might have more than one cap. Second, there is the question of whether, in accordance with the Asymmetry, one should accept a Capped Model for positive values or ideals, but reject a Capped Model for negative values or ideals, and whether one could give a principled, non-ad hoc justification for such a combination of views that is both consistent and avoids unacceptable implications. Third, I noted that if one adopts a Capped Model, one must address a host of difficult questions concerning the model's scope.

In section 7.4, "Neutrality Intuitions, Dominance Principles, and the Relative Normative Significance of People, Spaces, and Times," I took up a series of largely unexplored questions for practical reasoning that the field of population ethics opens up. In particular, I asked whether, setting aside cases involving special relations, we should be utterly neutral with respect to people, spaces, and times and, relatedly, whether we should treat people, spaces, and times the same for the purposes of practical reasoning. I offered numerous examples and considerations to suggest that we should not.

In particular, I suggested that temporal location may have a significance that spatial location lacks. I also suggested that it matters greatly that different temporal regions be filled with high quality sentient life, but that it matters much less, if at all, that different spatial regions be filled with high quality life. On my view, there are cases in which we should, in essence, give preference to people over times and spaces, and to times over spaces. However, controversially, I also believe that in certain cases we should, as it were, give preference to times over people. In essence, this is because I believe there is impersonal value in filling different temporal regions with high quality sentient life, and that such value can, at least in some cases, outweigh the personal disvalue associated with losses in individual wellbeing.

In section 7.5, "Some Open Questions Concerning a Capped Model of Ideals," I addressed one of the questions, raised at the end of section 7.3, concerning the scope of a Capped Model of Ideals. I considered four different approaches one might adopt: caps are set for the entire universe, caps are set for different temporal regions, caps are set for different spatial regions, or caps are set for both temporal and spatial regions. I noted how these approaches might account for different judgments that people might make regarding my examples. I also noted that the second and fourth approaches would provide a way of responding to Parfit's Absurd Conclusion, a position which implicitly adopts both the perspective that we should be neutral between different locations of the good in time and space, and the welfarist view that all goods are only good to the extent that they are good for sentient beings. I noted that my examples cast doubt on the first assumption, and that there are powerful reasons to doubt the second assumption as well, once one recognizes that, as noted in section 7.2, there can be impersonal ideals as well as personal ideals.

Importantly, any Capped Model that reflects the judgment that it is important that different temporal or spatial regions be filled with high quality sentient life will be attaching *impersonal* value to the filling of temporal or spatial regions. In other words, on such a view, there is a value to having different temporal or spatial regions be filled with high quality life that is *distinct* from the extent to which such situations are *good for* the sentient beings who inhabit those temporal or spatial regions.

I noted that any Capped Model is open to the charge of being arbitrary or ad hoc, since there seems to be no principled reason to set the cap for any given ideal at one place rather than another. I further noted that charges of being arbitrary, ad hoc, and implausible will especially plague those versions of the Cap Model that don't take the entire universe as their scope. This is because there is no principled reason for fixing the size of the relevant temporal or spatial regions one way rather than another, yet whatever sizes one chooses will significantly impact how good or bad an outcome is deemed to be. Relatedly, it may seem deeply implausible that adding new people, or greatly improving the quality of lives of a group of people, might have (virtually) *no* effect on the overall goodness of an outcome, or a *great* effect on the overall goodness of an outcome, depending on which side of a temporal or spatial boundary it happened to take place. Additionally, I noted that any Capped Model that applies caps to temporal or spatial regions smaller than the entire universe will, if there are a large number of such regions, face versions of the Repugnant Conclusion, unless one can come up with a plausible way of having different caps both within and across the different temporal and spatial regions. Since one of the reasons for moving to a Capped Model in the first place was to avoid implications such as the Repugnant Conclusion, it will be particularly damaging to any version of the Capped Model if it ends up facing an analog of the Repugnant Conclusion.

Overall, my discussion in section 7.5 suggested that much more thought needs to be given to the motivation, justification, and defense of different versions of the Capped Model or alternatives to it, and the general question of how best to aggregate both within and between different lives *and values* to determine the comparative goodness of different outcomes. This remains among the most important, vexing, and underexplored areas of population ethics, and practical reasoning more generally.

Let me end with the following observations. As noted in my introduction, when Parfit first began using his simple figures to explore various issues in population ethics, a common reaction was to ask "What do *boxes* have to do with ethics?" I think it is safe to say that that question has long since disappeared from the minds of Parfit's readers. Even so, however, I believe that Parfit's work opened up whole areas for philosophical exploration which remain largely underappreciated.

The fact is that Parfit's "box ethics" has ramifications that extend far beyond the topic of population ethics and our obligations to future generations. Indeed, Parfit's curiosity opened up its own Pandora's box of puzzles and problems that remain largely unsolved and deeply perplexing. It is part of Parfit's extraordinary legacy that many future generations of philosophers will need, and want, to contend with the many brilliant insights and complex issues that he has given us. I take some comfort in the thought that through his own unstinting, shining example, Parfit, like Pandora herself, has provided us with *hope* that if humankind manages to survive the next few generations, we may one day finally be up to the task of adequately coming to terms with the brilliant insights and deep paradoxes that Parfit has unleashed upon the world.[40]

---

[40] I'd like to express my gratitude to the Editors for all their hard work in bringing this volume to fruition and, especially, to Jeff McMahan, for his acute editorial comments on my chapter, and his indispensable role in making these volumes a reality and a fitting tribute to Derek Parfit. I'd also like to thank the members of my moral theory reading group, Shelly Kagan, Frances Kamm, and Jeff McMahan, for excellent feedback over many years on many of the topics discussed in this chapter. Finally, my biggest debt, by far, is to Derek Parfit, whose discussion with me of these topics, and others, over the course of forty years was an unending source of inspiration, excitement, and pure philosophical joy.

8
Totalism without Repugnance

Jacob M. Nebel

8.1 Introduction

According to

> **Totalism**: One distribution of well-being is better than another just in case the one contains a greater sum of well-being than the other.

Many philosophers, following Parfit (1984), reject totalism on the grounds that it entails

> **The Repugnant Conclusion:** For any number of excellent lives, there is some number of lives that are barely worth living whose existence would be better.

Consider, for example, a population of ten billion flourishing human beings. Totalism seems to imply that it would be better if there were instead some much larger number of psychologically simple creatures—e.g., oysters or newborn infants—whose short lives were filled only with mild pleasures. As Parfit (2016, 110) puts it, "There might be [a greater sum of happiness] in the lives of many people who each had very little happiness, just as there might be some greater mass of milk in a vast heap of bottles that each contained only one drop."

To avoid the repugnant conclusion, many philosophers have suggested alternatives to totalism. But these alternatives have consequences that seem even more implausible than the repugnant conclusion, and none of them can claim the allegiance of more than a handful of philosophers. The search for a plausible

---

My greatest debt is to Derek Parfit for supervising my BPhil thesis (Nebel 2015), from which this material is drawn, and for his encouraging and endlessly generous feedback. I would also like to thank Tim Campbell, Joe Carlsmith, David Clark, Kara Dreher, Jimmy Goodrich, Ben Holguín, Karsten Klint Jensen, Harvey Lederman, Jeff McMahan, Samuel Scheffler, Trevor Teitel, and Teru Thomas for helpful comments and discussion.

Jacob M. Nebel, *Totalism without Repugnance* In: *Ethics and Existence: The Legacy of Derek Parfit.* Edited by: Jeff McMahan, Tim Campbell, James Goodrich, and Ketan Ramakrishnan, Oxford University Press. © Oxford University Press 2022.
DOI: 10.1093/oso/9780192894250.003.0009

alternative to totalism may, to some, have the feel of a degenerating research program.

Some philosophers suggest that, in light of the failure to develop a plausible alternative to totalism, we should embrace the repugnant conclusion, claiming that its intuitive repugnance is misleading. Many of these philosophers surmise that we find the repugnant conclusion repugnant because we underestimate the value of a life that is barely worth living.[1] We think of the excellent lives as much like our own, and the barely-worth-living lives as very much worse than ours. But perhaps *our* lives, those of affluent Westerners, are barely worth living. If we have a sufficiently high standard for a life worth living, then we may no longer find the repugnant conclusion repugnant. And if we are willing to accept the repugnant conclusion, then perhaps we should embrace totalism after all.

There is, however, a negative analogue of the repugnant conclusion, which becomes even more repugnant as our standard for a life worth living increases. According to the *negative* repugnant conclusion, for any number of horrible lives, there is some number of people whose existence would be worse, even though each of their lives would be very nearly worth living.[2] This negative repugnant conclusion seems, to many people, no less repugnant than the original repugnant conclusion. But it is especially repugnant if we have a high standard for a life worth living.[3] If, for example, the lives of most affluent Westerners are barely worth living, then a life that is very nearly worth living might be only slightly worse than those of most affluent Westerners. But it seems repugnant that some population of people whose lives are only slightly worse than those of most affluent Westerners would be *worse* than one of, say, billions of people who are tortured for their entire lives.

Totalism seems to entail both the repugnant and negative repugnant conclusions. The repugnant conclusion seems very hard to avoid. And if we try to make the repugnant conclusion seem acceptable, the negative repugnant conclusion seems even worse. So it seems that totalism will have unacceptable implications no matter what.

In this chapter, I speculatively develop a version of totalism that avoids the repugnant conclusion, along with its negative analogue. I am not the first to suggest that totalism can avoid the repugnant conclusion. Griffin (1988, 340, n. 27) observes that arguments for the repugnant conclusion questionably assume that well-being is "measurable on a single continuous additive scale, where low numbers, if added to themselves often enough, must become larger than any initial, larger number." Others point out that, by rejecting this structural assumption, totalists can avoid the repugnant conclusion.[4] However, few philosophers

---

[1] For example, Tännsjö (2002); Ryberg (2004); Huemer (2008).
[2] See Blackorby et al. (1998); Carlson (1998).   [3] As Mulgan (2002) observes.
[4] See Crisp (1988); Portmore (1999); Kitcher (2000); Thomas (2018); and Carlson (forthcoming).

seem to have taken this suggestion very seriously. Most writers on population ethics simply assume that totalism entails the repugnant conclusion.[5] This assumption is reasonable because no one, to my knowledge, has developed a plausible version of totalism that makes good on Griffin's suggestion. It is far from clear how quantities of well-being can be aggregated and compared in a sensible way that allows totalism to avoid the repugnant conclusion. The main task of this chapter is to explore how that might be done.

The theory of welfare aggregation sketched in this chapter appeals to a kind of lexical superiority, which I motivate and relate to the repugnant conclusion in section 8.2. The idea that some goods might be lexically superior to others is not new, of course. It is at least as old as Mill (1863); some attribute it to Aristotle. But lexical superiority, as it is standardly developed and understood, is implausibly extreme and open to seemingly decisive objections. Even Rawls, who assigns lexical priority to the basic liberties in his theory of justice, thinks that "in general, a lexical order cannot be strictly correct" (1999, 40). What is most novel and important about the theory studied here is how it makes progress on these problems. I develop the theory and explain how it can help address some long-standing problems for lexical superiority in sections 8.3–8.5. Although my discussion focuses on lexical superiority in well-being, particularly in the context of population ethics, my strategy may be of independent interest, for example, to the growing literature on lexical tradeoff structures in decision theory.[6]

8.2 Well-Being

In this section, I explain how some number of excellent lives could contain a greater sum of well-being than any number of lives that are barely worth living (for brevity, *mediocre*). This may seem impossible because we tend to assume that well-being has a certain structure, which I describe below. This structural assumption leads totalism to the repugnant conclusion and its ilk. I explain how we can reject this assumption, thereby avoiding the repugnant conclusion and its negative analogue.

In discussions of population ethics, writers typically represent distributions of well-being via boxes or lists of real numbers, where the height of a box or the number in a slot represents the value of a life or lives. A neutral life, which marks the boundary between good lives and bad lives, is normalized to zero. The value of an excellent life might then be represented by a number greater than or equal to 100; the value of a mediocre life might be represented by a positive number less

---

[5] See, e.g., Arrhenius (2000); Cowen (1996); Huemer (2008); Parfit (2016); Sider (1991); Temkin (2012).
[6] See Tversky (1969); Luce (1978); Manzini and Mariotti (2012).

than or equal to 1. If our numbers faithfully represent these values, then this means that an excellent life is at least 100 times better than a mediocre life.

This kind of representation encourages the assumption that well-being is a scalar quantity—that is, a quantity that can be represented by a single real number. The assumption that well-being has the structure of the real numbers is significant. For the real numbers satisfy the Archimedean property: for any positive real numbers x and y, there is some natural number n such that $nx > y$. If the value of an excellent life and that of a mediocre life can be faithfully represented by positive real numbers, then, for any number of excellent lives, there must be some number of mediocre lives whose existence would contain more total value—no matter how little value is added by each mediocre life, and no matter how much value is added by each excellent life. (Recall Parfit's analogy to drops of milk.) Totalism therefore leads straight to the repugnant conclusion.

But well-being is not like milk: it has many dimensions and is not, as Sen (1980) puts it, a "homogeneous magnitude" (193). It is a substantive and controversial assumption that these distinct values, as they are realized in any life, can be reduced to a scalar quantity.

To illustrate the importance of this insight, consider a single-person analogue of the repugnant conclusion. McTaggart (1927, volume II: 452–53) imagines two lives. One life lasts for a million years and is excellent throughout with respect to "knowledge, virtue, love, pleasure, and intensity of consciousness." The other, "oyster-like" life has "very little consciousness," has "a very little excess of pleasure over pain," and is "incapable of virtue or love." McTaggart thinks that, if the oyster-like life is long enough, it would be better. Call this *McTaggart's conclusion*. As McTaggart predicts, many of us find this conclusion repugnant.[7]

It is a desideratum of a solution to the repugnant conclusion that it can be extended in a natural way to avoid McTaggart's conclusion. There are, of course, important differences between the two conclusions. For example, there is someone for whom an extended life is better, but, some philosophers believe, there is no one for whom an expanded population is better. Other things being equal, however, a uniform solution to the two problems seems preferable. To see this, consider what we might call the *mundane* conclusion: for any number of very long *oyster-like* lives, there is some number of very short oyster-like lives whose existence would be better. This conclusion is not repugnant or even implausible. If we are willing to accept the mundane conclusion but not the repugnant conclusion, then our diagnosis of the repugnant conclusion should appeal to the richer values that characterize excellent lives and distinguish them from mediocre (e.g., oyster-like) lives.

---

[7] See also McMahan (1981); Parfit (1986); Cowen (1989); Temkin (2012). McMahan (1985, 260–62) uses a single-life analogue of the repugnant conclusion to motivate a lexical view in population ethics.

McTaggart's conclusion might be avoided in a number of different ways. One possibility is that the marginal value of pleasure diminishes quickly enough that there is a finite upper bound on the value of a life that contains only pleasure. As the life gets arbitrarily long, its value approaches a finite limit, which might be less than the value of an excellent life of sufficient length.

I find it hard to believe that pleasure has diminishing marginal value for the person who experiences it. Pleasure might plausibly have diminishing marginal value for creatures who get bored, or who can remember their past experiences. But we can imagine that the oyster-like creature has neither of these features. Intuitively, the second half of this creature's life could add just as much value to its life as the first half. The two halves might even involve qualitatively identical experiences. But even if an appeal to diminishing marginal value were plausible in the intrapersonal case, it is less plausible in the interpersonal case. Appeals to diminishing marginal value violate the intuitive *separability* of lives.[8] The goodness of conferring some benefit on one person, or of bringing some people into existence, intuitively should not depend on how many other people enjoy that benefit or already exist—e.g., on distant planets. The separability of lives can neatly explain why, when making decisions that impact population size or well-being, we can ignore the welfare of unaffected people on distant planets. But if lives had diminishing marginal value, then a life's contribution to the value of an outcome would depend on how many other people exist, and on how well off they are. So, assuming that the effects of our choices on the value of outcomes sometimes bear on what we ought to do, facts about unaffected people on distant planets would sometimes bear on what we ought to do. That seems hard to believe. I, therefore, doubt that an appeal to diminishing marginal value is the best way to avoid McTaggart's conclusion.

It may seem impossible to avoid McTaggart's conclusion if additional pleasure always makes a life better, by some nondiminishing amount. That is what McTaggart thought. But the apparent impossibility relies on a scalar conception of well-being. Suppose that the value of any life can be represented by a real number, and that ingredients of well-being—the kinds of things that make life worth living—increase the value of that life by a nondiminishing amount. Let some positive real number y represent the value of an excellent life that lasts for a million years. And suppose that each year of the oyster-like life is good to degree x (where $0 < x < y$). There must, by the Archimedean property, be some natural number n such that $nx > y$. So an oyster-like life, if sufficiently long, could contain enough pleasure so that its value would exceed that of the excellent life.

Suppose, however, that we reject a scalar conception of well-being. We might follow Sen in viewing well-being as fundamentally a *vector* quantity—i.e.,

---

[8] Broome (2004); see also Mulgan (2001).

representable as a list of components. For simplicity, suppose that the ingredients of well-being can be reduced to two dimensions, which (following Kitcher 2000) we can call the important (i) and the trivial (t). Suppose that the values of both dimensions can be represented by real numbers with no upper or lower bound. I wish to remain neutral regarding the content of these dimensions of well-being. But, for purposes of avoiding McTaggart's conclusion, the important dimension might include things like virtue, knowledge, and friendship, with the trivial dimension being restricted to mild sensory pleasures.

These vectors might be ordered lexically—first, by their values along the important dimension and, second, by their values along the trivial dimension. More precisely, according to what we'll call the *standard lexical ordering*, $(i_1, t_1) \geq (i_2, t_2)$ iff either

1. $i_1 > i_2$, or
2. $i_1 = i_2$ and $t_1 \geq t_2$.

The standard lexical ordering entails that if one life is better than another along the important dimension, then it is better overall. Between two lives that are equally good along the important dimension, the better one is the one that is better along the trivial dimension. This ordering can easily be generalized to any number of dimensions.[9]

If the mild pleasures of an oyster-like life increase its value only along the trivial dimension, then the standard lexical ordering allows us to avoid McTaggart's conclusion. No matter how long the oyster-like life is, its value will never surpass a life that is good in the important ways.

Many conceptions of well-being fit this kind of structure. Mill is often held to believe that the higher "pleasures of the intellect, of the feelings and imagination, and of the moral sentiments" are lexically superior to the lower pleasures of "mere sensation" (1863, ch. 2). Ross places virtue "at a point higher on the scale of value than that which pleasure ever reaches" (1930, 150). And Gurney (1887) suggests that some duration of torture would be worse than any duration of moderate pain. On these views, some dimensions of well-being (or ill-being) have lexical priority over others, in the sense that at least some gain or loss along the more important dimensions outweighs any gain or loss along more trivial dimensions of value.

Some might characterize the difference in value as *infinite*. But, following Rabinowicz (2003), we should distinguish between infinite and lexical superiority. One reason is that, if some good is infinitely valuable, then the expected value of any act with nonzero probability of realizing that good is also infinite, so we cannot discriminate between the expected values of acts with different nonzero probabilities of realizing that good. Lexical views raise other problems in uncertain

---

[9] See Chipman (1960).

cases (as we'll see in section 8.5), but they avoid this one. Moreover, if some good is infinitely more valuable than another, then any dose of the higher good, however small, would outweigh any amount of the lower. That is true for the standard lexical ordering above, but we'll later consider a kind of lexical superiority that avoids this consequence. Before we depart from the standard lexical ordering, though, let's see how this kind of structure would allow totalists to avoid the repugnant conclusion.

Say that a life is neutral iff it is neutral in the important ways ($i = 0$) and in the trivial ways ($t = 0$), that a life is barely worth living iff it is neutral in the important ways ($i = 0$) and good in the trivial ways ($t > 0$), and that a life is excellent only if it is good in the important ways ($i > 0$). Vector quantities of well-being can be added by adding their components: the sum of $(i_1, t_1), ..., (i_n, t_n)$ is $(\Sigma_{k=1}^{n} i_k, \Sigma_{k=1}^{n} t_k)$. The resulting sums can be compared by the standard lexical ordering. Any population of excellent lives would then contain a greater sum of well-being than any population of lives that are barely worth living, because the latter will be worse along the important dimension.[10] Totalism would then avoid the repugnant conclusion.

This strategy can also allow totalists to avoid the negative repugnant conclusion that, for any number of horrible lives, there is some number of lives that are very nearly worth living whose existence would be worse. This conclusion can be avoided so long as a horrible life is negative in the important ways ($i < 0$), and a life that is nearly worth living is neutral in the important ways ($i = 0$) and negative in the trivial ways ($t < 0$). Any population of horrible lives would then contain a lower sum of well-being than any population of lives that are nearly worth living.

Some might be uncomfortable with my characterization of this strategy as consistent with totalism. I can see two possible reasons for this discomfort. The first is our conception of well-being as a vector quantity. But Sen (1980) makes a good case for why all proponents of "utility-supported moralities," on various theories of well-being, should prefer a vector conception of utility. And vector quantities can be summed, just like scalar quantities. The second is the lexical ordering of these vector quantities. But Chipman (1960, 221) goes so far as to *define* utility as "a lexicographic ordering, represented by a [...] vector with real components." And Mill is often interpreted as a utilitarian with something like a lexical view about pleasure. So restricting "totalism" to exclude a lexical ordering

---

[10] Cf. Kitcher (2000, 573). Kitcher describes but neither endorses nor defends this strategy; he emphasizes that it "may *just* be a formal solution" to his impossibility theorem. Nor does he apply it to the negative or single-life analogues of the repugnant conclusion. And, for reasons that emerge in sections 8.3–8.5, I reject the standard lexical ordering to which Kitcher appeals. Similar remarks apply to Thomas (2018) and Carlson (forthcoming), who use formalizations much like Kitcher's in response to Arrhenius's impossibility theorems. See also List (2004, 130), who considers an aggregation function much like Kitcher's in a very different context.

of vector-valued well-being levels seems to me unmotivated. The core commitment of totalism is preserved: the more well-being, the better.

We might, however, worry that other versions of the repugnant conclusion could still slip through the cracks.[11] This would be true if the important components of well-being could come in arbitrarily small amounts. For we could then imagine a vast population of people who barely instantiate the important goods. And it may be repugnant to conclude that some such population would be better than a smaller one in which people's lives are much better in the important ways.

A complete response to this objection would require a theory of well-being. This is because we would need to know what the important things are like in order to know whether they can come in arbitrarily small amounts, and whether it would be repugnant to conclude that some population of people whose lives are barely good in the important ways would be better than a smaller one in which people's lives are much better in the important ways. I wish to remain neutral about what makes life worth living. But there are, I believe, plausible theories of well-being on which the objection can be answered.

On some views, the important dimensions of well-being cannot take arbitrarily small values. The simplest cases involve binary dimensions. For example, the lives that are most worth living might be ones that are meaningful[12] or autonomous.[13] Although people can be more or less autonomous and have more or less meaningful lives, we might care most about whether we are (sufficiently) autonomous, or whether our lives are (sufficiently) meaningful. We might think that a world filled with enough free agents or meaningful lives, if they are sufficiently happy, contains more of what makes live worth living than a world filled with any number of unfree agents living meaningless lives, however happy they are. Such views could avoid seemingly repugnant conclusions along the important dimension.[14]

On other views, the important things can come in very small amounts, but a life that is barely good in such ways would have to be quite good overall. This might be true if the important dimension is a composite of other values. Griffin (1988, 86), for example, holds that a sufficiently long life with certain global properties—"satisfying personal relations, some understanding of what makes life worth while, appreciation of great beauty, the chance to accomplish something with one's life"—would be better than any length of life containing "just enough surplus of simple pleasure over pain to go on with it." If a positive i-value requires all of these

---

[11] This kind of objection is pressed by Ryberg (1996).
[12] Smuts (2013); see also Frankfurt (1999), Audi (2005), Wolf (2010).
[13] See Griffin (2002); Mulgan (2006).
[14] I supposed above that the important component can be represented by any real number. But, if we accept a view like the ones mentioned in this paragraph, we might instead restrict the important dimension to two (Kitcher 2000) or three (Manzini and Mariotti 2012) values. Mandler, Manzini, and Mariotti (2012) argue that sequences of such coarse-grained criteria can serve as the basis for surprisingly rich models of rational choice.

features, then it need not be repugnant to conclude that a vast population of lives with low i-value would be better than a smaller population in which people's lives are much longer and filled with even more of these goods. Many other philosophers have suggested similar views, which give great weight to combinations of various goods and holistic properties of lives.[15]

Sen's own conception of the good life can be understood as a sort of hybrid of the approaches I have mentioned, appealing to combinations of valuable properties with coarse-grained structure. Sen understands quality of life primarily in terms of "the capability to achieve valuable functionings" (Sen 1993, 31, 1985). Functionings are states and activities of a person—e.g., being well-nourished, being respected, working in meaningful ways, participating in public life. Sen places great weight—on some interpretations, lexical weight[16]—on one's ability and liberty to achieve those functionings. Although capabilities can come in degrees, we might care primarily about the presence or absence of a capability, so that arbitrarily small improvements in capability do not improve one's life along the important dimension. And, because many different kinds of functionings matter, many different capabilities matter. As Sen (1985, 202) recognizes, there is also a kind of interdependence between capabilities and functionings: some capability sets require valuable functionings in the first place, and some functionings can only be manifested by choice and ability. It is, therefore, plausible that if a person's capability set is sufficiently rich, so that her life is at all good in the important ways, then her life must be quite good all things considered. Sen's capabilities approach, so understood, may be able to avoid intuitively repugnant conclusions along the important dimension.

As these remarks suggest, totalism's avoidance of seemingly repugnant conclusions is no *fait accompli*. Much depends on what, in fact, makes life worth living. For example, hedonists who reject the lexical priority of any pleasures or pains cannot avoid the repugnant conclusion within the framework of totalism. But if totalists instead value combinations of goods, or properties with coarse-grained structure, then they can avoid seemingly repugnant conclusions along the important dimension. Some philosophers might hope for a solution to the repugnant conclusion that is neutral between all substantive theories of well-being.[17] But it seems to me that the plausibility of different methods of aggregating "the amount of whatever makes life worth living" (Parfit 1984, 387) should depend on what one thinks makes life worth living. We should not reject an otherwise attractive theory

---

[15] See, e.g., Broad (1938) on McTaggart's conclusion, and Dorsey (2009) on "lives for headaches."
[16] See Nussbaum (2000) and Pettit (2001).
[17] I suspect that this hope motivates Parfit (1986)'s appeal to *perfectionism*, according to which any loss of "the best things in life" makes things worse, no matter how much else is gained. Parfit doesn't claim that there is *less well-being* in a world with fewer of the best things in life, because this would rule out some plausible theories of well-being. Instead, he claims that such a world is *worse* even if it contains much more well-being.

of interpersonal aggregation just because it is less plausible according to certain theories of well-being. Indeed, it is progress to discover that different theories stand or fall together.

8.3 Lexical Thresholds

We have seen how a scalar conception of well-being leads totalism to the repugnant conclusion. I suggested that we follow Sen in viewing well-being as, fundamentally, a vector quantity. This picture of the structure of well-being, along with a lexical ordering of well-being vectors, would allow totalists to avoid the repugnant conclusion, the negative repugnant conclusion, and McTaggart's conclusion.

The standard lexical ordering, however, seems implausible. It entails that a single excellent life would be better than any number of mediocre lives. It entails that a single horrible life would be worse than any number of lives that are nearly worth living. And it entails that a person's life is improved by an arbitrarily small gain along the important dimension, no matter how much she loses along the trivial dimension. These consequences seem extreme. In this section, we'll consider a new view which avoids these consequences.

8.3.1 Superiority and Noninferiority

Arrhenius and Rabinowicz (2005) distinguish between two kinds of lexical superiority:

Strong Superiority: For any value-bearers x and y, x is strongly superior to y just in case any quantity of x would be better than any quantity of y.

Weak Superiority: For any value-bearers x and y, x is weakly superior to y just in case some quantity of x would be better than any quantity of y.

The standard lexical ordering implies that the important components of welfare are strongly superior to the trivial components. That seems implausibly extreme. Most proponents of lexical views in population ethics seem to have weak superiority in mind. Griffin, for example, suggests that "[p]erhaps it is better to have a *certain* number of people at a certain high level than a very much larger number at a level where life is just worth living" (1988, 340, emphasis mine). But it is not clear how totalists can maintain weak superiority without collapsing into strong superiority. Let me explain.

I mentioned earlier that lives are intuitively separable: the contribution that a life makes to the value of an outcome should not depend on the existence or welfare of other people in the outcome. According to

Separability: For any populations X, Y, and Z, X is at least as good as Y just in case adding X to Z would be at least as good as adding Y to Z—i.e., a population composed of X and Z would be at least as good as a population composed of Y and Z.

This principle allows us, when assessing the effects of our acts on the goodness of outcomes, to ignore the existence and welfare of people who are unaffected—e.g., people who are long dead or who exist on distant planets. But a problem arises if we accept, in addition to separability, the following two principles:

Transitivity: For any value-bearers X, Y, and Z, if X is at least as good as Y, which is at least as good as Z, then X is at least as good as Z.

Completeness: For any value-bearers X and Y, either X is at least as good as Y, or Y is at least as good as X.

On these assumptions, weak superiority collapses into strong superiority (Jensen 2008). Suppose that excellent lives are weakly but not strongly superior to mediocre lives. Then there must be some number of excellent lives—say, ten billion—whose existence would be better than any number of mediocre lives, but also some number of excellent lives—say, one—whose existence would not be better than some number of mediocre lives—say, one million. Completeness implies that one million mediocre lives would, therefore, be at least as good as one excellent life. We could then apply separability: adding one million mediocre lives to a population of one million other mediocre lives (i.e., two million mediocre lives) would be at least as good as adding a single excellent life to that same population (i.e., one million mediocre lives plus one excellent life); adding one million mediocre lives to a population of one excellent life (i.e., one million mediocre lives plus one excellent life) would be at least as good as adding a single excellent life to that same population (i.e., two excellent lives). By transitivity, two million mediocre lives would be at least as good as two excellent lives. We could then apply separability and transitivity again to conclude that three million mediocre lives would be at least as good as three excellent lives. This reasoning can be iterated to show that some number of mediocre lives would be at least as good as ten billion excellent lives. But that is inconsistent with our hypothesis that ten billion excellent lives would be better than any number of mediocre lives.

It does not matter which numbers we choose. If we accept separability, completeness, and transitivity, then the weak superiority of excellent lives entails their strong superiority.

Strong superiority seems implausible. And I take transitivity as sacrosanct. Some might reject separability. But, to the extent that the value of outcomes bears on what we ought to do, separability is very attractive. Separability lets us easily explain why, when making decisions that affect population, we can ignore the welfare of people who are long dead or who exist on distant planets. And it is a core feature of totalism. Without separability, it is hard to see how the value of a population could be understood as the *sum* of each individual's well-being. It is, at the very least, worth exploring possible views that maintain separability while avoiding strong superiority.

I propose that totalists reject completeness: some populations are neither better than, worse than, nor equally as good as some alternatives. Many people would independently reject completeness in other contexts. Consider the albums *Revolver* and *Rubber Soul*. Neither seems better than the other. Nor do they seem equally good. We can imagine that the Beatles added a great song to *Revolver*, resulting in *Improved Revolver*. Although *Improved Revolver* might be better than *Revolver*, this need not make *Improved Revolver* better than *Rubber Soul*. If *Revolver* and *Rubber Soul* were equally good, then *Improved Revolver* would be better than *Rubber Soul*. So *Revolver* and *Rubber Soul* must not be equally good. These two albums, many would argue, are *incommensurable* in value.

Similarly, totalists might judge some populations to be incommensurable with respect to their sums of well-being, and therefore with respect to their value.[18] This claim would allow totalists to maintain separability, transitivity, and the weak superiority of excellent lives, while rejecting their strong superiority. Again, some might resist my characterization of this package of views as consistent with totalism, on the grounds that incommensurable quantities of well-being cannot be summed. But, as we saw in section 8.2, vector quantities of well-being can be summed component by component; this can be done regardless of how the resulting sums are ordered (e.g., according to the standard lexical ordering or in some other way that violates completeness, as we'll soon see). Furthermore, totalists might reject completeness for reasons having nothing to do with population ethics. For example, interpersonal comparisons of well-being might be too

---

[18] Many others have appealed to the idea of incommensurability in population ethics (see Blackorby, Bossert, and Donaldson 1996; Qizilbash 2007, 2018; Rabinowicz 2009; Chang 2016; Parfit 2016; Frick 2017; Gustafsson 2019; Bader, forthcoming). What primarily distinguishes the present proposal is the particular *source* of incommensurability identified—i.e., in the structure of well-being—which raises independently interesting issues even in fixed-population ethics (see Nebel 2020). (Unfortunately, since writing this chapter, I have come to have serious doubts about the possibility of incommensurability; see Dorr, Nebel, and Zuehl 2021.)

imprecise, in principle, to yield a complete ordering, but this is compatible with additive aggregation (as Sen 1970b emphasizes). And many "ideal" utilitarians (e.g., Laird 1936, 256) reject completeness on the grounds that different goods are too heterogeneous to be compared with much precision.

Although totalists can deny that any number of excellent lives would be better than any number of mediocre lives, they cannot allow any number of excellent lives to be *worse* than any number of mediocre lives. We can distinguish between two kinds of *noninferiority*:

> **Strong Noninferiority:** For any value-bearers x and y, x is strongly noninferior to y just in case no quantity of x would be worse than any quantity of y.
>
> **Weak Noninferiority:** For any value-bearers x and y, x is weakly noninferior to y just in case some quantity of x would not be worse than any quantity of y.

Excellent lives are strongly noninferior to mediocre lives just in case no number of excellent lives would be worse than any number of mediocre lives. Excellent lives are weakly noninferior to mediocre lives just in case some number of excellent lives would not be worse than any number of mediocre lives.

The repugnant conclusion is that, for any number of excellent lives, some number of mediocre lives would be better. Avoiding this conclusion requires excellent lives to be weakly noninferior to mediocre lives. But if excellent lives are weakly noninferior to mediocre lives, then, given separability and transitivity, they must also be strongly noninferior to mediocre lives.[19] Suppose that excellent lives are *not* strongly noninferior to mediocre lives: there is some number m of mediocre lives whose existence would be better than some number n of excellent lives. We can show by induction that, for any natural number q, qm mediocre lives would be better than qn excellent lives. The base case, in which $q = 1$, is given: we have supposed that m mediocre lives would be better than n excellent lives. The inductive step is that, for any natural number q, if qm mediocre lives would be better than qn excellent lives, then $(q+1)m$ mediocre lives would be better than $(q+1)n$ excellent lives. To prove the inductive step, assume that qm mediocre lives would be better than qn excellent lives. By separability, $(q+1)m$ mediocre lives would be better than qn excellent lives plus m mediocre lives: it is better to add qm mediocre lives to a population of m mediocre lives than it is to add qn excellent lives to that same population. Moreover, the base case implies, by separability, that qn excellent lives plus m mediocre lives would be better than

---

[19] The proof follows the same strategy as Jensen (2008), although Jensen's assumes completeness and is concerned with superiority, not noninferiority.

$(q+1)n$ excellent lives. By transitivity, $(q+1)m$ mediocre lives would be better than $(q+1)n$ excellent lives. This proves the inductive step. So, by induction, for any natural number q, qm mediocre lives would be better than qn excellent lives. This would mean that excellent lives cannot be weakly noninferior to mediocre lives. For there would then be some q such that qn excellent lives would not be worse than any number, including qm, of mediocre lives. And we have just shown that, without strong noninferiority, this is impossible. Therefore, given separability and transitivity, weak noninferiority requires strong noninferiority.

If excellent lives are weakly noninferior to mediocre lives, then, given separability and transitivity, they must be strongly noninferior. But they needn't be strongly superior, so long as we reject completeness. If we were to assume completeness, then strong noninferiority would require strong superiority. For if no number of excellent lives would be worse than any number of mediocre lives, and if *not worse than* implied *at least as good as*, then, for any n and m, n excellent lives would be at least as good as m mediocre lives. Take $n = 1$. If a single excellent life would be better than any number of mediocre lives, then we have strong superiority. If a single excellent life would be *just as good* as m mediocre lives, then we are in trouble. For, according to totalism, if mediocre lives are worth living, then for any m, $m+1$ mediocre lives would be better than m mediocre lives. But if $m+1$ mediocre lives would be better than m mediocre lives, and if m mediocre lives would be just as good as a single excellent life, then $m+1$ mediocre lives would be better than a single excellent life. This contradicts strong noninferiority, according to which no number of mediocre lives would be better than any number of excellent lives. So the only option consistent with strong noninferiority when an excellent life is at least as good as m mediocre lives is for the excellent life to be better. Therefore, if totalists were to assume completeness, then strong noninferiority would collapse to strong superiority. By rejecting completeness, totalists can deny that any number of excellent lives would be better than any number of mediocre lives. But they cannot allow any number of excellent lives to be worse than any number of mediocre lives.

Some readers might balk at strong noninferiority. But it seems to me considerably more plausible than strong superiority. This is clearest in cases of risk, where (as we'll see in section 8.5) it seems hard for proponents of strong superiority to avoid absurd consequences. But it also seems to me independently reasonable to accept strong noninferiority while rejecting strong superiority. The difference between strong noninferiority and strong superiority may seem negligible when we consider the axiological claims in the abstract. But strong noninferiority and strong superiority differ greatly in their natural implications for what we ought to do. Let me mention a few examples to illustrate the difference. Suppose, in these cases, that the only relevant consideration is the goodness of outcomes, and that it is wrong to choose an outcome just in case it is worse than some alternative.

Suppose that some prisoner will be tortured for many years. We can either relieve a few hours of her agony or relieve the minor headaches of n people. If any amount of agony were worse than any amount of mild discomfort, then it would be wrong to relieve the headaches, no matter how large n is. But we might think that if n is large enough, it would not be wrong to relieve the headaches. Nor would it be wrong to relieve the few hours of torture, no matter how large n is. But if we could relieve the full duration of her torture, or even just a year of it, I think it would be wrong to relieve the mild headaches instead.

Or suppose that n people's lives are very nearly worth living, and that one person's life is excellent. We can benefit the n people by just enough to make their lives barely worth living, but this would have the side effect of transforming the single excellent life into a horrible life. If excellent lives were strongly superior to mediocre lives, and if horrible lives were strongly inferior to lives that are nearly worth living, then it would be wrong to benefit the n people, no matter how large n is. But we might think it permissible to benefit the n, if n is large enough, albeit not obligatory, no matter how large n is. However, if there were instead billions of excellent lives which would become horrible, it would seem to me wrong to bring about this side effect by benefiting the n people in trivial ways, no matter how large the n.

Or consider choices regarding a single life. Suppose that you have to make a decision on your friend's behalf. Her life will end in a few days, unless you put her in Nozick (1974)'s experience machine, where she would enjoy mild sensory pleasure for n years. If real-world goods were strongly superior to mild sensory pleasure, then it would be wrong to put her in the experience machine, no matter how large n is. But we might think it permissible—although not obligatory—to put her in the experience machine, if n is large enough. However, it would seem to me wrong to put her in the experience machine for *any* duration when the alternative is several decades of good life in the real world. This suggests that real-world goods are strongly noninferior, but not strongly superior, to mere sensory pleasure.

You might not share my judgments about these particular cases. The basic point, though, is that strong noninferiority is much less extreme than strong superiority because it leaves room for permissible tradeoffs between the important and trivial dimensions of well-being. I do not find it plausible that the most important components of well-being *ought* to be pursued at any trivial cost. But it may be more plausible that they are *worth* pursuing—i.e., that it is permissible to pursue them—at any trivial cost.

It is not enough, however, just to say that excellent lives are weakly superior and strongly noninferior, but not strongly superior, to mediocre lives. We need a model of how quantities of well-being can be compared in a way that makes good on these claims. That is our next task.

8.3.2 Multiple Thresholds

We are representing the sum of well-being in a distribution X as a vector (i_X, t_X), where i_X is the sum of the X-people's well-being in the important dimension(s), and t_X is the sum of the X-people's well-being in the trivial dimension(s). Some philosophers have considered the possibility of comparing distributions via the standard lexical ordering, according to which X is at least as good as Y iff either

1. $i_X > i_Y$, or
2. $i_X = i_Y$ and $t_X \geq t_Y$.

This ordering entails that important goods are strongly superior to trivial goods. If we reject strong superiority, we need a different way of comparing quantities of well-being.

We might begin by imposing a single *lexical threshold*, understood as the lowest value along the important dimension needed to outweigh any value along the trivial dimension.[20] Let us represent this threshold by Δ. Consider the view that quantitiy of well-being (i_X, t_X) is at least as great as quantity (i_Y, t_Y) just in case either

1. $i_X - i_Y > \Delta$, or
2. $i_X \geq i_Y$ and $t_X \geq t_Y$.[21]

This view is a generalization of the standard lexical ordering, which is obtained in the special case where $\Delta = 0$. I assume that Δ is a finite value that doesn't vary with the population or other features of the distribution. The lexical threshold makes it possible that neither of two populations is at least as good as the other, because one might have less of the trivial stuff but not sufficiently more of the important stuff to exceed the lexical threshold. Consider, for example, a population of one person whose life is excellent. This population might be incommensurable with, not better than, a vast population of mediocre lives.

However, the partial ordering above has counterintuitive consequences when some small gain along the important dimension is not enough to overcome the lexical threshold. Such a gain cannot outweigh any loss along the trivial dimension, however great or small. The "however great" side of this coin is, at least, more plausible than the analogous implication of the standard lexical ordering, which implies strong superiority. But the "however small" side has no appeal. Suppose,

---

[20] Mulgan (2006) uses "lexical threshold" to refer to something quite different. I believe that my concept also differs from Klocksiem (2016)'s notion of "threshold lexicality."

[21] Some might wonder why we should appeal to the *differences* in i-values at all. Some might suggest that X is better if i_X exceeds both i_Y and some threshold Δ. But that would violate separability: whether X is better than Y could depend on whether enough X-lives are excellent, even if those very same lives exist in Y.

for example, that A is better in the important ways than B, but not by enough to exceed the lexical threshold (e.g., our one-person population), and that B is barely better in the trivial ways (e.g., one short oyster-like life). The view under consideration says that A is not at least as good as B. But that seems wrong.

We can avoid this problem by imposing an additional threshold δ on the trivial dimension. We can represent B's trivial gain as $0 < t_B - t_A < \delta$. We might say that A's slight edge over B along the important dimension ($0 < i_A - i_B < \Delta$) outweighs this slight loss along the trivial dimension. But, if the trivial loss were much greater, so that it exceeded δ, then A would no longer be better than B, nor would A be worse. We can define δ as the greatest quantity along the trivial dimension that would be outweighed by a quantity of exactly Δ along the important dimension: $(\Delta, 0) > (0, \delta)$, but $(\Delta, 0) \not> (0, \delta + \epsilon)$, for any $\epsilon > 0$. We might then formulate the partial ordering as follows:

The Lexical-Threshold View: For any quantities of well-being (i_X, t_X) and (i_Y, t_Y), (i_X, t_X) is at least as great as (i_Y, t_Y) iff either

1. $i_X - i_Y > \Delta$, or

2. $i_X \geq i_Y$, and

   a. $t_X \geq t_Y$, or

   b. $\dfrac{i_X - i_Y}{t_Y - t_X} > \dfrac{\Delta}{\delta}$.[22]

Condition (1) says that if X is better than Y in the important ways by more than Δ, then X is at least as good as Y, no matter how much better Y is in the trivial ways. This secures weak superiority. (2) then states the two other ways in which X might be at least as good as Y. They both require X to be at least as good in the important ways. (2a) says that if X is also at least as good in the trivial ways, then X is at least as good as Y. (2b) matters when X is better than Y in the important ways by less than Δ, but worse than Y in the trivial ways. It asks us to compare the ratio of the differences along each dimension to the ratio of each dimension's threshold. If the ratio of the important gain to the trivial loss exceeds the ratio of Δ to δ, then X is at least as good as Y. This allows even small gains along the important dimension to outweigh minuscule losses along the trivial dimension.

---

[22] These ratios are meaningful so long as each dimension can be measured on a ratio scale. The different components of well-being needn't share the *same* scale, any more than density requires mass and volume to share the same scale.

The lexical-threshold view states conditions under which one quantity of well-being is greater than another. It is compatible with many different views about how the goodness of a distribution relates to its total quantity of well-being. *Lexical-threshold totalism* is the conjunction of the lexical-threshold view and totalism. The lexical-threshold view allows totalists to claim that some number of excellent lives would be better than any number of mediocre lives, and that, for any number of excellent lives, there is some *worse* number of mediocre lives, without claiming that *any* number of excellent lives would be better than any number of mediocre lives. Totalists can accept these claims—and analogous ones regarding negative well-being and length of life—by rejecting completeness and by imposing thresholds on multiple dimensions of well-being. In the next two sections, I argue that, by appealing to the lexical-threshold view, we can make progress on some of the most vexing problems that seem to afflict lexical views in any context, not just population ethics.

8.4 Marginal Differences, Incompleteness, and Vagueness

Lexical superiority (whether weak or strong) is most plausible when there are differences in kind, not merely of degree. But, as Parfit (1986, 20) observes, there are "fairly smooth continua" between excellence (e.g., Mozart) and mediocrity (e.g., muzak). If the difference between excellent lives and mediocre lives is one of degree, then it may be implausible to appeal to any kind of lexical superiority in well-being.

Consider a finite sequence of lives, ranging from the excellent (x_1) to the mediocre (x_n). Each life x_k might be qualitatively very similar to its successor x_{k+1}, seeming only slightly better with respect to each kind of thing that makes life worth living. Some philosophers argue that if x_1 were weakly superior to x_n—i.e., if some number of x_1-lives would be better than any number of x_n-lives—then some life x_k would have to be weakly superior to its successor x_{k+1}.[23] But it is implausible that some life should be so much better than a life that is qualitatively so similar to it. These philosophers, therefore, reject weak superiority.

These philosophers seem to endorse the following *sequence argument*:

Suppose that no life in the sequence is weakly superior to its successor. Then, for any number of x_k-lives, some number of x_{k+1}-lives must be better. By transitivity, for any number of x_1-lives, some number of x_n-lives must be better. So the x_1-lives couldn't be weakly superior to the x_n-lives. If the x_1-lives were weakly superior to the x_n-lives, then some life in the sequence would be weakly

---

[23] See Ryberg (2002); Arrhenius (2005).

superior to its immediate successor. But it is absurd that some life should be so much better than a life that is qualitatively so similar to it.

The sequence argument is an important challenge. But we can reasonably reject it. Proponents of the lexical-threshold view can accept a smoother picture of our sequence of lives by appealing, first, to incommensurability and, second, to the vagueness of lexical thresholds. Let me explain these points in turn.

First, the sequence argument slides from the rejection of weak superiority to the rejection of weak *noninferiority*. After supposing that no life in the sequence is weakly superior to its successor, we inferred that, for any number of x_k-lives, some number of x_{k+1}-lives must be better. This inference is good only if we assume completeness. But lexical-threshold totalists can reject completeness and allow for incommensurable values. So they can claim that no life in the sequence is even weakly superior to its successor.

That response is simple, and it highlights another way in which incommensurability is important. But it may not be entirely satisfying if we still have to admit that some life in the sequence is weakly *noninferior*—and therefore strongly noninferior, given separability—to its successor. For if no life is even weakly noninferior to its successor, then for any number of x_k-lives, there must be some number of x_{k+1}-lives whose existence would be better. We could then show that, for any number of x_1-lives, there must be some number of x_n-lives whose existence would be better, thereby undermining weak noninferiority. Given separability, we seem forced to admit that some life in the sequence is strongly noninferior to its successor, and that may still seem absurd.

My second response takes the form of a dilemma: either this conclusion is not absurd or we can reject it. My reasoning has to do with vagueness.

It is supposed to be absurd that some life is strongly noninferior to its successor because each life in the sequence is so similar to its successor. Each life should therefore be "only marginally worse" than its predecessor (Arrhenius and Rabinowicz 2005, 108). That is why, intuitively, for every k, x_k is not strongly noninferior to x_{k+1}. Call this *the key premise*. Compare the key premise to

THE Conditional Premise: For every k, if x_k is weakly superior to x_n, then so is x_{k+1}.

The key premise, given transitivity and separability, entails the conditional premise. For suppose that the conditional premise is false: for some k, x_k is weakly superior to x_n but x_{k+1} is not. So there is some number m of x_k-lives whose existence would be better than any number of x_n-lives. And suppose that the key premise is true, so that x_k is not strongly noninferior to x_{k+1}. By separability and transitivity, x_k cannot be weakly noninferior to x_{k+1}. So there is some number of

x_{k+1}-lives whose existence would be better than m x_k-lives. By transitivity, some number of x_{k+1}-lives would have to be better than any number of x_n-lives, which contradicts our hypothesis that x_{k+1} is not weakly superior to x_n.[24]

Assuming classical logic, however, we can derive from the conditional premise that either all or none of the lives in our sequence are weakly superior to x_n. Obviously not all of the lives are weakly superior to x_n. So, we might conclude, none of them are.

This reasoning, however, would be soritical, because it can be vague whether some x_k is weakly superior to x_n. This is because it can be vague what the values of our thresholds Δ and δ are, and whether some life is good in the important respects. For example, Griffin suggests that "we might wish to stop the slide [...] at that point along the line where people's capacity to appreciate beauty, to form deep loving relationships, to accomplish something with their lives beyond just staying alive [...] all disappear" (1988, 339). It can be vague whether some person has or lacks these capacities.

The point can be put more generally. Suppose that, for every k, x_k is weakly superior to x_n just in case x_k is *excellent*. It is surely vague whether a life is excellent. But the conditional premise then implies, assuming classical logic, that either all or none of the lives in the sequence are excellent. That is clearly false.

The exact upshot of this point depends on how we resolve the sorites paradox. On most theories that retain classical logic, the conditional premise is false. Those who prefer such theories can reject the key premise of the sequence argument. That some life in the sequence is strongly noninferior to its successor seems to me not much more implausible than that some life is excellent even though its successor is not. Others claim that sorites arguments have true premises but weaken classical logic so that the arguments are invalid. Those who prefer such nonclassical theories can apply their preferred logic to the sequence argument to avoid the seemingly absurd result.

I am not denying that the sequence argument raises a challenge. My claim is that this challenge is an instance of a more general one: the sorites paradox.[25] Some might find it objectionable for a moral theory to give such great weight to vague conditions.[26] Although there may be differences in kind between excellent and mediocre lives, between Mozart and muzak, the only axiologically relevant differences, some might think, are the differences in degree on which these kind-differences supervene. On this view, we should not give lexical weight to the

---

[24] Even if separability is rejected, we could derive the conditional premise from the key premise's analogue that, for every k, x_k is not *weakly* noninferior to x_{k+1}. Proponents of the sequence argument would, I suspect, accept this weaker premise. See also Pummer (2018), who argues that reasons to accept principles like the key premise also support principles like the conditional premise, which give rise to transitivity-less analogues of the spectrum arguments of Rachels (1998) and Temkin (1996).

[25] As I also claim, in Nebel (2018), of the Rachels–Temkin spectrum arguments against transitivity.

[26] Bacon (2018), for example, argues that we should not care intrinsically about vague matters.

seemingly arbitrary thresholds at which a life becomes excellent, an insight becomes profound, some pain becomes agony, or some creative work constitutes a work of genius. Goodness is a function only of the comparative, degree-based properties in virtue of which things satisfy these vague, absolute conditions.

Commonsense morality, however, gives great weight to properties with borderline cases.[27] It may be morally wrong to harvest one innocent person's vital organs in order to save two lives, but morally obligatory to do so for the sake of a million lives. We may have a duty to rescue a nearby child at little cost to ourselves, but no duty to donate nearly all our resources to save a greater number of children on another continent. It may be vague whether some act of consent was informed and freely given, and therefore, sufficient to make some act morally permissible. It may be vague what one knows or intends, and yet the differences between knowledge and ignorance, intent and foresight, may determine which actions are negligent, which are reckless, which are warranted, which are blameworthy, and which make one liable to be harmed.

These examples are deontic ones. It might be objected that although binary judgments about permissibility and wrongness may depend on such properties, axiological ones about goodness may not. But many conceptions of the good can be expected to raise similar cases. It may be borderline whether some life that contains both goods and evils is worth living or not. And plausible non-hedonic components of well-being—e.g., knowledge, friendship, and achievements—have borderline cases. We might also think that population size can be vague because of vagueness in personal identity, and that it can be vague whether something is painful. It seems that we will inevitably have to give great weight in our axiology to vague conditions, so this problem is not unique to the lexical-threshold view.

Here is one way to sharpen the point. Consider a standard totalist who appeals to a complete ordering of scalar quantities of well-being. Consider a sequence of lives from the excellent to the *horrible* where each life is only marginally better than its successor—e.g., because it contains one more nanosecond of mild pleasure. (For this to be true, all lives in this sequence must contain both good and bad components.) The standard totalist holds that any number of the first life would be better than any number of the last. She must conclude that, for some life in the sequence, any number of such lives would be better than any number of its successor lives, containing one less nanosecond of pleasure. That seems implausible. But the implausibility isn't the fault of their theory of aggregation; it's a general effect of vagueness. It seems absurd for a nanosecond of pleasure to make the difference between a life in this sequence that is worth living and one that isn't, since any consecutive lives in this sequence are extremely similar in terms of their balance of good and bad components. But if we cannot live with that consequence,

---

[27] These examples are based on Alexander (2008), though he seems to deny that there can be moral vagueness.

then we need some other solution to the sorites paradox, which we could reasonably expect to solve the present problem.

The lexical-threshold view's combination of vagueness and incommensurability suggests a smoother picture than the one characterized by the sequence argument. Excellent lives are weakly superior to mediocre lives. Had we assumed completeness, there would be some life along a finite sequence from excellent lives to mediocre ones that was weakly superior to its immediate successor. But if we reject completeness, this life may instead be only strongly noninferior to its successor. The vagueness of lexical thresholds explains why this result *seems* incredible, even though it is not much more incredible than there being a pair of extremely similar lives only one of which is excellent.[28]

8.5 The Problem of Risk

In this section, I discuss what seems to me the most serious problem for lexical views. The problem arises in cases of uncertainty. Essentially the same problem afflicts deontological theories that posit absolute moral prohibitions.[29] Such theories seem to yield absurd results when we are uncertain about whether our act constitutes the breaking of a promise, or the intentional killing of an innocent person. Huemer (2010) argues that this problem afflicts lexical views more generally—e.g., about well-being and population ethics.[30]

Imagine that we can donate some money to one of two charities.[31] The *trivial* charity would use our money to improve many people's lives in trivial ways. We know that with certainty. The trivial charity might, for example, supply minuscule tubes of anti-itch ointment or tasty lollipops to millions of people. And suppose we know that these goods will not lead to improvements in people's lives along the important dimensions. The *important* charity would, with probability p, use our money to bring about some important good whose value exceeds the threshold Δ. It might, for example, be an art school that, if better funded, would be more likely to train some number of artistic geniuses who would have otherwise gone unrecognized. Or it might be an organization that would, with probability p, free some number of enslaved children.

---

[28] Broome (2004, 174) argues that we cannot combine vagueness and incommensurability; see Carlson (2004, 2013) for counterexamples to Broome's "collapsing principle." Appeals to vagueness and incommensurability in responding to sequence arguments have been more recently criticized by Handfield and Rabinowicz (2017); see also Pummer (Chapter 18, this volume) against vagueness.

[29] See Jackson and Smith (2006).

[30] Here I focus on Huemer's objection, which involves interpersonal tradeoffs. In Nebel (2019) I discuss a risky, intrapersonal analogue of the mere addition paradox. The lexical-threshold view violates what I there call "minimal prudence," which I find very hard to reject.

[31] Huemer's example is targeted at Parfit's perfectionism. I have modified it to apply to the view sketched here.

Suppose that our only aim is to make things go best. If $p = 1$, then donating to the important charity would certainly make things better in the important ways, by enough to exceed the lexical threshhold. So lexical-threshold totalism says that we ought to donate to the important charity, no matter how many people would be aided by the trivial charity. Huemer then asks, "For what values of p would this remain true?" (2010, 338).

Huemer considers three possible answers. On one view, for any $p > 0$, we ought to donate to the important charity, regardless of how many people would be aided by the trivial charity. This seems to imply that we should donate all of our resources to organizations with vanishingly small probabilities of churning out artistic geniuses or freeing child slaves, rather than charities that are much more likely to help people, even if only marginally.

On a second view, for any $p < 1$, there is some number of people who would be aided by the trivial charity such that we ought to donate to that charity. But this would make our lexical view irrelevant to practical deliberation, because we can never be *certain* that an act would lead to the creation of artistic masterpieces or the freeing of child slaves.

On a third view, there is some probability $0 < p < 1$—call it the *risk threshold*—above which we ought to donate to the important charity, regardless of the number of people aided by the trivial charity, and below which we ought to donate to the trivial charity. But suppose that there are *two* important charities (call them A and B) in addition to the trivial charity (call it C). We know that each of A and B has a probability slightly less than p of realizing the important good. But if we were to donate to both A and B, the probability of realizing an important good would exceed the risk threshold p. On the view under consideration, we shouldn't donate to A, and we shouldn't donate to B, but we nonetheless should donate to them *both*. That may seem absurd; it "puts value and probability together in a way that leads to paradox" (Jackson and Smith 2006, 277).

Lexical-threshold totalism, however, suggests a different response. According to what might be called the *weak threshold view*, there is some risk threshold $0 < p < 1$—which depends on the magnitude of the possible tradeoffs along each dimension—above which we ought to donate to the important charity, and below which it can be permissible to donate to the trivial charity. But, for any $p > 0$, it is permissible to donate to the important charity.

The weak threshold view avoids the paradoxical result that we shouldn't donate to A, shouldn't donate to B, and yet should donate to both A and B. And it flows naturally from lexical-threshold totalism and the standard decision-theoretic obligation to maximize expected value, on a natural understanding of expected value. We simply apply lexical-threshold totalism's partial ordering to vectors of expected values along each dimension. That is, we represent the expected value of a prospect with probabilities $p_1, ..., p_n$ of realizing values $(i_1, t_1), ..., (i_n, t_n)$, respectively, with the vector $(\sum_{k=1}^{n} i_k p_k, \sum_{k=1}^{n} t_k p_k)$. The values of prospects can then be partially ordered according to lexical-threshold totalism. We can then claim that an act is permissible just in case no alternative has greater expected value. This gives us the weak threshold view.

Some might object that the weak threshold view still has paradoxical implications. It entails that there is no obligation to donate to *A* alone, that there is no obligation to donate to *B* alone, but that we ought to donate to both *A* and *B*. And it may seem absurd that we can permissibly refrain from donating to *each* charity, considered separately, if we ought to donate to them both.

This result, however, is not absurd. We ought to donate to both *A* and *B*. But suppose that we decide not to donate to *A*. Then we act wrongly. Is there any *additional* obligation to donate to *B*? Is our act more seriously wrong if, given our decision not to donate to *A*, we decide not to donate to *B* either, and instead give the entire sum to *C*? I do not see why that would have to be so. The claim is not that we do no wrong in donating to neither of the important charities. The claim is rather that we do no *additional* wrong in donating to neither of the important charities, given that we are already committed to doing wrong by not donating to them both.

More familiar cases instantiate this pattern of obligation. Suppose, for example, that you have two cookies. You've promised, to me, that you'd give them to my two children. You ought to give them both a cookie. But suppose you decide to eat one cookie. It might not be true that you do some additional wrong by eating the other cookie. You've already broken your promise to me, and there might be sufficient reason not to give a cookie to only one of my children. Or consider Quinn (1990)'s self-torturer, who receives $10,000 each time he increases his pain by a negligible amount. We might think that each increase is rational, but enough of them taken together are irrational. These examples suggest that there can be an obligation to do *A* and *B*, even if there is no independent obligation to do *A* and no independent obligation to do *B*.

Some might object that, even if the weak threshold view can avoid the absurd consequences faced by the other views we've discussed, it is nonetheless implausible that, for any probability *p* and any number of people aided by the trivial charity, it is permissible to donate to the important charity. That seems too permissive.[32]

Some might find this implication unpalatable on the grounds that, in practice, we always have some credence that an act could result in an important gain. But,

---

[32] On some understandings of incommensurable values, lexical-threshold totalism can secure the weaker verdict that every rational agent ought to have some risk threshold or other, below which she would donate to the trivial charity. This can be obtained by understanding the lexical threshold as the upper bound of a permissible range of thresholds, which extends arbitrarily close to 0, and by requiring each agent to have some threshold in that range. This would rule out a policy of donating to the important charity no matter how unlikely the important gain. But there would be no particular threshold below which everyone ought to donate to the trivial charity.

for that very reason, the case we are considering is unrealistic. In practice, seemingly trivial benefits to a person have some probability of yielding more important benefits, so that benefiting a very large number of people in seemingly trivial ways might have a greater probability of realizing an important gain than donating to a highly ineffective art school, for instance. So, although the weak threshold view's verdict about the charity case may be more permissive than seems plausible, it's not obvious that this implausibility translates to a serious practical problem.

That's not to say that the permissive implications of the weak threshold view are entirely welcome. But these implications seem to me implausible only when the probability of an important gain is minuscule. And it is well known that tiny probabilities raise serious puzzles for expected utility theory. Suppose, for example, that an evil demon forces you to choose between the following options. He will either

1. Create and torture 10^{301} people for their entire lives, or
2. Flip a fair coin until it lands heads, or until it has been flipped n times, whichever happens first. If the coin lands heads on the mth flip ($m \leq n$), he will create and torture 2^m people. If the coin lands tails n times, he will create and torture 2^{n+1} people.

Intuitively, it is at least *permissible* to choose option (2), for any n. Unless the coin lands tails a thousand times in a row, (2) would result in fewer people tortured than (1). But, on the plausible assumption that there is no upper limit to the badness of people being tortured, and if n is large enough, then (2) would be worse in expectation than (1). (For example, if the badness of torture is linear with respect to the number of people tortured, then let $n \geq 10^{301}$.) So, for some n, expected utility theory requires you to choose (1). That is counterintuitive.

My point is that the implausible implications of the weak threshold view may be instances of a more general difficulty for expected value maximization—namely, its counterintuitive verdicts when dealing with tiny probabilities—which I have simply applied to lexical-threshold totalism. If that's correct, then the axiology is not to blame. I have no solution to the paradoxes of decision theory. But some proposed solutions—e.g., discounting tiny probabilities down to zero[33]—would allow lexical-threshold totalism to avoid the difficulties we have considered. On the other hand, perhaps the counterintuitive implications of expected utility theory are to be embraced. But the permissive implications of the weak threshold view strike me as no less implausible than the demanding

---

[33] See, e.g., Shafer and Vovk (2006); Smith (2015); and Monton (2019). For critique, see, e.g., Parfit (1981) and Isaacs (2016).

implications of expected utility theory. Many people do, in fact, donate large sums of money to causes that have very little chance of realizing important values, rather than charities that could (with near certainty) improve many people's lives in more trivial ways. So the permissiveness of the weak threshold view may not be a decisive reason to reject lexical-threshold totalism.

Indeed, if we are committed to maximizing expected value, standard totalism may fare even worse than lexical-threshold totalism under uncertainty. For example, Arrhenius and Stefánsson (2020) point out that, given expected utility theory, standard totalism implies the "risky very sadistic conclusion": that, for any population of excellent lives, any population of horrible lives, and arbitrary high probability p, there is some population of mediocre lives such that, rather than guaranteeing the population of excellent lives, it would be better to create the horrible lives with probability p and mediocre lives with probability $1 - p$. This conclusion strikes me as even more implausible than the implications of lexical-threshold totalism under uncertainty.

8.6 Conclusion

Totalism leads to the repugnant conclusion and its negative analogue if we view well-being as a scalar quantity. But if we follow Sen in viewing well-being as a vector quantity, and if we respond to McTaggart's conclusion by giving lexical priority to some dimensions of well-being, then we can avoid these repugnant conclusions. By rejecting completeness and imposing lexical thresholds on the dimensions of well-being, totalists can also avoid the implausibly strong superiority of excellent lives, in a way that preserves the intuitive separability of lives. The resulting view—lexical-threshold totalism—can also mitigate the significance of seemingly marginal differences in well-being, and avoids the most paradoxical implications of standard lexical orderings in uncertain cases.

Ultimately, the plausibility of lexical-threshold totalism depends on whether a reasonable theory of well-being fits the structure of the lexical-threshold view. And I have not defended any particular view about what makes life worth living. This makes lexical-threshold totalism somewhat of a moving target: we cannot always say whether some implication of the theory is repugnant, because we don't know what the important and trivial dimensions are. It, therefore, seems to me that research in the theory of well-being is of crucial importance to the problems of population ethics.

What I find most attractive about the lexical-threshold view is its diagnosis of the repugnant conclusion's repugnance. The repugnant conclusion is repugnant because it oversimplifies what makes life worth living. Many philosophers compare the paradoxes of population ethics to Arrow's (1951) impossibility result in the theory of social choice.³⁴ The solution to Arrow's theorem, in the context of social welfare aggregation, is to require more information about each person's good: as Sen (1970a) emphasizes, we cannot get very far with merely ordinal, intrapersonal information about each person's good. We need a richer framework of well-being. The lexical-threshold view extends this insight to variable-population cases: we cannot get by with merely scalar information about each person's good, because no single cardinal scale can accommodate the complexities of what makes life worth living and the vast differences between lives of different qualities. Well-being is, in this way, unlike milk.

References

Alexander, Larry. 2008. "Scalar Properties, Binary Judgments." *Journal of Applied Philosophy* 25 (2): 85–104. https://doi.org/10.1111/j.1468-5930.2008.00401.x.

Arrhenius, Gustaf. 2000. "Future Generations: A Challenge for Moral Theory." Doctoral thesis, Uppsala University. http://urn.kb.se/resolve?urn=urn:nbn:se:uu:diva-787.

Arrhenius, Gustaf. 2005. "Superiority in Value." *Philosophical Studies: An International Journal for Philosophy in the Analytic Tradition* 123 (1/2): 97–114. https://doi.org/10.2307/4321574.

Arrhenius, Gustaf, and Wlodek Rabinowicz. 2005. "Millian Superiorities." *Utilitas* 17 (02): 127–46. https://doi.org/10.1017/S0953820805001494.

Arrhenius, Gustaf, and H. Orri Stefánsson. 2020. "Population Ethics under Risk." Unpublished manuscript. Institute for Futures Studies; Stockholm University. https://philpapers.org/archive/ARRPEU.pdf.

Arrow, Kenneth Joseph. 1951. *Social Choice and Individual Values.* New York: Wiley.

Audi, Robert. 2005. "Intrinsic Value and Meaningful Life." *Philosophical Papers* 34 (3): 331–55. https://doi.org/10.1080/05568640509485162.

Bacon, Andrew. 2018. *Vagueness and Thought.* New product edition. Oxford Philosophical Monographs Series, New York: Oxford University Press.

Bader, Ralf M. forthcoming. "Person-Affecting Utilitarianism." In *Oxford Handbook of Population Ethics*, edited by Gustaf Arrhenius, Krister Bykvist, Timothy, Campbell, and Elizabeth Finneron-Burns. Oxford: Oxford University Press, forthcoming.

Blackorby, Charles, Walter Bossert, and David Donaldson. 1996. "Quasi-Orderings and Population Ethics." *Social Choice and Welfare* 13 (2): 129–50. http://link.springer.com/article/10.1007/BF00183348.

Blackorby, Charles, Walter Bossert, David Donaldson, and Marc Fleurbaey. 1998. "Critical Levels and the (Reverse) Repugnant Conclusion." *Zeitschr. F. Nationalökonomie* 67 (1): 1–15. https://doi.org/10.1007/BF01227760.

---

³⁴ See Cowen (1996); Arrhenius (2000); Kitcher (2000).

Broad, C. D. 1938. *An Examination of McTaggart's Philosophy*. Vol. II. Cambridge: Cambridge University Press.

Broome, John. 2004. *Weighing Lives*. Oxford; New York: Oxford University Press.

Carlson, Erik. 1998. "Mere Addition and Two Trilemmas of Population Ethics." *Economics and Philosophy* 14 (02): 283. https://doi.org/10.1017/S0266267100003862.

Carlson, Erik. 2004. "Broome's Argument against Value Incomparability." *Utilitas* 16 (2): 220–4. https://doi.org/10.1017/S0953820804000548.

Carlson, Erik. 2013. "Intransitivity." In *International Encyclopedia of Ethics*. Oxford: Blackwell Publishing Ltd.

Carlson, Erik. forthcoming. "On Some Impossibility Theorems in Population Ethics." In *Oxford Handbook of Population Ethics*, forthcoming. https://www.york.ac.uk/media/philosophy/documents/events/Carlson%20On%20Some%20Impossibility%20Theorems%20in%20Population%20Ethics%20-%20Draft%2030%20January%202015.docx.

Chang, Ruth. 2016. "Parity, Imprecise Comparability and the Repugnant Conclusion." *Theoria* 82 (2): 182–214. https://doi.org/10.1111/theo.12096.

Chipman, John S. 1960. "The Foundations of Utility." *Econometrica* 28 (2): 193. https://doi.org/10.2307/1907717.

Cowen, Tyler. 1989. "Normative Population Theory." *Soc Choice Welfare* 6 (1): 33–43. https://doi.org/10.1007/BF00433361.

Cowen, Tyler. 1996. "What Do We Learn from the Repugnant Conclusion?" *Ethics* 106 (4): 754–75. http://www.jstor.org/stable/2382033.

Crisp, Roger. 1988. "Ideal Utilitarianism: Theory and Practice." DPhil Thesis, University of Oxford.

Dorr, Cian, Jacob M. Nebel, and Jake Zuehl. 2021. "The Case for Comparability." Unpublished manuscript. New York University; University of Southern California. https://philpapers.org/rec/DORTCF-2.

Dorsey, Dale. 2009. "Headaches, Lives and Value." *Utilitas* 21 (01): 36.

Frankfurt, Harry G. 1999. *Necessity, Volition, and Love*. Cambridge: Cambridge University Press.

Frick, Johann. 2017. "On the Survival of Humanity." *Canadian Journal of Philosophy* 47 (2–3): 344–67. https://doi.org/10.1080/00455091.2017.1301764.

Griffin, James. 1988. *Well-Being*. Oxford: Oxford University Press. http://www.oxfordscholarship.com/view/10.1093/0198248431.001.0001/acprof-9780198248439.

Griffin, James. 2002. "A Note on Measuring Well-Being." In *Summary Measures of Population Health: Concepts, Ethics, Measurement, and Applications*, edited by Christopher J. L. Murray. New York: World Health Organization.

Gurney, Edmund. 1887. *Tertium Quid: Chapters on Various Disputed Questions*. https://archive.org/details/tertiumquidchap00gurngoog.

Gustafsson, Johan E. 2019. "Population Axiology and the Possibility of a Fourth Category of Absolute Value." Economics & Philosophy 36: 81–110. https://doi.org/10.1017/S0266267119000087.

Handfield, Toby, and Wlodek Rabinowicz. 2017. "Incommensurability and Vagueness in Spectrum Arguments: Options for Saving Transitivity of Betterness." Philos Stud 175 (9). 2373–87. https://doi.org/10.1007/s11098-017-0963-9.

Huemer, Michael. 2008. "In Defence of Repugnance." *Mind* 117 (468): 899–933. https://doi.org/10.1093/mind/fzn079.

Huemer, Michael. 2010. "Lexical Priority and the Problem of Risk." *Pacific Philosophical Quarterly* 91 (3): 332–51. https://doi.org/10.1111/j.1468-0114.2010.01370.x.

Isaacs, Yoaav. 2016. "Probabilities Cannot Be Rationally Neglected." *Mind* 125 (499): 759–62. https://doi.org/10.1093/mind/fzv151.

Jackson, Frank, and Michael Smith. 2006. "Absolutist Moral Theories and Uncertainty." *The Journal of Philosophy* 103 (6): 267–83.

Jensen, Karsten Klint. 2008. "Millian Superiorities and the Repugnant Conclusion." *Utilitas* 20 (03): 279–300. https://doi.org/10.1017/S0953820808003154.

Kitcher, Philip. 2000. "Parfit's Puzzle." *Noûs* 34 (4): 550–77. https://doi.org/10.1111/0029-4624.00278.

Klocksiem, Justin. 2016. "How to Accept the Transitivity of Better Than." Philosophical Studies 173: 1309–34. https://doi.org/10.1007/s11098-015-0548-4.

Laird, John. 1936. *An Enquiry into Moral Notions*. New York: Ams Press.

List, Christian. 2004. "Multidimensional Welfare Aggregation." *Public Choice* 119 (1–2): 119–42. https://doi.org/10.1023/B:PUCH.0000024168.00362.af.

Luce, R. Duncan. 1978. "Lexicographic Tradeoff Structures." *Theory and Decision* 9 (2): 187–93. http://www.springerlink.com/index/V834703QQ8K3W874.pdf.

Mandler, Michael, Paola Manzini, and Marco Mariotti. 2012. "A Million Answers to Twenty Questions: Choosing by Checklist." *Journal of Economic Theory* 147 (1): 71–92. https://doi.org/10.1016/j.jet.2011.11.012.

Manzini, Paola, and Marco Mariotti. 2012. "Choice by Lexicographic Semiorders: Choice by Lexicographic Semiorders." *Theoretical Economics* 7 (1): 1–23. https://doi.org/10.3982/TE679.

McMahan, Jeff. 1981. "Problems of Population Theory." *Ethics* 92 (1): 96–127. http://www.jstor.org/stable/2380707.

McMahan, Jeff. 1985. *Problems of Population Theory*. PhD thesis, University of Cambridge.

McTaggart, J. Ellis. 1927. *The Nature of Existence*. Volume II. Cambridge University Press.

Mill, John Stuart. 1863. *Utilitarianism*.

Monton, Bradley. 2019. "How to Avoid Maximizing Expected Utility." *Philosophers' Imprint* 19 (18): 25.

Mulgan, Tim. 2001. "What's Really Wrong with the Limited Quantity View?" *Ratio* 14 (2): 153–64. https://doi.org/10.1111/1467-9329.00152.

Mulgan, Tim. 2002. "The Reverse Repugnant Conclusion." *Utilitas* 14 (03): 360. https://doi.org/10.1017/S0953820800003654.

Mulgan, Tim. 2006. *Future People: A Moderate Consequentialist Account of Our Obligations to Future Generations*. Oxford; New York: Clarendon Press; Oxford University Press.

Nebel, Jacob M. 2015. "Incommensurability in Population Ethics." B.Phil. Thesis, University of Oxford.

Nebel, Jacob M. 2018. "The Good, the Bad, and the Transitivity of Better Than*." *Noûs* 52 (4): 874–99. https://doi.org/10.1111/nous.12198.

Nebel, Jacob M. 2019. "An Intrapersonal Addition Paradox." *Ethics* 129 (2): 309–43. https://doi.org/10.1086/700085.

Nebel, Jacob M. 2020. "A Fixed-Population Problem for the Person-Affecting Restriction." *Philosophical Studies* 177: 2779–87. https://doi.org/10.1007/s11098-019-01338-5.

Nozick, Robert. 1974. *Anarchy, State, and Utopia*. New York: Basic Books.

Nussbaum, Martha Craven. 2000. *Women and Human Development the Capabilities Approach*. Cambridge; New York: Cambridge University Press. http://site.ebrary.com/id/10205240.

Parfit, Derek. 1981. "Correspondence." *Philosophy and Public Affairs* 10 (2): 180–1.

Parfit, Derek. 1984. *Reasons and Persons*. Oxford: Clarendon Press.

Parfit, Derek. 1986. "Overpopulation and the Quality of Life." In *Applied Ethics*, edited by Peter Singer, 145–64. Oxford Readings in Philosophy. Oxford: Oxford University Press.

Parfit, Derek. 2016. "Can We Avoid the Repugnant Conclusion?" *Theoria* 82 (2): 110–27. https://doi.org/10.1111/theo.12097.

Pettit, Philip. 2001. "Symposium on Amartya Sen's Philosophy: 1 Capability and Freedom: A Defence of Sen." *Economics and Philosophy* null (01): 1–20. https://doi.org/10.1017/S0266267101000116.

Portmore, Douglas W. 1999. "Does the Total Principle Have Any Repugnant Implications?" *Ratio* 12 (1): 80–98. https://doi.org/10.1111/1467-9329.00078.

Pummer, Theron. 2018. "Spectrum Arguments and Hypersensitivity." *Philosophical Studies* 175: 1729–44. https://doi.org/10.1007/s11098-017-0932-3.

Qizilbash, Mozaffar. 2007. "The Mere Addition Paradox, Parity and Vagueness*." *Philosophy and Phenomenological Research* 75 (1): 129–51. http://onlinelibrary.wiley.com/doi/10.1111/j.1933-1592.2007.00063.x/full.

Qizilbash, Mozaffar. 2018. "On Parity and the Intuition of Neutrality." *Economics & Philosophy* 34 (1): 87–108. https://doi.org/10.1017/S0266267117000281.

Quinn, Warren S. 1990. "The Puzzle of the Self-Torturer." *Philosophical Studies* 59 (1): 79–90.

Rabinowicz, Wlodek. 2003. "Discussion: Ryberg's Doubts about Higher and Lower Pleasures Put to Rest?" *Ethical Theory and Moral Practice* 6 (2): 231–35. https://doi.org/10.1023/A:1024447122558.

Rabinowicz, Wlodek. 2009. "Broome and the Intuition of Neutrality." *Philosophical Issues* 19 (1): 389–411. https://doi.org/10.1111/j.1533-6077.2009.00174.x.

Rachels, Stuart. 1998. "Counterexamples to the Transitivity of *Better Than*." *Australasian Journal of Philosophy* 76 (1): 71–83. https://doi.org/10.1080/00048409812348201.

Rawls, John. 1999. *A Theory of Justice*. Cambridge, MA: Belknap Press of Harvard University Press.

Ross, W. D. 1930. *The Right and the Good*, edited by Philip Stratton-Lake. Oxford: Clarendon Press (reprinted 2002).

Ryberg, Jesper. 1996. "Parfit's Repugnant Conclusion." *The Philosophical Quarterly* 46 (183): 202. https://doi.org/10.2307/2956387.

Ryberg, Jesper. 2002. "Higher and Lower PleasuresDoubts on Justification." *Ethical Theory and Moral Practice* 5 (4): 415–29. http://link.springer.com/article/10.1023/A:1021309407124.

Ryberg, Jesper. 2004. "The Repugnant Conclusion and Worthwhile Living." In *The Repugnant Conclusion*, edited by Torbjörn Tännsjö and Jesper Ryberg, 239–55. Library of Ethics and Applied Philosophy 15. Springer Netherlands. https://doi.org/10.1007/978-1-4020-2473-3_13.

Sen, Amartya. 1970a. *Collective Choice and Social Welfare*. San Francisco: Holden-Day San Francisco.

Sen, Amartya. 1970b. "Interpersonal Aggregation and Partial Comparability." *Econometrica* 38 (3): 393. https://doi.org/10.2307/1909546.

Sen, Amartya. 1980. *Equality of What?* The Tanner Lectures on Human Values.

Sen, Amartya. 1985. *Commodities and Capabilities*. Amsterdam: North-Holland.

Sen, Amartya. 1993. "Capability and Well-Being." In *The Quality of Life*, edited by Martha Nussbaum and Amartya Sen. Oxford University Press.

Shafer, Glenn, and Vladimir Vovk. 2006. "The Sources of Kolmogorov's Grundbegriffe." *Statistical Science* 21 (1): 70–98. https://doi.org/10.1214/088342305000000467.

Sider, Theodore. 1991. "Might Theory X Be a Theory of Diminishing Marginal Value?" *Analysis* 51 (4): 265–71. http://analysis.oxfordjournals.org/content/51/4/265.full.pdf.

Smith, Martin. 2015. "Evidential Incomparability and the Principle of Indifference." *Erkenntnis* 80 (3):605–16. https://doi.org/10.1007/s10670-014-9665-2.

Smuts, Aaron. 2013. "Five Tests for What Makes a Life Worth Living." *The Journal of Value Inquiry* 47 (4): 439–59. https://doi.org/10.1007/s10790-013-9393-x.

Tännsjö, Torbjörn. 2002. "Why We Ought to Accept the Repugnant Conclusion." *Utilitas*, November, 339–59. https://doi.org/10.1017/S0953820800003642.

Temkin, Larry S. 1996. "A Continuum Argument for Intransitivity." *Philosophy & Public Affairs* 25 (3): 175–210.

Temkin, Larry S. 2012. *Rethinking the Good: Moral Ideals and the Nature of Practical Reasoning*. Oxford Ethics Series. Oxford; New York: Oxford University Press.

Thomas, Teruji. 2018. "Some Possibilities in Population Axiology." *Mind* 127 (507): 807–32. https://doi.org/10.1093/mind/fzx047.

Tversky, Amos. 1969. "Intransitivity of Preferences." *Psychological Review* 76 (1): 31–48. https://doi.org/10.1037/h0026750.

Wolf, Susan R. 2010. *Meaning in Life and Why It Matters*. The University Center for Human Values Series. Princeton, NJ: Princeton University Press.

9
Context-Dependent Betterness and the Mere Addition Paradox

Johann Frick

9.1 Introduction

Population ethics is frequently described as a field littered with paradoxes. In this chapter, I outline a novel solution to one of the most venerable and interesting puzzles in this branch of moral philosophy: Derek Parfit's *Mere Addition Paradox*.[1] The paradox is of enduring interest for several reasons. For one, it can be read as one of the first "impossibility results" in population ethics. It suggests that many people's pre-theoretic judgments about population axiology, and by extension about how we ought to shape the size and quality of life of future generations, are in deep tension with one another. Worse than that, a natural extension of the paradox appears to push us into the arms of the Repugnant Conclusion—a result that strikes many as profoundly counterintuitive.

At the same time, the import of Parfit's paradox reaches far beyond the field of population ethics. Over the past three-and-a-half decades, philosophers' attempts to grapple with this problem have brought forth some of the most original and daring work in the theory of value—work that challenges some of our most fundamental assumptions about the nature of the good itself, in particular the notion that the "all-things-considered better than" relation is transitive.[2]

In this chapter, I aim to *dissolve* the Mere Addition Paradox. The paradox, I argue, trades on an ambiguity about the context of choice. Once this ambiguity is removed, we see that on one way of specifying the context of choice, there is in fact no tension between the three pairwise judgments that make up the paradox, whereas on another way of specifying the context of choice, we lose our basis for affirming one of these pairwise judgments. In neither case does Parfit's Mere Addition case threaten to take us to the Repugnant Conclusion. The lessons for value theory in general are also less dramatically revisionary than some had thought. Correctly understood, Parfit's Mere

---

[1] Though Parfit had discussed versions of the Mere Addition Paradox in a draft called "Overpopulation," circulated as early as 1973, his canonical presentation of the problem on which I draw in what follows is in Chapter 19 of *Reasons and Persons*.

[2] I am referring, of course, to the work of Larry Temkin. See his seminal article "Intransitivity and the Mere Addition Paradox" and his treatise *Rethinking the Good*.

Addition Case challenges not the transitivity of the "better than" relation, but instead a different, and less sacrosanct, idea, namely the so-called Independence of Irrelevant Alternatives principle. What Parfit's puzzle teaches us, I will argue, is that betterness is sometimes *context-dependent*: the relative goodness of two outcomes can depend on whether or not a third outcome could have instead been chosen.

9.2 The Mere Addition Paradox

Parfit presents the Mere Addition Paradox in the context of searching for "Theory X," by which he means a complete and satisfactory axiology for the field of population ethics.[3] Such a population axiology, if one could be found, could then be conjoined with a principle of beneficence, which would tell us, alone or in conjunction with other moral principles, how to act in shaping the number and quality of life of future people.

One very simple candidate for Theory X, which is embraced by classical utilitarianism, is what Parfit calls:

> **The Impersonal Total Principle**: "If other things are equal, the best outcome is the one in which there would be the greatest quantity of happiness—the greatest net sum of happiness minus misery."[4]

The Impersonal Total Principle implies that a loss in the *quality* of lives in a population can be compensated for by a sufficient gain in the *quantity* of lives that are lived, provided they are minimally worth living. However, this consequence of the Impersonal Total Principle gives rise to a well-known problem. It implies:

> **The Repugnant Conclusion**: "For any possible population of at least ten billion people, all with a very high quality of life, there must be some much larger imaginable population whose existence, if other things are equal, would be better, even though its members have lives that are barely worth living."[5]

This is a conclusion which most population ethicists, Parfit included, deem intuitively unacceptable.[6] Someone who embraces the Impersonal Total Principle, however, can be forced to the Repugnant Conclusion via a simple "Spectrum Argument," illustrated by Figure 9.1.

---

[3] Following Hilary Greaves, I understand a population axiology as "a betterness ordering of states of affairs, where the states of affairs include ones in which different numbers of persons are ever born." See Greaves, "Population Axiology," p. 1.
[4] Parfit, *Reasons and Persons*, p. 387.   [5] Parfit, *Reasons and Persons*, p. 388.
[6] For a dissenting voice, see Torbjörn Tännsjö, "Why We Ought to Accept the Repugnant Conclusion."

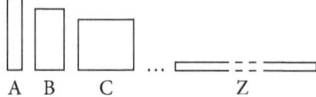

Figure 9.1 The Spectrum Argument for the Repugnant Conclusion.

Each block represents a different possible history of the world, with the width of the block representing the number of people who ever live and the height of the block their quality of life. Someone who accepts the Impersonal Total Principle must grant that B is better than A. For, while the people in B are *slightly* less happy than the people in A, there are sufficiently *more* of them to make B all things considered better than A. *Mutatis mutandis* for the comparison between C and B. Iterated application of this step, plus the transitivity of "all-things-considered better than," lead us to the Repugnant Conclusion that Z, an extremely large population made up of people whose lives are barely worth living, is better than A, a population of ten billion people with very happy lives.

It might be thought that we can easily escape this predicament by rejecting the Impersonal Total Principle. Many philosophers, myself included, are attracted to an alternative view, which John Broome has dubbed:

> **The Intuition of Neutrality**: It does not make the world go better, all else being equal, to add to it a life that is worth living. Rather, doing so is ethically neutral.[7]

The Intuition of Neutrality neatly dovetails with a deontic intuition about the morality of procreation, the so-called *Procreation Asymmetry*, which strikes many as powerfully attractive.[8] According to this intuition, if a future person would foreseeably have a life that is not worth living, this in itself gives us a strong moral reason to refrain from bringing this person into existence. By contrast, there is no moral reason to create a person whose life would foreseeably be worth living, *just because* her life would be worth living. If, on the other hand, we deny the Intuition of Neutrality and embrace the view that each additional happy life makes the world better all else equal, the Procreation Asymmetry seems hard to sustain. If creating a new happy life would make the world better, all else equal, shouldn't we have *some* moral reason to do so?

Rejecting the Intuition of Neutrality would have strongly revisionary implications in many other contexts as well. A nice illustration comes from John Broome. Considering the moral value of programs for improving people's safety, he writes:

---

[7] I explicate and defend the Intuition of Neutrality in my "On the Survival of Humanity."
[8] The Procreation Asymmetry was first discussed by Jan Narveson in "Utilitarianism and New Generations." The label is due to McMahan, "Problems of Population Theory." I defend the Procreation Asymmetry at length in my "Conditional Reasons and the Procreation Asymmetry."

CONTEXT-DEPENDENT BETTERNESS AND THE ADDITION PARADOX   235

When people's lives are saved, by making roads safer or in other ways, the wellbeing of the people who are saved is generally small in comparison to the wellbeing of all the new people, their descendants, who come into existence as a result. This is perfectly predictable. If all the descendants' wellbeing had to be counted too, that would enormously alter the value we attach to saving people's lives. But actually, in judging the value of safety on the roads, we routinely ignore all this wellbeing.[9]

If we accept the Intuition of Neutrality, then the Spectrum Argument toward the Repugnant Conclusion never gets off the ground, since we reject its very first step. If containing more happy lives does not make the world go better all else equal, there is no reason to accept that B is better than A (or that C is better than B, etc.). So the argument never gets going.

Parfit's Mere Addition Paradox, however, shows that avoiding the Repugnant Conclusion is not as simple as that. Even if we reject the Impersonal Total Principle and instead embrace the Intuition of Neutrality, there is a second argument that threatens to take us to the Repugnant Conclusion all the same. Consider Figure 9.2.

A represents a population of ten billion people, all with very happy lives. A+ consists of two groups. The first group consists of the *same* people as A (represented visually by the shading of the box), with the same high quality of life.[10] Let's call these the "A-people." A+ also contains a group of extra people, equal in number to the A-people. Let's call these the "new people." These new people are significantly worse-off than the A-people, but still have lives that are well worth living. Outcome B contains the same two groups as A+. Everyone in outcome B is equally well-off; everyone is worse-off than the people in A, but better-off than the new people were in A+. The average quality of life in B (and hence also the total wellbeing in B) is above that in A+.[11]

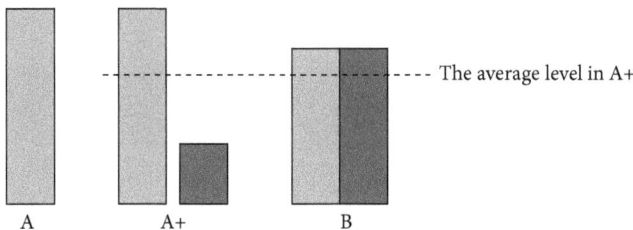

Figure 9.2 The Mere Addition Paradox.

---

[9] Broome, "Should We Value Population?," p. 402.
[10] Following a convention introduced by Larry Temkin in *Rethinking the Good*, two groups in different outcomes are represented by boxes with the same shading if and only if they contain the same individuals.
[11] This way of presenting the paradox, in which outcomes A+ and B contain the same two groups of people (the A-people and the new people) has become canonical in the subsequent literature. In particular, it is the version of the paradox that Temkin focuses on in "Intransitivity and the Mere Addition Paradox" and *Rethinking the Good*. It is also the version of the case I will initially presuppose

In *Reasons and Persons*, Parfit convincingly argues that each of the following three pairwise comparisons is extremely plausible:

(1) B is better than A+.
(2) A is better than B.
(3) A+ is not worse than A.

Let us briefly review the case for each of these three claims.

The intuition that B is a better outcome than A+ is for many people the most robust. It is supported by a number of distinct moral views: Total utilitarians, average utilitarians, telic egalitarians, and prioritarians all converge on the claim that B is a better outcome than A+.

The second claim, that A is better than B, also strikes many people as strongly intuitive. *Everyone* who exists in B is worse-off than everyone who exists in A (including the people who exist in both A and B). This verdict would, of course, be contradicted by proponents of the Total Principle. But as we have seen, the Total Principle itself is suspect, since it implies the Repugnant Conclusion. By contrast, for someone attracted to the Intuition of Neutrality, the claim that A is better than B should be *especially* plausible. For a move from A to B can be decomposed into two distinct effects, as Figure 9.3 illustrates.

First, there is a change in the wellbeing of the A-People. This is the move from A to B_1. B_1 is incontrovertibly worse than A. Second, there is the addition of the new people, B_2, to B_1. However, if the Intuition of Neutrality is correct, adding new lives worth living does not make the world go better. So, B, the union of B_1 and B_2, is not better than B_1. And B_1, we said, is worse than A. So, all things considered, B is worse than A.[12]

Finally, consider the comparison between A and A+, shown in Figure 9.4.

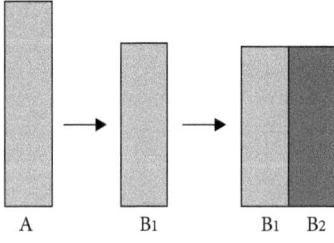

Figure 9.3 Decomposing the move from A to B.

in presenting my solution. In the Appendix to this chapter, I show how my solution can be extended to a version of the case in which the populations of A+ and B, while equal in size, do not contain the same people.

[12] Larry Temkin makes a version of this argument in *Rethinking the Good*, p. 415.

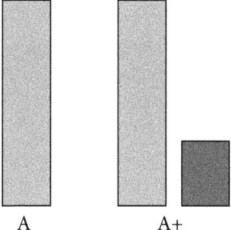

Figure 9.4 Comparing A and A+.

Relative to A, A+ involves what Parfit calls "mere addition," meaning that the existence of the New People in A+ does not affect anyone else's wellbeing, and that they have lives that are worth living.

If we reject the Impersonal Total Principle and accept the Intuition of Neutrality, we don't claim that the existence of some additional people with lives worth living makes the outcome *better* than A. But, at the same time, Parfit thinks it is very hard to see how merely adding a set of new people could make an outcome *worse*. He maintains that we should embrace:

The Mere Addition Principle: Merely adding a group of new people, all of whom have lives that are worth living, does not make an outcome worse.

This principle might be challenged: What about the fact that, as a result of adding the worse-off new people, there is *inequality* in A+, whereas there isn't in A? Couldn't this fact be thought to make A+ worse than A? To this *Objection from Inequality*, Parfit gives the following response: We should distinguish two kinds of case: If we can avoid inequality by making some existing people better-off, then avoiding inequality can make the outcome better. But if inequality can only be avoided if some people, who have lives worth living, never exist, then avoiding inequality does not make the outcome better. So, Parfit concludes, when inequality is produced by mere addition, it does not make the outcome worse. As he puts it: "We cannot plausibly claim that the extra people should never have existed *merely because [...] there are other people who are even better-off.*"[13] If this argument goes through, then the inequality in A+ gives us no reason to reject the claim that A+ is not worse than A. (An analogous response might be given to the claim that A+ is worse than A in virtue of having lower average wellbeing or of being the outcome in which the worst-off fare worse).

But now it seems we have a problem: We have affirmed that A is better than B, and that B is better than A+. By the transitivity of "better-than," it seems we are committed to the claim that A is better than A+. But the Mere Addition Principle

---

[13] Parfit, *Reasons and Persons*, p. 425.

denies this. We therefore have a set of three propositions, each of which is intuitively compelling, but which seemingly cannot all be true—a paradox.

By itself, this simple Mere Addition case is not enough to force us to the Repugnant Conclusion. For the *least* implausible revision to our three pairwise judgments, Parfit believes, is to revise the claim that A is *better than* B to the claim that B is *not worse* than A. We are then left with the following three pairwise judgments:

(1) B is better than A+.
(2) B is not worse than A.
(3) A is not worse than A+.

These three judgments are logically consistent, since the "not worse than" relation, unlike the "better than" or "worse than" relations is not transitive. For example, one might think that a career as a lawyer and a career as a musician are qualitatively sufficiently different to vitiate very precise evaluative comparisons. It may then be the case that a career as a lawyer earning $150k a year is not worse than a career as a musician earning $80k a year, and that a career as a musician earning $80k a year is not worse than a career as a lawyer earning $160k a year. But a career as a lawyer earning $150k a year *is* worse than a career as a lawyer earning $160k a year, all else equal. So, if we only affirm that B is *not worse than* A, this does not threaten to take us to the Repugnant Conclusion that Z is *better* than A. (Indeed, it does not even threaten to take us to the weaker conclusion that Z is *not worse* than A, since "not worse than" is not transitive.)

There is, however, a "supercharged" variant of the Mere Addition Paradox which does threaten to take us all the way to the Repugnant Conclusion. In what Parfit calls the "Up-Down Case," illustrated by Figure 9.5, the A-People are actually made *better*-off when we add the New People (hence the labeling of this outcome as "A++"). Of course, even in this case we are to assume that average utility in A++ is lower than in B, which in turn has a lower average utility than A.

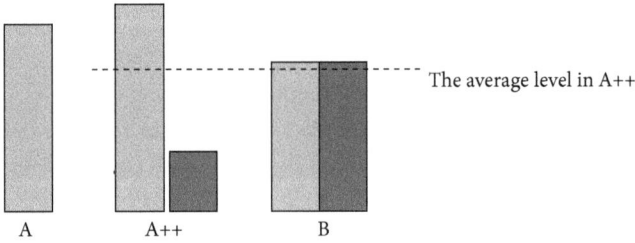

Figure 9.5 The Up-Down Case.

As in the original Mere Addition Case, Parfit thinks it is very plausible that:

(1) B is better than A++.
(2) A is better than B.

The same considerations in support of these claims that we just surveyed still apply.

However, in the Up-Down Case, not only is A++ not *worse* than A. We should affirm a stronger claim:

(3) A++ is *better* than A.

After all, Parfit reasons, had we chosen A instead of A++, this would have been *worse* for everyone who exists in A; and in addition, a second group of people, all of whom have lives that are well worth living, would never have existed. Given this, it is hard to see how A would not have been *worse* than A++.

So, in the Up-Down Case, it seems very plausible that A++ is better than A, and that B is better than A++. But since "better than" *is* a transitive relation, these two plausible judgments entail that B is *better* than A. And this reasoning can now be iterated. By the same two step Up-Down procedure, we can argue that B++ is better than B, that C is better than B++, and so on—all the way to the Repugnant Conclusion.

These, in brief, are Parfit's claims about the Mere Addition Paradox and the Up-Down Case. The significance of these problems for population axiology are self-evident: If Parfit's arguments about the Mere Addition Case are sound, Theory X will not be able to accommodate all our pre-theoretic convictions concerning population axiology, since these turn out to be inconsistent. Moreover, unless the challenge of the Up-Down Case can be met, we must abandon the hope of constructing a Theory X that avoids the Repugnant Conclusion.

9.3 Temkin on the Mere Addition Paradox and the Non-transitivity of "Better Than"

The Mere Addition Paradox, however, is far more than just a theoretical puzzle for population ethicists. In his seminal 1987 paper "Intransitivity and the Mere Addition Paradox" and carried further in his 2012 book *Rethinking the Good*, Larry Temkin forcefully argues that fully coming to grips with this problem should prompt us to reexamine some of our most fundamental assumptions about the nature of the good itself.

Temkin contends that, besides accepting that at least one of the intuitively compelling pairwise judgments (1) through (3) is false, there is a fourth possible solution to the paradox that needs to be considered. This is to reject the idea that the "all-things-considered better-than" relation is transitive.

To many, of course, this proposal will seem a non-starter. Surely, if there is anything we know about the nature of the good, it is that "better than" is transitive.[14]

Temkin concedes that this idea will seem rationally undeniable, if we accept a certain picture of the nature of our moral ideals—what he calls the "**Internal Aspects View of Outcome Goodness.**" According to this view,

> [r]oughly, for each outcome, O, how good that outcome is all things considered depends solely on how good it is with respect to each moral ideal that is relevant for assessing the goodness of outcomes, and on how much all of the relevant ideals matter vis-à-vis each other, where these depend solely on O's internal features. Moreover, for any two outcomes, O_1 and O_2, O_1 will be better than O_2 all things considered if and only if the extent to which O_1 is good all things considered, as determined solely on the basis of O_1's internal features, is greater than the extent to which O_2 is good all things considered, as determined solely on the basis of O_2's internal features.[15]

If all our moral ideals which together determine the goodness of an outcome conform to the Internal Aspects View, then we can assign each outcome a goodness "score," which is *solely* a function of its "internal," or intrinsic, properties. And then the goodness of outcomes surely *must* be transitive. If outcome 1 has a higher goodness score than outcome 2, and outcome 2 has a higher goodness score than outcome 3, and these scores are solely a function of the intrinsic features of these three outcomes, then the score of outcome 1 must also be higher than that of outcome 3.

However, Temkin argues that if we are truly compelled by Parfit's reasoning in support of each of the three pairwise judgments that compose the Mere Addition Paradox, then this should lead us to question the Internal Aspects View. What may underlie and justify our non-transitive intuitions in the Mere Addition Paradox, Temkin argues, is the fact that certain of our moral ideals, such as the ideal of equality, may be what he calls "essentially pairwise comparative." For instance, Temkin maintains that on the view suggested by Parfit's claims about the badness of inequality, it is true that "*[e]quality is [c]omparative*, not merely in the ordinary sense—that it involves judgments about how some fare relative to others—but in the sense that our judgment about a situation's inequality depends

---

[14] See, for instance, Voorhoeve, "Vaulting Intuition."
[15] Temkin, *Rethinking the Good*, p. 370.

on the alternative it is being compared to."[16] On this view about equality, Temkin writes, "the *relevant and significant* factors for comparing A and A+ regarding inequality differ from those for comparing A+ and B in a sense connected with inequality being *essentially pairwise comparative*."[17] Thus, "[t]here is no fact of the matter as to how bad the inequality in A+ *really* is considered just by itself. How bad it is depends upon the alternative compared to it. Compared to B, A+ is bad; compared to A, it isn't."[18,19]

Hence, according to Temkin, if we accept Parfit's reasoning about the Mere Addition Paradox, this suggests the following lesson: Rather than being a function only of an outcome's intrinsic aspects, the overall goodness of an outcome is often essentially comparative or as I will say *comparison-dependent*: Depending on which alternative it is being compared to, an outcome will do better or worse in terms of certain moral ideals, such as equality. And since these ideals are part of what makes an outcome better or worse *all-things-considered*, the *all-things-considered* goodness of outcomes will often be comparison-dependent as well. If all this is true, we should not expect the "all-things-considered better than" relation to be transitive.

Temkin does not claim that our intuitions about the Mere Addition Paradox *require* us to give up on the transitivity of "all-things-considered better than." We may instead choose to give up one of our considered judgments about the Mere Addition Paradox and preserve the transitivity of the "better than" relation. What Temkin maintains is that *if* we do embrace certain deeply plausible ways of thinking about the Mere Addition Paradox (among them Parfit's claims in *Reasons and Persons* about when inequality makes an outcome worse and when it doesn't, which we surveyed above, but also certain forms of Maximin, as well as the Narrow Person-Affecting view), then this would force us to deny that the "all-things-considered better than" is transitive. As he writes:

> *If* one accepts an Essentially Comparative View, Parfit's three judgments regarding A, A+, and B may well be undeniable, but they will no longer be incompatible, since, as we have seen, given an Essentially Comparative View, either transitivity may fail for the "all-things-considered better than" relation [...] or the "all-things-considered better than" relation may fail to apply across different sets of alternatives, including, as it turns out, Parfit's alternatives.[20]

---

[16] Temkin, "Intransitivity and the Mere Addition Paradox," p. 147.
[17] Temkin, "Intransitivity and the Mere Addition Paradox," p. 149.
[18] Temkin, "Intransitivity and the Mere Addition Paradox," p. 150.
[19] It should be noted that this is not Temkin's *own* view about the badness of inequality. On Temkin's own view, set out in his 1993 book *Inequality*, equality is *not* essentially pairwise comparative, and is indeed compatible with the Internal Aspects View.
[20] Temkin, *Rethinking the Good*, p. 398.

I believe that Temkin's remarks on the Mere Addition Paradox contain, at once, a deep insight and an important error. I think Temkin is right that if we take Parfit's claims about the Mere Addition Paradox seriously, they present a potent challenge to the Internal Aspects View of Outcome Goodness. However, we should depart from the Internal Aspects View in a different way than Temkin suggests. The lesson of the Mere Addition Paradox, I will argue, is *not* that the goodness of outcomes is often *comparison*-dependent, but that it is *context*- or *choice-set* dependent. Accordingly, we will see that what the Mere Addition Paradox challenges is not the transitivity of "better than," but a different principle of rational choice: the Independence of Irrelevant Alternatives.

9.4 A Crucial Ambiguity

The Mere Addition Paradox, I claim, trades on an ambiguity about the context of choice. As others before me have remarked, the three pairwise comparisons that Parfit makes in constructing the paradox implicitly assume a particular context of choice, namely one in which the feasible set contains *only* the two options being compared.[21] Let us call this a *two-possible* choice.

That Parfit must be making this assumption is evident from the way he deals with the Objection from Inequality against the claim that A+ is not worse than A (or indeed better than A, in the Up-Down Case). Parfit's response to this objection, recall, was that if the only way of removing the inequality between the A-people and the new people is for the latter group never to exist, then the inequality is not a bad-making feature of A+. This is true in a *two-possible* choice between A and A+, and supports the judgment that, in *that* case, A+ is not worse than A. To cite one of Parfit's examples, we might imagine that the new people in A+ are all born blind, in a world in which there is no cure for blindness.

By contrast, in a *three-possible choice*, where A, A+, and B are all in the feasible set, this argument would not get a purchase. For here there *does* exist a way of removing the inequality between the A-people and the new people other than by preventing the new people from coming into existence – namely option B. To borrow Parfit's example, imagine that the new people are born blind into a society which does have a cure for blindness. If the seeing (the A-people) were willing to sacrifice some of their resources, the blind could all be cured of their disability.

Accordingly, I claim that there is a sense in which *all three* intuitive judgments about Parfit's Mere Addition Case are true, namely as pairwise comparisons in *two-possible* cases. Thus, it seems to me true that:

---

[21] See, in particular, Boonin, "Don't Stop Thinking about Tomorrow"; Roberts, "Temkin's Essentially Comparative View, Wrongful Life and the Mere Addition Paradox"; and Cusbert, "Acting on Essentially Comparative Goodness."

(1′) B is better than A+, when the option set is Q = {A+, B};
(2′) A is better than B, when the option set is R = {A, B};
(3′) A+ is not worse than A, when the option set is T = {A, A+}.

The air of paradox arises from the assumption that, if these three pairwise rankings are true in two-possible choices, they all carry over to the *three-possible* case, in which the feasible set contains, at once, all three outcomes.[22] It would then be true that

(1*) A is better than B, when the option set is S = {A, A+, B};
(2*) B is better than A+, when the option set is S = {A, A+, B};
(3*) A+ is not worse than A, when the option set is S = {A, A+, B}.

This would spell big trouble, since (1*), (2*), and (3*) would together constitute an instance of what I call "non-transitivity *within an option set*," as opposed to the "non-transitivity *across different option sets*" that we witness in propositions (1′), (2′), and (3′). From the perspective of practical reason, failures of transitivity *within* an option set would be much the worse problem, since it could imply contradictory instructions and paralyze choice. This is clearest in cases where the outcomes within an option set are ranked in a *cyclical* fashion (as in the Up-Down Case). In that case, for each outcome that we could bring about, there is a better outcome that we could bring about instead. But even if the betterness ranking within an option set is not cyclical but *merely* non-transitive, this could imply contradictory instructions: (2*) suggests that, if I aim to do what will produce the best outcome, I have more reason to bring about B than A+, whereas (1*) and (3*) together suggest the opposite. We therefore have strong reason to want to deny that the outcomes within an option set can, in an intelligible sense, be non-transitively ordered. By contrast, non-transitivity *across* different option sets seems far more innocuous from the point of view of practical reason. Since, by assumption, we are not talking about the same context of choice in (1′), (2′), and (3′), this combination of claims cannot imply contradictory instructions or lead to rational dilemmas.[23]

Fortunately, I submit, we are not forced to this conclusion. As the arguments of the following sections will establish, it is a mistake to assume that the pairwise

---

[22] In section 9.9, I will consider cases involving a sequence of choices where, although the agent can choose between only two alternatives at any given point in time, all three alternatives are available *over time*.

[23] One might worry that having a betterness ranking which is non-transitive across option sets could prove problematic in contexts of *dynamic* choice, in particular by opening the agent up to the possibility of being "money-pumped" in a sequential presentation of the Up-Down case. This worry is taken up in section 9.9.

rankings in the two-possible cases all carry over to the three-possible case. Specifically, I will argue, in the three-possible case proposition (3*) is false.

9.5 Doubts about the Independence of Irrelevant Alternatives

Parfit, of course, *does* assume that his three judgments about the two-possible cases would all carry over to the three-possible case. This is because he accepts an idea often referred to as the "Independence of Irrelevant Alternatives."[24] Here is the version of this principle that I shall have in mind in what follows:

The Independence of Irrelevant Alternatives (IIA): If outcome O_1 is better than outcome O_2 when the option set is $S = \{O_1, O_2, \ldots, O_n\}$, then O_1 must still be better than O_2 when the option set is contracted to T, where T is a *subset* of S that contains O_1 and O_2. (*Contraction consistency*) Likewise, if O_1 is better than O_2 when the option set is T, then O_1 must be better than O_2 when the option set is expanded to S. (*Expansion consistency*)

To some philosophers this principle captures a basic truth about the nature or goodness, almost as unassailable as the claim that the "better than"-relation is transitive. Parfit is one of them. In *Reasons and Persons*, he writes: "The relative goodness of two outcomes cannot depend on whether a third outcome, that will never happen, might have happened."[25] If the Independence of Irrelevant Alternatives principle is correct, then how A+ compares evaluatively to A *could not* depend on whether we are in a two-possible case, in which these are the only two possible outcomes, or a three-possible case, where outcome B was also in the feasible set. Hence, any judgement that we make about the relative goodness of A and A+ in a two-possible case would necessarily carry over to the three-possible case.

However, while Parfit finds the Independence of Irrelevant Alternatives principle intuitively compelling, it is in fact far from secure. To help us see this, it will pay to approach the question obliquely. Instead of asking straightaway whether the presence of B in the feasible set could affect the relative *goodness* of A+ compared to A, let us investigate first whether the presence or absence of B from the feasible set could make a difference to the *moral permissibility* of *choosing* A+ over A. That is, we are asking not an "axiological" but a "deontic" question.

---

[24] For two seminal discussions of this principle, see Sen, "Internal Consistency of Choice"; and Anand, "The Philosophy of Intransitive Preference."
[25] Parfit, *Reasons and Persons*, p. 429.

To this question, the answer is emphatically "yes." In a two-possible choice, where the only alternative to A+ is A, the choice of A+ is morally innocuous. Admittedly, opting for A+ creates an outcome in which there is inequality: the new people are worse-off than the A-people, and this fact may be regrettable in itself. Yet, at the same time, their lives are well worth living, and they are the best lives that the new people could feasibly have. It is hard to see how, under these circumstances, creating the new people by choosing A+ could be wrong.

The permissibility of choosing A+ changes entirely if option B is added to the feasible set. It can now no longer be said to the new people that, although they are significantly less well-off than the A-people, their lives are going as well as they could have gone. Given that outcome B is also available in this scenario, this is no longer the case. There now exists a way of avoiding the inequality between the A-people and the new people other than by preventing the new people from coming into existence.

Moreover, there is no adequate justification for choosing A+ rather than B. Compared to A+, we argued above, B is better on egalitarian, on utilitarian, and on prioritarian grounds. Hence, in the three-possible case, the new people have an *unanswerable complaint* if A+ obtains and would be victims of *injustice*, whereas neither is true if the feasible set contained only A and A+. In a three-possible choice, while it continues to be permissible to choose A (we are not required by morality to create the new people), *if* we are going to bring about an outcome in which the new people exist, our only permissible course of action is to choose B.

This sensitivity of normative properties such as "is unjust" or "is impermissible" to the context of choice is a common phenomenon in ethics. Consider another example:

Employment:

A multi-national corporation is considering whether to open a new factory in a developing country, with high rates of poverty and unemployment. It must decide among three options:

(1) Don't hire anyone.

(2) Hire 1000 workers, who have very little bargaining power, and pay them very little (though still enough to make working for the corporation at this wage worth their while).

(3) Hire the same 1000 workers and pay them a decent wage.

Many would judge that, while (1) and (3) are both morally permissible, option (2) is wrong, on account of being *exploitative*.

But what *makes* option (2) exploitative, or at least *wrongfully* exploitative? I submit that it is the presence of option (3) in the feasible set. To exploit someone, very roughly, is to take unfair advantage of their vulnerability or weak bargaining position, usually by extracting a bigger surplus than they would receive in a fair transaction.[26] This is the case when the corporation *could* be paying its workers a decent wage but uses their weak bargaining position to instead pay them a pittance.

Suppose, by contrast, that the feasible set is different: the world market for the good being produced by the corporation is *so* competitive that only by paying its workers a very low wage can the company be economically viable. The option of paying a decent wage is simply not available. The feasible set contains only options (1) and (2). I claim that, while it would still, of course, be morally regrettable that the company isn't able to pay its workers a decent wage, option (2) would not, under these circumstances, constitute *wrongful exploitation*. This could make it permissible to choose option (2).

My strategy in what follows will be to argue that this sensitivity of normative properties on the context of choice has *axiological* implications. It seems to me that whether an outcome constitutes wrongful exploitation bears, not just on the question whether it is morally permissible to bring it about, but also on its *goodness*. Likewise, I will make the case that, since in Parfit's Mere Addition Case the presence or absence of option B alters whether A+ is *unjust*, this *eo ipso* affects the goodness of A+ compared to A. If this is so, then we cannot conclude, as Parfit does, that since A+ is not worse than A in the two-possible case, the same must be true in the three-possible case as well. The path would then be clear to a solution of the Mere Addition Paradox.

9.6 A Digression: The Fine-Grained Individuation Gambit

It might be interjected that I am misapplying the Independence of Irrelevant Alternatives principle. The principle states that how two outcomes O_1 and O_2 compare in terms of relative goodness cannot depend on whether some third outcome O_3 was also possible, or not. This presupposes that the two outcomes O_1 and O_2 are, in the relevant sense, the *same* outcomes, whether or not O_3 is in the feasible set.

But, the objection goes, it is unclear that this is the case, either in the Mere Addition Paradox or in the Employment case I just discussed. In both instances I argued that the presence or absence of the third outcome makes a difference to the normatively significant properties of the second (whether it is unjust; whether it is exploitative). This may suggest that outcomes need to be individuated in a more *fine-grained* manner. In the Mere Addition Paradox, A+, when chosen from

---

[26] For an account of wrongful exploitation along these lines, see Horton, "The Exploitation Problem."

option set T = {A, A+} and A+, when chosen from option set S = {A, A+, B} are not, in the relevant sense, the *same* outcome, since the latter outcome has a normative property that the former lacks, namely that of being unjust.[27]

I think that, whatever the merits of this fine-grained individuation gambit may be as way of defending the Independence of Irrelevant Alternatives principle, it fails entirely to rebut my challenge to Parfit's assumption that our judgments about the three two-possible cases should all carry over to the three-possible case. Recall the dialectical context: It is *Parfit* who needs to invoke the Independence of Irrelevant Alternatives principle in order to make the case that A+ is not worse than A—not just in the two-possible case (where this claim is supported by his response to the Objection from Inequality) but in the three-possible case as well (where his response to the Objection from Inequality does not get a purchase). Hence, if the Independence of Irrelevant Alternatives principle could not, in fact, be applied across these two contexts of choice, because A+ isn't in the relevant sense the *same* outcome across these two contexts of evaluation, then Parfit's argument does not even get off the ground.

More generally, it seems to me that while the strategy of individuating options more fine-grainedly (out of a recognition that the context of choice may alter their morally significant properties) may help to preserve the "letter" of the Independence of Irrelevant Alternatives principle, it already concedes the fundamental philosophical point, namely that the context of choice in which a pairwise evaluative comparison is being made is often crucial in making this comparison. The *intended* upshot of the Independence of Irrelevant Alternatives principle is that the choice set in which outcomes occur does not matter to their relative goodness. However, by resorting to the fine-grained individuation strategy, we accept that context *does* matter. We accept that, in order to know how two outcomes compare, we often need information about what other outcomes are in the option set. Indeed, we can only know *which* two outcomes it is that we are comparing in the first place, and what their normatively relevant properties are, by considering facts about the choice set in which these outcomes are situated.

So, it seems that the fine-grained individuation strategy can only "immunize" the Independence of Irrelevant Alternatives principle against the problem cases I am considering by already conceding what is really at issue, namely that the wider context of choice often matters in evaluating the relative goodness of two outcomes. Once this fundamental point is acknowledged, it is of relatively little interest whether we choose to uphold the letter of the Independence of Irrelevant Alternatives principle by fine-grainedly individuating options according to the option set in which they occur. The version of the principle that is philosophically

---

[27] For a defense of the idea that putative counterexamples to the Independence of Irrelevant Alternatives Principle can be dealt with by individuating the relevant outcomes or alternatives in a more fine-grained manner, see Neumann, "Choosing and Describing."

substantive and interesting is the one that does not depend on such fine-graining. For this reason, I will, in what follows, continue to treat A+ in the two-possible case and A+ in the three-possible case as the same outcome.

9.7 Why Injustice Makes an Outcome Worse

Section 9.5 argued for the claim that, A+ is unjust when chosen in the three-possible case, whereas it isn't when chosen in the two-possible case. It is very plausible, I argued, that this can make a difference to whether it is permissible to bring this outcome about in these two different contexts of choice. This, however, is a *deontic* question, concerned with how we ought to act or choose. What we are ultimately interested in, however, is an *axiological* question: do things *go worse* if A+ obtains in a three-possible case than if A+ obtains in a two-possible case?

In *Reasons and Persons*, Parfit himself cautions against attempts to solve the Mere Addition Paradox by reducing it to a question about how we ought to act. He writes:

> It may [...] be said: "Suppose that these outcomes [in the Mere Addition Paradox] were the predictable effects of different possible acts. If we ask what we ought to do, we solve the Paradox. Assume that we could bring about either A, or A+, or B. It would be wrong to bring about A+. This would be wrong since there is a better outcome, B, that we could have brought about. But it would also be wrong to bring about B, since there is a better outcome: A."[28]

In response to this proposal, Parfit argues that attempting to resolve the Mere Addition Paradox by appeal to what we ought to do is not a solution to the paradox but "merely ignores it." The Mere Addition Paradox, he insists, is a puzzle of axiology, about the relative goodness of outcomes, not a deontic question about what we ought to do:

> Most of our moral thinking may be about what we ought to do. But we also have views about the relative goodness and badness of different outcomes. As I have said, these are not views about moral goodness or badness, in the sense that applies to acts or to agents. If an earthquake kills thousands, this is not morally bad in this sense. But it is bad in a sense that has moral relevance. Our views about the relative goodness of different outcomes sometimes depend upon our views about what we ought to do. But such dependence often goes the other way. [...] [S]ome of our beliefs about what we ought to do depend upon our beliefs

---

[28] Parfit, *Reasons and Persons*, p. 429.

about the relative goodness of outcomes. Since these latter beliefs form the basis of some of our morality, we cannot refuse to consider an argument that is about these beliefs.[29,30]

These remarks, however, do not cut against the solution I am about to propose. I am not making the mistake of viewing axiological questions about the relative goodness of outcomes as equivalent, or reducible, to the deontic question of which outcome to bring about. What my solution depends on, rather, is the thought that the deontic fact that it is unjust or morally wrong to bring about some outcome *bears on* the axiological question how well the world goes if that outcome is brought about. (As we will see, this is a claim which neither Parfit nor Temkin are in a position to deny, since they have in fact explicitly defended it elsewhere.) That is, having already argued that:

(1) The presence of B in the feasible set gives outcome A+ a property in the three-possible case—that of being *unjust*—which it does not possess in the two-possible case.

I will now make the case that:

(2) The fact that A+ is unjust in the three-possible case makes it *worse*, all else equal, than when the only alternative is A.

If this second claim were also true, it would provide an explanation for how it could be that:

(3) While A+ is not worse than A in a two-possible case, A+ *is* worse than A in the three-possible case.

One might initially be skeptical of (2) on the basis of the following line of reasoning: The fact that A+ is unjust when chosen in the three-possible case, whereas it isn't when chosen in the two-possible case, can certainly make a difference to how one ought to *act* in either case. Agents who bring about A+ in the former case may be acting wrongly, whereas agents who bring about A+ in the two-possible case may have done nothing wrong. But why also believe that the world *goes worse* if A+ obtains in a three-possible case than if A+ obtains in a two-possible case? Or, to put the same question a different way: supposing we know

---

[29] Parfit, *Reasons and Persons*, p. 429.
[30] Similar claims are at the heart of Parfit's response to David Boonin, who in "Don't Stop Thinking about Tomorrow" had discussed the Mere Addition Paradox in exclusively deontic terms. See Parfit, "Acts and Outcomes."

that A+ obtains, do we have reason to hope that we are in a two-possible rather than a three-possible case, because then A+ would not be unjust, and therefore a better outcome? By assumption, there is no difference in the *levels of wellbeing* that people enjoy in A+ in the three-option and in the two-option case. But if the injustice of an outcome doesn't make things *worse for* anyone, then why should the presence of injustice matter in itself to the evaluation of the outcome? It is one thing, we might say, to avoid the injustice of A+ by doing B instead. That would actually make things better for the victims of injustice. But how could it be thought to make a difference if the only reason why A+ does not contain injustice is because B, the morally superior alternative, is not *feasible*?

This skeptical worry would be well-taken if we thought that our only reason for caring whether there is injustice or wrongdoing was out of a concern for the bad *effects* of injustice of wrongdoing, in terms of people's wellbeing. But I submit that this is not what we really believe. We can bring this out with what I call the Argument from the News-Value of Wrongdoing.

Consider the following case:

Bystanders:
You read in the newspaper of a young child who drowned in a shallow pond. You surmise from the story that the child must have stumbled into the pond while unattended, with no-one present to rescue it. As you go on reading, however, you learn to your horror that your initial assumption was mistaken. There were, in fact, numerous bystanders, each of whom could have easily rescued the child, but who instead stood by and did nothing.

If you are like me, finding out that you are a situation which contained two feasible outcomes, namely:

(1) The child drowns.
(2) Bystanders rescue the child.

instead of a situation in which the latter outcome wasn't possible, is *bad news*. Whereas the death of a young child is a tragedy in any event, learning that what actually occurred was that people stood by and watched the child drown is horrifying. What has happened here is not just a misfortune but a *moral catastrophe*.

For a second illustration, return to our earlier Employment Case. Suppose you learn of a company which is operating a factory in a developing country with high rates of poverty and unemployment, and is paying its workers very little for long and arduous hours of work. Since unfortunately such things are common, you assume that what we have here is a typical case of economic exploitation: in other words, you assume that the company *could* be paying its workers a more decent wage, but is taking advantage of their vulnerability and weak bargaining position to pay them a pittance instead. However, you subsequently learn that your pessimistic supposition was, in fact, mistaken. The workers are not being exploited. The company is operating in an extremely tough international market with profit margins that are razor thin. Even by paying its workers as little as it is, it is barely breaking even. With the best will in the world, the option of paying its employees a higher wage is simply not available if the company is to remain economically viable.

If you are like me, you are *relieved* to learn this. What you have found out changes nothing about the fact that the workers are being paid very little for long hours of work. But learning that they are not, after all, the victims of unjust exploitation strikes us as good news in its own right.

These intuitions about the news-value of information about the presence (or absence) of injustice or wrongdoing lend credence to the view that we care about whether there is wrongdoing *independently* of caring about avoiding the bad *effects* of wrongdoing.

As a matter of fact, neither Parfit nor Temkin would disagree with this claim. Indeed, that is greatly understating matters: In other contexts, both Parfit and Temkin explicitly endorse the notion, which they label "deontic badness," according to which an outcome can be worse, all else equal, because it contains wrongdoing or injustice.[31] Indeed (as I discovered subsequent to writing a first draft of this chapter), Parfit even makes an argument in support of the notion of deontic badness which appeals to the "news-value" of finding out that an outcome was, or was not, produced by wrongdoing:

> Suppose [...] we believe that P hates Q, and that P has poisoned Q's coffee. We cannot intervene, since we are too far away. We might later learn that [(1)] though our beliefs are true, Q is immune to P's poison, and is unharmed. We might instead learn that [(2)] our beliefs about P were false. P does not hate Q, and P was merely adding milk to Q's coffee. In both these versions of Case Five, the best news may be that Q has not been killed. But [(2)] would be significantly better news than [(1)]. If what we learnt was [(1)], the moral badness of P's attempt would still be there. It would be much better if [(2)] were true, so that no moral badness would be there.[32]

So neither Parfit nor Temkin are in a position to gainsay the possibility that, in the three-possible case, A+ is made *worse* by the fact that to bring it about would be unjust and wrong.

---

[31] See Temkin, *Rethinking the Good*, chapter 7.4; and Parfit, *On What Matters*, section 180.
[32] Parfit, *On What Matters*, p. 468.

Of course, we still need a justification for *why* this should be the case. What reasons do we have to care whether we, or others, are behaving justly or unjustly, once we prescind from the good or bad effects on people's wellbeing of our so acting?

The contemporary philosopher who has seen most deeply into this question is T.M. Scanlon. For Scanlon, the requirements of morality are "not just formal imperatives; they are aspects of the positive value of a way of living with others."[33] Behaving morally toward others, not treating them unjustly, allows us to realize a valuable form of *relationship* with them, a form of *mutual recognition*. It is constituted by living with others on terms that they could not reasonably reject insofar as they also are motivated by this ideal.

Indeed, Scanlon argues that much of our motivation to be moral stems from the appeal of standing in this valuable relationship of mutual recognition with others:

> [W]hat is particularly moving about charges of injustice and immorality is their implication for our relations with others, our sense of justifiability to or estrangement from them. [...] [W]hen we look carefully at the sense of loss occasioned by charges of injustice and immorality we see it as reflecting our awareness of the importance for us of being "in unity with our fellow creatures."[34]

If Scanlon is right, the reason to avoid treating others unjustly is not reducible to avoiding the bad effects of injustice. Injustice has a significance of its own that goes beyond that of causing suffering, or producing other bad effects. By acting unjustly toward others, we violate the terms of a relationship of *mutual regard*. By treating them in ways that they could reasonably reject, we fail to accord them a certain form of respect. This puts ourselves in a very different relation to our fellows.

A society or a group of individuals whose dealings are tainted by injustice thus fails to realize a valuable form of interpersonal relationship. That, I think, gives us a grounds for not wanting to relate to one another on unjust terms, quite independently of avoiding the bad effects that injustice often has. That is why, all else equal, we have reason to want, or hope for, outcomes that are not marred by injustice—even if the absence of injustice does not, otherwise, make people better-off.

If these arguments are sound, we are now in a position to assert:

(2) The fact that A+ is unjust in the three-possible case makes it a *worse*, all else equal, than when the only alternative is A.

Now, by itself, this is not enough to establish that:

---

[33] Scanlon, *What We Owe to Each Other*, p. 162.
[34] Scanlon, *What We Owe to Each Other*, p. 163.

(3) While A+ is not worse than A in a two-possible case, A+ *is* worse than A in the three-possible case.

For it certainly isn't the case that *whenever* an outcome is unjust, it is necessarily worse than one an agent could permissibly bring about. There are many counter-examples to that claim. In our earlier Employment case, for instance, a morally motivated observer may well hope that, if the corporation doesn't employ the workers on fair terms (although it could), then it will at least employ them on exploitative terms, even if doing so is wrong. That way, workers will still be spared from the worst ravages of poverty.[35]

But the Mere Addition Case seems to me different, for the following reason: In the Employment case, outcome (2) is clearly better than outcome (1) in one respect—there are people, namely the company's would-be employees, who will be *worse-off* if outcome (1) is chosen. This may make it the case that, despite the fact that exploitation is a *bad-making feature* of this outcome, this badness can be *outweighed*, all things considered, by the fact that people are spared from a worse fate in (2).

Crucially, no such thing is true in the Mere Addition Paradox. If we choose A rather than A+, this will not be worse for *anyone* who ever lives. Moreover, recall that Parfit's Mere Addition argument is directed at people like myself who embrace the Intuition of Neutrality, and who therefore believe that merely adding happy lives to an outcome does not make the world go better *in any other sense* either.

If we accept the Intuition of Neutrality, we therefore think that A+ is *in no respect* better than A. Hence, if in the three-possible case the presence of injustice makes A+ worse than A *in some respect*, this is enough to make A+ worse than A *all things considered*. We should reject the Mere Addition Principle, which denies this possibility.

If all this is true, we can claim to have solved the Mere Addition Paradox. In the three-possible case, we can affirm the following transitive ranking over the three options: A is better than B is better than A+. This blocks the argument toward the Repugnant Conclusion. At the same time, we have seen that this ranking in the three-possible case is consistent with all three pairwise judgments that Parfit affirms in constructing the Mere Addition Paradox, so long as these are understood as evaluative judgments about *two-possible* cases.

Essentially the same claims could, I believe, be plausibly made about the Up-Down Case as well. Granted, in this case if we choose A rather than A++, there *are* people for whom this will be worse (namely the A-people). Consequently, it is less obvious than in the Mere Addition Case that the injustice of A++ in the three-

---

[35] For a view of this kind, see Alan Wertheimer's discussion of 'mutually beneficial exploitation' in his *Exploitation*. See also Horton, "The Exploitation Problem."

possible case would make A++ worse than A *all-things-considered*. Given how extremely unappealing the alternatives are, however, my main task is simply to show how it could *possibly* be the case that we can render a verdict about the three-possible case that respects transitivity and at the same time avoids the Repugnant Conclusion. The argument from injustice accomplishes that. The claim that, in the three-possible case, A++ is *all things considered* worse than A is rendered attractive by how implausible the alternatives are. To the victor the spoils.

9.8 Comparison-Dependent vs Context-Dependent Goodness

Temkin is right that the Mere Addition Paradox has an important lesson to teach us about the nature of our moral ideals: it challenges the Internal Aspects View of Outcome Goodness. We should reject the Internal Aspects View, because some evaluative features of outcomes, such as whether the outcome contains injustice, are not a function of that outcome's intrinsic properties alone.

However, Temkin errs when he suggests that the Mere Addition Paradox gives us grounds to reject the Internal Aspects View in favor of a view on which the goodness of an outcome may be *comparison*-dependent, differing chameleon-like depending on which outcome we are comparing it to. If this were indeed the case, then how A+ compares to A in terms of inequality wouldn't differ depending on whether or not B was also in the option set or not. Rather, in *both* a two-possible and a three-possible choice, A+ would not be worse than A in terms of equality, whereas the inequality in A+ would a bad-making feature of A+ *when compared to B*. In that case, however, our non-transitive judgments in two-way choices *would* carry over to a three-way choice between A, A+, and B, thus raising the specter of non-transitivity *within* an option set.

Fortunately, Temkin is mistaken that Parfit's views about the badness of inequality support the claim that how A+ is to be judged in terms of equality is a function of the alternative it is being compared to, as opposed to the option set as a whole. Our basis for thinking that A+ is not worse than A in a two-possible case is that the inequality between the A-people and the new people could only be eliminated by preventing the new people from coming into existence. But crucially, this rationale no longer applies in a three-possible case. Here, there *is* a way of avoiding the inequality in A+ that makes the new people better-off. Hence, not availing ourselves of this option and producing outcome A+ is an injustice; and this, in turn, makes A+ worse, not just in relation to B but in relation to A as well.

Thus, on a Parfitian view about the inequality, the goodness of A+ is *not*, as Temkin maintains, essentially *comparison*-dependent, but rather *context*-dependent: it is a function of what the other feasible alternatives *are*, not of which of these feasible alternatives it is being *compared* to. This, as we saw, supports the view that while the correct pairwise judgments in two-possible choices are non-transitive *across* option sets, in a three-possible choice between A, A+, and B, we obtain a transitive ranking. Temkin's belief that the Mere Addition Paradox poses a *deep* challenge to the transitivity of the "all-things-considered better than" relation thus draws the wrong lesson from this case.

Similar remarks apply to Temkin's discussion of the Mere Addition Case in terms of the ideal of "maximin." Arguing that "maximin" is essentially comparative, Temkin writes: "while usually it is morally regrettable if the worst-off fare worse in one situation than another, this is not always so, and, in particular, is not if it results from mere addition."[36] Therefore, A+ is not worse than A in terms of maximin, though it is worse than B in terms of maximin.

Again, however, these remarks overlook the importance of the option set. If our concern is that the worst-off not fare worse than they otherwise *might*, this does not support the thought that maximin could never judge a situation bad if it is produced by mere addition. What matters are the *available alternatives*. So, a move from A to A+, even though it is just 'mere addition' could be criticized on grounds of maximin, provided outcome B was also available. It would be innocuous only in a two-possible case where option B was absent.

In fairness to Temkin, he does, at other points in *Rethinking the Good*, consider the possibility that some of the challenges to the transitivity of the "all-things-considered better than" relation that his book raises might be addressed by giving up the Independence of Irrelevant Alternatives principle instead (though curiously Temkin never explicitly discusses this possibility with regard to Parfit's Mere Addition Paradox itself).[37] In that sense, my discussion can be seen as exploring in greater depth a possibility that Temkin himself had already schematically sketched out. My main point contra Temkin, however, is that, at least as far as Parfit's Mere Addition Paradox is concerned, these two theoretical options are not on a par. I have argued that, whether we look at it through the lens of a Parfitian view about the badness of inequality or the ideal of maximin, there is nothing about the Mere Addition Paradox that lends support to rejecting the transitivity of betterness (at least *within* an option set). What consideration of the Mere Addition Paradox supports is instead the far less radical notion that the relative goodness of two outcomes can depend on whether or not a third outcome could have instead been chosen.[38]

---

[36] Temkin, "Intransitivity and the Mere Addition Paradox," p. 151.

[37] See, in particular, the brief discussions in Temkin, *Rethinking the Good*, chapter 11, section 4, and chapter 13, section 5.

[38] In *Rethinking the Good*, Temkin presents many other examples from outside the domain of population ethics which, he believes, also show that the transitivity of "all-things-considered better than" is in deep tension with some of our considered judgments. (See, in particular, the "spectrum of ordeals" cases from chapter 5 of this book.) Although I find these cases fascinating and suggestive, I lack the space to discuss them here. For two able critiques of Temkin's arguments, see Nebel, "The Good, the Bad, and the Transitivity of Better Than" and Voorhoeve, "Vaulting Intuition."

9.9 Dynamic Choice and Worries about Money-Pumping

There is one more loose end to tie up. Even though I have shown that we should not accept that A, A+, and B are non-transitively ranked in the *three-possible* case, I do accept each of Parfit's pairwise judgments when understood as judgments about *two-possible* cases. For this reason, I am committed to accepting a weaker form of non-transitivity, namely non-transitivity *across* different option sets.

One might worry that this could lead to problems in contexts of dynamic choice, in particular to the possibility of being "money-pumped" in a sequential version of the Up-Down Case. Suppose that I am first presented with a choice between A and A++; then a choice between A++ and B; and finally a choice between B and A. At each step, I must pay a small sum of money if I wish to choose the latter option. The worry is that, given my evaluative judgments in the three two-possible cases, I should prefer to do so, at each step. Yet the overall effect of making these three trades is to return me to my starting point, only poorer. Surely, the objection goes, there must be something rationally defective with a set of evaluative judgments that would support such a pattern of choice.[39]

To put this worry to rest, we must distinguish two versions of the money-pump scenario.[40] The first, which we can call the "foresight scenario," is one where I am aware, in making my choice between A and A++, that if I pay to choose A++, I will subsequently be offered the second choice between A++ and B, and that, if I pay to choose B, I will subsequently be offered a third choice, to pay to choose A over B.

This is a scenario, I claim, in which the evaluative truths about A, A++, and B do not, in fact, support my being money-pumped, and moreover I know this. For in a situation where I will, sequentially, be offered a choice between all three options, their ethical properties do not differ from those in a three-option case, in which all three options are *simultaneously* available to me. In particular, if choosing option A++ would be morally unjustifiable in a three-option case, because the presence of option B gives the new people an unanswerable complaint against A++, then the same would be true of choosing A++ *and then sticking with it* in the sequential case. The fact that B is not *immediately* available as an alternative to A++ is irrelevant to the question whether it is morally justifiable to remain with A++ once the option of moving to B has become available.

Hence, in confronting the initial choice between A and A++, I know that if I pay to choose A++, I can subsequently bring about one of three outcomes, each of which is worse than sticking with A in the first place: (i) I could trade to A++ and

---

[39] The money-pump objection to intransitive preferences was first presented by Davidson, McKinsey, and Suppes, "Outlines of a Formal Theory of Value."

[40] As is common in this literature. See for instance Rabinowicz, "Money Pump with Foresight."

then stick with this option. But this is worse than remaining with A, on account of the injustice of A++. (ii) I could trade to A++ and, once given the opportunity, pay to trade to B (as I morally ought to), and then subsequently stick with B. But in that case, I have paid twice over to end up with an option that is worse than A. Finally, (iii) I could pay to go from A to A++, from there to B, and thence back to A. In that case, I have paid three times over, only to end up with the same option that I began with. I conclude that, in a scenario with foresight, a rational agent will not be money-pumped.

Suppose, by contrast, that I do *not* know from the start what my options will be. In deciding whether to pay to choose A++ over A, I am not aware that, once I have made this choice, I will subsequently be offered a choice between A++ and B, and so on. Can I now be money-pumped? Yes, I can, given my evaluative judgements about the three two-possible cases. The question is whether this need indicate any rational defect on my part.

I submit that it does not. There are situations where even a perfectly rational agent can be led around in a cycle, paying at every step, without this indicating anything problematic about the structure of her underlying preferences or evaluative judgments. Consider the following example:

Change of Plans:

A single woman is deciding whether to try and become pregnant. Because of a medical issue, she must resort to *in vitro* fertilization. In addition, she is informed that due to an abnormality in her genotype, any child she will be able to conceive, now or at any point in the future, will suffer from a congenital malady, Condition X, which will restrict its life expectancy to about 45 years. There is currently no known treatment for Condition X. However, other than its shortened life expectancy, her child's quality of life will be unaffected and overall it will have a life that is well worth living. The woman has the following preferences:

(1) In the absence of a cure for Condition X, she prefers having a child with Condition X to remaining childless.

(2) If she has a child with Condition X and a cure for this condition becomes available, the woman believes that she is morally required to provide this cure to her child, even if it is very expensive, and so she prefers this.

(3) However, if the cost of providing a cure for Condition X to her child would be very high, the woman would prefer remaining childless to having a child and paying for the cure.

At time t_1, believing correctly that no cure for Condition X currently exists, the woman pays a fertility clinic to start a procedure of *in vitro* fertilization. Shortly after, at t_2, she learns that a cure for Condition X has been found, but that it is very expensive. Believing that it is too late to call off her pregnancy, the woman makes a down payment to sign her future child up for the cure.[41] Finally, at t_3, the woman learns that the procedure of *in vitro* fertilization has not yet yielded a viable embryo but that it soon will; so she pays a small administrative fee to cancel the procedure and ensure that she remains childless.

The woman has paid to trade in a circle. But I can detect no irrationality in doing so. The woman's preferences, both individually and taken as a set, are both reasonable and morally permissible. What makes her pay thrice over only to end up where she began is not some defect in the structure of her preferences, but the fact that, at each but the last step of the cycle, she was operating with incomplete information about what her total option set over time would look like. Sometimes life springs surprises on us. And in responding to these surprises, we may rationally depart from the pattern of choice that a rational agent would have adopted *ex ante*, had he possessed perfect foresight.

9.10 Conclusion

In this chapter, I have proposed a new solution to Derek Parfit's Mere Addition Paradox. I argued that the paradox trades on an ambiguity about the context of choice. There is a sense in which *all three* intuitive judgments about Parfit's case are true, namely as pairwise comparisons in *two-possible* cases. The air of paradox arises from the assumption that these pairwise judgments carry over to a *three-possible* case, in which all three outcomes are possible. But this, I argued, is not the case. In a three-possible case, there is a complaint of *injustice* against option A+ and this, I argued, makes it a worse outcome, not only than B but also than A. This solves the Mere Addition Paradox and blocks the argument toward the Repugnant Conclusion. While there are still many impossibility theorems lurking in the field of population ethics,[42] the threat—if not the philosophical interest—of the Mere Addition Paradox is more apparent than real.

Appendix: Extending the Solution to "Non-Overlapping" Cases

The solution to the Mere Addition Paradox that I have presented in this chapter has focused on a version of the problem in which outcomes A+ and B contain the same two groups of people (the "A-people" and the "new people"). Here, I briefly sketch how my solution can be extended to two variations of the Mere Addition Case that relax this assumption.

Consider, first, a version of the problem, illustrated by Figure 9.6, in which the populations of A+ and B, while equal in size, consist of entirely different individuals.

---

[41] In this stylized case, assume that killing an embryo, *in vitro* or *in utero*, is not legally an option.
[42] For an impressive compendium, see Arrhenius, *Population Ethics*.

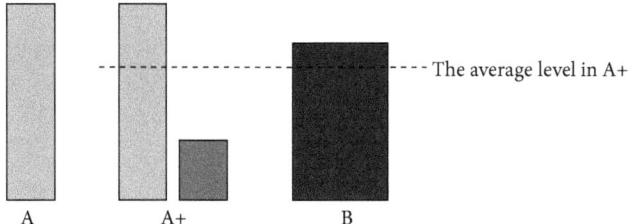

Figure 9.6 A Mere Addition Case with different individuals in A+ and B.

The crucial difference concerns the pairwise comparison of A+ and B. In the version of the paradox discussed in the body of the article, choosing A+ when B was also available was *worse for* someone, namely the "new people," who exist in both these outcomes. By contrast, in the "non-overlapping" case we are now considering, choosing A+ is worse *for* no-one. The people who exist in A+ are numerically non-identical with those in B; hence, choosing B could not have been better for them. Everyone who exists in A+ has a life worth living and is as well-off as it is feasible for them to be. As a result, choosing A+ over B would give no person a *personal* complaint of *injustice*. There is no-one with a legitimate moral claim that has been violated. No-one has been *wronged*.

This does not mean, however, that choosing A+ over B would be morally unproblematic. Indeed, most philosophers, Parfit included, have the confident intuition that it would be morally wrong to choose A+ over B. Granted, if we accept Parfit's claim in *Reasons and Persons* that inequality only makes an outcome worse if can avoid inequality by making some existing people better-off, then the inequality in A+ is not a bad-making feature of this outcome. Nonetheless, anyone with utilitarian or prioritarian leanings should support the verdict that it is wrong to choose A+ over B, given that average and total wellbeing are higher in B and the worst-off are better-off. Injustice, in the sense of riding roughshod over people's legitimate moral claims, is not the only modality of wrongdoing. Choosing A+ over B is wrong in virtue of its *moral opportunity cost*: we could have brought about an outcome in which the same number of people ever live, and the people who exist fare considerably better in the aggregate. (In this sense, the non-overlapping version of the Mere Addition Paradox is akin to another of Parfit's celebrated problem cases in population ethics: the Non-Identity Problem.)

Can 'victimless wrongdoing' of this kind support a claim of deontic badness?[43] Could it make A+, when chosen in a three-option case, a *worse outcome* than it is in a case where the feasible set contains only A and A+?

---

[43] For the notion of victimless wrongdoing and its application to the Non-Identity Problem, see my "Zukünftige Personen und Schuld ohne Opfer." An English translation of this text is available on my homepage.

I believe so. While victimless wrongdoing does not involve the mistreatment of other people, and therefore does not produce the kind relational impairment and estrangement from one's victims that is the result of acting *unjustly*, it is by no means morally neutral whether we act wrongly in this sense. In acting wrongly, the agent still willfully disregards relevant moral considerations. Insofar as we believe that we have reason to take morality seriously and to avoid acting wrongly, we can hardly regard it as a matter of indifference whether people's actions, in a given case, were morally wrong or not. Indeed, as Parfit remarks in *On What Matters*, volume 3: "If there was no deontic badness, it would not in itself matter whether people acted wrongly. What would matter would be only the non-deontic badness of these acts and their effects."[44] Moreover, while choosing A+ over B does not violate the claims of any particular person, doing so fails to respond appropriately to the value and importance of persons in general. As I argue elsewhere, it is precisely because for each person, conditional on her existence, we have reason to want her life to go as well as possible in an absolute sense that in deciding *whom* to create, we should aim to create those persons whose life we expect to go absolutely best (either individually or in the aggregate).[45]

For these reasons, learning that A+ was chosen in a context where B was also available, and where doing so was therefore morally wrong, would be "bad news," even in this non-overlapping scenario. Hence, while A+ is not worse than A in a two-possible case, it *is* worse in a three-possible case, in virtue of the deontic badness of this outcome. The paradox once again dissolves once the context of choice is clarified: each of the three pairwise judgments—that B is better than A+; that A is better than B; and that A+ is not worse than A—comes out as true, if understood as claims about a two-possible case. But in a case where all three outcomes are feasible, we should affirm the following transitive ranking: A is better than B and A+, and B is better than A+.

Consider, finally, the variation of the Mere Addition Case illustrated by Figure 9.7.[46]

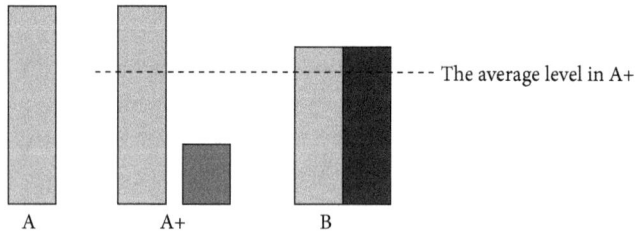

Figure 9.7 A Mere Addition Case with different extra people in A+ and B.

---

[44] Parfit, *On What Matters*, p. 468.
[45] See my "Conditional Reasons and the Procreation Asymmetry."
[46] I thank Jeff McMahan for prompting me to think about this case.

This is a version of the problem in which the A-people exist in all three outcomes, but where the extra people in outcomes A+ and B, while equal in number, are distinct from one another. (Call them, respectively, the "+-people" and the "B-people.") In this case, A+ would not be worse for, or unjust to, the +-people, for they would not exist in either of the other two outcomes. So that reason for thinking that A+ would be worse than A does not apply here. It is true that the +-people would be worse-off than the B-people. And that, on my view, constitutes a *pro tanto* reason for choosing B over A+, if we are to produce either of these two outcomes. However, this reason may not be decisive, all things equal. Notice that in the three-possible choice among A, A+, and B, only B would be worse for the A-people, who will exist in all three possible outcomes. So, if the actual outcome is B, the A-people will have a complaint: they will be worse-off than they would have been if the outcome had been A or A+. By contrast, if the outcome is A+, no-one will have a complaint. The question then is whether the moral reason to cause better-off additional people to exist rather than less well-off people, *if* we are going to cause additional people to exist, outweighs the narrow person-affecting reason not to do what will be worse for the independently existing A-people (people who will exist however we choose). If we think that the reason to avoid people having complaints (by doing what is *worse for* people) is in general stronger than the reason to cause better-off people to exist rather than less well-off people, then it may be not only not unjust to choose A+ but also not wrong.[47] This depends, of course, on the number of individuals and their comparative levels of wellbeing. But in this case, the number of additional people in A+ is the same as the number in B and the difference in their levels of wellbeing is not much greater than the difference between the level of wellbeing of the A-people in A+ and their level of wellbeing in B. I conclude that, plausibly, choosing A+ would *not* be wrong in this variation of the Mere Addition Case, and, hence, that no deontic badness attaches to this option. Consequently, unlike in the other two versions of the Mere Addition Case considered above, there is no reason for the axiological judgment that A+ is worse than A.

Would this verdict make trouble for the solution to the Mere Addition Paradox that I have presented in this essay? If we must concede that, at least in this variation of the case, there truly is no way of avoiding the verdict that A+ is not worse than A, then could we be lead from there to the Repugnant Conclusion after all?

I believe not. The verdict that, in this case,

(1) A+ is not worse than A, even in a three-possible case (since choosing A + is *neither* unjust nor impersonally wrong, all things considered)

---

[47] Two philosophers who have explicitly defended this view are Jeff McMahan and Michael Otsuka. See McMahan, "Causing People to Exist and Saving People's Lives" and Otsuka, "How it Makes a Moral Difference that One is Worse Off than One Could Have Been."

would only make trouble if, as before, we also had reason to affirm that:

(2) B is better than A+.

However, the very considerations that give us reason to endorse (1), in this variation of the Mere Addition Problem, also undermine the case for (2). In fact, I believe that, at least for some values of A+ and B, A+ is *better* than B in this case. As I said, I believe that our narrow person-affecting moral reasons not to do what will be worse for independently existing people can outweigh our reasons to cause better- rather than worse-off additional people to exist, if we are going to cause any additional people to exist. Given this, it would not just permissible to choose A+ rather than B. In fact, failing to do so would be morally wrong. Moreover, it might be said to *wrong* the independently existing people. Independently existing people, I think, have a claim not to be made worse-off in order to create better-off rather than worse-off new people, if there is also the option of not creating any new people at all. And the *deontic badness* of wrongly choosing B over A+, and thereby wronging the independently existing people, can make it the case that, all things considered, B is a *worse outcome* than A+.

Thus, the same kind of consideration—deontic badness—that I appealed to in order to solve the original Mere Addition Paradox, by arguing that A+ is worse than A in the three-possible case, can help us solve this variation of the problem as well—but this time by supporting the judgment that B is worse than A+.[48]

References

Anand, P., "The Philosophy of Intransitive Preference," *The Economic Journal* 103/417 (1993): 337–46.

Arrhenius, G., *Population Ethics: The Challenge of Future Generations* (unpublished manuscript).

Boonin, D., "Don't Stop Thinking about Tomorrow: Two Paradoxes about Duties to Future Generations," *Philosophy & Public Affairs* 25/4 (1996): 267–307.

Broome, J., "Should We Value Population?," *The Journal of Political Philosophy* 13/4 (2005): 399–413.

Cusbert, J., "Acting on Essentially Comparative Goodness," *Thought* 6/2 (2017): 73–83.

Davidson, D., McKinsey, J., and Suppes, P., "Outlines of a Formal Theory of Value," *Philosophy of Science* 22 (1955): 140–60.

---

[48] For extremely valuable comments on earlier drafts of this chapter, I would like to thank Alisabeth Ayars, Ralf Bader, Tim Campbell, Joseph Carlsmith, Tom Dougherty, Tomi Francis, Hilary Greaves, Mark Johnston, Michal Masny, Jeff McMahan, Jake Nebel, Melinda Roberts, Larry Temkin, as well as the participants of the 2019 Princeton Workshop on Procreation and Population Ethics. My biggest debt of gratitude is owed to my former teacher and mentor Derek Parfit, who first kindled in me a fascination for population ethics, and who set, for all of us, an example of philosophical rigor and imagination that we can only strive to emulate.

Frick, J., "On the Survival of Humanity," *Canadian Journal of Philosophy*, 47/2–3 (2017): 344–67.

Frick, J., "Zukünftige Personen und Schuld ohne Opfer," in M. Rüther and S. Muders (eds.), *Worauf es ankommt. Derek Parfits praktische Philosophie in der Diskussion* (Felix Meiner Verlag, 2017), 113–45.

Frick, J., "Conditional Reasons and the Procreation Asymmetry," *Philosophical Perspectives: Ethics* 33/2 (2020): 53–87.

Greaves, H., "Population Axiology," *Philosophy Compass* 12/11 (2017): 12:e12442.

Horton, J., "The Exploitation Problem," *The Journal of Political Philosophy* 27/4 (2019): 469–79.

McMahan, J., "Problems of Population Theory," *Ethics* 92/1 (1981): 96–127.

McMahan, J., "Causing People to Exist and Saving People's Lives," *Journal of Ethics* 17/1–2 (2013): 5–35.

Narveson, J., "Utilitarianism and New Generations," *Mind* 76 (1967): 62–72.

Nebel, J., "The Good, the Bad, and the Transitivity of Better Than," *Noûs* 52/4 (2018): 874–99.

Neumann, M., "Choosing and Describing: Sen and the Irrelevance of Independence [sic] Alternatives," *Theory and Decision* 63 (2007): 79–94.

Otsuka, M., "How it Makes a Moral Difference that One is Worse Off than One Could Have Been," *Politics, Philosophy & Economics* 17/2 (2018): 192–215.

Parfit, D., *Reasons and Persons* (Oxford University Press, 1984).

Parfit, D., "Acts and Outcomes: A Reply to Boonin-Vail," *Philosophy & Public Affairs* 25/4 (1996): 308–17.

Parfit, D., *On What Matters*, volume 3 (Oxford University Press, 2017).

Rabinowicz, W., "Money Pump with Foresight," in M.J. Almeida (ed.), *Imperceptible Harms and Benefits* (Springer, 2000), 123–54.

Roberts, M., "Temkin's Essentially Comparative View, Wrongful Life and the Mere Addition Paradox," *Analysis* 74/2 (2014): 306–26.

Scanlon, T.M., *What We Owe to Each Other* (Belknap, 1998).

Sen, A. "Internal Consistency of Choice," *Econometrica* 6/3 (1993): 495–521.

Tännsjö, T., "Why We Ought to Accept the Repugnant Conclusion," *Utilitas* 14/3 (2009): 339–59.

Temkin, L., "Intransitivity and the Mere Addition Paradox," *Philosophy & Public Affairs* 16/2 (1987): 138–87.

Temkin, L., *Inequality* (Oxford University Press, 1993).

Temkin, L., *Rethinking the Good: Moral Ideals and the Nature of Practical Reasoning* (Oxford University Press, 2012).

Voorhoeve, A., "Vaulting Intuition: Temkin's Critique of Transitivity," *Economics and Philosophy* 29/3 (2013): 409–25.

Wertheimer, A., *Exploitation* (Princeton University Press, 1996).

10
Saving Posterity from a Worse Fate

Niko Kolodny

10.1 Introduction

Suppose we must choose among different outcomes, in which people fare better or worse.[1] Suppose different numbers of people, or at least different people, would ever exist in such outcomes. That is, suppose our choice affects the growth of the population, or the identities of future people. Which outcomes are wrong for us to choose?

Consider the simplest sort of case. Suppose that Eleanor, but no one else, will exist whatever we choose. What's up to us is merely whether her neighborhood will be the Good Place, where she will flourish, or the Medium Place, where she will get by. It would be wrong, we might think, to put her in the Medium Place.

Some qualifications right away. First, the fact that someone will flourish or get by or suffer, fare well or so-so or badly, if we make a choice is a less compelling reason, if any reason at all, when they will fare badly only because of their own choices, despite our best efforts to provision them, to present them with good opportunities, to put them in a position to fare well, should they make the right choices. When I speak in this chapter of our choice affecting how people fare, therefore, it should be understood as shorthand for affecting how people are provisioned, what opportunities they have access to. That, rather than how they ultimately fare, is what makes a claim on us.

Second, of course, we may have agent-relative reasons to give greater weight to ourselves, to our projects, and to our relationships. We may be prohibited from taking certain means to otherwise desirable outcomes. And there may be impersonal values—such as the progress of art and science, biodiversity and the health of natural ecosystems—that bear on our choice, apart from their effects on how people fare. But let's set these aside for the moment. Restricting our attention to how people fare in the outcomes that we might choose, which outcomes are wrong for us to choose?

---

[1] Thanks to audiences at Universitat Pompeu Fabra, Princeton University, Queens University, and the 2019 Society for Applied Philosophy Conference at Cardiff University, as well as written comments from Tom Dougherty, Johann Frick, Andrew Lister, Véronique Munoz-Dardé, Philip Pettit, Ketan Ramakrishnan, Kieran Setiya, and Jay Wallace. I am especially indebted to two of the editors of this volume, Jimmy Goodrich and Jeff McMahan, for extensive and probing comments.

Third, we might well think that it isn't wrong to put Eleanor in the Medium Place, if she wouldn't be too badly off there: if, to put it crudely, she would be above a threshold of sufficiency so that failing to raise her even higher, even at no cost to us, would be at most supererogatory. But suppose that she would be below that threshold in the Medium Place, although she's above the threshold of being glad to have been born.[2]

Granting that it is, intuitively, wrong to put Eleanor in the Medium Place, why is it? There are two broad ways of thinking about it. The more familiar way might be called "Benefit Thinking." Benefit Thinking explains why it is wrong to put Eleanor in the Medium Place by pointing out that we benefit people (in this case, Eleanor) more by putting her in the Good Place than we benefit people (again, still just Eleanor) by putting her in the Medium Place.

It's another way of thinking about it, which might be called, "Worse-Fate Thinking," that I want to explore. Worse-Fate Thinking explains why it would be wrong to put Eleanor in the Medium Place by pointing out that people in the Medium Place (namely, Eleanor) are left to a worse fate in the Medium Place. Put another way, the people in the Medium Place (namely, Eleanor) have reason to prefer how things are for people (not necessarily themselves, but in this case, as it happens, herself, Eleanor) in some alternative outcome that we might choose: namely, the Good Place. Put still another way, leaving Eleanor in the Medium Place is wrong because it increases, relative to some alternative that we might choose, the number of people fated to exist a lower level of well-being. If we choose the Good Place, the number of people at every level less than whatever level of flourishing obtains at the Good Place is zero. If we choose the Medium Place, by contrast, the number at some level less than that level of flourishing increases to one.

One's first thought may be that the second answer—that we are saving people from something worse—has greater moral force. Isn't it more urgent to save people from something worse than merely to benefit them? But one's second thought may be to discount the first thought, as an illusion or artifact of framing. Surely benefitting Eleanor by putting her in the Good Place rather than the Medium Place comes to the same thing as saving her from the worse fate of the Medium Place by putting her in the Good Place. So Worse-Fate Thinking is no different from Benefit Thinking.

---

[2] It might also be said that, while the fact that people would fare better or worse can be a reason for action, it is in many contexts not a reason of individual morality, which might tend to make a private person's choice wrong, but instead a reason of administrative morality, which would tend instead to make the choice of some public agency wrong or in some other sense incorrect. Or it might be said that it is not a moral reason at all, but instead an "extramoral" reason. For powerful arguments for these alternative interpretations of the significance, in many contexts, of the fact that people would fare better or worse, see Wallace (2019). It may be that this chapter is best understood as an account of administrative morality or extramoral reasons.

It is true that Worse-Fate Thinking and Benefit Thinking deliver the same verdicts in the ordinary, same-people choices with which we are most familiar, where neither the number nor the identities of people are affected by what we choose. But Worse-Fate Thinking delivers different verdicts from Benefit Thinking in more exotic choices that affect the numbers or identities of people.

The key difference between Worse-Fate and Benefit Thinking might be put this way. Suppose our choice is whether to cause Eleanor to exist at the Good Place or not to cause anyone to exist. In this case, choosing that no one exist does not save people from a worse fate. This is because existing with a life worth living is not a worse fate than not existing. Someone who exists with a life worth living does not have reason to prefer how things are for people when no people exist. So Worse-Fate Thinking finds no grounds to count as wrong causing Eleanor to exist. Benefit Thinking agrees, insofar as causing someone to exist with a life worth living benefits them. However, Eleanor's existing also does not save from a worse fate. Not to exist is not to suffer a worse fate worse than a life worth living. It's not a condition someone is in at all and so not a condition such that in it someone has reason to prefer how things are for people in some alternative. So Worse-Fate Thinking also finds no grounds to count as wrong not causing Eleanor to exist. Here Benefit Thinking disagrees, since not causing Eleanor to exist passes up a chance to benefit someone.

I will argue that the principle, "Worse-Fate," that I formulate to represent this alternative to Benefit Thinking gives intuitive answers to many of the questions of population ethics. To indulge in some jargon that will be familiar to the initiated, but that will have be explained in what follows, Worse-Fate accounts for the "procreation asymmetry," avoids the "repugnant choice," and delivers plausible results in "mixed same-number" cases.

What's the catch? One catch, it might be said, is that Worse-Fate implies that a choice may not be required, and may even be wrong, when it benefits people more. But this is just to say that Worse-Fate Thinking diverges from Benefit Thinking. And it is surprisingly hard to come up with non-question-begging grounds for the conclusion that our concern for how people fare reflects Benefit Thinking rather than Worse-Fate Thinking. After all, if we restrict our attention to ordinary, same-people choices, they seem to have equal title to represent our concern for how people fare, since they deliver precisely the same verdicts. If, once we consider the more exotic choices, which do affect numbers and identities, Worse-Fate Thinking delivers more intuitive verdicts, then why not conclude that Worse-Fate Thinking best represents our concern for how people fare? Why not conclude that we misinterpret ourselves when we suppose that our intuitions in the original case of Eleanor express Benefit Thinking? Why not conclude that our intuitions are in fact guided by Worse-Fate Thinking? Or, to consider an alternative hypothesis, perhaps both Worse-Fate and Benefit Thinking are operative in our concern for how people fare in ordinary, same-people choices. We just don't notice the difference in ordinary, same-people choices, since they deliver the same practical verdicts. To represent our concern for how people fare, we must have a principle that does justice to both Worse-Fate and Benefit Thinking. In that case, Worse-Fate can be amended, into a principle I call "Worse-Fate-Pareto." That avoids the most persuasive counterexamples (or, as it seems to me, apparent counterexamples) to Worse-Fate.

A second catch is that Worse-Fate gives practical verdicts that pattern in seemingly "incoherent" ways, such as violating "transitivity." However, I don't see a compelling reason to assume that practical verdicts must be "coherent" in the alleged ways. So long as we can state a principle that explains the intuitively correct verdicts and that has an attractive rationale, we secure the sort of coherence that matters.

Worse-Fate implies that a choice to cause someone to be can be wrong even though it leaves no particular person worse off than that person would have been in any alternative. Suppose that our choice is either to cause Mindy to be in the Medium Place or to cause Eleanor to be in the Good Place. According to Worse-Fate, it would be wrong to cause Mindy to be in the Medium Place. But Mindy is not worse off than she would be in the alternative. How then can she complain? And if no one can complain, how can it be wrong? This is Parfit (1984)'s "non-identity problem."

However, Worse-Fate can be seen as part of a more complex view, Worse-Fate-As-Answer, where Worse-Fate functions as an answer to a person's putative complaint about having been caused to be. On this view, people can complain about choices that cause them to be, even when those choices do not make them worse off, on the grounds that such choices harm or invade them, without their consent. One thing that can answer such a putative complaint is that the choice saved people from a worse fate. However, when a choice to cause someone to be failed to save people from a worse fate, the people caused to be have an unanswered complaint against that choice. So Mindy in the Medium Place has a complaint if she is caused to be that Eleanor in the Good Place lacks if she is caused to be.

Whether we can accept any of these ideas, Worse-Fate, Worse-Fate-Pareto, or Worse-Fate-As-Answer, I don't know. Perhaps we are committed, and rightly so, to Benefit Thinking. But if so, then this chapter at very least sets up a collision with error that gives us a sharper appreciation of that deep truth.

10.2 Taxonomy

Some labels will help us to keep things straight. Say that someone is "contingent" relative to a choice set if whether that person ever exists depends on the choice we make: there's at least one choice in the set where that person exists at some time, and at least one other choice in the set where that person never exists. Someone is "non-contingent" relative to a choice set if in every choice in the set, that person (like Eleanor) exists at some time. A "same-people" choice set involves only non-contingent persons. A "contingent" (or in Parfit's terms, "pure") choice set involves only contingent persons. A "mixed" choice set involves some contingent and some non-contingent persons. In a "same-number" choice set, the same number of persons exist no matter what choice we make. In a "different-number" choice set, the number varies with the choice we make.

Observe that in different-number choice sets, at least some people who exist in the choice with the higher number must be contingent. So that leaves us with five categories, represented in Table 10.1. Our strategy for covering all of these categories proceeds in four steps. We begin with "pairs": choice sets with only two options. First, we assume trade-off rules that tell us which option it is wrong to choose in same-people pairs, insofar as we seek to avoid consigning people to worse fates. Second, we argue that since such trade-off rules are not sensitive to whether people are contingent, the rules that tell us what it is wrong to choose in same-people pairs also tell us what is wrong to choose in contingent and mixed same-number pairs, insofar as we seek to avoid consigning people to worse fates. Third, we propose a way to transform different-number pairs into same-number pairs, so that the rules tell us which option it is wrong to choose in different-number pairs as well. Finally, we generalize to choice sets with more than two options by saying that it is wrong to choose an option given that choice set if it would be wrong to choose that option given a pair of that option and another option in the set.

I assume throughout that we have full information about what will happen if we make a choice, including what choices will then be available to us. I assume that a choice A that is available to us in the future, if we make some choice B now, is a choice that we can make now: that is, we can make the composite choice of making B now and A later.

10.3 Same-People Choices

Let's start with same-people choices. They are our theoretical base camp, where our moral judgment feels most at home (or at least as at home as anywhere else).

Table 10.1 Categories of Choices

	None contingent	All contingent	Some contingent, some not
Same number	Same people	Contingent same number	Mixed same number
Different number	[Not possible]	Contingent different number	Mixed different number

10.3.1 Trade-off Rules

The first matter to consider is trade-offs. Saving some people from worse fates may have the opportunity cost of failing to save other people from worse fates. How should we make such trade-offs? We make the "prioritarian" assumption that, other things equal, we have more reason to save people from, as it were, worse worse fates: lower lower levels. And we allow some aggregation. Other things equal, we have more reason to save more people rather than fewer people from a worse fate.

Consider, in Figure 10.1, a choice in which, if we opt for Most Better, one person drops[3] from 101 to 100, but 99 rise from 101 to 200. Arguably, it isn't wrong to choose Most Better. On the one hand, we give some, but not absolute, priority to reducing (perhaps to zero) the number who occupy lower levels: to saving people from worse worse fates. The fact that All Equal has one fewer at 100 than Most Better has counts more in All Equal's favor than that Most Better has one fewer at 101 than All Equal has counts in Most Better's favor, since 100 is a lower level than 101. On the other hand, we give weight to how many fewer people occupy lower levels: to saving more people rather than fewer from a worse fate. Since Most Better saves so many more from 101 than All Equal saves from 100, this second effect, arguably, swamps the first.

Without presuming to specify what the trade-off rules are, let's assume that there are some trade-off rules such that for any same-people pair $\{A, B\}$, the rules tell us either that A is not wrong or that B is not wrong, given $\{A, B\}$, at least

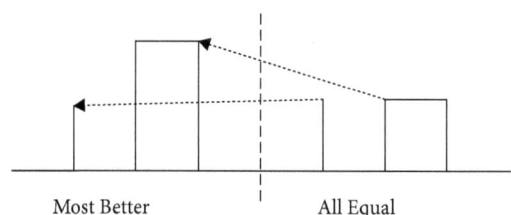

Figure 10.1 Reasonable Trade-Off.

Note: As usual in such diagrams, the width of the bar represents the size of the population, whereas the height represents how well off the people in that population are. The first "bar" or line in this particular diagram just represents a single person. The dotted arrows indicate the trade-offs. If Most Better is chosen, one person is at a lower level, indicated by the downward sloping line, whereas the rest are at a higher level, indicated by the upward sloping line.

---

[3] Here and throughout I ignore the possibility of status-quo effects: for example, that other things equal there is more reason to keep things as they are than to make a change. The examples should be read in such a way that no option represents the status quo, even if, for convenience, I sometimes use expressions that suggest a status quo, such as "drops."

insofar as saving people from worse fates is concerned. This leaves a lot open, of course. But the aim of this chapter is not so much to tell us how to treat same-people choices as it is to tell us, once we have decided how to treat same-people choices, to extend that treatment to the other, more exotic choices. So far, then, we have just a kernel of a Worse-Fate principle, which tells us at least when choices are wrong given same-people pairs.

10.3.2 Zero Embargo

Although, in the examples so far, all of the people in question had lives worth living (represented by positive levels) in every outcome, Worse-Fate and the trade-off rules should also be understood to cover cases where people have lives such that they have reason to prefer never to have been brought into existence (with negative levels): where people have lives, to use a somewhat unfortunate phrase, not for them worth living. For example, in Figure 10.2, it is wrong to choose All Negative, even though the fate for a single person of being at −101 in One Negative is worse than the fate for a single person of being at −100 in All Negative.

Among the trade-off rules may be Zero Embargo, which gives absolute priority to improving things for people below zero before improving things for people above zero. Zero Embargo can be stated more exactly, to reflect the point that to save from a worse fate is always to reduce the number of people who occupy a lower level, which, in same-people cases, is also to increase the number who occupy a higher level. Zero Embargo gives absolute priority to reducing the numbers at lower levels below zero—to "raising" people below zero closer to zero—over reductions in numbers at lower levels above zero—to "raising" people already at zero or above even higher.

> Zero Embargo: Given the choice of an outcome with exactly n people each at some positive level, it is wrong to choose instead an outcome of $n - m$ people (no matter how many) each at some positive level (no matter how high) and m

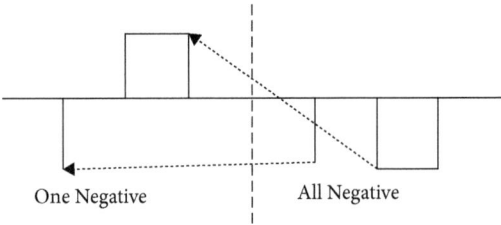

One Negative | All Negative

Figure 10.2 Reasonable Trade-Off (Negative).

people (no matter how few) each at some negative level (no matter how close to zero).

Zero Embargo claims that there is a discontinuity at zero, such that gains below zero may not be traded off against gains above zero. There is a ban on exchanges, as it were, across the boundary that divides lives that are not worth living from lives that are. I myself am drawn to Zero Embargo. Why should anyone have to be consigned to a life not worth living just so others, who already have a life worth living, should be even better off? However, I will not assume Zero Embargo in this chapter. I will instead indicate where assuming it makes a difference.

10.3.3 Sufficiency

These trade-off rules may imply a sufficiency threshold or thresholds. That is, the trade-off rules may be such that, first, no choice that leaves everyone above some threshold is wrong. In other words, above that threshold, how we make "trade-offs" is not of moral concern. Second, the trade-off rules may be such that any choice that leaves someone below the (same or different) threshold is wrong when the other choice in the pair leaves everyone above that threshold. In effect, Zero Embargo is such a threshold, located at zero.

10.3.4 Equality and "Leveling Down"

The trade-off rules tell us how to triage, when saving some people from worse fates has the opportunity cost of failing to save others from worse fates. These rules do not express a preference for equality as such. Indeed, insofar as the trade-off rules are such rules of triage, they not only do not require, but moreover prohibit, "leveling down." At least, this is so for any case of leveling down such that most will agree (or at least feel defensive about not agreeing) that it should be prohibited, or at least not be required. Given a same-people pair $\{A, B\}$, if B differs from A only in that the number in a higher occupied level H in A is reduced by n and the number at some lower occupied level L in A is increased by n, and all are below the level of sufficiency, then B is wrong. B simply assigns those additional n to the worse fate of L (rather than H), while offering nothing in return as far as saving from worse fates is concerned. This is not meant to rule out the possibility of reasons of a different kind, independent of saving from worse fates, for equalizing as such. Perhaps a more equal state of affairs is, in that respect, impersonally better. I find that hard to credit, though. It seems like a fetish for a certain kind of cosmic pattern. At any rate, it is a different sort of reason.

10.3.5 Ties

Suppose the trade-off rules leave a tie; more than one outcome is not wrong. However, everyone is below the threshold, if there is one, above which any "trade-offs" are not of moral concern. And a lottery is possible. Then we should give each person who might be better off if the tie is resolved in a certain way the highest chance of the tie being resolved in that way, compatible with fairness to others. So if in *A*, Ada is at 10 and Bill is at 11 and in *B*, Ada is at 11 and Bill is at 10, then we should decide between *A* and *B* by tossing a fair coin. That gives Ada the highest chance of the eleventh unit, namely a 0.5 chance, compatibly with fairness to Bill. To give any higher chance to Ada would mean giving a lower chance to Bill. That would be unfair to Bill, since he is in the same situation. I will view this as not itself part of Worse-Fate, but as an independent Highest Fair Chance Principle which is engaged when Worse-Fate leaves a tie.

10.3.6 Levels Not Losses

When evaluating how well one outcome saves people from worse fates relative to the alternatives, I believe, we should consider only the number of people at each level, whoever they may be, at that outcome as compared with the number of people at each level in the alternative outcomes. We should not consider how much better or worse *particular people fare* at that outcome as compared with how *they themselves fare* at some alternative. In a slogan, we should consider "levels not losses." Requiring that our Worse-Fate principle consider levels not losses will have similar consequences to allowing it not to be "narrowly person-affecting," in Parfit's terminology. To be sure, this maneuver—to follow Parfit in allowing principles not to be narrowly person-affecting—is no great innovation. If there is something new to say here, it is this. While the rejection of a requirement of narrow person-affectingness is usually motivated by exotic choices, in which the choice affects the identities or numbers of people, there is already reason to consider levels not losses even if we consider only garden-variety, same-people choices.

A focus on levels not losses is closely related to what we might call "outcome-anonymity." A principle is outcome anonymous just when once we know, for each outcome, how many people are at which level in that outcome, attaching names—that is, learning who is at which level in which outcome—provides no further information relevant to applying the principle. For example, if in *A*, Ada is at 10 and Bill is at 11 and in *B*, Ada is at 11 and Bill is at 10, then either neither outcome should be wrong or both should be, since they differ only in the names attached to the people at the relevant levels. As far as our Worse-Fate principle is concerned, the two outcomes amount to the same thing: one person at 10, one person at 11.

Table 10.2 Outcome Anonymity

	Ada	Bill
A	10	11
B	11	10
C	13	1

Outcome-anonymity blocks sensitivity to losses: to how much better or worse a particular person, such as Ada, is relative to another outcome. For example Table 10.2, outcome-anonymity requires A and B to be equivalent even though A differs from B with respect to, say, how much Ada loses relative to C. In A she loses 3, in B she loses 2. If outcome-anonymity is independently plausible, then it provides some support for a focus on levels not losses.[4]

A further argument for considering levels not losses is that a principle that considers losses will have difficulty avoiding the following result: that a tie between outcomes that differ only in a permutation of names can be broken by introduction of an outcome that it would be wrong to choose. Suppose that it would be wrong to choose C. Then, one might think, neither A nor B is wrong. Invoking the Highest Fair Chance Principle, we should flip a coin. But now consider a principle that considers losses rather than levels, such as the Minimax Loss Principle, which says that it is wrong to choose an outcome that fails to minimize the maximum difference between someone's level in that outcome and that person's highest level in any outcome (compare Meacham 2012). According to that principle, the introduction of C, which again is wrong to choose, would make A wrong. This is because in A Ada is 3 below her maximum of 13, whereas in B Bill is only 1 below his maximum of 11.

Why is this result to be avoided? To begin with, there is the intuition that the privileging of B is unfair to Bill. If, when confronted with just A and B, we would think that we should give Bill a 0.5 chance at the eleventh unit, why should the introduction of C lead us to think that giving Bill any chance at the eleventh unit would be wrong? A proponent of the Minimax Loss Principle, presumably, will reply that Ada should be compensated for the additional units she loses by our not choosing C, which would have given her 13. However, this reply violates what we might call the Wrongful Gain Principle: If it would be wrong for someone to have something, then the fact that some choice makes it the case that they go without

---

[4] That said, the argument for outcome-anonymity may seem stronger than it really is if it is mistaken with what we might call "choice-anonymity": that changing the names at the top of the columns, reversing Ada's and Bill's levels at every outcome, makes no difference. A principle can be choice anonymous without being outcome anonymous, as is the case with the Minimax Loss Principle presently discussed. So it overstates the case to say that a violation of outcome-anonymity is a violation of impartiality or moral equality. For this reason, I worry that Frick (2017, 356) overstates the case when he labels the axiological analogue of outcome-anonymity the "Principle of Impartiality."

that thing cannot make that choice wrong. What the master loses in manumitting his slave, what the thief forgoes in not stealing a purse, what the candidate fails to attain in not being the beneficiary of a third party's rigging the election, and so forth are not things for which they are owed compensation. Since Ada would only have the additional units under C if we chose wrongly, the fact that she must be forgo them is likewise not something for which she is owed compensation.

10.4 Contingent Same-Number Cases

Insofar as Worse-Fate considers levels not losses, it treats contingent same-number cases in precisely the same way as same-people cases. So Worse-Fate implies, intuitively, the deontic equivalent of Parfit (1984)'s "Same Number Quality Claim or Q" at least as restricted to contingent cases: that it is wrong to cause a group of contingent people, the Lows, to live lives at a lower level, still worth living, when we could cause instead the same number of entirely distinct contingent people, the Highs, to live lives at a higher level. (Parfit's "Depletion" and "The 14-Year-Old Girl" are the canonical cases.)

True, if we choose the Lows, we do not make those particular people worse off than they would be if we chose the Highs. But again Worse-Fate considers levels not losses; it is insensitive to how particular people fare relative to another outcome. And, as we saw, there is already reason in same-people cases to favor a principle that considers levels not losses, even before considering exotic cases, in which identities change.

10.5 Mixed Cases

Mixed cases involve both contingent people, whose existence depends on our choice, and non-contingent people, who will exist no matter what we choose. Since Worse-Fate considers levels not losses, it again treats contingent people just like non-contingent people. So it implies that an option in a mixed same-number case is wrong just when the corresponding option in a corresponding same-people (or contingent same-number) case would be.[5]

This gives us intuitive results in mixed same-number cases. Consider Parfit (2017)'s "Case Four" (Table 10.3):

---

[5] Contrast Voorhoeve and Fleurbaey (2016) and Otsuka (2018). McMahan (2013) explores the possibility that it may depend on what happens in other outcomes on the grounds that it entitles people to regret what might have been.

Table 10.3 Parfit's Case Four

	Tom	Dick	Harry
A	50 years of pain		One day of pain
B		One day of pain	Two days of pain

Table 10.4 Parfit's Case Four Modified.

	Dummy	Harry
A'	50 years of pain	One day of pain
B'	One day of pain	Two days of pain

As Parfit observes, a view that favored non-contingent people, such as Harry, perhaps on the ground that Harry would otherwise have been worse off, might make it wrong, counterintuitively, to choose B.

Worse-Fate, by contrast, because it considers levels not losses, implies that it is wrong to make a choice in a mixed case that would be wrong in the corresponding same-people case. To construct such a case, we simply shift cells to the right to fill in any empty cells, as in Table 10.4. Since A' is wrong and B' isn't given {A', B'}, A is wrong and B isn't in Case Four.

Having said this, mixed choices may still differ from same-people or contingent choices, because there may be other differences between contingent and non-contingent people that are morally relevant. One such difference concerns the objections that they have to what we choose. If we choose B, then does not non-contingent Harry have a *pro tanto* objection, on his own behalf, that he could have been better off had we chosen A? By contrast, if we choose A, then contingent Tom has no objection of this kind: no objection that he could have been better off if we had chosen B. In section 10.15, we will consider a different objection that Tom might still have. But for now let us assume that Tom has no objection. Suppose that the only thing that can answer a person's objection to a choice, so that they do not have a complaint about it, so that we do not wrong them by making it, is that others would have had objections at least as strong to any alternative. It would then follow that we wrong someone by making a choice to which they have an objection when we could have chosen an alternative to which no one would have had any objection. It would then follow that we wrong Harry by choosing B.

However, I think that we should say instead that, insofar as someone's objection to a choice is that they would have been better off had we made a different choice, the fact, if it is a fact, that any other choice would have left people to a worse fate can answer their objection. This is what we can say to Harry when we choose B. The alternative, A, would have left someone to a worse fate; there would have been someone with fifty years of pain, whereas at B there is only someone with two days of pain. This, it seems to me, reasonably expresses our intuitive disquiet about choosing A, why we feel that Harry's objection has little force in this context. This does not deny that there is a morally relevant asymmetry between contingent Tom and non-contingent Harry. Harry has an objection at one outcome, whereas Tom has no objection at any outcome. But this asymmetry makes no difference to the verdict in this case, since Harry's objection can be answered, by citing that the alternative would have meant a worse fate for someone.

It is compatible with this, however, that Harry's non-contingency can be a tie-breaker. Change the case so that Tom in A^*, like Harry in B, will suffer two days of pain. Then choosing B does not save anyone from a worse fate. In that case, perhaps Harry does have an unanswered objection to our choosing B, in which case we wrong Harry by choosing B. Note that this is compatible with the Wrongful Benefits Principle. The gain of another day free of pain in A^* is not something that it would be wrong for Harry to have.[6]

Here's another line of thought to a similar conclusion. Another distinguishing feature of a contingent person, apart from the fact our choosing differently cannot make them better off, is that we cannot *give* a contingent person a chance of existence. We can only *make it the case that* there is a chance that they exist. This may mean that the Highest Fair Chance Principle applies to mixed and same-people cases in different ways. Consider again the choice between A^* and B, which apart from issues of contingency is symmetrical. Should we give Harry only a 0.5 chance of A^*? If we can't give Tom any chance, then Harry may truly say that we can give Harry a better than 0.5 chance of A^*, without thereby reducing the chance we give Tom of B. So perhaps 1 chance of A^* is the highest chance we can give Harry without unfairly depriving anyone else, such as Tom, of a better chance. So, by another route, the fact that Harry is non-contingent is a tie-breaking reason to choose A^* over B.

10.6 Contingent Different-Number Cases Below Zero

Now let us consider how to extend Worse-Fate to (contingent and mixed) different-number cases. Before getting lost in the details, let us remind ourselves of the basic strategy. First we transform different-number cases into same-number cases. Then we apply to the transformed cases whatever trade-off rules that we

---

[6] If non-contingency is a tie-breaker, then we should choose Pregnancy Testing over Pre-Conception Testing in Parfit (1984, 367), and so resist Parfit's "No-Difference View." Thanks to Andrew Williams for pointing this out.

have already decided are appropriate for same-number cases. The transformations are not ad hoc manipulations to deliver intuitive verdicts. They have an underlying rationale. This is to save people from a worse fate, in light of certain observations about what counts as a worse fate: a condition such that in it one would have reason to prefer how things are for people in the alternative. The two most important observations will be, first, that someone's existing with a life worth living does not save from a worse fate where the alternative is non-existence. Second, non-existence does save from a worse fate where the alternative is someone's existing with a life not worth living.

How we transform different-number cases depends on whether we are considering people in "negative territory," with lives below zero, or people in "non-negative territory," with lives at or above zero. Let's begin by considering cases in which anyone who exists will be in negative territory.

Let's also suppose, for the moment, that at most one person exists. Other things equal, we save people from a worse fate by replacing a person at a lower level, say, -100, with someone at a higher level, say, -50. The best that we can do by way of saving people from a worse fate, however, is simply not to bring anyone into existence. So long as someone comes to be, we are assuming, they will be below zero. So they will have reason to prefer how things are for people in an outcome in which no one exists: "how things are for people" being that no people exist. If the alternative is no one's existing, it is a worse fate to exist below zero.

Now let's suppose that more than one person may exist, while continuing to suppose that anyone who exists is below zero. Bringing one fewer person into existence (by supposition at some negative level) prevents one more person from the worse fate of existing at some negative level.

This licenses the following accounting fiction: treat bringing one fewer person into existence (by supposition at some negative level) as equivalent to replacing a person (at that negative level) with someone at zero. Replacement by someone at zero, like not being brought into existence at all, saves one person (who would otherwise be at some negative level) from a worse fate.

By doing this, we can transform a different-number case into a same-number case. Each fewer person brought into existence becomes, as it were, a person brought into existence at zero. Once we have reduced it to a same-number case, then we can apply whatever trade-off rules we would apply in a same-number case. More generally:

> If outcome A in a pair $\{A, B\}$ has fewer people than outcome B (all of whom, recall, are below zero) add people at zero to A until the groups are the same size, making a new outcome A'. Then apply the trade-off rules to the resulting pair, $\{A', B\}$, to determine which, if either, is wrong. A is wrong given $\{A, B\}$ iff A' is wrong given $\{A', B\}$. B is wrong given $\{A, B\}$ iff B is wrong given $\{A', B\}$.

This explains why we should choose Parfit's "Hell One" with a few below zero over "Hell Two" with vastly many only slightly better off (Parfit 1984, 406). The comparison becomes one between Hell Two and, as it were, Hell One', where people are added at zero to equalize the numbers. Assuming plausible trade-off rules, given {Hell One', Hell Two}, Hell Two is wrong and Hell One' isn't. So given {Hell One, Hell Two}, Hell Two is wrong and Hell One isn't.[7]

10.7 Contingent Different-Number Cases Above Zero

Now let's consider cases in which anyone who exists will be in non-negative territory. Let's begin, as before, by supposing that at most one person exists.

In such cases, no one's existing would not save anyone from a worse fate. Existing at some level at or above zero is not a worse fate than not existing. It's not a condition such that someone in it would have reason to prefer how things are for people—namely, not existing—at the alternative. Nor does someone's existing save anyone from a worse fate. Not existing is not a worse fate than existing at a level at or above zero. Indeed, it makes little sense to describe non-existence as a "condition" such that someone "in that condition" would have reason to prefer existing at a level at or above zero.

This is perhaps the key difference between Worse-Fate and Benefit Thinking. While seeking to prevent people from suffering worse fates would not give us any reason to create people with lives worth living—to "prevent people from not existing"—seeking to benefit people would give us reason to create people with lives worth living, at least if we benefit people by creating them with lives worth living.

Now let's suppose that more than one person may exist, while continuing to suppose that anyone who exists is at or above zero. Given that anyone who exists will be at or above zero, we should not, in contrast to the approach of previous subsection where everyone was in negative territory, treat one fewer person at a positive level as equivalent to replacing a person at a positive level with a person at zero. Being at zero rather than at some positive level is a worse fate. But simply not existing rather than being at some positive level, which is what we are actually considering, is not a worse fate.

So I suggest an alternative way of reducing such different-number cases to same-number cases. This is simply to ignore the best-off people in the more populous outcome. First I illustrate how this would work. Then I try to justify it.

---

[7] As Alex Voorhoeve pointed out to me, this accounting fiction—adding a person at zero for each fewer person—is more questionable if we hold that equality itself matters. Hell One' has significant inequality, whereas Hell One does not. While some may be troubled by this, I am not. As I noted in section 10.3.4, I do not think that equality itself matters.

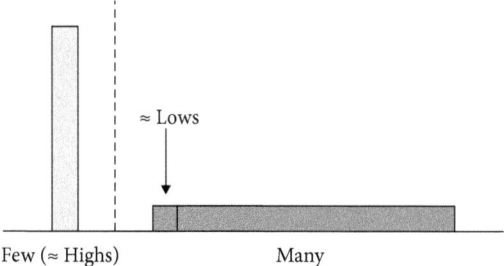

Figure 10.3 Repugnant Choice.

If outcome A in a pair $\{A, B\}$ has more people than outcome B (all of whom, recall, are at or above zero) subtract from A the best-off people from A until the groups are the same size, making a new outcome A'. Then, as before, apply apply the trade-off rules to the resulting pair, $\{A', B\}$, to determine which, if either, is wrong. A is wrong given $\{A, B\}$ iff A' is wrong given $\{A', B\}$. B is wrong given $\{A, B\}$ iff B is wrong given $\{A', B\}$.

Worse-Fate thus implies that it is wrong to make the repugnant choice: to bring it about that the Many exist with lives barely worth living, rather than that the Few exist with better lives Parfit (1984) (Figure 10.3).

We subtract a sufficient number from the Many (any of whom counts as among the "best off" in Many) so as to equalize numbers with the Few.[8] We are then left with a contingent same-number case like the choice between the Highs and the Lows, where the Few have become the Highs and the Many have become the Lows. We have already agreed that it would then be wrong to choose the Lows over the Highs. So, likewise, it would be wrong to choose the Many over the Few.[9]

Now on to justification. To explain how this approach embodies Worse-Fate Thinking, why it is an appropriate generalization of the single-person case with which we began this subsection, we proceed by cases. As shorthand, say that A "loses" to B iff A is wrong given $\{A, B\}$ and B isn't wrong given $\{A, B\}$.

First, suppose B does not lose, according to the trade-off rules, to A', the reduced outcome with the surplus, best-off population removed. Could B somehow lose to A, the unreduced outcome with the surplus population restored? Or suppose that A' loses to B. Could A somehow not lose to B? (Figure 10.3 "Repugnant Choice" illustrates both possibilities.) In other words, could the

---

[8] In the diagrams, different fill patterns in the bars indicate different people. So, this diagram represents a contingent different-number case, in which none of the people in Many exist in Few.

[9] Another strategy for avoiding the Repugnant Choice is to appeal to the loss of impersonal values (see section 10.10.2.2) that the Many entail and, perhaps, to deny Negative Transitivity (see section 10.11.2). Compare Parfit (2016).

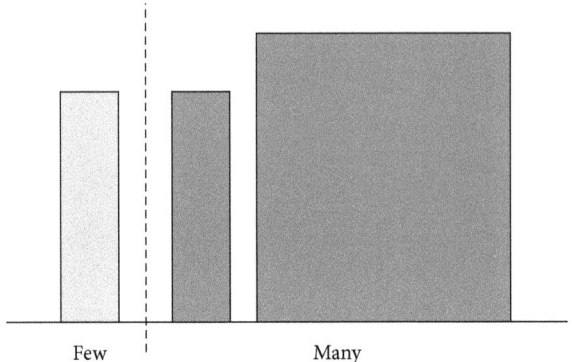

Figure 10.4 Ignoring the Best Off.

unreduced *A* somehow do better against *B* than does the reduced *A*'? It is hard to see how. For *A* merely adds to *A*' people at some levels or other. Adding people at one level can't reduce the number of people at some other level. And saving people from a worse fate requires reducing the number at some level.

The next sort of case: Suppose that *B* loses to *A*', the reduced outcome with the surplus, best-off population removed. And suppose that all of the surplus best off subtracted from *A* were at or above the highest level in *B*. Can *B* somehow not lose to *A*? Or suppose that *A*' does not lose to *B*. Can *A* somehow lose to *B*? (Figure 10.4 "Ignoring the Best Off," illustrates this second possibility.) In other words, could *B* somehow do better against the unreduced *A* than against the reduced *A*'? Not given our supposition that all of the surplus best off subtracted from *A* are at or above the highest level in *B*. *B* does not save from a worse fate any of the best off "added back" to *A*, since each person added back is at least as well off as anyone in *B*.

In the final sort of case, *B* again loses to *A*', or *A*' does not lose to *B*, but now not all of the best off subtracted from *A* were at or above the highest level in *B*. It's less clear what to say about such cases. With an admittedly weaker rationale, and perhaps only as a placeholder, however, I will say that *B* still can't do better against *A*. The weaker rationale is that the advocate of *A* can say, against the advocate of *B*, "Choose from *A* any population same in number to *B*, even the worst off in *A*, and *A* does more to save the members of that population from worse fates than does *B*."

Whether or not we accept this rationale, we can treat this approach as a placeholder for some more nuanced treatment of such cases. None of the cases that we have cause to consider in this chapter are of this form. That is, to address classic examples such as the Repugnant Choice, Mere Addition, and so on, we only need to consider cases in which the best off subtracted from *A* are all better off than the best off in *B*.

10.8 Contingent Different-Number Cases Above and Below Zero

To address contingent different-number pairs with people above and below zero, we combine the two approaches. To address choice sets with more than two options, we say that an outcome is wrong given a set if it is wrong when paired with another option in the set. We can now state Worse-Fate, our formalization of Worse-Fate Thinking, in a more general form.

> Worse-Fate: Given a choice set, S, consider each pair of outcomes, $\{A, B\}$ in S. First step: Take whichever outcome, if any, has fewer people below zero. Add dummy zeros to that outcome until the number of people below zero and dummy zeros at that outcome is the same as the number of people below zero in the other outcome. So, suppose that A has no more people below zero than B. Construct A' by adding people at zero to A until the number of people below zero and dummy zeros at A is the same as the number of people below zero in B. Rechristen B as B'. Second step: Having done that, take the resulting outcome, if any, that has more people at or above zero (ignoring dummy zeros). Subtract the best-off people from that outcome until the number of people at or above zero at the two outcomes is the same. Suppose that B' has no fewer people at or above zero than A'. Construct B'' by subtracting the best-off people in B' until the number of people at or above zero in B'' is the same as the number of people at or above zero in A'. Rechristen A' as A''. Third step: Apply the trade-off rules to the resulting same-number choice set $\{A'', B''\}$ to determine which, if either, is wrong. If and only if A'' loses to B'', then A loses to B (and vice versa). Abstracting from considerations other than how the people in question fare, it is then wrong, given S, to choose an outcome X in S if and only if X loses to some Y in S.

Worse-Fate delivers the right answers in a stylized version of the procreation asymmetry. Given a choice between GOOD, with a child with a life worth living, and NO, with no child, neither choice is wrong. We subtract the child in GOOD so as to make the two populations equal: i.e., equally zero. That leaves us with two equivalent options, neither of which loses to the other. Given a choice between BAD, with a child with a life not worth living, and NO, BAD is wrong. We add a dummy zero to NO so as to make the two populations equal: i.e., equally one. Since it is better to be at zero than below it, BAD loses to NO.

We can put the point another way, to bring out that Worse-Fate doesn't just deliver the right results, but moreover explains the procreation asymmetry. According to Worse-Fate Thinking, it is wrong to leave people to a worse fate, a condition such that they would have reason to prefer how things are for people in some alternative. This is why BAD over NO is wrong. The person who exists in

BAD has reason to prefer how things are in NO. By contrast, NO over GOOD is not wrong. No one is left to any fate in NO. There is no person with reason to prefer how things are in GOOD.[10]

The stylized procreation asymmetry assumes a possibly artificially limited choice set, where one cannot instead make, say, a non-contingent child even better off, but not as well off as the child one would have. If one had such a choice, then Worse-Fate implies that, as far as concerns how people fare, one should make it. This does not necessarily mean, however, that it is wrong to have a child when one could instead make a non-contingent child better off. One might have other reasons, such as agent-relative reasons, to have one's own child.

Note that Benefit Thinking, on its own, does not explain why it is wrong to choose to bring someone into existence with a life not worth living when the alternative is not bringing anyone into existence. This is because not bringing someone into existence does not benefit anyone. So Benefit Thinking must be supplemented with a principle that implies that it is wrong to bring someone into existence with a life not worth living when the alternative is not bringing anyone into existence. By contrast, Worse-Fate Thinking gives a unified answer to different-number cases below and above zero. In all cases, we seek to avoid consigning people to worse fates.

10.9 Conflicts with Benefit Thinking

So far, so good for Worse-Fate. But now objections rush in.

10.9.1 Benefit Requires

Recall Figure 10.4 "Ignoring the Best Off." Some may object that in Ignoring the Best Off, while Worse-Fate permits us to choose the Many over the Few, it does not require us to. Is this acceptable?

The traditional utilitarian answer is no, because is always wrong to fail to bring about a greater sum of happiness. The familiar reply is to deny that we have reason to bring about a greater total quantity of happiness. What matters is making people happy, not making happy people.

A sophisticated proponent of benefit thinking, however, can retrench and say, more plausibly, the following. First, it net benefits a particular person to cause them to be with a life worth living, even if they would not have been worse off

---

[10] This brings out an important structural similarity to the "Variabilism" of Roberts (2011) and the "SHMV" of Meacham (2012). An important difference, though, is that these alternative approaches consider losses not levels, and so deliver, to my mind, implausible or undermotivated verdicts.

otherwise (Parfit 2017). Second, we have reasons, bearing on permissibility, to benefit people, for their sake, not to increase the sum of happiness. In a stronger form, the claim would be:

> Benefit Requires: If B net benefits people more than A, then it is wrong to choose A given a choice set that includes A and B.

"Net benefits people more" can be understood in at least two different ways. The first is straightforward:

> Sum: B sum net benefits people more than A iff B has a higher sum total of (possibly priority-weighted) net benefits than A.

The second way is something like a generalization of the Pareto criterion familiar from same-people cases: that we can make one person better off without making anyone else worse off. Consider a choice between putting Eleanor in the Good Place or putting Eleanor and Chidi in the Good Place. The latter doesn't benefit Eleanor any less and it additionally benefits Chidi. So it is something like Pareto superior to the former. More generally, we say:

> Pareto: B Pareto net benefits people more than A just when we can pair each person in A with exactly one "counterpart" in B, such that every B-counterpart is at least as well off as their A-counterpart, anyone in B without an A-counterpart is above zero, and either there some B-counterpart who is better off than their A-counterpart or there is someone in B who has no A-counterpart and who is above zero. (More precisely, let $Pop(A)$ be the population at outcome A. B Pareto net benefits people more than A iff there exists an injective "counterpart" function $C : Pop(A) \mapsto Pop(B)$ such that (1) for each $i \in Pop(A)$, $C(i)$ is net benefitted in B at least as much as i in A, (2) for each "counterpartless" $j \in Pop(B)$ (that is, each j such that there is no i such that $j = C(i)$), j is above zero, and (3) either (a) there is some $k \in Pop(A)$ such that $C(k)$ is net benefitted in B more than k in A or (b) there is some counterpartless $j \in Pop(B)$.)

Because a person's counterpart need not be herself, even when she exists in both outcomes, this criterion is in one way weaker than the familiar Pareto criterion. It allows, whereas the familiar criterion does not, that B might Pareto net benefit more than A even when there is someone, Lesser, who is worse off in B than Lesser is in A. This can happen if there is an appropriate counterpart function that assigns Lesser in B a counterpart in A who is not Lesser herself.

There is reason to reject Benefit Requires, on either interpretation. On the sum interpretation, Benefit Requires requires us to make the repugnant choice. After all, the sum of the benefits we give to the Many is greater than the sum of those we give to the Few. And if we accept priority, that reasons to provide increments of net benefit to a person diminish as those increments bring the person to a higher level, then the case only becomes stronger.[11] On the Pareto interpretation, Benefit Requires requires us to choose GOOD, over NO, in the procreation asymmetry.

10.9.2 Benefit Permits

There is, however, a weaker version of Benefit Thinking. Consider a choice set containing just Few and Add in Figure 10.5 (ignoring Equalize for the time being). Once we subtract the better off people in Add, i.e., the first bar, the Few become like the Highs in a contingent same-number case, and the worse off people in Add, i.e., the second bar, become like the Lows. Thus, as it is wrong to choose the Lows over the Highs, it is wrong to choose Add over Few.

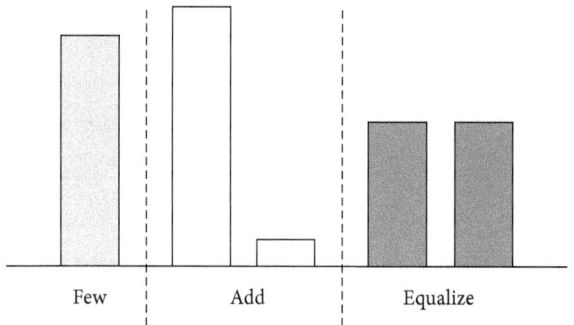

Figure 10.5 Mere Addition.

---

[11] Parfit (2017) at footnote 21 seems to suggest that we might avoid the repugnant choice by appealing to a deontic version of Temkin (2012)'s Consolidate Additional Benefits principle: that there is reason to give a few large benefits instead of giving many smaller benefits, even when the sum of benefits to the many is greater and the many are worse off. So there is reason to give large benefits to the Few, instead of smaller benefits to the Many. But, first, it is not clear that CAB applies to the repugnant choice. Temkin (2012) writes that "many find CAB compelling, at least for those cases where if many people have their burdens increased a little this would have relatively little overall impact on their lives, whereas if a few people have their burdens increased substantially this would have a substantial impact on their lives" (pp. 69–70). But the benefit of existence, even a lower level, would seem to have a substantial impact on one's life. Second, CAB may not save us from the repugnant choice. Suppose CAB argues for choosing the Few over the Many in a choice between the two. Nevertheless, CAB should allow us to add n Manys at L while lowering n Few by L (since the same number of benefits, of the same size, go to people with less). So, we ought to take each step down, but once we reach the Many, we ought rather to choose the Few. So, we have cycling. Suppose we then say, as I will say in section 10.11.4, that, when presented with just the choices in that cycle, any choice is permissible. Then it is permissible to choose the Many from a set that includes the Few.

Is this acceptable? No, one might answer, on the grounds of:

Benefit Permits: If B net benefits people more than A, then it is not wrong to choose B given $\{A, B\}$.

This is another, weaker expression of Benefit Thinking.

On the sum interpretation, we again have reason to reject Benefit Permits. It permits the repugnant choice.

But what about Pareto Permits: i.e., Benefit Permits interpreted by Pareto? As I argue in section 10.10, it isn't clear to me that there is a compelling argument, beyond the intuition that Add over Few is not wrong, for any form of Benefit Permits. However, if we like, we can incorporate Pareto Permits into Worse-Fate, by revising the definition of "loses." Recall how Worse-Fate works. It begins by looking at each pair of choices $\{A, B\}$ in the choice set. It transforms each such pair into a same-number choice $\{A'', B''\}$ (by adding zeros to equalize numbers in negative territory and subtracting the best off to equalize numbers in non-negative territory). If and only if A'' is wrong and B'' isn't wrong, we say that A "loses" to B. It is then wrong to choose an X in the set that loses in this sense to some Y in the set. To incorporate Pareto Permits, we change the definition of "loses" to read:

If and only if A'' is wrong and B'' isn't wrong and A does not Pareto net benefit people more than B, A loses to B.

In other words, a choice that Pareto benefits can always, as it were, force a draw. Even if a choice would otherwise lose to another, it doesn't so long as it Pareto benefits. Call the principle that results from Worse-Fate by so revising "loses": "Worse-Fate-Pareto."[12]

This might seem ad hoc, but it can be given a rationale. The thought would be that our judgments about ordinary, same-people choices, such as that of Eleanor, are driven simultaneously by two impulses: Worse-Fate Thinking and Pareto Benefit Thinking. We are permitted to save from a worse fate, and we are permitted to Pareto benefit. However, we fail to realize that these are different impulses, because in ordinary same-people cases they drive in the same direction. Given any same-number pair, the choice, if there is one, that Pareto net benefits, such as putting Eleanor in the Good Place, will also save people from a worse fate.

---

[12] Some might contend that it is wrong to choose Add over Few if a non-contingent person ends up worse off: that is, if there is a non-contingent person in the second bar in Add. To prevent this from counting as a Pareto benefit, we might require the counterpart function to map to oneself when possible: i.e., that $C(i) = i$ where $i \in Pop(B)$. This would be another instance in which non-contingency can break a tie. See the end of section 10.5.

It's only given exotic, different-number choice sets that a choice that Pareto net benefits may not save people from a worse fate. In such a case, the appropriate extension of our judgments about ordinary, same-people choices is to permit either. That is how we do justice to both impulses: to save from worse fates and to Pareto benefit.

10.9.3 The Sadistic Choice

A further worry about Worse-Fate is that it may lead to what Arrhenius (2000) calls a:

> Sadistic Choice: A differs from B only in that A has a group all at or above zero whereas B has a group all below zero, but A loses to B.[13]

The Sadistic Choice is implied by views that hold it against a choice that it adds people above zero but below some positive "critical level" (Blackorby and Donaldson 1984; Blackorby, Bossert, and Donaldson 1995). In Figure 10.6, the thick lines represent welfare levels as usual.[14] Since the critical level is 50, a rule that tells us to minimize aggregate shortfall would tell us to choose A, which has a total shortfall (shaded) of 100, over B, which has a total shortfall of 120. However, B differs from A only in that A has a group all below zero and B has a group all above zero. (Compare Parfit (1984, 415)'s (A).)

Average utilitarianism (and principles, such as Hurka (1983)'s and Ng. (1989)'s, that approximate average utilitarianism at some population levels) also leads to a Sadistic Choice (Figure 10.7). Since the average in B is lower, average utilitarianism tells us to choose A. However, A differs from B—that is, ignoring the last bar in both—only in that A has a group all below zero and B has a group all above zero.

---

[13] Arrhenius proves, roughly and translated into deontic terms, that any theory that accepts all four of Negative Transitivity, Dominance, Addition, and Non-Priority Principles cannot avoid permitting the instantiation of at least one of the Repugnant, Anti-Egalitarian, and Sadistic Choices.

- Dominance Principle: If A has the same number as B, and every person in A is better off than any person in B, then A beats B.
- Addition Principle: If when we create B simply by adding to A people all with lower welfare, A beats B, then when we create C simply by adding to A more people with even lower welfare, A beats C.
- Minimal Non-Extreme Priority Principle: There is always some n such that if A has one person below zero and $n - 1$ others at very high welfare, whereas B has n people at low but positive welfare, B does not beat A.
- Anti-Egalitarian Choice: A has higher average welfare than B and A is perfectly equal whereas B is unequal, but B beats A.
  However, we reject Negative Transitivity and, if we accept Zero Embargo, we reject the Minimal Non-Extreme Priority Principle.

[14] Assume that the people are different, although this isn't indicated by a change of pattern.

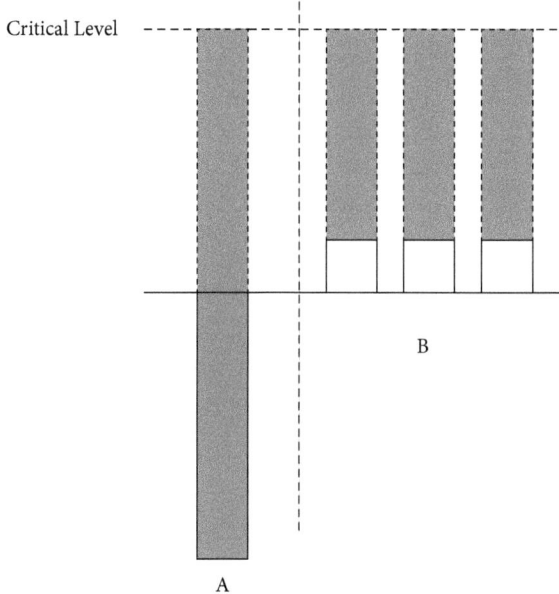

Figure 10.6 Sadistic Choice: Critical Level.

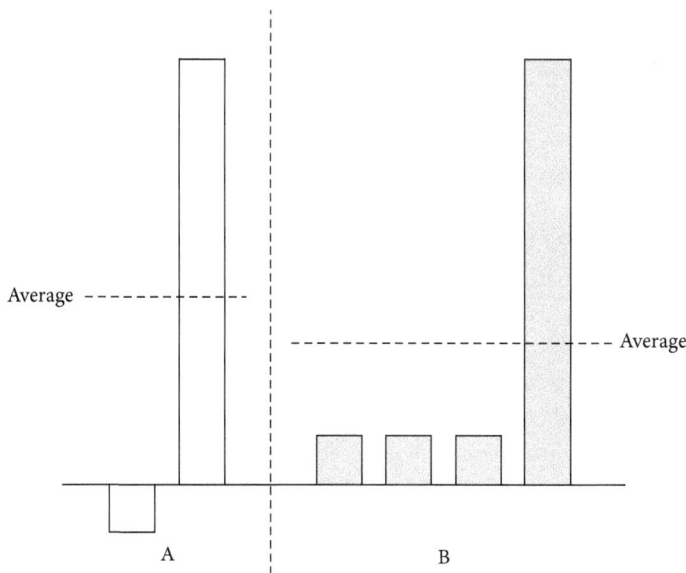

Figure 10.7 Sadistic Choice: Average Utilitarianism.

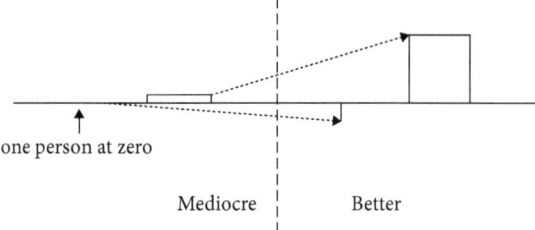

one person at zero

Mediocre   Better

Figure 10.8 Constructing a Sadistic Choice: Step 1.

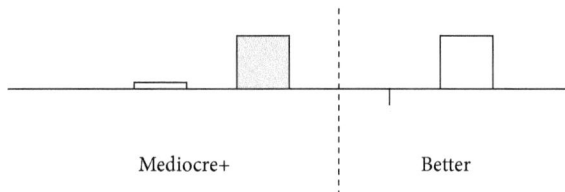

Mediocre+   Better

Figure 10.9 Constructing a Sadistic Choice: Step 2.

Can Worse-Fate lead to a sadistic choice? Yes, so long as we reject Zero Embargo, We start, in Figure 10.8, with an outcome, Mediocre, that has just one person at zero and several others all at some equal, positive, Mediocre level. So long as we reject Zero Embargo, we should be able to find an outcome such as Better that beats Mediocre by the trade-off rules. In Better, the person at zero is now slightly negative, and all the rest are at some much higher positive, equal level. By making the second bar of Better sufficiently high, we should eventually be able to make Better beat Mediocre, again so long as we reject Zero Embargo.

Now consider a new choice. In Figure 10.9, Mediocre is replaced by Mediocre+ which adds a new population equivalent to the second bar of Better and subtracts the person at zero. If we apply Worse-Fate to this choice, Mediocre+ loses to Better. First, we add a dummy zero to Mediocre+. Second, we subtract the second bar of Mediocre+. In other words, we reduce Mediocre+ to Mediocre. But we have assumed that Mediocre loses to Better. So, according to Worse-Fate, it is wrong to choose Mediocre+ over Better. But the choice of Better over Mediocre+ satisfies the definition of a Sadistic Choice. Mediocre+ differs from Better—that is, ignoring the last bar in both—only in that Better has one person below zero and Mediocre+ has a group all above zero: namely, the first bar.

Should we be troubled by Sadistic Choices of this kind? I don't think so. My sense is that anxiety about Sadistic Choices stems from one of three sources. First, there is the thought that it is clearly not wrong to choose an outcome in which no one is negative over an outcome in which everyone is negative. However, Worse-Fate does not imply that it is wrong. In a choice between just the first bar of Mediocre+ and the first bar of Better (that is, the one person below zero), Worse-Fate implies that it would be wrong to choose the first bar of Better. Instead, Worse-Fate implies that it can be wrong to choose an outcome that differs from another only in that one adds a population in which all are positive whereas the other adds a population in which all are negative. (The latter claim would imply the former claim if we had reason to accept Separation, discussed in section 10.11.1. But we have independent reason to reject Separation.)

The second source of anxiety is Benefit Thinking. The choice of Better over Mediocre+ is like the choice of Few over Add, in that it passes up an opportunity to Pareto net benefit. Mediocre+ Pareto net benefits people more than Better, just as Add Pareto net benefits people more than Few. What gives the choice of Better over Mediocre+ a "sadistic" character that the choice of Few over Add lacks is that, without the benefit, one person is below zero. But that may be a red herring. Perhaps the anxiety is just that Mediocre+ loses to Better even though it Pareto net benefits. If this is what troubles one, then one can simply accept Worse-Fate-Pareto.

"No," someone may reply, "the problem is not that we are passing up an opportunity to benefit people. The problem is that we are leaving someone in negative territory, when we have an alternative that leaves no one in negative territory. That's what makes it sadistic, rather than simply inefficient or wasteful." This is the third source of anxiety about Sadistic Choices. I am sympathetic to it. But the more one stresses that leaving someone in negative territory is objectionable in a way in which merely failing to lift someone still further in positive territory is not, the closer one comes to accepting Zero Embargo: that is, that we should not consign people to lives not worth living merely to benefit people with lives worth living. Yet if we accept Zero Embargo, then we avoid Sadistic Choices in the first place. For if we accept Zero Embargo, then it is not wrong to choose Mediocre over Better to begin with.

10.10 Arguments for Benefit Thinking

We have discussed reasons to reject Benefit Thinking: namely, that, in certain forms, it requires or permits the repugnant choice, or requires GOOD over NO in the procreation asymmetry. If we wish, by opting for Worse-Fate-Pareto, we can incorporate a certain degree of Benefit Thinking into Worse-Fate, without these consequences. But the question remains whether there are any grounds to accept

Benefit Thinking. Two main grounds appear time and again in the literature. But, on reflection, they have surprisingly little force.

The first is that only Benefit Thinking can explain the intuitive verdicts in same-number cases. This is simply false. Worse-Fate explains them just as well.

The second ground is that only Benefit Thinking can explain why we have reason to ensure the survival of humanity. This too is false. There are other reasons, albeit ones mostly independent of Worse-Fate.

10.10.1 Same-Number Cases

For some time, I (like others, e.g., Ng. 1989, 237) felt compelled to accept not only Benefit Permits, but also Benefit Requires by the following reasoning:

> Clearly, in ordinary, same-people cases it is not only not required, but moreover wrong, say, to put Eleanor in the Medium Place, when we could instead put her in the Good Place! How are we to explain this, if not by appeal to Benefit Thinking? The same goes for contingent same-number cases. Doesn't the correct verdict in the choice between the Highs and the Lows require Benefit Thinking?

But as an argument for Benefit Thinking over Worse-Fate Thinking, this argument has no force. For Worse-Fate on its own explains the correct verdicts. It is wrong to put Eleanor in the Medium Place, or to create the Lows, not because we fail to bestow more benefits, but instead because we leave the worst off to a worse fate.

10.10.2 The End of Humanity

Another argument for Benefit Thinking, which Frick (2017), in criticism, calls the "argument from additional lives," runs as follows:

> Not only is it not wrong to postpone the end of humanity, but moreover it is wrong, in some cases, not to postpone it. What reason is there to postpone the end of humanity but to provide future people with the benefit of being caused to be with lives worth living? But once we accept this, aren't we forced to the Benefit principles? Indeed, aren't we pressed even to Benefit Requires and even to the sum interpretation? (Bennett 1978; Ng. 1989, 237; Temkin 2012, 414; McMahan 2013, 26; Parfit 2017, 119)

The reply is that there are other reasons to postpone the end of humanity, besides the benefits that we would thereby confer on future humans.

10.10.2.1 Interests of Non-contingent People

What are these reasons? First, the fact that non-contingent people (mostly those dead or already alive) would be worse off if humanity were to end earlier may argue for postponing the end of humanity. In following Worse-Fate, we will be, to some extent, responsive to such reasons. Postponing the end of humanity may save non-contingent people from a worse fate.

10.10.2.2 Impersonal Values

Second, impersonal values may argue for postponing the end of humanity. The things of impersonal value in question range from the general to the specific: sentient life, valuing, humanity, art and science, and so on. What matters is that the impersonal values have the following four properties.

(1) The things of impersonal value give rise to reasons to ensure that they continue to be instantiated into the future. Perhaps this is because we have reasons to preserve existing things of value (Frick 2017; Scheffler 2018). Perhaps it is because what is of value is, in part, a certain development, or narrative, or career through time, which the premature end of humanity would cut short (Bennett 1978). Perhaps it is simply because the premature end of humanity would prevent things of impersonal value from being instantiated: certain discoveries never made, certain works of art never given shape. (Reasons of this last kind are not only reasons for us to postpone the end of humanity, but also reasons for a creator to create humanity.)

(2) Postponing the end of humanity plays an important, perhaps essential, role in ensuring that these things of impersonal value continue to be instantiated into the future.

(3) These things of impersonal value give us reasons independently of their effects on how anyone fares. Of course, partaking of these impersonal values is what makes people's lives worth living, and so whether these values are available for people to partake of bears on how people fare, which in turn gives us reasons. But these reasons, derived from how people fare, differ from reasons derived from the impersonal values themselves.[15] Indeed, the interests of people provide reasons that weigh against the

---

[15] Discussions of these issues often blur the distinction between interest-based and impersonal-value-based reasons.

> As long as extinction can be deferred, human life, and posthuman life, can continue indefinitely, with unimaginable numbers of people enjoying the goods of life, which might in time become vastly superior to the goods accessible to human beings thus far, just as the goods accessible to us are vastly superior to those that were accessible to our remote evolutionary ancestors. To most of us, it is appalling to think that instead of this incalculable number of people enjoying these incalculable benefits, there might instead be only the emptiness of a world devoid of consciousness. (McMahan 2013, 26)

reasons derived from impersonal values. It may be wrong to purchase a future for those values at the price of human suffering.

(4) The reasons deriving from impersonal values are more holistic and less additive than reasons deriving from the interests of people.

I find it implausible that the reason to be concerned for how a person fares weakens as additional people are added to an outcome. Why should that reason weaken simply because there are more other people, even people distant in time and space? Accordingly, I find it implausible to think that, if we accept that there are reasons to benefit, we can avoid the repugnant choice by saying that, as more people are added, the reason to benefit each additional person diminishes.[16] By contrast, it is entirely plausible that the contribution of, say, each additional verse to the flourishing of letters, or each additional painting to the flourishing of the visual arts, diminishes. This is why we do not face a repugnant choice for impersonal values, where we sacrifice a few Dutch Masters for a multitude of velvet Elvises. And there are other holistic, non-additive effects of contributions to impersonal values (some of which are implicit in the very description of the values). Temporal extent matters in a way that spatial extent does not (Bennett 1978; Lenman 2002). Sequence and narrative structure may matter. Continuity may matter.

Offhand, the indefinite continuation of "human" and "posthuman life," the deferral of "the emptiness of a world devoid of consciousness," would seem to be values independent of people's levels of well-being.

> We can first distinguish between the quality of people's lives and the quantity of well-being per person. These might diverge. The best things in your life might be of a higher quality than the best things in mine, and your life might go worse than mine only because you would have many fewer of these best things. (Parfit 2016, 117)

On the one hand, Parfit treats "quality," roughly, as a dimension that, multiplied by "duration," gives the "quantity of well-being." On the other hand, he treats "quality" as something that, while still important qua contribution to well-being, independently weighs against the quantity of well-being. But this seems like odd double counting. It seems that when we view quality as something with independent weight, we are not viewing quality as something that is important qua contribution to well-being, but are instead viewing quality as important qua realization of impersonal values. Indeed, that is how Parfit seems to describe it later in the same paper: "There would be no art, or science, no deep loves or friendships, no other achievements, such as that of bringing up our children well, and no morally good people" (p. 123). That would be a loss in itself, presumably, even if other contributions to well-being somehow more than made up for it.

[16] For such an approach to the repugnant choice, see Hurka (1983) and Temkin (2012) on "capped ideals." In fact, what seems to drive Hurka to claim that increasing the population matters more as the population approaches zero is not the thought that each person's well-being counts for more as the population approaches zero, but instead that each person's existence contributes more to the impersonal value of humanity's existence or survival as the population approaches zero. If so, then his population principle amalgamates two quite different moral concerns: the well-being of persons and "a special value in the existence of animal species" (p. 496).

A further problem for supposing that there is a limit to what Parfit calls the "positive value of quantity" is that if the limit applies to quantity at a given time, then we court Parfit (1984, 410–11)'s Absurd Conclusion.

10.10.2.3 Agent-Relative Reasons

Finally, we, the people making the choice, may have various agent-relative reasons to postpone the end of humanity (Bennett 1978; Lenman 2002). Scheffler (2018), in particular, describes "attachment-based" reasons of "interest," "love," "valuation," and "reciprocity." These agent-relative reasons may be closely related to the non-contingent-interest-based and impersonal-value reasons already mentioned. They may simply be reasons based in the interests of non-contingent people, but magnified since we are the non-contingent people. Or what appear to be agent-relative reasons may simply be the reasons that impersonal values give us, in light of what we, in our moment in time, are in a position to affect.[17]

In choices that affect future generations, we should take account of, on the one hand, these reasons of impersonal value and (insofar as they are distinct) these agent-relative reasons, and, on the other, the reasons to save people from worse fates. One possibility is that we should choose in two steps. First, we rule out choices that, by hastening the end of humanity, would be insufficiently responsive to these reasons of impersonal value and these agent-relative reasons. Second, of the choices left, we rule out those that Worse-Fate (or Worse-Fate-Pareto) judges to be wrong. It would then be wrong, or otherwise insufficiently supported by reason, to make any of the choices thus ruled out.

10.11 Incoherence

Another source of resistance to Worse-Fate is that it issues patterns of practical verdicts that are said to be somehow "incoherent." In brief, my reply is that we have no good reason to assume that practical verdicts must be "coherent" in the alleged ways. Granted, it would be a problem if accepting Worse-Fate committed us to a logically inconsistent set of beliefs. (We would then know that there is something in Worse-Fate that we should revise, at least if we could identify what it was.) And, granted, if Worse-Fate implies patterns of, say, intransitive practical verdicts, and if we also assume that practical verdicts are transitive, then we are committed to a logically inconsistent set of beliefs. But the question is why we should assume that practical verdicts are transitive in the first place, especially if the intuitively correct practical verdicts pattern in intransitive ways and if we have a principle that explains why they pattern as they do.

---

[17] If so, then a Martian who stumbled into our history, without any of our agent-relative reasons, would nevertheless have impersonal reason to help us keep ourselves around long enough, say, to ratify the Equal Rights Amendment.

10.11.1 Separation

Worse-Fate violates:

Separation: Thinking of outcomes as sets of pairs of persons and levels, where $A' \subseteq A$ and $B' \subseteq B$, if A' is wrong and B' is not given $\{A', B'\}$ and if $B \setminus B'$ is not wrong given $\{A \setminus A', B \setminus B'\}$, then B is not wrong given $\{A, B\}$.

The reasoning behind Separation might be put this way. If B' over A' is a good change, and if $B \setminus B'$ over $A \setminus A'$ is a neutral change, then how can both changes together—B over A—amount to a bad change?[18]

But is Separation compelling? Recall the earlier Figure 10.1 Reasonable Trade-Off (Figure 10.10 repeats Figure 10.1). Let $B' = B$ and $A' =$ the first bar of A. According to Worse-Fate, A' loses to B', $B \setminus B' (= \emptyset)$ does not lose to $A \setminus A'$ (= the second bar of A), but B loses to A. This is a violation of Separation, but anyone who accepts the procreation asymmetry should find this pattern of judgments intuitive.

10.11.2 Negative Transitivity

Worse-Fate and Worse-Fate-Pareto also violate:

Negative Transitivity: If A is not wrong given $\{A, B\}$ and B is not wrong given $\{B, C\}$, then A is not wrong given $\{A, C\}$.

Suppose the outcomes are: NO child, child with a GOOD life, and a child with a GREAT life.[19] According to Worse-Fate, GOOD does not lose to NO. It's

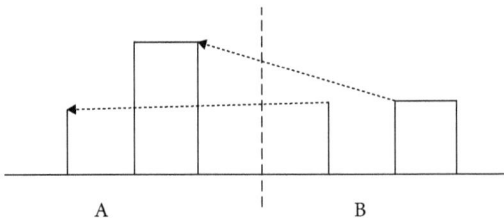

Figure 10.10 Reasonable Trade-Off.

---

[18] Compare Frick (2021)'s argument for why Equalize is not better than Few and Broome (2005)'s puzzlement about the "greediness of neutrality," although the latter concerns, I think, Negative Transitivity, rather than Separation.

[19] The choice between NO and GOOD is like that facing "Sarah" and the choice between GOOD and GREAT or, perhaps, among NO, GOOD, and GREAT is like that facing "Clare" in Parfit (2017).

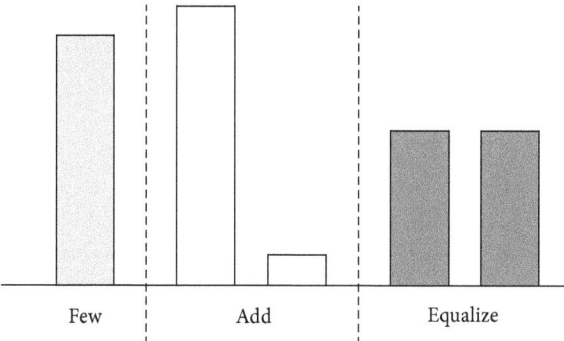

Figure 10.11 Mere Addition.

permissible to have a child with a good life, if the only alternative is not to have a child. That is not for the child to suffer a worse fate. NO does not lose to GREAT. It's permissible not to have a child even if one could have a child with a great life. That is not to suffer any fate at all. But it is not the case that GOOD does not lose to GREAT. It would be wrong to choose to have a child with a good life rather than a great life. In that case, the child does suffer a worse fate.[20]

But why should this be a problem? The intransitive pattern of practical verdicts that Worse-Fate implies is precisely the intuitive pattern! Worse-Fate implies that when both GOOD and GREAT are options, it is wrong to choose GOOD. No other choice from all three, or any two, is wrong.[21]

It is because of the failure of negative transitivity that Worse-Fate-Pareto blocks the "mere addition" argument for the permissibility of the repugnant choice (Parfit 1984, 2016). Recall the earlier Figure 10.5 "Mere Addition" (Figure 10.11 repeats Figure 10.5). Suppose that it is not wrong to choose Add over Few. It does not seem wrong to choose Equalize over Add. By repeating the sequence of adding and equalizing, the population increases and the level declines until we reach the Many.

---

[20] Compare (Frick 2020b), which suggests other cases in which, intuitively, Negative Transitivity is violated.

[21] McMahan (2013) appears to use this case to argue for, roughly, Benefit Thinking. If we assume that there is weaker reason for GOOD than for GREAT, and that there is not weaker reason for NO than for GREAT, then it should follow that there is weaker reason for GOOD than for NO. But surely there isn't weaker reason for GOOD than for NO. So, McMahan concludes, there must, in fact, be weaker reason for NO than for GREAT. But I don't see any reason to accept this pattern of judgments. Worse-Fate explains the pattern of judgments that needs to be explained: namely, that any choice is permissible, except GOOD when given the option of GREAT.

Worse-Fate blocks this argument at the start, by saying that it is wrong to choose Add over Few. Worse-Fate-Pareto blocks it later, by violating Negative Transitivity.

- Given {Equalize, Add}, Equalize is not wrong, since Equalize saves from a worse fate (and Add is wrong because it does not Pareto benefit).
- Given {Add, Few}, Add is not wrong, since Add Pareto benefits.
- Given {Equalize, Few}, Equalize is wrong, since Few saves from a worse fate and Equalize does not Pareto benefit.

This violates Negative Transitivity. Note also that:

- Given {Few, Add, Equalize} only Few is not wrong (since Add loses to Equalize and Equalize loses to Few).

10.11.3 Choice-Set Independence

Worse-Fate and Worse-Fate-Pareto violate:

Choice-Set Independence: If A is wrong given $\{A, B\}$ then A is wrong given $\{A, B, C\}$.

Begin by noting that there is nothing incoherent, in general, in the idea that the permissibility of a choice can change as the choice set is expanded. For example, consequentialism straightaway violates the converse of Choice-Set Independence, where "not wrong" replaces "wrong." Suppose C brings about a better outcome than A which brings about a better outcome than B. In that case, A is not wrong given $\{A, B\}$ but A is wrong given $\{A, B, C\}$.

So why should there be anything troubling about a pattern of verdicts that violates Choice-Set Independence, so long as those verdicts are intuitive? Consider in Table 10.5, Greaves (2017)'s illustration of how "necessitarianism"—the view that considers only the well-being of non-contingent people—violates choice-set independence. Given $\{A, B\}$, Y is non-contingent. Since Y's well-being counts along with X's A is wrong. Given $\{A, B, C\}$, Y is contingent. Since Y's well-being no longer counts, A is not wrong. I agree that this is a compelling counterexample to necessitarianism. But what compels? Opposition to choice-set dependence itself? Or simply recognition that necessitarianism gives the wrong answer— choose $A!$—given $\{A, B, C\}$? Worse-Fate, it is worth noting, gives the right answer—choose $B!$—given $\{A, B\}$, $\{B, C\}$ or $\{A, B, C\}$.

Table 10.5 A Problem for Necessitarianism

	X	Y
A	100	1
B	90	90
C	50	

10.11.4 Acyclicity

Finally, Worse-Fate and Worse-Fate-Pareto violate:

Acyclicity: If A is not wrong and B is wrong given $\{A, B\}$ and B is not wrong and C is wrong given $\{B, C\}$, then it is not the case that C is not wrong and A is wrong given $\{A, C\}$

It follows that Worse-Fate and Worse-Fate Pareto also violate:

Positive Transitivity: If A is not wrong and B is wrong given $\{A, B\}$ and B is not wrong and C is wrong given $\{B, C\}$, then A is not wrong and C is wrong given $\{A, C\}$

The example below in Figure 10.12 shows how Worse-Fate violates Acyclicity. A beats B, even though we ignore the first bar of A, and B beats C, since we ignore the first bar of C. But C beats A, since we consider both bars, and the loss in the second bar in C relative to A is, let's suppose, outweighed by the huge gain in the first bar of C relative to A.[22]

How troubling is this? Worse-Fate can still issue verdicts even when such cycles are present, if we add a clause to the final sentence:

Abstracting from considerations other than how the people in question fare, it is then wrong, given S, to choose an outcome X in S if and only if X loses to some Y in S and it is not the case that Y loses to some Z_1, which loses to some Z_2, which loses to..., which loses to Z_n (all in S), which loses to X.

---

[22] According to Worse-Fate Pareto, by contrast, B does not beat C, since C Pareto benefits. If we add the indented clause below, the one that begins "Abstracting from considerations," then C is the only choice given $\{A, B, C\}$ that is not wrong. For a case in which Worse-Fate Pareto violates Acyclicity, consider a case in which the second bar of C is in negative territory but C still beats A by the trade-off rules. This is to assume that Zero Embargo does not hold. Since C would "add new people" below zero, C would not Pareto benefit relative to B, and so B would beat C even according to Worse-Fate Pareto. Even if Zero Embargo does hold, Worse-Fate Pareto can violate Positive Transitivity. In Mere Addition, Few beats Equalize, and Equalize beats Add, but Few does not beat Add, since Add Pareto benefits.

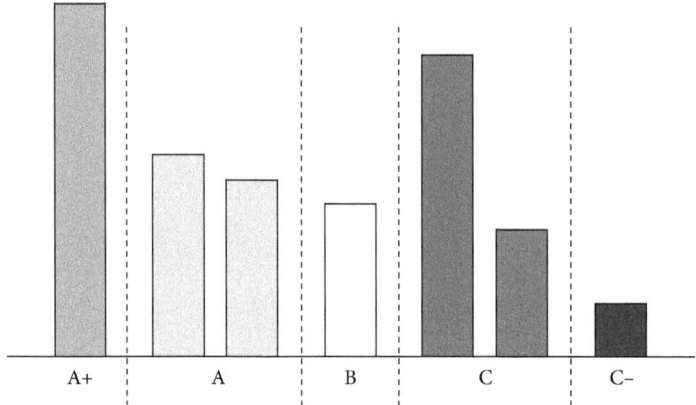

Figure 10.12 Cycling.

Given $\{A+, A, B, C, C-\}$, any choice other than $A+$ is wrong. Given $\{A, B, C, C-\}$, only $C-$ is wrong. Given $\{A, B, C\}$, no choice is wrong. Insofar as we are guided by Worse-Fate Thinking, we may well feel that something is wrong with the choice of A, B, or C. Whichever we choose, some alternative would have saved some people from a worse fate. True; it's just that, in light of that fact, the best we can do is just choose one.[23]

10.11.5 The Deontic and the Axiologic

"Incoherence" of the kind that we have been discussing may be problematic for axiological claims, about which outcomes would be better or worse than others. Consider Choice-Set Independence. Whether one outcome is better than another, one might say, should not depend on what other options it is compared with (although Temkin (2012) argues formidably that it does). However, the claims that we are considering are deontic claims, about which outcomes it would be wrong to choose. No one denies that what it is wrong to choose depends on the choices one has.

Of course, if deontic claims about what it would be wrong to choose require an axiological ordering of outcomes as better or worse, then these problems cannot

---

[23] As far as I can see, this need not expose us to "money pumps," where we would pay some morally relevant cost x to trade C for B given just those two options, then pay x to trade B for A given just those two options, and then pay x to trade A for C given just those two options. On the assumption of full information, including information about future choices available to us, we can never face such a series of choices. We have all of the choices available to us now: $\{C, B - x, A - 2x, C - 3x\}$. Given that set, every choice but C is wrong.

be avoided. And Greaves (2017) assumes that any moral theory (at least any sane one, that takes the consequences of choices seriously) needs an ordering of outcomes as better or worse. But I don't see why. To be sure, a moral theory needs to say when and why choices can be wrong because of properties of the outcomes that they bring about. But, as Worse-Fate shows, that theory need not say anything about whether one outcome is better or worse than another. (And even if it does, one may suspect that it is simply reporting judgments about which outcomes one ought to choose, given a choice.) Indeed, talk of better and worse outcomes seems at best an unnecessary, and at worst a distorting, intermediate layer. Why say that choosing this outcome is wrong because (i) it is wrong to produce a worse outcome, (ii) this outcome is worse, and (iii) it is worse because of its properties and the properties of alternative outcomes? Why not cut out the middleman and just say that this choice is wrong, because of the properties of the outcome it would produce and of alternative outcomes?

It might be said that we still need an ordering of outcomes to be able to say such things as, "The outcome will be worse if the hurricane makes landfall," where no choice is involved. But I don't see why we need to say such things at all. To be sure, we have reason to hope that the hurricane does not make landfall and to regret it if it does. But an ordering of outcomes is just as superfluous in accounting for reasons for hope and regret as it is in accounting for reasons for action. Why not say that we have reason to hope for this outcome and will have reason to regret the alternative because of the relevant properties of those outcomes: that is, those properties to which we appeal when we, mistakenly in my view, seek to order the outcomes as better or worse?

10.12 Do We Need a Principle?

I have proceeded as though we need a principle that tells us how to take account of how future people fare. But it might be said that we need no such principle. Scheffler (2018), for instance, seems to suggest that we can avoid the thicket of population ethics by recognizing simply that the "positive...attachment-independent reasons of beneficence may be...reasons to ensure that the chain of human generations is extended into the indefinite future under conditions conducive to human flourishing."

I'm not sure what he has in mind, but let us suppose that Scheffler is suggesting that so long as a choice leaves everyone above some sufficiency threshold, it is not wrong—at least not wrong because of its effects on how people fare—no matter what the size of the population.

Worse-Fate is certainly compatible with such a view. Indeed, Worse-Fate implies such a view when the trade-off rules reflect a sufficiency threshold.

But worries linger. Scheffler's formula is silent about how we should choose when not everyone can be above the threshold. Such silence is less of a problem, of course, if the threshold is lower and so there is less chance that we will ever be forced to leave people below it. However, if the threshold is higher, there is more chance that we will be forced to leave someone below it and so need guidance that the mere appeal to a threshold of sufficiency does not provide.

If the sufficiency threshold that applies to future people is the same threshold that applies to same-people cases, however, the threshold seems, to judge from intuitions about same-people cases, rather high. What level of healthcare provision for the current population is it, for example, such that trade-offs are no longer a matter of concern?

Now perhaps Scheffler has in mind a sufficiency threshold applying to future people that is different from the sufficiency threshold (if any) applying in same-people cases. But to say that a different threshold applies to future people seems to me hard to defend. Why should the well-being of future people count for less (or more)? People are people.

In any event, the threshold for future people, even if different from the threshold for present people, would also be, intuitively, rather high. Suppose that it costs us nothing at all to excavate ore here rather than there. If we excavate here, as a kind of side-benefit, we prevent some future miasma from being released. If it is released, then people in the future, each of whom enjoys the healthcare, education, etc., of a idealized Scandinavian social democracy, would have to spend a month of afternoons over their lifetime indoors, to avoid the harmless but unbearable unpleasantness until the miasma dissipates. Is it absurd to think that it would be wrong for us, made fully aware of this, to excavate there, rather than here?

10.13 Ignoring the Unaffected

In a way that we have so far suppressed, the letter of Worse-Fate is at odds with its spirit. The issue is how Worse-Fate counts "unaffected" people. A person is "unaffected" relative to a choice set just when that person is at the same level of well-being at every choice in the set. Those who died long before we make our choice, for example, may be such unaffected people. Of course, any contingent person is affected; their very existence varies with the choice we make. But some non-contingent people may also be affected; although their existence does not vary with our choice, their well-being may. The letter of Worse-Fate makes it sensitive to the unaffected, whereas, according to its spirit, it should be insensitive to the unaffected.

To illustrate what is at stake, consider Parfit (1984, 420)'s objection to average utilitarianism:

Whether this would be bad, on the Average Principle, depends on facts about all previous lives. If the Ancient Egyptians had a very high quality of life, it is more likely to be bad to have a child now. It is more likely that this child's birth will lower the average quality of the lives that are ever lived. But research in Egyptology cannot be relevant to our decision whether to have children.

Parfit is here assuming a version of average utilitarianism that is sensitive to the unaffected. With respect to the choice whether to have a child now, it takes the average utility not simply of those people who will be affected by that choice, but of all people, including the Ancient Egyptians who are not affected by it. However, a version of average utilitarianism that is sensitive only to the affected would avoid this objection. Since this version of average utilitarianism would not consider the utility of the unaffected Ancient Egyptians in computing the averages, research in Egyptology would have no bearing on our decision whether to have children now.

To tighten this up a bit: For any outcome A in a choice set S, let A^*, the affected counterpart of A, be an outcome that differs from A solely in that every person in A who is unaffected relative to S has been removed. Let S^*, the affected counterpart of S, be the set that replaces each element in S with its affected counterpart. Say that a principle is insensitive to the unaffected just when according to that principle, A is wrong (given S) iff the affected counterpart A^* is wrong (given the affected counterpart S^*).

Read without qualification, many principles are sensitive to the unaffected. First, any principle that gives (sufficient) weight to equality is sensitive to the unaffected. In Figure 10.13, the unaffected are marked by dashed lines. Whereas A is more egalitarian than B, B^*, with the unaffected removed, is just as egalitarian as A^*.

As we have seen with Parfit's Egyptians, average utilitarianism, read without qualification, is also sensitive to the unaffected. Recall Figure 10.7 "Sadistic Choice: Average Utilitarianism." Suppose that the unaffected, marked by dashed lines in Figure 10.14, are the last bar of each choice. Whereas A has a higher average than B, A^* has a lower average than B^*, where the unaffected are removed.[24]

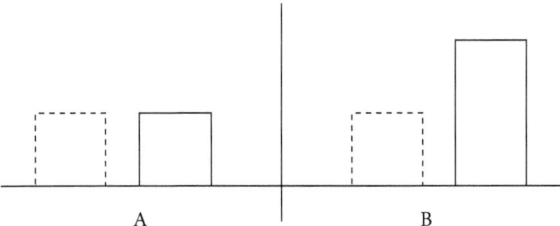

Figure 10.13 Ignoring the Unaffected: Equality.

---

[24] Yet another example of a view that is sensitive to the unaffected is the suggestion in section 10.10.2.2 that a person's well-being counts for less as the size of the population increases.

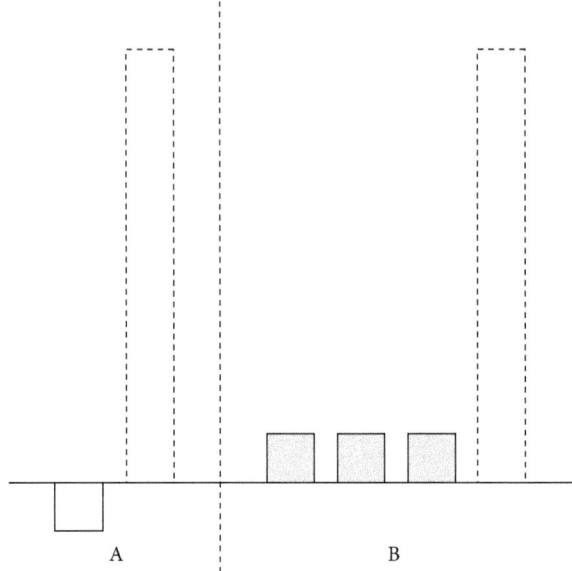

Figure 10.14 Ignoring the Unaffected: Average.

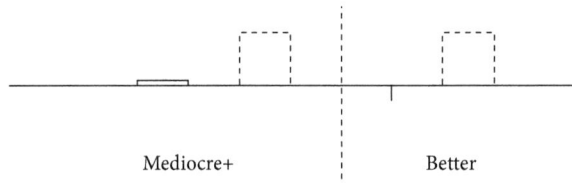

Figure 10.15 Ignoring the Unaffected: Sadistic Choice.

As it stands, Worse-Fate is also sensitive to the unaffected. Suppose that the last bar in Mediocre+ and Better, marked by dashed lines in Figure 10.15, are unaffected. Worse-Fate holds that Mediocre+ is wrong. But Worse-Fate does not hold that the affected counterpart of Mediocre+—i.e., the last bar removed—is wrong.

Worse-Fate should not be sensitive to the unaffected. Indeed, Worse-Fate should ignore the unaffected. After all, Worse-Fate cares simply about saving people from worse fates, and no choice can save unaffected people from worse fates. Accordingly, we should modify Worse-Fate so that it judges outcomes only by their affected counterparts. We can now state it in its full generality:

Worse-Fate[-Pareto] Final Version: Given a choice set, S, consider each pair of outcomes, $\{A, B\}$, in the affected counterpart, S^* of S. Suppose A has no more people below zero than B. Construct A' by adding people at zero to A until the number of people below zero and dummy zeros in A' is the same as the number below zero in B. Rechristen B as B'. Suppose that B has no fewer people at or above zero than A. Construct B'' by subtracting the best-off people in B' until the number of people at or above zero in B'' is the same as the number of people at or above zero in A. Rechristen A' as A''. Then apply the trade-off rules to the resulting same-number choice set $\{A'', B''\}$ to determine which, if either, is wrong. If and only if A'' is wrong and B'' isn't [and A does not Pareto net benefit people more than B] then A loses to B (and vice versa). Abstracting from considerations other than how the people in question fare, it is then wrong, given S, to choose an outcome X in S if and only if X^*, the affected counterpart of X in S^*, loses to some Y^* in S^* and it is not the case that Y^* loses to some Z_1^*, which loses to some Z_2^*, which loses to ..., which loses to Z_n^* (all in S^*), which loses to X^*.

Worse-Fate-Pareto differs from Worse-Fate only in including the bracketed clause.

10.14 Comparison with Frick

It is worth distinguishing this account from that given in recent work by Johann Frick. Frick (2020a) proposes to explain the positive side of the procreation asymmetry by suggesting that reasons to benefit someone are conditional on the existence of that person. There is no unconditional reason to cause someone to exist, even if they will live a life worth living. However, if someone will exist, then one has reason, for their sake, to benefit them. In choosing NO over GOOD, there is no child for whose sake one fails to benefit. Why, then, isn't it permissible to choose GOOD when one has the options of GREAT and NO? Frick suggests that one will better satisfy the standard of benefitting the child in GREAT for that child's sake, if one chooses GREAT, than one will satisfy the similar standard of benefitting the child in GOOD for that child's sake, if one chooses GOOD. And Frick suggests that, when other things are equal, one has more reason to choose what will better satisfy a relevant standard.

One worry about Frick's account is that it is incomplete. Frick offers no guidance on how it is to generalize. First, it is unclear how it generalizes to contingent same-number pairs where neither choice is (in our sense) Pareto superior to the other (such as a contingent version of Reasonable Trade-off). Second, it is unclear how it generalizes to mixed same-number pairs where, considering just the contingent people, neither choice is Pareto superior to the other. Finally, it is unclear how it generalizes to different-number pairs where some in the larger population are worse off than some in the smaller. Consider {Few, Add}. On the one hand, the standard introduced by creating the people in the first bar of Add is better satisfied than the standard introduced by creating the people in the sole bar of Few. On the other hand, the standard introduced by the creation of the people in the second bar of Add is worse satisfied than the standard introduced by the creation of the people in the sole bar of Few. Is Few required, merely permitted, forbidden? For each answer, one can see a plausible argument that it represents the natural extension of what Frick says about the simpler case of {NO, GOOD, GREAT}. (However, Frick (2021) suggests that, intuitively, Add should not be forbidden given {Few, Add}, whereas Add should be forbidden given {Few, Add, Equalize}.

Another worry about Frick's account is that its appeal to conditional reasons is unnecessary. We can explain the positive side of the procreation asymmetry by observing, first, that our judgments in ordinary, same-people cases at least as plausibly reflect Worse-Fate as Benefit Thinking, and, second, that given {NO, GOOD}, Worse-Fate Thinking permits NO and permits GOOD, since neither saves anyone from a worse fate. The person who exists in GOOD does not have reason to prefer how things are in NO, and there is no one in NO who has reason to prefer how things are in GOOD.

A further, related worry about Frick's account is that it implies that our reasons with respect to contingent people are different from our reasons with respect to non-contingent people. When people are non-contingent, we have reason to choose for their sake. When people are contingent, we have reason to choose so as to ensure that we will best satisfy whatever standards that will apply to us. If these reasons are so different, then why suppose that we will get the intuitively correct answers in mixed cases: namely, the choices that would be wrong are just those that would be wrong in the corresponding same-people case? In Case Four, why not suppose that the non-contingent person, Harry, should be favored, so that Tom is consigned to fifty years of pain to save Harry from one day?

10.15 Who Can Complain?

Recall the choice whether to create the contingent Lows or the contingent Highs. Each of the Lows has a life worth living. And each would not have existed otherwise. Suppose we accept both:

> No Wrong without Complaint: Abstracting from considerations other than how the people in question fare, it is wrong to choose an outcome only if someone who exists in that outcome can complain about the choice.
>
> No Complaint when Benefitted: Someone can complain about a choice only if they are not net benefitted by the choice.

Then it is not wrong to choose the Lows over the Highs. And yet it seems that it is wrong, as Worse-Fate implies. So something has to give. This is the "non-identity problem."

Moreover, even if one is not ready to accept these premises in their full generality, one may at least find it intuitive that the Lows could complain about our choice. At least my first reaction to these cases was (and the first reaction of many of my students is) that the Lows do have a complaint. That is, my first reaction was to think: "If we continue to degrade the environment, what will we tell our grandchildren?"

The first point to make is that Benefit Thinking is no better placed to solve the non-identity problem. Granted, a proponent of Benefit Thinking can simply reject No Wrong without Complaint. But then so too can a proponent of Worse-Fate Thinking.

The second point is that Worse-Fate can be part of a more complex view, which sustains the idea that the Lows can complain, whereas the Highs cannot, in part by rejecting No Complaint when Benefitted.

10.15.1 Complaint although Benefitted

On what basis can someone complain about a choice that net benefits them? One might complain that the choice was ill willed, or negligent, or took excessive risks one's behalf. But when one is caused to be with a life worth living, there needn't be ill will, or negligence, or excessive risk-taking.

Nevertheless, there may be other grounds to complain about being caused to be with a life worth living. One ground for complaint is that the choice may expose you to or cause you to suffer some specific harm (Shiffrin 1999; Harman 2004). A specific harm is a deprivation, bad experience, etc., abstracted from its effect on net well-being. For example, if we view pain as a specific harm, then causing someone to exist with some pain causes them to suffer a specific harm even if they have a life worth living on balance.[25]

It may suffice to answer this complaint that you consented. But when you are caused to be, you did not consent, because you could not consent. Now, even where you did not consent, because you could not consent, it may suffice to

---

[25] Harman (2004) suggests that it may be wrong to choose B because it involves greater aggregate specific harm than A, even if B also involves greater aggregate specific benefit, and so greater net benefit, than A. But I worry that this will imply that B would lose to A even though each person in B has a life worth living, is better off than every person in A, and suffers less specific harm than anyone in A. This is because, if the population in B is larger than in A, then the aggregate specific harm in B, although much smaller for each person in B than for each person in A, will outweigh the aggregate specific harm in A. Compare Parfit (1984, 407)'s Ridiculous Conclusion.

answer this complaint that it saves you from a graver specific harm (Shiffrin 1999). But causing you to be does not save you from a graver specific harm.

Another basis for complaint is that the choice intervenes in something that is yours: something that by all accounts you have a special claim to control. It may suffice to answer this complaint that you consented. And, even where you did not consent, because you could not consent, it may suffice to answer this complaint that it saves you from a graver specific harm. For example, suppose, finding you anesthetized, I see my one chance to surgically remove a fatal tumor. If I wait for your consent, it will be too late. This seems permissible, because the surgery saves you from a graver specific harm. Now suppose that the surgery only improves your vision: saves you from having to replace your glasses with a stronger prescription, for example. While the surgery benefits you overall, it does not save you from a graver specific harm. Do you have no grounds for complaint if I take the initiative? Perhaps you do. And if optical surgery counts as an "intervention," perhaps causing you to be is also an intervention—perhaps a far more significant one?

Of course, you may welcome being benefitted overall (Wallace 2013). So, you may feel conflicted about complaining. Indeed, you may have become attached to what was brought about, in which case the conflict may be particularly acute. However, the fact that you feel conflicted does not mean that I can adequately answer your complaint about what I did.

10.15.2 Worse-Fate-as-Answer

Suppose, then, that in causing even the Highs to be, they have some such basis for complaint. How might we answer it? We can say that had we not caused the Highs to be, we would have caused other people, the Lows, to be, and the Lows would have suffered a worse fate than the Highs. This seems a sufficient answer to the Highs' complaint. "If it wasn't you, it would have been the Lows, and they would have suffered a worse fate. Whatever complaint you have, their complaint would have been yet stronger."[26]

After all, this sort of justification seems to answer complaints about causing someone to be with a life not worth living. Suppose we have to choose between causing Bad to be, with a life so bad as not to be worth living, and someone, Worse, with a life still worse. Were Bad to complain, we could tell Bad: "But the alternative would have been even worse for Worse. Whatever complaint you have, Worse would have had an even stronger complaint. What would we have told him?"

---

[26] We are assuming that the Highs and the Lows are the only options. There is no option, or no permissible option, of not causing anyone to exist. For reasons why it might be impermissible to cause no one to exist, see section 10.10.2.2.

If we can answer the Highs' complaint in this way, then this suggests a different explanation of why it is wrong to choose the Lows. It is that we can tell the Highs, but not the Lows: "If we had chosen the alternative, there would have been people, instead of you all, with stronger complaints than you all have. What would we have told them?" This vindicates the thought that the Lows do, as it first seems, have an unanswered complaint about our choice, even though they would not have existed otherwise. "What will we tell our grandchildren?" isn't confused, on this view. It's the right (albeit rhetorical) question to ask.

Consider the following principle:

Answer: Even if a person has an objection on their own behalf to a choice, they do not have a valid complaint against it—that is, they are not wronged by it—if (i) that choice saves from a worse fate or (ii) avoids objections that are at least as strong. One or the other fact answers their objection.

Clause (i) suffices to answer the complaints of the Highs. But clause (ii) may bind when more than one choice is not wrong according to Worse-Fate. There are two kinds of complaints that might be avoided. Both kinds can be illustrated by Figure 10.4 "Ignoring the Best Off," where neither the Few nor the Many is wrong according to Worse-Fate.

First, if there are contingent people among the Few, then we cause someone to be if we choose the Few. Of course, we also cause someone to be if we choose the Many, since the Many has more people than the Few. So whether we choose the Few or the Many, we give someone a complaint about being caused to exist. This very fact, according to (ii), answers the objection of the Many. We can say, to the Many: "No matter what we chose, someone would have had the sort of objection that you have." This would mean that we do not wrong anyone by choosing the Many.

Second, recall from section 10.5 that non-contingent people, such as Harry, may have a complaint about choices that leave them worse off, which can be a tie-breaking reason. So, returning to Figure 10.4 "Ignoring the Best Off," suppose that (even if there are no contingent people among the Few) there is a non-contingent person among the second, better-off bar of the Many, who also exists, at a lower level, in the Few. That non-contingent person would have an objection about choosing Few, since Few leaves him worse off. Perhaps, then, his objection can answer the objection of a contingent person whom we cause to be by choosing the Many, by saying: "Had we not made that choice, some particular person would have been worse off."

This gives us the following:

Worse-Fate-As-Answer (or, alternatively, Worse-Fate-Pareto-As-Answer): Relative to a choice set, S, it wrongs a contingent person x to choose an A

where x exists, unless (abstracting from considerations other than how the people in question fare) A is not wrong (relative to S) according to Worse-Fate (or, alternatively, Worse-Fate-Pareto) and for every B in S such that B is not wrong and x does not exist at B, either (a) some y exists at B who does not exist at A or (b) some y who exists at A is worse off in B.[27]

If there is a contingent person among the Few, then clause (a) would mean that (at least as far as Worse-Fate is concerned) it does not wrong anyone among the Many to choose the Many over the Few in Figure 10.4 "Ignoring the Best Off." Similarly, the Pareto version would mean that it does not wrong anyone in Add to choose Add over Few in Figure 10.5 "Mere Addition," so long as there is some contingent person among the Few. If there is a non-contingent person among the second better-off bar in the Many, then clause (b) would mean that it does not wrong anyone among the Many to choose the Many over the Few in Figure 10.4 "Ignoring the Best Off."

Worse-Fate-As-Answer might provide a deeper explanation of Worse-Fate. The root question is how we can justify our choice to the people whom we create. It is a sufficient justification that, had we not created them, we would have created other people, and they would have had stronger objections to our choice. Population ethics can thus be brought entirely within the framework of a morality rooted in objections that people have on their own behalf, according to which a choice is wrong just when there are stronger objections to it than to some alternative.

Worse-Fate-As-Answer might also provide a deeper explanation of the Pareto addendum. Suppose we choose Add over Few where there is some contingent person among the Few. It may be a sufficient justification to the Adds to say the following.

> Had we not created you, we would have created someone with complaints like yours. Moreover, one of you can point to how things are even for best-off person among the Few, another of you can point to how things are even for next best person among the Few, and so on, and all of you Adds can jointly say that you prefer how things actually are for you.

Even so expanded, Worse-Fate-As-Answer would imply that, in the stylized procreation asymmetry, we wrong the child created by the choice of GOOD. Although GOOD is not wrong given {GOOD, NO}, neither (a) nor (b) is satisfied. NO does not cause anyone else to exist, and NO does not make any particular, non-contingent person worse off.

---

[27] It's a further question whether it not only wrongs someone, but also is wrong, to choose to A.

However, in less stylized versions of the procreation asymmetry, non-contingent people, such as the parents, are made worse off by the choice of NO. And Worse-Fate-As-Answer explicitly abstracts from agent-relative reasons or impersonal reasons. Perhaps, once those reasons are considered, they can answer the complaints of the child caused to be by GOOD.

That being said, we can of course stipulate cases in which there are no such reasons. Take a case of Figure 10.4 "Ignoring the Best Off" in which all of the Few are non-contingent and all of the second-bar of Many are contingent. In such cases, the verdict of Worse-Fate-As-Answer, that we wrong each person in the second bar of the Many by choosing the Many, might seem to have all the sense of the suicide note of Thomas Hardy's Little Father Time: "Done because we are too menny."

References

Arrhenius, G. 2000. "An Impossibility Theorem for Welfarist Axiologies." *Economics and Philosophy*, 247–66.

Bennett, J. 1978. "Maximising Happiness." In *Obligations to Future Generations*, edited by R. I. Sikora, 61–73. Philadelphia: Temple University Press.

Blackorby, C., and D. Donaldson. 1984. "Social Criteria for Evaluating Population Change." *Journal of Public Economics* 25: 13–33.

Blackorby, C., W. Bossert, and D. Donaldson. 1995. "Intertemporal Population Ethics: Critical-Level Utilitarian Principles." *Econometrica* 63: 1303–20.

Broome, J. 2005. "Should We Value Population?" *Journal of Political Philosophy* 13: 399–413.

Frick, J. 2017. "On the Survival of Humanity." *Canadian Journal of Philosophy* 47: 344–67.

Frick, J. 2020a. "Conditional Reasons and the Procreation Asymmetry." *Philosophical Perspectives* 34: 53–87.

Frick, J. 2020b. "Future Persons and Victimless Wrongdoing." In *Worauf Es Ankommt. Derek Parfits Praktische Philosophie in Der Diskussion*. Hamburg: Felix Meiner Verlag.

Frick, J. 2021. "Context-Dependent Betterness and the Mere Addition Paradox." In *Ethics and Existence: The Legacy of Derek Parfit*, edited by Jeff McMahan, Tim Campbell, James Goodrich, and Ketan Ramakrishnan, 232–263. Oxford: Oxford University Press.

Greaves, H. 2017. "Population Axiology." *Philosophy Compass* 12: 1–15.

Harman, E. 2004. "Can We Harm and Benefit in Creating?" *Philosophical Perspectives* 18: 89–113.

Hurka, T. 1983. "Value and Population Size." *Ethics* 93: 496–507.

Lenman, J. 2002. "On Becoming Extinct." *Pacific Philosophical Quarterly* 83: 253–69.

McMahan, J. 2013. "Causing People to Exist and Saving People's Lives." *The Journal of Ethics* 17: 5–35.

Meacham, C. 2012. "Person-Affecting Views and Saturating Counterpart Relations." *Philosophical Studies* 158: 257–87.

Ng, Y-K. 1989. "What Should We Do About Future Generations?" *Economics and Philosophy* 5: 235–53.

Otsuka, M. 2018. "How It Makes a Moral Difference That One Is Worse Off Than One Could Have Been." *Politics, Philosophy, and Economics* 17: 192–215.

Parfit, D. 1984. *Reasons and Persons*. Oxford: Oxford University Press.

Parfit, D. 2016. "Can We Avoid the Repugnant Conclusion?" *Theoria* 82: 110–27.

Parfit, D. 2017. "Future People, the Non-Identity Problem, and Person-Affecting Principles." *Philosophy and Public Affairs* 45: 118–57.

Roberts, M. 2011. "The Asymmetry: A Solution." *Theoria*, no. 77: 333–67.

Scheffler, Samuel. 2018. *Why Worry About Future Generations?* Oxford: Oxford University Press.

Shiffrin, S. 1999. "Wrongful Life, Procreative Responsibility, and the Significance of Harm." *Legal Theory* 5: 117–48.

Temkin, L. 2012. *Rethinking the Good*. Oxford: Oxford University Press.

Voorhoeve, A., and M. Fleurbaey. 2016. "Priority or Equality for Possible People?" *Ethics*, 929–54.

Wallace, R. J. 2013. *The View from Here*. Oxford: Oxford University Press.

Wallace, R. J. 2019. *The Moral Nexus*. Princeton, NJ: Princeton University Press

11
Against Large Number Scepticism

Andreas L. Mogensen

11.1

One of the central questions in population ethics is whether we should endorse the *Total View*, according to which one population is better than another just in case the total welfare is higher (all else being equal). The key objection to this view is well-known. Parfit notes that the Total View entails:

The Repugnant Conclusion: For any possible population of at least ten billion people, all with a very high quality of life, there must be some much larger imaginable population whose existence, if other things are equal, would be better, even though its members have lives that are barely worth living.[1]

Most people, Parfit included, find the Repugnant Conclusion unacceptable. No matter how large the second population is imagined to be, the first seems better.

The literature on interpersonal aggregation contains similar cases involving a trade-off between a smaller quantity of some very significant good and vast quantities of very minor goods. Consider Larry Temkin's *Lollipops for Life* case:

Suppose there were two alternative universes. In one, countless people would each receive many licks of different lollipops over the course of their lives. Unfortunately, there would also be one innocent person who suffered unbearable agony for fifty years before eventually dying a slow, lonely, torturous death. In the second universe, each of the countless people would receive *one* less lick of a lollipop over the course of their lives, but the innocent person would be spared the agony and instead live a full, rich life. Which universe would be better?[2]

Many feel that the value of saving the one from agony and death outweighs the value of allowing each of the countless people to experience this trivial good, no matter how many people we can benefit in this way.

---

[1] Parfit, *Reasons and Persons*, 388.   [2] Temkin, *Rethinking the Good*, 34.

Our judgements about the Repugnant Conclusion and Lollipops for Life are surprisingly difficult to maintain with much confidence. That's because there exist well-known impossibility theorems indicating that these verdicts are inconsistent with other intuitively compelling moral principles.[3] Where several intuitively compelling principles turn out to be mutually inconsistent—as they so often do in philosophy—there are different ways to proceed. One increasingly popular strategy is to look for rescue from beyond philosophy. The hope is that we can find psychological explanations that debunk one or more of our intuitions, while leaving others standing, now unopposed.[4] This chapter looks at the application of this strategy to the cases we've discussed. Specifically, I will look at the suggestion that we should distrust the intuitions I've highlighted because we can't adequately grasp the very large numbers involved.[5] Following Theron Pummer, I'll refer to this as *large number scepticism*.[6]

I'm going to argue that the case for large number scepticism is unconvincing. In doing so, I won't try to provide positive evidence for the reliability of the intuitions that interest us. I presume a form of *phenomenal conservatism*.[7] I take it that a person has a reason for believing *p* just by virtue of having the intuition that *p*, absent the existence of a so-called *undercutting defeater*: a discrediting explanation for why they have that intuition. The question that concerns us here is whether we have a defeater of that kind when it comes to our intuitions about the Repugnant Conclusion or Lollipops for Life, where the discrediting explanation is one that appeals to our inability to adequately grasp very large numbers. I argue that a defeater of that kind is unforthcoming.

There are two objections that I will use repeatedly in critiquing the arguments used to support large number scepticism. I call these the *Upper Bound Objection* and the *Mode of Evaluation Objection*.

I'll start by outlining the Upper Bound Objection. We can think of this as an attempt to flesh out the following remark from Parfit, about large number scepticism in respect of the Repugnant Conclusion: "Even if we cannot adequately imagine very large numbers, we understand the belief that there is no number of such people whose existence would be better."[8] The core idea is that if we want to show our intuitions about the Repugnant Conclusion and Lollipops for Life to be

---

[3] Arrhenius, 'An Impossibility Theorem'; Ng, 'What Should We Do About Future Generations?'; Norcross, 'Comparing Harms'; Parfit, *Reasons and Persons*, 419–42; Rachels, 'Counterexamples to the Transitivity of Better Than'; Temkin, 'A Continuum Argument for Intransitivity'; Temkin, *Rethinking the Good*. But see Carlson, 'Aggregating Harms' and Thomas, 'Some Possibilities in Population Axiology.'

[4] Greene, 'The Secret Joke of Kant's Soul'; Huemer 'Revisionary Intuitionism'; Singer, 'Ethics and Intuitions'.

[5] Broome, *Weighing Lives*; Cureton, 'Moral Intuitions about Large Numbers'; Greene, 'A Psychological Perspective'; Horton, 'Aggregation, Complaints, and Risk'; Huemer, 'In Defence of Repugnance'; Norcross, 'Comparing Harms'.

[6] Pummer, 'Intuitions about Large Number Cases'.   [7] Huemer, *Ethical Intuitionism*.

[8] Parfit, 'Can We Avoid the Repugnant Conclusion?', 111.

untrustworthy, it's not enough to show that intuitions about large numbers are unreliable in some respect or other. Suppose, for example, that we systematically underestimate just how much good is present in aggregate when asked to consider very large numbers of very minor goods. In and of itself, this wouldn't explain why we say that no number of minor goods is large enough to outweigh a more concentrated quantity of some very significant good. By analogy, there is evidence that people systematically underestimate the number of dots on a page.[9] Thus, if they knew how much ink was required to print a dot, we should expect that they would systematically underestimate the ink required to print a certain array of dots. But in spite of that, we do not expect people to say things such as that there is no number of dots such that the ink required to print them would be enough to fill the Grand Canyon. We would need some other kind of evidence to support a prediction of that kind. Similarly, for it to be expected that we would perceive no number of very minor goods at all as great enough to outweigh a more concentrated quantity of some very significant good, it is not enough to show that we systematically underestimate just how much good is present in aggregate when asked to consider very large numbers of very minor goods. We would seem to need evidence that our responsiveness to increasingly larger numbers is characterized by some inappropriate upper bound. The Upper Bound Objection insists that we don't have evidence for the existence of such an upper bound.

Let's now consider the Mode of Evaluation Objection. The core idea here is that we can't adequately support large number scepticism by drawing on experiments or surveys that consider how people respond to increasing numbers using methods that require different people to evaluate different items in isolation, as opposed to evaluating paired items side-by-side. Alternatives can end up being ranked very differently if considered in isolation by different people or by the same person at different times (*separate evaluation* or *SE*) as opposed to when evaluated jointly by one and the same individual (*joint evaluation* or *JE*).[10] For example, Christopher Hsee found that people were willing to pay more for a set of dinnerware containing twenty-four intact pieces versus another containing forty intact pieces plus a few broken pieces, but only if these options were considered in SE. In JE, subjects were not willing to pay more for less.[11] One leading hypothesis is that preference reversals of this kind occur because JE facilitates the evaluability of attributes whose significance it is difficult to assess in isolation.[12] This suggests that judgements elicited in JE are generally more trustworthy. As I'll try to show, a lot of the evidence used to support large number scepticism looks at studies involving SE. However, the key intuitions elicited by the Repugnant Conclusion and Lollipops for Life involve JE. Since SE and JE elicit different rankings and invoke different modes of response, evidence derived from

---

[9] Krueger, 'Perceived Numerosity'.   [10] Zhang, 'Joint Versus Separate Modes of Evaluation'.
[11] Hsee, 'Less is Better'.   [12] Hsee, 'The Evaluability Hypothesis'.

SE designs provides limited support for large number scepticism. So says the Mode of Evaluation Objection.

My aim in this chapter is to pick apart the case for large number scepticism, using the two objections just noted as well as a host of other more specific criticisms. The chapter is structured as follows. Section 11.2 will consider the support for large number scepticism offered by John Broome. Section 11.3 will criticize a number of arguments put forward by Michael Huemer. Thereafter, I will focus on more empirically grounded arguments due to Joshua Greene and Adam Cureton. Section 11.4 will consider what we can learn from evidence of scope insensitivity in contingent valuation. Section 11.5 will assess the significance of people's diminishing sensitivity to increasing numbers of lives lost or saved. In section 11.6, I'll consider whether well-established limitations of the mind/brain's core number systems support large number scepticism. Section 11.7 will consider what we should make of evidence that people are more moved by single victims than by groups. In each case, I'll try to show that the argument for large number scepticism proves unconvincing.

11.2

Probably the best-known discussion of large number scepticism occurs in John Broome's *Weighing Lives*. According to Broome, intuitions about very large numbers "are often wrong, because our imagination is not able to grasp just how big numbers can be."[13] By way of support for this claim, Broome notes that "many people's intuition tells them that the process of natural selection, however many billions of years it continued for, could not lead from primordial slime to creatures with intelligence and consciousness."[14]

Broome doesn't provide supporting references for this observation, but I think we should be sceptical that people who doubt the capacity of Darwinian evolution to produce creatures like us are really driven by the thought that no amount of time will suffice. That's because doubts about the age of the Earth have played a key role in attacks on evolutionary theory. Lord Kelvin famously challenged Darwin by drawing on physical estimates indicating that the Earth was no older than a hundred million years—too little time for Darwin's theory to work. Although now disproven, Kelvin's estimates continue to be cited by creationists.[15] In fact, many creationists treat the age of the Earth as a pivotal issue in their attacks on the scientific consensus.[16] This is hard to make sense of if Broome is right: it presumably wouldn't matter whether the Earth is younger than a hundred million years or older than 4.5 billion years if any amount of time is perceived by

---

[13] Broome, *Weighing Lives*, 58. [14] Ibid., 58. [15] Bird, *Philosophy of Science*, 5.
[16] Cotner, Brooks, and Moore, 'Is the Age of the Earth One of Our "Sorest Troubles"?'.

those who doubt the Darwinian consensus as insufficient for natural selection to do its work.

That having been said, there may be people who are confident that no amount of time could allow natural selection to yield creatures with *intelligence* and *consciousness* if they hold dualist convictions about the nature of the mind. There is something astonishing about the idea that sufficient tinkering with biochemistry will cause thoughts and feelings to arise out of a mindless, slimy world. But these intuitions tell us less about our ways of grasping big numbers, and more about the intuitive appeal of mind-body dualism.[17] So there's little, if any, support for large number scepticism here.

11.3

Michael Huemer is another prominent defender of large number scepticism.[18] Huemer's argument has a number of semi-independent stages, each intended to bolster the case for doubting our intuitions about the Repugnant Conclusion. I'll argue that Huemer fails to mount a convincing case for disregarding these intuitions.

Huemer first illustrates our deficiency in grasping very large numbers by asking us to reflect on the oddity of the audience member's reaction in the following vignette. An astronomer is giving a public lecture. She mentions that the sun is expected to die in five billion years. A member of the audience becomes noticeably agitated. The astronomer tries to reassure him, stressing that the sun won't burn out for five *billion* years. The audience member sighs with relief, exclaiming: "Phew! I thought you said five *million* years."

I agree it would be pretty surprising to find someone reacting so differently to these estimates. However, this probably reflects something specific to our expectations about how people value the far future. We might expect that people exhibit either a form of pure time preference in light of which all events in the very distant future are discounted to the point of insignificance, or else a form of temporal neutrality on which events five billion years from now are no less significant than those five million years from now, all else being equal. A person who is indifferent to events in the former category but very concerned about the same event when re-described so as to fit into the latter category would therefore be rather puzzling. This need not imply a general limitation in our ability to appreciate morally significant differences between very large numbers of the kind mentioned in the vignette. Consider what happens if we put these numbers in a context where the passage of time is not at issue. Suppose war between the US and China is

---

[17] See Forstmann and Burgmer, 'Adults are Intuitive Mind-Body Dualists'.
[18] Huemer, 'In Defence of Repugnance'.

inevitable. It would be one thing to learn that five million people will die in the ensuing conflict. I would feel very differently if told that the expected causalities are as high as five *billion*.

Continuing his case, Huemer notes that in trying to imagine a billion years, our mental state is virtually the same as when trying to imagine a five million years. He writes: "If promised a billion years of some pleasure, most of us would react with little, if any, more enthusiasm than we would upon being promised a million years of the same pleasure."[19]

As before, I think it's hard to rule out the hypothesis that this can be explained in terms of something specific to our attitudes about time, as opposed to how we react to large numbers generally. As well as the point about discounting noted previously, we should keep in mind that quite a few philosophers have argued that extreme longevity is undesirable.[20] It certainly doesn't take much ingenuity to appreciate the worry that a very long life could be plagued with boredom—especially if we have to keep on having the same experience for one billion years! So it's not clear what we can infer from the fact that most people aren't more enthused by the promise of a billion years of some pleasure than by a million years.

As another illustration of our numerical fallibility, Huemer asks us to imagine a very large and very thin piece of paper, with a thickness of one-thousandth of one inch. For every time it gets folded in half, the paper doubles in thickness. When asked to consider how thick the paper will be after fifty folds, Huemer reports that most people expect it to be less than 100 feet. Actually, the answer is approximately 18 million miles.

As before, I don't think we can infer very much from this. The thickness of the paper in this example is an exponential function of the number of folds. But no one thinks it would be sensible to model the aggregate intrinsic value of the very many minor goods involved in the Repugnant Conclusion or Lollipops for Life via an exponential function of their number. According to the Total View, we should use a linear function. The fact that we're very bad at estimating just how quickly an exponential function grows therefore seems neither here nor there. Exponential growth is famously counter-intuitive, whereas children at a young age are able to make correct predictions about linear growth. Mirjam Ebersbach and Friedrich Wilkening note: "Mental representation of nonlinearity appears to be an important cognitive concept, the understanding of which may require a quite different way of thinking from that of linearity."[21]

As specific evidence of our fallibility in compounding small numbers, Huemer highlights a paper by Paul Slovic and colleagues assessing people's willingness to

---

[19] Ibid., 908.
[20] Agar, *Humanity's End;* Kass, 'Ageless Bodies, Happy Souls'; Williams, 'The Makropulos Case'.
[21] Ebersbach and Wilkening, 'Children's Intuitive Mathematics', 296.

use seat-belts when driving.[22] These results are supposed to illustrate our fallibility in appreciating the cumulative significance of small risks. In my view, there are two key problems with drawing on Slovic et al. to support large number scepticism.

Firstly, the experimental design used by Slovic et al. makes it hard to say anything meaningful about how people actually evaluate the cumulative significance of small risks. Slovic et al. divided participants randomly into two groups. Those in the first group were told the probability per car trip of a fatal accident or injury and given an accompanying statement asserting that because the probability per trip is so very small, wearing a seatbelt isn't worth it. Those in the second group were told the estimated lifetime probability of a fatal car accident or disabling injury and were given an accompanying statement asserting that because the risk is so high, wearing a seat-belt is very important. Those in the second group were more likely to report that their use of seat-belts would change and to support mandatory seat-belt laws. Participants were subsequently shown both sets of materials and asked which they found more convincing: 80% selected the pro seat-belt argument that drew on the lifetime risk of accident or injury from driving.

This survey design isn't a very good one if you're interested in assessing people's ability to compound risk values. Slovic et al. were in fact studying the effects of different approaches to risk communication. It's hard to say to what extent the lower support for seat-belt laws in the first group reflected a failure to correctly evaluate the accumulated risk over the course of a lifetime of driving, as opposed to people's willingness to go along with the statement they received, telling them confidently that the risk was insignificant. We can't say whether people's responses were driven by their own efforts to assess the cumulative risk or by deference.

Even granting that people fail to appreciate just how high the risk of an accident becomes when the small per-trip risk is compounded, this needn't support large number scepticism. This is where the second problem comes in: namely, the Upper Bound Objection. It's one thing to say that people don't grasp the full magnitude of the accumulated lifetime risk of fatality or disabling injury when compounded over tens of thousands of car trips, and quite another to say that people don't appreciate that the overall risk goes up and up insofar as people take increasingly larger numbers of trips and can in principle get arbitrarily high given sufficiently many trips per lifetime. The design adopted by Slovic et al. provides no meaningful test of that hypothesis, and so their results provide no meaningful evidence for the existence of a normatively inappropriate upper bound.

---

[22] Slovic, Fischhoff, and Lichtenstein, 'Accident Probabilities and Seat Belt Usage'.

Before I close out this section, let me quickly address the following concern. Some may think that Huemer's case for large number scepticism survives the objections I have been making, because whereas I may be able to suggest competing explanations for the various phenomena to which Huemer appeals in making his case, Huemer can provide a common explanation for these phenomena, whereas I cannot. Large number scepticism may be thought to win out on grounds of parsimony.

In reply, I deny that these phenomena are suitably alike that a common explanation is appropriate. Or, rather, I deny that this holds true across the board. In some cases, it is plausible that a common explanation is called for. For example, pure time preference may explain both our reactions to the astronomer vignette and our relative indifference at being promised one billion years of some pleasure, as opposed to one million years. Nonetheless, it is clear that the broad assertion that we are bad at responding to large numbers paves over key nuances, and that we need to disaggregate. For example, I have noted that we are not insensitive to the difference between millions and billions of war deaths in the way that we seem to be insensitive to the difference between millions and billions of years in the future. To insist on parsimony here would be procrustean. We need a range of different explanatory tools to account for the different ways in which we respond to the moral significance of very large numbers.

11.4

Joshua Greene supports large number scepticism by highlighting examples of *scope insensitivity* in the literature on *contingent valuation*,[23] as do Lucius Caviola and colleagues.[24] I'll argue that the contingent valuation literature fails to provide convincing support for large number scepticism.

Contingent valuation is a method used to assign monetary values to various goods that don't ordinarily have market prices, typically by asking people how much they're willing to pay to protect or provide the good in question. Its use is especially prominent in assessing the 'existence value' of environmental goods: i.e., the value that people assign to the existence of these goods over and above the benefits derived from their direct use. Various methodological concerns have been raised about contingent valuation.[25] The one that matters for us is *scope insensitivity*: the phenomenon whereby people's willingness-to-pay for various goods doesn't increase appropriately in response to an increase in the quantity or scope of the good in question.

---

[23] Greene, 'A Psychological Perspective'.
[24] Caviola, Savulescu, and Faulmüller, 'Cognitive Biases'.
[25] See Haab et al. 'From Hopeless to Curious?'; Hausman, 'Contingent Valuation'.

The *locus classicus* for this concern is a phone survey conducted by Daniel Kahneman. Kahneman asked some respondents about their willingness-to-pay to clean the lakes in one named region of Ontario, whereas others were asked about their willingness-to-pay to clean all lakes in the province of Ontario. Kahneman found that "people seem to be willing to pay almost as much for any one region as for all Ontario together."[26] Another widely cited example of scope insensitivity is a study by William Desvousges and colleagues.[27] Respondents were asked for the most their household would agree to pay each year in higher prices for wire-net covers to save a certain number of birds from drowning in uncovered waste-oil holding ponds. One group of respondents were asked about their willingness-to-pay to prevent 2,000 birds dying each year. A second were asked how much they were willing to pay to save 20,000 birds. A third group were asked about their willingness-to-pay to prevent 200,000 birds from drowning per year. The sample means for the three groups were $80, $78, and $88, respectively. The sample median was $25 in each group.

These results may seem to support large number scepticism, but I think that appearance is mostly illusory. Considered as a basis for large number scepticism, there are three significant limitations of the contingent valuation literature.

First of all, I'm not acquainted with clear evidence that scope insensitivity is tied specifically to large numbers. Obviously, the survey by Desvousges et al. asked subjects to focus on relatively large numbers, but some of the classics don't. No large numbers were used in Kahneman's phone survey, so far as I can tell: the key contrast was between cleaning the lakes in one named region versus all of Ontario. Similarly, Peter Diamond and colleagues found that they couldn't reject the hypothesis that respondents' willingness-to-pay was the same when asked to consider preserving one, two, or three wilderness areas out of the fifty-seven total found in Colorado, Idaho, Montana, and Wyoming.[28] The authors themselves at one point highlight "the small range in the number of areas to be preserved".[29]

Admittedly, these cases aren't so clear cut. There are around 250,000 lakes in Ontario. Respondents in the surveys conducted by Diamond et al. were given information about the acreage of the wilderness areas under consideration, which are in the range 700,000–1,200,000 acres. So large numbers were involved in some way, even if they weren't focal. For that matter, it's equally true that small numbers were in play in the study by Desvousges et al. and may have played a greater role than is immediately apparent. As well as indicating the absolute number of birds that could be saved, respondents were told what percentage of the population this number represents: 2,000 birds was "much less than 1% of the 8.5 million

---

[26] Kahneman, 'Comments', 233.
[27] Desvousges et al., 'Measuring Natural Resource Damages'.
[28] Diamond et al., 'Does Contingent Valuation Measure Preferences?'. [29] Ibid., 60.

migratory waterfowl in the Central Flyway"; 20,000 was "less than 1%"; and 200,000 represented "about 2%". We should remember Frege's observation that there is no uniquely correct way to number some collection of objects: any given number can "at most [be said] to belong to it in view of the way in which we have chosen to regard it".[30] Whether Desvousges et al. forced individuals to reckon with the moral significance of large numbers depends on whether they took individual birds or fractions of total populations as the unit of moral significance. There is some evidence to suggest that individuals were responding principally to the latter when expressing their willingness-to-pay.[31]

Here's a second limitation of the contingent valuation literature. By and large, contingent valuation studies do pass a basic scope test that indicates greater willingness-to-pay for increasing quantities of the good being assessed. Reviewing the literature in the late 1990s, Richard Carson observed: "There are over 30 studies with direct split-sample tests of the scope insensitivity hypothesis which reject it. In contrast, there are only a handful of studies in which the hypothesis is not clearly rejected."[32] Writing some fifteen years later, Catherine L. Kling and colleagues note: "Meta-analyses show that scope effects are typically present in well executed studies."[33] Contemporary controversy focuses less on whether there is a statistically significant effect of scope on willingness-to-pay, and more on whether responses pass more stringent tests of normative adequacy, such as the *adding-up test*, which requires that willingness-to-pay for A and for B when A is assumed to be already secured should equal willingness-to-pay for A and B together.[34]

In light of the Upper Bound Objection, I think we should regard evidence of scope insensitivity in contingent valuation studies as supporting large number scepticism only insofar as such evidence indicates the existence of some normatively inappropriate upper bound on our responsiveness to the quantity of the good being assessed. The results reported by Desvousges et al. can seem to exemplify this phenomenon: willingness-to-pay hardly budged even as the number of birds that could be saved went up by orders of magnitude. But those results aren't quite as representative as many people believe. The fact is that respondents are typically sensitive to scope in contingent valuation studies. The significance of the fact that people can't pass the adding-up test seems unclear, at best, when considering whether to trust our intuitions about the Repugnant Conclusion or Lollipops for Life. The adding-up test concerns consistency in the valuation of parts and wholes and does not have any obvious bearing on the existence of a

---

[30] Frege, *Foundations of Arithmetic*, §22. [31] See Carson, 'Contingent Valuation', 34–5.
[32] Carson, 'Contingent Valuations Surveys', 132.
[33] Kling, Phaneuf, and Zhao, 'From Exxon to BP', 19.
[34] Desvousges, Mathews, and Train, 'Adequate Responsiveness'; Haab et al. 'From Hopeless to Curious?'; Hausman, 'Contingent Valuation'.

normatively inappropriate upper bound on people's ability to respond to the moral significance of number.

Thirdly, to the extent that people are insufficiently responsive to scope in contingent valuation studies, this may be explained (at least in part) by the fact that contingent valuation studies ask people for their willingness-to-pay money or accept financial compensation, and by the fact that they typically rely on SE as opposed to JE.

Consider the hypothesis proposed by Daniel Kahneman and Jack Knetsch.[35] They provide evidence that responses to contingent valuation studies express respondents' willingness to acquire a feeling of 'moral satisfaction' by contributing to the provision of a public good. They hypothesize that 'moral satisfaction' is weakly related, if at all, to the size of the good to which one contributes. Clearly, this points to a specific issue related to willingness-to-pay estimates, and one that shouldn't be expected to bias the moral intuitions that interest us. Baron and Greene provide evidence against the explanation hypothesized by Kahneman and Knetsch, but also report results that support the same general point I'm making here.[36] In particular, they find that sensitivity to number can be enhanced if subjects are asked to make a 'good-good' trade-off, as opposed to a 'good-money' trade-off. Subjects in the 'good-money' condition were asked what increase in personal taxes they would be willing to pay in order to prevent certain US government programmes from being cut. Subjects in the 'good-good' condition were asked what reductions in other programmes they would be willing to make in order to avoid the ten proposed cuts. The latter condition elicited significantly greater sensitivity to quantity. Insofar as either of these conditions is similar to the kind of judgements that we're asked to make in thinking about the Repugnant Conclusion or Lollipops for Life, it would seem that the 'good-good' condition is more comparable.

More importantly, there's the Mode of Evaluation Objection. The elicitation of scope insensitivity in contingent valuation studies may be due to the prevalence of SE designs. Evidence suggests that people rely on affect to a greater extent when making assessments in SE, whereas JE is more likely to elicit cognitive evaluations that are sensitive to number.[37] It shouldn't be surprising, then, that scope insensitivity of the kind observed by Desvousges et al. is hard to reproduce in JE. As noted by Jiao Zhang, "dramatic scope-insensitivity effects occur only when different scopes are presented in SE and disappear when presented in JE."[38] The moral intuitions elicited when we're asked to consider

---

[35] Kahneman and Knetsch, 'Valuing Public Goods'.
[36] Baron and Greene, 'Determinants of Insensitivity to Quantity'.
[37] Ritov and Baron, 'Joint Presentation Reduces the Effect of Emotion on Evaluation of Public Actions'.
[38] Zhang, 'Joint Versus Separate Modes of Evaluation', 228. See also Carson, 'Contingent Valuation Surveys'.

the Repugnant Conclusion or Lollipops for Life clearly involve JE: the relevant alternatives are assessed side by side. Evidence of insensitivity to scope elicited via SE therefore provides poor evidence for discounting these intuitions.

In sum, there's no clear evidence that scope insensitivity is tied specifically to large numbers, well-designed contingent valuation studies typically find scope effects, and instances of scope insensitivity in contingent valuation studies can be explained by factors that shouldn't be expected to bias the moral intuitions that interest us.

11.5

David Fetherstonhaugh and colleagues and Stephan Dickert and colleagues provide evidence that people's responses to saving lives can be described in terms of a pattern called *psychophysical numbing*, whereby people become less sensitive to increasing losses of life.[39] As the authors note, this is just what we would expect if our attitudes towards lives lost and/or saved can be modelled via *prospect theory*.[40] Adam Cureton argues that results of this kind support large number scepticism.[41] I think Cureton's argument is undermined by the Upper Bound Objection.

Let me begin with a brief, informal statement of prospect theory. Prospect theory is a descriptive theory of decision-making under uncertainty. It is characterized by a particular kind of value function, which relates gains and losses to perceived value. Prospect theory assumes that agents adopt a reference point and assess potential outcomes as gains or losses relative to that reference point. The value function is steeper for losses than it is for gains. It is steepest for both nearer the reference point and is concave for gains and convex for losses, indicating diminishing sensitivity. Thus, otherwise equivalent changes in the absolute amount gained or lost should be perceived as less significant when considered in respect of gains or losses that are already high as opposed to low in absolute terms.

For example, as applied to lives saved and/or lost, Fetherstonhaugh et al. note that a reduction in the number of deaths from 2,000 to 1,000 should be perceived as more valuable than reducing the number of deaths from 99,000 to 98,000. More generally, interventions that save a greater proportion of potential victims should be perceived as more valuable, even if they don't save more people overall. And that's exactly what we find. For example, Fetherstonhaugh et al. observed that people are more supportive of a programme that would save 4,500 lives at risk

---

[39] Fetherstonhaugh, Slovic, and Friedrich, 'Insensitivity to the Value of Human Life'; Dickert, et al., 'Scope Insensitivity'.
[40] Kahneman and Tversky, 'Prospect Theory'.
[41] Cureton, 'Moral Intuitions about Large Numbers'.

from cholera if this intervention is described as directed towards a refugee camp containing 11,000 people at risk as opposed to 250,000 people.

Clearly, our diminishing sensitivity to lives lost is normatively inappropriate. That isn't just the philosopher's view. Dickert et al. asked participants to consider different value functions and found a higher preference for a linear function relating victim number to aid response, as opposed to the decelerating curve corresponding to psychophysical numbing. Notably, people's preference for the linear function turned out to be inconsistent with the overall trend when participants were asked to choose between concrete charitable projects: their behaviour was more consistent with psychophysical numbing.

Since the distorting effects of diminishing sensitivity are felt most severely for very large numbers, Cureton takes results like this to support large number scepticism. Highlighting the potential for diminishing sensitivity to bias our moral intuitions, he writes: "it seems to me that once this tendency is pointed out, many of us will, on reflection, think it best to search for other grounds on which to base our judgements about large groups of people."[42]

I don't think we should go along with this. Since Dickert et al. observed evidence of psychophysical numbing even when people were asked to choose between different charitable projects, the phenomenon can't be dismissed via the Mode of Evaluation Objection. However, the Upper Bound Objection applies with full force. Of itself, the existence of diminishing sensitivity only indicates that our subjective response to increasingly larger numbers is attenuated relative to what it should be, and more so for higher values. This doesn't explain why we feel there is no number of minor goods capable of outweighing a more concentrated quantity of very significant goods, as opposed to simply needing to be presented with a figure that is exaggerated. To revisit an example used in section 11.1, note that perceived numerosity in dot estimation tasks is also found to be a concave function of objective numerosity.[43] Nonetheless, we do not expect people to report that there is no number of dots such that the ink required to print them would fill the Grand Canyon. In general, a concave function may be monotonically increasing with no upper bound: e.g., the function $f(x) = \ln x$.

11.6

I think the Upper Bound Objection also applies to another example of large number unreliability highlighted in Cureton's discussion.

The current paradigm in the study of numerical cognition maintains that our knowledge of number arises from two core systems, each believed to be innate and

---

[42] Ibid., 11–12. [43] Krueger, 'Perceived Numerosity'.

present in other animal species.⁴⁴ The *object tracking system* provides precise representations of small numerosities and allows us to quickly and exactly enumerate arrays of up to three elements. The *approximate number system* is able to represent larger numbers, albeit with increasing imprecision. We'll focus on the approximate number system.

To illustrate its workings, consider how people perform in numerical discrimination tasks.⁴⁵ Firstly, our ability to discriminate between numerosities is characterized by a *distance effect*. When asked to consider arrays of dots, we can more easily distinguish between two distant numerosities, such as eighty and a hundred, than two proximate numerosities, such as eighty-one and eighty-two. Secondly, we're subject to a *magnitude effect*, whereby the ease of discriminating between numerosities with a fixed absolute distance declines as numerosities increase. Thus, we are better able to discriminate thirteen dots from ten dots than twenty-three dots from twenty dots. Effects of this kind aren't confined to estimation tasks involving dot arrays. They also occur when people are asked to discriminate between the values of Arabic numerals.

Why do we observe effects of this kind? It is hypothesized that the approximate number system can be characterized as representing numerosities in terms of a normally distributed spread of mental activation imposed on a compressed mental number line, corresponding to a logarithmic scale, with equivalent widths for the bell curves associated with different numerosities and peaks centred on the target values.⁴⁶ The distributed spread of activation means that any given numerosity is likely to evoke nearby sections of the number line, making it difficult to discriminate between close values. The compression of the internal number line introduced by logarithmic scaling means the spread of activation covers greater absolute distances for larger values, making numerical discrimination more difficult at higher magnitudes.

Results like those highlighted above are discussed by Cureton principally because they seem to explain why we show diminishing sensitivity to number in the way discussed in section 11.5. But the increasing imprecision exhibited by the approximate number system in dealing with ever greater numerosities might of itself be thought to provide support to large number scepticism, and some of Cureton's remarks may be read in this way. For example, he writes: "Our numerical representations are more precise for smaller numbers, but they become fuzzier for large numbers. We are almost useless at perceiving large numbers."⁴⁷

As I see it, the fact that we are worse at discriminating between neighbouring values for ever larger numerosities doesn't of itself give any clear indication of why

---

⁴⁴ Dehaene, *The Number Sense*; Feigenson, Dehaene, and Spelke, 'Core Systems of Number'.
⁴⁵ Dehaene, *The Number Sense*, 59–64.
⁴⁶ Dehaene, *The Number Sense*; Feigenson, Dehaene, and Spelke, 'Core Systems of Number'; Viarouge, et al., 'Number Line Compression'.
⁴⁷ Cureton, 'Moral Intuitions about Large Numbers', 16.

we have the intuitions we do about the Repugnant Conclusion and Lollipops for Life. A version of the Upper Bound Objection applies. The fact that large number representations are very imprecise should lead us to expect that we would have great difficulty in recognizing the exact number of very many minor goods needed to outweigh the more concentrated but very significant good, but it's not clear why it should lead us to expect that we would think that no number at all is great enough. Consider the following comparison. If you asked me how many marbles we would need to assemble to have a collection that weighed as much as the Empire State Building, I would be at a loss to offer any kind of precise estimate. Should it be millions, tens of millions, billions? I have no idea. But there is nothing counterintuitive about the thought that some sufficiently large number will do the trick. Why don't I respond similarly when asked how many licks of a lollipop are sufficient to outweigh the value of sparing someone from agony and premature death?

11.7

According to the Upper Bound Objection, a convincing case for large number scepticism needs to show that our responsiveness to increasingly larger numbers is characterized by some normatively inappropriate upper bound, falling at the right point on the number line.

There is one body of evidence indicating a morally inappropriate upper bound to people's responsiveness to number, but one whose existence turns out to provide very little, if any, support for large number scepticism. Here I have in mind evidence of *compassion fade* or *psychic numbing* for numbers of victims greater than one: a phenomenon whereby increasing the number of people in need above a threshold of one leads to diminished affective responses and/or lower willingness to contribute to beneficial interventions.[48] For example, Tehila Kogut and Ilana Ritov found that people were willing to pay more if asked to help save a single child than if asked to help save eight children.[49] Those participants who were presented with the opportunity to help a single child also reported experiencing more distress. Feelings of empathic concern did not differ across the two conditions. Similar results were obtained in a recent set of studies by Daniel Västfjäll and colleagues, who conclude that "affective feelings about charitable causes were strongest for a single endangered person and began to decline as the number in danger grew larger."[50]

---

[48] Cameron and Payne, 'Escaping Affect'; Hsee and Rottenstreich, 'Music, Pandas, and Muggers'; Kogut and Ritov, 'The "Identified Victim" Effect'; Västfjäll et al., 'Compassion Fade'.
[49] Kogut and Ritov, 'The "Identified Victim" Effect'. [50] Västfjäll et al., 'Compassion Fade', 7.

These results are obviously disturbing, but they don't support large number scepticism.

Firstly, although they indicate the existence of a certain kind of upper limit in our responsiveness to the moral significance of number, that limit is the smallest positive integer, and not some enormous number. Introspectively, we may be struck by the difficulty of empathizing with victims numbered in the thousands or millions, but it turns out that we go off the rails already at the point where the numbers are greater than one. These results therefore don't indicate any specific deficiency in responding to very large numbers.

It could be argued that they nonetheless support large number scepticism. Lollipops for Life involves a choice between benefiting a single victim or a larger group of people. If single individuals elicit an inappropriately high level of distress or concern relative to groups of individuals for numbers as low as one versus eight, this of itself might suggest that how we respond to Lollipops for Life is likely to be off-target, regardless of whether we're especially bad at responding to very large numbers.

However, there is a second objection to using evidence of compassion fade to support large number scepticism: the Mode of Evaluation Objection. In the study noted above, Kogut and Ritov found compassion fade by eliciting willingness-to-pay estimates using SE. They subsequently tested whether subjects would continue to value the life of the single victim more than that of a group of victims in JE. They did not.[51] It seems that compassion fade is specific to SE designs and so can't be used to support large number scepticism without falling foul of the Mode of Evaluation Objection.

11.8

This completes my review of the existing evidence and arguments taken to support large number scepticism. If all has gone to plan, I'll now have convinced you that the case for large number scepticism is wanting. The considerations to which philosophers have appealed in making the case that we should distrust our intuitions about large number cases are insufficient to discount our intuitions about the Repugnant Conclusion or Lollipops for Life. Assuming that these intuitions are to be treated as credible unless proven otherwise, they retain their default plausibility and cannot simply be set aside.

I'm not saying that our intuitions about large numbers are perfectly reliable. As my discussion has made clear, they are in fact unreliable in a number of ways. The fact that our intuitions about large numbers exhibit these different kinds of

---

[51] Kogut and Ritov, 'The Singularity Effect'.

unreliability arguably provides *some* reason to doubt the reliability of our intuitions about the Repugnant Conclusion or Lollipops for Life. Nonetheless, I have emphasized the ways in which the distinctiveness of these intuitions significantly limits the support to be derived for large number scepticism in this way. We do not have sufficient evidence that these intuitions are unreliable in the specific way required to meet the Upper Bound Objection and/or the Mode of Evaluation Objection.

If that's right, we'll need to work a bit harder than we might have hoped if we want to make progress in moral philosophy. We can't appeal to the existing psychological literature to clear away the dust we've kicked up. To make progress, we might try soldiering on in the way philosophers are used to, hoping that the search for reflective equilibrium will lead us to a solution. We could otherwise leave the armchair and try to expand the evidence base in relevant psychological sub-disciplines, hoping that further research with a more direct plan-of-attack will clinch the case for large number scepticism. Either way, we have work to be getting on with.[52]

References

Agar, N., *Humanity's End: Why We Should Reject Radical Enhancement* (MIT Press, 2010).

Arrhenius, G., 'An Impossibility Theorem for Welfarist Axiology', in *Economics and Philosophy* 16/2 (2000): 247–66.

Baron, J., and Greene J., 'Determinants of Insensitivity to Quantity in Valuation of Public Goods: Moral Satisfaction, Budget Constraints, Availability, and Prominence', in *Journal of Experimental Psychology: Applied* 2/2 (1996): 107–25.

Bird, A., *Philosophy of Science* (Routledge, 1998).

Broome, J., *Weighing Lives* (Oxford University Press, 2004).

Cameron, C. D. and Payne, B. K., 'Escaping Affect: How Motivated Emotion Regulation Creates Insensitivity to Mass Suffering', in *Journal of Personality and Social Psychology* 100/1 (2011): 1–15.

Carlson, E., 'Aggregating Harms—Should We Kill to Avoid Headaches?', in *Theoria* 66/3 (2000): 246–55.

Carson, R. T., 'Contingent Valuation Surveys and Tests of Insensitivity to Scope', in R. J. Kopp, W. W. Pommerehne, and N. Schwartz (eds.), *Determining the Value of*

---

[52] For valuable comments on previous drafts of this chapter I'm grateful to the audience at the Derek Parfit Memorial conference held in Oxford in May 2018 and to the seminar audience at the Institute for Future Studies, Stockholm, to whom I presented this chapter in September 2018. I'd especially like to thank Ketan Ramakrishnan for his comments on the chapter during the editing process for this volume.

Non-Market Goods: Economic, Psychological, and Policy Relevant Aspects of Contingent Valuation Methods (Kluwer, 1997), 127–63.

Carson, R. T., 'Contingent Valuation: a Practical Alternative When Prices Aren't Available', in *Journal of Economic Perspectives* 26/4 (2012): 27–42.

Caviola, L., Mannino, A., Savulescu, J. and Faulmüller, N., 'Cognitive Biases Can Affect Moral Intuitions about Cognitive Enhancement', in *Frontiers in Systems Neuroscience* 8 (2014), Article 195.

Cotner, S., Brooks, D. C., and Moore, R., 'Is the Age of the Earth One of Our "Sorest Troubles"? Students' Perceptions about Deep Time Affect Their Acceptance of Evolutionary Theory', *Evolution* 64/3 (2010): 858–64.

Cureton, A., 'Moral Intuitions about Large Numbers', Presentation at the 2009 Southern Society for Philosophy and Psychology Conference, Savannah, GA.

Dehaene, S., *The Number Sense: How the Mind Creates Mathematics. Updated and Revised Edition* (Oxford University Press, 2011).

Desvousges, W. H., Johnson, F. R., Dunford, R. W., Hudson, S. P., Wilson, K. N., and Boyle, K. J., 'Measuring Natural Resource Damages With Contingent Valuation: Tests of Validity and Reliability', in J. A. Hausman (ed.), *Contingent Valuation: A Critical Assessment* (North Holland, 1993), 91–164.

Desvousges, W. H., Mathews, K., and Train, K., 'Adequate Responsiveness to Scope in Contingent Valuation', in *Ecological Economics* 84 (2012): 121–8.

Diamond, P. A., Hausman, J. A., Leonard, G. K., and Denning, M. A., 'Does Contingent Valuation Measure Preferences? Experimental Evidence', in J. A. Hausman (ed.), *Contingent Valuation: A Critical Assessment* (North Holland, 1993), 41–83.

Dickert, S., Västfjäll, D., Kleber, J., and Slovic, P., 'Scope Insensitivity: The Limits of Intuitive Valuation of Human Lives in Public Policy', *Journal of Applied Research in Memory and Cognition* 4/3 (2015): 248–55.

Ebersbach, M. and Wilkening, F., 'Children's Intuitive Mathematics: The Development of Knowledge about Nonlinear Growth', in *Child Development* 78/1 (2007): 296–308.

Feigenson, L., Dehaene, S., and Spelke, E., 'Core Systems of Number', in *Trends in Cognitive Neuroscience* 8/7 (2004): 307–14.

Fetherstonhaugh, D., Slovic, P., Johnson, S. M., and Friedrich, J., 'Insensitivity to the Value of Human Life: A Study of Psychophysical Numbing', in *Journal of Risk and Uncertainty* 14/3 (1997): 283–300.

Forstmann, M., and Burgmer, P., 'Adults Are Intuitive Mind-Body Dualists', in *Journal of Experimental Psychology: General* 144/1 (2015): 222–35.

Frege, G., *The Foundations of Arithmetic: A Logico-Mathematical Enquiry into the Concept of Number*, transl. Austin (Northwestern University Press, 1980).

Greene, J. 'A Psychological Perspective on Nozick's Experience Machine and Parfit's Repugnant Conclusion', Presentation at the 2001 Society for Philosophy and Psychology, Annual Meeting, Cincinnati, OH.

Greene, J., 'The Secret Joke of Kant's Soul', in W. Sinnott-Armstrong (ed.), *Moral Psychology. Volume 3. The Neuroscience of Morality: Emotion, Brain Disorders, and Development* (MIT Press, 2008), 35–80.

Haab, T. C., Interis, M. G., Petrolia, D. R., and Whitehead, J. C., 'From Hopeless to Curious? Thoughts on Hausman's "Dubious to Hopeless" Critique of Contingent Valuation', in *Applied Economic Perspectives and Policy* 35/4 (2013): 593–612.

Hausman, J., 'Contingent Valuation: From Dubious to Hopeless', in *Journal of Economic Perspectives* 26/4 (2012): 43–56.

Hsee, C. K., 'The Evaluability Hypothesis: An Explanation for Preference Reversals Between Joint and Separate Evaluation of Alternatives', *Organizational Behavior and Human Decision Processes* 67/3 (1996): 247–57.

Hsee, C. K., 'Less is Better: When Low-Value Options Are Valued More Highly than High-Value Options', in *Journal of Behavioral Decision Making* 11/2 (1998), 107–21.

Hsee, C. K., and Rottenstreich, Y., 'Music, Pandas, and Muggers: On the Affective Psychology of Value', in *Journal of Experimental Psychology: General* 133/1 (2004): 23–30.

Huemer, M., *Ethical Intuitionism* (Palgrave, 2005).

Huemer, M., 'In Defence of Repugnance', in *Mind* 117/468 (2008): 899–933.

Huemer, M., 'Revisionary Intuitionism', in *Social Philosophy and Policy* 25/1 (2008): 368–92.

Horton, J., 'Aggregation, Complaints, and Risk', in *Philosophy & Public Affairs* 45/1 (2017): 54–81.

Kahneman, D., 'Comments', in R. G. Cummings, D. S. Brookshire, and W. D. Schulze (eds.), *Valuing Environmental Goods: An Assessment of the Contingent Valuation Method* (Rowman and Allanheld, 1986), 185–94.

Kahneman, D., and Knetsch, J. L., 'Valuing Public Goods: The Purchase of Moral Satisfaction', in *Journal of Environmental Economics and Management* 22/1 (1992): 57–70.

Kahneman, D., and Tversky, A., 'Prospect Theory: An Analysis of Decision Under Risk', in *Econometrica* 47/2 (1979): 263–91.

Kass, L. 'Ageless Bodies, Happy Souls: Biotechnology and the Pursuit of Perfection', in *The New Atlantis: A Journal of Technology and Society* 1/1 (2003): 9–28.

Kling, C. L., Phaneuf, D. J., and Zhao, J., 'From Exxon to BP: Has Some Number Become Better Than No Number?', in *Journal of Economic Perspectives* 26/4: 3–26.

Kogut, T., and Ritov, I., 'The "Identified Victim" Effect: An Identified Group, or Just a Single Individual?', in *Journal of Behavioral Decision Making* 18/3 (2005): 157–67.

Kogut, T., and Ritov, I., 'The Singularity Effect of Identified Victims in Separate and Joint Evaluations', in *Organizational Behavior and Human Decision Processes* 97/2 (2005): 106–16.

Krueger, L. E., 'Perceived Numerosity', *Perception and Psychophysics* 11 (1972): 5–9.

Ng, Y. K., 'What Should We Do About Future Generations? Impossibility of Parfit's Theory X', in *Economics and Philosophy* 5/2 (1989): 235–53.

Norcross, A., 'Comparing Harms: Headaches and Human Lives', in *Philosophy and Public Affairs* 26/2 (1997): 135–67.

Parfit, D., *Reasons and Persons* (Oxford University Press, 1984).

Parfit, D., 'Can We Avoid the Repugnant Conclusion?', in *Theoria* 82/2 (2016): 110–27.

Pummer, T. 'Intuitions about Large Number Cases', in *Analysis* 73/1 (2013): 37–46.

Rachels, S., 'Counterexamples to the Transitivity of Better Than', in *Australasian Journal of Philosophy* 76/1 (1998): 71–83.

Ritov, I., and Baron, J., 'Joint Presentation Reduces the Effect of Emotion on Evaluation of Public Actions', in *Cognition and Emotion* 25/4 (2011): 657–75.

Singer, P., 'Ethics and Intuitions', in *The Journal of Ethics* 9/3–4 (2005): 331–52.

Slovic, P., Fischhoff, B., and Lichtenstein, S., 'Accident Probabilities and Seat Belt Usage: A Psychological Perspective', in *Accident Analysis and Prevention* 10/4 (1978): 281–5.

Temkin, L. S., 'A Continuum Argument for Intransitivity', in *Philosophy and Public Affairs* 25/3 (1996): 175–210.

Temkin, L. S., *Rethinking the Good: Moral Ideals and the Nature of Practical Reasoning*. (Oxford University Press, 2012).

Thomas, T., 'Some Possibilities in Population Axiology', in *Mind* 127/507 (2018): 807–32.

Västfjäll, D., Slovic, P., Mayorga, M., and Peters, E., 'Compassion Fade: Affect and Charity Are Greatest for a Single Child in Need', in *PLOS One* 9/6 (2014): e100115.

Viarouge, A., Hubbard, E. M., Dehaene, S., and Sackur, J., 'Number Line Compression and the Illusory Perception of Random Numbers', in *Experimental Psychology* 57/6 (2010): 446–54.

Williams, B., 'The Makropulos Case: Reflections on the Tedium of Immortality', in his *Problems of the Self* (Cambridge University Press, 1973), 82–100.

Zhang, J., 'Joint Versus Separate Modes of Evaluation: Theory and Practice', in G. Keren and G. Wu (eds.), *The Wiley Blackwell Handbook of Judgment and Decision Making* (John Wiley and Sons, 2013), 213–38.

12
Are We Living at the Hinge of History?

William MacAskill

12.1 Introduction

In the final pages of *On What Matters*, Volume II (2011), Derek Parfit made the following comments:

> We live during the hinge of history. Given the scientific and technological discoveries of the last two centuries, the world has never changed as fast. We shall soon have even greater powers to transform, not only our surroundings, but ourselves and our successors. If we act wisely in the next few centuries, humanity will survive its most dangerous and decisive period. Our descendants could, if necessary, go elsewhere, spreading through this galaxy.[1]

These comments hark back to a statement he made twenty-seven years earlier in *Reasons and Persons* (1984):

> the part of our moral theory... that covers how we affect future generations... is the most important part of our moral theory, since the next few centuries will be the most important in human history.[2]

He also subsequently made the same claim in even stronger terms during a talk sponsored by Giving What We Can at the Oxford Union in June 2015:

> I think that we are living now at the most critical part of human history. The twentieth century I think was the best and worst of all centuries so far, but it now seems fairly likely that there are no intelligent beings anywhere else in the observable universe. Now, if that's true, we may be living in the most critical part of the history of the universe... [The reason] why this may be the critical period in the history of the universe is if we are the only rational intelligent beings, it's only we who might provide the origin of what would then become a galaxy-wide civilisation, which lasted for billions of years, and in which life was

---

[1] Parfit (2011, p. 616).
[2] Parfit (1984, p. 351). I thank Pablo Stafforini for reminding me that Parfit made this comment.

much better than it is for most human beings. Well, if you look at the scale there between human history so far and what could come about, it's enormous. And what's critical is that we could blow it, we could end it.[3]

The claim that we live at the most important time in history is striking. But, despite the clear influence it had on his thought, in his written work Parfit simply asserts this claim, in the context of discussing other topics; he does not canvass arguments either for or against.[4]

In this chapter, I try to make the hinge of history claim more precise, give arguments in favour and against, and assess whether it is true. Ultimately, I argue that the claim (as I construe it, which might be quite far from any claim Parfit would endorse) is quite unlikely to be true, and that this fact can serve as part of an argument for the conclusion that impartial altruists should generally be investing their resources, rather than trying to do good immediately.

In section 12.2, I give some background by sketching two worldviews that might motivate the claim that we live at the hinge of history. In section 12.3, I make the claim more precise, choosing to define my terms so that they are action-relevant, bearing on the question of whether to 'give now or give later'. In sections 12.4 and 12.5, I give two arguments against the hinge of history claim, and in section 12.6, I discuss two counterarguments in favour. I conclude that there are some strong arguments for thinking that this century might be unusually influential, but that these are not strong enough to make the hinge of history claim likely.[5]

12.2 Two Worldviews

I know of two worldviews that might motivate the idea that we live at the most important period in history. Both of these worldviews rely on a perspective that is

---

[3] 'We are living in the most crucial moment in the history of the Universe—Derek Parfit—Oxford talk' (available at https://youtu.be/j9Y26XUwtQQ).

[4] I say this with one caveat. In the talk he gives one argument, as follows: "There are many ways in which human history might be ended soon, probably nuclear war isn't one of them, but there are various others. The simplest is a really large asteroid. To guard against quite a lot of these dangers, we need to start colonising other parts of space. Need to put a few people on earthly planets and then go further. That's why, when we have spread out, it'll be less critical. That's why this is the most dangerous period." I'll come back to this argument in section 12.6.

[5] This chapter is indebted to many people: those who have been particularly influential include Nick Beckstead, Phil Trammell, Toby Ord, Aron Vallinder, Allan Dafoe, Matt Wage, and, especially, Holden Karnofsky and Carl Shulman. I also thank the many insightful commenters who responded to an early blog post version of this chapter, 'Are we living at the most influential time in history?' *Effective Altruism Forum*, Sep 2019 (available at https://forum.effectivealtruism.org/posts/XXLf6FmWujkxna3E6/are-we-living-at-the-most-influential-time-in-history-1). As I mention in that blog post, these ideas have been discussed in the effective altruism community for some time and I don't claim originality for any of them, though their development and the resulting mistakes are my own.

impartial and longtermist:[6] they assess the importance of an event 'from the point of view of the universe', rather than from our own parochial perspective; and they assume that, in expectation, the vast majority of value occurs in the very long-run future, appreciating that civilization might persist for billions of years, spreading to the stars and potentially settling trillions of solar systems.

The first worldview is the *Time of Perils* view: that we live at a period of unusually high risk of human extinction. The term comes from Carl Sagan, who I believe was an influence on Parfit:

> It might be a familiar progression, transpiring on many worlds—a planet, newly formed, placidly revolves around its star; life slowly forms; a kaleidoscopic procession of creatures evolves; intelligence emerges which, at least up to a point, confers enormous survival value; and then technology is invented. It dawns on them that there are such things as laws of Nature, that these laws can be revealed by experiment, and that knowledge of these laws can be made both to save and to take lives, both on unprecedented scales. Science, they recognize, grants immense powers. In a flash, they create world-altering contrivances. Some planetary civilizations see their way through, place limits on what may and what must not be done, and safely pass through the time of perils. Others, not so lucky or so prudent, perish.[7]

On this view, with the invention of nuclear weapons, we entered an era where we had the technological power to destroy ourselves. Similarly, as we improve technologies like synthetic biology, we will soon develop the ability to create novel pathogens that could infect and kill the entire world population. These technologies pose unprecedented risks to the continued survival of humankind. Within a few centuries, however, wisdom will have caught up with technological progress, and we'll take action to reduce the risks; alternatively, we will have spread out among the planets, and civilization will not be so fragile.[8]

The 'unusual' is important on the Time of Perils view. Perhaps extinction risk is high at this time period, but will be even higher at some future times. In which case those future times might be even more important than today. Or perhaps extinction risk is high, but will stay high indefinitely, in which case in expectation we do not have a very long future ahead of us, and the grounds for thinking that extinction risk reduction is of enormous value fall away.[9] What's more, what's

---

[6] For discussion of the idea of 'longtermism' see my blog post 'Longtermism', Effective Altruism Forum, Jul 2019 (available at https://forum.effectivealtruism.org/posts/qZyshHCNkjs3TvSem/longtermism). For a defence of 'strong longtermism', see Greaves and MacAskill (ms), 'The Case for Strong Longtermism'.
[7] Sagan (1994, pp. 305–6). I thank Pablo Stafforini for this quote.
[8] Ord (2020) stakes out this viewpoint in considerable depth.
[9] For more on the importance of the exogenous risk of extinction to the value of the long-term future, see Tarsney (2019).

really crucial is not that we live at a period of unusually high extinction risk, but that we live at a period where we can do an unusual amount to reduce extinction risk. If extinction risk were high, but there was nothing we could do to reduce it, then the Time of Perils view would be of historical interest, but would not be of interest from the perspective of figuring out what we ought to do.

The second worldview that could motivate the hinge of history idea is what I'll call the *Value Lock-In* view: that we are coming to a point in time where we will invent a technology that will enable the agents alive at that time to maintain their values indefinitely into the future, controlling the broad sweep of the entire rest of the future of civilization. The most prominent example of this worldview, most closely associated with the work of Nick Bostrom and Eliezer Yudkowsky, identifies greater-than-human-level artificial intelligence (AI) as the key technology determining when value lock-in will happen. These authors are quite aware that they are, therefore, claiming that the invention of greater-than-human-level intelligence will be the most important event in history. In the Preface to *Superintelligence*, Bostrom describes his view as follows:

> In this book, I try to understand the challenge presented by the prospect of superintelligence, and how we might best respond. This is quite possibly the most important and most daunting challenge humanity has ever faced. And—whether we succeed or fail—it is probably the last challenge we will ever face.

Later in the book he expands on this idea:

> it may be reasonable to believe that human-level machine intelligence has a fairly sizeable chance of being developed by mid-century, and that it has a non-trivial chance of being developed considerably sooner or much later; that it might perhaps fairly soon thereafter result in superintelligence; and that a wide range of outcomes may have a significant chance of occurring, including extremely good outcomes and outcomes that are as bad as human extinction...[10]

And later he summarizes part his discussion on the powers of superintelligence as follows: "the first superintelligence might well get a decisive strategic advantage. Its goals would then determine how humanity's cosmic endowment will be used."[11] On this Bostrom-Yudkowsky view, in the coming decades or centuries, we will invent an artificially intelligent agent that has the power to improve its own intelligence, which then will give it greater powers to improve its own intelligence further. Through this process of recursive self-improvement, that agent might

---

[10] Bostrom (2014, p. 21).
[11] Bostrom (2014, p. 115). 'Cosmic endowment' refers to all accessible resources in the universe.

rapidly—perhaps over the course of days or weeks—develop intelligence greater than that of all of the rest of humanity combined. At that point, it will have the power to do what it wants with the human species, and will be able to spread to the stars and use the resources in the accessible universe in whatever way it wants. If, however, we are able to control this superintelligence, and align it with human values, then our preferences would determine how all of the resources in the accessible universe would be used. Either way, how this transition goes will determine the entire future of the universe.

On either of these views, we live at, or are approaching, the hinge of history. Let's now turn to making this claim more precise.

12.3 Making the Hinge of History Claim Precise

The claim that we are at the most 'important' or 'critical' time in human history is vague. There are various ways of making this idea more precise, and in this I will choose only one way of doing so. To be clear, I don't take myself to be undertaking exegesis of Parfit's views—this may or may not be the concept that Parfit had in mind, and other definitions of the concept could result in other interesting discussions.

The concept in this area that I will focus on is *how much expected good one can do with the direct expenditure (rather than investment) of a unit of resources at a given time*. I will call this the *influentialness* of a time. On my interpretation, then, the 'hinge of history' claim is that we live at the most influential time ever.

'Influentialness' is an interesting concept because it connects closely to an action-relevant issue: namely, whether as impartial altruists we should be trying to do good now, or whether we should be trying to invest resources in order that we (or people we pass our resources onto) can do more good at a later date. In particular, if we are longtermists—that is, we have a particular concern for ensuring that the long-run future goes well[12]—then there is a *prima facie* presumptive argument in favour of the idea that we should be investing[13] in order to have more impact at a later date. As Parfit notes, civilization might last for billions of years. Given this, if our aim is to influence the value of the long-term future, we have only lost a tiny proportion of that value if we delay the point at which we take action by a few centuries, passing on our philanthropic resources to younger people who share our values, who would then later do the same, passing those resources onto younger people who share their values. But over that time, those

---

[12] MacAskill (2019).
[13] Here I use 'investment' to refer to both financial investment, and to using one's time to grow the number of people who are also impartial altruists. So the idea of investment, here, is not limited merely to money.

resources would have grown enormously. At a 5% real rate of return, over 200 years our invested financial resources would be 17,000 times as large. What's more, because the rate of return on investment exceeds the growth rate,[14] these resources would also be much larger as a proportion of the world economy: if the rate of return is one percentage point larger than the growth rate of the world economy, after 200 years the invested resources would be seven times as large, when measured as a fraction of the world economy. Other things being equal, greater resources would allow us (or our inheritors) to do much more good. So there seems to be a strong *pro tanto* reason for impartial and longtermist altruists to invest their resources rather than donating now.

However, if now is a particularly influential time, then there is a potential response to this argument. If we have very unusually good opportunities for doing good now that we won't have in the future then, even though we would have greater resources in the future, nonetheless we might plausibly be able to have more of an impact now, with these very unusual opportunities. So assessing whether we are at a particularly influential time is crucial for assessing the decision of whether to try to have an impact now, or to invest and give later.

We can make this concept of 'influentialness' more precise in the context of Philip Trammell's work on the optimal timing of philanthropy.[15] In Trammell's basic model, the expected good that one does at a time is given by three factors. First, is simply the amount of philanthropic resources one uses at that time. Second, is how quickly philanthropic resources diminish in their returns.[16] Third is a scale factor: at different times, because of the opportunities available at the time, the same amount of resources, if well-spent, will generate more or less expected value. This scale factor is the idea of 'influentialness' that I refer to.[17]

However, for the purposes of true action-relevance, the influentialness of a time is not quite what we're looking for. Even if we assume that now is the most influential *time*, because there are available opportunities to safeguard the long-run future, a rural farmer in Central African Republic would simply not be able to access those opportunities, and so for that person the question of how influential the present time is is neither here nor there. So we can generalize Trammell's model slightly by talking about person-times rather than times: rather than being indexed to a particular time, each term in his model should be indexed to a particular person-time. This means the model could generate conclusions not just about *when* our resources should be used to generate impact, but also *who* we should give those resources to in order to generate impact.

---

[14] Piketty (2013).   [15] Trammell (ms).

[16] As is standard in economic theory, Trammell models this using an isoelastic utility function.

[17] Trammell himself refers to this as 'hingeyness', in reference to Parfit's claim. However, I worry that this term sounds too unserious, so I prefer 'influentialness'.

Four features of the concept of influentialness are worth emphasizing. The first is that one's influentialness is given by how much expected good one *can* do at a time. It is not given by how much (expected) good one *actually* does. So, hypothetically, someone who in 1910 knew what Hitler would go on to do, and had the opportunity to discourage him from ever moving into politics, but chose not to discourage him, would count, on this definition, as highly influential, even though as a matter of fact they did not change the course of human history in any way.

The second notable feature of this concept is that the influentialness of a person at a time is dependent on the level of knowledge and understanding of that person at that time. Imagine, for example, that some hunter-gatherer had an opportunity to shape the entire course of the future of the human race, but was not able to know, or be in a position to know, that this was possible. That hunter-gatherer would have been at what we might call an unusually 'pivotal' time, but they would not have been at a particularly *influential* time, because they would not have been able to turn resources into enormous amounts of (expected) value. Applying this to our own case: we could fail to be at a particularly influential time either because there are no unusually impactful opportunities to do good available to us, or because we lack the understanding necessary to take advantage of those opportunities. It may well be the case that, even if future opportunities are worse than they are today, future people will be more influential because they have much better scientific and moral knowledge than we have today.

The third feature of this concept that I want to highlight is that the probability distribution that goes into the idea of 'expected value' in the definition of influentialness is our own. This can be confusing when we are considering people in the future who might have much better (or worse) evidence than us, and therefore have different probability distributions. But we can think about it using the standard analysis of the 'value of information'. In the standard analysis, the value of gaining information (including imperfect information, which might be misleading) is given by the expected value of making the best decision given the new information minus the expected value of making the best decision without that information. So, for example, if you currently believe you have a 60% chance of making the right decision about how to spend your resources, which would generate 1 unit of value if you make the right decision, but believe that if you gained some piece of new evidence you would have an 80% chance of making the right decision, then you should try to get that evidence, and indeed you should be willing to forego up to 0.2 units of value in order to get that evidence.[18]

---

[18] Plugging these numbers into the formula: Expected value of best decision given new information—Expected value of best decision given no new information = (0.8*1 + 0.2*0) − (0.6*1 + 0.4*0) = 0.2.

Although value-of-information analysis is typically limited to a single decision-maker over time, we can use the same analysis to think about passing resources across multiple decision-makers over time. If you think you have a 60% chance of making the right decision about how to use a unit of resources, with value 1 if you do make the right decision and 0 otherwise, whereas some other future person has an 80% chance of making the right decision about how to use a unit of resources, with value 1 if they make the right decision and 0 otherwise, then you should pass your resources onto this other person. (Indeed, you should be willing to forego up to 0.2 units of value in order to pass on those resources.)

The same analysis applies, moreover, if one believes that the *option-set* might be different in the future. If your best option, with a unit of resources, generates 1 unit of value, and you believe that there's a 50% chance that a particular future person will have a new best option worth 2 units of value, and a 50% chance of a best option worth only 0.5 units of value, then you should pass resources on to that future person. Alternatively, if you thought this future person would have only a 10% chance of having a best option worth 2 units of value, and a 90% chance of a best option worth 0.5 units of value, then you should spend the resources yourself.[19]

In general, in this context we can usefully, though somewhat cold-heartedly, think of future people (including ourselves at later times), who we might pass resources on to, simply as machines for converting resources into good outcomes. If we think that such people will in expectation, and by our own lights, be better than us at converting resources into good outcomes then we should pass our resources on to those people.

The fourth feature of the concept I want to highlight is that it refers only to direct expenditure of resources, or what economists would call 'consumption', rather than investment. This is crucial because the issue I am primarily addressing is whether we should spend our resources now, or invest them for a later date. This means that we need to be careful. If investment can reliably compound at a positive rate over time, then there is always an argument for thinking that earlier generations can do more good than later generations: if the later generation is more influential, then the earlier generation can invest the money and give a larger sum to the later generation. So when I later claim that previous generations were less influential than we are today, I am meaning that they could do less good with direct expenditure; I am not also making the claim that, had they invested the money, passing on those resources to today, they would still have done less good.

---

[19] For more discussion of the idea of 'option value', including in the application to moral learning over time, see MacAskill (ms).

With all this on board, we can turn now to stating the Hinge of History claim. The version of the claim that I wish to assess is the claim we are at an enormously influential moment out of a vast future. That is, not merely are we among the most influential people ever, but we are among the most influential people ever out of a civilization that will one day take to the stars. So I can state the claim as follows:

> HH: We are among the very most influential people ever, out of a truly astronomical number of people who will ever live.

In HH, the phrase 'among the very most influential' is vague. Nothing too significant rests on this vagueness; we could make it more precise by interpreting it as saying, for example, that you and I are among the million most influential people ever.

Parfit himself would not necessarily claim that HH is very likely. But what he would endorse, I think, is the conditional claim that *if* civilization survives the next few centuries, then we are among the very most influential people ever, out of trillions upon trillions of people who will ever live. And, though to my knowledge Parfit does not state his views on whether we will survive the next few centuries, it seems hard to believe it's extremely likely that we'll destroy ourselves. If Parfit agreed with that, then he would have assigned quite a significant likelihood (greater than 10%) to HH being true.

Note that, in representing the claim the way I do, I am considering a somewhat bolder claim than the one that Parfit himself makes. He claims that the next few centuries are the most important ever, whereas I am considering primarily the claim that *we today* are among the most influential people who ever live. I do this, again, to make the discussion as action-relevant as possible. For the purposes of action today, it does not much matter whether the most influential time is one century or one thousand years away. Either way, we have an argument for saving. It's only if now—our own lifetimes—are far more influential than times after we die that we have, instead, an argument for trying to have an impact right away rather than growing our resources and passing them on to subsequent generations.

Having now defined the claim that I consider, I turn to assessing its plausibility. In the next two sections, I give two arguments against having a significant degree of belief in HH.

12.4 The Base Rates Argument against HH

The first argument I want to marshal against HH is simply that our prior in HH should be very low, and the evidence we have in favour of it is not sufficiently strong to overcome this low prior.

A natural prior is given by what Bostrom called the *Self-Sampling Assumption*. I'll use the formulation of this assumption given by Thomas (ms):

> A rational agent's priors locate him uniformly at random within each possible world.[20]

An implication of this principle is that, for any property F, your prior should be such that if there are n people in a population, the probability that you are in the m most F people in that population is m/n. This principle seems compelling as a way of setting priors. The *a priori* probability that I am in the top 100 funniest people in Scotland today is 100 out of 5.4 million; the *a priori* probability that I am in the top 1000 strongest people in the UK today is 1000 out of 66.4 million. I believe that, among those who study anthropic reasoning, the self-sampling assumption (as stated in some form similar to Thomas's formulation) is widely accepted: the major question is whether to *also* accept further principles, like the 'self-indication assumption'.[21]

If we set our priors this way, we assign a very low prior probability to HH. If we don't go extinct in the next few centuries, then there are plausibly a vast number of people in the future. The Earth will remain habitable for something on the order of a billion years. Even if current population levels reduced to a tenth of what they are today (i.e. to about one billion people per century), that would mean that there would be 10,000 trillion people to come. If, as Parfit suggests, we would subsequently take to the stars, that number would get far higher: there are one hundred billion stars in the Milky Way; settling just 0.1% of them with the same population as on Earth would mean that there are a trillion trillion people to come. If we consider also the eight billion other galaxies that we could access,[22] the numbers get correspondingly higher again.

For the purposes of my argument, what matters is not these precise numbers, but that any of them are astronomical. If there are a trillion trillion people to come, then the *a priori* probability that we are among the million most influential people

---

[20] Note that this is the 'very rough' formulation given by Thomas. His paper ultimately spells out a much more precise formulation, but this will not be necessary for our purposes. Bostrom (2002, p. 57), states the principle as follows: "(SSA) One should reason as if one were a random sample from the set of all observers in one's reference class."

[21] Thomas (ms) states the self-indication assumption (very roughly, before making it more precise) as: "A rational agent is proportionally more confident *a priori* in worlds with large populations than in worlds with small populations, all else equal." Bostrom (2002, p. 66) states the self-indication assumption as: "Given that you exist, you should (other things equal) favor hypotheses according to which many observers exist over hypotheses on which few observers exist." Note, moreover, that the argument I make is not merely a version of the Doomsday argument. Even if we accept the self-indication assumption (as I believe we should), which neutralizes the Doomsday argument, there is a further question about whether we are among the most influential people ever. See Mogensen (2019) for an in-depth explanation of this.

[22] Ord (ms).

ever is one in a million trillion. This is about the same probability as dealing a Royal Flush from a well-shuffled pack of cards three times in a row. But even if we assume that there are only a hundred trillion people to come, the *a priori* probability of being among the million most influential people ever is still one in a hundred million—about as likely as winning the lottery.

An alternative, more visual, way of seeing the same argument is to think about all the ways that influentialness might vary over time. (Here, in order to be able to represent this on a two-dimensional graph, I'll just look at influentialness over time, rather than influentialness over person-times.) Some ways in which we might *a priori* expect influentialness to vary are as in Figure 12.1. However, at least on the Value Lock-In view, none of these represent how influentialness varies over time. Instead, the graph looks like the one displayed in Figure 12.2.[23]

That is, on the Value Lock-In view, almost everything of importance that happens for the fate of the universe occurs over the course of just a few decades or a century—what is essentially a single point in time. What's more, on this view, that point in time is essentially now. This is an astonishing claim to make. It's not so clear that the Time of Perils view would have this same exact implication. But Parfit's comments that we might be living at the "most critical part of the history of the universe" suggests that the broad picture is roughly similar.

That we should have a very low prior in HH doesn't yet tell us that we should have a very low posterior in HH. Sometimes we should update from extraordinarily low priors to significant posteriors. For example, if I shuffle a pack of cards and then deal them out face up in a row, and there is a random-seeming sequence of cards in front of you, your posterior that the cards are in the sequence they seem to be in should be reasonably high. However, your prior that the cards would be in that sequence should have been astronomically low: 1 in 52!, or 1 in 10^68.

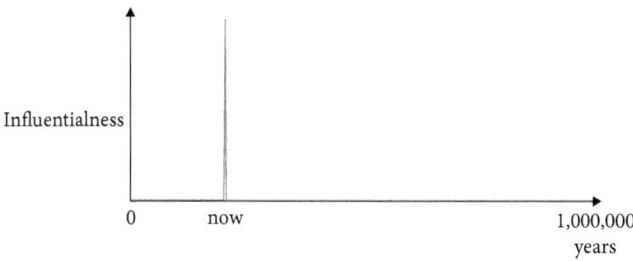

Figure 12.1 The value lock-in view.

---

[23] This, of course, is an approximation. Occasions prior to the lock-in event could still be very influential, if they gave the opportunity to prevent an extinction event, or if they gave the opportunity to shape the values of those who are alive during the lock-in event.

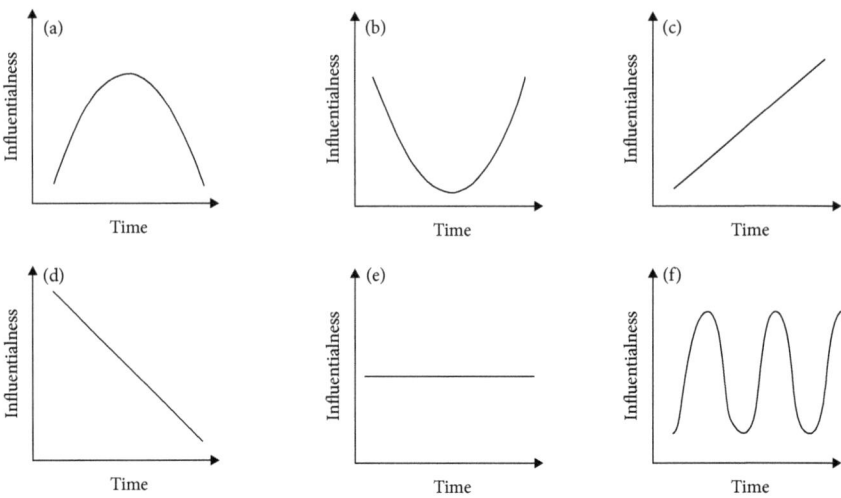

Figure 12.2 How influentialness may vary over time.

However, HH is not merely *a priori* extremely unlikely. It's also *fishy*. It's less like believing that I just dealt a random-seeming sequence of cards from a well-shuffled pack, and more like believing I dealt a sequence of cards in perfect order (two to Ace of clubs, then two to Ace of diamonds, etc.) from a well-shuffled pack. Being fishy is different than just being unlikely. The difference between unlikelihood and fishiness is the availability of alternative, not wildly improbable, hypotheses, on which the outcome or evidence is reasonably likely.[24] If I deal the random-seeming sequence of cards, I don't have reason to question my assumption that the deck was shuffled, because there's no alternative somewhat plausible background hypothesis on which the random-seeming sequence is a likely occurrence. If, however, I deal the deck of cards in perfect order, I do have reason to significantly update that the deck was not in fact shuffled, because the probability of getting cards in perfect order if the cards were not shuffled is reasonably high. That is: P(cards not shuffled)P(cards in perfect order|cards not shuffled) >> P(cards shuffled)P(cards in perfect order|cards shuffled), even if my prior credence was that P(cards shuffled) > P(cards not shuffled). So I should update towards the cards having not been shuffled.

Similarly, if it seems to me that I'm among the most influential people who have ever or will ever live, this gives me good reason to suspect that the reasoning process that led me to this conclusion is flawed in some way, because P(I'm reasoning poorly)P(seems like I'm living at the hinge of history|I'm reasoning

---

[24] Horwich (1982, p. 94), though he talks about an event being 'surprising' rather than a claim being 'fishy'.

poorly) >> P(I'm reasoning correctly)P(seems like I'm living at the hinge of history|I'm reasoning correctly).

The strength of this argument depends in part on how confident we are of our own reasoning abilities in this domain. But it seems to me there's a strong risk of bias in our assessment of the evidence regarding how influential our time is. One reason for thinking this is *salience*. It's much easier to see the importance of what's happening around us now, which we can see, than it is to assess the importance of events in the future, involving technologies and institutions that are unknown to us today, or (to a lesser extent) the importance of events in the past, which we take for granted and involve unsalient and unfamiliar social settings.[25]

A second reason for thinking this is *confirmation bias*. For those of us, like myself and like Parfit, who would very much like for the world to be taking much stronger action on extinction risk mitigation (even if the probability of extinction is low), it would be a good outcome if people who do not have altruistic and longtermist values think that the risk of extinction is high, even if it's low. So we might be biased (subconsciously) to overstate the case in favour of taking action to mitigate extinction risk. And, in general, people have a tendency towards confirmation bias: once they have a conclusion ("we should take extinction risk a lot more seriously"), they tend to marshal arguments in favour of that conclusion, rather than carefully assess arguments on either side. Though we try our best to avoid such biases, it's hard to overcome them.

In general, if you accept that you should have a very low prior in HH, you need to be very confident that you're good at reasoning about the long-run significance of events (such as the magnitude of risk from some new technology like artificial intelligence or synthetic biology), and our ability to have leverage over them, in order to have a significant posterior credence in HH, rather than concluding, instead, that we're mistaken in some way. But we have no reason to believe that we're very reliable in our reasoning in these matters. We don't have a good track record of making predictions about the importance of historical events, and some track record of being badly wrong. So, if a chain of reasoning leads us to the conclusion that we're living at the most influential time ever, we should think it more likely that our reasoning has gone wrong than that the conclusion really is true. Given the low base rate, and given our unreliable tools for assessing the claim, the evidence in favour of HH is almost certainly a false positive.

---

[25] One example of this salience bias in action, with respect to the 'influentialness' claim, comes from Qin Dynasty philosopher Li Si: "With the might of Qin and the virtues of Your Highness, in one stroke, like sweeping off the dust from a kitchen stove, the feudal lords can be annihilated, imperial rule can be established, and unification of the world can be brought about. This is the one moment in 10,000 ages. If Your Highness allows it to slip away and does not press the advantage in haste, the feudal lords will revive their strength and organize themselves into an anti-Qin alliance. Then no one, even though he possess the virtues of the Yellow Emperor, would be able to annex their territories" (De Bary and Bloom, 1999, p. 208).

Finally, we can assess the quality of the arguments given in favour of the Time of Perils or Value Lock-in views, to see whether, despite the *a priori* implausibility and fishiness of HH, the evidence is strong enough to give us a high posterior in HH. It would take us too far afield to discuss in sufficient depth the arguments made in *Superintelligence*, or *Pale Blue Dot*, or *The Precipice*. But it seems hard to see how these arguments could be strong enough to move us from a very low prior all the way to significant credence in HH. As a comparison, a randomized controlled trial with a p-value of 0.05, under certain reasonable assumptions, gives a Bayes factor[26] of around 3 in favour of the hypothesis;[27] a Bayes factor of 100 is regarded as 'decisive' evidence.[28] In order to move from a prior of 1 in 100 million to a posterior of 1 in 10, one would need a Bayes factor of 10 million—extraordinarily strong evidence.

But the evidence we currently have for either the Value Lock-In view or the Time of Perils view are merely informal arguments. They aren't based on data (because they generally concern future events) nor, in general, are they based on trend extrapolation, nor are they based on very well-understood underlying mechanisms, such as physical mechanisms. And the range of deep critical engagement with those informal arguments, especially from 'external' critics, has, so far, been limited. So it's hard to see why we should give them much more evidential weight than, say, a well-done randomized controlled trial with a p-value at 0.05, let alone assign them an evidential weight three million times that amount.

Of course, a full treatment of this would involve assessing at length the arguments that Bostrom and Ord and others give for their position, which it's not the purpose of this chapter to do. But it's hard to see how, even if the arguments in those texts seemed compelling, they could be strong enough to move us all the way from a tiny prior to a sufficiently large posterior.

I'll now consider two responses to the argument I have just made. The first response is to accept that we don't have good reasons for thinking that we're at the *most* influential time in history. Instead, we could just consider the idea that we're at an enormously influential time. And very little changes whether you think that we're at the most influential time ever, or merely at an enormously influential time.

However, I don't think this response is a good one, for two reasons. First, the Bostrom-Yudkowsky view on superintelligence is inconsistent with the idea that we're merely at an enormously influential time. On their view, the development of artificial general intelligence is the decisive moment for the entire rest of civilization. But if you find the claim that we are among the very most influential people ever hard to swallow, then you have, by *modus tollens*, to reject the Bostrom-Yudkowsky story of the development of superintelligence. So there is a material

---

[26] Where the Bayes factor is P(hypothesis|evidence)/P(not-hypothesis|evidence).
[27] Benjamin et al. (2018). [28] E.g. Jeffreys (1962, p. 432).

difference in the views we should hold, depending on whether we believe we're at the most influential time ever, or merely an enormously influential time.

Second, even if we're at some enormously influential time right now, if there's some future time that is even more influential, then an obvious strategy for longtermist altruists to pursue would be to send resources to that time in the future. So the question of whether we're at the most influential time, or a merely enormously influential time, is directly action-relevant.

A second counterargument that one could make is that, for the purposes of action-relevance, we do not need to consider how influential this time is compared to times in the past, or times in the distant future.[29] All that matters is the relative influentialness of now compared to any time we can (in expectation) pass resources on to, which might be the next 1000 years or so, but not much longer than that.

In response, I'll note again that some views, such as the Bostrom-Yudkowsky view, are inconsistent with the claim that we're merely at the most important time in the next 1000 years—on their view, we are at the most important time ever. And if, in considering the question of influentialness over time, we come to have less confidence in the Bostrom-Yudkowsky view, that could lead us to take very different actions than we would otherwise have taken. Moreover, understanding how influentialness may or may not have varied in the past is useful if we want to think about how it might vary in the future. (If, for example, we come to believe that the formation of the world religions were a particularly influential moment in the past, that might lead us to think that the points in time when new ideologies are formed in the future will also be particularly important.)

But the point that, ultimately, what we should care about is the action-relevant concept is well-taken. If some people and times in the past were enormously influential, that does not matter to us, today, for the purposes of action. Nor does it matter if people in a million years' time have enormous opportunities to have an impact, if we are certain that we cannot pass resources that far into the future.[30]

So one might instead defend a restricted claim:

Restricted-HH: We are among the very most influential people, out of the very large number of people who will live over the coming 1000 years.

---

[29] Greg Lewis raises this point in the comments section of my blog post, 'Are we living at the most influential time in history?'.

[30] Though we should be careful about claiming that we are 'certain' that we cannot pass resources even further into the future than 1000 years' time. Given how enormous your influence would be if you were able to invest those resources over such large timespans (perhaps ending up with a significant fraction of global wealth), even a very low probability of attaining that outcome could have very great expected value.

In this statement, 'very large' might refer to the billions to hundreds of billions of people who are to come over the next 1000 years. (Which is small compared to the trillions upon trillions of people who would live if we took to the stars.)

This claim is *much* weaker than the original HH, and is therefore much more plausible *a priori*. However, a similar line of argument can be made against Restricted-HH as can against HH. It's *a priori* unlikely that, of all the people and times to come over the next 1000 years, it is we, today, who can do the most good in expectation with a unit of resources.[31] Moreover, as we shall see in section 12.6, it's much harder to come up with a convincing argument for the claim that we, now, are far more influential than people in the centuries to come, than it is to make arguments for the claim that those in the coming millennium are far more influential than those in the millenia that follow. The arguments that I'll cover in section 12.6—that we are unusually early on in history, on a single planet, and at a period of unusually high economic and technological growth—would plausibly support the idea that any time in the next few centuries is as influential as today is.

12.5 The Inductive Argument against HH

In addition to the base rates argument against HH, which relies on priors and claims we shouldn't move drastically far from those priors, there's a positive argument against HH, which gives us evidence against HH, whatever our priors. This argument is based on induction from past times, as follows:

> P1. The influentialness of comparable people in the past has been increasing over time, with increasing knowledge and opportunities being the most important factor.
> P2. We should expect our knowledge and opportunities to continue into the future.
> C. So we should expect the influentialness of those future people who we can pass resources on to be greater, too.

Let's begin with the first premise: that the influentialness of comparable people in the past has been increasing over time, with increasing knowledge and opportunities being the most important factor. I think it's relatively clear, for example, that we should prefer that a well-educated European living in 1600 pass philanthropic resources to us, today, rather than attempting to directly do good with those resources. At least three considerations support this view. First, the opportunities

---

[31] This claim also is not a reasonable interpretation of Parfit's comments. Parfit's claim was that the next few centuries are unusually important: if the claim was merely that they were unusually important out of the next 1000 years, that would not be a very strong claim at all.

available to this person in 1600 were in general less high-leverage than the opportunities available to us today.[32] In particular, they would have had few opportunities to shape the long-run future: most of the existential risks that someone faced in 1600, such as an asteroid collision or supervolcanic eruption, were not known of at the time, and would have been impossible to do anything about even if they were known. Second, and even more importantly, was their impoverished scientific understanding. A well-educated European in 1600 still believed, for example, that witches could summon storms, that werewolves could be found in Belgium, that mice are spontaneously generated in piles of straw, that a murdered body will bleed in the presence of the murderer, and that the sun revolves around the Earth.[33] They did not have the modern scientific method, physics, biology, chemistry, or social science, and instead their worldview was theocentric. They could not have known about the vastness of the future nor make reasonable guesses about how to positively influence the long-run future.

Finally, and most importantly of all, is moral progress. Those in 1600 believed that women and people of other races and religions are of lesser moral standing than European Christian men. Intense social hierarchy, inequality, and slavery were regarded as the natural and just way of things. Homosexuality and premarital sex were regarded as deeply immoral. The idea of liberalism had not been developed. Torture was commonplace and celebrated, as were cruel punishment and violence against heretics. In general, the moral beliefs that were widespread at the time were grounded in a narrow understanding of Christian doctrine that we would now deplore.[34] For these reasons, the altruistic priorities of someone in 1600 would have been radically different from what we would think today.

When we look over a shorter timespan—say, looking back to 1970, or to 1920— the argument is not quite as clear-cut. In particular, possible existential risks from new technology were knowable at those times.[35] But even still, there is a good argument for thinking that we are in a much better position to have a positive impact today than we could during those times. Again, our opportunities are better today than they were before—there was little that one could do decades ago to work on risks from misaligned artificial intelligence or synthetic biology. Our scientific knowledge is considerably better, including our understanding of the nature of existential risks: the idea of a nuclear winter was only developed in the 1980s, and the scientific consensus regarding anthropogenic climate change was only developed over the 1970s to 1990s. We have only learned of the impressive success of deep learning as paradigm for progress in artificial intelligence

---

[32] An exception might have been the opportunity to shape the values of the time, which are plausibly persistent for a long time period, including via religious institutions.
[33] These facts are taken from Wootton (2005, p. 6).
[34] For more on moral change over time, see Pinker (2011, esp. chapter 4) and Morris (2015).
[35] For example, possible risks from artificial intelligence were identified by the pioneers of computer science, such as Alan Turing and I.J. Goode.

(and therefore learned more detail on the shape that technical artificial intelligence safety work ought to take,[36] in the event that deep learning leads to artificial general intelligence) in the last decade. And moral progress has continued, too. Cosmopolitanism has continued to become more widespread, and rights for women, minorities, and people of all sexual identities have been progressively secured. On the intellectual side of moral progress, most notable is that population ethics only became a serious field of inquiry after the publication of *Reasons and Persons* in 1984. But without that work it's hard to believe that someone would have reliably prioritized existential risk reduction over other altruistic activities.

So, just as we concluded with longer timespans, it seems that our influentialness has increased since 1920 or 1970. And the primary driver of this increased influentialness is our increasing scientific and moral knowledge. But we should strongly expect this increase in knowledge to continue into the future. As a general matter, people in the future, who we could pass our resources to, will plausibly be far smarter and more informed than even the most brilliant minds of today: they may be the beneficiaries of enhancement technologies, more powerful intelligence-augmenting tools like computers and artificial intelligence, better educational methods, and better nutrition. And they will very likely have a radically larger edifice of scientific knowledge to base their decisions on, with decades or centuries of further moral progress, including on the very particular question of how best to use resources to make the world better.[37]

But, as well as the general point, we also can identify specific, crucial gaps in our current understanding. On the empirical side, we still don't know how developments in synthetic biology and AI will play out; we have a very poor understanding of how resilient civilization is, in terms of both how large a disaster would be required to kill everyone, or how likely civilization would be to recover after a major but non-existential catastrophe; and we have very limited understanding of good forecasting practices beyond a few years. On the moral side: we have no good theoretical understanding of how to evaluate tiny probabilities of enormous amounts of value; nor do we have a compelling account of how to deal with the possibility of creating infinite amounts of value; there has been very little work trying to understand the expected value of the continuation of human civilization; and we have very limited understanding of how to correctly make decisions in the face of normative uncertainty. Insights on these questions could all significantly change how we would choose to prioritize our altruistic efforts. And this list I've

---

[36] See Amodei et al. (2016).

[37] Might one worry that such reasoning would lead one *never* to use one's resources philanthropically? I don't think so. The pace at which we are improving our understanding of the world will inevitable slow, and may indeed have already been slowing over the course of the last fifty years. Once we are reaching the plateau, we might well want to spend significant proportions of our resources at particularly pivotal moments in time. What's more, with every generation we wait, we have less future to be able to positively influence; this is a cost, and at some point in time, the cost of delay will outweigh any benefits thereby gained. This is explored more thoroughly in Trammell (ms).

given is just a tiny subset of all the crucial questions that are still unanswered.[38] But if we should expect our knowledge and understanding to significantly increase over the coming decades and centuries, just as it has over the previous decades and centuries, and that knowledge and understanding is typically the dominant factor in terms of how much good an individual can do with a unit of resources, then we should think that future people will be more influential than we are.

The claim that we're at the hinge of history (at least as I have defined this idea) is therefore in tension with another view of Parfit's: that we may be at just the beginning of intellectual and moral progress. In the final paragraph of *Reasons and Persons*, Parfit commented that:[39]

> There could clearly be higher achievements in the struggle for a wholly just world-wide community. And there could be higher achievements in all of the Arts and Sciences. But the progress could be greatest in what is now the least advanced of these Arts or Sciences. This, I have claimed, is Non-Religious Ethics. Belief in God, or in many gods, prevented the free development of moral reasoning. Disbelief in God, openly admitted by a majority, is a recent event, not yet completed. Because this event is so recent, Non-Religious Ethics is at a very early stage. We cannot yet predict whether, as in Mathematics, we will all reach agreement. Since we cannot know how Ethics will develop, it is not irrational to have high hopes.

I agree with Parfit's optimism here. But if there is a good chance that future generations will have discovered many ways in which we are misguided, scientifically and morally, then we have a strong argument for thinking that they will be able to spend resources in higher-value ways than we can, and are therefore more influential than we are. Indeed, if we are morally mistaken enough, perhaps even our best-intended efforts today could be doing harm.

In the discussion above, I looked at how the value of opportunities to shape the long-run future (in particular by reducing existential risks) have changed over time. I believe this is the most relevant question for an inductive argument, because I believe that opportunities that shape the long-run future tend to be the highest value opportunities.

But, as a sanity check, we could also ask how influentialness has varied over time if we just restrict ourselves to attempts for a person to make their own time better. This should seem to be a more favourable case for the idea that influentialness is going down over time, because the world has become so much richer over time, and we have made so much progress on so many of the social problems that affect the people of the day.[40] But, even so, I think that the opportunities we have

---

[38] For a longer list, see Greaves et al. (2019). [39] Parfit (1984, p. 454). [40] Pinker (2011).

to benefit individuals alive at the present time are far better than the opportunities that were available in 1970 to benefit people alive in 1970, those that were available in 1920 to benefit people alive in 1920, and similarly for 1600 and indeed for any other time in the past.

Again, the two principal factors that have caused this are increasing technology (allowing us to purchase a wider variety of goods) and increasing scientific knowledge. Since the 1970s we have a far greater understanding of how to improve the lives of those in poor countries, as a result of improvements in epidemiology, public health, economic theory, and the randomista movement. And, especially since the 1920s, we have far more and better opportunities to benefit very poor people, especially via medical technology. In the 1920s, we simply did not have the technology to provide cheap lifesaving medicines to the poorest people in the world. In the 1970s we did, and in some cases the cost-effectiveness of the opportunities available (such as smallpox eradication) were enormous. But it's not clear at all that we could have identified these opportunities *ex ante*: we could not have known that global health would have been the enormous success that it was, and the long history of failures in aid spending suggests that altruistically minded individuals of the time were not able to reliably identify the actions that would turn out *ex post* to have enormous positive impact.

12.6 Some Arguments for HH

So far I've given two arguments against having a significant degree of belief in HH. This section will consider two additional arguments that one might raise in favour of HH.[41] I think that these arguments are fairly strong, and they caveat my

---

[41] One argument I won't consider here is that there is an annual risk of human extinction or lock-in, so earlier centuries are more likely to have people in them, and to be prior to some lock-in event. We of course need to take that into account, but in Trammell's model, that is taken into account in the 'δ' term, which represents our 'rate of pure time preference', rather than in the influentialness of a time. I also won't discuss further the question of how to set fundamental priors in this context. For more discussion of that, see the comments from Toby Ord, and my replies, on my blog post 'Are we living at the most influential time in history?'. Ord proposes using a Jeffreys prior to model the chance that we are among the most influential people. I don't discuss Ord's proposal simply because it would involve a long digression into a proposal that I ultimately think is a red herring. I think there are reasons for thinking that people at earlier times are more likely to be influential, but these are given by the arguments I present in this section and shouldn't be built into one's fundamental prior. Moreover, Ord's proposal faces technical issues: on his account, the prior one chooses for being among the most influential people is highly sensitive to the reference class chosen; without further modification, it would generate inconsistent probability assignments to multiple hypotheses; it would have predicted that the most influential people were very likely in the past; and it involves treating the superlative 'most influential' very differently from other arbitrary superlatives, like 'most beautiful', 'funniest', and so on. I also won't discuss the fact that we can affect the future but not the past, so those who live later on simply have fewer future lives that they can affect. So for this reason, we should expect earlier people to have more influence than later people. I don't discuss this in the body text because, though it is clearly true, it will not make a major difference to the argument: the first person who ever lives will only have

12.6.1 Living on a Single Planet

We currently live in a civilization that exists on a single planet. If, in the future, we take to the stars and form an interstellar civilization, then the vast majority of people who ever live will be part of a multiplanetary civilization. So this is a clear and objective way in which the present time is very unusual. Moreover, there are a number of reasons for thinking that times when we live on a single planet are unusually influential. First, as Parfit mentions in his talk at the Oxford Union, civilization's period on a single planet might be one of unusually high existential risk. A single planet means a single point of failure. So, for example, a collision between Earth and a large asteroid could end human life on this planet, but it would not pose a risk to human life on other planets. Second, it means we are at a period of unusually low population and economic power (compared to a vast interstellar civilization), so any resources we have are an unusually large fraction of total resources at the time, which might give us an unusual ability to influence the course of civilization as a whole. Third, it means that any one person is able to communicate almost instantaneously with almost anyone else in civilization. In contrast, once a civilization is interstellar, communication with other solar systems will take many years: the closest solar system to our own is four light-years away, the galaxy is 100,000 light-years across, and the distances between galaxies is measured in the millions of light-years. Again, this gives individuals alive during the present time an unusual potential opportunity to influence civilization as a whole.

This is an important argument—in particular in the form that emphasizes how small civilization is, today, compared to future civilization—and I believe it should cause a major update in favour of HH, away from our prior.

However, its strength should not be overstated. First, the reduction in existential risk in virtue of being interplanetary may be relatively small. For example, even absent any technological intervention, the annual risk from an asteroid collision without any human action is about one in a hundred million. What's more, we have now detected all of the near-Earth asteroids over 10km in size, over 95% of near-Earth asteroids larger than 1km, and there are numerous methods by which we could deflect one if detected. Moreover, even if there were a major asteroid collision, it doesn't seem very likely that it would cause the extinction of the

---

twice as many lives ahead of her as the median person, who, on the scenarios we are considering, had many trillions of people before her. So taking this consideration into account would not make a significant difference to our assessment of HH.

human race. Many mammal species survived the Chicxulub impactor (which caused the extinction of the dinosaurs), as did many reptiles and fish, and humans have an enormous population, with one hundred times the biomass of any large wild animal that's walked the Earth,[42] spread out across a wide diversity of environments, with the technological and scientific capability to weather a long period of global cooling following an asteroid impact.[43]

Instead, those who work on existential risk tend to believe that the most likely risks come from *omnicidal agents*, in particular from omnicidal superintelligence. In *The Precipice*, for example, Toby Ord gives an estimate of total existential risk this century as being at about one in six, with almost two-thirds of that coming from risks from misaligned superintelligence.[44] For this risk, there is not much additional benefit from being an interplanetary civilization: though it would be harder for a misaligned superintelligence to eliminate all human life across two planetary systems than one, it would not be much harder. Similar considerations would hold for other existential risks, such as those from perennial totalitarianism, convergence on the wrong moral view, and from sufficiently powerful doomsday cults.[45]

Second, the period where civilization is close together enough that it is easy for one individual or group to influence the whole rest of civilization may be quite prolonged. We do not know how hard it will be to become a truly interstellar civilization. But when we think about future progress we should bear in mind that the last 250 years of rapid technological and economic progress is a historical anomaly, which could well slow into the future. Indeed, we have already some data that frontier growth is slowing,[46] and demographic changes predict a slowing or even negative growth rate by the end of the coming century.[47] We may well therefore be primarily Earthbound for many thousands or tens of thousands of years to come.

---

[42] Wilson (2002, p. 29).

[43] Might it be the case that the *existential* risk from asteroid collision is much higher than the extinction risk from asteroid collision, because of the possibility that an asteroid impact destroys advanced civilization, and we never recover? I do think that the probability of unrecovered civilizational collapse from an asteroid impact is higher than the probability of extinction. But I think that, even if advanced civilization were destroyed, it is very likely that we would recover. Agriculture was developed independently in several different locations within a short time period, suggesting that it was not a bottleneck; and it took merely thousands of years (which is a short period of time compared to the typical mammalian species lifespan of around half a million years) for us to move from agricultural to industrial civilization. Over the course of the agricultural era we also saw sustained (though slow) economic growth and technological development, the rate which seemed to be continually accelerating: for more discussion, see Roodman (2020). One might worry that we have used up so many fossil fuels that we could not rely on them to re-industrialize, but this is not true. For example, the 1.2 billion tons of recoverable coal in the US's North Antelope Rochelle mine alone is more than total global coal use between 1770 and 1830. This issue is explored in much more depth by Rodriguez (ms).

[44] Ord (2020). [45] Toby Ord discusses this more in *The Precipice*, chapter 7.

[46] See, for example, Gordon (2017) and Vollrath (2020). [47] Jones (2020).

What's more, even when we start settling areas outside of Earth, we may well be primarily confined to the solar system for considerably longer again. And while we are still primarily limited to our solar system, it is still comparatively easy for one individual or group to communicate with and influence the rest of civilization: for example, it takes only one hour for light to traverse even the full diameter of the asteroid belt.[48]

12.6.2 Unusually Fast Economic and Technological Progress

The world growth rate is around 3.5% per year.[49,50] It is not plausible that we can sustain such a high growth rate indefinitely into the future. To see this, suppose that in the future the world economy will grow by (merely) 2% per year indefinitely. If so, then after 10,000 years there would be 10^19 times present-day GDP for every atom in the galaxy. This is not a plausible outcome.

I believe that this appeal to rapid economic and technological progress is the strongest argument in favour of thinking that we live at an unusually influential time. The present time is certainly highly *distinctive* in terms of its growth rate. And even if you only think it 10% likely that the most influential time is at a period of unusually high economic growth, then you should give at least a 10% credence to the idea that we are among the most influential 10,000 years. And there are positive arguments for thinking that we should expect the most influential times to be those of unusually fast technological progress: in particular, if the fate of the future is determined by how we manage the invention and deployment of particular technologies (such as artificial intelligence or particularly dangerous weapons), then at periods of unusually fast technological progress, we are moving faster through the space of all technological inventions, and are therefore more likely to discover one of the critical technologies.

However, there are still caveats that need to be made. First, crucially, though this argument indicates a way in which the present time is very unusual, and therefore potentially very unusually important, it doesn't give us grounds for thinking that the present time is the very most important time, rather than some future century over the coming few millennia. And that is the action-relevant question.

Second, there's an argument for expecting longtermist altruists to be *less* influential during periods of fast economic growth. In a very stable environment, it is easier to make and fund very long-term projects. And, in a world where most people only care about the short term (especially the period when they live), we

---

[48] Where the asteroid belt is around 3 Astronomical Units from the sun, with one AU being 8 light-minutes.
[49] This argument originally comes from Hanson (2009).   [50] See, for example, Roser (2020).

should expect that projects that only have long-term payoffs will be the most neglected, and there would be low hanging fruit for longtermists to pick in this area. But if we live at a period of rapid change, that advantage that longtermists have is lost: it's much harder, or impossible, to have reliable long-term plans, because doing so would involve being able to predict inherently unpredictable changes in the technological landscape.[51]

12.6.3 Summing Up

We have seen that there are some compelling arguments for thinking that the present time is unusually influential. In particular, we are growing very rapidly, and civilization today is still small compared to its potential future size, so any given unit of resources is a comparatively large fraction of the whole. I believe these arguments give us reason to think that the most influential people may well live within the next few thousand years. But these arguments are far from watertight, and they do not give us very strong reasons for thinking that we, now, are among the most influential people ever, rather than people in the centuries or millennia to come. But we do have positive reasons—namely, our predictably increasing knowledge and opportunities, as canvassed in my inductive argument—for thinking that the most influential people are yet to be born.

12.7 Conclusion

Because civilization has such a long future ahead of it, and because resources grow over time (both in absolute terms and as a fraction of the world economy), there is a strong *prima facie* case for impartial altruists to invest their resources, passing them on to future people to use philanthropically. However, if we thought that the present time was exceptionally influential—or even the most influential time—this would be a strong counterargument. Parfit seemed to believe this, as he indicated in his comments in *Reasons and Persons*, *On What Matters*: Volume 2, and in a talk for Giving What We Can. Assessing whether this is true is crucially important, deserving of far more attention than I have been able to give it in this chapter. There are some good arguments for thinking that our time is very unusual, if we

---

[51] More fundamentally, there are also serious questions about how to make quantitative comparisons of economic power over such long timescales. There are very many things that the rich can buy today that people in the past could not, but there are also some things that people in the past could buy that those in the present could not. (Someone with an overwhelmingly strong preference for dodo meat would regard some people in the past as far richer than we are today.) So we could try to instead pick some objective indicator of economic growth, such as energy capture. But any such indicator seems to have problems. For example, over the last twenty years the US economy has grown by about 50%, but it has not increased its energy consumption, because it has become more energy efficient over time.

are at the start of a very long-lived civilization: the fact that we are so early on, that we live on a single planet, and that we are at a period of rapid economic and technological progress, are all ways in which the current time is very distinctive, and therefore are reasons why we may be highly influential too. But the claim that we are among the *most* influential people is considerably stronger again, and does not seem warranted. I have given two arguments for scepticism about this stronger claim: first, that our prior on this claim should be very low, and that the evidence we have from moving away from this prior is not sufficiently strong; second, that if we look at how influentialness has been changing over time, we should expect it to continue into the future as our knowledge and understanding improves over time.

In *On What Matters*: Volume 2, Parfit comments that:

> Life can be wonderful as well as terrible, and we shall increasingly have the power to make life good. Since human history may be only just beginning, we can expect that future humans, or supra-humans, may achieve some great goods that we cannot now even imagine. In Nietzsche's words, there has never been such a new dawn and clear horizon, and such an open sea.

In Parfit's discussion, 'open sea' refers to the space of possible goods that future humans or supra-humans could enjoy. And, though it is undoubtedly true that life to date has sampled from only a tiny corner of the menu of possible experiences, the even more important 'open sea' that Nietzsche himself referred to[52] is the newfound potential for knowledge given our liberation from a theocentric worldview.

We are only just starting out on this intellectual voyage. There is still far more to learn and understand. Over time we should expect to radically change our understanding of the good, and of how to promote it. Just as our powers to grow crops, to transmit information, to discover the laws of nature, and to explore the cosmos have all increased over time, so will our power to make the world better— our influentialness. And given how much there is still to understand, we should believe, and hope, that our descendents look back at us as we look back at those in the medieval era, marvelling at how we could have got it all so wrong.

References

Dario Amodei et al. Concrete Problems in AI Safety. arXiv preprint arXiv:1606.06565 (2016).

Daniel J. Benjamin et al. (2018). Redefine Statistical Significance. *Nature Human Behaviour*. 2(1): 6–10.

---

[52] Nietzsche (2001, p. 199, aphorism 343).

Nick Bostrom (2002). *Anthropic Bias: Observation Selection Effects in Science and Philosophy.* New York: Routledge.

Nick Bostrom (2003). Astronomical Waste: The Opportunity Cost of Delayed Technological Development. *Utilitas* 15(3):308–14.

Nick Bostrom (2014). *Superintelligence: Path, Dangers, Strategies.* Oxford: Oxford University Press.

W.M. Theodore de Bary and Irene Bloom (1999). *Sources of Chinese Tradition*, Volume 1. *From Earliest Times to 1600.* New York: Columbia University Press.

Robert J. Gordon (2017). *The Rise and Fall of American Growth: The US Standard of Living since the Civil War.* Princeton, NJ: Princeton University Press.

Hilary Greaves and William MacAskill (ms), The Case for Strong Longtermism.

Hilary Greaves, William MacAskill, Rossa O'Keeffe-O'Donovan and Philip Trammell (2019). A Research Agenda for the Global Priorities Institute. Available at https://globalprioritiesinstitute.org/wp-content/uploads/gpi-research-agenda.pdf.

Robin Hanson (2009). Limits to Growth. *Overcoming Bias.* Available at http://www.overcomingbias.com/2009/09/limits-to-growth.html

Paul Horwich (1982). *Probability and Evidence.* Cambridge: Cambridge University Press.

Harold Jeffreys (1961). *The Theory of Probability.* Oxford: Oxford University Press.

Charles I. Jones (2016). Life and Growth. *Journal of Political Economy* 124(2):539–78.

Charles I. Jones (2020). The End of Economic Growth? Unintended Consequences of a Declining Population. Available at https://web.stanford.edu/~chadj/emptyplanet.pdf.

William MacAskill (2019). 'Longtermism'. *Effective Altruism Forum.* Available at https://forum.effectivealtruism.org/posts/qZyshHCNkjs3TvSem/longtermism.

William MacAskill (ms). Moral Option Value.

Andreas Mogensen (2019). Doomsday Rings Twice. Available at https://globalprioritiesinstitute.org/wp-content/uploads/2019/Mogensen_doomsday_rings_twice.pdf.

Ian Morris (2015). *Foragers, Farmers, and Fossil Fuels: How Human Values Evolve.* Princeton, NJ: Princeton University Press.

Friedrich Nietzsche (2001). *The Gay Science.* Edited by Bernard Williams. Cambridge: Cambridge University Press.

Toby Ord (ms). The Edges of our Universe.

Toby Ord (2020). *The Precipice: Existential Risk and the Future of Humanity.* London: Bloomsbury.

Derek Parfit (1984). *Reasons and Persons.* Oxford: Clarendon Press.

Derek Parfit (2011). *On What Matters*, Volume 2. Oxford: Oxford University Press.

Thomas Piketty (2013). *Capital in the Twenty-First Century.* Cambridge, MA: Harvard University Press.

Steven Pinker (2011). *The Better Angels of Our Nature*. London: Penguin.

Luisa Rodriguez (ms). On Civilisational Collapse and Recovery.

David Roodman (2020). Modeling the Human Trajectory. OpenPhilanthropy.org. Available at https://www.openphilanthropy.org/blog/modeling-human-trajectory

Max Roser (2020). Economic Growth. OurWorldInData.org. Available at https://ourworldindata.org/economic-growth.

Carl Sagan (1994). *Pale Blue Dot: A Vision of the Human Future in Space*. New York: Random House.

Christian J. Tarsney (2019). The Epistemic Challenge to Longtermism. Available at https://globalprioritiesinstitute.org/wp-content/uploads/2019/Tarsney_Epistemic_Challenge_to_Longtermism.pdf.

Teru Thomas (ms). Self-Location and Objective Chance.

Philip Trammell (ms). Discounting for Patient Philanthropists. Available at https://philiptrammell.com/static/discounting_for_patient_philanthropists.pdf.Dietrich Vollrath (2020). *Fully Grown: Why a Stagnant Economy Is a Sign of Success*. Chicago: University of Chicago Press.

Edward O. Wilson (2002). *The Social Conquest of Earth*. New York: Liveright.

David Wootton (2015). *The Invention of Science: A New History of the Scientific Revolution*. Harmondsworth: Penguin UK.

13
On Theory X and What Matters Most

S. J. Beard and Patrick Kaczmarek

> I regret that, in a book called *On What Matters*, I have said so little about what matters. I have been trying to defend the belief that some things really do matter. I hope to say more about what matters in what would be my Volume Four.
>
> (Derek Parfit, *On What Matters*, Volume 3)

At the time of his death in 2017 it is clear that Derek Parfit was still working on the problems of population ethics that had concerned him for over forty years. He described the book mentioned in the above quote (in a book that would come out three weeks after he died) as a rewrite of Part 4 of his groundbreaking 1984 book *Reasons and Persons*, and he also indicated that it would contain a "longer and revised version" of a talk he gave in Stockholm in 2014. It is possible that this would have fulfilled his plan, described in a letter to his sister Theadora Ooms in 1996 and read at his memorial symposium, to write a book "if I survive... that will address truth, evil, time, and the sublime". Sadly, we will never get to see this book, and as far as the authors have been able to determine, no version of it survives in his lengthy correspondence and drafts, which are currently in the possession of Larry Temkin and Jeff McMahan. However, we believe that by reading across the breadth of Parfit's work, both published and unpublished, it is possible to determine a trajectory for some of his ideas that we can use to glean what this book might have defended. In order to stimulate further discussion and scholarly attention to the late work and manuscripts of Parfit, and to help those who are less interested in such minutia to actually understand and apply the theories contained in it, we here offer a summary of our conclusions about this trajectory and its likely destination.

The portion of Parfit's work that we will focus on deals with the field of population axiology, which concerns the evaluation of outcomes that differ in terms of the size or composition of populations. According to Parfit, a satisfactory theory of population, which he labelled 'Theory X', "must solve the Non-Identity Problem, avoid the Repugnant and Absurd Conclusions, and solve the Mere

Addition Paradox".[1] Since he first suggested these criteria, many philosophers have attempted to prove the impossibility of meeting these requirements, and thus the non-existence of Theory X. Notable amongst these have been Gustaf Arrhenius, Stewart Rachels, and Tyler Cowen.[2] Others have argued that one or more of these criteria should not be regarded as so inviolable as Parfit suggests, so that theories that fail to meet all of them might still be satisfactory. Notable amongst these have been John Broome, Torbjörn Tännsjö, and Michael Huemer regarding the Repugnant Conclusion, Larry Temkin regarding the Mere Addition Paradox, and David Boonin regarding the Non-Identity Problem.[3,4]

Despite this, Parfit continued searching for Theory X and devoted much time in his final years to writing a lengthy paper, "Towards Theory X" (Parts 1 and 2), in which he developed many new lines of argument concerning it. While this remains unpublished, Parfit did publish two shorter works that explicitly considered how to satisfy the conditions for Theory X.[5] In doing so he sketched three principles: the Wide Dual Person-Affecting Principle, the Simple View, and the Imprecise Lexical View. These combine a unique approach to evaluating the wellbeing of variable populations with a broader axiological pluralism that is also concerned about people's Quality of Life.[6]

In this chapter, we consider these principles in light of the whole range of Parfit's writings and argue that they can, collectively, satisfy all the criteria that Parfit set himself, so that, although he never lived to say so, his search for Theory X may have been nearing an end. We also begin the next important step of developing this theory by applying these principles to the global challenges that Parfit maintained "mattered most".[7]

13.1 Background

13.1.1 The Absurd Conclusion

Let us begin with the criteria for Theory X that has received the least attention, and which he was able to satisfy first, and most directly. The Absurd Conclusion is implied by the view that the number of people who exist at any time is less important than the length of time over which people continue to exist because the value of adding extra people diminishes as instantaneous population size

---

[1] (Parfit 1984, 443).   [2] (Cowen 1996; Arrhenius 2000, 2003, 2011; Rachels 2004).
[3] (Temkin 1987; Tännsjö 2002; Broome 2004; Boonin 2014).
[4] The Absurd Conclusion has received comparatively little discussion in the literature.
[5] See (Parfit 2016 and 2017b).
[6] Although Parfit himself did not capitalize the phrase 'Quality of Life', throughout this chapter we do so (except when quoting or paraphrasing Parfit) because, we believe, it helps highlight that we are using this phrase in a very specific way.
[7] (Parfit 2017a, 436–7).

increases, but the value of adding future generations does not.[8] At one point Parfit appears to have found this view attractive. However, he ultimately rejected it. He argued that it would be wrong for us to believe that the value of adding a person with a bad life, such as one plagued by unbearable suffering and containing little or no good things, should ever be diminished. However, if the value of adding people with good lives at one point in time diminished, while the value of adding people with bad lives did not, then this would imply the following:

> *Absurd Conclusion.* In one possible outcome, the future would consist of a single century with an enormous number of people, "[n]early all of [whom] would have a quality of life far above that enjoyed by most of the Earth's actual population" while one in ten billion would "have a life that was not worth living". In a second possible outcome "there would be the same enormous number of extra future people, with the same high quality of life for all except the unfortunate one in each ten billion" but these would exist across ten billion future centuries, rather than occupying only one. "[T]he first outcome would be very bad [and] the second very good even though, in both outcomes, there would be the very same number of extra future people, with the very same high quality of life for all except the unfortunate one in each ten billion."[9]

There is certainly something absurd about this conclusion, especially if one reflects on the fact that space and time, while being experienced in distinctively different ways by human beings, are very similar according to the current best laws of Physics. However, Parfit never explicitly defines the nature of this absurdity.

One possibility, which Parfit does not explore, is that this conclusion is absurd because the implied asymmetry between space and time is absurd. If this were so, then we could avoid it simply by accepting the principle that the value of good, but not bad, lives diminishes as population size increases, regardless of how this population is distributed across space or time. This is not a position that Parfit himself adopts, and it seems to us that this is likely because this move would have other implications that are hardly less absurd than that specifically mentioned by Parfit. Consider:

> *Another Absurd Conclusion.* For a population with a certain number and distribution of lives that is very good, the mere addition of groups with the same number and distribution of lives can make it worse, and could eventually make it very bad.

---

[8] Parfit attributes this view primarily to Peter Singer. See (Parfit 1976).   [9] (Parfit 1984, 410–1).

For instance, a population in which almost everybody enjoys a very high quality of life and only a tiny minority of people live bad lives might be very good when the size of the population was relatively small but could become very bad as it grew, even where the proportion of good and bad lives remain unchanged, if the value of these good lives diminished with population size while that of the bad lives did not. This conclusion would strike us as being equally as absurd as that described by Parfit in his *Reasons and Persons*, even though it relies on no asymmetry between space and time.

To put this another way, if we simply try to avoid the Absurd Conclusion by prohibiting different aggregation methods for the value of lives based on their location in space and time, we might still be left with theories that would imply that it may be good that there was life on Earth, even though there is also some suffering on Earth, but that it would be bad if there were also life on many other planets, even if none of these planets, though also containing some suffering, had a population with lives that were any worse than those on Earth.

However, Parfit's response to the Absurd Conclusion is equally able to handle both these sorts of absurdity. He sought to avoid the Absurd Conclusion by rejecting the view that "while there is no limit, in any period, to the disvalue of quantity, there is a limit to its value".[10] He would later formalize his position as:

The Simple View. Anyone's existence is in itself good if this person's life is worth living. Such goodness has non-diminishing value, so if there were more such people, the combined goodness of their existence would have no upper limit.[11]

13.1.2 The Repugnant Conclusion

While avoiding the Absurd Conclusion, the Simple View makes it harder to avoid another problem; namely, the:

Repugnant Conclusion. Compared with the existence of many people who would all have some very high quality of life, there is some much larger number of people whose existence would be better, even though these people would all have lives that were barely worth living.[12]

Indeed, Parfit noted that if one accepts the Simple View, then the only way to avoid this conclusion is to deny the principle that "a sufficiently large number of lives that all made the world better must, together, contribute more to the value of an outcome than a set number of other lives even if these were all, individually,

[10] (Parfit 1984, 411–12).   [11] (Parfit 2016, 112).   [12] (Parfit 2016, 110).

much better".[13] Parfit was not the first to observe this conclusion;[14] however, he was the first to name it, draw attention to it, and to explore its numerous ramifications.[15]

It is important to note that Parfit's description of the Repugnant Conclusion differed in some important ways from other philosophers who shared his concerns, both before and since.[16] The most notable of these is that, for Parfit, the Repugnant Conclusion was specifically, and always, a conclusion about people's Quality of Life, or the extent to which someone's life is *worth living*. 'Quality of Life' is a term that Parfit coined to describe the broadest possible conception of the value of a life, and one he intended to be broader than traditional conceptions of a person's welfare, wellbeing, or utility and to capture more than simply that person's self-interest or what made their life go best.[17]

This leads to, and helps explain, another difference between Parfit's Repugnant Conclusion and that of many other philosophers. For Parfit:

> When we are most concerned about [the Repugnant Conclusion], our concern is only partly about the value that each life will have for the person whose life it is. We are also concerned about the disappearance from the world of the kinds of experience and activity which do most to make life worth living.[18]

Parfit, therefore, did not merely seek to incorporate one of the numerous, brilliant axiologies that have sought alternative means of aggregating value across lives,[19] but rather saw the Repugnant Conclusion as demanding a substantial account of what he called the 'qualitative differences' in the value of different lives. If it is to avoid the Repugnant Conclusion, therefore, Theory X must describe a broader axiological pluralism, evaluating outcomes according to both the wellbeing they contain and other facts that contribute to people's Quality of Life, and not simply propose an alternative method of aggregating value.[20]

Parfit's initial efforts to produce such a theory focused on a concern for the value of the *Best Things in Life*.[21] According to this view, which he labelled 'Perfectionism', "even if some change brings a great net benefit to those who are affected, it is a change for the worse if it involves the loss of one of the Best Things

---

[13] (Parfit 2016, 112).

[14] Perhaps the closest antecedent can be found in (McTaggart and McTaggart 1927). Similar observations can be found in (Sidgwick 1907), who notably did not find this conclusion implausible.

[15] (Parfit 1982, 142). [16] Cf. (Masny 2019). [17] See (Parfit 1982, 117–18; 2016, 117).

[18] (Parfit 1986, 161).

[19] These are too numerous to mention. However, some notable examples include (Hurka 1983; Blackorby et al. 2005; Thomas 2017).

[20] We do not mean to imply that Parfit was the only person who shared this view, although he seems to have been in the minority. For other sources, see (Crisp 1992; Cowen 1996).

[21] The Best Things in Life "are the best kinds of creative activity and aesthetic experience, the best relationships between different people, and the other things which do most to make life worth living" (Parfit 2016, 161).

in Life".²²,²³ The correct way to evaluate these goods, according to Perfectionism, is to view them pluralistically, considering both how they contribute to people's welfare as well as what Parfit sometimes referred to as their 'perfectionist value'. Thus, whether lives contain both kinds of value or whether they are valuable only because of the welfare they contain is more than a quantitative difference, it is a difference in quality. The potential loss of perfectionist value that only these Best Things in Life can bring justifies our belief that enough high-quality lives might be more valuable than any number of other lower-quality lives, allowing us to avoid the Repugnant Conclusion.

Yet, Parfit believed that Perfectionism in this form faced many objections and even called it "crazy".²⁴ Two of these objections are that it had elitist implications because it gave insufficient consideration to eliminating suffering (a point we will return to in section 13.3) and that it could not clearly differentiate between the different kinds of good, or between their values.²⁵ Thus, while his earlier writings provide us with some of the ingredients necessary for his Theory X, these still require substantial elaboration.

13.2 Parfit's Final Papers

13.2.1 The Non-Identity Problem

A commonly held intuition is that one of two outcomes cannot be worse if this outcome would be worse for no one.²⁶ However, Parfit famously demonstrated that this leads to a head-on collision with another well-worn intuition in variable population cases.

> *Non-Identity Problem.* That where different people existed in different outcomes, one of these outcomes could be clearly worse, for instance because the people in that outcome lived worse lives, even though it was worse for nobody, because these people did not exist in the other outcome.²⁷

For much of his life, Parfit thought that the only way to avoid this problem was to endorse the impersonal view that it should make *no difference* whether an outcome was better or worse for any particular people.²⁸

---

[22] (Parfit 2016, 163).
[23] Parfit may have held a similar view about rationality, arguing that a creator's desire for "his creation to be as good as possible" or a scientist's desire "to make some fundamental discovery" would be rational "even if this person knows that his act is against his own self-interest" (Parfit 1984, 192).
[24] (Parfit 1986, 164). [25] (Parfit 2016, 163–4).
[26] Parfit dubbed this the 'Narrow Telic Principle' (Parfit 2017b, 118).   [27] (Parfit 1984, 359).
[28] (Parfit 1984, 363–80).

However, in a paper published posthumously, Parfit suggested that he considered this conclusion to have been mistaken. He maintained that, while the Non-Identity Problem constitutes a strong objection to narrow person-affecting views, which appeal to comparative harms or benefits, there were other *wide* person-affecting views that could avoid this difficulty by appealing to whether an outcome was merely good, or bad, for people instead. According to these principles, I am benefited if you do what is good for me, even if I do not 'fare better' relative to some other outcome, where the degree to which an outcome is good for me depends only on how well I fare in that outcome. Choosing an outcome in which somebody does not exist can therefore be seen as denying that person a benefit that was ours to provide. Even if we can't quite describe this as a harm, because such an outcome is in no way bad for this person, the total lack of value for them is still an evaluative feature of this outcome, indicating that choosing it, rather than an outcome in which they exist with a good life, means choosing not to do what would have been good for this person.

In this way, we can avoid the Non-Identity Problem while still accepting principles like the:

Wide Principle. One of two outcomes would be in one way worse if this outcome would be less good for people, by benefiting people less than the other outcome would have benefited people.[29]

Such principles permit more sophisticated approaches to evaluating the lives of future people, which can avoid the worst excesses both of impersonal views (e.g., that we must give these people equal weight in our moral consideration) and of other person-affecting views (e.g., that, in non-identity cases, these people's well-being may not matter at all). This is because they do not necessarily imply that *existential benefits*, benefits of coming into existence with a life that is good for one, are always of equal worth to *comparative benefits*, benefits of being better off given that one already exists.[30]

One difference between existential benefits and comparative benefits is that, other things being equal, existential benefits change the number of persons who exist. Parfit saw this as an important difference, and argued that we should accept wide person-affecting principles that account for it. In particular, we ought to accept the:

---

[29] (Parfit 2017b, 129).

[30] Parfit credits Jeff McMahan with these terms. In earlier work, he referred to these two kinds of benefits as 'comparative' and 'non-comparative' and argued that acknowledging the existence of non-comparative benefits helps to bridge the gap between consequentialist and contractualist accounts of why we should care about future generations (Parfit 2011b). See also (Beard and Kaczmarek 2020).

Wide Dual Person-Affecting Principle. One of two outcomes would be in one way better if this outcome would together benefit people more, and in another way better if this outcome would benefit each person more.[31]

According to this dual principle, the addition of lives that are worth living would always be in one way good, and this value is non-diminishing as the Simple View implies. However, the value of adding lives is different to that of providing comparative benefits in that it might increase the total sum of benefits without benefiting any person more. Thus, for any fixed quantity of benefits, this principle prefers an outcome where this is concentrated in fewer people to one where it is shared between more people; the benefits to each person being greater in the first outcome while the benefits to all would be the same. As Parfit put it "though existential benefits are just as good for the people who receive them as similar comparative benefits, these benefits do less to make outcomes better when and because more people exist, since there would then be fewer benefits per person".[32]

However, it is less clear what this principle should say about two outcomes that involve a tradeoff between the quantity of wellbeing and the number of people. For instance, suppose we must choose between:

A = n people at level 100; and
B = 2n people at level 75

In this case, choosing A would still benefit each person more, because all the people in A are better off than they would be in B, but choosing B can be said to 'together benefit people more' because it involves a larger quantity of benefits. Parfit offers no arguments for how this tradeoff should be made, and indeed in his draft paper, "Towards Theory X: Part Two", he provides some lines of argument suggesting that no precise tradeoff between these two ways in which outcomes could be better may be possible due to 'different-number-based imprecision'.[33]

---

[31] (Parfit 2017b, 154).   [32] (Parfit ms3, 20).
[33] These arguments can be found in (Parfit ms2, 8–14). Different-number-based imprecision involves the claim that "[when] two possible worlds would contain different numbers of people, this fact makes these worlds less precisely comparable". He develops arguments for the view based on two sets of competing principles. Firstly, the 'Total-and-Average View', that:

> It would always be in one way better if (1) the people who exist would together have a greater total sum of well-being, and in another way better if (2) because this total sum of well-being would come to fewer people, there would be a greater average sum of well-being per person.

And, secondly, the 'Total View' and the 'Part-Whole Principle', that:

> If world T would contain more people than World S, and it is true both that everyone who would exist in S would either also exist in T and be better off, or would have some counterpart in T who would be better off, and that everyone else who would exist in T would have a life that is clearly worth living, these facts strongly support the view that T would be better than S.

On the other hand, Parfit was also keen to stress that there are some cases in which such tradeoffs between the value of these two kinds of benefit should be made. For instance, if the difference between the wellbeing levels of people across two outcomes were very great, the existence of many more people at the lower level would be worse than the existence of fewer people at the higher level even if it meant more wellbeing, and hence a greater collective benefit.[34]

Parfit argued that his Wide Dual Person-Affecting Principle would agree since it "would often imply that one of two outcomes would be better though the people who exist would have a much smaller total sum of benefits".[35] However, he conceded that the principle might still form part of a view that implied the Repugnant Conclusion. Yet, he did not believe that this would be the case for his Theory X because: "We might also justifiably believe that great losses in the quality of people's lives could not be outweighed by any increase in the sum of benefits, if these benefits came in the lives of people whose quality of life would be much lower."[36]

This brings us to the final component of Theory X.[37]

13.2.2 The Mere Addition Paradox

In the above quote, Parfit was almost certainly alluding to his 2016 paper "Can We Avoid the Repugnant Conclusion?", in which he sets out to defend the Simple View with the following:

> *Imprecise Lexical View.* If many people exist who all have some high quality of life, that would be better than if there existed any number of people whose lives, though worth living, would be, in certain ways, much less good.[38]

However, it's not clear that Parfit actually believed any of these principles and views. Both the lines of argument he developed and the implication of different-number-based imprecision, came in for significant criticism; see e.g., (Arrhenius 2016). Parfit acknowledged that his claims "are hard to prove, since it makes sense to claim that all such truths are precise" and these lines of argument were dropped from later work, such as (Parfit 2016). However, there is at least anecdotal evidence that he continued believing in different-number-based imprecision and hoped to revise his arguments and respond to his critics in later work.

[34] (Parfit 2017b, 155-6). [35] (Parfit 2017b, 157). [36] (Parfit 2017b, 157).

[37] We have focused on only one kind of difference between the value of existential and comparative benefits that Parfit's Wide Principle might allow. Yet, he acknowledged that there may be others. In particular, this principle might allow us to say that we have strongest reason to provide a comparative benefit though providing an existential benefit would produce a better outcome. For instance, he writes that it is both plausible and defensible to believe that "we ought to give some benefits to presently existing people rather than giving some greater benefits to future people" (Parfit 2017b, 148-9). This difference is also discussed at greater length in (Parfit ms3, 18-19). However, note that despite these differences between the moral significance of existential and comparative benefits, Parfit continued to defend a version of his 'No Difference' view, that: when our choice and acts would greatly lower the quality of life of future people "[t]hese choices and acts would make things go much worse, and would be wrong. It would make no moral difference... that these choices and acts would be worse for no one" (paraphrased from Parfit 2017a, 122-3).

[38] (Parfit 2016, 115).

The proposed view contains two related principles, only one of which is explicitly stated here. The first of these, which is left implicit in the above statement, is the principle that many evaluative judgements cannot be made precisely, even if one is aware of all the underlying facts. Parfit's acceptance of this principle appears closely related to his value pluralism since one of the key sources he gives for this normative imprecision is that outcomes can differ in terms of the many features that determine people's Quality of Life. As previously alluded to, Parfit saw these features as being distinct from, and broader than, those that determined people's wellbeing. Because of this distinctiveness, we cannot evaluate all these features on a common scale; this leads to the conclusion that we may not be able to produce a precise ordering of outcomes that contain these lives. As Parfit puts it:

> There can be fairly precise truths about the relative value of some things. One of two painful ordeals, for example, might be twice as bad as the other, by involving pain of the same intensity for twice as long. However, in most important cases relative value does not depend only on any such single, measurable property. When two painful ordeals differ greatly in both their length and their intensity, there are no precise truths about whether, and by how much, one of these pains would be worse. There is no scale on which we could weigh the relative importance of intensity and length. Nor could five minutes of ecstasy be precisely 7.6 times better than ten hours of amusement.[39]

In many cases, such as these, "when two things are qualitatively very different", outcomes containing them may be *roughly comparable*; meaning that it is "impossible either that one of these things is better than the other by some precise amount, or that both things are precisely equally good".[40] However, sometimes the qualitative differences between two outcomes, or the lives they contain, make them *utterly incommensurable* because there is simply no way in which the value of these outcomes can be compared on a single common scale, even roughly.

This, we contend, is where the second explicit feature of Parfit's view comes in, which is the analogue of his earlier Perfectionism. Where the qualitative difference between two goods, P and Q, reaches a point where their values are incommensurable, and yet P is still better than Q, the evaluative relation of lexical superiority and inferiority.[41] As Parfit defines this, "though the existence of more Qs would always be non-diminishingly better, the existence of some sufficient number of Ps

---

[39] (Parfit 2016, 113). [40] (Parfit 2016, 113).
[41] Parfit says little about his conception of lexicality. His fullest account appears to be the following passage from "Towards Theory X: Part One":

> The most important sense of 'good' and 'bad' are, I believe, reason-implying. One of two things is relevantly better if this thing has features that does or might give us stronger reasons to choose this thing, or to respond to this thing in other positive ways. If some things are lexically better than others in this reason implying sense, the strength of these

would be better than the existence of any number of Qs".[42] In the case of wellbeing and the Best Things in Life, this means that:

> [If in one world] there would be no art, or science, no deep loves or friendships, no other achievements, such as that of bringing up our children well, and no morally good people [, that world] would be much worse than [some other worlds] in what we can call qualitative or perfectionist terms... This great qualitative loss would, I believe, make [this world] in itself a worse world, even [if it] would give, to the same number of people, a greater and more equally distributed sum of well-being.[43]

As we saw in section 13.1.2, the Imprecise Lexical View does not require both imprecision and lexicality simply to avoid the Repugnant Conclusion, perfectionist lexicality alone would suffice. However, the combination of both these features can overcome at least one of the objections Parfit raised against this earlier Perfectionism, that the difference between the Best Things in Life and other goods could not be precisely defined. This second view also performed better than his earlier Perfectionism in relation to certain versions of the Mere Addition Paradox.

One of these versions of the Mere Addition Paradox, which both appeared especially troubling to Parfit and was the last version he considered, concerns the following case:

World A = N people at level 100;
World Raised A Plus = N people at level 101 and a million times as many other people at level 95;
World B = the same number of people as in Raised A Plus but all at level 99.

These worlds, together with the Z population from the Repugnant Conclusion, are illustrated in Figure 13.1.

> reasons could not be represented by using either a scale or numbers. Though there would be no limit to the combined strength of our possible reasons to choose certain things, we would have stronger reason to choose certain other things.
>
> Such claims may seem to make no sense. If there is no limit to the combined strength of certain reasons, it may seem impossible that certain other reasons could be stronger. But this objection assumes that the strength of all our reasons must correspond to different positions on some scale, or be able to represented by numbers. As before, that is not so. It may help to mention here what Raz calls exclusionary reasons. These are reasons to ignore, or give no weight to, certain other reasons. Suppose, for example, that I am judging who deserves to win some prize, and one of the contestants is my best friend. Though I have a reason to want my best friend to win, my role as a judge gives me an exclusionary reason to ignore this friendship-based reason. This exclusionary reason doesn't defeat my friendship-based reason merely by being stronger. Excluding is not the same thing as outweighing. Even if we doubt the claim that there are such exclusionary reasons, we should admit that this claim makes sense. (Parfit ms1, 15–16)

[42] (Parfit 2016, 112).   [43] (Parfit 2016, 123).

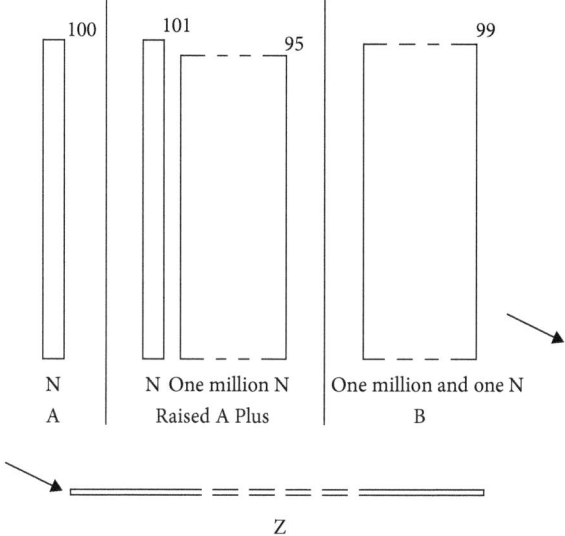

Figure 13.1 Mere Addition Paradox
Source: (Parfit 2016, 117).

Parfit claims that somebody might argue:

(H) Since N of the people in Raised A Plus would have a higher quality of life than all of the N people in A, and everyone else in Raised A Plus would have a quality of life that would not be much lower, Raised A Plus would be better than A.

(I) Since World B would contain as many people as Raised A Plus, and these people would together have, in B, a greater and more equally distributed sum of well-being, B would be better than Raised A Plus.

Therefore:

(J) B would be better than A. Compared with the existence of N people at level 100, it would be better if there existed instead a million times as many people all at level 99.[44]

However, if this was so, then it would seem that we could apply the same kind of argument to another three populations, taking B as our starting point and arguing that a Raised B Plus would be better than B and that C would also be better than Raised B Plus, and hence than A, despite everyone in C having a lower Quality of Life than those in B. Continuing down this chain of reasoning would produce the

---

[44] (Parfit 2016, 124).

inevitable conclusion that World Z is better than World A. This is paradoxical because it implies the Repugnant Conclusion.[45]

According to the perfectionist part of this view, we can reject the conclusion of this chain of reasoning because the transition from A to Z involves the loss of the Best Things in Life. Yet, on its own, this argument gives us no reason to refute any of the individual steps in this chain, and at each of these steps, the judgement that will inevitably lead to the Repugnant Conclusion seems more plausible than its alternative, making the denial of any of these steps appear crazy. However, Parfit's Imprecise Lexical View can counter this objection because it creates a new, more reasonable, way in which we can reject (I), namely we can claim that B and Raised A Plus are not precisely comparable. As Parfit puts it, "though World B would be better than Raised A Plus in utilitarian and egalitarian terms, B would be worse in qualitative terms, since the best things in people's lives would be worse in B".[46] This leads him to conclude that:

> (K) given the conflict between these values, Worlds B and Raised A Plus are only imprecisely comparable, and would be imprecisely equally good.

Parfit notes that, on its own, (K) may still appear less plausible than (I) as the qualitative difference between the people in Raised A Plus and B would be very slight. However, though B is in many ways better than Raised A Plus, there is at least this one way in which Raised A Plus is better, and since we cannot precisely weigh the relative strength of these different kinds of value, we should not accept (I), but can only say that B would be imprecisely equally good as Raised A Plus. Furthermore, Parfit claims, if we overlook the potential importance of this qualitative difference between Raised A Plus and B, by assuming that such a small difference must be trivial in comparison to the many ways in which B is better than A, then this will lead to the Repugnant Conclusion. As he puts it:

> (K) seems implausible because, in a change from Raised A Plus to B, there would be only a slight qualitative loss. The best lives would fall only from level 101 to 99. It may be hard to believe that this slight qualitative loss could make Raised A Plus not better than B, but only imprecisely equally good. But it would be much harder to believe that, compared with the existence of many people whose quality of life would be very high, it would be better if there existed instead some vast number of people whose lives were barely worth living. Since (K)'s way of rejecting premise (I) is less implausible than the Repugnant Conclusion, this argument fails. By appealing to this Imprecise Lexical View, we can justifiably reject this conclusion.[47]

---

[45] But see also (Temkin 1987). [46] (Parfit 2016, 126). [47] (Parfit 2016, 126–7).

This gives us reason to reject (I), and hence to avoid even this especially troubling version of the Mere Addition Paradox while still avoiding the Repugnant Conclusion.

Hence, we see how combining the Imprecise Lexical and Simple Views with the Wide Dual Person-Affecting Principle can produce a theory capable of meeting the four criteria for Theory X.

13.3 Applying Theory X

The previous sections outlined the basic principles of Theory X and how these met the theoretical conditions that Parfit wanted it to satisfy. In this section, we continue to explore this moral theory by applying it to the global challenges that Parfit argued mattered most.

13.3.1 Ensuring Humanity's Survival

Parfit addresses the question of 'what matters most?' in *Reasons and Persons*, *On What Matters*, Volume 1, and *On What Matters*, Volume 3. Here is what he says in *On What Matters*, Volume 3:

> What now matters most is how we respond to various risks to the survival of humanity. We are creating some of these risks, and we are discovering how we could respond to these and other risks. If we reduce these risks, and humanity survives the next few centuries, our descendants or successors could end these risks by spreading through this galaxy.[48]

This echoes a concern that goes back *Reasons and Persons*, and a thought experiment about the costs of nuclear war. He writes:

> I believe that if we destroy mankind, as we now can, this outcome will be much worse than most people think. Compare three outcomes:
>
> (1) Peace.
> (2) A nuclear war that kills 99% of the world's existing population.
> (3) A nuclear war that kills 100%.

---

[48] (Parfit 2017a, 436).

(2) would be worse than (1), and (3) would be worse than (2). Which is the greater of these two differences? Most people believe that the greater difference is between (1) and (2). I believe that the difference between (2) and (3) is very much greater... The Earth will remain habitable for at least another billion years. Civilization began only a few thousand years ago. If we do not destroy mankind, these few thousand years may be only a tiny fraction of the whole of civilized human history. The difference between (2) and (3) may thus be the difference between this tiny fraction and all the rest of this history.[49]

Theory X supports this conclusion. This is because, according to its principles, all potential future lives should be counted equally (the Simple View) and their wellbeing will contribute to the goodness of outcomes as much as our own, in one way at least (the Wide Dual Person-Affecting Principle).

However, as we have seen, these are not the only principles that Theory X contains and, while its other principles do not undermine this conclusion, they do imply that this is not the only feature of human extinction that would be bad. This is best illustrated by another thought experiment from the end of Part 4 of his *Reasons and Persons*, concerning another version of the Mere Addition Paradox. Parfit asks us to consider the following possible futures for our species:[50]

> When the A+-Future begins, everyone enjoys an extremely high quality of life. After a thousand years, the surface of the earth becomes inhospitable, lowering everyone's quality of life. After another thousand years, the surface of the earth becomes uninhabitable, thereby ending human history.
>
> In the A-Future, the first two thousand years go even better. Everyone has a quality of life that is higher than that of the best-off people in the A+-Future. Near the end of this period, scientists predict that the earth's surface will shortly become uninhabitable, so people decide to dig deep caves, enabling humanity to survive. However, while life in these caves is worth living, it is far less good than it had been on the Earth's surface. Throughout the years lived in the caves, people's quality of life is very low, and their lives are only barely worth living. Yet, since the A-Future would be in no way worse than the A+-Future, and in at least one way better, it seems that the A-Future would be better.
>
> In the B-Future, people in the first two thousand years have decided, at a slight cost to their quality of life, to prepare the caves by stocking them with long-lasting resources that provide a great increase in the quality of life of everyone who lives during the first two thousand years in these caves, before these

---

[49] (Parfit 1984, 453–4).   [50] Closely paraphrased from (Parfit 1984, 438ff).

resources are exhausted, and their lives become barely worth living. People's quality of life would be the same for the first four thousand years. Although those living in the first two thousand years, would have a slightly lower quality of life, they would lose very much less than would be gained by as many people in the next two thousand years. This would seem to be an even better outcome.

Similar remarks apply to the C-Future, in which people decide, at a slightly greater cost to themselves, to prepare the caves by stocking them with even longer lasting resources that provide a slightly lower benefit to the people who will live in these caves, but will last for an additional four thousand years before they become exhausted. The people in the first four thousand years would be slightly worse off in terms of their quality of life, but there would be a very much greater gain for the people in the next four thousand years. Hence, this outcome seems even better.

By the same reasoning, so would the D-Future, and the E-Future, and so on. Therefore, the best of all these possible histories would seem to be the Z-Future. In this future, the people living in the first two thousand years decide, at very great cost to themselves, to prepare the caves by stocking them with extremely long-lasting resources that might only provide a tiny benefit to those who would live in these caves, but which would not be exhausted for millions of years, providing by far the greatest total benefit overall. In this outcome, throughout the rest of human history, the quality of life would not be much above what it would have been in the caves in the A-Future, and everyone would have lives that are barely worth living. This is the Repugnant Conclusion.

These futures are illustrated in Figure 13.2.

As should be clear from the previous section, Theory X, because it contains the Imprecise Lexical View, would only be committed to the first step in this chain of reasoning, and would imply that even the transition from the A-Future to the B-Future would not be a precise change for the better but rather, at most, a change between two outcomes that are only roughly comparable. Though the B-Future would be better than the A-Future regarding its total sum of benefits, the B-Future would be worse in qualitative terms, given that people's Quality of Life would be lower in the B-Future than in the A-Future. Hence, the B-Future would be no better than the A-Future.

Thus, while Theory X gives us reason to seek to save humanity from extinction on the grounds of astronomical waste, it does not imply that we should place the maximization of future wellbeing ahead of all other concerns. For instance, if we find ourselves at the pinnacle of human history, facing a future in which things will only get worse (though they may never get bad), ensuring our species' future may not be worthwhile if it meant making certain sacrifices that

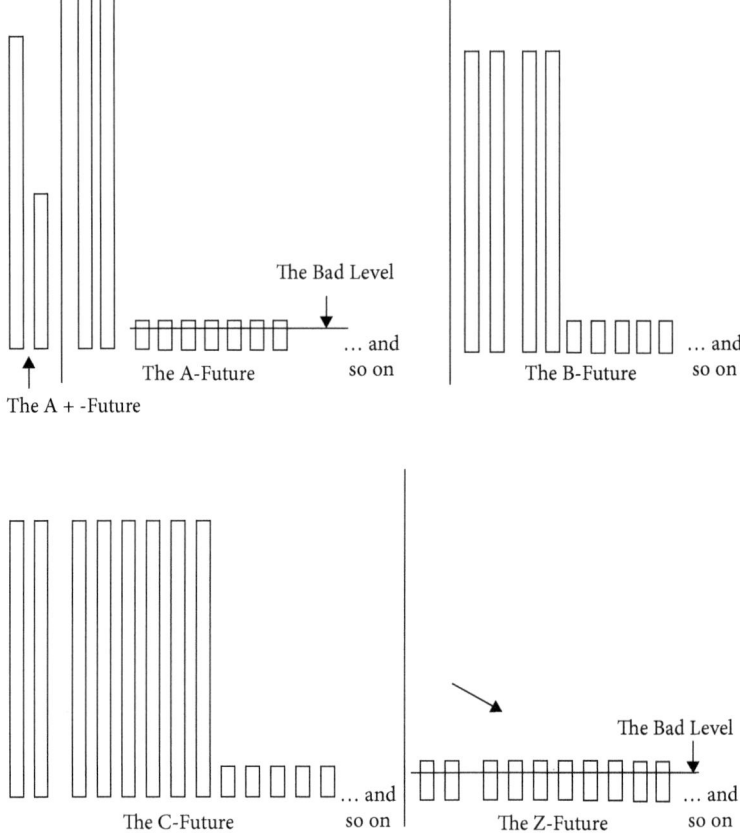

Figure 13.2 Another Version of the Mere Addition Paradox
Source: (Parfit 1984, 438–9).

would worsen this pinnacle, for instance by removing some of the Best Things in Life.

Of course, this is not the kind of future that Parfit imagines; indeed, his view is that in the future people will enjoy more of the Best Things in Life. As he puts it:

> Life can be wonderful as well as terrible, and we shall increasingly have the power to make life good. Since human history may be only just beginning, we can expect that future humans, or supra-humans, may achieve some great goods that we cannot now even imagine.[51]

---

[51] (Parfit 2017a, 436).

Suppose, then, that some of the details of Parfit's nuclear war example change. Life is still good until nuclear war erupts, killing 99% of humanity and destroying our civilization. For several hundred years, the survivors manage to keep warm in tight-knit tribes during the longest winter on human record only to inherit what Tim Mulgan calls a 'broken world'.[52] Though humanity may continue to survive for millions of years, future people's lives will forevermore be only barely worth living. Thus, while human extinction would still involve the loss of a very large quantity of wellbeing, since no amount of wellbeing could ever be as valuable as the loss of the Best Things in Life it is now the shift from peace to war that constitutes the greater total loss of value and the difference between these two would be greater than that between human survival and extinction.

While never explicitly stated by Parfit, the idea that there may be something even more important than the mere survival of humanity is reflected in his work. For instance, when discussing the badness of nuclear war, Parfit says:

> [Some] people believe that there is little value in the mere sum of happiness. For these people, what matters are what Sidgwick called the 'ideal goods'—the Sciences, the Arts, and moral progress, or the continued advance towards a wholly just world-wide community. The destruction of mankind would prevent further achievements of these three kinds. This would be extremely bad because what matters most would be the highest achievements of these kinds, and these highest achievements would come in future centuries.[53,54]

At this time Parfit made no pronouncement of whether he counted himself amongst these people or amongst those who cared most about the future quantity of wellbeing. However, as we have seen, his subsequent writings suggest that Theory X gives greater importance to something like these ideal goods.

Hence, according to Theory X, while the avoidance of human extinction may be what matters most, it is avoiding the loss of the Best Things in Life that contributes most to this fact. Seen in this light, we may be said to currently care far less than we should for the preservation of what is best about our civilization, as well as the preservation of our species. Let us call such a potential loss of perfectionist value a 'P-catastrophe', and the risk of such catastrophes 'P-risks'. According to Theory X, P-risks present a morally significant and neglected area of concern.

13.3.2 Managing Global Catastrophic Risk

However, Theory X does not only have interesting implications about the value of human survival but also how to respond to risk and uncertainty. For instance,

---

[52] (Mulgan 2015, 93).   [53] (Parfit 1984, 453–4).
[54] Sidgwick discusses the subject at (Sidgwick 1907, 114–15).

when we do not know if the survivors of a nuclear war would recover and rebuild a flourishing civilization. For ordinary people in the real world, who have no crystal ball and cannot know what the future holds, important decisions must invariably be made under such conditions.

Despite stressing the primary practical importance of risk and uncertainty, Parfit did little to address this pressing issue directly. For instance, one of his best-known thought experiments from *Reasons and Persons* asked readers to consider:

> *The Risky Policy.* As a community, we must choose between two energy policies. Both would be completely safe for at least three centuries, but one would have certain risks in the further future. This policy involves the burial of nuclear waste in areas where, in the next few centuries, there is no risk of an earthquake. But since this waste will remain radio-active for thousands of years, there will be risks in the distant future.[55]

Yet, at no point does he describe how we should respond to this risk; preferring, in cases like this, to assume that a negative outcome either obtains or does not.[56]

Parfit comes closest to setting out his reasons for this omission in the following passage from *On What Matters*, Volume 1:

> It is of great practical importance what we ought to do in cases that involve risk or uncertainty. These questions have been well discussed by many philosophers, decision theorists, and others. Certain other questions about reasons, though more fundamental, have been less well discussed. These are also questions about which people disagree more deeply.[57]

And later: "Given the difference between these two sets of questions, they are best discussed separately. So I shall often suppose that, in my imagined cases, everyone would know all of the relevant facts."[58] While acknowledging that Parfit could not possibly have dealt with every aspect of moral theory in his work, we believe that this omission was unfortunate and that his Theory X has more to offer to discussions about risk and uncertainty than he apparently realized. This is because it helps to address the difficult issue of how theories involving lexical superiority, or other forms of axiological absolutism, handle situations under risk.

One's knee jerk reaction may be that such theories are unduly insensitive to uncertainty and risk. That, on the one hand, it appears that any chance, no matter

---

[55] (Parfit 1984, 371).
[56] At least one associate of Parfit's maintains that this was simply because he was too bad at mathematics to work directly on cases involving probability.
[57] (Parfit 2011a, 37).   [58] (Parfit 2011a, 162).

how small, of preserving a lexically superior good would be morally more important than even the certainty of losing a very large quantity of lesser goods. On the other hand, however, it would also seem that any chance, no matter how small, that this superior good might be lost would also be morally more important than even the certainty of gaining a very large quantity of lesser goods. A handful of philosophers argue that implications like this constitute decisive objections to such theories as being too demanding in the priority they give to higher goods and their insensitivity to risk, while efforts to make them less demanding, for instance by setting a threshold probability below which lexical superiority no longer applies, lead to paradoxical implications.[59]

However, other philosophers have found ways to counter these arguments. Seth Lazar and Chad Lee-Stronach, for instance, have recently shown how lexical and other absolutist axiologies can provide a coherent and undemanding response to cases involving risk and uncertainty, so long as they avoid assigning infinite value to superior goods, but rather posit that the value of lesser goods cannot exceed an upper bound. Orthodox Expected Utility Theory would then allow tradeoffs between superior and lesser goods under some conditions, but not others, without this having any paradoxical implications.[60]

They suggest that the most obvious way to achieve this is if "[any lesser good] has diminishing marginal value, which decreases asymptotically towards zero, so that the total value approaches a limit beneath the value of a single token of [a superior good]".[61] Reducing the probability of creating (or preserving) a superior good will then make it possible for a sufficient quantity of the lesser good to exceed its value, despite this diminishing tendency. So, for instance, we might believe that the value of adding to the total sum of benefits in an outcome decreases as the sum of benefits increases, so that there is a maximum value for the total quantity of welfare. We might represent this as a utility score of 10. Now, if a single instance of one of the Best Things in Life had a utility score of 20, this would explain why the loss of one of these things would be bad, no matter how much additional welfare was added. However, merely accepting a 25% risk that one of the Best Things in Life could be lost would only have an expected utility score of −5, meaning that there could still be some amount of welfare that would make accepting this risk worthwhile.

Since it includes the Simple View, that the value of additional good lives does not diminish, Theory X specifically excludes this approach. However, Lazar and Chad Lee-Stronach acknowledge this is not the only approach we can take to avoid these problems, and indeed there remains a significant problem with their proposed solution. This is that it can provide different assessments of groups of choices, depending on whether they are considered individually or together. For

---

[59] See for example (Huemer 2010).   [60] (Lazar and Lee-Stronach 2017).
[61] (Lazar and Lee-Stronach 2017, 100).

instance, if the above gamble were considered morally acceptable once, then it would seem no less acceptable to make it multiple times. However, if considered as a group accepting three separate 25% risks to one of the Best Things in Life would have an expected utility score of more than -13, meaning that there should be no quantity of wellbeing worth making this sacrifice for. The difficulty for lexical, and other absolutist, axiologies is how to decide whether to evaluate each of these gambles on their own, rendering them permissible, or collectively, rendering them impermissible.[62]

Parfit referred to this kind of problem as an 'each-we' dilemma and designed his theories specifically to address them.[63]

So, what approach might Theory X take to solving these challenges? We can start by considering some passages in which Parfit sets out a unique approach to the description of risk. On his view:

> To decide which of our possible acts would make things go expectably-best, we take into account both how good the effects of the different possible acts might be, and the probabilities, given our beliefs or the available evidence, that these acts would have these effects. When what matters is only the number of lives that are saved, some act's outcome would be expectably-best if this is the act that would save the greatest expectable number of lives. The expectable number that some act would save is the number of lives that this act might save, multiplied by the chance that this act would save these lives.[64]

He adds two clarificatory notes to this passage, pointing out that: "Rather than talking of the expectable goodness of these outcomes, many people talk of their expected goodness. But that word is misleading, since such expectable goodness is often not goodness that either is, or should be, expected."[65] And that:

> Expectabilists need not assume that the expectable goodness of outcomes depends only on the expectable sum of benefits. As Broome and Kamm suggest, for example, it may also matter how these benefits, or people's chances of getting these benefits, are distributed between different people... And we might have reasons to be risk-averse, giving somewhat greater weight to avoiding the worst outcomes.[66]

Given that the language of expected value is standard across the literatures of ethics, economics, and decision theory, this choice of terminology may appear pedantic. However, when seen in the light of his Imprecise Lexical View, we believe its importance becomes clearer.

---

[62] (Lazar and Lee-Stronach 2017, 105–7). [63] (Parfit 1984, 91). [64] (Parfit 2011a, 160).
[65] (Parfit 2011a, 462). [66] (Parfit 2011a, 462–3).

According to Orthodox Expected Utility Theory, one should evaluate cases of risk merely by multiplying the value of each possible outcome by the probability of that outcome given one's choice. Such an approach can make good sense when all values are representable on a single scale. However, it makes less sense when they are not. For instance, Expected Utility Theory would say that we should treat a situation in which there is a 50% chance of losing all the Best Things in Life in the same way as we would a situation in which we would expect to lose 50% of the Best Things in Life. However, according to the Imprecise Lexical View, a situation in which 50% of the Best Things in Life would be retained would still be lexically superior to a situation in which all were lost, while having a value comparable with preserving all the Best Things in Life, because the existence of these goods matters far more than their quantity.

In considering how we should respond to a situation in which the expectable outcome involves a risk to the Best Things in Life, we need to find a better way of representing this intermediate state in our axiology. The Imprecise Lexical View provides just such a way, because outcomes that are truly intermediate between lexically superior and inferior alternatives are not precisely comparable with either, but roughly comparable with both. This allows us to construct a framework that will be functionally like Lazar and Lee-Stronach's, but where it is not the value of a lesser good (here, wellbeing) that has an upper bound, but rather its comparability to the value of superior goods (the Best Things in Life). As we reduce the probability that superior good will exist, we effectively make the value of an outcome more comparable to one in which a lower good exists with certainty and less comparable to one in which a higher good exists with certainty. Depending on the degree of qualitative difference between these two goods, there will be a range of thresholds, representing the points at which this probabilistic good becomes increasingly incomparable with the certainty of a superior good and comparable with the certainty of a lesser good.[67]

---

[67] Parfit sometimes used a five-tier hierarchy of thresholds to describe such increasing incomparability (Parfit ms1, 23 and 26). This could be adapted for cases involving risk and uncertainty along the following lines:

1. Where both the qualitative differences between the two goods are very small and the probability of receiving the superior good is very low, then there's some quantity of the lesser good that would be better.
2. As the qualitative differences between the two goods either increases and/or the probability of receiving the superior good increases, then:

   (a) first it would become indeterminate whether there is some quantity of the lesser good that would be better or whether any quantity of the lesser good would at most be roughly comparable;
   (b) then any quantity of the lesser good would at most be roughly comparable;
   (c) and then it would become indeterminate whether any quantity of the lesser good would at most be roughly comparable or would be worse.
3. Finally, where either the qualitative differences between the two goods are very great or the probability of receiving the superior good is very high, any quantity of the lesser good would be worse.

On this framework, we might say that it would not be worse to sacrifice a small chance of preserving some of the Best Things in Life in order to increase the overall level of wellbeing, but it would still be, at most, a matter of rough comparability. Since, as we described in section 13.2.2, rough comparability is not a transitive notion, there is no contradiction between believing that one person did no wrong by choosing between two roughly comparable options, but that many people together did great wrong by selecting a lexically inferior option, thus avoiding the each-we dilemma implied by Lazar and Lee-Stronach's approach. This seems to us like a promising proposal, and we believe that further work on this aspect of Theory X is needed.[68]

13.3.3 Alleviating Poverty and Suffering

While preventing human extinction is what Parfit thought mattered most, he also believed that it mattered a great deal that we do more to counteract the worst cases of human suffering and poverty in the world. As he puts it:

> One thing that greatly matters is the failure of we rich people to prevent, as we so easily could, much of the suffering and many of the early deaths of the poorest people in the world. The money that we spend on an evening's entertainment might instead save some poor person from death, blindness, or chronic and severe pain. If we believe that, in our treatment of these poorest people, we are not acting wrongly, we are like those who believed that they were justified in having slaves.[69,70]

Claims such as this are not hard to defend on purely utilitarian grounds and seem consistent with the principles in Parfit's Theory X. However, it is hard to miss the notion that there is something especially bad about suffering, which is not

---

[68] Some may object to the introduction of yet more imprecision into our evaluation of outcomes under risk and believe that, from being too demanding, this makes Theory X not demanding enough because we might plausibly do what we wish if we cannot precisely determine which of two outcomes would be best. However, Parfit was clear that he did not believe this was the correct response to such imprecision. For instance, in response to a different objection along similar lines, he writes that:

> we can reply that, if global warming would kill many people, and have other bad effects, making the world in some ways worse, and these bad effects would also predictably be greater than any good effects, that would be enough to make global warming a bad thing, which it might be our duty to try to prevent, or limit. Such claims would not be undermined if we can also predict that... these two possible futures would be less precisely comparable, so that neither future would be worse all things considered. (Parfit ms2, 15–16)

Thus, while it may weaken the absolute precision with which we can say that certain outcomes would be bad, this imprecision may not weaken our reasons for working to avoid them.

[69] (Parfit 2017a, 436).

[70] Parfit continues: "We ought to transfer to these people... at least ten percent of what we inherit or earn" and provides an endnote with practical advice about the most effective ways of doing this.

captured merely in its negative effect on individuals' wellbeing. This sense is brought into focus when one considers Parfit's specific reference to the wrongness of keeping slaves, something that he had previously discussed in his unpublished "Towards Theory X: Part 2". Here he writes:

> The ancient Greeks had amazing achievements in poetry, drama, architecture, sculpture, history, philosophy, mathematics, and some kinds of science. These achievements were in part made possible by slavery and unjust inequalities. When we consider these facts, we may...believe that these ancient Greeks acted wrongly, and ought to have abolished slavery and these inequalities, even if that would have prevented most of these great achievements. We may also believe that, though these ancient Greeks ought to have acted in these ways, these morally required acts would have made history go in ways that would not have been better, but only imprecisely equally as good. On this view, when we compare these ways in which history actually went and might have gone, there would be no precise truths about the relation between the perfectionist value of these great achievements, and the badness of Greek slavery and the other injustices on which these achievements were partly based.[71]

For some people, this passage may seem troubling and highlight what is wrong with the perfectionist implications of Parfit's view—that it gives insufficient weight to suffering. How could the harm of slavery be considered imprecisely equally as important as the achievements of the ancient Greeks?

However, this reply misses an important implication of this passage. As we have seen, Parfit's Imprecise Lexical View implies that, all else being equal, the loss of any of the Best Things in Life, such as the achievements of the ancient Greeks, would be a change for the worse no matter how much additional wellbeing this created. Yet, in this case, he suggests that this is not so and that the loss of these things would only make our history imprecisely equally as good (or in his later terminology 'roughly comparable') to what it has been. There is thus no contradiction between Parfit's Imprecise Lexical View and his belief that this form of slavery was an inexcusable crime.[72] If this is so, then it follows that the badness of slavery is not only a function of its negative effect on people's wellbeing but must also involve qualitative changes to the value of outcomes that are in some way comparable to those of losing the Best Things in Life.

---

[71] (Parfit ms2, 29).

[72] The nature of this crime is not considered further by Parfit but would seem to depend on the distinction he sometimes draws between the goodness of outcomes and what we ought to do. It would thus be similar to our potential obligations to benefit presently existing people, even when we could give a greater benefit to future people (discussed in footnote 37), and to do what would have predictably the best results, even if we cannot make precise judgements of the relative value of our choices (discussed in footnote 67). Since these do not relate to the goodness of outcomes, they do not form part of Theory X.

Parfit briefly addresses this issue at two other points in his work. Firstly, as we have seen, it is related to his earlier belief that Perfectionism appeared elitist and that we should reject "the Nietzschean view that the prevention of great suffering can be ranked wholly below the preservation of creation of the best things in life".[73] While at first he saw rejecting this concern as 'irrelevant' to his considerations, he appears to have returned to the issue again in 2016, noting that "if we care greatly about the quality of life, being in this sense Perfectionists, that would not make us elitists, who care most about the wellbeing of the best-off people".[74] We have already seen that Parfit saw the Quality of Life as being a broader notion than wellbeing. However, this assertion that his Imprecise Lexical View would not be elitist seems to suggest that its breadth may well incorporate more than simply wellbeing and the Best Things in Life.[75]

The other place in Parfit's work where he seems to connect the value of the Best Things in Life and the badness of suffering comes right at the end of *On What Matters*, Volume 3, where he chooses to close his argument for the moral importance of avoiding human extinction with the following observation:

> If we are the only rational beings in the Universe, as some recent evidence suggests, it matters even more whether we shall have descendants or successors during the billions of years in which that would be possible. Some of our successors might live lives and create worlds that, though failing to justify past suffering, would have given us all, including those who suffered most, reasons to be glad that the Universe exists.[76]

We, therefore, believe that, though he never stated this clearly, a special concern for the alleviation of suffering may be a feature of Parfit's Imprecise Lexical View, and hence of Theory X. Again, we believe that further work on this aspect of Theory X is needed.[77]

---

[73] (Parfit 1986, 20).   [74] (Parfit 2016, 117).

[75] Indeed, elitism is not the only charge that can be levelled against a purely perfectionist account of Quality of Life. Despite his statements to the contrary, Perfectionism on its own may also be unable to avoid the Repugnant Conclusion and may imply a version of Parfit's Ridiculous Conclusion, while more sophisticated accounts of the Quality of Life can also avoid these troubling implications as well— see esp. (Beard 2019).

[76] (Parfit 2017a, 437).

[77] In this section, we have only considered how Theory X might account for the badness of suffering in terms of its impact on people's Quality of Life. Another aspect of Theory X on which further work is needed is how it fits in with Parfit's views on distributive ethics. Parfit famously argued against egalitarianism as a distributive principle and in favour of what he called 'The Priority View', according to which "we have stronger reasons to benefit people the worse off these people are" (Parfit 2012, 401).

However, it is not clear how this view relates to existential benefits. On the one hand, Parfit argued that "[it] is sometimes claimed, for example, that we have prioritarian reasons to have children, since we would thereby benefit some of the possible people who would otherwise be badly off, by never

13.4 Conclusion

In this chapter, we have argued that, although he did not live long enough to complete it, Parfit's work contains all the components necessary to construct a Theory X that would fulfill the requirements of his lifelong search. The combination of a Wide Dual Person-Affecting Principle, concerning the value of well-being, and his Simple and Imprecise Lexical Views, which place this into a wider pluralism about the value of lives, can avoid the Absurd and Repugnant Conclusions, solve the Non-Identity Problem, and escape the Mere Addition Paradox. This combination can also be applied to those cases that Parfit asserted mattered most, and support his conclusions about them.

---

existing... But when we apply these distributive principles, we should not include, among the people who are badly off, possible people who never exist. Like the Principles of Personal Good, or Pareto Principles, the Prioritarian Principles that I have considered cannot be applied to cases in which, in the different possible outcomes, different people would exist" (Parfit 2012, 440).

On the other hand, in an unpublished draft of the paper that would become (Parfit 2017b), he begins considering a version of the priority view that would apply to these people. He writes:

> Suppose instead that the possible outcomes are these:
>
> A: Tom's total will be negative 100, Dick's total will be 100
> C: Tom and Dick will never exist
>
> Though having zero well-being is different from never existing, this difference seems unimportant here. Most of us would believe that A would be worse than C. If someone's total level of well-being would be below zero, this person's life would be bad to live, and worse than lives that are not worth living. It would be better if such lives are not lived because such people never exist. In defending our belief that A would be worse than C, we could not appeal to the simplest version of the Priority View... We could appeal, however, to another version of the Priority View. We could claim that
>
> (J) the badness of someone's being existentially harmed is greater than the goodness of someone's receiving an equally great existential benefit.
>
> If someone is existentially harmed by being caused to have a life that is intrinsically bad, this person would be worse off than someone who is existentially benefited by being caused to have a life that is intrinsically good. Since benefiting people does more good the worse off these people are, preventing people from being existentially harmed does more good than giving people equally great existential benefits. That is why A would be worse than C (Parfit ms3, 5).

Parfit does not make it clear whether he endorses this latter view. However, he appears to view it more sympathetically than the alternative view he is considering at this point in the paper, that there is a fundamental asymmetry between existential benefits and existential harms. Our view is that Parfit may have wished to incorporate prioritarianism into his theory, so long as he could do so in a way that would not give us additional reasons to have children. One proposal towards this end would be to apply the priority view to Parfit's Wide Individual Principle but not his Wide Collective Principle, yielding the following:

> *Prioritarian Dual Wide Person-Affecting Principle.* One of two outcomes would be in one way better if this outcome would together benefit people more, and in another way better if this outcome would benefit each person more, where benefiting each person matters more the worse off these people are.

Another proposal towards this end would be to apply the priority view only to people whose lives are bad but not those whose lives are good.

Naturally, in combining these principles and applying them to these cases, we have come across issues in need of further work. Yet, these represent not only problems for this theory to overcome but also opportunities to break fresh ground in moral philosophy. Thus, while the search for Theory X may not quite be over, we believe that Parfit has laid the foundations for a truly innovative, insightful, and compelling approach to assessing and responding to the global challenges we now face. If it is not presumptuous for us to say, we feel that, for Parfit, as for Sidgwick before him, the words of F. W. H. Myers are appropriate:

> He pointed to a definite spot; he vigorously drove in the spade; he upturned a shining handful; and he left us as his testament, *Dig Here*.[78,79]

References

Arrhenius, G., An Impossibility Theorem for Welfarist Axiologies, in *Economics and Philosophy* 16/2 (2000): 247–66.

Arrhenius, G., The Very Repugnant Conclusion, in K. Segerberg and R. Sliwinski (eds.), *Logic, Law, Morality: Thirteen Essays in Practical Philosophy in Honour of Lennart Åqvist* (Uppsala University, 2003), 167–80.

Arrhenius, G., The Impossibility of a Satisfactory Population Ethics, in E. Dzhafarov and L. Perry (eds.), *Descriptive and Normative Approaches to Human Behavior* (World Scientific, 2011), 51–66.

Arrhenius, G., Population Ethics and Different-Number-Based Imprecision, in *Theoria* 82/2 (2016): 166–81.

Beard, S. Perfectionism and the Repugnant Conclusion, in *The Journal of Value Inquiry* 54 (2019): 119–40.

Beard, S. and Kaczmarek, P., The Wrongness of Human Extinction, in *Argumenta* 5/1 (2020): 85–97.

---

[78] (Schultz 2004, 719).

[79] We would like to thank the editors of this volume, Jeff McMahan, Tim Campbell, James Goodrich, and Ketan Ramakrishnan. Jeff McMahan and Tim Campbell also provided feedback on earlier drafts of this work, as did Larry Temkin, Michael Otsuka, Shlomi Segall, and participants at the workshop "Evaluating Extreme Technological Risk", hosted by the Centre for the Study of Existential Risk at the University of Cambridge, as well as colleagues at a work in progress seminar, all of whom we gratefully acknowledge. S. J. Beard worked on this chapter while a Visiting Scholar at the Centre for Philosophy of Natural and Social Science at the London School of Economics. Patrick Kaczmarek received support during the writing of this chapter from the Berkeley Existential Risk Initiative and the Effective Altruism Foundation. This publication was made possible through the support of a grant from Templeton World Charity Foundation, Inc. The opinions expressed in this publication are those of the author(s) and do not necessarily reflect the views of Templeton World Charity Foundation, Inc.

Blackorby, C., Bossert, W. and Donaldson, D., *Population Issues in Social Choice Theory, Welfare Economics, and Ethics* (Cambridge University Press, 2005).

Boonin, D., *The Non-Identity Problem and the Ethics of Future People* (Oxford University Press, 2014).

Broome, J., *Weighing Lives* (Oxford University Press, 2004).

Cowen, T., What Do We Learn from the Repugnant Conclusion?, in *Ethics* 106/4 (1996): 754–75.

Crisp, R., Utilitarianism and the Life of Virtue, in *The Philosophical Quarterly* 42/167 (1992): 139–60.

Huemer, M., In Defence of Repugnance, in *Mind* 117/468 (2008): 899–933.

Huemer, M., Lexical Priority and the Problem of Risk, in *Pacific Philosophical Quarterly* 91/3 (2010): 332–351.

Hurka, T., Value and Population Size, in *Ethics* 93/3 (1983): 496–507.

Lazar, S. and Lee-Stronach, C., Axiological Absolutism and Risk, in *Noûs* 53/1 (2017): 97–113.

Masny, M., On Parfit's Wide Dual Person-Affecting Principle, in *The Philosophical Quarterly* 70/278 (2020): 114–39.

McTaggart, J. and McTaggart, E., *The Nature of Existence*, Volume II (Cambridge University Press, 1927).

Mulgan, T., Utilitarianism for a Broken World, in *Utilitas* 27/1 (2015): 92–114.

Parfit, D., On Doing the Best for Our Children, in M. Bayles (ed.), *Ethics and Population* (Schenkman Pub. Co., 1976), 100–15.

Parfit, D., Future Generations: Further Problems, in *Philosophy & Public Affairs* 11/2 (1982): 113–72.

Parfit, D., *Reasons and Persons* (Oxford University Press, 1984).

Parfit, D., Overpopulation and the Quality of Life, in P. Singer (ed.), *Applied Ethics* (Oxford University Press, 1986), 145–64.

Parfit, D., *On What Matters*, Volume 1 (Oxford University Press, 2011).

Parfit, D., *On What Matters*, Volume 2 (Oxford University Press, 2011).

Parfit, D., Another Defense of the Priority View, in *Utilitas* 24/3 (2012): 399–440.

Parfit, D., Can We Avoid the Repugnant Conclusion?, in *Theoria* 82/2 (2016): 110–27.

Parfit, D., *On What Matters*, Volume 3 (Oxford University Press, 2017).

Parfit, D., Future People, The Non-Identity Problem, and Person-Affecting Principles, in *Philosophy & Public Affairs* 45/2 (2017): 118–57.

Parfit, D., *Towards Theory X: Part One* (unpublished ms1).

Parfit, D., *Towards Theory X: Part Two* (unpublished ms2).

Parfit, D., *The Non-Identity Problem* (unpublished ms3).

Rachels, S., Repugnance or Intransitivity: A Repugnant But Forced Choice, in T. Tännsjö and J. Ryberg (eds.), *The Repugnant Conclusion* (Springer, 2004), 163–86.

Schultz, B., *Henry Sidgwick—Eye of the Universe: An Intellectual Biography* (Cambridge University Press, 2004).

Sidgwick, H., *The Methods of Ethics*, Seventh Edition (Hackett Publishing Company, 1907).

Tännsjö, T., Why We Ought to Accept the Repugnant Conclusion, in *Utilitas* 14/3 (2002): 339–59.

Temkin, L., Intransitivity and the Mere Addition Paradox, in *Philosophy & Public Affairs* 16/2 (1987): 138–87.

Thomas, T., Some Possibilities in Population Axiology, in *Mind* 125/507 (2017): 807–32.

PART III
EVALUATIVE IMPRECISION, INCOMMENSURABILITY, AND VAGUENESS IN VALUE

14
How to Avoid the Repugnant Conclusion

Ruth Chang

I propose a way to defuse continua arguments that exploit normative predicates like 'stronger reason', 'better', 'more choiceworthy', 'preferable to', 'best', and the like in order to generate puzzles or paradoxes of normativity. The most famous of these is Parfit's continuum argument for the Repugnant Conclusion (Parfit 1984).[1,2] According to that argument, we can create a continuum of outcomes varying only by population size and quality of life such that each successive outcome is intuitively better than its predecessor until we arrive at an outcome in which there is a very large number of people, each with a life barely worth living. Given the transitivity of 'better than', it follows that this world, with a vast number of people with lives barely worth living, is better than the first world in the continuum, one with a large number of people all of whom are leading excellent lives. This is the Repugnant Conclusion.

Parfit thought his continuum argument was significant because it placed a challenging constraint on normative theorizing: the correct normative theory must be able to avoid the Repugnant Conclusion, but it is unclear how it is to be avoided. Indeed, the last (finished) paper Parfit published (Parfit 2016) before his unexpected death was an attempt to answer the challenge he himself had made so famous.

Curiously, Parfit's argument has made little impact on mainstream normative theorizing; instead it has given birth to—or at least breathed new life into—the branch of practical ethics now known as 'population ethics'. This seems to me doubly unfortunate. First, there's more to population ethics than contemplating the well-being and size of future populations; there is also the value of human existence, the importance of continuity in what we care about, what we owe to

---

[1] Thanks to Timothy Campbell, Jimmy Goodrich, Theron Pummer and Wlodek Rabinowicz for helpful comments on an earlier draft of this chapter, and to audiences at the Oxford Nuffield Political Theory Workshop, the Conference on Incommensurability and Non-Standard Value Relations in Sweden, and the Warwick Centre for Ethics and Law, especially Ralf Bader and Victor Tadros, for helpful discussion. Research assistance was provided by Laura Callahan, Carolina Flores, and Stacy Topouzova. Without Derek Parfit, this chapter, and, indeed, my life as a philosopher, would not exist.

[2] A version of which is sometimes known as the 'Mere Addition Paradox' (Parfit 1984). Note that the argument does not involve a 'continuum' in a strict mathematical sense, and such arguments are sometimes also referred to as 'spectrum' arguments. Since some of the arguments made here also, I believe, apply to at least some strict continua arguments, I follow Parfit's original terminology.

future persons and our species from our situated perspective, and various deontic considerations that, arguably, cannot be simply 'added' down the line to purely nondeontic conclusions. Samuel Scheffler's *Why Worry?* (2018) provides a salutary example of how the field might be taken in new directions. Other issues relevant to the ethics of populations, beyond discussion of person-affecting views, impossibility arguments, and continua arguments inspired by Parfit's writings include individual responsibility for creating new lives, the application of theories of justice to future generations, animal population ethics, gamete donation, disability and equality, climate change, and normative uncertainty, to name a few.[3]

Second, it seems to me even more unfortunate that Parfit's continuum argument has been largely neglected by mainstream normative theorists. It has been taken seriously by a cadre of those with a non-deontic bent (sometimes self-styled 'pluralists'), but it has been pretty much ignored by deontologists, virtue theorists, perfectionists, and other nonconsequentialists, perhaps because it has been mistakenly thought to be 'a mere puzzle' based on suspect consequentialist assumptions. As I want to suggest in this chapter, thinking and worrying about Parfit's argument bears interesting, highly generalizable fruit. It gives us reason to doubt assumptions we make about the very warp and weave of normativity itself, and as such may have profound implications for any normative theory.

The continua arguments of interest proceed in broad outline as follows (further features to come). Start with an item that instantiates a mix of two contributory factors relevant to its evaluative assessment. Generate a second item that appears to stand in a transitive comparative relation, R, to the first. Continue to generate successive items along the continuum by modifying each predecessor through a small diminution in one factor and a large enhancement in the other so that R appears to hold between each item and its predecessor. Iterate. By the transitivity of R, it follows that the last item is R-related to the first item. But, it is intuitively clear that the last item is *not* R-related to the first item. Hence the puzzle.

I propose what I will call a 'structural' solution to such arguments.[4] Despite initial appearances, the structure along the continuum is not uniform; the R-relation, say, 'better than', does *not* hold between each item and its predecessor. A break in structure halts the slide to the repugnant conclusion. All structural solutions deny that the R-relation, such as 'better than', holds between each item and its successor.

The challenge for structural solutions is to specify and defend the supposed change in structure as one moves along the continuum. As it turns out, appeal to

---

[3] See the forthcoming *Oxford Handbook on Population Ethics* (OUP) eds. Timothy Campbell, Gustaf Arrhenius, et al., which covers many of these issues.

[4] One advantage of a structural solution is that it does not depend on the subject matter of the claims that generate the puzzle and so may have wide application.

any of three natural, possible accounts of structural change, namely *incommensurability, incomparability, or indeterminacy*, either will not allow us to avoid the repugnant conclusion or suffers from other grave difficulties. And a fourth possible 'i' explanation, namely Parfit's own appeal to (lexical) *imprecision*, is also problematic; at best it fails to provide an answer to some continua arguments, including, arguably, a version of Parfit's own.[5]

Instead, we must recognize that somewhere along the continuum, there is a qualitative shift among items such that successive items are not better than their immediate predecessors but *on a par*. Parity is a fourth, *sui generis* way in which two items can be compared beyond being better, worse, or equal to one another. If parity holds somewhere along the continuum, the slide to the repugnant conclusion is halted, and continua arguments are thereby defused.

This proposed solution is perfectly general and so in principle applies to all continua arguments, such as such as those that counsel walking across the grass (Harrison 1953), having another cigarette, self-torture (Quinn 1984[6]), opting for a year's worth of torture over a lifetime of minor pains (Rachels 2001; Temkin 2012), and even, perhaps, calling a red patch blue (Graff 2001).[7] In this chapter, I focus on Parfit's argument in population ethics, but the application to other continua arguments can be more or less readily made.

None of this is to say that *no* continua arguments can be avoided by appeal to one of the 'i' explanations; the point is rather that none of these explanations can provide a general solution to *all* of them. Anyone looking to respond to continua arguments *writ large* must appeal to the parity solution to solve at least *some* continua arguments. I believe that parity provides a solution to the most

---

[5] A fifth 'i' explanation is *ignorance*; perhaps there is some point along the continuum at which an item is not better than its successor but we just do not know where. I endorse this explanation but with a twist: there is a zone of items, each on a par with its predecessor, but sometimes we do not know where this zone begins or ends. Our ignorance concerns parity, not some trichotomous relation. I have offered some arguments against 'trichotomous ignorance' doing work of this sort elsewhere (Chang 2002a).

[6] The specified features of the continua arguments of interest exclude those involving indiscernible differences as Quinn's does; it must seem that the next item in the continuum is better than its predecessor. But Quinn's argument could be reformulated so that the difference in pain is just discernible, and so reformulated would be included in the target class of arguments.

[7] More work would be required to apply this solution to *non*normative continua arguments, but my suspicion is that at least some such arguments would be amenable to such treatment. So, for example, in Parfit's (1984) continuum of identity starting with Parfit and ending with the conclusion that Greta Garbo is identical to Parfit (via the transitivity of identity), there will be a zone of items in which items are on a par with respect to being identical. The same goes for continua arguments involving indiscernible differences in color (Graff 2001); while indeterminacy can play a role in such continua, in order to get from, say, red to blue along a continuum, there might well be a zone in which items are on a par with respect to being identical in color. This is controversial and could be nonsense. More apparently plausible might be a continuum of items with respect to bulkiness; I have suggested that a bicycle is on a par with a 2 × 4 plank in bulkiness (Chang 2002b) and perhaps a continuum argument could be generated for bulky items, which could then be avoided by an appeal to parity. For general discussion of different types of continua arguments, see Wibren van der Burg (1991) and Anali Jefferson (2014).

interesting and compelling continua arguments, like Parfit's in population ethics, Quinn's self-torturer, and Rachels/Temkin pain cases. If my arguments are correct, those sceptical of parity must find some other, *nonstructural*, solution to challenges posed by such arguments.[8]

If the 'parity solution' to continua arguments is right, then our commonplace understanding of value, reasons and choice require reexamination. We should no longer assume that actions, events, and things can be only better, worse, or as good as one another, that one duty can be only more significant, less or as significant as another, or that the reasons for choice can only be stronger (or trump, exclude, bracket, cancel, or silence), less strong, or as strong as one another.[9] Actions and states of affairs can be on a par in value; our obligations can be on a par with respect to what we ought to do; and our reasons to choose or to have some attitude can be on a par in normative significance. The possibility of parity in turn gives rise to a different way of thinking not only about value, reasons, and choice but also about what it is to be a rational agent. This is a case, I believe, in which thinking about 'a mere puzzle' can open up new ways of thinking about fundamental aspects of the normative world and our place in it.

---

[8] Two main nonstructural 'solutions' to continua arguments have been proposed. (For a persuasive dispatching of some other proffered solutions, see Parfit 2016.)

First, Rachels (2001) and Temkin (2012) have suggested that 'better than, simpliciter' or (what is treated synonymously) 'all-things-considered-better-than' are nontransitive relations. (Their solution is not structural because they allow that each item is better than its predecessor but that since better than is nontransitive, the Repugnant Conclusion does not follow.) I believe that there are two issues that can be raised about their arguments:

i) There is no genuine *substantive* relation, 'better than, simpliciter' or 'all-things-considered-better-than' whose transitivity we should expect. Such relations are, I have proposed instead, 'placeholder relations'—not themselves substantive relations but formal relations that hold the place of *substantive* relations, such as 'better than with respect to justice' or 'better than with respect to honoring/maximizing social well-being' (Chang 2004a,b, 1997). As placeholders for substantive relations, they cannot properly be thought to be in themselves transitive or nontransitive. There is related discussion in Kamm (1996, fn 34 pp. 350ff) and Thomson (2001) (there is no goodness, simpliciter).

ii) Even if Rachels and Temkin can dispose of the puzzle formulated with their stipulated relation, they also need to deal with the puzzle as formulated in terms of the familiar 'better than' relation, which is transitive. My suggestion is that we should accept a structural solution to such arguments. See also Parfit (2017) (even if there is some stipulated relation of betterness that is 'essentially comparative', the relation we use in these arguments and predominantly in ordinary life involves comparing 'intrinsic aspects' of items (though it seems plausible that the ordinary betterness relation cuts across this distinction between 'essentially comparative' and 'intrinsic aspect' approaches to comparisons)).

Second, Gustaf Arrhenius (2011) has argued for an impossibility result—there is no way of resolving problems raised by continua arguments without giving up certain plausible assumptions. The 'solution', then, is that the paradox is genuine, admitting of no solution (and is therefore nonstructural since it does not deny that each item is better than its predecessor). If I have understood Arrhenius correctly, one his assumptions is what I call *Trichotomy*, discussed below, which of course is consistent with partial orderings that allow for (trichotomous) incomparability or indeterminacy. The arguments of this chapter, if correct, suggest that we should give up this assumption.

[9] For an argument that seemingly noncomparative relations among reasons or values depend on comparative relations, see Chang (2016b).

14.1 The Continuum Argument for the Repugnant Conclusion

Parfit asks us to consider a continuum of possible worlds or outcomes in which each successive world involves a slight decrease in the well-being of its people but some large addition of people leading lives with that diminished quality of well-being. All else is stipulated as irrelevant or equal. It seems that each successive world is better than its predecessor; after all, it seems that a sufficiently large increase in the quantity of lives worth living can compensate for the small diminution in quality of life that obtains in each successor world. And if 'better than' is transitive, it follows that a world at the end of the continuum, Z, in which there are vast numbers of people whose lives are barely worth living, is better than a world at the beginning of the continuum, A, in which there is a smaller but still significant number of people all leading excellent lives. But that is a repugnant conclusion. Parfit's continuum is depicted in Figure 14.1.

There are three assumptions of Parfit's argument worth noting, two of which we can set aside in order to make continua arguments as broad in scope and as challenging as possible. First, Parfit—and others who have put forward continua arguments—assume that an increase in quantity of lives at a fixed quality maps onto an evaluative difference in quantity. If you add a hundred lives at quality q, you add more goodness than if you add only eighty. A suitably large increase in the quantity of lives, then, should be understood to entail a suitably large increase in the goodness of the outcome. This assumption is not problematic for our purposes.

Second, Parfit sometimes discusses his continua argument as if comparative judgements about the goodness of worlds issue from a god's-eye point of view, impartial goodness, all-things-considered-goodness or goodness simpliciter. That there is such a viewpoint is highly controversial, and I suggest that we instead understand comparisons along the continuum as proceeding with respect to an

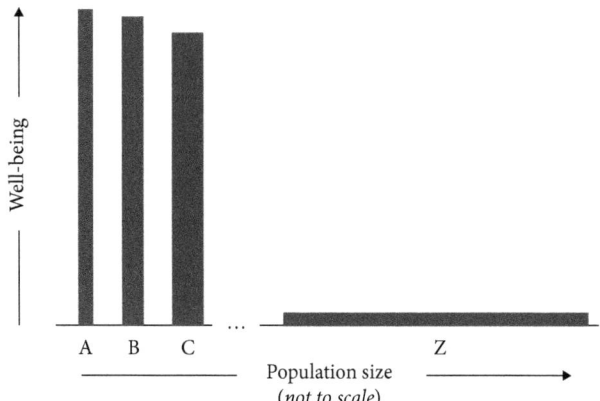

Figure 14.1 Parfit's continuum.

ordinary substantive 'covering consideration', call it 'V', such as 'social well-being', 'beneficence', 'justice', etc., in terms of which each world is putatively better than its successor. For our purposes, we can simply assume, for the sake of argument, that there is some V, understood as a unity or a collection of familiar considerations, in terms of which Parfit's, and other continua arguments, can proceed.[10]

Third, Parfit seems to assume that only consequentialist covering considerations are relevant to assessing how items on the continuum compare, and correspondingly that outcomes are the only items out of which a problematic continuum might be formed. Some proponents of such arguments defend this assumption by claiming that, at the very least, these consequentialist considerations are *a part* of the truth about how the outcomes compare. But Parfit's argument goes much deeper than that response allows. His continuum argument may well hold for actions and ways of being that differ in terms of some deontological V such as 'doing one's duty' or some perfectionist excellence. You might, for example, have an imperfect duty to give to charity. Facts about the comparative normative significance of giving one amount rather than another are relevant to the determination of what you have a duty to do. More controversially, when duties themselves conflict, they might be said to have respective 'strengths' or 'significances' that stand in comparative relations, especially since it is a mistake to think that comparative relations necessarily suppose aggregation, summation, cardinality, rates of trade-off or any of the crude representational features with which they are often unfairly saddled (Chang 2016b). At the very least, we should leave open the possibility that continua arguments present a challenge to non-consequentialist theories.[11]

The plausibility of a continuum argument rests on the plausibility of three imprecisely specified conditions obtaining, each of which is in principle neutral between different normative theories:

(i) the covering consideration, 'V', has at least two significant contributory factors that are 'bi-directional', that is, in some cases, one factor favors one item on the continuum while the other factor favors the other item;

---

[10] Although I assume a suitable V for Parfit's argument, if you find this assumption problematic, you can throughout substitute a paradigmatic continuum involving painful experiences with the covering consideration being 'painfulness'.

[11] See also Kamm (2007: 484ff) and Arrhenius, Chapter 16, this volume, but compare Boonin (1996) who argues that the continuum argument holds only for values and not duties. Note that theories that eschew normative comparative assessment *altogether* would be immune from continua arguments, but such theories are patently implausible. So long as a theory allows notions such as trumping, being more significant than, being less important than, and so on, it may be open in principle to continua arguments. I have argued that comparisons transcend the usual divide between axiology and deontology and that the question of value and the question of what one ought to do can be treated under the same rubric of comparisons with respect to an appropriate—deontological or axiological—covering consideration (Chang 2016b).

(ii) each successive item on the continuum is generated by diminishing slightly one (particular) significant contributory factor of its predecessor while enhancing greatly the (particular) other so that these changes appear to make it R-related to its predecessor; and

(iii) a significantly 'unbalanced' package of these contributory factors of V—for example, one factor instantiated in a nominal (or notable) way relative to the other—is not R-related to a significantly *less* unbalanced package of these contributory factors.

I restrict my attention to continua that meet these three conditions. Going forward, I will assume that there is always a 'V' with respect to which a comparative claim is made even if not explicitly stated and, for simplicity, that 'V' has only two relevant contributory components, both of which make important contributions to V-ness. To simplify even further, I will assume that the two factors are quantity and quality of V-ness (though continua could also be generated by two bi-directional *qualities* of V-ness).

Parfit's continuum argument (as well as all standard ones relativized to a V) meets the three conditions. It proceeds by trading off two bi-directional contributory factors of V in the same way: a small diminution in quality of V for a large increase in quantity of V. As we move along the continuum, each item involves a small diminution of quality which, it seems, can be compensated for by a large increase in quantity so that each item is better than its predecessor. At the start of the continuum, world A is, relatively speaking, a 'balanced' package of quantity and quality of V-ness—a good number of people leading excellent lives—while Z, at the end of the continuum is, relative to A, an 'unbalanced' package of V-ness—a googol of people with lives barely worth living.

Now a key assumption of continua arguments is that a small diminution in quality in conjunction with a sufficient enhancement in quantity does not make a *qualitative difference that makes a difference* to how the items compare. That is, all continua arguments assume:

Uniformity: The R-relation holds between every item and its predecessor on the continuum because there are no qualitative differences between any two adjacent items that makes a difference to how they R-relate.

Structural solutions to continua arguments deny that Uniformity holds; they posit a 'break' somewhere along the continuum where there is a qualitative difference that makes a difference to how the items compare.[12]

---

[12] Theron Pummer (2018) points out that even some nonstructural solutions, like those that deny transitivity, must posit a break of sorts along the continuum, not between adjacent items but in what is true of each item with respect to the first item. Eventually, there will be an item along the continuum that is not better than A but whose predecessor is. That is not the sort of break of interest here. Note too

Could the break in structure be given by a single point? Perhaps, depending on how the continuum is constructed. But if the continuum is sufficiently fine-grained, a single break point will be implausible; how could there be a single item along the continuum before which all worlds are better than their predecessors but after which all worlds are not better than their predecessors, or a single item that is not better than its predecessor but which is followed by worlds each of which is better than their respective predecessors? For any putative structural break point, it seems plausible that we can construct worlds around it that would appear to be part of the structural break, too. To finesse this issue, I am going to assume that a plausible structural solution will posit a *zone* of items along the continuum that form a break in the structure along the continuum, in principle compatible with there being only one item in 'The Zone'. There could in principle be many such zones scattered throughout the continuum but I will focus on the first such zone. In Parfit's continuum, we might suppose that The Zone begins around, say, world P and ends around, say, world S (though of course these are arbitrarily selected). I say 'around' because The Zone might in principle be surrounded by indeterminacy. Within The Zone, at least one item is not better than its predecessor and thus the slide to the Repugnant Conclusion is halted. The idea of a structural solution positing a zone of break points is depicted in Figure 14.2.

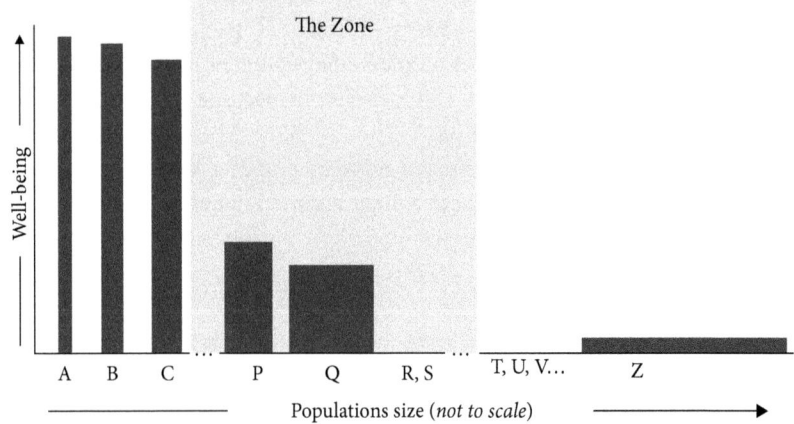

Figure 14.2 The Zone.

that a possible 'solution' according to which every item along the continuum is on a par with its predecessor would count as nonstructural; such a solution strikes me as not plausibly applicable to continua that *prima facie* lead to repugnant conclusions (if A is plausibly on a par with B which is plausibly on a par with C, we would never arrive at the putative repugnant conclusion that Z is better than A or even that Z is on a par with A since betterness is not at issue and parity is nontransitive). Thanks to Jimmy Goodrich for raising this question.

For a structural solution to succeed, it must explain and defend the claim that there must be some world in The Zone— suppose Q—for which it is not true that it is better than its predecessor—P. But there are a number of ways in which this could be so. In the next section, we examine and reject three seemingly natural possibilities.

14.2 Three Standard Structural Solutions to Continua Arguments

14.2.1 Incommensurability

Two items are *incommensurable* with respect to V if there is no common cardinal scale of units by which their *V-ness* can be represented or measured. For example, the pleasure you get from watching a comedic television sitcom cannot plausibly be measured by hedonometers or some unit of well-being that also measures the satisfaction you achieve from attaining a life-long goal of, say, writing a best-selling novel. A cardinal unit of measure can give rise to either a ratio scale, as inches or pounds give rise to a scale of length or weight, or an interval scale, as degrees Fahrenheit or Celsius give rise to a scale of temperature. Two items are incommensurable with respect to V if their *V-ness* cannot be represented by either an interval or ratio scale.

Suppose that P is a world with a large population that is doing just fine— 'middle class' we might say by way of rough (if icky) shorthand. Q is a world with 50% more people all of whom enjoy very slightly less good middle-class lives than those enjoyed by people in P. Suppose now that Q and P are incommensurable with respect to V: there is no cardinal unit of *V-ness* by which we might ascertain that the *V-ness* of world P is 4.56 units worse or .876 times better than the *V-ness* of world Q. Is the slide to the repugnant conclusion thereby blocked?

The answer is a definitive 'no'. One might think that some kind of cardinal scale is required to have trade-offs and that all trade-offs must be conceived in numerical terms. But this is not so. Even if there is no cardinal unit by which achieving a life-long goal better conduces to your well-being than watching your favourite television programme, achieving the life-long goal might be better *ordinally*, that is, by a ranking that does not admit of (nonderivative) cardinal differences in your well-being. Thus while there may be no ratio or interval scale according to which Q might be more V than P, Q might nevertheless be better than P in *V-ness* in a merely ordinal ranking. And if Q is better than P, the slide to the Repugnant Conclusion is not halted since Q is better than P, R is better than Q ... and so on. In short, incommensurability is no solution to continua arguments because incommensurability is compatible with comparability.

This is not to say that incommensurability does not hold in The Zone. It will if there is no numerically specifiable rate of trade-off among the factors that contribute to the comparison of outcomes with respect to V, a condition that will plausibly hold of the continua of interest: could the goodness of the addition of a certain number of good lives really be worth 1.214 times the small drop in the well-being of the entire population? A structural solution to continua arguments, then, should countenance incommensurability in The Zone. But incommensurability itself is a non-starter as a solution to continua arguments.

14.2.2 Incomparability

If Q and P are *incomparable* (with respect to V), then the slide to the Repugnant Conclusion is halted. Is incomparability the right structural response to continua arguments? Some have so suggested (Handfield 2014).[13]

Much turns on how we understand 'incomparability'. We should not, as many economists, philosophers, and decision theorists do, define, or assume incomparability to be the failure of the one item to be better, worse, or as good as the other (with respect to V). As I've argued elsewhere, *which* relations exhaust the conceptual space of comparability between two items is a substantive matter open to debate (Chang 1997, 2002a, 2016a). 'Better than', 'worse than', and 'equally good' are three such relations, but there could be more. So we should instead understand 'incomparability' neutrally—without prejudging what basic, positive value relations exhaust the conceptual space of comparability between two items—as the failure of *any* basic, positive value relation—whichever those might be—to hold between them.

Are Q and P incomparable with respect to V? It is worth noting, as a first pass, that there is a dearth of strong arguments for the existence of incomparability. As I have argued elsewhere, the seven arguments in the extant literature each suffer from compelling problems (Chang 1997). Of course, it does not follow that there is no incomparability, only that establishing incomparability is not as straightforward as it might seem.

Even if incomparability holds between some items, there is good reason to doubt that it holds between Q and P. Suppose that P is a large number of people with middle-class lives. Q is an even larger number of people with slightly less good lives. (It does not matter how we characterize them so long as they conform to the pattern for generating consecutive items on the continuum, viz., a small diminution in quality of V and a large increase in quantity of V relative to its predecessor). Now consider P+ and Q-. P+ is identical to P in quality of lives but identical to Q in the quantity of lives. Q- is identical to Q in quality but identical to P in quantity. See Figure 14.3.

---

[13] Although Handfield (2014) appears to assume that if x and y are neither better than one another nor equally good, they are incomparable, we can excise the implication of incomparability and understand his proposal instead as consistent with the parity solution offered below.

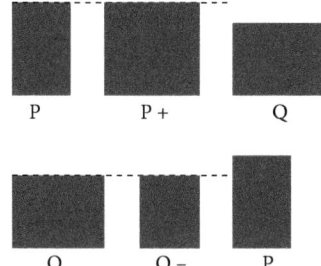

Figure 14.3 Against incomparability.

P+ is comparable with both P and Q: it is better than each of them as it is identical with each in one respect and an enhancement of each in the other respect (modulo organic unities and the like, but in any case they are comparable). Similarly, Q- is comparable with both P and Q—it is worse than both of them since it is identical with each in one respect and a diminution of each in one respect. Both P+ and Q- are each comparable with P and Q. So how could P and Q be incomparable with one another? To think that they could is to deny:

The Small Uni-Dimensional Difference Principle ("Difference Principle"): A small unidimensional (that is, single-factor) evaluative difference between two items cannot trigger incomparability between those items if they are comparable without that difference.[14]

Since P+ differs from Q by a small evaluative difference in one contributory factor and P+ is comparable with P, then according to the principle, a small difference in one contributory factor—the difference between P+ and Q—cannot trigger incomparability where before there was comparability. The same goes for Q-. The argument against incomparability goes as follows:

1. P is comparable with P+ (modulo organic unities and the like, P+ is better since it is evaluatively identical to P in quality but better in quantity).
2. Q differs from P+ by a small evaluative difference in one contributory factor (Q has a slightly lower quality of well-being than P+).
3. Difference Principle: A small evaluative change in one contributory factor cannot trigger incomparability where before there was comparability.
4. Since P is comparable with P+ (by 1), and the difference between P+ and Q is a small evaluative change in one contributory factor (by 2), and a small evaluative change in one contributory factor cannot trigger incomparability where before there was comparability (by 3), P is comparable with Q.
5. Therefore, P and Q are not incomparable.

---

[14] See Chang (2002a), which restricts two ways in which this principle does not universally hold, neither of which are relevant here. The principle does not entail completeness.

The Difference Principle has intuitive support. If the principle did not hold, the continuum would be subject to a very strange pattern of comparison. At the beginning of the continuum, each successor is better than its predecessor. As we progress through the continuum, we reach a zone in which items can no longer be compared with their predecessors. Moving beyond The Zone, the items might then return to the same pattern before, viz., each item is better than its predecessor. The incomparabilist would have us believe that a continuum could display this pattern of comparison even though each item differs from its predecessor in exactly the same way: by only a small diminution in quality and a large enhancement in quantity. A structural solution challenges Uniformity, but incomparability seems like overkill.

There is a further, more theoretical, reason to think that P and Q are not incomparable with respect to V. It would be natural for there to be a correspondence between a comparative relation that holds between two items on a continuum and an appropriate practical response in a choice situation in which V-ness is all that matters and one must choose between those items. Of course, comparative merit and choice need not be so connected, but it would be highly attractive if we could 'read off' an appropriate practical response to two items from their comparative value and *vice versa*. I can think of no reason to doubt that there is such a correspondence.

If there were, then we might imagine a god faced with a choice between possible worlds along the continuum, where *V-ness* is what matters in determining which world to actualize. Since B is better than A, they should actualize B, but since C is better than B, they should actualize C, and so on, working their way through the continuum. Now suppose they reach P, which is better than O, and Q which, by hypothesis, is incomparable with P. Which world should they actualize? If two alternatives are incomparable, there can be no justified choice between them; we are stuck with existential plumping rather than rational choosing. But surely a god's choice of which world to create is guided by the value of the worlds they can create. In any case, we can substitute worlds with humdrum alternatives between which we mere mortals choose in the course of leading rational lives. Our choices along such continuum are not plausibly beyond the scope of justification.

Thus incomparability does not appear to be the right sort of phenomenon to hold in The Zone.[15]

---

[15] For a different argument against incomparability, see Toby Handfield and Wlodek Rabinowicz (2018). I discuss their argument in section 14.4. For an argument as to why rational choice is not possible among incomparables but is among items that are on a par, see Chang (2016b and 2017).

14.2.3 Indeterminacy

We left open in principle the possibility that The Zone, whatever relations may hold within it, could be surrounded by indeterminacy. But what of the suggestion that indeterminacy holds *in* The Zone? The break in the continuum might consist in items that are indeterminately better or worse than or indeterminately equal to or comparable with their immediate predecessors with respect to V (Broome 1997; Qizilbash 2005, 2014; Knapp 2007; Thomas, Chapter 17, this volume). Perhaps The Zone is a zone of indeterminacy.

It is surprisingly difficult to arrive at an uncontroversial definition of indeterminacy (Greenough 2003; Taylor 2018). We do not have to settle the matter here, although as we will see, indeterminacy has one essential feature that will be important for our purposes.

There is a quick argument against indeterminacy as a solution to continua arguments.[16] If classical logic holds, then any structural solution must *deny* that one item on the continuum is better than its predecessor. This is because continua arguments proceed by asserting that each item is better than its predecessor, and so any structural solution must negate this premise, which is equivalent to maintaining that some item is *not better* than its predecessor. Now on a natural assumption (to be questioned later), if one item, say, Q, is *not better* than its predecessor, say, P, it must be incomparable with it, equally as good, or worse. We can dismiss incomparability given the arguments above. We can also dismiss evaluative equality since, presumably, if Q and P are equally good, then we can just increase the quantity of Q more (or diminish its quality less) and end up with an item that is better than P, leaving the continua argument intact. So it seems that the only possibility is that Q is worse than P. But this seems highly implausible. By diminishing the quality of P ever so slightly but enhancing the quantity significantly, could the resulting item really be *worse* than P? The indeterminist 'softens the blow' by offering that Q is not determinately worse than P but only indeterminately worse than P. But it is very unclear how, given that is so implausible that Q is worse than P, adding the thought that it is only indeterminately so makes indeterminacy an attractive solution.

There is a deeper and I think much more interesting problem with the indeterminacy solution. That will be my focus here.

---

[16] Theron Pummer (Chapter 18, this volume) offers some defence against the idea that certain continua arguments, like those that lead to Parfit's Repugnant Conclusion, can be understood as sorites arguments. The arguments explored here, if successful, do the same but indirectly.

We can start by distinguishing two sorts of indeterminacy, although the problem with them will be the same. In semantic indeterminacy (due to vagueness), there is indeterminacy in the application of a predicate; it is indeterminate whether 'bald' applies to Herbert, whose cranial hairs, we can imagine, are spare and non-uniformly distributed. Sometimes this idea is taken to be a matter of the sentence 'Herbert is bald' being neither determinately true nor determinately false, or the idea that 'bald' admits of certain 'tolerances', or that there are multiple legitimate 'sharpenings' of the predicate not all of which agree on whether Herbert is or is not bald, or that Herbert is a 'borderline' case of being bald, and so on.

If it is semantically indeterminate whether Q is better than P with respect to V, there is vagueness somewhere in the predicate 'better than with respect to V' such that the sentence, 'Q is better than P' is semantically indeterminate. And if it is indeterminate whether Q is better than P (and perhaps indeterminate whether R is better than Q, and so on), then, as we go along the continuum, we cannot assert 'Z is better than A' since the chain of betterness inferences has been interrupted, and thus the slide to the Repugnant Conclusion is halted.

In metaphysical indeterminacy, there is indeterminacy in the way the world is rather than in our words. A property or relation, such as identity or part-whole, may indeterminately hold of an item; it may be indeterminate whether, after undergoing fission or some other operation, the resultant person(s) are identical to me, and it may be indeterminate whether this clump of rock in Tanzania is a part of Mount Kilimanjaro. One way of cashing out the idea holds that there are multiple fully determinate worlds, some in which this patch of dirt is part of Mount Kilimanjaro and some in which it is not, but it is indeterminate which world is actual. (Akiba 2004; Barnes 2010; Williams 2010).

If it is metaphysically indeterminate whether Q is better than P, then although in every world it is determinate whether Q is better than P—in some worlds it is and in some worlds it is not—it is indeterminate which of these worlds is actual. If it is indeterminate whether Q is better than P, then Q is not determinately better than P and so gain, it might be thought that the slide to the Repugnant Conclusion is halted.

But indeterminacy—whether due to vagueness in our words or indeterminacy in the facts—does not provide a good structural solution to continua arguments. To see why, we start with semantic vagueness. Due to vagueness in the word 'bald', it is neither true nor false that Herbert is bald. Suppose that we must *resolve* the indeterminacy; we must sort Herbert into one of two camps—the 'bald' or the 'not-bald'—and that this resolution must be based solely on how Herbert stands to the word 'bald'. Extrinsic factors, such as the fact that if you resolve the indeterminacy one way rather than another you will receive Herbert's gratitude, must be put aside. Basing our resolution only on facts about how Herbert stands to the semantic item, 'bald', we can resolve the indeterminacy only *arbitrarily*. We might 'precisify' the word 'bald' to include Herbert or we might not. The precisification we choose must be arbitrarily chosen.¹⁷ In short, we can resolve the matter of whether 'bald' applies to Herbert by the flip of a coin. But it would be odd to think that continua arguments could be defused by making an arbitrary linguistic stipulation (Chang 2001; Schoenfield 2015).¹⁸

The same goes for metaphysical indeterminacy. Suppose it is metaphysically indeterminate whether this clump of rock is part of Mount Kilimanjaro. There are fully determinate worlds in which Kilimanjaro includes within its boundaries the clump of rock and fully determinate worlds in which it does not, but it is indeterminate which world is the actual world. Suppose now that we must draw a map that specifies whether the clump is a part of Mount Kilimanjaro. Again, we stipulate that no extrinsic factors are relevant to the case; we simply need to determine whether this clump of rock is part of Kilimanjaro solely on the basis of the facts about whether the mountain stands in the part-whole relation to the clump of rock. As far as these facts go, there is nothing to be said in favour of drawing the map one way as opposed to another since it is indeterminate whether the clump is a part of the mountain. The resolution of how to draw the map must be *arbitrary*; we are permitted arbitrarily to select a world in which the clump belongs or a world in which it does not belong. Resolution under indeterminacy is, as R.J. Williams puts it, a matter of "randomly and groundlessly" making a judgement call (Williams 2016). In short, whether the clump is a part of Kilimanjaro can be settled with the flip of a coin.

Now consider Parfit's continuum. Q is a world like P except that there are many more people leading slightly less good lives. Is Q better than P with respect to V? The question is a *substantive* one on which we should bring to bear substantive arguments concerning, for instance, the question of whether a doubling in quantity of lives in P more than compensates for the slight loss in quality of life in P. Suppose P is a world of ten million people leading solidly middle-class lives. If we double the number of people and diminish the quality slightly, do we have a better world? This is a question to be argued over by substantive debate—the kind of debate that forms the bread and butter of first-order normative theorizing. It is not a question to be settled by 'random and groundless' fiat. Indeed, if a god had to choose which world to create, it would be odd to think that the choice could be properly resolved by the flip of a coin.

---

¹⁷ Indeterminists who go in for degrees of truth might suggest that it could be 'more true' that Herbert is bald than that he is not bald if, say, there are more sharpenings that favour his being bald. But appealing to a ratio of possible sharpenings to resolve the indeterminacy is to appeal to something extrinsic to the facts about how Herbert stands to the word 'bald', such as 'majority rule'. Moreover, there may still be an arbitrary choice when it is between options whose degree of truth is ½.

¹⁸ In Chapter 17, this volume, Teruji Thomas suggests that we can avoid this difficulty by supposing that each precisification of a value relation such as 'better than' is itself a real relation in the world. This then brings us to the discussion of metaphysical indeterminacy below. My objection there, I believe, applies to Thomas' suggested solution in terms of metaphysical indeterminacy.

Of course, *some* substantive matters are up for arbitrary resolution: if two items are equally good, then a resolution in favour of one can be determined by the flip of a coin. But P and Q are not equally good. If they were, then the continuum argument could be reformulated with Q+, which is better than P, in place of Q. Moreover, a small improvement in one of them need not make it thereby better, which it must if they were equally good (Chang 1997, 2002a).

The problem with indeterminacy as a structural solution to continua arguments is that the question of whether items in The Zone, or for that matter, throughout the continuum, are better than their predecessor is a substantive matter not appropriately resolved by arbitrary stipulation. If we arbitrarily stipulate that Q is not better than P, we are left with 'resolutional remainder'—the substantive question at issue remains open rather than settled (Chang 2002a). Things are different when confronted with indeterminacy; it is always permissible to resolve the indeterminacy arbitrarily.

It might be countered that arbitrarily resolving that, say, Q is better than P leaves resolutional remainder only because it is *important* whether Q is better than P; any appearance that the substantive question has not been settled by an arbitrary fiat is due to uncertainty or anxiety over, for instance, whether one has judged the matter correctly (Williams 2016). Perhaps *any* 'high stakes' case will leave resolutional remainder in the wake of arbitrary judgement (Constantinescu 2012; Williams 2016).

Resolutional remainder is not psychological anxiety over whether one has employed the right epistemic procedure in coming to a judgement nor is it concern about the fact that epistemic peers may arbitrarily resolve the indeterminacy in different ways. It is the normative fact—left in place after arbitrary fiat—that the substantive question of whether Q *is* better than P remains open. And there may be resolutional remainder even when the matter at hand is of low stakes. Suppose you are to judge which of two poems should win the Woodbury Junior High School poetry prize. Perhaps one poem has great rhythm while the other has an arresting tone. If you flip a coin to decide between them, the substantive question of which is better is not thereby settled. Or you might have to adjudicate the relative aesthetic merits of two tea services, one delicate and muted while the other is graphic and bold. If you arbitrarily stipulate that one is more beautiful, you do not thereby settle the question of which is in fact more beautiful—the question remains. You may, of course, arbitrarily stipulate that one is more beautiful than the other on extrinsic grounds—you do not want to waste time working out the substantive truth of the matter—and 'settle' the question in a pragmatic sense. But the substantive issue on the merits remains.

The indeterminist might now shift his position, accepting that it is not only high stakes cases that involve resolutional remainder but insisting that *any normative* case will have resolutional remainder after arbitrary resolution (where equality does not hold) (Constantinescu 2012). Normative questions—

apart from cases of equality—are not the sort of questions that can be resolved by arbitrary stipulation. Another way to put this point, borrowing from Gallie (1956), is to say that semantic questions about the application of normative predicates and metaphysical questions about the normative facts are *essentially contested* matters that are by their nature always open to substantive debate. Arbitrary stipulation, will thus always leave resolutional remainder. But notice that if the indeterminist maintains that there can be indeterminacy about normative matters, such as whether Q is better than P, they have shifted ground by abandoning indeterminacy as it is usually understood. It is essential to indeterminacy, whether semantic or metaphysical, that there can be arbitrary—'random and groundless'— resolution among the permissible ways of resolving the indeterminacy. The permissibility of arbitrary resolution is essential to what indeterminacy *is*.

None of this is to say that normative matters are never vague. It is plausibly vague whether certain things are good—is a life filled with a great deal of suffering and a single moderate achievement a good one? Exactly where we 'draw the line' of a good life may be an arbitrary matter. The same goes for many normative predicates; is a shiny beetle beautiful? And, although a trickier matter, there might also be indeterminacy in normative comparisons. It could be indeterminate which of two poems is better; the poems might be identical but for an extra comma that alters the rhythm very slightly—making it not better or worse but just very slightly different. It could be perfectly in order arbitrarily to resolve the indeterminacy by stipulating that one is better. The same goes for 'high stakes' cases, although examples of such cases will be more controversial because of the 'noise' created by their importance. Indeterminacy in comparison most plausibly holds only if the items are extremely similar in all contributory factors, and yet the difference is so marginal as to make it indeterminate what relation holds. Items on a continuum do not follow this paradigm; while appearing similar in quality, they are very different in quantity.

I suggest that indeterminacy, like incomparability, is not the right sort of phenomenon to defuse continua arguments.

14.3 Parfit's Solution: Imprecise Lexicality

Some philosophers have suggested that the solution to Parfit's continua argument lies in lexicality: there is a point along the continuum at which an item is lexically superior to each of its successors. At that point, we reach a threshold quality of life such that any diminution in that quality, however small (but not diminishingly so), makes the outcome inferior, no matter the number, even a googol, of people living that quality of life. So, for example, you might think that a world with a sufficient number of people enjoying an upper-class life, say, with the music of Beethoven and the artwork of Picasso, is lexically superior to any number of people leading middle-class lives, say, with the music of Supertramp and some stellar limericks. Or that a world with a sufficient number of people living at subsistence is lexically superior to a world with any number of people living lives below subsistence. Any drop from an upper-class life to a middle-class life, or from subsistence to below subsistence, is so significant a qualitative difference that it marks a lexicality: no number of lives at the lower quality of life can be better (or equal) to a sufficient number of lives at the higher quality.

The trouble with lexicality is a specific version of the problem already encountered in thinking that there could be a single break point along the continuum: it is hard to believe that there is a point on the continuum which is better than all possible successors. Suppose that P is such a point. We can imagine a world, Q, which involves a small diminution in quality of life relative to P and an enormous increase in the number of people leading such lives. It would be hard to maintain that P is better than Q let alone that P is *lexically* better than Q—i.e., that P would be better even if there were any, even a googol, number of people leading lives at the slightly lesser quality of life. For any putative point of lexical superiority, it seems that we can generate an item that involves a small diminution in quality of life and a large enhancement in quantity such that it would be hard to believe that the first is lexically superior to the second. It is this implausibility that has led most to abandon lexicality as a solution to continua arguments.[19]

Parfit (2016) offers an ingenious response on behalf of lexicalists. His defence of lexicality starts with a distinction between two kinds of comparability—precise and imprecise. When things can be compared precisely, there is a cardinal unit—analogous to inches or degrees Celsius—by which you can measure the goodness of each item. In other words, precisely comparable items are commensurable—there is a cardinal scale by which the values of the two items can be measured. When things can only be compared imprecisely, by contrast, there is no 'precise' cardinal unit (or level) by which their value can be measured. Perhaps there is an 'imprecise' cardinal unit, or, what might amount to the same thing: an imprecise cardinal scale with 'units' perhaps given by interval ranges or something like probability distributions, which measures the value of items. Imprecisely comparable items are incommensurable but comparable. Parfit did not put things quite this way. He talked instead of a linear scale of value, like a number line, and suggested that imprecisely comparable items cannot be put on such a scale.[20] It is

---

[19] Note that if the arguments in the previous section are correct, an appeal to indeterminacy will not help the lexicalist with this difficulty.

[20] Here is what Parfit writes: "Many people assume that, when there are truths about the relative goodness of different things, these truths must be precise, though we may not know what these truths are. There is one way of thinking which can make this seem the only possible view. If things of some kind can be better or worse than others, and by more or less, it may seem that the goodness of these things corresponds to their positions on some line or scale of value. On this *Linear Model*, truths about goodness must be precise because positions on a line are precise... But when two things

not entirely clear whether Parfit meant to include mere ordinality within imprecise comparability—perhaps merely ordinal rankings are the most imprecise rankings of all—but for present purposes we can set mere ordinality aside since it is not relevant to Parfit's solution. We can think of Parfit as offering *six* ways two things could be (more-than-merely-ordinally) comparable: precisely better, precisely worse, precisely equal, imprecisely better, imprecisely worse, and imprecisely equal. Whether we have precise comparability or imprecise (sometimes he called it 'rough'; Parfit 1984: 461) comparability depends entirely on whether there is a cardinal ratio or interval scale by which the value of the two items can be measured.

Parfit thought that lexicality is the right sort of solution to the continua argument he made famous, but not lexicality as it is ordinarily understood. Assuming precision in comparisons, if P is lexically superior to Q, there is some number representing the value of P (or more accurately, some function unique up to affine transformations), say 100, such that a diminution in the quality of life in Q, however small, cannot be compensated for by an increase in the quantity of such lives in Q, no matter how large. But how could this be, Parfit thought, if, as is plausible, the addition of lives worth living in Q each adds value to Q? With enough such lives, Q's value should surpass 100. The same holds for any putative point of lexicality. Parfit thought that the presumed precision is the problem.

---

are qualitatively very different, that could not be true. So when we think about the goodness of such things, we should reject this Linear Model. Nor could the goodness of such things correspond to different real numbers, since such numbers are also precise. Nor could some of these things be better than others by some imprecise amount or to some imprecise degree, since the concepts of an amount or a degree also imply precision. We should think only about *differences* between the value of these things, since the concept of a difference does not imply precision" (Parfit 2016: 114). It is perhaps worth noting that from conversations with Parfit over the years, it became clear to me that Parfit's key point in introducing imprecise or rough comparability was that the value of an individual item could not be located on a linear scale of value. This seems to me a very important point and can be captured by the idea of items being incommensurable. The last two sentences of Parfit's explanation may seem jarring to the reader as Parfit moves from a claim about measuring the goodness of individual items to a claim about *differences* between items. When Parfit was preparing for his Schock Prize lecture, he asked me whether I thought he should add in this chapter reference to *differences* between items since he knew that I understood the related idea of 'parity' in terms of evaluative differences. I urged him to do so in order to (i) make clear that his concern was not with mere ordinality, (ii) move imprecise comparability away from the difficult idea of 'imprecise' cardinal units, and (iii) bring the idea of imprecise equality closer to parity. Still, for Parfit, the foundational idea concerns how to represent the value of individual items, and the upshots for evaluative differences come down the road. I have suggested that this explanatory priority should be reversed: we should understand comparisons between incommensurables in terms of features of the *differences* between items first, and what follows about how to represent the value of individual items being compared is of less importance. I explore other differences between parity and imprecise equality in Chang (2016c), the main one being that Parfit is still thinking 'trichotmously', i.e., that 'better than', 'worse than', and 'equally good' form the foundation of comparisons, while I favour 'tetrachotomy', to be explored below.

Once we give up the idea that the value of P could be represented by some number on a cardinal scale, we can save lexicality.[21]

We should, Parfit argues, understand comparisons along the continuum as *imprecise* rather than precise. As we move along the continuum, each item is imprecisely better than its predecessor. Eventually we reach a point, P, which, while imprecisely better than its predecessor, O, is also *imprecisely lexically better* than every item beyond The Zone—U, V...Z. An item *x* is imprecisely lexically better than an item *y* just in case *x* is imprecisely better than *y* and no increase in the quantity of *y*, even a googol, could change this fact. But the transition from P, the lexically superior item, to U, a lexically inferior item, is not implausibly abrupt. In between, there are a number of items comprising The Zone in which each item is *imprecisely equally as good* as its predecessor. Thus, there is a gradual transition from P, the lexical threshold, to U, the first item beyond The Zone, through a series of items that are imprecisely equally as good as their immediate predecessor. And, Parfit adds, there can be indeterminacy around The Zone. Since the chain of betterness is broken, the slide to the Repugnant Conclusion is halted. Parfit's solution is depicted in Figure 14.4.

There are two worries we might have about Parfit's solution.

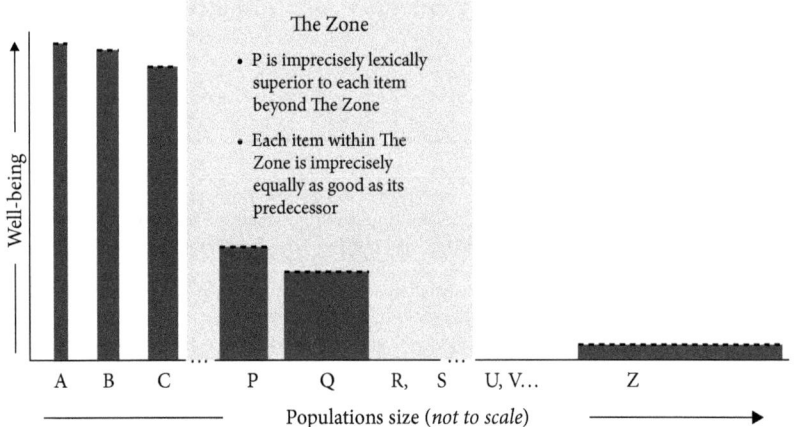

Figure 14.4 Parfit's Imprecise Lexicality Solution.

---

[21] Parfit rejects the idea that each additional life in Q has diminishing marginal value because he holds what he calls the 'Simple View': "Anyone's existence is in itself good if this person's life is worth living. Such goodness has non-diminishing value, so if there were more such people, the combined goodness of their existence would have no upper limit" (Parfit 2016: 112). But we could modify the Simple View to be more plausible and understand it as the claim that the addition of each life worth living adds overall value to an outcome without insisting that the value is non-diminishing. In that case, while each additional life in Q adds overall value, the V-ness of Q might only asymptotically approach the value of P. Insofar as this possibility is plausible, it may remove some of the motivation for Parfit's introduction of imprecision to save lexicality. (Indeed, when Parfit first introduces the Simple View, he describes it in a way that is compatible with diminishing marginal value: he writes: "On what I shall call

First, it is unclear how an appeal to imprecise equality helps Parfit's lexical solution. If imprecise equality is a form of equality (equality without precise cardinal measurability) just as imprecise betterness is a form of betterness (betterness without precise cardinal measurability), then for each item in The Zone of imprecise equality, we can presumably improve the item sufficiently to achieve imprecise betterness. If R is imprecisely equally as good as Q, then why not just make sufficient improvements to R so that R+ is now better than Q? We could then reconstitute the continuum with R+ instead of R. The Zone of imprecise equality would then become The Zone of betterness. But if P is imprecisely lexically superior to every item beyond The Zone, then the other members of The Zone, Q, R, and S, each of which is, by hypothesis, better than its predecessor, must also be lexically superior to every item beyond The Zone since each is better than P. Once again, we are left with an implausibly abrupt transition from an item, S (the last item in The Zone), that is putatively imprecisely lexically superior to its successor, T (the first item beyond The Zone). In this way, Parfit's appeal to imprecision may not avoid the original difficulty with a precise lexical solution. If Parfit's solution is to succeed, it must do so by relying on the claim that there is at least one item, S, that is imprecisely lexically superior to its successor, T. That is how the continuum argument can be stopped.[22] Whether the solution is plausible will then turn on whether imprecise lexicality is plausible.[23]

The second worry concerns the scope of Parfit's solution. If imprecise lexicality and imprecise equality exist and are not a mere chimera, *some* continua arguments could surely be constructed that surreptitiously exploit this fact, and thus pointing out an imprecise lexical threshold with a buffer zone of imprecisely equally good items could defuse such arguments. But lexicality, whether precise or imprecise, as a solution to continua arguments has limited scope. This is because lexicality is a very strong condition, and continua arguments can be generated without it.

---

the Simple View: Anyone's existence is in itself good, and makes the world in one way better, if this person's life is good to live, or worth living" (p. 110).) For a useful discussion of diminishing marginal value in the context of thinking about continuum arguments, see Arrhennius and Rabinowicz (2005). Yet another, perhaps less plausible, possibility here is that the increase in overall value of each additional life beyond a certain point is infinitesimal.

[22] In this way, I believe that Rabinowicz's characterization of Parfit's solution as one according to which none of the usual trichotomy of relations 'better than', 'worse than', or 'equally good' holds— what he calls 'incommensurability'—is potentially misleading. Instead, we might understand Rabinowicz' solution as an argument in support of the parity solution. See Rabinowicz, Chapter 15, this volume. I discuss Rabinowicz' solution in fn 41 below, though it deserves a fuller discussion than I can give it here.

[23] In the alternative, Parfit might allow, as he sometimes seems to suggest (Parfit 2016, 120), that *every* item beyond The Zone is imprecisely equally as good as its predecessor; that is, that The Zone occupies all worlds of the continuum after the world that provides the threshold of lexical superiority. But this suggestion, too, leaves Parfit with a sharp boundary between P, which is by hypothesis lexically superior to all subsequent items in the continuum, and Q, which is only imprecisely equally as good as P but not lexically superior to R.

Parfit's argument begins with a world, A, with a large number of people living excellent lives and ends up with a world, Z, with a googol people leading lives barely worth living. What gives the appearance that lexicality is relevant to avoiding the Repugnant Conclusion is that it is plausible to think that A is lexically superior to Z—it does not matter how many people there are with lives barely worth living, a world with a sufficient number of exquisite lives will always be better. The same goes for the Rachels/Temkin continua arguments involving pain—a sufficient amount of torture is plausibly lexically inferior to any number of years of mosquito bites—and Quinn's self-torturer argument—mild pain for any length of time is plausibly lexically superior to some period of excruciating pain. Apparent lexicality between the first and last items on the continuum has been so common a feature of continua arguments that some authors treat it as a fixed feature of such arguments (Handfield and Rabinowicz 2018).

Might it be possible to generate continua arguments without apparent lexicality? One strategy might be to take standard continua and simply remove all items that appear to stand in lexical relations. In some cases, there would be nothing left, if, for instance, each item on the continuum represents one seemingly lexical superior item relative to its successor. In most cases, however, a continuum could remain that leads to a false, if perhaps not repugnant, conclusion. Continua leading to false conclusions need avoiding, too. So appeals to lexicality will not help. Once we recognize that we need some other solution for such continua arguments, we might also see that this alternative solution holds even for continua where there is apparent lexicality. Or so I will suggest in the final section.

It is difficult to generate continua that *clearly* lead to false conclusions while at the same time not relying on lexicality because all such continua trade on controversial substantive claims. But we can offer an example and an abstract argument for thinking that such continua exist.

Suppose world A_1 contains 1000 people leading upper-class lives. Its successor, A_2, involves a slight diminution in quality of life but also one extra life. If the diminution is sufficiently small, it can be traded off against the value of a whole extra life. Everyone in A_2 leads nearly as good lives as they do in A_1, and there is a whole extra person enjoying that excellent level of well-being. Thus, we suppose, A_2 is better than A_1. (If you don't agree, jigger the numbers until you do.[24]) A_3 then involves a slight diminution in the quality of life in A_2 and the addition of another life such that A_3 is better than A_2. The same for A_4 until we arrive at A_{50}, which involves, suppose, 1050 people leading lower-class lives. In fifty small steps

---

[24] Jiggering the numbers in any way will not necessarily lead to a plausible continuum argument, however. My claim is existential; there are plausibly *some* continua arguments that don't involve even apparent lexicality between the first and last items of the continua.

we move from an upper-class to a lower-class quality of life, but with each successive world containing an extra life. Since the change in quality of lives is so slight, each successor is better than its predecessor. By the transitivity of 'better than with respect to V', 1050 people leading lower-class lives is better than 1000 people leading upper-class lives. While perhaps not exactly repugnant, the conclusion seems false. Could fifty extra people leading lower-class lives make A_{50} better than a world where nearly everyone is leading significantly better upper-class lives? Suppose our covering consideration, V, is beneficence. It seems more beneficent for a god to create world A_1 with 1000 people leading excellent upper-class lives than to create world A_{50}, a world with an extra fifty people but everyone leading much worse lower-class lives. Nonetheless, it does not seem correct to think that A_1 is lexically superior to A_{50}; a sufficiently large, perhaps a googol, number of people leading lower-class lives might be thought to be clearly better than a mere 1000 people leading upper-class lives. A god would be elitist to think otherwise. If these claims are correct, we have a continua argument leading to a false conclusion but no lexicality between the any of the items along the continuum.

There is a general, abstract argument for thinking that there are many such continua, despite the fact that any given continuum will be open to challenge and controversy. Suppose a covering consideration, V, admits of hierarchical categories of quality of V-ness. Take, for instance, the very general categories of quality: excellent, very good, good, mediocre, and poor—most naturally understood as occupying some region on some (perhaps imprecise) cardinal scale. Some things might be of an excellent quality with respect to V while others might be a poor quality with respect to V. Now perhaps some sufficient amount of the excellent will be lexically superior to some amount of the poor; that is, a sufficient amount of the excellent will always be better than any, even a googol, amount of the poor (though the plausibility of this will depend on the 'V' at stake). But it is less plausible to think that a sufficient amount of the excellent will always be superior to any amount of the very good or the mediocre. Lexicality does not plausibly hold between the excellent, on the one hand, and the very good or even the mediocre, on the other.

When a continuum is generated by having successive items move from one qualitative category to a hierarchically near one, lexicality is less plausible. At the same time, such a continuum could plausibly lead to a false conclusion, e.g., some relatively large quantity of mediocrity is better than some sufficiently small quantity of excellence. These considerations suggest that, insofar as there are many such Vs with hierarchical qualitative categories, there could be many continua arguments that do not involve apparent lexicality. Thus Parfit's solution, even if successful, will not provide an answer to the general problem raised by continua arguments.

14.4 Parity

I propose that we avoid false and repugnant conclusions from continua arguments by recognizing that each item in The Zone is *on a par* with its predecessor.[25] 'On a par' is a fourth positive value relation beyond the usual trichotomy of 'better than', 'worse than', and 'equally good' that can hold between two items with respect to V. It is nontransitive (if x is on a par with y with respect to V and y is on a par with z with respect to V, it does not follow that x is on a par with z with respect to V), symmetric (if x is on a par with y then y is on a par with x), and irreflexive (x is not on a par with itself; x is equally V as itself). According to the parity solution, we can defuse continua arguments leading to false or repugnant conclusions by allowing that somewhere along the continuum, there is a zone of items in which each item is on a par with its predecessor. Because the chain of betterness is broken by parity, we avoid the conclusion that the last item is better than the first. The Parity Solution is depicted in Figure 14.5.

If parity holds, then we must reject what I have elsewhere called 'Trichotomy':

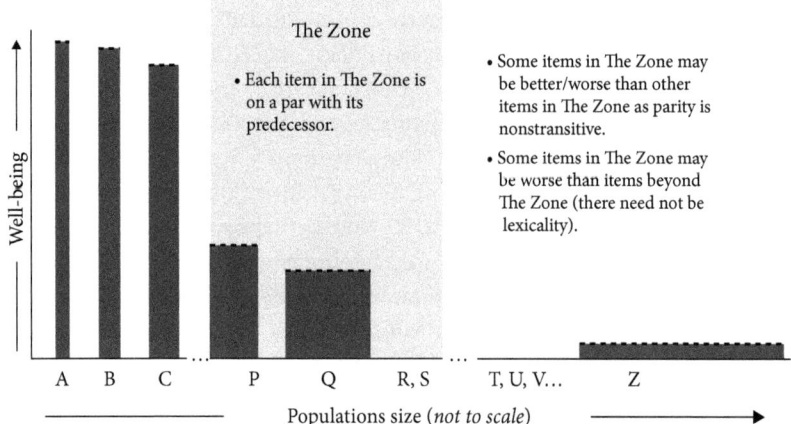

Figure 14.5 The Parity Solution.

---

[25] Mozaffar Qizilbash (2007) proposes that 'parity' can be a solution to Parfit's Repugnant Conclusion argument, but what he means by 'parity' is what most would consider 'incomparability'. So, for example, he urges that the 'mark' of parity is susceptibility to the 'Small Improvement Argument', but that argument was first used to establish what many consider incomparability, that is, the failure of any of the usual trichotomy of positive value relations to hold. Without argument that this trichotomy fails to exhaust the space of comparability between items, what he calls the 'mark' of parity in fact is the 'mark' of incomparability. Joseph Raz (1986), for instance, thinks that this is so. Qizilbash instead defines 'incomparability' as holding when no matter how much we improve one of two incomparable items, neither will be better than the other (p. 134). But this is an implausible account of incomparability. Most incomparabilists would want to allow that although a mediocre musician and a mediocre physicist may be incomparable in creativity, improve the creativity of the physicist enough, and the resulting Einstein will be more creative than the musician.

Trichotomy: If two items can be compared with respect to some V, one must be better or worse than the other or the two must be equally good. So if none of these relations holds, the items are incomparable with respect to V.

We should instead accept 'Tetrachotomy':

Tetrachotomy: If two items can be compared with respect to some V, one must be better or worse than the other, the two must be equally good, or they must be on a par with one another. So if none of these relations holds, the items are incomparable with respect to V.

If parity is the right solution to continua arguments, then we have misunderstood the structure of value—and of normativity more generally. Values do not have the same structure as nonevaluative considerations and nor can their qualitative dimensions be resolved or represented in terms of the trichotomy of better, worse, and equal, whether precise or imprecise. Moreover, just as values can stand in parity relations, so too can reasons—reasons can be stronger, weaker, and equally as strong as one another but they can also be on a par. This has implications for normative theories—consequentialism, certain forms of deontology, virtue theory, perfectionism, and pluralism—that implicitly assume trichotomy among their elements in answering the question of how one ought to live. I have argued for the possibility of parity and its intuitiveness, suggested an informal model of it, and given examples of the work it can do elsewhere (Chang 1997, 2002a, 2016a, 2017). I have also distinguished parity from imprecise equality (Chang 2016c). I will not repeat those arguments here. Instead, I want to suggest answers to two questions: (1) *Why* should we think that parity solution holds as opposed to any other structural solution? And, (2) *How*, on a tetrachotomous view of value, could parity hold?

Why should we think the parity solution holds? As already noted, Trichotomy is not definitional of our ordinary notion of comparability but a substantive thesis that must be won by argument. Since our concept of comparability leaves open the possibility of a fourth basic value relation, then the arguments of this chapter can be seen to comprise an argument for parity by elimination: incommensurability, incomparability, indeterminacy, and lexical imprecision are not good solutions to continua arguments and so we are left with the parity solution. And if parity is a better solution than the others, we should, as far as structural solutions go, opt for parity as the best way to defuse continua arguments.

Is parity a better solution? There is a significant reason to think that parity *is* better than the other solutions. Parity is the only structural solution that can respect the compelling intuition that lies at the heart of continua arguments, namely:

Compensation: A small diminution in quality can be compensated for by a large enhancement in quantity.[26]

Compensation explains why, when we slightly diminish the quality of lives in a world but significantly enhance the quantity of such lives, we end up with a world that seems better than its predecessor. It is the pre-theoretic and intuitive idea that when we start with something and we diminish it in one way, we can bring it up to at least where it was before without removing it from the sphere of comparability with how it was with the diminishment.

Suppose you make a mean chocolate cake. Your recipe calls for a teaspoon of pure vanilla extract but you are all out. You could compensate for the diminution in the tastiness of the cake that results from the lack of vanilla by adding orange essence instead. You succeed in compensating for the diminution in taste by making the cake not worse than it was before but still comparable with the tried and true version. In the same way, continua arguments crucially rely on this intuitive idea of compensation. A diminution in quality of lives can be compensated by a sufficient increase in quantity of such lives, making the new item, B not worse and still comparable with A. Most continua arguments assume that the way a sufficient quantity compensates for a diminution in quality is by making the item *better*. Iterated application of the principle gives rise to continua arguments. Without Compensation, we could not have Parfit's (or Rachels', Temkin's, Quinn's, etc.) continua argument. But making *better* is only one way in which enhancing the quantity can compensate for a loss in quality.

The intuitive strength of Compensation makes the problem posed by continua arguments deep and difficult. A solution that allows us to keep the principle while still avoiding false or repugnant conclusions is significantly better than ones that require us to reject it. As it turns out, only parity allows us to maintain Compensation while incomparability, indeterminacy, and imprecise lexicality require us to reject it. If this is right, the mistaken assumption of continua

---

[26] A generalized version would hold that a small diminution in one contributory factor can be compensated for by a large enhancement in another. Neither the original nor the generalized versions necessarily hold *tout court*—for example, a small diminution in a very significant contributory factor may not always be compensable by a large increase in a very insignificant one and there is always the further possibility of organic unities—but the principles must be plausible in the context of generating continua arguments since they are what permit the generation of problematic continua upon which such arguments rely. Of course, a competing compensation principle might hold that enough of an enhancement in quantity can always compensate by making the enhanced item *better*, which would preclude the first advantage of the parity solution discussed below. But such a principle is arguably false; to take just one possible case, a doubling in some number of crummy lives is not obviously better than that number of lives only slightly worse in quality. At any rate, for continua arguments to be as strong as possible, they must appeal to principles that are as plausible and widely applicable as possible. Compensation, as I understand it, holds that a sufficiently enhanced quantity can always make a small diminution in quality *not worse and still comparable*. Thanks to Jimmy Goodrich and Theron Pummer for inviting me to say more about why I understand Compensation as I do.

arguments is Trichotomy. Once we abandon Trichotomy for Tetrachotomy, we can defuse continua arguments while maintaining Compensation.

Consider world A with, say, 1000 people leading upper-class lives. To mark the quality of their lives, we can call it '100', though nothing of cardinal significance should be attached to this number. We might represent A as (100, 1000), where the first number in the ordered pair represents the quality of V-ness and the second the quantity of V-ness.

Now consider world B, which is identical to A except for a slight diminution in quality. We might represent B as (99, 1000). B – (99, 1000)—is worse than A – (100, 1000)—since it is identical in all respects and worse in one (we can assume that a Pareto criterion holds in the case). Thus the *relative position* of B to A is that the former is worse. By Compensation, we should be able to improve B's relative position to A by compensating for the small diminution in quality by a large enhancement in quality.

According to Trichotomy, there are only two ways we can do this. We can compensate, that is improve the relative position of B to A, by making B equally as good as A or by making it better.

Consider B+, which we might represent as (99, 1500). Suppose, for the sake of argument, that B+ is equally as good as A. (Note that nothing turns on whether there is such a B+). But if there is some enhancement in quantity that makes B equally as good as A, we can always find a larger enhancement that makes it better. Any improvement in an item that is equally as good as another makes it better. So we might have B++, which is represented as (99, 1501). B++ is better than A. In this way, Compensation in conjunction with Trichotomy allows us to generate a continuum of items, each of which is better than its predecessor, until we end up with an item at the end of the continuum which is clearly not better than the first. It is this trichotomous form of compensation that generates continua that lead to false or repugnant conclusions.

If, however, we reject Trichotomy and adopt Tetrachotomy, we can avoid the problems posed by continua arguments. According to Tetrachotomy, there are *three* ways an enhancement in quantity can compensate for a diminution in quality: it can make an item equally good, better, or *on a par*. We deny that there is B+ that is equally as good as A and maintain that both B+ and B++ are on a par with A. The enhancement in quantity compensates for the loss in quality not by making the item equal or better but by making it on a par. We improve the relative position of B to A changing it from being worse to being on a par. And if B is on a par with A, the chain of betterness is broken and the slide to a false or repugnant conclusion is halted. Thus the parity solution allows us to defuse continua arguments while maintaining the principle of Compensation.

The incomparability solution requires us to reject Compensation because it holds that when we reach The Zone, the enhancement in quantity does *not* compensate; instead an item becomes incomparable with its predecessor—there is *no* positive relation that holds between them.²⁷ The same holds for indeterminacy; there is no compensation, only an indeterminate failure of compensation. Imprecise lexicality also denies that Compensation holds throughout the continuum; at some point an item will be lexically superior to all items beyond The Zone—indeed, an increase in quantity expressly *fails* to compensate for a drop in quality for that is what it is to be lexically inferior. Finally, although incommensurability, since it is compatible with betterness, allows Compensation to hold throughout the continuum, it is a non-starter because it makes no progress whatsoever in providing a solution to continua arguments. Only parity allows us both to maintain Compensation and to defuse continua arguments. In this way, parity is superior to any of its structural rivals. We thus have strong reason to prefer it.

But we haven't yet explained *how* parity might hold. To see how items in The Zone could be on a par, we need to step back and examine value as seen through tetrachotomous eyes. Doing so will have an important upshot: it allows us to see how the parity solution provides theoretical underpinning for a common, 'on the street', untutored response that many have to continua arguments.²⁸

On a trichotomous view, values can be understood as dividing into 'categories', 'levels', 'divisions', 'leagues', and so on—for example, 'outstanding', 'excellent', 'very good', 'good', 'mediocre', 'poor'—where each category occupies some rough region on a trichotomous, hierarchical, perhaps imprecise, cardinal or ordinal scale. With respect to justice, something can be excellent or poor; with respect to tastiness, fantastic or mediocre; with respect to beneficence, great or just okay. There will be multiple ways to carve up categories of V-ness, but crucially categories are hierarchically related as better, worse, or equal to one another— the fantastic is a better category of V-ness than the okay, which is better than the terrible (e.g., Andreou 2015). This way of thinking about values is, I believe, mistaken.

Rather than think of values as dividing into hierarchical categories, we should instead think of them as demarcated by different *neighbourhoods* of V-ness. According to a tetrachotomous view of value, values can be marked out by different neighbourhoods of that value. When we understand values as falling into neighbourhoods, as opposed to hierarchical categories of value, we focus not on the amount or extent or degree of V-ness, as categories suggest, but rather on the *significance* of V-ness. Values have different 'significances', that is, there are ways of being V-significant, and these need not be hierarchically ordered as better, worse, or equal to one another. Neighbourhoods or 'significances' do not occupy regions of a trichotomous cardinal or ordinal scale of value. They are distinct ways

---

²⁷ It would be like trying to compensate for the lack of vanilla by adding a ton of cement instead, turning the product into something arguably incomparable in tastiness with the cake-without-vanilla.
²⁸ From unscientific polling of non-philosophers and philosophers alike.

in which a value can have evaluative significance that need not be better, worse, or equal to one another but can be on a par.

Consider, by way of analogy, literal neighbourhoods—the kind in which people live. Surely with respect to being a good place to live, some neighbourhoods are better than others. Hunts Point in the South Bronx is worse than Hell's Kitchen in New York City. Moreover, some neighbourhoods will be excellent, while others only mediocre. But many neighborhoods are not so hierarchically structured. Is the Upper West Side better, worse, or equally as good as Soho? (To convince yourself that they are not equally good, just run the Small Improvement Argument—adding an extra coffee bar makes a neighbourhood better, but adding an extra coffee bar to the Upper West Side does not make it better than Soho.) Neighborhoods are often just *different* with respect to being a good place to live without being representable as occupying hierarchical regions on a cardinal scale. I suggest that the right thing to say is that, with respect to being a good place to live, Soho and the Upper West Side are *on a par*. Different neighbourhoods can represent different ways in which being a good place to live has evaluative significance without one significance being better than another.

The demarcation of neighbourhoods is a profoundly tricky matter (and of course could be vague), but for our purposes, we can dodge this question (nothing I say below about neighbourhoods below presupposes that they are not vague or indeterminate in some other way) and focus instead on how neighbourhoods might help support the parity solution.[29]

Neighbourhoods allow us to vindicate a common intuitive response to continua arguments. It is natural to think that continua arguments go wrong because they ride roughshod over what is clearly a qualitative change along the continuum. The quality of items at the beginning and end of the continuum are very different, so there must be some qualitative shift somewhere along the continuum that explains why it is no longer true that an item is better than its predecessor.

One way to flesh out this intuition is to think that the qualitative shift is a change in the *quality of V-ness*; we move, for example, from upper-class qualities of life to middle-class ones, and somehow that shift explains why the continuum argument is mistaken. The trouble with this way of understanding the intuition is that it runs afoul of *Compensation*, according to which every small diminution in quality can be compensated for by a large increase in quantity. As we slowly diminish the quality of lives from upper-class ones to middle-class ones, each diminution can be compensated by an increase in quality. Under the assumption of Trichotomy, the compensation makes the item better than its predecessor. So an appeal to the change in *quality* of V-ness—from upper-class quality lives to

---

[29] Neighbourhoods should *not* be understood as clumpy regions on a trichotomously ordered scale of value (for understandings of parity along these tricthomous lines, see Hsieh 2005 and Andreou 2015).

middle- or even lower-class quality lives—does not vindicate the intuition; on the contrary it allows the continua argument to proceed as usual.

If instead we understand the intuitive response as one about *neighbourhoods* of value, that is, as noting a qualitative change in the *significance* of V-ness as we move along the continuum, and we accept Tetrachotomy instead of Trichotomy, we can vindicate the intuition and defuse the argument.

At the beginning of the continuum, we have items each of which involves a large number of people leading upper-class lives. Although each successive item involves a slight diminution in quality, the resulting lives are still upper-class and all such items belong to the same neighbourhood of V-ness, what we might call the 'large numbers of upper-class lives' neighbourhood. Note that this neighbourhood is marked by both quantities and qualities of life—the number of lives must be large and the quality must be upper-class. As we progress through the continuum, eventually we come upon a different neighbourhood of V-ness, where we have significantly larger numbers of people with middle-class lives, what we might call the 'very large numbers of middle-class lives' neighbourhood. Again each of those items, although involving successively slight diminutions in quality, are nevertheless middle-class lives and in very large quantities. By hypothesis, as we move along the continuum, each item is better than its predecessor. By the transitivity of betterness, every item in the 'very large numbers of middle-class lives' neighbourhood is better than every item in the 'large numbers of upper-class lives' neighbourhood. We can account for this fact by noting that the former neighbourhood is better than the latter. If a god had to create either a world from the 'large number of upper-class lives' neighbourhood or a world from the 'very large numbers of middle-class lives' neighbourhood, they should create a world from the second neighbourhood, since the neighbourhood, and consequently all worlds belonging to it, are better than all of those belonging to the first.

Thus, if one neighbourhood is better than another, then all items belonging to the better neighbourhood are better than all items in the worse neighbourhood. Think of the analogue with a necessarily hierarchical category: every item belonging to the category of the 'excellent' will be better than every item belonging to the category of the 'mediocre'. Neighbourhoods can, but crucially need not, be hierarchical; they can be on a par. This means that if two neighbourhoods are on a par, then every item belonging to the one neighbourhood is on a par with every item belonging to the other.

Now as we progress further along the continuum, we might reach another neighbourhood, the 'extremely large numbers of lower-class lives' neighbourhood that is once again, suppose, hierarchically related to the previous two neighbourhoods by being better. Of course, you might disagree with this evaluation—the substantive judgements about these neighbourhoods are subject to dispute and will depend upon various factors including the role of perfectionism in V-ness.

What is important is the thought that eventually we will reach a neighbourhood that is not better than its predecessor neighbourhood but on a par with it.

Let us suppose that following the 'extremely large numbers of lower-class lives' neighbourhood, we reach the 'vast numbers of lives-at-subsistence' neighbourhood and that those neighbourhoods are on a par. In the 'vast numbers of lives-at-subsistence' neighbourhood, each person has a life worth living but has only the minimum needed to survive in an industrialized Western democracy—in 2016, the U.S. Department of Labor estimated this to be an annual income of $12,228.[30] Vast numbers of such people mark an evaluative significance that is not better than the significance marked by extremely large people enjoying lower-class lives, but on a par with it. If the neighbourhoods are on a par, then every item belonging to the 'extremely large numbers of lower-class lives' neighbourhood is on a par with every item belonging to the 'vast numbers of lives-at-subsistence' neighbourhood. And since they are, by hypothesis, adjacent neighbourhoods, the last item in the former neighbourhood will be on a par with first item in the latter neighbourhood. We can allow, moreover, that neighbourhoods overlap; it may be indeterminate where one neighbourhood ends and another begins; nonetheless, adjacent items can still be on a par since the neighbourhoods are on a par.[31] We thus have two adjacent items that are on a par; the one item is not better than its predecessor. Hence the slide to the false or repugnant conclusion is halted. And it is halted for precisely the untutored, intuitive reason continua arguments are thought to be fishy: there is a qualitative change along the continuum that defuses the argument. That qualitative change is a change in a neighbourhood of value not being better than its predecessor neighbourhood but on a par with it.[32]

Toby Handfield (2014) has shown, on certain natural assumptions, if there is a failure of the trichotomy of relations, which is true of parity, that failure must occur at more than one point.[33] So we should think of the parity solution involving a zone of items, each of which is on a par with its predecessor. There may be many

---

[30] https://www.bls.gov/opub/reports/working-poor/2016/home.htm#technical-notes

[31] It would be a mistake to think that because there is indeterminacy as to where a neighbourhood begins and ends that it follows that the relations between items in that indeterminate zone are themselves indeterminately related. The indeterminacy at issue is as to where a neighbourhood begins and ends, not as to how to adjacent items in that zone compare.

[32] Tom Parr, Sam Bagg, and Jimmy Goodrich suggested to me that if parity holds, we might even insist that parity holds throughout the continuum since all the neighbourhoods that could be drawn are on a par. I believe they are right for some continua. But consider the most difficult case for a parity solution, one in which Compensation holds at the beginning of the continuum by each successor item being *better than* its predecessor, and then shifting to a zone in which each successor item is on a par with its predecessor.

[33] Handfield's proof applied to the parity solution would run as follows. Suppose A, the first item in the continuum, is better than Z, the last item on the continuum. Suppose too that P is on a par with Q, and that everywhere else on the continuum, each item is better than its predecessor. By the transitivity of 'better than (with respect to V)', P is better than A and Z is better than Q (since P occurs further down the continuum from A and Z occurs further down the continuum from Q). But if P is better than A, which is better than Z, which is better than Q, it would follow that P is better than Q. But P is supposedly on a par with Q. Thus we need more than one point at which items are on a par.

such zones along a continuum. But all such zones will include items that comprise the border between two neighbourhoods that are on a par.

We end by examining a challenge posed by Toby Handfield and Wlodek Rabinowicz (2018; Rabinowicz, Chapter 15, this volume) to *any* solution to continua arguments that posits both the failure of the usual trichotomy of relations to hold between adjacent items and a lexical relation between the first and last items on the continuum.[34] (Their argument applies not just to determinate failures but also to indeterminate ones, though I discuss only the former since it is relevant to parity.) As we have suggested, not all continua arguments need to involve lexicality, but since parity purports to be in principle available as a solution all continua arguments, their challenge must be addressed.

Handfield and Rabinowicz argue that any failure of the usual trichotomy to hold between two adjacent items on the continuum must, if it is to stop the chain of betterness along the continuum, be 'radical' or 'persistent', that is, it must continue to hold no matter how much the quantity of the successor item is increased. Consider P with, say, 1000 people living excellent lives and Q with, say, 2000 people living slightly less excellent lives. If Q is not better, worse, or equally as good as P, then it must be so no matter how many additional lives we add to Q. This is because if by adding a large number of lives to Q we can make Q better than P, then we will not have broken the chain of betterness—Q is be better than P and the continua argument proceeds as usual. This is an important argument that helps to underscore a key difference between a trichotomous and tetrachotomous understanding of value.

I believe that Handfield and Rabinowicz are right that the persistence of the failure of trichotomy is a problem if we assume Trichotomy. But is it a problem if we assume Tetrachotomy? On the assumption of Trichotomy, the failure of the usual trichotomy entails *incomparability*. We have already argued that since adjacent items differ by a small diminution in quality and large enhancement in quality, it is implausible to think that they are incomparable. Assuming for the sake of argument that they are, Handfield and Rabinowicz's argument shows that

---

[34] There is another possible objection to the parity solution that is worth mentioning here. If A is a pretty great world and Z is a pretty bad one, we need an explanation of how we get such a drastic change in value through parity. This objection, I believe, involves misconceiving of parity as a kind of rough equality. I explain why parity is not in Chang (2002b, 2016a). We explain the drastic change in value by appealing to the very large change in quality from A to Z, most plausibly through multiple parity zones and perhaps by a single parity zone. As we move from A along the continuum, there is, as it were, a 'first' item that is worse than A. That 'first' item represents a qualitative shift that emerges from a zone of parity. There may be many such qualitative shifts in serial diminutions in quality along the continuum, each emerging from a zone of parity or perhaps a single shift from which Z emerges. Put another way, parity can operate in continua arguments either as successive terraces, each with successively less overall value, or as a steep cliff. Which model is more plausible depends on the details of the continuum at issue. Note that their objection also helps to highlight how the parity solution provides a potential solution to a wide range of continua arguments, not just those in which the first item is lexically superior to the last. Many thanks to Victor Tadros and Ralf Bader for raising the worry.

they must be incomparable no matter how much we enhance the quantity of the successor item; the incomparability must be persistent. If P – 1000 people living middle-class lives—is incomparable with Q – 2000 people living only slightly less excellent lives—then no matter how many people we add to Q, P and Q must remain incomparable. It is hard to believe, however, that a googol of people leading only slightly diminished excellent lives is incomparable with 1000 people leading only slightly better lives. Persistent incomparability is indeed a cost of an incomparabilist solution.

On the assumption of Tetrachotomy, however, the failure of the trichotomy of relations (and no other failure) entails a form of comparability, *parity*. If parity holds between adjacent items in The Zone, then, by the Handfield/Rabinowicz argument, parity must continue to hold no matter how much we increase the quantity in Q.[35] Is such 'persistent' parity plausible?

It is not plausible in general; it is not the case that for *any* two items on a par that differ by one being a slight diminution in quality and a large enhancement in quantity, that no matter how much we increase the quantity, the items will remain on a par—two careers may be on a par, but if we increase the salary of one of them enough, it can be better. But in the case of items in The Zone, I now want to suggest, persistent parity is plausible.[36]

Whether parity persists depends on the character of the neighbourhood(s) to which the items that are on a par belong. In the case discussed above, we suggested that the 'extremely large numbers of lower-class lives' neighbourhood is on a par with the 'vast numbers of lives-at-subsistence', and thus, that there would be a zone of items at the transition between such neighbourhoods, each of which would be on a par with its predecessor. Let us zero in on two such items, say P and Q. Suppose P belongs to the first neighbourhood and Q to the second.

---

[35] A quick informal proof: If increasing the quantity in Q makes P and Q equally good, then any further quantitative enhancement in Q makes Q better than P—by the logic of equality and the assumption at the outset (and one needed for continua arguments to get going) that an increase in quantity makes for an evaluative increase in quantity of V-ness, entailing that there are no organic unities present. In either case, the chain of betterness would not be halted. Increasing the quantity in Q could make Q tetrachotomously incomparable with P, but for the reasons given above, this would be highly implausible. Therefore, the right conclusion to draw from the Handfield/Rabinowicz argument is that parity continues to hold.

[36] In this way, parity does not have what Qizilbash (2018) thinks is the 'mark' of parity—viz., that a large enough improvement always breaks the parity into betterness. Qizilbash appears to understand parity as 'rough' or imprecise equality so that enough of an improvement guarantees that the improved item will be better. While I think this is often true of items that are on a par, it need not be true. Unsurprisingly, whether it is true depends on the values at stake. Note, too, that just because some arguments for parity allow that enough of an improvement can 'break' the parity, e.g. my Chaining Argument (Chang 2002), it does not follow that it is feature of parity that whenever there is a sufficiently significant improvement in one item, the improved item is better. Indeed, the main principle on which the Chaining Argument relies, the 'Uni-dimensional Difference Principle' explicitly does not hold universally but is subject to what I called the 'Aristotleian' and 'Hegelian' provisos. Anders Herlitz (forthcoming) helpfully underscores the point that parity, if it is to block continua arguments, must sometimes persist as Handfield and Rabinowicz argued.

Would Q remain on a par with P even if we increased the quantity of lives at subsistence to a googol? Since a googol of people at subsistence would still belong to the neighbourhood of 'vast numbers of lives-at-subsistence', Q would still belong in the same neighbouroood as it did before and so would remain on a par with P. So there would be no problem with parity's persistence in this case.

But what about other cases? Is parity along the continuum restricted to neighbourhoods of value in which, beyond a certain threshold, an increase in quantity does not change the parity relation that otherwise holds? The answer is, 'yes', and I now want to explain why this result is both expected and perfectly natural.

There are two ways in which increasing the quantity of a value can make no difference to whether two items are on a par. They both have to do with the character of the neighbourhood to which the items belong. First, as we have just seen, sometimes, a value is significant in a way that is marked by a certain quantity, e.g., 'vast numbers of lives-at-subsistence' so that any increase in quantity leaves the item in the same neighbourhood. But, second, some neighbourhoods do not mark any quantity of V; beyond a certain threshold of quantity and quality, it is the *quality* of V-ness that determines the relation between items belonging to the neighbourhood. In this case, the qualitative aspect of a neighbourhood becomes critical.

Consider pain. There is a way in which pain could have evaluative significance, what we might call '*life-debilitating*', that is, pain so intense and severe that it prevents you from having anything like a normal human life. There are, of course, substantive matters for dispute as to which pains belong to such a neighbourhood, the contours of such a neighbourhood, how that neighbourhood overlaps with other neighbourhoods, and so on, but there will be some fixed points: a lifetime of excruciating torture would certainly belong to his neighbourhood. So too would 65 years of such torture—or so I will suppose. Sixty-five years of excruciating torture leaves you a shell of a person unable to have anything approximating a normal human life.

Now consider 70 years of slightly less excruciating torture. Let us suppose this experience also belongs to the neighbourhood of 'life-debilitating' pain; while the painfulness is discernibly less awful, 70 years of it still leaves you a shell of a person with no prospect of leading a normal human life. Is 70 years of slightly less excruciating pain worse than 65 years of slightly more excruciating pain? It might seem obvious that 70 years of only slightly less excruciating torture is worse—after all, it involves an extra 5 years of excruciating torture. But that judgement ignores the *significances* of such pains. Sixty-five years of excruciating torture leaves you a shell of a person; seventy years of slightly less excruciating torture makes no difference in this regard; you are still left a shell of a person. The evaluative quantity of the pain is greater, but the *significance* of the experience of painfulness remains the same. Psychologists suggest that short-lived intense trauma can be like this—they can make leading certain kinds of lives going forward impossible. Different traumas have different evaluative significances. Excruciating torture for 65 years or slightly less excruciating torture for 70 has the same significance: your prospects for a normal life have been ruined.

Are the experiences, then, equally painful? The Small Improvement Argument shows that they are not; if we improve the 65-year experience by decreasing the intensity of the pain slightly but discernibly, the improved 65-year experience, 65+, is better than the original experience, 65. However, 65+ is not better than 70. Both 65+ and 70 are still in the same neighbourhood of lifetime debilitating painfulness. Of course the same is true of 65 and 65+, but the qualitative improvement in 65+ renders 65+ better than 65. The point here is that being in the 'lifetime debilitating' neighbourhood of pain is what we might call a '*quantity swamper*'; once the pain debilitates you for life, that is, meets a certain threshold of quantity and quality, increasing the quantity doesn't make the experience worse and nor does decreasing it make it better; the fact that the pain debilitates you for life 'swamps' the badness of the additional quantity of such pain. The phenomenon of swamping is a familiar one in axiology. Here we apply it to trade-offs between quantities and qualities.

Belonging to a neighbourhood that is a quantity swamper does not entail that membership in the neighbourhood *qualitatively* swamps; you can make a qualitative improvement to a painful experience, thereby making it better than it was before. The swamping, then, is specifically a swamping of *quantitative* improvements or detractions. In this way, 65+ can be better than 65 while not being better than 70, while all three nevertheless belong to same quantity swamping neighbourhood of 'lifetime debilitating' pain. Since 65+ can be better than 65 and not better than 70, it follows, by the principle of the substitutability of equally good items, that 65 and 70 are not equally good.

I suggest that, because 70 years is not worse than 65 years, could not be better, and yet nor are they equally painful, the right thing to say is that they are on a par in painfulness. Crucially, they remain on a par no matter how much the quantity of pain is increased. Quantity swamping is a feature of some neighbourhoods in which, beyond a certain threshold of quantity and quality, the fact of belonging to that neighbourhood 'swamps' any quantitative improvement so that whatever evaluative relation held before will continue to hold despite the quantitative improvement. 'Lifetime debilitating' is a neighbourhood of pain that has this feature.[37]

---

[37] Note that none of this is to say that belonging to the same neighbourhood precludes one item being better than the other. The point is rather that *some* neighbourhoods of value, such as 'life-debilitating painfulness' are ones in which at a certain threshold level of quantity and quality of painfulness, the addition of quantity won't make a difference to how items in the neighbourhood compare.

The same goes for other values, such as 'social well-being'. There are neighbourhoods of social well-being, understood as some combination of quantity of lives and quality of lives, where, at a certain threshold of quantity of quality, the character of the neighbourhood swamps any increases in quantity in determining how the items belonging to that neighbourhood compare. Take for instance, the 'vast numbers at subsistence' neighbourhood of the value of social wellbeing. One way social well-being can be significant is by being instantiated by vast swathes of humanity living at the minimal level for survival in an advanced industrialized nation—still with lives worth living—as we saw, earning \$12,228 or less per annum. Suppose there are a billion people living at subsistence. Compare that world to another with a billion plus one hundred thousand people living at subsistence. Is the second world better than the first? I suggest that such worlds belong to the 'vast subsistence' neighbourhood of social well-being and are on a par with respect to social well-being. The additional one hundred thousand people with lives worth living adds value, but the fact that the neighbourhood of value is that of 'vast numbers at subsistence' swamps the quantitative value added to ensure that the items remain on a par. And since 'vast numbers at subsistence' is a neighbourhood that, beyond a certain threshold of number of lives and quality of lives, quantitatively swamps, the second world will be on a par with first no matter how many additional lives are added. A billion lives at subsistence will be on a par with any number of lives at subsistence so long as they belong to the same quantitative swamping neighbourhood of social well-being.

If this is right, then we have explained how two items belonging to the same quantity-swamping neighbourhood of value can be on a par and remain on a par no matter how much the quantity is increased. And once we have shown this, it readily follows that the parity that holds between an item, P, belonging to a predecessor neighbourhood, and an item, Q, belonging to the successor *quantity swamping* neighbourhood, will also persist. If we increase the quantity of Q even to a googol, the fact of membership in the neighbourhood will swamp the quantitative value added and the items will remain on a par. The persistence of parity can be explained by appeal to features of neighbourhoods of value.

Of course it remains to be shown that *every* continuum of *every* continua argument will involve either (i) a neighbourhood of value where vastness of quantity is a mark of that neighbourhood and items in that neighbourhood are on a par with their immediate predecessors, *or* (ii) parity among items that belong to a quantity swamping neighbourhood. But I believe the prospects are good. After all, for continua arguments to minimize controversy over each step, they will need to involve vast numbers. And many such arguments do seem to invoke neighbourhoods of value where, beyond a certain threshold, quantity may be swamped, e.g. many years of torture, vast numbers of lives at poverty, very long periods of mild pains, etc. Rather than a bug, the persistence of parity is a feature of a tetrachotomous understanding of value.[38,39]

14.5 Conclusion

A structural solution to continua arguments posits a break in the chain of betterness (or worseness) relations that putatively hold throughout the continuum: somewhere along the continuum there is a zone of items, each of which is not better than its predecessor. We examined and raised significant difficulties for four such possible solutions: incommensurability, indeterminacy, incomparability, and Parfit's own solution, imprecise lexicality. Some of these solutions fail to defuse continua arguments (incommensurability); others provide formal solutions but suffer from serious substantive flaws (indeterminacy and incomparability); and some may, at best, successfully defuse only a small class of continua arguments (imprecise lexicality).

We proposed instead that the chain of betterness relations is broken by a zone of *parity*. Being *on a par* is a fourth basic way items can compare beyond being 'better than', 'worse than', or 'equally as good as' one another. If parity holds then the slide to a false or repugnant conclusion is halted. We offered two reasons for

---

[38] That values have such significances is, strictly speaking, a defence against the charge of 'persistence' that even Trichotomists could help themselves to. However, unless neighbourhoods are understood *not* as regions of a trichotomous cardinal or ordinal scale of value, the thought that neighbourhoods could have this quantitative swamping feature is hard to defend.

[39] It is perhaps worth noting that the parity solution does not require giving up Parfit's modified Simple View, viz., the view that adding lives worth living adds value to an outcome. The parity solution allows that the modified Simple View may be true but cautions that that value can be swamped by the fact that the items in question belong to a quantity swamping neighbourhood of value. Wlodek Rabinowicz suggests an alternative solution that grows out of his elegant modelling of parity in terms of permissible fitting attitudes to have towards values and their bearers. His idea is that sometimes it is permissible to have an attitude towards an item in The Zone that favours, say, Q over P, while it is also permissible to have an attitude that favours P over Q, and that when these conditions obtain, Q and P are on a par. He argues that these attitudes can continue to be permissible no matter how much one increases the quantity of Q because there are multiple substantive views about value that deliver different rankings of P and Q no matter how much we increase the quantity of Q. If some of those rankings tell us that P is better than Q and some tell us that Q is better than P no matter how much we increase the quantity of Q, parity persists between P and Q even if we increase the number of people in Q to a googol. My worry about his solution is that the range of substantive approaches to values that he must countenance to account for the persistence of parity will undermine the otherwise elegant model of value relations he proposes more generally: we might think that some item X is clearly better than some item Y with respect to V, but because the range of eligible weightings of the contributory aspects of V that Rabinowicz must countenance in order to explain the persistence of parity in continuum arguments is so broad, those weightings must also be eligible in cases when we are contemplating the comparative relation between X and Y. And although intuitively it will be clear that X is better than Y with respect to V, Rabinowicz's permissiveness about weightings of contributory factors of V-ness will require us to say instead that X and Y are on a par since on some eligible weightings, Y will be better than X while on others X will be better than Y. Moreover, Rabinowicz's solution requires us to reject the Simple View, a view Parfit did not want to reject, while the parity solution allows us to maintain the Simple View.

accepting parity in preference to other possible solutions. Unlike other structural solutions, parity allows us to maintain the strong intuition at the heart of all continua arguments, the idea that a slight diminution in quality can be compensated for by a large increase in quantity. Moreover, parity gives theoretical expression to a common, untutored response to continua arguments: as we move along the continuum, there is a qualitative shift that halts the slide to the false or repugnant conclusion. The parity solution offers an attractive way to explain that shift.

Accepting the parity solution requires rejecting a 'trichotomous' view of value according to which two items that are comparable with respect to some value must be related by 'better than', 'worse than', or 'equally good'. We explored some features of an alternative 'tetrachotomous' view and noted that values have *significances* or 'neighbourhoods', akin to categories or levels or leagues of value, that can be on a par. These neighbourhoods of value help to support the parity solution by explaining how parity might hold between adjacent items on a continuum.

In this way, thinking about what might seem to be a 'mere puzzle' in ethics opens up an alternative way of understanding the very structure of values and of normativity more generally.

References

Akiba, Ken, 'Vagueness in the World'. *Nous* 38,3 (2004): 407–29.

Andreou, Chrisoula, 'Parity, Comparability, and Choice'. *Journal of Philosophy*, 112,1 (2015): 5–22.

Arrhenius, Gustaf, 'The Impossibility of a Satisfactory Population Ethics'. *World Scientific Review* 20,54 (2011): 1–26.

Arrhenius, Gustaf, 'Impossibility Theorems in Population Ethics: Values, Norms, and Non-Transitivity'. In the *Oxford Population Ethics Handbook*, ed. Gustaf Arrhenius, Krister Bykvist, and Timothy Campbell (Oxford: Oxford University Press, forthcoming).

Arrhenius, Gustaf, and Wlodek Rabinowicz, 'Millian Superiorities'. *Utilitas*, 17 (2005): 127–46.

Barnes, Elizabeth, 'Ontic Vagueness: A Guide for the Perplexed'. *Nous* 44,4 (2010): 601–27.

Boonin-Vail, David, 'Don't Stop Thinking About Tomorrow: Two Paradoxes about Duties to Future Generations'. *Philosophy and Public Affairs* 25,4 (1996): 267–307.

Broome, John, 'Is Incommensurability Vagueness?' In *Incommensurability, Incomparability, and Practical Reason*, ed. Ruth Chang (Cambridge, MA: Harvard University Press, 1997).

Chang, Ruth, 'Introduction'. In *Incommensurability, Incomparability, and Practical Reason* (Cambridge, MA: Harvard University Press, 1997).

Chang, Ruth, 'Against Constitutive Incommensurability, or, Buying and Selling Friends'. *Philosophical Issues* (annual special issues supplement to *Nous*), 11 (2001): 33–60.

Chang, Ruth, 'The Possibility of Parity'. *Ethics*, 112 (2002a): 659–88.

Chang Ruth, *Making Comparisons Count* (New York: Routledge, 2002b).

Chang, Ruth, 'All Things Considered'. *Philosophical Perspectives*, 18 (2004a): 1–22.

Chang, Ruth, 'Putting Together Morality and Well-Being'. in *Practical Conflicts*, ed. Monika Betzler and Peter Baumann (Cambridge: Cambridge University Press, 2004b).

Chang, Ruth, 'Practical Reasons: The Problem of Gridlock'. In *Companion to Analytical Philosophy*, ed. Barry Dainton and Howard Robinson (London: Bloomsbury Press, 2013).

Chang, Ruth, 'Transformative Choices'. *Res Philosophica*, 92 (2015): 237–82.

Chang, Ruth, 'Parity: An Intuitive Case'. *Ratio* 29,4 (2016a): 395–411.

Chang, Ruth, 'Comparativism: The Grounds of Rational Choice'. In *Weighing* Values, ed. Errol Lord and Barry Maguire (New York: Oxford University Press, 2016b).

Chang, Ruth, 'Parity, Imprecise Comparability, and the Repugnant Conclusion'. *Theoria* 82 (2016c): 183–215.

Chang, Ruth, 'Hard Choices'. *Journal of the American Philosophical Association*, 92 (2017): 586–620.

Constantinescu, Cristian, 'Value Incomparability and Indeterminacy'. *Ethical Theory and Moral Practice* 15,1 (2012): 57–70.

Dougherty, Tom, 'Moral Indeterminacy, Normative Powers and Convention'. *Ratio*, 29,4 (2016): 448–65.

Gallie, W.B., 'Essentially Contested Concepts'. *Proceedings of the Aristotelian Society* (1956): 167–98.

Greenough, Patrick, 'Vagueness: A Minimal Theory'. *Mind*, 112,446 (2003): 235–81.

Graff, Delia, 'Phenomenal Continua and the Sorites'. *Mind*, 110,440 (2001): 905–35.

Handfield, Toby, 'Rational Choice and the Transitivity of Betterness'. *Philosophy and Phenomenological Research*, 89 (2014): 584–604.

Handfield, Toby and Rabinowicz, Wlodek, 'Incommensurability and Vagueness In Spectrum Arguments: Options for Saving Transitivity of Betterness'. *Philosophical Studies*, 175 (2018): 2375–87.

Harrison, Jason, 'Utilitarianism, Universalisation, and Our Duty to be Just'. *Proceedings of the Aristotelian Society*, 53 (1953): 105–34.

Herlitz, Anders, 'Spectrum Arguments, Parity, and Persistency'. *Theoria* (forthcoming, 2020).

Hsieh, Nien-he. 'Equality, Clumpiness, and Incomparability'. *Utilitas*, 17, 2 (2005): 180–204.

Jefferson, Annali, 'Slippery Slope Arguments'. *Philosophy Compass*, 9/10 (2014): 672–80.

Kamm, Frances, *Morality, Mortality*, Volume 2 (Oxford: Oxford University Press, 1996).

Knapp, Christopher, 'Trading Quality for Quantity'. *Journal of Philosophical Research*, 32 (2007): 211–34.

Parfit, Derek, *Reasons and Persons* (Oxford: Oxford University Press, 1984).

Parfit, Derek, 'Can We Avoid the Repugnant Conclusion?'. *Theoria*, 82,2 (2016): 110–27.

Parfit, Derek, 'Future People, the Non-Identity Problem, and Person-Affecting Principles'. *Philosophy and Public Affairs*, 45 (2017): 119–56.

Qizilbash, Mozzafar, 'Transitivity and Vagueness'. *Economics and Philosophy*, 21 (2005): 109–31.

Qizilbash, Mozzafar, 'The Mere Addition Paradox, Parity, and Vagueness'. *Philosophy and Phenomenological Research*, 75,1 (2007): 129–51.

Qizilbash, Mozzafar, '"Incommensurability" and Vagueness: Is the Vagueness View Defensible?'. *Ethical Theory and Moral Practice*, 17,1 (2014): 41–54.

Qizilbash, Mozzafar, 'Parity and the Intuition of Neutrality', *Economics and Philosophy*, 34 (2018): 87–108.

Quinn, Warren, 'The Puzzle of the Self-Torturer'. *Philosophical Studies* 59,1 (1990): 79–90.

Rabinowicz, Wlodek, 'Value Relations'. *Theoria*, 74,1 (2007): 18–49.

Rabinowicz, Wlodek, 'Value Relations Revisited'. *Economics and Philosophy* 28,2 (2012): 133–53.

Rachels, Stuart, 'A Set of Solutions to Parfit's Problems'. *Nous*, 35,2 (2001): 214–38.

Raz, Joseph, *The Morality of Freedom* (Oxford: Clarendon Press, 1986).

Scheffler, Samuel, *Why Worry About Future Generations?* (Oxford: Oxford University Press, 2018).

Schoenfield, Miriam, 'Decision Making in the Face of Parity'. *Philosophical Perspectives* (supplement to *Nous*), 28,1 (2014): 263–77.

Schoenfield, Miriam, 'Moral Vagueness is Ontic Vagueness'. *Ethics*, 126,2 (2015): 257–82.

Taylor, David, 'A Minimal Characterization of Indeterminacy'. *Philosophers Imprint*, (2018): 1–25.

Temkin, Larry, *Rethinking the Good* (Oxford: Oxford University Press, 2012).

Thompson, Judith Jarvis, *Goodness and Advice* (Princeton: Princeton University Press, 2001).

U.S. Department of Labor, 'A Profile of the Working Poor', Bureau of Labor Statistics, 2016, at https://www.bls.gov/opub/reports/working-poor/2016/home.htm#technical-notes.

van der Burg, Wibren, 'The Slippery Slope Argument'. *Ethics*, 102,1 (1991): 42–65.

Williams, J. Robert, 'Ontic Vagueness and Metaphysical Indeterminacy'. *Philosophy Compass*, 3/4 (2008): 763–88.

Williams, J. Robert, 'Decision Making Under Indeterminacy'. *Philosopher's Imprint*, 14 (2014): 1–34.

Williams, J. Robert, 'Indeterminacy, Angst and Conflicting Values'. *Ratio*, 29 (2016): 412–33.

15
Can Parfit's Appeal to Incommensurabilities in Value Block the Continuum Argument for the Repugnant Conclusion?

Wlodek Rabinowicz

15.1 Introduction

Starting with *Reasons and Persons* (1984), Parfit repeatedly grappled with the Repugnant Conclusion. His last published attempt, "Can We Avoid the Repugnant Conclusion?," was published as late as 2016. It appeared in a special issue of the Swedish international philosophy journal *Theoria*. The issue collected contributions from a symposium held in Stockholm in 2014 on the occasion of Parfit being awarded the Rolf Schock Prize in Logic and Philosophy by the Swedish Academy of Sciences. Having chaired the prize symposium I have long been tempted by the idea of investigating Parfit's proposal in some detail. This Festschrift in his memory provides a welcome opportunity to do so.

In his *Theoria*-paper, Parfit attempts to block the "Continuum Argument" for the Repugnant Conclusion by an appeal to "imprecise equalities" in value.[1] My aim is to assess this attempt. By "imprecise equality" Parfit means something very close to *incommensurability*—a relation that holds between two items if and only if none of them is better than the other nor are they (precisely) equally as good.[2] Or, at least, imprecise equality is meant to entail incommensurability:

---

[1] The "continuum" label for the argument, which Parfit seems to have taken over from Temkin (1996), is a misnomer. The argument sets up a *discrete* and indeed finite sequence of larger and larger populations, with gradually decreasing wellbeing levels. That this sequence is discrete, and thus not a continuum, is essential for the argument. While I here retain Parfit's label, "the Sequence Argument" or "the Spectrum Argument" are more adequate names for this form of reasoning.

[2] To prevent misunderstandings, the reader should be warned that this definition of incommensurability, while nowadays quite common among value theorists (probably due to the influence of Raz 1986), is very different from how this notion has been traditionally understood. On the traditional understanding, two items are incommensurable in value if their value cannot be measured on a common cardinal scale. Now, obviously, cardinal measurability of value is a strong requirement. It is

Precisely equal is a transitive relation. [...] But if X and Y are imprecisely equally good, so that neither is worse than the other, these imprecise relations are not transitive. [...] Two things are imprecisely equally good if it is true that, though neither thing is better than the other, there could be some third thing which was better or worse than one of these things, though not better or worse than the other. (Parfit 2016, pp. 14f)

Is the comparison with "some third thing," which is better or worse than one of two items but not better or worse than the other, intended to be a part of the definition of imprecise equality? Or is it rather meant to be a useful (partial) test of the relation Parfit has in mind, as it implies that X and Y are not precisely equal in value? Here, I will assume the latter. Indeed, until further notice, I will assume that imprecise equality is the same thing as incommensurability.[3] Like Joseph Raz (1986), I take the comparison with "some third thing" as a (partial) test, or "mark," of incommensurability, but not as a part of its definition.[4,5]

The Continuum Argument is meant to establish that for any population, however large, that consists of people with excellent lives, there is a better population in which everyone has a drab life, barely worth living. The argument proceeds by constructing a finite sequence of populations of rapidly increasing size and slowly decreasing life quality, the same for all individuals in a given population. While the lives of the individuals get worse and worse, they remain worth living. The argument assumes—and this assumption is not questioned by Parfit—that:

Adding people with lives worth living and of the same quality as those of all the others always makes the world better.[6]

---

therefore not surprising that Chang (2016a), who interprets incommensurability in this traditional way, denies that Parfit's imprecise inequality is the same thing as incommensurability. Two items might well be incommensurable in this traditional sense without being imprecisely equal. Indeed, one of them might be better than the other. By contrast, on my definition, what is required for incommensurability is something stronger: the absence of a common *ordinal* scale on which the value of both items can be measured.

[3] This assumption will be slightly qualified later on. I will consider the possibility that Parfit by imprecise equality means something more specific than mere incommensurability; he might mean something like Ruth Chang's "parity." I am indebted to Mozaffar Qizilbash for pressing this point.

[4] "We have here a simple way of determining whether two options are incommensurate given that it is known that neither is better than the other. If it is possible for one of them to be improved without thereby becoming better than the other, or if there can be another option which is better than the one but not better than the other, then the two original options are incommensurate. I shall call this feature the *mark of incommensurability*. But remember that it is not its definition. While being, for most purposes, perfectly sufficient as a test of incomparability, it is not in fact a necessary condition of incomparability" (Raz 1986, pp. 325f; Raz's own emphasis).

[5] James Goodrich has suggested to me a third option: That something is better or worse than X but not better or worse than Y might be a "ground" of X and Y not being precisely equal and thereby a partial ground their incommensurability (and not part of the definition of this concept). It is an interesting suggestion in itself, but—as far as I can see—there is no sign that Parfit has been thinking along these lines.

[6] While in this chapter I go along with Parfit and take the above assumption for granted, it certainly is not uncontroversial. More generally, it could be argued that additions of lives worth living are axiologically neutral, i.e., that they do not make the world either better or worse. Instead, they might make it incommensurable with the world without these additions. (See Rabinowicz 2009a for an extended discussion.)

Indeed, Parfit accepts what he calls the *Simple View*, according to which the marginal value of such additions is not only always positive, but it also never diminishes (Parfit 2016, p. 112).

The first population in the Continuum Argument's population sequence is large (as large as one pleases, according to the argument) and consists of people with excellent lives. Each successive population is much larger than the preceding one, but the lives of its members are slightly worse. At each step, a large increase in size is meant to compensate for a small decrease in life quality: Each successive population is thus supposed to be better than the preceding one. The last, huge population consists of people with drab lives, of the muzak-and-potatoes variety. Such lives still are worth living, but only barely so.[7] By the transitivity of betterness, this last population is better than the first one.

For Parfit, this is a Repugnant Conclusion.[8] Indeed, he believes that a sufficiently large population of people with excellent lives is better than any population, however large, of people with drab lives.

To block the argument, Parfit suggests that, at some points in the population sequence, we will encounter an incommensurability (an "imprecise equality"): the next population will be incommensurable with the immediately preceding one, instead of being better as the Continuum Argument requires.

As we shall see, blocking the argument in this way carries a considerable cost. The kind of incommensurability Parfit needs to posit has to be very thoroughgoing: It must persist however much the next population in the sequence is increased in size (and thereby improved). While highly atypical and seemingly counter-intuitive, this persistency can, I believe, be justified if incommensurability is interpreted on the lines of the fitting-attitudes analysis of value, as permissibility of divergent preferential attitudes regarding the compared items. (Cf. Rabinowicz 2008, 2012, for this account.) But even if the worry about persistency can thus be allayed, the conclusion will be that one of Parfit's substantive value assumptions—his Simple View regarding the marginal value of increases in population size—might need to be rejected.

---

[7] Here is how Parfit describes this last population in the sequence, the "Drab Z": "there would be nothing in people's lives that would be bad, but there would also be very little that was good. The only good features, I suggested, might be muzak and potatoes. But that description is too simple. If the people in Drab Z would be in other ways like us, we could not plausibly assume that these people's lives would contain nothing bad, but very little that was good. Even if we lost most external goods, some of us would have inner mental resources with which we could make our lives fairly good, by composing long poems, for example, or thinking about some intellectual problems. [...] we can suppose that lives in Drab Z would be only barely worth living, not because they would be lived by people like us who were in such deprived conditions, but because these lives would be lived by beings who would be psychologically much simpler than us." (Parfit 2016, p. 118)

[8] More generally, the Repugnant Conclusion is the claim that for any population in which everyone's life is as good as one pleases, there is a better population in which everyone's life is barely worth living.

15.2 Preparing the Ground—Informal Discussion

The following principle expresses the key idea behind the Continuum Argument:

Compensation: Small losses in quality can always be compensated, and indeed outweighed, by sufficiently large increases in quantity.

In the Continuum Argument, as one moves forward in the population sequence, small losses in life quality are supposed to be outweighed, in each step, by increases in quantity—in the population size. Each population in the sequence is therefore supposed to be better than the immediately preceding one.

On the other hand, the argument's conclusion contravenes the intuition that compensation of quality losses by quantity increases has limits:

Limits to Compensation: Large losses in quality cannot always be compensated by increases in quantity.

There are positive levels of quality such that the loss involved in the move from such level to another, much lower one, cannot be compensated by any increase in quantity, however large. This intuition lies behind the claim that the starting-point of the population sequence is better than its end-point.

Large quality losses cannot be compensated by increases in quantity in cases of *weak superiority*, i.e., cases in which some quantity of the good of the higher quality is better than any quantity of the good of the lower quality. In the case Parfit focuses on, the higher good is an excellent life, while the lower good is a drab life.

"Weak superiority" as the label for this relation between types of good was introduced in Arrhenius and Rabinowicz (2005, 2015). There are other labels that have been in use for the same relation: "discontinuity in value" (Griffin 1986), "radical superiority" (Handfield and Rabinowicz 2018), and "lexical superiority" (Parfit 2016). Parfit's label—"lexical superiority"—is potentially misleading, which is why I here abstain from using it. To say that a type of good is lexically superior to another type of good might suggest that *any* quantity of the former would be better than any quantity of the latter. In Arrhenius and Rabinowicz (2015), this more demanding relation is referred to as *strong superiority*. Griffin (1986) calls it "trumping." Strong superiority is not at issue in the case we consider: While Parfit is a perfectionist, he does not suggest that even a single excellent life would be better than any number of drab lives.[9]

---

[9] Tim Campbell (in private communication) has made me aware that I might have been too categorical on this point. As he notes, "Parfit [also] wanted to avoid the Single-Life Repugnant Conclusion. No matter how long a single drab life, L, is, a single excellent life, L*, with sufficiently

To block the Continuum Argument we have three options. We can (1) deny that it is possible to construct the requisite finite sequence of types of lives leading from an excellent life all the way to a drab life by small quality decreases; (2) deny the transitivity of betterness in the sequence of populations; (3) deny that small quality losses can always be compensated by increases in quantity.

Option 1: One might question whether the large quality distance between an excellent life and a drab life can be scaled in a finite number of small steps—a finite number of small decreases in quality. Small relative to what? What counts as a small decrease diminishes in absolute size as the quality of a life goes down. But then we might never reach a drab life from an excellent life, in this way. Indeed, if we increase the number of steps ad infinitum, a drab life might not even be the limit of such an infinite sequence. Any sequence in which each step is small might instead converge to a life of a higher quality.

This objection is plausible, but not compelling. Defenders of the Continuum Argument might respond that even if decreases in life quality must be small at each step—small in relation to the quality of life that at this step is being decreased, they could still get us all the way down to a life that is barely worth living. Suppose, for example, that in this life sequence each quality decrease, from one type of life to the next, is of the same absolute size, but this size is chosen in such a way as to be counted as small even when the quality of a life is already very low.[10] Then such decreases will be counted as small, indeed, even smaller relatively speaking, at all the steps at which the life quality is higher. This construction would guarantee that a drab life can be reached from an excellent life in a finite number of small steps of equal size, provided that the quality distance between these two types of life is not infinitely large. Any finite distance can be traversed by a finite number of equal-sized steps.

Admittedly, this response makes strong assumptions about measurability of life quality: Unless the latter can be measured on an interval scale, it doesn't make sense to talk about equal-sized quality decreases.[11] But still, such a reply cannot be dismissed out of hand. To the extent that we do have intuitions about life quality

---

many high-quality goods would be better than L." But then, Campbell conjectures, "whatever Parfit would say about the comparison of L and L*, he would also say about the comparison of L* and the set of drab lives that, together, have the same duration as L." Note that this set of drab lives can be as large as you wish, since L can be as long as you wish.

Is Campbell right in his conjecture? I am not sure. Parfit might have thought that a multitude of shorter drab lives is better, and perhaps even much better, than a single extremely long life of this kind, even if the total duration of both were the same. But if Campbell's conjecture is correct, then, as we shall see, this would undermine the *ad hominem* force of an objection that Jensen (2020) has recently raised against Parfit's Simple View. I will present Jensen's objection in section 15.7 below.

[10] To put it a bit more precisely, let L and L′ be two types of lives such that L′ a drab life and L is a life that is only slightly better than L′. Then we can consider a sequence of types of lives decreasing in quality in which each quality decrease is of the same size as that between L and L′.

[11] This measurability assumption is especially problematic in view of the fact that for Parfit life quality is not reducible to wellbeing level. It is a more specific concept. When we consider the Repugnant Conclusion, reducing the quality of a life to its wellbeing level would have unwelcome

losses or gains being relatively small or large, we do seem to be prepared to measure such losses and gains on something like a (rough) interval scale.

Note that rejecting option 1 and thus accepting that

(i) we can reach a drab life from an excellent life by a series of small decreases in quality,

does not mean that we need to accept that

(ii) there is a finite series of small quality decreases going from an excellent life to a drab life and such that each decrease in the series can be outweighed by a sufficient increase in population size.

Clearly, (i) does not imply (ii). Indeed, we can accept (i) and still reject (ii) even if we also accept that

(iii) for each type of life, there is *some* small decrease of its quality that can be outweighed by a sufficient increase in population size.

(iii) doesn't mean that *every* small quality decrease is so outweighable. While small, it might not be small enough to be outweighable by an increase in quantity. Consequently, if one starts off with an excellent life and then constructs a descending sequence of types of life in which each quality decrease can be outweighed by an increase in quantity (= in population size), it might turn out that no such sequence ever reaches the level of a drab life. The limit to which it converges might lie considerably higher.

Option 2: One might want to deny the transitivity of betterness. Larry Temkin, who champions this proposal, suggests that we should interpret betterness all-things-considered as an "essentially comparative" concept (see, for example, Temkin 2012). Therefore, in comparing alternative outcomes, we should not start with assessing how good or bad each outcome is in itself. Instead of assessing outcomes in isolation, we should evaluate them relative to each other. Given this Essentially Comparative View, there is no guarantee that betterness is going to be

---

consequences. Parfit allows that a drab life might have the same overall level of wellbeing as, say, a "roller-coaster" life in which highs alternate with lows, if in in such a life the highs only barely outweigh the lows. In Parfit's view, the Repugnant Conclusion is truly repugnant only when it is a claim about drab lives—lives that "contain nothing bad, but very little that was good." What is repugnant is that a population of drab lives could be better than a population of excellent lives. An analogous claim about roller-coaster lives or about happy lives of extremely short duration (stretching over "one happy day, or one ecstatic hour") would not be (so) repugnant (Parfit 2016, p. 118). He emphasizes that "there are important differences between the quality of people's lives and the amount of well-being per person" (ibid.). He apparently allows that two lives can have the same "amount of wellbeing" but still their quality might differ.

transitive. In different pairwise comparisons different aspects or considerations might come to the fore, one aspect in the comparison of A with B, another in the comparison of B with C, and yet another when C is compared with A. This variation in perspectives might well lead to violations of transitivity. Temkin contrasts such an essentially comparative approach to evaluation with the Internal Aspects View, according to which value comparisons are secondary to intrinsic evaluations of outcomes. On the latter view, the transitivity of betterness is guaranteed. (Cf. Temkin 2012, sections 7.6, 7.7.) But then, if it is the essentially comparative conception that should be used in evaluation of different outcomes such as alternative populations, we can block the Continuum Argument by denying that betterness is transitive. Indeed, we can claim that the argument's population sequence forms a betterness cycle: Each population in the sequence is better than its immediate predecessor, but the last population is worse than the one we have started with.

In a posthumously published paper, Parfit (2017) admits that betterness can be understood in these two different ways, but he nevertheless insists that it is (something like) the Internal Aspects View that is appropriate when it comes to assessing alternative outcomes:

> Temkin rightly assumes that the phrase "better than" can be used in different senses, which refer to different relations. Temkin argues that, though some outcomes are intrinsically better than others in a sense that is transitive, such claims may apply to only a "severely limited part of the normative realm." I believe that many outcomes, and many other things, are intrinsically good or bad, in ways that make them better or worse than others. Such goodness or badness is not essentially comparative, since it does not consist in being related in certain ways to other things. (Parfit 2017, p. 139)

This is one way in which option 2 might be opposed, but there is also another, more satisfactory way. One might accept that Temkin is right in his insistence that evaluations of outcomes should be essentially comparative rather than intrinsic, but argue that he does not go far enough in this comparative approach. When two outcomes are compared, we need to consider not just how they relate to each other, but also how they relate to other possible outcomes in the domain. It is only by such extended comparisons that their values can be adequately assessed, In this way, the reference class with respect to which the value assessment is being made—the domain as a whole—is the same as one moves from one pairwise comparison to another. There is thus no variation in perspectives and the argument for non-transitivity breaks down. I will later show how this holistic approach to value comparisons can be developed.

Option 3: This is Parfit's preferred alternative. The other two options are discarded; he assumes that the relation of betterness between populations is transitive and that it is possible to construct a finite life sequence that leads by small quality decreases from an excellent life to a drab life. What he denies is that such small quality losses can always be compensated by increases in quantity. At some points in the Continuum Argument's population sequence $X_1, \ldots, X_n$, we will encounter incommensurabilities: For some i < n, the next population, X_{i+1}, will not be better than the immediately preceding one, X_i, as the Continuum Argument requires. Instead, the two populations will be incommensurable ("imprecisely equal"). This makes it possible to reject the repugnant implication that X_n must be better than X_1, and indeed it makes it possible to insist on the opposite being the case: X_1, a sizeable population of people with excellent lives, is better than X_n, a population of people with drab lives, barely worth living, however large the latter population might be.

As an aside, it should be pointed out that bringing in incommensurability at just one point in the population sequence, say, between X_i and X_{i+1}, is not a viable option. If for every j < n distinct from i, X_{j+1} were better than X_j, the transitivity of betterness would imply that (i) X_i is better than X_1 unless i = 1, and that (ii) X_n is better than X_{i+1}. Since Parfit claims that (iii) X_1 is better than X_n, it follows from (i) and (iii), by the transitivity of betterness, that (iv) X_i is better than X_n. But then, again by the transitivity of betterness, (iv) and (ii) imply that X_i is better than X_{i+1}, contrary to the assumption that that these two populations are incommensurable.

As was shown in Handfield (2014), this inconsistency can be avoided if we postulate that there are *at least two* points of incommensurability in the sequence.[12] And indeed, Parfit seems to think that incommensurability ("imprecise equality") might well come in at *every* point in the population sequence:

[Continuum] arguments assume that [...] any slight loss of quality could be outweighed by a sufficient gain in quantity. If we assumed precision, it would be hard to reject these arguments. We would have to claim that *any* slight loss of quality would outweigh any gain in quantity.[13] As several writers claim, that would be very implausible. Compared with the existence of some number of people, it would not always be worse if instead there existed many more people

---

[12] A simple example shows that two such points can suffice for a sequence of an arbitrary length n > 2: Suppose that, for some i such that 1 < i < n, X_i is incommensurable both with X_{i-1} and with X_{i+1}. With these two exceptions, for all other adjacent pairs, the second population in the pair is better than the first, as in the Continuum Argument. But still, contrary to the conclusion of this argument, the first population in the sequence is better than the last one. By the transitivity of betterness it then follows that X_{i-1} is better than X_{i+1}, but this implication does not create any inconsistency. To see this, we need to complete the construction. By the transitivity of betterness, it is determined how all the populations distinct from X_i are related to each other. We also know how X_i relates to its immediate neighbors, X_{i-1} and X_{i+1}, but we need to specify how it relates to other populations in the sequence. So, let us assume, for simplicity, that X_i is incommensurable not only with its neighbors but also with the other populations in the sequence. Clearly, this construction is consistent.

[13] This is clearly a mistake on Parfit's part. Given precision, i.e., given that incommensurabilities are excluded, critics of the Continuum Argument would only have to posit that *some* slight quality losses would outweigh any gains in quantity. This would be enough for the conclusion that the first population in the sequence is better than the last, however large the latter might be.

who would have a slightly lower quality of life. But we should deny that such truths would be precise. We should then claim that *no* slight loss in quality would either be outweighed by, or outweigh, any such gain in quantity. It would not be better if there existed many more people whose quality of life would all be lower, since two such worlds would at most be imprecisely equally good.

(Parfit 2016, p. 120, my emphasis)

Parfit's suggestion that *no* slight loss in quality would be outweighed by any gain in quantity seems unnecessarily radical. As pointed out above, to block the Continuum Argument it is enough if incommensurability intervenes at a couple of points in the population sequence. At other points, the next population may well be better than its immediate predecessor.

Let's put this matter aside, however. Parfit's central suggestion, I take it, is that at least some adjacent populations in the Continuum Argument's population sequence will be incommensurable. To assess this proposal, I will first prepare the ground by setting up a simple formal framework. This will be done in the next section.

15.3 Preparing the Ground—Formal Framework

The domain that we are going to consider consists of populations in which everyone's life is worth living and which are homogeneous in life quality—everyone has the same type of life. ("Type of life" and "life quality" are here used interchangeably.) We refer to types of life as $L, L', \ldots$, and to quantities—population sizes—as $k, k', \ldots$, etc. Thus, in what follows, kL will stand for a population of k people with lives of type L. We do not distinguish between populations on the basis of the personal identity of its members. This is not needed for the discussion that follows.

For any L such that the domain contains some L-population, we take it that any quantity of L can form a population: If the domain contains a population kL for some k, then it contains L-populations of every size. This implies, in particular, that there is no upper limit on population sizes.

There are two kinds of betterness relations we need to consider: one between types of life and the other between populations. To distinguish between them I use the T-subscript for the former relation (T for "type"). Thus, $L \succ_T L'$ stands for the claim that L is a better type of life than L', while $kL \succ k'L'$ states that a population of k people with lives of type L is better than a population of k' people with lives of type L'.

The two relations are closely connected. Indeed, the first relation can be defined in terms of the second (for this suggestion, see Jensen 2020):

$$L \succ_T L' =_{df} 1L \succ 1L'.$$

In other words, a type of life L is better than another type of life L' whenever a life of type L is better than a life of type L'.[14] In what follows, we shall therefore freely move from betterness claims regarding types of life to betterness claims regarding lives.

As for the relation of betterness among populations, I assume that this relation is asymmetric and transitive.

Asymmetry: If $kL \succ k'L'$, then $k'L' \not\succ kL$.
Transitivity: If $kL \succ k'L'$ and $k'L' \succ k''L''$, then $kL \succ k''L''$.[15]

Indeed, I shall in addition assume that betterness and worseness (= the converse of betterness) are *transitive across equal goodness*, i.e. that every population that is better (worse) than kL must also be better (worse) than $k'L'$ if kL and $k'L'$ are (precisely) equally good. Thus, letting $\approx$ stand for the transitive, symmetric and reflexive relation of equal goodness, I assume, as part of the condition of Transitivity, that:

(i) if $k''L'' \succ kL$ and $kL \approx k'L'$, then $k''L'' \succ k'L'$
and
(ii) if $kL \succ k''L''$ and $kL \approx k'L$, then $k'L' \succ k''L''$.

A much more economical representation that entails all these standard conditions on $\succ$ and $\approx$ starts from the relation $\succeq$ of being *at least as good*. This relation, which is taken as primitive, is assumed to be reflexive and transitive. That is, a "quasi-order" (or a "pre-order," as it also sometimes is called). Betterness and equal goodness are then defined as the asymmetric and the symmetric parts of $\succeq$, respectively:

$kL \succ k'L' =_{df} kL \succeq k'L'$ and $k'L' \not\succeq kL$; $kL \approx k'L' =_{df} kL \succeq k'L'$ and $k'L' \succeq kL$.

Now comes a value assumption that will be very important in what follows. Since we only consider populations of people with lives worth living, I assume, following Parfit, that the larger a population is the better it is, if life quality is kept constant.

---

[14] Analogously, L and L' are equally good iff life L is equally as good as life L', and they are incommensurable iff life L is incommensurable with life L'. It is often assumed that wellbeing levels form a linear ordering: if two such levels are distinct, then one is higher than the other. But this view can be questioned. And anyway, as we have seen above, the type (= quality) of a life is not reducible to its wellbeing level. Thus, it should be possible for distinct L and L' to be equally good or even incommensurable. The ordering of types of life need not be linear, nor even need it be complete.
[15] By the definition of $\succ_T$ in terms of $\succ$, these conditions imply that the betterness relation between types of life is also asymmetric and transitive. Note, by the way, that the transitivity of the latter relation has not been questioned in the discussion of the Continuum Argument. It is the transitivity of the betterness relation between populations that has been a subject of some dispute.

Principle of Quantity: For all k, k′ and L, kL ≻ k′L if k > k′.[16]

Here, > stands for the relation "greater than" between quantities. Since quantities form a linear ordering and ≻ is an asymmetric relation, the Principle of Quantity immediately implies its converse:

For all k, k′ and L, kL ≻ k′L only if k > k′.

As we remember, according to Parfit, an excellent life is weakly superior ("lexically superior" in his terminology) to a drab life. The relation of weak superiority between types of life can easily be defined in our framework:

L is *weakly superior* to L′ =$_{df}$ For some k, kL ≻ k′L′ for all k′.

That is, L is weakly superior to L′ if some (sufficiently large) quantity of L is better than any quantity of L′.

Let me now introduce another concept that will be useful in what follows.

L is *exchangeable* for L′ =$_{df}$ For every k, there is some k′ such that k′L′ ≻ kL.

That is, L is exchangeable for L′ if for every quantity of L there is a quantity of L′ that is better.[17]

As we have seen, the main assumption behind the Continuum Argument is Compensation: Small losses in quality can always be outweighed by sufficiently large increases in quantity. In our current terminology, this means that a type of life is exchangeable for a worse type of life if the quality difference between them is small.

Now, suppose there is a sequence of types of life, $L_1, L_2, \ldots, L_n$, such that L_1 is weakly superior to L_n. Thus, for some quantity k_1, k_1L_1 is better than any quantity of L_n. (Think of L_1 as an excellent life and of L_n as a drab life.) Then it *cannot* be true that every type L_i in this sequence is exchangeable for its successor L_{i+1}.

---

[16] As the reader might recall, I have some qualms about this assumption; cf. footnote 6 above.

But what about the mirror assumption, which we might call the Principle of Quality? It says that better life quality makes the population better as long as its size is kept constant:

Principle of Quality: For all k, L and L′, kL ≻ kL′ if L ≻$_T$ kL′.

This principle looks very plausible, but I have no use for it in what follows, so I won't assume it. Also, while seemingly so plausible, the Principle of Quality might be questioned if one allows that the marginal value of added lives could decrease and that it could decrease at different rates for different types of life. If it would decrease faster for L than for L′, then for large k, kL′ might be better than kL despite the fact that L is a better type of life than L′. (I am indebted for this cautionary observation to Karsten Klint Jensen.)

[17] Note that exchangeability on this definition is a non-symmetric relation (which might not be how we use this term in ordinary language). Thus, L might be exchangeable for L′ without L′ being exchangeable for L. To illustrate this, let one type of life be drab and the other excellent.

Otherwise, it would be possible to construct a sequence of populations starting with k_1L_1:

$$k_1L_1, k_2L_2, \ldots, k_nL_n$$

in which each population is better than its immediate predecessor. By the transitivity of betterness, it would then follow that k_nL_n is better than k_1L_1. But given the asymmetry of betterness, this is incompatible with k_1L_1 being better than any quantity of L_n.

We can also put it this way: If all types in the sequence leading from an excellent life to a drab life are exchangeable for their immediate successors, then we have a Repugnant Conclusion on our hands. Since exchangeability is a transitive relation, for every quantity of excellent lives there is some quantity of drab lives that is better. Parfit cannot accept it.

But then, if some L_i in the sequence is not exchangeable for L_{i+1}, how can these types of life be related instead?

One possibility is that L_i is weakly superior to L_{i+1}.[18] But how can this be if we suppose that at each point in the sequence the next type of life is only slightly worse than its immediate predecessor?

To make sense of this, we might appeal to the idea of *the diminishing marginal value of quantity*. It might be that k_iL_i is better than any quantity of L_{i+1} because increases in the quantity of L_{i+1} so steeply diminish in their marginal value that no quantity of L_{i+1} can ever reach the value of k_iL_i. (Cf. Arrhenius and Rabinowicz 2005, 2015. See also Jensen 2008.)

Parfit (2016, p. 112) finds this option implausible; he rejects the Diminishing Value View. The argument he uses appeals to the analogy between goodness and badness:

> The existence of [...] wretched people would not have a badness that would diminish as the number of such people grew, so that it mattered less and less whether more such people exist. The badness of more such suffering would never decline. [...] we cannot plausibly either apply some Diminishing Value View to lives that are bad, or restrict this view to lives that are good.

But is it a convincing argument? Why can't we restrict the Diminishing Value View to good lives only, i.e. accept diminishing value but reject diminishing

---

[18] Indeed, it is the only available possibility as long as the betterness relation between populations is supposed to be *complete*, i.e., as long as we do not allow for incommensurabilities. In Arrhenius and Rabinowicz (2005, 2015) it was shown (within a somewhat different formal framework) that, given this completeness condition, any sequence $L_1, \ldots, L_n$ such that L_1 is weakly superior to L_n must contain some L_i that is weakly superior to its immediate successor in the sequence. (To be more precise, this was shown not specifically for types of life, but more generally, for all quantifiable goods.)

*dis*value? Indeed, as Parfit himself admits, "there are some asymmetries between suffering and happiness, and some of the other things that can make lives good or bad" (ibid.). So why cannot there be an asymmetry (i.e., a disanalogy) between goodness and badness in this respect as well?[19]

Be that as it may. In any case, Parfit is not willing to allow that the marginal value of good lives can ever diminish. He accepts what he calls the *Simple View*: "the Simple View claims: Anyone's existence is in itself good if this person's life is worth living. Such goodness has non-diminishing value, so if there were more such people, the combined goodness of their existence would have no upper limit" (ibid., p. 112).[20]

This leads him to reject the suggestion that at some point in the sequence $L_1, \ldots, L_n$ we could encounter a type of life, L_i, that is weakly superior to the next type L_{i+1}, in spite of it being only slightly better than the latter.

As the Simple View is literally stated, it only denies that the marginal value of added lives can diminish. But what about the possibility that this marginal value could sometimes *increase*? For example, that the value of a population could radically increase upon reaching a certain size, perhaps even increase to infinity? Parfit might have wanted to reject this possibility as well. He seems to have been attracted to the view that the value added by a life to a population is just the value that this life has in itself. Thus, if the added life does not affect the life quality of other population members, it never adds more value to the population, or less value, than what it is intrinsically worth. (Or, at least, this is so as long as everyone in a given population has life of the same quality, so that adding more people with lives of that quality does not make the population either more or less equal.) This, I think, is what the Simple View amounts to.

---

[19] As I have been reminded by Tim Campbell (in private communication), there is a more challenging criticism of such an asymmetric view in Parfit's *Reasons an Persons*, ch. 18 ("The Absurd Conclusion"). If the marginal value of good lives diminishes, while bad lives have a non-diminishing marginal disvalue, then, if the size of a population increases while the percentage of bad lives remains constant in this growing population, the combined disvalue of bad lives must sooner or later overtake the combined value of good lives. This might seem counter-intuitive.

Whether it is counter-intuitive is not obvious to me. But, on the other hand, one might perhaps simply bite the bullet and assume that the marginal disvalue of bad lives can also diminish. For just as the diminishing value of good lives would help us to avoid the Repugnant Conclusion, the diminishing marginal disvalue of bad lives would help in avoiding the Reverse Repugnant Conclusion—the mirror image of the Repugnant Conclusion in the domain of populations composed of people with bad lives. Intuitively, it seems that a sizeable population in which everyone has a terrible life is worse than any population, however large, in which everyone's life is only barely bad (barely worth not living). But if the marginal disvalue of such barely bad lives is not diminishing, it is difficult to uphold this view—just as it is difficult to resist the Repugnant Conclusion if the marginal value of barely good lives (lives barely worth living) does not diminish. (I owe this observation to James Goodrich. The Reverse Repugnant Conclusion was formulated by Carlson 1998.)

[20] Note, though, that earlier in his paper Parfit offers a different, much weaker formulation of the Simple View—one that does not require the marginal value of good lives to be non-diminishing: "the *Simple View*: Anyone's existence is in itself good, and makes the world in one way better, if this person's life is good to live, or worth living" (Parfit 2016, p. 110).

I will come back to the Simple View later on, in the last section. Now let us just take it as given that Parfit is not prepared to allow that a type of life can be weakly superior to another type of life that is only slightly worse.

But then, if the types of life in the sequence leading by small steps from an excellent life to a drab life cannot *all* be exchangeable for their immediate successors, as this would lead to the Repugnant Conclusion, and if none of these types can be weakly superior to its immediate successor, what other possibility is left?

15.4 Enter Incommensurability

What is left is the possibility that for some pairs L_i and L_{i+1} of adjacent types in this sequence that by small steps leads from an excellent life to a drab life, the relation between L_i and L_{i+1} admits of *incommensurability*. And indeed, that it admits of incommensurability of a very thoroughgoing sort, which I will call *persistent*. By this I mean that some quantity k_i of L_i is such that while L_{i+1} is worse than k_iL_i in smaller quantities, it is incommensurable with k_iL_i in *all* larger quantities. Thus, if k_iL_i isn't better than $k_{i+1}L_{i+1}$, then these two populations are incommensurable and this incommensurability would persist however much the quantity of L_{i+1} were increased. Consequently, the Continuum Argument could not be repaired by increasing the quantity of L_{i+1}. No quantity of L_{i+1}, however large, could do the job, since no quantity of L_{i+1} would be better than (or equally as good as) k_iL_i.

Here's the definition of this relation between types of life:

L admits of *persistent incommensurability* with L' $=_{df}$ For some quantity k of L, there is a quantity k' of L' such that kL is incommensurable with every quantity of L' at least as large as k'.[21]

As is easy to see, if the above holds for some quantity k of L, then kL will be better than every quantity of L' that is commensurable with kL.[22] Thus, no quantity of L' will be better than kL. Which means that L is not exchangeable for L'. In smaller quantities, L' is worse than kL and it is incommurable with kL in all larger quantities.

---

[21] Note that this is not a symmetric relation. If L admits of persistent incommensurability with L', it doesn't follow that L' admits of persistent incommensurability with L. Indeed, it might well be the case that L' is exchangeable for L.

[22] Suppose that k*L' is commensurable with kL (i.e. either better or worse than, or equally as good as kL) and that kL is incommensurable with every quantity of L' at least as large as k'. We want to show that kL is better than k*L'. Proof: By the definition of persistent incommensurability, k* will have to be smaller than k'. But then k*L' cannot be better than or equally as good as kL. For then, by the Principle of Quantity and Transitivity, k'L' would be better than kL, contrary to the hypothesis. Consequently, if kL is commensurable with k*L', it must be better than k*L'.

As for weak superiority, if L admits of persistent incommensurability with L′, this certainly does not imply that L is weakly superior to L′, but it does not exclude it either: Even though kL is incommensurable with every sufficiently large quantity of L′, some larger quantity of L might be better than any quantity of L′. We can, however, exclude this possibility if we stipulate that persistent incommensurability with L′ extends to all quantities of L at least as large as k. We can define this more demanding relation as follows:

> L admits of *strictly persistent incommensurability* with L′ $=_{df}$ There is a quantity k of L such that for every quantity k^+ of L at least as large as k, there is some k′ such that k^+L is incommensurable with every quantity of L′ at least as large as k′.

But, one might ask, does the incommensurability between the populations instantiating two adjacent types of life have to be so thoroughgoing for the Continuum argument to be blocked by an appeal to incommensurability? The answer is yes, it is necessary. The following can be proved:

> **Trilemma:** For any two types of life L and L′, exactly one of the following three relations must obtain: (i) L is exchangeable for L′, (ii) L is weakly superior to L′, or (iii) L admits of strictly persistent incommensurability with L′.

The proof of the Trilemma is provided in the Appendix, where Trilemma is proved in a generalized form, not just for lives worth living but for all types of goods. The proof relies on Transitivity and the Principle of Quantity.[23]

Thus, to block the Continuum Argument by an appeal to incommensurability, Parfit needs to postulate incommensurability that is extremely thoroughgoing.

As will be argued in the next section (15.5), positing such persistent incommensurability is quite problematic (though perhaps not unacceptable, see section 15.6). But will it at least be sufficient?

This might be questioned. Let's consider for a moment the dialectics of a hypothetical debate between Parfit and a proponent of the Continuum Argument.[24] Parfit, who wants to insist that an excellent life (L_1) is weakly superior to a drab life (L_n), might be asked to specify a number k_1 of L_1-lives that in his view would be better than any number L_n-lives. If he does come up with a definite answer, which might not be that easy, the proponent of the Continuum Argument needs to counter this proposal. Thus, she needs to present an appropriate population sequence: a sequence of (what she claims) better-and-better

---

[23] In Handfield and Rabinowicz (2018), a very similar trilemma, though formulated in somewhat different terminology and with weak inferiority replacing weak superiority, was proved for types of bads, more specifically, for harms of varying intensity. Here, in the Appendix, I prove it for types of goods, with types of lives worth living being instances of types of goods.

[24] I am indebted to John Broome for making me think harder about this issue.

populations in which everyone's life is getting worse-and-worse, but the number of people increases. This sequence must start with k_1L_1 and end with k_nL_n, for some k_n that may be as large as she pleases. To come up with a *prima facie* plausible sequence of this kind might not be easy.

But, if this demand is met, then it is up to Parfit to try to find a fault in his opponent's proposal: He needs to point to some populations in the offered sequence that are incommensurable with their immediate successors, instead of being worse as his opponent claims.[25] This might not be easy. What's more, the incommensurabilities need to be persistent, to prevent the opponent from repairing the population sequence by increasing the sizes of successor populations.

Even if Parfit would manage to do it, it would not be the end of the matter. The proponent of the Continuum Argument could come back and offer *another* population sequence starting with k_1L_1 and continuing all the way to some quantity k_n of L_n, but involving intermediate types of life that differ from those in her original proposal. Parfit would then again need to find faults in this new sequence, and so on and so on. It is not clear how this debate could be conclusively resolved. Note that both sides have their respective burdens of proof, as both come up with positive, though opposing, claims.

In what follows, I gloss over the complexity of this dialectics and instead focus on the very concept of persistent incommensurability. What I am going to say will also apply to the stronger notion of strictly persistent incommensurability.

15.5 Assessing the Costs

Persistent incommensurability is a strange creature. In the standard cases that are used in the literature to illustrate incommensurability, one of the incommensurable items is better than the other in some relevant respects and worse in other relevant respects. All things considered, taking all the relevant respects into consideration and considering how they might be admissibly weighed against each other, none of the two items is better overall, nor are they equally good. The

---

[25] Alan Hájek has questioned this (in private communication). Why should there be this requirement on Parfit? To give an analogy, a critic of the *sorites* need not specify the number of grains of sand at which heaps begin. And while it may be indeterminate (vague) which number it is, the critic is not obliged to delimit this zone of indeterminacy. I think, though, that there is an important dialectical difference between these two cases: While everyone agrees that the conclusion of the *sorites* is absurd, not everyone finds the Repugnant Conclusion repugnant. Critics of the *sorites* are therefore in a much stronger dialectical position. They need not be as specific in their critique as the critics of the Continuum Argument.

Still, while imperfect, this analogy is instructive. In both cases, it might be indeterminate where exactly the relevant break point(s) of the argument is (are) located. In particular, it might well be indeterminate which populations in the Continuum Argument's population sequence are incommensurable with their immediate successors. I do not consider the possibility of indeterminacy in this chapter, but a model in which incommensurabilities are allowed to be indeterminate is developed in Rabinowicz (2009b).

same applies to the case we focus on, in which the compared items are (homogeneous) populations and the relevant respects, or dimensions of comparison, are quality and quantity: type of life and population size. The preceding population is better in quality and the succeeding one is better in size. However, in the standard cases of multidimensional comparisons, if two items are incommensurable, this incommensurability is not supposed to be persistent: A sufficiently large improvement (worsening) of one of the items in any of the relevant dimensions will make it all-things-considered better (worse) than the other.

In the well-known *small-improvement argument* for incommensurability, one starts with two items, X and Y, neither of which is better than the other. (This is taken to be established independently.) The aim of the argument is to prove that they are not (precisely) equally good either and thus that they must be incommensurable. To that end, one considers a small improvement of one of the items, say, Y, in some relevant respect. This slightly improved variant of Y, Y^+, is better than Y. But if it still is not better than X, this shows that X and Y cannot be equally good, since betterness is transitive across equal goodness. If the two items were equally good, then anything better than Y would be better than X.

It is significant that this argument relies on a *small* improvement. Given that X isn't better than Y, it would strain credulity to think that *no* improvement of Y in the relevant respect under consideration could make it better than X. Therefore, if $k_i L_i$ isn't better than $k_{i+1} L_{i+1}$, it strains credulity to think that no increase, however large, in the quantity of L_{i+1} could make the L_{i+1}-population better than $k_i L_i$. This is especially strange if, as the Simple View has it, the marginal value of added L_{i+1}-lives never diminishes. But even if this value were allowed to diminish, it is still possible that large increases in quantity should considerably increase the value of L_{i+1}-population. Thus, to put it mildly, it seems that the persistence of incommensurability, which Parfit needs to block the Continuum Argument, is something higly atypical. This puts his proposal under pressure.[26]

Let me develop this line of thought a little further. Ruth Chang has made an influential suggestion that in cases of of multidimensional comparisons between items falling under the same covering value, if neither item is better than the other and they are not equally good, the two items are *on a par*. They are incommensurable (in the sense in which I am using the term), but still in the same league, so

---

[26] This worry about persistency of incommensurability was first raised in Handfield and Rabinowicz (2018), in connection with our discussion of the well-known Temkin-Rachels Spectrum Argument against the transitivity of betterness. (In that paper, strictly persistent incommensurability is referred to as "radical" incommensurability.) To block the Spectrum Argument by an appeal to incommensurabilities also requires these incommensurabilities to be strictly persistent. Which is not surprising, since that argument is a close cousin of the Continuum Argument. In the next section, I am going to suggest how the worry about persistency could be put to rest. Thus, this chapter might be seen as an attempt to solve the problem posed in my earlier paper with Handfield.

to speak.[27] They are not incomparable: for Chang, parity is a *sui generis* form of comparability, which is distinct from the three other, standard, forms (better, worse, and equally good). It is plausible, I think, to suppose that Parfit's "imprecise equality" is just this relation of parity.[28] Items that are imprecisely equal are incommensurable but nevertheless on a par; they are not incomparable with each other.

Now, it is often taken to be a feature of parity, as opposed to incomparability, that if two items are on a par, and it is possible to considerably improve one of them, then this considerable improvement will make that item better than the other. In other words, parity is not supposed to be persistent.

Indeed, Qizilbash (2018) takes such lack of persistency to be the "mark of parity." On his interpretation of this relation, parity is what he calls "rough equality" and rough equality is sensitive to significant unilateral changes in value:

> On this view [= the rough-equality view], when parity holds between items [...] while some slight change in value may not tilt the balance in favour of one of them, any significant increase in the value of one of the items will make it better, and any significant reduction in the value of one will make it worse, than the other. This feature of parity is the 'mark of parity' on the rough equality view. [...] this mark [...] is implied by a central component of the rough equality view: the assumption that while parity is a form of equality and a distinct relation, it is not precise equality. The mark of parity also distinguishes parity from "incomparability". If there were "incomparability", on this view, while one is not better than the other even some significant increase (or reduction) in the value of one option would not make it better (worse) than the other.
>
> (Qizilbash 2018, p. 90)

He contrasts this rough-equality account of parity with the one I myself have put forward in Rabinowicz (2008, 2012) and argues that the latter account fails to entail that parity must have this mark of impersistence. He is right. My account does not have this implication.

Here comes a brief sketch of my proposal. It takes its departure from the *fitting-attitudes analysis* of value but allows that in some cases there might exist a range of

---

[27] "Parity typically holds between items that bear very different aspects of V and yet are nevertheless 'in the same neighbourhood' of V-ness" (Chang 2016a, p. 193). V here refers to the "covering value"— the covering consideration, with respect to which the items in question are being compared. Aspects of V are different relevant respects, or dimensions, of comparison. "Being 'in the same neighbourhood' of a value is being in the same 'rank', 'league', 'division', 'category', or 'level'"(Chang 2016b, p. 405).

[28] When I wrote in the Introduction that "[b]y 'imprecise equality' Parfit means something very close to *incommensurability* [...] Or, at least, imprecise equality is meant to entail incommensurability," I had this interpretation of imprecise equality as parity in mind.

Chang (2016a) makes the same suggestion, though she questions whether Parfit himself would agree. Nevertheless, she argues that it is the best account of the relation that is targeted by Parfit when he talks about "imprecise equality."

different permissible (not unfitting) attitudes towards an item. The attitudes I focus on are preferences. I analyze value relations that obtain in a domain of items under consideration. All these relations are defined in terms of the class K of permissible preference orderings of the items in a given domain. An item X is *better* than another item Y iff it ought to be preferred to Y, i.e., iff every ordering in K ranks X above Y. They are *equally good* iff every ordering in K ranks them equally, or, what amounts to the same, iff one ought to be indifferent between X and Y. Every ordering in K is a quasi-order, i.e. a reflexive and transitive relation. This implies that the relation $\succeq$ of being at least as good (= better or equally as good) is also a quasi-order, just as we have assumed it to be.

Incommensurability arises when it is permissible for preferences to diverge. In particular, X and Y are *on a par* iff some orderings in K rank X above Y, but some other orderings in K rank Y above X. That is, they are on a par iff it is permissible to prefer X to Y but also permissible to have the opposite preference.

The orderings in K might, or might not, contain gaps in some places. We do not assume that they must be complete. Preference gaps between some items in the domain might well be permissible. It should be noted that allowing for incomplete preference orderings in K makes room for incommensurabilities that do not depend on divergence in permissible preferences. Indeed, given my definitions of betterness and equal goodness, it is enough that in a single preference ordering in K there is a preference gap between X and Y for these two items to be incommensurable in value. (Though, as we have seen, more is required for them to be on a par.) A radical form of this kind of incommensurability obtains if there is a gap between X and Y in *every* ordering in K. This is how I interpret incomparability. Thus, X and Y are *incomparable* iff it is impermissible to prefer one of these items to the other or to be indifferent. What is required is a preferential gap. Needless to say, this account makes incomparability between items belonging to the same ontological category a rare phenomenon, something we encounter perhaps only in cases of genuine moral dilemmas. That a gap in preferences between X and Y might be permissible does not seem problematic. But that it is required—that every permissible preference ordering contains such a gap—must be very unusual.

Orderings in K are meant to represent permissible *overall* preferences, i.e. preferences that take into account all the relevant respects of comparison. Parity will typically arise in cases of multidimensional comparisons, if one item ranks higher in some respects and the other item ranks higher in other respects. The overall preference regarding such items will then depend on how the different respects (dimensions) are weighted against each other. It is unrealistic to expect that there is a unique correct assignment of weights to dimensions. Different weight assignments will normally be admissible. Therefore, it might well be the case that an overall preference for one item and an overall preference for the other item will both be permissible, due to different admissible weighings of dimensions. As a result, the two items will be on a par.[29]

Now, Qizilbash suggests that this account, unlike his own, does not *exclude* that parity might be persistent. He is right, of course. However, even on my proposal, parity typically is not going to persist if one of the items in a parity pair is significantly improved in some relevant respect. When the improvement becomes large enough, the preference for the other item will typically stop being permissible, which will put an end to parity.[30]

Nevertheless, it is an important feature of my account that it at least in principle allows for persistent (and indeed strictly persistent) parity. In the next section, I will demonstrate how this possibility can arise.

15.6 Accounting for Persistence

First, let me sketch how my general account of value relations applies to value comparisons between populations.

The domain of items we consider in this case is, as previously, the set of possible populations, with different sizes and different types of life, the same for every person in a population, and worth living. There is no upper limit on size. K is the class of permissible preference orderings of that domain. Every such ordering P of populations induces the associated ordering P_T of types of life by the definition:

P_T ranks L higher than L' $=_{df}$ P ranks 1L higher than 1L'.

L is better than L' iff for every permissible preference ordering P, P_T ranks L higher than L'.

We may assume, if we wish, that all orderings in K induce the same ordering of types of life: for all orderings P and Q in K, $P_T = Q_T$. In a more general setting, however, this assumption should not be made. Indeed, there are good reasons not

---

[29] But of course, there will be many cases in which X comes up higher than Y on every admissible assignment of weights to relevant respects. In such cases, X will be ranked above Y in every permissible ordering. This might be the case even if Y is better than X in some of relevant respects. It might not be admissible to give these respects as much weight as is needed to tip the overall preference in favor of Y.

[30] Impersistency of parity is also to be expected on another recent account of that relation, due to Chrisoula Andreou (Andreou 2015). On her account, two items are on a par with respect to some covering value V iff they belong to the same category (the same "league") with respect to V, but nevertheless are mutually incommensurable with respect to V, i.e., neither is a better specimen of V nor are they equally good specimens of V. Categories of a given value are supposed to be linearly ordered from higher to lower: excellent specimens of V, good specimens, mediocre ones, etc. Unless the categories are very broad, if X and Y are on a par, a significant improvement (worsening) of one of the items will move it to a higher (lower) category. Thus, it won't any longer be on a par with the other item. Indeed, it will be better (worse) than that other item. Thus, even on this account parity typically isn't going to persist.

to make it, if we think of life types as multidimensional. Permissible rankings of types of life can then vary, depending on how the dimensions of a life are weighed.[31] But in the model at hand, we might just as well assume, for simplicity, that different orderings in K agree on how they rank types of life. What they disagree about is the relative weight they give to the type of life (quality) as compared to the size of the population (quantity).[32]

By contrast, other assumptions we make about the model are crucial. Thus, we assume that orderings in K satisfy the preferential versions of the conditions previously imposed on the relation of betterness between populations: Permissible preferences are asymmetric and transitive (also across indifference, which is assumed to be an equivalence relation), and they obey the preferential version of the Principle of Quantity:

Preferential Principle of Quantity: For all orderings P in K, all L, k and k', P ranks kL above k'L if k > k'.

In this principle, "if" may be replaced by "iff," since the ordering > of quantities is linear and the preference relation is asymmetric.

Given my analysis of betterness and equal goodness in terms of permissible preferences, these conditions on K imply the corresponding conditions on betterness and equal goodness: Betterness is asymmetric and transitive (also across equal goodness, which is an equivalence relation), and it satisfies the Principle of Quantity.

Two preferential relations will be useful in the following discussion: the preferential variants of weak superiority and exchangeability. Suppose that P is an ordering of possible populations. We define P-exchangeability and weak P-superiority as follows:

L is *P-exchangeable* for L' $=_{df}$ For every quantity of L, there is a quantity of L' that P ranks higher.
L is *weakly P-superior* to L' $=_{df}$ There is a quantity of L that P ranks higher than every quantity of L'.

I now move to the question how strictly persistent parity can arise in this model.

---

[31] In this more general setting, it will be possible to have types of life that are mutually incommensurable in their value. See Rabinowicz (forthcoming) for a modeling of this kind.
[32] Weights that are assigned to different dimensions of comparison between populations need not be simple coefficients that add up to one. The weighting system might be much more complicated. For some suggestion as to how it could look like in the case at hand, see footnote 35 below.

L admits of *strictly persistent parity* with L' =$_{df}$ There is a quantity k of L such that for every quantity k$^+$ of L at least as large as k, there is some k' such that k$^+$L is on a par with every quantity of L' at least as large as k'.

Lemma: If K contains orderings P and Q such that L is weakly P-superior to L' and Q-exchangeable for L', then L admits of strictly persistent parity with L'.

Proof of the Lemma: If L is weakly P-superior to L', then for some k, (i) P ranks kL higher than every quantity of L'. Consider any k$^+$ ≥ k. If L is Q-exchangeable for L', then for some k', (ii) Q ranks k'L' higher than k$^+$L. By the transitivity of permissible preferences and the Preferential Principle of Quantity, (i) implies that (iii) P ranks k$^+$L higher than every quantity of L', while (ii) implies that (iv) Q ranks every quantity of L' at least as large as k' higher than k$^+$L. Together, (iii) and (iv) imply that (v) for every k$^+$ ≥ k, there is some k' such that k$^+$L is on a par with every quantity of L' at least as large k'. This means that L admits of strictly persistent parity with L'. Q.E.D.[33]

---

[33] Is there any other way in which strictly persistent parity can arise in my model? The Lemma assumes that K contains at least one permissible ordering P such that L is weakly P-superior to L'. That such an ordering is permissible might, however, be questioned if L' is only slightly worse than L. If one, like Parfit, is unwilling to allow that L could be weakly superior to L' in such a case, i.e., that L could be weakly P-superior to L' in *every* permissible ordering P, then one might perhaps also be unwilling to allow that this could hold in *any* permissible ordering. Which gives rise to the question: Could L admit of strict persistent parity with L' even if in every permissible preference ordering P, L is P-exchangeable for L'?

I believe it is possible, though it would require K to contain an infinite number of orderings. The idea would be that for every quantity k$^+$ of K at least as large as some k and for every quantity of L' at least as large as some k', some ordering in K ranks this quantity of L' higher than k$^+$L while some other ordering in K still ranks it lower. (In the latter ordering it would take a larger quantity of L' to be ranked higher than k$^+$L.) As a result, k$^+$L is on a par with any quantity of L' at least as large as k'. Thus, L admits of strictly persistent parity with L'. This is compatible with L being P-exchangeable for L' in every permissible ordering P. (This shows, by the way, that in such infinite models P-exchangeability in all permissible orderings P does not entail exchangeability, even though the converse holds. Likewise, weak P-superiority in all permissible P does not entail weak superiority, even though the converse holds.) Whether such a modelling is possible, as I believe it is, would have to be checked, of course.

But while some type L in the Continuum Argument's life sequence can in this way admit of strictly persistent parity with its successor, despite being P-exchangeable for the latter in every permissible ordering P, this is not the end of the matter. If we don't want to allow any ordering P in which a type of life is weakly P-superior to a slightly worse type a life, then how can we prevent that *each* type of life in the Continuum Argument's life sequence is P-exchangeable for its successor? And we must prevent it, if we don't want the first type in this sequence to be P-exchangeable for the last type.

P-exchangeability is a transitive relation. On Parfit's view, the first type in this sequence is weakly superior to the last type, which entails, of course, that it is weakly P-superior to, and not P-exchangeable for the last type. The solution—the only possible solution—would be to posit preferential gaps in all permissible orderings. And the gaps have to be strictly persistent. More precisely, we must posit for every permissible ordering P that there are some (at least two) types in the sequence such that P admits of a strictly persistent preference gap between these types and their immediate successors. That this is the only possible solution follows from the preferential version of the Trilemma: For every permissible preference ordering P and for all types L and L', either L is weakly P-superior to L' or P-exchangeable for L', or it admits of a strictly persistent preference gap with regard to L'. The proof of this result is exactly analogous to the proof of Trilemma provided in the Appendix. It rests on the preferential versions of Transitivity and Principle of Quantity.

It is not difficult in this model to provide an example of a sequence of types, $L_1, \ldots, L_n$, in which no type is weakly superior to its immediate successor, but L_1 is weakly superior to L_n. Clearly, if the latter holds, then it cannot be that every type in this sequence is exchangeable for its successor. (Remember that exchangeability is a transitive relation, and if L_1 is weakly superior to L_n then it cannot be exchangeable for L_n.) Therefore, by the Trilemma, for some L_i in $L_1, \ldots, L_n$, L_i must admit of strictly persistent incommensurability with L_{i+1}. Indeed, there must be at least two types of life in this sequence that are like this. If there were only one such type, then—by the Trilemma—all other types in the sequence would be exchangeable for their immediate successors. Consequently, it would be possible, on the basis of this type sequence, to construct a sequence of populations in which incommensurability would appear at just one point, while at every other point the next population would be better than its immediate predecessor. We already know that this is impossible, since betterness is transitive and the first population is supposed to be better than the last one (see section 15.2).

Here is the simplest possible example of a type sequence that satisfies the above requirements. This sequence consists of just three types, L_1, L_2, and L_3. Suppose that for some permissible orderings P and Q,

L_1 is weakly P-superior to L_2 and L_3, while L_2 is P-exchangeable for L_3,
and
L_1 is Q-exchangeable for L_2, and both L_1 and L_2 are weakly Q-superior to L_3.

By the Lemma above, these conditions imply that L_1 admits of strictly persistent parity with L_2 (since it is weakly P-superior to L_2 and Q-exchangeable for L_2), while L_2 admits of strictly persistent parity with L_3 (since it is weakly Q-superior to L_3 and P-exchangeable for L_3).

If we in addition suppose that orderings P and Q exhaust class K of permissible orderings (remember, we want the example to be as simple as possible), it can be proved that L_1 is weakly superior to L_3, as required.[34]

We can think of this example as follows: L_1 is an excellent life, while L_3 is a drab life. L_2 is an intermediate type of life: worse than L_1 and better than L_3. When one moves from an excellent life to a drab life, by decreasing life quality in each step, one must at some point cross the line between lives worth *striving for* and those

---

[34] *Proof:* To prove that L_1 is weakly superior to L_3, we need to show that some quantity of the former is better than every quantity of the latter. Since L_1 is weakly P-superior to L_3, there is some k such that (i) P ranks kL_1 above every quantity of L_3. Similarly, since L_1 is weakly Q-superior to L_3, there is some k' such that (ii) Q ranks $k'L_1$ above every quantity of L_3. Now, either k = k' or one of these two quantities is larger than the other. Without loss of generality, assume that $k \geq k'$. Then, by the transitivity of permissible preferences and the Preferential Principle of Quantity, (ii) implies that (iii) Q ranks kL_1 above every quantity of L_3. Therefore, by (i) and (iii), both P and Q rank kL_1 above every quantity of L_3. Since P and Q exhaust class K, this implies that kL_1 is better than every quantity of L_3.

More generally, it can be proved in this way that in a model with just a *finite* number of preference orderings in K, L is weakly superior to L' if it is weakly P-superior to L' in every ordering P in K.

that are not (even though they still are worth living). Where this line is drawn varies between different permissible preference orderings; there is an optionality to this choice. This variation can be expected especially if the types of life in the area where the line plausibly can be drawn don't differ much in quality. But the line must be drawn somewhere, since an excellent life is worth striving for and a drab life definitely is not. At the point at which a given preference ordering draws the line, we get a sudden drop in the ordering: the types of life above the line are preferentially weakly superior to those below. In the toy example above, P draws the line between L_1 and L_2, while Q draws it between L_2 and L_3.[35]

It might be noted that nothing would change if we allowed for yet another permissible preference ordering, R, which is cautious and thus avoids adjudicating between P and Q. It avoids the decision as to where exactly the line should be drawn. The price of this avoidance is incompleteness: an ordering that avoids this decision must contain gaps. R can be defined as the intersection—the common part—of P and Q. Allowing for such cautious orderings seems reasonable. But if R is the common part of P and Q then adding it to K would not affect any of the conclusions we have reached above. (The proof is left to the reader.)[36]

Thus, our model makes room for type sequences of the kind Parfit requires. In principle, we can have a type sequence that starts with an excellent life and ends with a drab life, and in which no type of life is weakly superior to its immediate successor but the first type is weakly superior to the last one. For this to be possible, some of the adjacent types in the sequence must admit of strictly persistent incommensurability. We have now seen how to account for it. Indeed, we have seen how to account for such a sequence in which adjacent types admit of strictly persistent parity. Parity can be persistent, after all.

15.7 Are We Home Then?

Not quite. The abstract model described in the preceding section makes room for type sequences of the requisite kind and thus shows that Parfit was on the right track. But I don't think that there is a way to square this model with some of Parfit's substantive value assumptions, and more specifically with his Simple

---

[35] Different orderings in K disagree about the relative weight they give to the type of life (quality) as compared to the size of the population (quantity). These weights might also vary for different population comparisons. To account for the example I have provided we can assume that for each ordering, its weight assignment depends on where it draws the line between the lives that are worth striving for and those that are not. In a comparison between two populations in both of which people's lives are above the line, the weight given to population size is relatively large. The same applies if people's lives in both populations are below the line. But if lives in one population are above the line and they are below the line in the other population, then in this comparison the importance of quality is much more decisive: When the size of the population above the line becomes large enough, then from that point onwards it is only the difference in quality that matters. Cf. Hájek and Rabinowicz (2021).

[36] Could we have a model in which *all* permissible orderings avoid deciding where the line is to be drawn? Yes, we can. In such a model all permissible orderings will be gappy.

View. According to the Simple View, adding more and more lives of the same type to a population has a non-diminishing value. Parfit relies on this assumption when he denies that a type of life can be weakly superior to another type that is only slightly worse. In the sequence that leads, by small quality decreases, from an excellent life to a drab life, no type of life is supposed to be weakly superior to its immediate successor. But, in my modeling of such sequences, I still postulated the existence of permissible *preference* orderings in which some types are *preferentially* weakly superior to their immediate successors. Can orderings of this kind be permissible if it is out of the question that the value of added lives could diminish? This might well be questioned.[37]

However, Parfit's Simple View is itself questionable: It can be shown to have counter-intuitive implications. In a recent paper, Karsten Klint Jensen (2020) has proved the following result: If an excellent life is weakly superior to a drab life, as Parfit would have it, then the Simple View implies that no population of drab lives, however large, could be better than even a *single* excellent life.[38] It is difficult to accept this conclusion, unless one adheres to a rather extreme form of perfectionism. To be sure, Parfit did have strong perfectionist sympathies, but it may be doubted that he would have been willing to push his perfectionism that far.[39] Consequently, Jensen's advice to Parfitians is that they should give up the Simple View.

Thus, the following seems to be a fair assessment of Parfit's proposal: His appeal to incommensurabilities is worth serious consideration. Arguably, any plausible

---

[37] Actually, there are two different ways in which one could account for one type L being preferentially weakly superior to another type L', which is only slightly worse than L. If, for some preference ordering P, L is weakly P-superior to L', this might be either because the marginal impact of adding more and more L'-lives steeply decreases and converges to zero at the limit, or because the L-population becomes radically upgraded in P-ranking upon reaching a certain threshold in size. If, upon reaching some threshold, the L-population becomes "infinitely" more preferred in P than L'-populations, this would also account for P ranking this L-population higher than any L'-population, however large. But in the latter case we would still have to assume, I think, that a *further* increase in the size of the L-population would have a lower marginal impact. Which again would imply that, in P, the marginal impact of increase in size will at some point have to diminish.

[38] In this proof, Jensen does not directly rely on the Simple View. Instead, he formulates a condition that intuitively follows from the Simple View but unlike the latter avoids the controversial assumption that values of lives and of populations can be quantified—an assumption which Parfit himself in other contexts rejects. To formulate this condition, Jensen considers a larger domain of possible populations than the one I have been working with. In his framework, this domain also includes non-homogeneous populations, in which people have lives of different types. His condition can then be formulated as follows:

> For every L and L', if L is better than L', then for every k, adding to kL another person with an L-life results in a better population than adding to kL a person with an L'-life.

Intuitively, if the value of adding more and more L-lives were diminishing, then—at least for some L' that are worse than L—it would be better at some point to add an L'-life to an L-population instead of a yet another L-life.

[39] I am no longer sure that I am right in this conjecture. In view of Tim Campbell's comments mentioned in footnote 9 above, one might argue that Parfit would, after all, have been willing to go that far. But this doesn't mean *we* should be willing to accept such a radical form of perfectionism.

attempt to block the Continuum Argument might need to bring in incommensurabilities at some point. As we have seen (cf. the Trilemma above), these incommensurabilities will have to be strictly persistent and thus, if they are meant to be cases of parity, they will be highly atypical. Still, such persistency phenomena can be accounted for if we rely on the modeling of value relations in which parities are analyzed in terms of opposing permissible preferences. But in order to account for the persistence of parity, we have postulated that it is permissible for a type of life to be preferentially weakly superior to another life type that might be only slightly worse.[40] This gives us a reason to reject Parfit's Simple View. We should no longer insist that the marginal value of added lives never diminishes.[41] This, however, we have reason to do anyway. As Jensen (2020) has shown, we need to discard the Simple View if we want to avoid excessive forms of perfectionism in population axiology. Thus, we should allow for some holistic value effects that can arise when population size increases. We need to allow for diminutions in the marginal value of added lives and perhaps also for its increases upon reaching some thresholds. What sorts of phenomena of this kind it might be plausible to assume remains to be seen. We need to know more about the range of permissible preferences regarding populations. Thus, there is work that remains to be done.[42]

---

[40] See, however, footnote 33 above where I tentatively sketch an alternative construction which avoids making this assumption.

[41] But even if we accept that the marginal impact of added lives does diminish in some permissible preference orderings, we need not assume that it diminishes at the same rate and in the same way in all of them. In particular, we need not allow that a type of life can be weakly superior to another type of life that is only slightly worse. This would be the case only if the former type were preferentially weakly superior to the latter in *all* permissible orderings (and even this would not be enough in infinite models). But we don't need to allow this. As we have seen in the preceding section, in cases of strictly persistent parity involving two types, L and L', L is preferentially weakly superior to L' in some permissible orderings but preferentially *exchangeable* for L' in other permissible orderings.

[42] One issue that might be considered is what happens if one weakens the Principle of Quantity and allows that the marginal value of added lives can drop all the way to zero. Thus, suppose we only accept:

Weak Principle of Quantity: For all k, k' and L, $kL \succeq k'L$ if $k > k'$.

In other words, increasing the size of the population, while keeping the life quality constant, need not make the population better; we only assume that it will be at least as good.

Given this weakening, there is room for a weakening of the concept of exchangeability:

L is *weakly exchangeable* for L' $=_{df}$ For every k, there is some k' such that $k'L' \succeq kL$.

Given the Principle of quantity, weak exchangeability implies exchangeability. But if the Principle of Quantity is weakend, this implication no longer holds.

Now, as it is easy to see, if in a life type sequence the first type of life is weakly superior to the last one, then it cannot be true that every type in the sequence is weakly exchangeable for its successor. Since weak exchaneability is a transitive relation, this would mean that the first type of life is weakly exchangeable for the last one, which it cannot be if it is weakly superior to it. Consequently, some types in the sequence cannot be weakly exchangeable for their immediate successors. If we do not want to allow that they can be weakly superior to them (because the sequence has been set up in such a way that differences between all adjacent life types are small), the only remaining possibility is that these types must admit of strictly persistent incommensurability with their immediate successors. This follows from what we might call the Second Trilemma:

Appendix

Here we broaden our perspective and generalize the kind of approach we have taken in this chapter. We apply it to *all types of quantifiable goods*, G, G', etc. Lives worth living (quantifiable by their numbers within each type) are examples of such goods, but there are of course many other examples as well. We focus on on all types of quantifiable goods that satisfy the Principle of Quantity: the more goods there are of a given type, the better.

Principle of Quantity: For all G and all quantities k, k' of G, if k' < k', then k'G $\succ$ kG.

$\succ$ stands for "is better than." This relation is assumed to be asymmetric and transitive. It is also transitive across equal goodness: if kG and k'G' are equally good, then whatever is better than one of them is better than the other.

Quantities can be understood in any way we please, for example as integers or as real numbers. They are linearly ordered by the relation <. It is *not* assumed that the way in which one type of goods is quantified is the same as that in which we quantify another type of goods. The ways in which different types of goods are quantified may be quite diferent. We do assume that, for any type of goods G we consider and for any quantity k of that type, there can exist some quantity k' of G such that k < k'. In other words, for every quantity of G a larger quantity of G is possible.

Definitions

G is *weakly superior* to G' $=_{df}$ For some quantity k of G, kG $\succ$ k'G' for all quantity k' of G'.

G is *exchangeable* for G' $=_{df}$ For every quantity k of G, some quantity k' of G' is such that k'G' $\succ$ kG.

G admits of *strictly persistent incommensurability* with G' $=_{df}$ There is a quantity k of G such that for every quantity k^+ of G that is at least as large as k, there is some quantity k' of G' such that k^+G is incommensurable with every quantity of G' at least as large as k'.

Trilemma: For any two types of goods G and G', exactly one of the following three relations must obtain between them: (i) G is exchangeable for G', (ii) G is weakly superior to G', or (iii) G admits of strictly persistent incommensurability with G'.

Proof

We want to prove that if G is neither exchangeable for G' nor weakly superior to G', then it admits of strictly persistent incommensurability with G'. This will establish that the three

> **Second Trilemma:** For any two types of life L and L', exactly one of the following three relations must obtain: (i) L is weakly exchangeable for L', (ii) L is weakly superior to L', or (iii) L admits of strictly persistent incommensurability with L'.
>
> The proof of the Second Trilemma rests on the transitivity of $\succeq$ and the Weak Principle of Quantity. I omit it here, since it is closely similar to the proof of Trilemma that I provide in Appendix.
> Thus, even if the marginal value of added lives is allowed to go down all the way to zero, we still have a need for strictly persistent incommensurabilities.

horns of the Trilemma are jointly exhaustive. That they are mutually exclusive should be obvious.

If G is not exchangeable for G', here must be some quantity k of G such that:

(1) No quantity of G' is better than kG.

But if G is not weakly superior to G', then there is some quantity k' of G' such that:

(2) kG is not better than k'G'.

There are three possible cases to consider that fall under (2):

(i) k'G' is better than kG.

But this contradicts (1).

(ii) k'G' is equally as good as kG.

Let k" be any quantity of G' larger than k'. By the Principle of Quantity, k"G' is better than k'G'. But then, by the transitivity of betterness across equal goodness, (ii) implies that k"G' is better than kG, which again contradicts (1).

(iii) k'G' is incommensurable with kG.

Only (iii) is compatible with both (1) and (2).

Thus, k'G' is incommensurable with kG. What about the quantities of G' that are larger than k'? How do they relate to kG?

Given (1), no quantity k" of G' larger than k' is better than kG. Nor can it be equally as good as kG (cf. the reasoning above for case (ii)). Can kG be better than k"G'? Surely not, given the transitivity of betterness, since by the Principle of Quantity, k"G' is better than k'G', but kG is not better than k'G'; it is incommensurable with k'G'.

Thus, kG is incommensurable not just with k'G' but also with every quantity k" of G' larger than k'.

This means that:

(3) kG is incommensurable with every quantity of G' at least as large as k'.

In other words, kG is incommensurable with every sufficiently large quantity of G' (and better than every smaller quantity of G').[43]

---

[43] If kG were worse than or equally as good as some quantity of G', then, by the Principle of Quantity and transitivity of ≻, it would be worse than all the larger quantities of G', contrary to (1). Consequently, kG must be better than every quantity of G' with which it is commensurable.

The same conclusion can be established for any quantity k^+ of G larger than k. By the Principle of Quantity and the transitivity of betterness, (1) implies:

(1^+)   No quantity of G′ is better than k^+G.

For then this quantity of G′ would also be better than kG, which contradicts (1).
And, since G is not weakly superior to G′, there must be some quantity k′ of G′ such that:

(2+) k^+G is not better than k′G′.

But then, by the similar argument as above, k^+G must be incommensurable with k′G′ and with every quantity of G′ that is larger than k′. Thus,

(4)   For every k^+ larger than k, k^+G is incommensurable with every quantity of G′ at least as large as some k′.

In other words, for all quantities k^+ of G larger than k, k^+G is incommensurable with every sufficiently large quantity of G′ (and better than every smaller quantity of G′).
(3) and (4) imply that:

(5)   G admits of strictly persistent incommensurability with G′.

Q. E. D.

Acknowledgements

This chapter was prepared for a conference in the memory of Derek Parfit, held in Oxford in May 2018. I wish to thank its organizers, Joseph Carlsmith, Jeff McMahan, and Ketan Ramakrishnan. Later, in October that year, I presented it at a conference on Real Values in Neuchâtel and Zurich, and then in December the same year in Stockholm, at a conference on climate change and population axiology. It was also discussed, in 2018 and 2019, at the philosophy seminars at the Australian National University in Canberra, Lund University, and University of Sydney. I much enjoyed these discussions and want to thank the audiences for criticisms and helpful suggestions. Gustaf Arrhenius, John Broome, Tim Campbell, James Goodrich, Alan Hájek, Toby Handfield, Karsten Klint Jensen, and Mozaffar Qizilbash have all sent me very useful and challenging comments, for which I am grateful. Toby Handfield deserves special credit; the worry about persistency of incommensurability, which I attempt to dispel in this chapter, was first raised and discussed in my earlier work with Toby. Special credit is also due to Al Hájek: In my joint work with Al, we have developed a degree-theoretic approach to commensurability and applied it to construct an error theory for the seemingly compelling intuitions that drive one to the Repugnant Conclusion. Finally, I wish to thank Joy Mellor, the copy-editor for Oxford University Press, for her meticulous work with my contribution to this volume.

References

Andreou, Ch., 2015, "Parity, Comparability, and Choice," *The Journal of Philosophy* 112: 5–22.

Arrhenius, G., and Rabinowicz, W., 2005, "Millian Superiorities," *Utilitas* 17: 127–46.

Arrhenius, G., and Rabinowicz, W., 2015, "Value Superiority," in I. Hirose and J. Olson (eds.), *The Oxford Handbook of Value Theory*, Oxford: Oxford University Press, 225–48.

Carlson, E., 1998, "Mere Addition and Two Trilemmas of Population Ethics," *Economics and Philosophy* 14: 283–306.

Chang, R., 2016a, "Parity, Imprecise Comparability, and the Repugnant Conclusion," *Theoria* 82: 182–214.

Chang, R., 2016b, "Parity: An Intuitive case," *Ratio* 29: 395–411.

Griffin, J., 1986, *Well-Being: Its Meaning, Measurement and Moral Importance*, Oxford: Clarendon Press.

Hájek, A., and Rabinowicz, W., 2021, "Degrees of Commensurability and the Repugnant Conclusion," published on-line in *Noûs*.

Handfield, T., 2014, "Rational Choice and the Transitivity of Betterness," *Philosophy and Phenomenological Research* 89: 584–604.

Handfield, T., and Rabinowicz, W., 2018, "Incommensurability and Vagueness in Spectrum Arguments: Options for Saving Transitivity of Betterness," *Philosophical Studies* 175: 2373–87.

Jensen, K. K., 2008, "Millian Superiorities and the Repugnant Conclusion," *Utilitas* 20: 279–300.

Jensen, K. K., 2020, "Weak Superiority, Imprecise Equality and the Repugnant Conclusion," *Utilitas* 32: 294–315.

Parfit, D., 1984, *Reasons and Persons*, Oxford: Oxford University Press.

Parfit, D., 2016, "Can We Avoid the Repugnant Conclusion?," *Theoria* 82: 110–27.

Parfit, D., 2017, "Future People, the Non-Identity Problem, and Person-Affecting Principles," *Philosophy and Public Affairs* 45: 119–56.

Qizilbash, M., 2018, "On Parity and the Intuition of Neutrality," *Economics of Philosophy* 34: 87–108.

Rabinowicz, W., 2008, "Value Relations," *Theoria* 74: 18–49.

Rabinowicz, W., 2009a, "Broome and the Intuition of Neutrality," *Philosophical Issues* 19: 389–411.

Rabinowicz, W., 2009b, "Incommensurability and Vagueness," *Proceedings of the Aristotelian Society*, Supplementary Volume 83: 71–94.

Rabinowicz, W., 2012, "Value Relations Revisited," *Economics and Philosophy* 28: 133–164.

Rabinowicz, W., forthcoming, "Getting Personal—The Intuition of Neutrality Reinterpreted," forthcoming in *The Oxford Handbook of Population Ethics*, ed. by G. Arrhenius, K. Bykvist and T. Campbell, Oxford: Oxford University Press.

Raz, J., 1986, *The Morality of Freedom*, Oxford: Clarendon Press.

Temkin, L. S., 1996, "A Continuum Argument for Intransitivity," *Philosophy & Public Affairs* 25: 175–210.

Temkin, L. S., 2012, *Rethinking the Good: Moral Ideals and the Nature of Practical Reasoning*, Oxford: Oxford University Press.

16
Population Ethics and Conflict-of-Value Imprecision

Gustaf Arrhenius

16.1 Introduction

Derek Parfit's infamous "Repugnant Conclusion" can be stated as follows:

The Repugnant Conclusion: For any population consisting of people with very high positive welfare, there is a better population in which everyone has very low positive welfare, other things being equal.[1]

In Figure 16.1, the width of each block represents the number of people whereas the height represents their lifetime welfare. Dashes indicate that the block in question should be much wider than shown, that is, the population size is much larger than shown.

These populations could consist of all the past, present, and future lives (a possible world), or all the present and future lives, or all the lives during some shorter time span in the future such as the next generation, or all the lives that are causally affected by, or consequences of, a certain action or series of actions, and so forth.[2]

---

[1] Here's how Parfit (1984), p. 388, formulates the conclusion: "For any possible population of at least ten billion people, all with a very high quality of life, there must be some much larger imaginable population whose existence, if other things are equal, would be better, even though its members have lives that are barely worth living." Hence, my formulation is more general than his. The *ceteris paribus* clause in the formulation is meant to imply that the compared populations are roughly equal in all other putatively axiologically relevant aspects apart from individual welfare levels. Although it is through Parfit's writings that this implication of Total Utilitarianism has become widely discussed, it was already noted by Henry Sidgwick (1907), p. 415, in the first edition 1874. For other early sources of the Repugnant Conclusion, see McTaggart (1927), pp. 452–3; Narveson (1967); and Broad (1979), pp. 249–50.

[2] More exactly, a population is a finite set of lives in a possible world. A, B, C, ... $A_1, A_2, ..., A_n$, A∪B, and so on, denote populations of finite size. We shall adopt the convention that populations represented by different letters, or the same letter but different indexes, are pairwise disjoint. For example, A∩B = $A_1 \cap A_2$ = Ø. We shall assume that for any natural number n and any welfare level X, there is a possible population of n people with welfare X (for a discussion of this *No-Limit Assumption*, see Arrhenius (2000b), ch. 3, (forthcoming)).

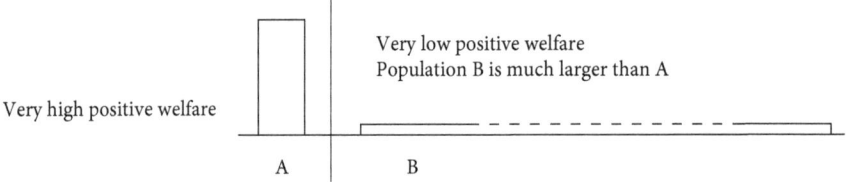

Figure 16.1

All the lives in Figure 16.1 have positive welfare, or, as we also could put it, all the people have lives worth living. The A-people have very high welfare whereas the B-people have very low positive welfare.[3] The reason for this could be that in the B-lives there are, to paraphrase Parfit, only enough ecstasies to just outweigh the agonies, or that the good things in those lives are of uniformly poor quality, e.g., eating potatoes and listening to Muzak.[4] However, since there are many more people in B, the total sum of welfare in B is greater than in A. Hence, a theory like Total Utilitarianism, according to which we should maximize the welfare in the world, ranks B as better than A—an instance of *the Repugnant Conclusion*.[5]

Notice that problems like *the Repugnant Conclusion* are not just problems for total utilitarians or those committed to welfarism, the view that welfare is the only value that matters from the moral point of view, since we have assumed that other axiologically relevant aspects are roughly equal. Hence, other values and considerations are not decisive for the value comparison of populations A and B. Thus, *the Repugnant Conclusion* is a problem for all moral theories according to which welfare matters at least when all other things are equal, which arguably is a minimal adequacy condition for any moral theory.

The Repugnant Conclusion highlights a problem in an area that has become known as *population ethics*. It involves foundational questions regarding axiology and our duties to future generations. The main problem in population ethics has been to find an adequate theory about the value of outcomes where the

---

[3] We shall say that a life has *neutral welfare* if and only if it is equally as good for the person living it as a neutral welfare component, and that a life has *positive* (*negative*) welfare if and only if it has higher (lower) welfare than a life with neutral welfare. A welfare component is neutral relative to a certain life x if and only if x with this component has the same welfare as x without this component. A hedonist, for example, would typically say that an experience which is neither pleasurable nor painful is neutral in value for a person and as such doesn't increase or decrease the person's welfare. The above definition can of course be combined with other welfarist axiologies, such as desire satisfaction and objective list theories. Moreover, there are a number of alternative definitions of a neutral life in the literature, many of which would also work fine in the present context. For a discussion, see Parfit (1984), pp. 357–8 and appendix G; Broome (1999), (2004); Arrhenius (2000b), (forthcoming), chs. 2 and 9); and Bykvist (2007), p. 101. Notice also that we actually don't need an analysis of a neutral welfare in the present context but rather just a criterion, and the criterion can vary with different theories of welfare.

[4] See Parfit (1984), p. 388, and (1986), p. 148. For a discussion of different interpretations of *the Repugnant Conclusion*, see Parfit (1984), (2014), (2016); and Arrhenius (2000b), (forthcoming).

[5] Throughout this chapter, "better" means "better, all things considered" if not otherwise indicated.

number of people, the quality of their lives, and their identities may vary. Since any reasonable moral theory has to take these aspects of possible outcomes into account when determining the normative status of actions, the study of population ethics is of general import for moral theory. Through his pioneering and seminal contributions, Parfit can rightly be said to be the founding father of this important field.[6]

As the name indicates, Parfit finds *the Repugnant Conclusion* unacceptable and most philosophers seem to agree. However, it has been surprisingly difficult to find a theory that avoids *the Repugnant Conclusion* without implying other very counterintuitive conclusions.[7] Actually, it is impossible to avoid *the Repugnant Conclusion* (or even worse conclusions) without violating some intuitively very convincing conditions. We know this for sure through a number of so-called impossibility theorems.[8] The proofs of these theorems show that there is no theory that fulfils a number of intuitively compelling adequacy conditions—conditions which everyone seems to agree that a reasonable moral theory must fulfil. Examples of such conditions are that one future is better than another if everyone is better off in the former as compared to the latter, or that it is better to create happy rather than unhappy people. The question as to how *the Repugnant Conclusion* should be dealt with has become one of the cardinal challenges of modern ethics and the inquiry into what it shows about the nature of ethics has opened up many new avenues for research. Population ethics has proved a very fruitful area of research, having implications for all areas of moral and political philosophy. This is all thanks to Parfit's ground-breaking work in this area.

Parfit has suggested a novel way of avoiding *the Repugnant Conclusion* by introducing what he calls "imprecision" in value comparisons.[9] He suggests that in a range of important cases, outcomes are only imprecisely comparable. In such cases, transitive relations such as "equally as good as" are not applicable. Instead, we have to make use of imprecise relations that are non-transitive. This imprecision is not due to any cognitive or epistemic limitations but a fact about the value comparisons of certain types of outcomes.

In his Rolf Schock Prize Lecture, he suggested that "[w]hen two possible worlds would contain different numbers of people, this fact makes these worlds less precisely comparable."[10] From this "Different-Number-Based Imprecision", as he called it, follows that many of the comparisons of different future populations will involve imprecise comparisons and transitivity of the involved relations might fail. Parfit suggests that this feature will open up a way of avoiding the Repugnant

---

[6] Another pioneer is Jan Narveson. See Narveson (1967), (1973), (1978).
[7] For a summary, see Arrhenius (2000b), (2013b), (forthcoming); Arrhenius, Ryberg, & Tännsjö (2014).
[8] See, e.g., Parfit (1984), (1986); and Arrhenius (2000b), (2000a), (2003), (2004), (2009b), (2011), (forthcoming).
[9] Parfit (2014), (2016).   [10] Parfit (2014).

Conclusion without implying other very counterintuitive conclusions, or at least less counterintuitive than *the Repugnant Conclusion*, and thus solve one of the major challenges in ethics.

Parfit and I had many exchanges about this proposal in which I, among other things, tried to convince him to instead go for what I called "Conflict-of-Value Imprecision" (to be explained below). Our presentations at the *Rolf Schock Prize Symposium in Logic and Philosophy in honour of Derek Parfit* were scheduled to appear in the same special issue of the journal *Theoria*. Mine, focusing on the idea of Different-Number-Based Imprecision, appeared unaltered but at the last minute Parfit changed his view and, surprisingly, went for Conflict-of-Value Imprecision instead of Different-Number-Based Imprecision.[11] So in the charming absent-minded way so characteristic of him, he completely wrongfooted me. As he graciously wrote to me later, he had had to change his talk (of which his article was a transcript) because of the criticism in my paper. I'm happy but also sad now. Parfit has left us and we no longer can have those delightful and insightful exchanges that I miss so much. But I'm happy to be able at last to reply to his revised proposal and consider whether it will help us with the paradoxes in population ethics, as he had hoped.

16.2 Imprecision and Conflict-of-Value Imprecision

Here's an example of what Parfit means by imprecision in value comparisons:

> Suppose that I ask you whether Einstein or Bach was a greater genius, or achieved more. You may first assume that this question couldn't have an answer, since it makes no sense to compare the genius, or achievements, of scientists and composers. But I might then point out that Bach was clearly a greater genius than many bad scientists, and Einstein was a greater genius than many bad composers. When you realize that there *can* be truths of this kind, you would not suddenly come to believe that as geniuses, or in their achievements, Einstein and Bach might be precisely equally as great. As you would see, the truth could be only that one of these people was imprecisely greater than the other, or more plausibly, that they were imprecisely equally as great.[12]

"Equally as good as" is transitive: If A is equally as good as B, and B is equally as good as C, then A is equally as good as C. "Imprecisely equally as good as", however, is non-transitive: Even if A is imprecisely equally as good as B, and B is imprecisely equally as good as C, A might not be imprecisely equally as good as C. For example, that Einstein and Mozart are imprecisely equally as good and Mozart

---

[11] Arrhenius (2016); Parfit (2016).   [12] Parfit (2014).

and Bohr are imprecisely equally as good is compatible with Einstein being greater than Bohr. According to Parfit, "[s]uch imprecision is not the result of our lack of knowledge, but is part of what we would know if we knew the full facts."[13]

That there are non-transitive value relations of this kind seems likely. A well-known case is "not better than". As Parfit puts it:

> If your life could go in different ways, it might be true that your being a writer would not be better than your being a doctor, which would not be better than your being a slightly less successful writer. But your being a writer would be better than your being a slightly less successful writer. Not better than would not here be a transitive relation.[14]

But how should this help us with the paradoxes in population ethics? Parfit adds another important assumption which I shall call "Conflict-of-Value Imprecision": "We might claim that...given the conflict between...values, [w]orlds are only imprecisely comparable, and would be imprecisely equally good."[15] So the idea is that imprecision may arise from weighing different values against each other, such as perfectionist values versus total welfare or equality. The values Parfit has is mind are the quality of people's lives and the quantity of welfare:

> we can...distinguish between the quality of people's lives and the quantity of well-being per person. These might diverge. The best things in your life might be of a higher quality than the best things in mine, and your life might go worse than mine only because you would have many fewer of these best things.[16]

What does Parfit have in mind when he talks about "quality of life" and the "the best things in life"? He doesn't say so much about it in Parfit (2016) but in a comment on one of the cases he discusses, he clarifies it a bit:

> Some people in Alpha would have a much higher quality of life than anyone in Y, since this quality would be at level 200 rather than at level 2. This higher quality of life, we should assume, would not be merely a difference in the amount of well-being per person. At level 200, the best things in life would be very good, and lives at level 2, in World Y, would not include any of these good things. *There would be no art, or science, no deep loves or friendships, no other achievements, such as that of bringing up our children well, and no morally good people.* World Y would be much worse than Alpha in what we can call *qualitative or perfectionist terms*. In

---

[13] Parfit (2014). His idea is similar to, but not the same as, Ruth Chang's (2002), (2005) proposal that there is a forth value-relation: "on a par". On a par is also a non-transitive relation.
[14] Parfit (2014).   [15] Parfit (2016), p. 126.   [16] Parfit (2016), p. 126.

one version of this case, lives at levels 1 and 2 would be like the lives of never-developing one-year-old and two-year-old children.[17]

Much more needs to be said about Parfit's idea of the quality of welfare components and how they contribute to the welfare of a life and the value of a population. However, the above will suffice for our discussion here I think. Parfit's central idea, as I take it, is that such qualitative difference in welfare components in people's lives contributes to the value of worlds or populations in addition to how they contribute to people's welfare, and might make populations imprecisely comparable.

This source of imprecision is very much along the lines of what I suggested to Parfit in our discussion: It is much more likely with imprecision arising from weighing different values against each other than from populations differing in size. Importantly, with Conflict-of-Value Imprecision we could get imprecision also in same number cases, not only in different number cases as with Different-Number-Based Imprecision. Hence, this imprecision could potentially undermine the same number conditions in the impossibility theorem such as Non-Elitism and Non-Extreme Priority (more on this below).

How could Conflict-of-Value Imprecision help us with the impossibility results in population ethics? Let's first look at some derivations of *the Repugnant Conclusion* and see whether imprecision can help us blocking some step in them.

16.3 The Quantity Sequence

There are other axiologies apart from Total Utilitarianism that imply *the Repugnant Conclusion*. These can be characterized by a set of conditions. Consider the following condition:

Quantity: For any pair of positive welfare levels **A** and **B**, such that **B** is slightly lower than **A**, and for any number of lives *n*, there is a greater number of lives *m*, such that a population of *m* lives at level **B** is better than a population of *n* lives at level **A**, other things being equal.[18]

Quantity has some intuitive plausibility and should appeal to those thinkers that find some truth in the saying "the more good, the better". However, it implies

---

[17] Parfit (2016), p. 123 (my emphasis). On p. 118 he gives the example of "the earliest sentient animals who had lives that were just worth living, because these animals had enough slight pleasures like those of cows munching grass or lizards basking in the sun".

[18] A welfare level is an equivalence class on the set of all possible lives with respect to the relation "has at least as high welfare as". For an exact statement of this principle, see Arrhenius (2000b), (forthcoming), where this condition is formulated in terms of "at least as good as".

the Repugnant Conclusion together with the following reasonable assumption regarding welfare levels:

Finite Fine-grainedness: There exists a finite sequence of slight welfare differences between any two welfare levels.

The idea here is that one can get from one welfare level to another in a finite number of steps of intuitively slight welfare difference. Examples of such welfare differences could be some minor pain or pleasure or a shortening of life by a minute or two.[19] These differences don't have to be of the same size or type. Let's say that a life of type *a* has higher welfare than a life of type *b*, and suppose that you are successively making *a* slightly worse, perhaps by shortening it by a minute or two or by adding some minor pain. *Finite Fine-grainedness* implies that there is a finite (but possibly great) number of such slight worsenings from *a* to another type of life *c* such that a life of this type will have the same welfare or lower welfare than a life of type *b*. It is quite hard to deny the intuitive force of this assumption.[20]

Consider the sequence in Figure 16.2 of populations for an informal demonstration that these two conditions together imply *the Repugnant Conclusion*:[21]

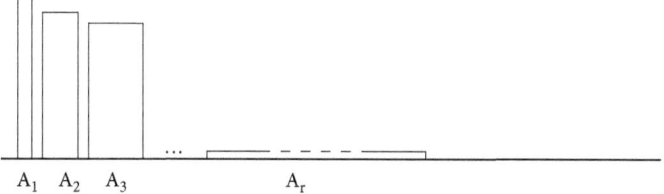

Figure 16.2 The Quantity Sequence

Assume that A_1 in Figure 16.2 is a population with very high welfare and that A_r is a population with very low positive welfare (again, the width of the blocks represents the number of lives in the population, the height represents their lifetime welfare; dashes indicates that the block in question should intuitively be

---

[19] For a precise definition of "slight welfare difference", see Arrhenius (2000b), (2011), (forthcoming).
[20] Notice that Finite Fine-grainedness doesn't imply that all sequences of slight welfare differences between two welfare levels are finite, just that there exists at least one such sequence. It is compatible with the welfare ordering being continuous as well as discreet. It just rules out that there are, so to speak, big "jumps" or "holes" in the order of welfare levels. For a discussion of Finite Fine-grainedness and possible theories of welfare that violate this condition, see Arrhenius (2005), (forthcoming); Arrhenius & Rabinowicz (2015). For an interesting effort to challenge Finite Fine-grainedness (in light of the impossibility theorems in population ethics), see Thomas (2018) and Carlson (forthcoming). Actually, a complete discussion of Parfit's new ideas on imprecision would have to involve a more detailed discussion of Finite Fine-grainedness but due to space restrictions, this will have to wait to another time.
[21] For an exact proof, see Arrhenius (2000b), (forthcoming). Parfit (2016) informally derives *the Repugnant Conclusion* with this kind of sequence argument.

much wider than shown). According to *Quantity*, there is a population A_2 with slightly lower welfare than A_1 and which is better than A_1; a population A_3 with slightly lower welfare than A_2 and which is better than A_2; and so forth. We can assume that the welfare levels in this sequence of populations satisfy Finite Fine-grainedness. Hence, we will finally reach population A_r with very low positive welfare. By transitivity, A_r is better than A_1. Since A_1 is an arbitrary population with very high welfare, this shows that for any population with very high welfare, there is a population with very low positive welfare which is better, that is, *the Repugnant Conclusion*.

Here's Parfit suggestion for how an appeal to imprecision can block this derivation:

> [This] assume that any slight loss in the quality of people's lives could be outweighed by a sufficient gain in the number of people who would exist and have lives that would be slightly less worth living. As we can more briefly say, any slight loss of quality could be outweighed by a sufficient gain in quantity. If we assumed precision, it would be hard to reject these arguments.—But we should deny that such truths would be precise... It would not be better if there existed many more people whose quality of life would all be lower, since two such worlds would at most be imprecisely equally good. Though the larger of these worlds would not be worse, this relation is not transitive. So we could claim that it would be worse if, in other, larger worlds, everyone's quality of life would be much lower.[22]

So the idea is that A_2 is not better than A_1 but only imprecisely equally as good "since two such worlds would at most be imprecisely equally good". Likewise for A_3 and A_2, and so on. Since "imprecisely equally as good as" is non-transitive, *the Repugnant Conclusion* doesn't follow. Actually, it doesn't even follow that A_1 is imprecisely equally as good as A_r which would be a slightly weaker version of *the Repugnant Conclusion*. This result is compatible with A_1 being better than A_r, which is what most people seem to believe. This appeal to imprecision implies, of course, a rejection of Quantity. However, it is compatible with a weaker version formulated in terms of "imprecisely equally as good as".

Is this argument convincing? Well, given that we can claim that there is a loss of the best things in life when we move down the sequence, this might work. Not obvious, however, since it is not clear why there couldn't be the same amount of the best things in life in A_1 and A_r but much more pain and suffering in A_r (more on this below). Moreover, there are other derivations of *the Repugnant Conclusion* that are trickier to deal with.

---

[22] Parfit (2016), p. 120.

16.4 The Sequential Dominance Addition Paradox

The next derivation is based on two principles. Here's the first one:

Dominance Addition: An addition of lives with positive welfare and an increase in the welfare of everyone in the original population makes a population better, other things being equal.[23]

The idea is that you don't make a population worse by adding lives worth living and increasing the welfare of the individuals in the original population. It is a logically weaker and intuitively more compelling version of the more well-known *Mere Addition Principle*: An addition of people with positive welfare does not make a population worse, other things being equal.[24] Yet, although it might seem a compelling principle at first glance, it is controversial. Several authors have rejected it, some for quite good reasons.[25] One might, for example, object to it on egalitarian grounds since a mere addition can introduce great inequality in an otherwise perfectly equal population.[26] Likewise for Dominance Addition albeit then the disvalue of the introduced inequality also has to be weighed against the positive value of the increased welfare of the lives in the original population, not only against the possible positive value of more lives with positive welfare. However, we shall set this aside for now since we are here interested in how imprecision might help us with the paradoxes in population ethics.

The next condition is a weak egalitarian condition:

Inequality Aversion: For any triplet of welfare levels A, B, and C, A higher than B, and B higher than C, and for any population A with welfare A, there is some larger population C with welfare C such that a perfectly equal population B of the same size as A∪C and with welfare B is better than A∪C, other things being equal.[27]

Another way of stating Inequality Aversion is to say that for any welfare level of the best off and worst off, and for any number of best off lives, there is some

---

[23] See Arrhenius (2000b), (forthcoming).
[24] Cf. Hudson (1987); Ng (1989); Sider (1991); and Parfit (2014), p. 420ff, Cf. fn. below.
[25] Ng (1989), p. 244; Blackorby, Bossert, & Donaldson (1995), p. 1305; Blackorby, Bossert, & Donaldson (1997), pp. 210–11; and Fehige (1998). Ng (1989), p. 238, ascribes to Parfit the view that a population axiology should satisfy the Mere Addition Principle, and one might get that impression from Parfit (2014), p. 420ff. In personal communication, however, Parfit has expressed doubts about the Mere Addition Principle in cases where the added people are much worse off than the rest of the population. See also Kavka (1982); Feldman (1997) ch. 10; and Carlson (1998), pp. 288–9.
[26] See Arrhenius (2009a), (2013a), (forthcoming).
[27] For an exact statement of this principle, see Arrhenius (2000b), (forthcoming), where this condition is formulated in terms of "at least as good as". I've here formulated it in terms of "better than" to simplify the exposition.

(possibly much) greater number of worst off lives such that it would be better to have an equal distribution of welfare on any level higher than the worst off, other things being equal.

It is a very weak egalitarian condition since it can be satisfied by a theory which demands that the total welfare must be greater for a population with perfect equality to be better than an unequal population of the same size. Moreover, it is also compatible with principles that give much greater weight to the welfare of the best off as compared to the welfare of the worst off. For example, a theory which requires that to compensate for one person falling from twenty to ten units of welfare, a hundred people have to be moved from zero to ten units, is compatible with Inequality Aversion. In that sense, its name is a bit misleading since it is compatible with quite non-egalitarian theories. Roughly, Inequality Aversion only rules out theories that imply that we should always or sometimes give some kind of "lexical priority" the best off.[28] A simple example of such a theory is "Maximax": Maximize the welfare of the best off.

Now consider the populations in Figure 16.3. All the people in population A enjoy very high welfare. In A+, we have added a second group of lives with positive welfare a bit lower than the lives in A, and increased the welfare of the original group in A. In B, which is of the same size as A+, we have equalized the welfare at a level higher than the +-lives but lower than the A-lives. We can assume that A+ and B fulfil the antecedent of Inequality Aversion.[29]

The Dominance Addition Principle implies that A+ is better than A. Inequality Aversion implies that B is better than A+. Likewise for populations B, B+, and C, and so forth until we finally reach population Z with very low positive welfare. By transitivity, Z is better than A, that is, *the Repugnant Conclusion.*

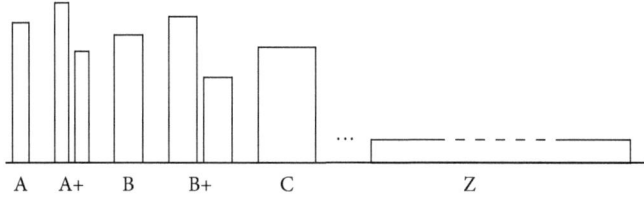

Figure 16.3 The Sequential Dominance Addition Paradox

---

[28] There are some more subtle theories that violate Inequality Aversion, such as theories that invoke some form of superiority in value. See Arrhenius (2005) and Arrhenius & Rabinowicz (2005), (2015), for a discussion. As we shall discuss below, Inequality Aversion can be derived from an even more intuitively compelling condition, Non-Elitism.

[29] If welfare is measurable on at least an interval scale, we could also assume that the total and average welfare in B is higher than in A+.

Here's Parfit's take on this case:

> Though World B would be better than [A+] in utilitarian and egalitarian terms, B would be worse in qualitative terms, *since the best things in people's lives would be worse in B*. We might claim that (K) *given the conflict between these values, Worlds B and [A+] are only imprecisely comparable, and would be imprecisely equally good*. This claim would not be in itself plausible.—(K) seems implausible because, in a change from [A+] to B, there would be only a slight qualitative loss. The best lives would fall only from level 101 to 99. It may be hard to believe that this slight qualitative loss could make [A+] not better than B, but only imprecisely equally good. But it would be much harder to believe that, compared with the existence of many people whose quality of life would be very high, it would be better if there existed instead some vast number of people whose lives were barely worth living.[30]

So the idea is that B is not better than A+ but, because of Conflict-of-Value Imprecision, B is instead imprecisely equally as good as A+. Given this, transitivity fails and we cannot derive that Z is better than A. Hence, in this case imprecision makes it possible for us to hold onto Dominance Addition but still avoid *the Repugnant Conclusion*. We can still hold on to the belief that A is better than Z. This appeal to imprecision implies, of course, a rejection of Inequality Aversion. However, it is compatible with a weaker version formulated in terms of "imprecisely equally as good as". We would also have to accept (K) which is quite counterintuitive but Parfit's idea is that this is less implausible than accepting *the Repugnant Conclusion*.[31]

Here's a first problem with this line of argument, however. Parfit claims that "the best things in people's lives would be worse in B". But the best things in life could be better for the extra people in a move to B (which explains their rise in welfare from 95 to 99). Moreover "in a change from [A+] to B, there would be only a slight qualitative loss" since "[t]he best lives would fall only from level 101 to 99". So in this case we have to weigh a small decrease in the quality of the best thing in life for the best off, against both a bigger increase in the quality of best things in life for the worst off, and a total and average increase of the best things in life. Hence, there doesn't seem to be a conflict of different values in this case.

Here's a second problem. Pace Parfit, it could be the same quality and amount of the best things in life in A+ and B but the bad things (pains, suffering) are more equally distributed in B. Hence, the same quality and amount of the best things in

---

[30] Parfit (2016), emphasis added.
[31] Of course, even if we grant Parfit that (K) is less implausible than *the Repugnant Conclusion*, that doesn't suffice to show that of all the counterintuitive conclusions we could accept, we should accept (K). That is, without further argument, it isn't clear that the view entailing (K) is the least counterintuitive way of avoiding *the Repugnant Conclusion*. Thanks to Jimmy Goodrich for drawing my attention to this point.

each life in A+ and B but in A+ there is an unequal distribution of the bad things whereas in B, these are equally distributed. And it is this that explain the different welfare pattern in A+ and B. Again, there would be no conflict of value.

A rejoinder would be to claim that this is possible when comparing A+ and B but not further down the sequence. To get to a life barely worth living, the quality and amount of the best things in life have to go down at some point, one might argue.

This raises an essential question for the appeal to Conflict-of-Value imprecision in population ethics that Parfit unfortunately never discusses: Could the best things in life be the same in a life with very high positive welfare and a life with very low positive welfare?

I think this is true since we are discussing lifetime welfare and one could just add more bad things to a life to move it from very high welfare to very low positive welfare (or further down) albeit with the same best things as a life with very high positive welfare. For example, to a life which is splendid for the first sixty years, involving the best things in life, we could add horrible suffering for the next twenty years. It seems intuitive that such a life would have very low positive lifetime welfare although it involves the best things in life.

Actually, Parfit agrees that such lives are possible and seems to have realized that this possibility limits the reach of an appeal to imprecision as a solution to the paradoxes when he writes:

> in Roller-Coaster Z, everyone would live as long as everyone in World A, and all of the good things in these people's lives would be just as good, but these people's lives would be barely worth living because their lives would also contain much that was very bad. This version of Z also raises questions that I shall not discuss here.[32]

One possibility is that Parfit's idea was that Conflict-of-Value Imprecision could only help us with one special version of *the Repugnant Conclusion*, namely one that involves "Drab Z, [in which] there would be nothing in people's lives that would be bad, but there would also be very little that was good. The only good features... might be muzak and potatoes" or some versions of this kind of Z-population, such as the ones that involve "the earliest sentient animals who had lives that were just worth living, because these animals had enough slight pleasures like those of cows munching grass or lizards basking in the sun."[33] He might then argue that other versions of *the Repugnant Conclusion*, albeit counterintuitive, are "significantly less repugnant" and that we could accept these versions of *the Repugnant Conclusion*. He never claims this about Roller-Coaster Z but he does

---

[32] Parfit (2016), p. 118.   [33] Parfit (2016), p. 118.

make that claim about "Short-Lived Z, [in which] our imagined people would live for only as long as some flowers bloom".[34]

There is, however, a problem with this solution to the Drab Z-version of *the Repugnant Conclusion*.[35] If we accept the Roller-Coaster Z-version of *the Repugnant Conclusion*, we cannot avoid the Drab Z-version without violating an adequacy condition which is as uncontroversial as it gets in population ethics. Consider a Roller-Coaster Z with very low positive welfare. We can then take a Drab Z version in which everyone also has very low positive welfare but everyone is better off than in the Roller-Coaster Z. It is very hard to deny that the former population is better than the latter and it follows from the following uncontroversial condition:

Egalitarian Dominance: If population A is a perfectly equal population of the same size as population B, and every person in A has higher welfare than every person in B, then A is better than B, other things being equal.

Hence, if an appeal to Conflict-of-Value Imprecision cannot block a derivation of the Roller-Coaster Z-version of *the Repugnant Conclusion*, then it cannot block the Drab-Z-version.

One could try to deny that there exists a Drab Z in which everyone has higher welfare than in Roller-Coaster Z but that would be very counterintuitive for the same reasons that we discussed above with respect to the question whether the best things in life could be the same in a life with very high positive welfare and a life with very low positive welfare. Just consider the possibility of a Roller-Coaster Z- in which everyone has slightly negative welfare since the bad things just outweighs the very good things in life. Such a Z is surely worse than Drab Z. Then consider a version of Roller-Coaster Z- where the lives are slightly improved by some extra happy days so that all lives are just barely worth living. Surely such a population could be worse than a version of Drab Z.[36]

16.5 Non-Elitism

In the Sequential Dominance Addition Paradox we made use of Inequality Aversion and Parfit's way out was to deny this condition by an appeal to imprecision. The application of this condition may involve comparisons of a few great losses against a greater number of small gains—another intuitive source for imprecision. However, that wasn't how we applied Inequality Aversion in the Sequential Dominance Addition Paradox. We just had roughly equally big gains

---

[34] Parfit (2016), p. 118. [35] I'm grateful to Tim Campbell for pointing this out.
[36] Cf. fn. 20.

and losses throughout the sequence. This shows that the paradox can be derived with a weaker condition that never involves comparisons of a few greater losses against a greater number of small gains. Hence, the Sequential Dominance Addition Paradox doesn't need to involve comparisons that could work as a source of imprecision. Here's the condition:

> *Non-Elitism*: For any triplet of welfare levels **A**, **B**, and **C**, **A** slightly higher than **B**, and **B** higher than **C**, and for any one-life population A with welfare **A**, there is a population C with welfare **C**, and a population B of the same size as A∪C and with welfare **B**, such that, for any population X consisting of lives with welfare ranging from **C** to **A**, B∪X is better than A∪C∪X, other things being equal.[37]

The intuition which this fairly densely formulated condition tries to capture is simply and roughly that there is some (possibly great) number of worst off people such that a slight decrease in welfare (from **A** to **B**) for *one* of the best off persons can be compensated for by an at least as great increase in welfare (from **C** to **B**) for all those worst off people to the effect that the involved people enjoy the same level of welfare (**B**).

Figure 16.4 provides an illustration. It shows two populations of the same size. Population A consists of a number of best off lives, $a_1, a_2, \ldots, a_n$, and a number of worst off *groups* of lives, $\alpha_1, \alpha_2, \ldots, \alpha_m$. In population B, one of the best off lives (a_1) has been replaced with a life (b_1) enjoying welfare just lower than the welfare of the best off. Moreover, one of the worst off groups of lives (α_1) has been replaced by a same sized group of lives (β_1) with the same welfare as life b_1. Population B is then better than A according to Non-Elitism.

By repeated application, Non-Elitism will yield that B is better than A+ in the Sequential Dominance Addition Paradox.[38] Hence, since the application of

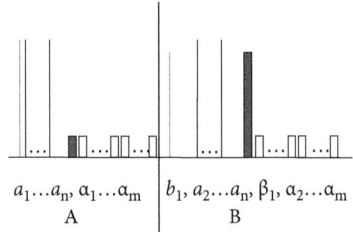

$a_1 \ldots a_n, \alpha_1 \ldots \alpha_m$ | $b_1, a_2 \ldots a_n, \beta_1, \alpha_2 \ldots \alpha_m$
A | B

Figure 16.4

---

[37] For an exact statement of this principle, see Arrhenius (2000b), (2011), (forthcoming), where this condition is formulated in terms of "at least as good as". I've here formulated it in terms of "better than" to simplify the exposition.

[38] This result presumes Finite Fine-grainedness. Actually, Inequality Aversion can be derived from Non-Elitism, see Arrhenius (2000b), (2003), (2011), (forthcoming).

Non-Elitism doesn't involve any comparisons of a few great losses against a greater number of small gains, an appeal to imprecision based on such comparisons won't help here. In Non-Elitism, the gains and losses for each involved individual is either of roughly the same size, or the gains for the worst off individuals are greater than the slight loss for the best off individual.

Another related point is that it would be counterintuitive if the zone of imprecision wasn't limited but "greedy".[39] Even if (and that is indeed a big "if" in this case) we could get imprecision when we weigh one best off person slight loss against one worst off person's gain of roughly the same size or greater, we should get out of the zone of imprecision at some point if we increase the number of people that gain. Non-Elitism is compatible with this idea since it talks about some, possibly great number of worst off people such that a slight decrease in welfare for *one* of the best off persons can be compensated for by an at least as great increase in welfare for the, possibly many more, worst off people.[40]

References

Arrhenius, G. (2000a). An Impossibility Theorem for Welfarist Axiologies. *Economics and Philosophy*, 16(02), 247–66.

Arrhenius, G. (2000b). *Future Generations: A Challenge for Moral Theory*. Retrieved from http://www.diva-portal.org/smash/record.jsf?pid=diva2:170236

Arrhenius, G. (2003). The Very Repugnant Conclusion. In *Logic, Law, Morality: Thirteen Essays in Practical Philosophy in Honour of Lennart Åqvist* (Vol. 51, pp. 167–80). Uppsala: Department of Philosophy, Uppsala University: Uppsala Philosophical Studies.

Arrhenius, G. (2004). The Paradoxes of Future Generations and Normative Theory. In Jesper, Ryberg & T. Tännsjö (Eds.), *The Repugnant Conclusion: Essays on Population Ethics* (pp. 201–18). Dordrecht: Kluwer Academic Publishers.

Arrhenius, G. (2005). Superiority in Value. *Philosophical Studies*, 123(1/2), 97–114. https://doi.org/10.1007/s11098-004-5223-0.

Arrhenius, G. (2009a). Egalitarianism and Population Change. In A. Gosseries & L. Meyer (Eds.), *Intergenerational Justice* (1st edition, pp. 325–49). Oxford: Oxford University Press.

---

[39] Broome (2004), ch. 12, uses the term "greedy" to describe incomparability that spreads way beyond its intuitive limitations. See also Handfield & Rabinowicz (2018); Herlitz (2020); Arrhenius (forthcoming), ch. 9.

[40] I would like to thank Andrea Asker, Krister Bykvist, Jimmy Goodrich, Anders Herlitz, Jeff McMahan, Julia Mosquera, Joe Roussos and especially Tim Campbell for helpful discussions. Thanks also to the audiences at the Moral Philosophy Seminar, Oxford, 16 May, 2016; Franco-Swedish Program in Philosophy and Economics Final Conference, Uppsala, 8 June, 2015; and the workshop Incommensurability: Vagueness, Parity and other Non-Conventional Comparative Relations, IFFS, Stockholm, 6–7 December 2019, for useful questions and comments. Financial support from Riksbankens Jubileumsfond (grant M17-0372:1) is gratefully acknowledged.

Arrhenius, G. (2009b). One More Axiological Impossibility Theorem. In L.-G. Johansson, J. Österberg, & R. Sliwinski (Eds.), *Logic, Ethics and All That Jazz: Essays in Honour of Jordan Howard Sobel* (Vol. 57, pp. 23–37). Uppsala: Department of Philosophy, Uppsala University: Uppsala Philosophical Studies.

Arrhenius, G. (2011). The Impossibility of a Satisfactory Population Ethics. In H. Colonius & E. N. Dzhafarov (Eds.), *Descriptive and Normative Approaches to Human Behavior, Advanced Series on Mathematical Psychology* (pp. 1–26). Singapore: World Scientific Publishing Company.

Arrhenius, G. (2013a). Egalitarian Concerns and Population Change. In O. Frithjof Norheim, N. Eyal, S. A. Hurst, & D. Wikler (Eds.), *Inequalities in Health: Concepts, Measures, and Ethics* (pp. 74–91). Oxford: Oxford University Press.

Arrhenius, G. (2013b). Repugnant Conclusion. In *The International Encyclopedia of Ethics* (pp. 4560–63). Oxford: Blackwell Publishing Ltd.

Arrhenius, G. (2016). Population Ethics and Different-Number-Based Imprecision. *Theoria*, *82*(2), 166–81. https://doi.org/10.1111/theo.12094.

Arrhenius, G. (forthcoming). *Population Ethics: The Challenge of Future Generations.* Oxford University Press.

Arrhenius, G., & Rabinowicz, W. (2005). Millian Superiorities. *Utilitas*, *17*(2), 127–46. https://doi.org/10.1017/S0953820805001494.

Arrhenius, G., & Rabinowicz, W. (2015). Value Superiority. In I. Hirose & J. Olson (Eds.), *The Oxford Handbook of Value Theory* (pp. 225–48). New York: Oxford University Press.

Arrhenius, G., Ryberg, J., & Tännsjö, T. (2014). The Repugnant Conclusion. In E. N. Zalta (Ed.), *The Stanford Encyclopedia of Philosophy* (Spring 2014, pp. 1–30). Retrieved from http://plato.stanford.edu.ezp.sub.su.se/archives/spr2014/entries/repugnant-conclusion/.

Blackorby, C., Bossert, W., & Donaldson, D. (1995). Intertemporal Population Ethics: Critical-Level Utilitarian Principles. *Econometrica*, *63*(6), 1303–20. https://doi.org/10.2307/2171771.

Blackorby, C., Bossert, W., & Donaldson, D. (1997). Critical-Level Utilitarianism and the Population-Ethics Dilemma. *Economics and Philosophy*, *13*(02), 197–230. https://doi.org/10.1017/S026626710000448X.

Broad, C. D. (1979). *Five Types of Ethical Theory* (1st edition). London: Routledge.

Broome, J. (1999). *Ethics out of Economics.* Cambridge: Cambridge University Press.

Broome, J. (2004). *Weighing Lives.* Oxford: Oxford University Press.

Bykvist, K. (2007). The Good, the Bad, and the Ethically Neutral. *Economics and Philosophy*, *23*(01), 97–105. https://doi.org/10.1017/S0266267107001253.

Carlson, E. (1998). Mere Addition and Two Trilemmas of Population Ethics. *Economics and Philosophy*, *14*(02), 283–306.

Carlson, E. (forthcoming). *On Some Impossibility Theorems in Population Ethics.* Mimeo, Department of Philosophy, Uppsala University.

Chang, R. (2002). The Possibility of Parity. *Ethics, 112*(4), 659–88.

Chang, R. (2005). Parity, Interval Value, and Choice*. *Ethics, 115*(2), 331–50.

Fehige, C. (1998). A Pareto Principle for Possible People. In C. Fehige & U. Wessels (Eds.), *Preferences* (pp. 508–43). Berlin: W. de Gruyter.

Feldman, F. (1997). *Utilitarianism, Hedonism, and Desert: Essays in Moral Philosophy.* Cambridge: Cambridge University Press.

Handfield, T., & Rabinowicz, W. (2018). Incommensurability and Vagueness in Spectrum Arguments: Options for Saving Transitivity of Betterness. *Philosophical Studies, 175*(9), 2373–87. https://doi.org/10.1007/s11098-017-0963-9.

Herlitz, A. (2020). Spectrum Arguments, Parity and Persistency. *Theoria, 86*(4), 463–81. https://doi.org/10.1111/theo.12249.

Hudson, J. L. (1987). The Diminishing Marginal Value of Happy People. *Philosophical Studies, 51*(1), 123–37. https://doi.org/10.1007/BF00353967.

Kavka, G. S. (1982). The Paradox of Future Individuals. *Philosophy & Public Affairs, 11* (2), 93–112.

McTaggart, J. M. E. (1927). *The Nature of Existence.* Cambridge: Cambridge University Press.

Narveson, J. (1967). Utilitarianism and New Generations. *Mind, 76*(301), 62–72.

Narveson, J. (1973). Moral Problems of Population. *The Monist, 57*(1), 62–86.

Narveson, J. (1978). Future People and Us. In R. I. Sikora & B. Barry (Eds.), *Obligations to Future Generations* (pp. 38–60). Cambridge: White Horse Press.

Ng, Y.-K. (1989). What Should We Do about Future Generations? *Economics and Philosophy, 5*(02), 235–53.

Parfit, D. (1984). *Reasons and Persons* (1991st edition). Oxford: Clarendon.

Parfit, D. (1986). Overpopulation and the Quality of Life. In P. Singer (Ed.), *Applied Ethics* (1st edition, pp. 145–64). Oxford: New York: Oxford University Press.

Parfit, D. (2014). *How We Can Avoid the Repugnant Conclusion.* Mimeo, University of Oxford, Faculty of Philosophy.

Parfit, D. (2016). Can We Avoid the Repugnant Conclusion? *Theoria, 82*(2), 110–27. https://doi.org/10.1111/theo.12097.

Sider, T. R. (1991). Might Theory X Be a Theory of Diminishing Marginal Value? *Analysis, 51*(4), 265–71.

Sidgwick, H. (1907). *The Methods of Ethics.* London: Macmillan.

Thomas, T. (2018). Some Possibilities in Population Axiology. *Mind, 127*(507), 807–32. https://doi.org/10.1093/mind/fzx047.

17
On Evaluative Imprecision

Teruji Thomas

17.1 Introduction

In some of Parfit's last work on population ethics he proposed what he called an *imprecisionist lexical view* (Parfit, 2016). I'm going to present three arguments about how to understand this view, and in particular how to understand one of the central ideas, the idea of *evaluative imprecision*.

First, Parfit claims that his view is incompatible with thinking about goodness in terms of positions on a scale of value. I find this claim mysterious. I'm going to explain an important sense in which it seems to be untrue.

Second, insofar as its interpretation is up for grabs, I'll argue that imprecision is usefully understood as ordinary vagueness.

I will, third, defend against Schoenfield (2015) the claim that even robust moral realists can understand evaluative vagueness or imprecision as a purely semantic phenomenon.

Given the occasion, I'm presenting these arguments in the context of Parfit's work, but the point of the project is not primarily interpretive. Perhaps in the end I am offering an alternative to Parfit's view, rather than an interpretation of it. The real question is: if you're attracted to a view in broadly the neighbourhood of the imprecisionist lexical view, what should that view look like? On the other hand, there are also good reasons to be sceptical of the imprecisionist lexical view and anything like it. I will explain one of them in the conclusion.

17.2 The Imprecisionist Lexical View

I begin by recalling what the imprecisionist lexical view is all about.

The first component is a *lexical* view, which can be characterized by the following two claims (and here I'm just paraphrasing Parfit, 2016, p. 112).

[1] The more good lives the better, and the value contributed by each additional life of a given kind does not diminish as the number of them grows.

[2]   Certain very good lives are *lexically better* than certain drab lives of low but still positive value.

'Lexically better' means that it would be better for there to be some number of people, all with the first, very good kind of life, than for there to be any number of people, all with lives of the second, much less valuable kind. Claim [2] is just the denial of the well-known 'Repugnant Conclusion'; avoiding the Repugnant Conclusion, and thus vindicating claim [2], is one of Parfit's main goals in his paper.

The second part of the imprecisionist lexical view is the claim that there is such a thing as evaluative imprecision. Parfit writes:

> If we compare different ways in which our life might go, when choosing between different careers, for example, or deciding whether to have children, there are only imprecise truths about which of these possible lives would be better or worse. And there are only imprecise truths about the relative goodness of many different acts or outcomes, such as ones that would greatly benefit a few people, or give lesser benefits to many others.   (p. 113)

Parfit is especially interested in the idea that two outcomes may be only 'imprecisely equally good'; he appeals to the analogous idea that Einstein and Bach are 'imprecisely equally great' in their genius.

Now, this example and similar ones are very familiar and have admitted a number of different diagnoses. Chang (2002), for example, would want to say that Einstein and Bach are *on a par* with regards to greatness; Broome (1997) would want to say that it's *vague* which one is greater; and others talk about *incommensurability* or *incomparability*. I'm not going to take a stand on these interpretive questions in general. In particular, everything I'm going to say is compatible with the notion of parity, and the view that Einstein and Bach are on a par, and so on. The question for me is what notion in this vicinity is most helpful in the context of the imprecisionist lexical view—and, in particular, in the context of spectrum arguments, to which I'll come later on. As far as *that* goes I'm going to side with Broome in suggesting that the most relevant notion of imprecision is ordinary vagueness.

17.3 Scales of Value

First, though, I want to consider another line of thought which will help to explain a little how Parfit is thinking about imprecision and where I disagree with him. Parfit makes the following claims.

(a) The lexical view is incompatible with thinking of goodness in terms of positions on a scale of value (p. 116).
(b) Evaluative imprecision is *also* incompatible with thinking about goodness in this way (p. 113).

Parfit introduces claim (a) as a *prima facie* objection to the lexical view. As I understand it, the point of (b) is that, once we recognize the existence of evaluative imprecision, we have an independent reason to avoid thinking of goodness in terms of positions on a scale. Therefore (a) provides no objection to the lexical view.

In any case, I find both of these claims rather mysterious. They make the imprecisionist lexical view seem much more conceptually radical than I think it really is. I also think that, in discussing these claims, there's a real danger of falling into a merely verbal dispute about what counts as 'a scale of value'. I don't want to enter into that merely verbal dispute, but as an act of clarification, I do want to explain an important sense in which both (a) and (b) appear to be incorrect.

On my way of thinking, a scale of value is an abstract object, a collection of points. These points together have a certain structure, and there might be different versions of this structure suitable for different purposes. For my purposes, it is certainly enough if the points on the scale are partially ordered (i.e. some are higher than others); if they can be added and subtracted (so that we can look at sums and differences in value); and if they can be multiplied and divided by real numbers (so that we can talk about average value and expected value). To think about goodness in terms of positions on a scale of value will then mean assigning points on the scale to the various objects of evaluation.

This picture suffices for almost everything that we ever want to do with a scale of value. For example, it is just what we need to be able to say, 'The difference in value between A and B is 21.6 times the average value of C and D'.

17.3.1 The Lexical View

When Parfit says that the lexical view is incompatible with thinking about goodness in terms of positions on a scale of value, what does he mean? As far as I can tell, he has something like the following argument in mind.

Consider a population A consisting of a suitable number of very good lives, as mentioned in claim [2], and a population Z consisting only of drab lives. It appears that, on the lexical view, the population A of very good lives must be infinitely many times more valuable than the population Z. Why is that? Well, we're told that the value contributed by the lives in Z does not diminish as the number of them grows. What that means, on the usual understanding, is that if we doubled the size of Z then we would double the value of the population. But according to the lexical view, A would still be better than this doubled population. So we see that A is more than twice as good as Z. If instead we triple the size of Z, we see by the same logic that A is more than three times as good as Z. And in general, for any finite number n, we see that A is more than n times as good as Z. And that's just what I mean by saying that A is infinitely many times more valuable than Z.

So what? The claim must be that you can't have a positive value on a scale that is infinitely many times higher than another.

However, this claim does not follow from my notion of a scale. For example, one could use the so-called surreal numbers as a scale, in which some quantities have magnitudes infinitely greater than others (see Chen and Rubio, 2018). I'll give another example below.

It is true that one can require, as an additional premiss, that no positive value is infinitely many times higher than another. Indeed, you may feel that it is implausible that some value could be infinitely many times higher than another, and you may back that up with arguments. But those are substantive arguments against the lexical view, not arguments that the lexical view is conceptually incompatible with thinking about goodness on a scale of value. Alternatively, you may think it's part of the very idea of a scale of value that no positive value is infinitely higher than any other. That is the uninteresting verbal dispute I alluded to earlier.

Mainly, then, I am just making the following positive claim: the lexical view is conceptually compatible with thinking about goodness in terms of a scale of value in the specific sense that I described.

For the technically inclined, there is a mathematical theory of the kinds of structures I identified as scales of value. I mentioned that it should be possible to compare values, to add and subtract them, and to rescale them by real numbers. Under some plausible assumptions about how these possibilities fit together, this means that the scale of value is what's called a *partially ordered vector space*. The set of real numbers is one example of a partially ordered vector space, as is the class of surreal numbers. Besides being conceptually natural, partially ordered vector spaces allow for generalizations of many well-known results from decision theory and formal ethics.[1]

Instead of giving a formal definition, I will just give one example that illustrates how a partially ordered vector space can be used to represent both lexicality and, to be as general as possible, parity as well. The points on the scale will just be triplets of real numbers, (x_1, x_2, x_3). Define (x_1, x_2, x_3) to be at least as

---

[1] See McCarthy et al. (2019) for a recent discussion. The use of partially ordered vector spaces to represent lexicality goes back at least to Hausner (1954); for recent examples in the context of population ethics, see Carlson (2007), Thomas (2018), and Gustafsson (2020), the latter focusing on parity. The slightly more general notion of a partially ordered abelian group has also been used in this context (Pivato, 2014; Thomas, 2022).

great as (y_1, y_2, y_3) just in case $x_1 \geq y_1$ and either $x_2 > y_2$ or else $x_2 = y_2$ and $x_3 \geq y_3$. We can add and subtract values one component at a time: $(x_1, x_2, x_3) + (y_1, y_2, y_3) = (x_1 + y_1, x_2 + y_2, x_3 + y_3)$, for example. And we can think of $(2x_1, 2x_2, 2x_3)$ as being twice as good as (x_1, x_2, x_3). Some points on this scale are infinitely greater than others: $(0, 1, 0)$ is infinitely greater than $(0, 0, 1)$, insofar as it is greater than $(0, 0, n)$ for every n. And some points on the scale are on a par: comparing $(0, 0, 0)$ with $(1, -1, 0)$, neither is at least as good as the other.[2]

17.3.2 Imprecision

Now let me turn to the issue of imprecision. Parfit writes:

> [I]t may seem that the goodness of...things corresponds to their positions on some line or scale of value. On this Linear Model, truths about goodness must be precise because positions on a line are precise. So when we think about the goodness of such things, we should reject this Linear Model...Nor could some of these things be better than others by some imprecise amount, or to some imprecise degree, since the concepts of an amount or a degree also imply precision. (p. 114)

I find the argument here rather opaque. So think about a different example for a moment: height. I don't have a precise height. Optimistically, there may be a precise whole number of millimeters to which my height is closest. But not a precise whole number of nanometers, or femtometers. That's because it's not a precise matter which atoms are part of me, and anyway it's not a precise matter how big the atoms are, quite setting aside more esoteric questions of fundamental physics. Nonetheless, there's no harm in saying that, for example, I'm about 178 cm tall, I'm about 12 cm taller than my wife, I'm less than twice as tall as my son. These statements are perfectly sensible and true, and they invoke amounts and degrees of height. This shows that the concept of an amount or degree does not imply precision, as ordinarily conceived. The idea of an imprecise amount is perfectly cogent.

Moreover, it is one thing to suppose that each object of evaluation has a position on the relevant scale, and another thing to suppose that this position is precise. There are many ways of spelling out this idea. One possible move is to

---

[2] Here I'm assuming that all the points on the scale are comparable, in Chang's sense, so that if neither of x and y is at least as good as the other, then they are on a par. This seems natural when talking about scales of value, but one could also have a more complicated framework in which only some pairs of points are comparable with each other.

think of the position of an object on the scale as an interval or region rather than a single point. That is one way of thinking about imprecise positions. But there is another way of thinking, which is sometimes better. Yes, the position of an object on the scale is a single point, but it is an imprecise matter, or it is indeterminate, *which* point it is. My height is some number of centimeters, but it is indeterminate which number. There is a smallest number of grains that makes a heap, but it is indeterminate which number. This is a standard way of talking about vague matters like heights and heaps, and it is plausibly spelled out using a supervaluationist theory of vagueness, about which I will say more in the next two sections.

17.4 Imprecision as Vagueness

Now let me turn to my second argument, that imprecision—in the context of the imprecisionist lexical view—is helpfully understood as a form of vagueness.[3]

17.4.1 The Spectrum Argument

I have to explain the puzzle that leads Parfit to combine lexicality and imprecision in the first place.

Recall the following 'spectrum argument' for the Repugnant Conclusion—that is, against condition [2]. Take a population consisting of any number you like of very good lives—the kind of lives mentioned in that assumption. From now on I'll say that lives like this are at level 100. (The 'levels' are nothing more than labels to help keep track of the different kinds of lives.) Next we consider a population with slightly lower quality of life, say at level 99, but with many more people; the claim is that if there are sufficiently many more people, then this second population is better than the first. Then we lower the quality of life a little to level 98, and greatly increase the size of the population; again, if this third population is sufficiently large, then it will be better than the one before, and therefore better than the original population. We continue in this way, generating a sequence of populations, decreasing the quality of life in small steps, and massively increasing the number of people. After (let's say, for the sake of concreteness) ninety-nine steps, we get to a potentially enormous population of drab lives, at level 1. This last population, if it's sufficiently large, will be better than the one before, and therefore better than the original population of very good lives. So, contrary to condition [2], the very good lives are not lexically better than the drab ones.

---

[3] For a more thorough discussion of the ideas in this section, see Thomas (2021). I refute there some prominent objections to the view that spectrum arguments can be defused by vagueness.

The key premiss in this argument is what's often called the Quantity Condition (Arrhenius, 2000). On the supposition that lives at levels n and $n-1$ are sufficiently similar,

(QC) Level $n-1$ *eventually beats* level n; that is, for any number of lives at level n, it would be better to have sufficiently many lives at level $n-1$.

The spectrum argument shows that this Quantity Condition, along with some background assumptions which I won't discuss, entails the Repugnant Conclusion.

The puzzle is how to reconcile the attractiveness of the Quantity Condition with the repugnance of the Repugnant Conclusion. Since Parfit is vehemently opposed to the Repugnant Conclusion, it seems he must concede that some instance of the Quantity Condition is untrue. The main point of introducing imprecision in this context is that it allows us to make this concession in a relatively modest or conservative way. The situation may be easiest to think about in terms of a concrete sequence of populations, $P_{100}, P_{99}, \ldots, P_1$, with each P_n consisting of lives at level n, and P_{n-1} so much larger than P_n that we are inclined to think that P_{n-1} is better than P_n. To block the argument that P_1 is better than P_n, it must nonetheless, for some n, turn out to be untrue that P_{n-1} is better than P_n. In fact, at some point, it must even turn out to be untrue that P_{n-1} is *at least as good* as P_n. Counterintuitive as this may be, Parfit thinks we can reconcile ourselves to this concession as long as it is *also* untrue that P_{n-1} is *worse* than P_n. And here's where imprecision may provide some help.

How so? On Parfit's way of thinking, imprecision entails the existence of a fourth value relation, that of imprecise equality: given two populations, they may be equally good, or the first may be better than the second, or the first may be worse than the second, or—as a distinct possibility—they may be imprecisely equally good.[4] So, if P_{n-1} and P_n are imprecisely equally good, it will indeed be untrue that P_{n-1} is at least as good as P_n, and also untrue that P_{n-1} is worse than P_n. We will have to give up the corresponding instance of the Quantity Condition, but we can still maintain that, for any number of lives at level n, it would be *at least imprecisely equally good* to have sufficiently many lives at level $n-1$ (that is: either imprecisely equally good or better).

That's how Parfit uses imprecision. However, it is not obvious that imprecision, as ordinarily conceived, entails the existence of a fourth value relation. Indeed (as I'll explain below) it *doesn't* if imprecision is the same as vagueness. Moreover, I think a stronger position is available if we think of imprecision in

---

[4] Thus, on this reading, imprecise equality is very much like parity; see Chang (2016 and Chapter 14, this volume) for analysis.

this second way.[5] While a fourth value relation, like parity or incommensurability, may well have an important role to play, vagueness is especially well suited to explaining the paradox raised by the spectrum argument.

17.4.2 The Spectrum Argument—Repackaged

To see why, note that we can repackage the spectrum argument in the following form. Here is a first premiss:

(A1)   Level 100 eventually beats level 100.

This is just to say that, for any population at level 100, a sufficiently large population at that same level would be better. Now add a second premiss:

(A2)   If level n eventually beats level 100, then level $n - 1$ eventually beats level 100.

This is because, according to the Quantity Condition, level $n - 1$ eventually beats level n. So if level n eventually beats level 100, then level $n - 1$ also eventually beats level 100. Finally, if we apply A2 many times—as I've set things up, ninety-nine times—we reach the Repugnant Conclusion:

(RC)   Level 1 eventually beats level 100.

Now here is the key idea. If one is committed, as Parfit is, to denying the conclusion RC, and one thinks that the Quantity Condition and the closely related A2 seem compelling, then one thinks that the repackaged spectrum argument (A1, A2, RC) looks just like a sorites argument. It is a sorites argument for the predicate 'eventually beats level 100'. At least, it has the form of a sorites argument, and the same paradoxical nature.

We know what to say about sorites arguments. The existence of a sorites argument is at least *prima facie* evidence (and for some authors, like Bueno and Colyvan (2012), it is *conclusive* evidence) that the relevant predicate is vague. Here, the relevant predicate is 'eventually beats level 100', and underlying that, 'better than'. Since the spectrum argument can be repackaged into the form of a sorites argument, vagueness—and not a fourth value relation—is the most natural

---

[5] Parfit, to be sure, writes: 'imprecision is not the result of vagueness in our concepts, or our lack of knowledge, but is part of what we would know if we knew the full facts' (p. 113). This is at least compatible with the view that evaluative imprecision is a form of metaphysical vagueness, an idea I'll consider later in this chapter.

diagnosis. Moreover, a central goal of theorizing about vagueness is to explain the fact that the premisses of a sorites argument seem compelling in isolation, even if the argument is unsound. So too, if we take vagueness properly into account, we'd *expect* A2 and, relatedly, QC to seem compelling; we'd therefore *expect* a suitably chosen P_{n-1} to seem better than P_n. In contrast, the claim that P_{n-1} and P_n stand in a fourth value relation does not explain these intuitions.

Now, as I emphasize in Thomas (2021), vagueness can productively coexist with parity or incommensurability; I'll explain a little more at the very end of this section. So I am not strongly disagreeing with those like Chang (Chapter 14, this volume), and arguably Parfit, who think that a fourth value relation is in the air. But when it comes to understanding the paradox presented by a sorites argument like (A1,A2,RC), vagueness, not parity, provides the key.

17.4.3 Supervaluationism

To get a clearer sense of what a vagueness-based view might actually look like, we have to choose a particular theory of vagueness. I'll focus on supervaluationism (Fine, 1975; Keefe, 2000), which, although far from universally accepted, is probably the best-known view. This will also help to set up my discussion of semantic vagueness in the next section.

Take 'tall' as an example, applied to people. According to supervaluationists, we can think about the meaning of 'tall' in terms of a range of *precisifications*, roughly glossed as admissible ways of making our language precise. One way of thinking about this is that, on each precisification, 'tall' picks out a different precise property (for some suitably abundant notion of property). On the simplest picture, there's one precisification on which 'tall' picks out the property of being at least 182 cm in height, and another on which it picks out the property of being at least 182.3 cm in height, and so on.[6] The properties picked out in this way I will call *precisifications of tallness*; on the simplest picture, they are the properties of being at least x cm tall, for each x in a certain range. 'Jan is tall' is *true* (and I'll say that Jan is definitely tall) just in case it would be true on each precisification, or in other words just in case Jan has each and every one of the relevant properties; 'Jan is tall' is *false* (and I'll say that Jan is definitely not tall) just in case Jan has none of the relevant properties; 'Jan is tall' is *indeterminate* or *borderline* (and I'll say that Jan is borderline tall) just in case Jan has some but not all of these properties. On some varieties of supervaluationism (see especially Edgington, 1996), it also makes sense to ask *on what proportion* of precisifications 'Jan is tall' would come out true;

---

[6] While this illustrates the basic idea, it can't quite be the right thing to say, since the meaning of 'at least 182 cm in height' is itself vague. How to think about precisifications is one of the key interpretive issues within supervaluationism; see Keefe (2000, ch. 7) for discussion.

if the answer is 'on all of them, or almost all of them', then we can say Jan is *almost definitely* tall.

A key feature of this supervaluationist treatment of 'tall' is that there's some number x such that people above x cm in height are tall, and people below x cm in height are not tall. After all, there is some such x for each precisification. It's just indeterminate which x it is, in the sense that different xs work for different precisifications. For short, I will say that 'tall' *refers indeterminately* to the various precisifications of tallness. So too, if 'better' is semantically vague, we should think that there is a range of relations to which the word 'better' indeterminately refers; these are the precisifications of betterness.

Now back to the spectrum argument. Recall that Parfit retreats to the claim that, for any number of lives at level n, it would be *at least imprecisely equally good* to have sufficiently many lives at level $n - 1$. And, in terms of the sequence of populations, he concedes that, for some n, P_{n-1} and P_n are imprecisely equally good. The supervaluationist view I am discussing, either as a reinterpretation of Parfit's view or as an alternative to it, says instead: for any number of lives at level n, it would be *at least borderline better* to have sufficiently many lives at level $n - 1$: either borderline better or definitely better. In fact, if we accept the variety of supervaluationism mentioned above, it would be *almost definitely better* to have sufficiently many lives at level $n - 1$. So too, for each n, P_{n-1} is almost definitely better than P_n.

As this sketch indicates, the interpretation of imprecision as vagueness can be reconciled with Parfit's own view to the extent that we can identify his notion of imprecise equality with that of borderline betterness. If P_{n-1} is only borderline better than P_n, then, in a sense, P_{n-1} and P_n are imprecisely equally good. However, contrary to Parfit's way of spelling things out, the possibility of borderline betterness does not in itself entail the existence of a fourth value relation. In a case of borderline betterness, it still may be true that either P_{n-1} is better than P_n, or P_{n-1} is worse than P_n, or P_{n-1} and P_n are equally good; borderline betterness can arise because it is indeterminate which of these three disjuncts obtains.

On the other hand, borderline betterness does not rule out parity. In the face of the spectrum argument, we could hold, for example, that P_{n-1} is almost definitely better than P_n, *and* that it is either better than P_n or they are on a par. Such a claim combines the most attractive features of both parity- and vagueness-based views.

17.5 Vagueness as Semantic

One reason why it's attractive to appeal to vagueness is that everyone agrees that vagueness is a real phenomenon; in fact, practically all our language is vague, and it's not terribly surprising that that includes our evaluative language. We have to defuse sorites arguments *somehow*; on this view there's *no extra cost* to defusing the basic spectrum argument. We don't, for example, have to embrace the intransitivity of betterness. Appealing to vagueness is, in that sense, theoretically conservative, and that's a great virtue of the view.

However, this line of thought is most compelling if 'better than' is vague in *the same way* that 'tall' and 'red' are vague. The most common view is that the vagueness of these terms is a semantic phenomenon: there is a kind of looseness in the way that they pick out properties in the world. (The supervaluationist view sketched above is meant to be a view of this kind.) But on closer inspection there is something puzzling about thinking of evaluative vagueness in this ordinary way. Indeed, Schoenfield (2015) has argued that if a robust form of moral realism is true, then moral vagueness is not merely semantic, but 'ontic' or metaphysical. To understand this claim, we are supposed to imagine a metaphysician's 'perfect', joint-carving language, containing exactly the predicates needed to provide a complete and accurate description of how things are fundamentally. By 'robust moral realism', Schoenfield means the view that such a language would contain moral predicates. By the claim that 'moral vagueness is ontic' she means (citing Barnes, 2014) that even in the perfect language these moral predicates would be vague. So, given the existence of moral vagueness, and given that the perfect language would contain moral predicates, the thesis is that at least some of those moral predicates would be vague.

Schoenfield is mainly concerned with the vagueness of permissibility, but her arguments seem to apply to betterness as well, and what we might call robust *evaluative* realism. They seem to suggest that, if 'better' is vague, and the perfect language contains evaluative predicates, then some of those predicates must be vague. The view that evaluative vagueness is ontic vagueness is troubling because, despite much recent work (see e.g. Barnes and Williams, 2011, Wilson, 2016, Wasserman, 2017, for three quite different approaches) there is widespread scepticism about the very idea of ontic vagueness; it is certainly not something to which everyone feels committed.

I want to set aside questions of whether this form of robust moral or evaluative realism is really plausible, and whether this conception of ontic vagueness is really problematic. (My inclination is 'no' to both!) I just want to illustrate how one could deny the thesis as stated. Although the view I will describe in the rest of this section is extremely speculative, I think it has a number of interesting features that deserve further exploration.[7]

---

[7] Similar ideas were discovered independently at around the same time and developed more systematically in an excellent paper by Sud (2019). My discussion will add value by focusing on betterness (where Sud focuses on wrongness); by suggesting a new way to think about the conceptual role of betterness; and by spelling out in somewhat more concrete terms, and in the context of the spectrum argument, one particular view in the family he considers.

17.5.1 The Basic Proposal

Recall that, if 'better' is semantically vague, then (on a supervaluationist view) there is a range of relations to which the word 'better' indeterminately refers; these are the precisifications of betterness. In order to get a version of robust evaluative realism, we might suppose that these precisifications are the fundamental evaluative relations, and that the perfect language would have a name, like 'betterness$^\sharp$', for each of them.

Let me address two initial objections as best I can. First: the obviously strange thing about the picture I'm offering is the proliferation of evaluative relations—not just a *fourth* one, like parity, but a different fundamental evaluative relation for each precisification of betterness. It would be difficult to entirely dispel the sense of strangeness, but it is worth bearing in mind that, unlike parity, these evaluative relations are not alternatives to betterness. Just as Jan can be both tall and at least 185 cm in height, X can be both better than Y and better$^\sharp$ than Y. Indeed, by design, if X is better$^\sharp$ than Y, then X is at least borderline better than Y.

Second: if the *precisifications* of betterness are the fundamental things, why do we speak in terms of betterness at all? An analogy may help. We're always thinking in terms of tables and chairs and heaps and organisms and tallness so on. And all of these concepts are terribly vague, and unlikely fundamental. The perfect language, rather plausibly, would not have words for tables and chairs as such; it would be more like the language of fundamental physics, referring in precise terms to such things as (perhaps) elementary particles, wave functions, position, mass, and charge. We sometimes think and talk about such things as well, but, given our physical and cognitive limitations, we could hardly navigate the world in just those terms. For everyday purposes, and indeed for many theoretical purposes, using higher-level, summary, vague concepts is what works best. I suggest thinking of betterness in an analogous way. There are fundamental, precise evaluative relations. But understanding and navigating the world in just those terms (regulating our pro-attitudes, deciding what to do) would be an intractable task for beings like us. For our everyday purposes, and indeed for most theoretical purposes, thinking in terms of a higher-level, summary, vague relation—betterness—is what works best.

That's the basic proposal, on behalf of the robust moral realist. However, what I've said so far doesn't speak directly to Schoenfield's biggest objection to semantic accounts of evaluative vagueness. I'll turn to that objection now.

17.5.2 Shiftiness

As Schoenfield points out, paradigmatic vague predicates are, in a specific sense, arbitrary in their meanings. For example, it seems we could get along just as well if we used the word 'tall' in a slightly more precise way. Suppose Jan is 185 cm in height. Although (let's suppose) we hesitate to say that Jan is tall, or to say that Jan is not tall, we can imagine a community (let's call them the Tallists), who are like ourselves in almost every way, except that their standards for applying 'tall' are looser than ours; they confidently assert 'Jan is tall'. And we can imagine another community (let's call them the Anti-Tallists), who confidently assert 'Jan is not tall'. We would be disinclined to think that there is any substantive disagreement between the Tallists and the Anti-Tallists, or between them and ourselves. Instead, most plausibly, the meaning of the word 'tall' in each community's mouths is shifted to make true and appropriate their way of speaking.

This *shiftiness*, as Schoenfield calls it, makes it seem unreasonable to assign any fundamental importance to the property (or range of properties) that *our* word 'tall' happens to pick out, rather than the property picked out by the word 'tall' in the mouths of these hypothetical communities. But, in contrast, we *do* care very much, and reasonably so, about the properties picked out by morally relevant evaluative predicates like 'better' or 'good'. If these evaluative predicates were similarly shifty, it would seem (from the moral realist's point of view) quite implausible to claim that *our* usage happened to be normatively privileged.[8]

To the extent that shiftiness is characteristic of semantic vagueness, one might straightforwardly conclude that evaluative predicates are not semantically vague. But the relationship between semantic vagueness and shiftiness is not entirely clear, and we should instead think of this as providing a challenge. A moral realist who thinks that 'better' is semantically vague has to explain the semantics in a way that allows for vagueness while not rendering our preoccupation with betterness unreasonably arbitrary.

17.5.3 Conceptual Role Semantics

There may be a few ways one might try to meet this challenge, but for concreteness I'll sketch an approach based on conceptual role semantics (Wedgwood, 2001). This is in fact one of the options Schoenfield considers in her paper (and it is the option considered by Sud; see fn. 7). She concedes that conceptual role semantics can avoid any problematic shiftiness (although I'll suggest that some *un*problematic shiftiness may remain). She claims, however, that conceptual role semantics rules out semantic vagueness, and that's where I disagree. In fact, conceptual role

---

[8] Schoenfield's specific complaint is that it would seem inappropriate to consult linguistic surveys to figure out what one ought to do, even as one might well consult facts about usage to figure out whether we are the Tallists and therefore whether Jan is tall. See Bacon (2018) for general discussion of the subtly different senses in which we might or might not care about vague properties.

semantics suggests a particular (and in some ways attractive) view about the precisifications of betterness—the relations which I've proposed are fundamental.

According to Wedgwood, the meaning of 'better' is characterized by a certain conceptual role. The rough idea is that betterness is whatever makes an attitude of preference fitting or correct. He is primarily concerned with the case where X and Y are acts, and betterness is a matter of whether it's all-things-considered better (for a particular agent at a particular time) to do X rather than to do Y; he takes the relevant sense of preference to be one of conditional intention. For the purposes of this chapter, I'm interested in potentially different senses of betterness and preference. I'm interested in the sense of betterness used to compare populations in the spectrum argument, which may or may not be directly related to what it would be all-things-considered better for an agent to do. Similarly, I don't want to be tied to the notion of preference as conditional intention. I unfortunately don't have much to say about what the relevant notion of preference actually is; but it has often been assumed that there is *some* kind of preference—some sort of 'pro-attitude', or attitude of approval—such that (in a sense to be made precise) it is appropriate to prefer X to Y just in case X is better than Y.[9] I am talking about that same kind of thing.

How, then, to formulate the connection between betterness and preference more precisely? Wedgwood focuses on the notion of validity of practical reasoning. To provide an interesting alternative (which I find somewhat clearer), I instead suggest a formulation in terms of requirements of rationality.[10] Namely:

(PLATITUDE) Necessarily, rationality requires that, if you believe X is better than Y then, if anything, you prefer X to Y.

The 'if anything' requires some explanation. It signals that, at least as far as PLATITUDE goes, rationality permits you to believe X is better than Y while not having any preference-like attitude between them. But it rules out believing X is better than Y while preferring Y to X, or being indifferent between them. It also rules out any other attitudes that are exclusive alternatives to a preference between X and Y, like perhaps a positive attitude of suspended judgement, or a strong feeling of ambivalence. The reason for including the 'if anything' is that I'm inclined to think that most of the time rationality requires us to avoid conflicting attitudes, rather than requiring us to have all the attitudes to which we are implicitly committed. For example, there's a sense in which believing that p is true and believing that if p then q is true commits one to believing that q is true.

---

[9] See Rabinowicz (2012) for a general theory of the connection between evaluative relations and preference-like attitudes that includes a careful treatment of parity.

[10] My way of thinking about such requirements is heavily influenced by Broome (2013).

But it's OK, as far as rationality goes, if one simply hasn't got around to forming a belief about q.[11]

It's clear that PLATITUDE partly ties down the concept of betterness.[12] For example, if we substituted 'worse' for 'better', then PLATITUDE wouldn't come out true. But we could substitute 'X is much better than' for 'X is better than Y' and PLATITUDE would still be plausible. So what I'm going to suggest is that the concept of betterness is *the most general* concept that makes PLATITUDE true. In a slogan, betterness is the correctness condition for preference.

To get a handle on this view, let us look more closely at what it suggests about shiftiness. There are two interesting cases.[13] In the first case, imagine a community that applies the predicate 'better' to a slightly different range of cases than we do, but use 'preference' (and its cognates) to cover the same range of mental states that we do. Suppose that they still affirm PLATITUDE, though, and typically prefer the things they judge (in their mouths) to be 'better'. Then a natural diagnosis is that their talk about 'betterness' has the same conceptual role as ours, and so has the same meaning. 'Better' means *better*: there is no shift here, and we have a substantive disagreement with them about which cases are better than which others.

The second case is more interesting. Imagine a community that uses both the word 'better' and the word 'prefers' in a shifted way. Suppose further that they go around affirming what *sounds* like PLATITUDE, and that it is in fact typically true that, in their mouths, they 'prefer' what they judge to be 'better'. Then a natural diagnosis is that both 'better' and 'prefer' in their mouths shift in meaning to pick out slightly different notions, better* and prefer*. Indeed, it is natural to guess that betterness* is the correctness condition for preference*, not for preference.

Now, the original worry was that it would be unreasonable and arbitrary to care about betterness, if 'better' is shifty. However, this second case, which indicates a certain kind of shiftiness, does not raise that worry. It is not unreasonable to care about betterness, if what we mean by that is *preferring* what is better. Nor is it unreasonable for *them* to care about betterness*, if what we mean by that is *preferring** what is better*. Crucially, preferring* what is better* is compatible with preferring what is better.

---

[11] Here I am following Broome (2013, §9.3). To be clear, there may be any number of ways of modifying or supplementing PLATITUDE, but I expect that most of what I say can be adapted.

[12] I talk about the *concept* of betterness here to emphasize that 'better' appears in PLATITUDE in a hyperintentional context, the context of belief. So, for example, if it turned out to be a necessary truth, but not a conceptual truth, that X is better than Y if and only if X contains more happy people than Y, it would still be impossible to substitute 'contains more happy people' for 'better' in PLATITUDE while preserving its truth. Thus PLATITUDE directly constrains the concept of betterness and only indirectly the meaning in any more extensional sense.

[13] Schoenfield and Sud characterize 'better' as non-shifty or *stable*. I think this disagreement (especially in Sud's case) is shallow: they have in mind the first kind of case, below, rather than the second. We're agreed, anyway, that conceptual role semantics can eliminate any *problematic* shiftiness. But it's still interesting to see that there a form of shiftiness remains, as we might expect in a case of semantic vagueness.

The conclusion is that when we accept conceptual role semantics, 'better' and 'prefer' can shift together in the way that we might expect from semantically vague terms, but the shiftiness is unproblematic.

17.5.4 Precisifications of Betterness

As I have mentioned, Schoenfield argues that conceptual role semantics rules out evaluative vagueness. I won't go into her argument here, but will just point out what I think it misses. The basic point is this. Conceptual role semantics emphasize the close connection between betterness and preference. Given that 'prefer' and its derivatives—ordinary non-evaluative terms—are semantically vague, it would actually be surprising if 'better' were not vague too.

Concretely, we might suppose that PLATITUDE is true for every admissible way of simultaneously making 'better' and 'prefer' precise.[14] To recall, each precisification determines precisifications preference$^{\sharp}$ and betterness$^{\sharp}$ of preference and betterness respectively; the suggestion is that the concept of betterness$^{\sharp}$ is the most general one making the following principle true:

(PLATITUDE$^{\sharp}$) Necessarily, rationality requires that, if you believe X is better$^{\sharp}$ than Y then, if anything, you prefer$^{\sharp}$ X to Y.

In short, betterness$^{\sharp}$ is the correctness condition for preference$^{\sharp}$. Besides illustrating how conceptual role semantics can allow for, and even *suggest* semantic vagueness, this principle gives some meaning to the claim that the precisifications of betterness, which I have proposed to be fundamental evaluative properties, are evaluative at all.

17.5.5 The Spectrum Argument, Revisited

Let me conclude this discussion by returning to the spectrum argument. Suppose we accept the imprecisionist lexical view and interpret imprecision as supervaluationist vagueness. I've suggested that, as we move down the sequence of populations, each is at least borderline better than the one before (indeed, almost definitely better), and the first is definitely better than the last.

---

[14] This is *almost* obvious; after all, if PLATITUDE is true, it should come out true on every precisification. The subtlety is that I'm *not* precisifying the other terms in PLATITUDE, notably 'rationality' and 'believe'; so I am suggesting a somewhat bolder principle that emphasizes the special connection between betterness and preference.

The elaborated conceptual role semantics yields an additional claim about the attitudes it would be appropriate to have when contemplating the various populations. Suppose that P_{n-1} is only borderline better than P_n. So P_{n-1} would count as better than P_n on most but not all ways of making 'better than' precise. On my view, it would be appropriate (in the sense spelled out by PLATITUDE$^\sharp$) to be in most but not all of the states of preferring$^\sharp$ P_{n-1} to P_n, and thus to be in a state that would count as preferring P_{n-1} to P_n on most but not all ways of making 'prefer' precise. This state is (of course) not a state of definite preference (it's a state of *almost* definite preference), but it is still more like favouring P_{n-1} over P_n than the other way around.[15]

This makes a happy contrast with a version of Chang's view on which some P_n and P_{n-1} end up being definitely on a par (or, in Parfit's terms, imprecisely equal in value). On such a view, the relationship between P_n and P_{n-1} is (so far as I can tell) fundamentally symmetric, and there is no sense in which it is appropriate to favour P_{n-1} over P_n rather than the other way around. For example, Rabinowicz (2012) suggests that, if P_n and P_{n-1} are definitely on a par, then it would be entirely appropriate to have an outright preference for either one.[16]

17.6 Conclusion

Let me summarize the arguments so far.

First, I explained an important sense in which evaluative imprecision, as well as lexicality, is compatible with thinking about goodness in terms of positions on a scale of value.

Second, I suggested that, insofar as its interpretation is up for grabs, we can fruitfully think of imprecision as a form of vagueness. At least, the spectrum argument can be repackaged in the form of a sorites argument, and this suggests specifically that vagueness is at work.

Third, I sketched how an elaboration of conceptual role semantics might be compatible with robust moral or evaluative realism, while simultaneously denying that evaluative vagueness is metaphysical. Even robust moral realists can recognize imprecision as a merely semantic phenomenon.

---

[15] What is a borderline case of preference actually like? That's a good question; answering it would require more careful thought about the relevant notion of preference. But here's an attempt at illustration. Preferring X over Y can still involve a little bit of ambivalence, but not too much. How much is too much? There's no precise limit. But borderline cases of preference involve ambivalence that is borderline excessive. Stronger ambivalence might be appropriate in cases of parity, although this differs from the view of Rabinowicz (2012) mentioned below. See Peterson (2006) and Williams (2014) for some alternative views about borderline cases.

[16] Hájek and Rabinowicz (2021) emphasize that (nonetheless) *most* permissible systems of preference will include a preference for P_{n-1} over P_n. This breaks the symmetry, but I am not convinced it adequately captures the psychology of the case.

Nonetheless, I don't think that one should be especially sanguine about the lexical imprecisionist view, even interpreted in the way I have suggested. Lexicality has problems that imprecision is impotent to cure. I conclude by explaining one of them.

Let A be the world in which many people exist with very good lives, at level 100, and Z a world with even more people, but whose lives are drab. Let Z^+ be like Z, but with ten times as many people. Imagine a scenario in which either Z or A might arise by chance (call this 'the Risky Scenario'), and compare it to a scenario in which Z^+ will arise for sure (call this 'the Safe Scenario'). Which of these scenarios is better? Z^+ is better than Z, by condition [1], and this counts in favour of the Safe Scenario. On the other hand, Z^+ is worse than A, by condition [2], and this counts against the Safe Scenario. How do these things weigh up? In general it may not be clear, but suppose that the chance that A will arise in the Risky Scenario is only one chance in a billion, or one chance in a trillion, or one chance in a trillion trillions. Thus it is all but certain that the Risky Scenario will result in an outcome significantly worse than the outcome of the Safe Scenario. It is hard for me to believe that the Risky Scenario is not worse than the Safe Scenario, if the chance of A is sufficiently small.

Suppose, for concreteness, that the Risky Scenario is worse than the Safe Scenario when the chance of A is one in one hundred. Then it is safe to say that the value difference between A and Z is less than a million times greater than the value difference between Z^+ and Z. Otherwise, the small chance of A would still easily make the Risky Scenario better than the Safe Scenario. On the other hand, according to Parfit's formulation of the lexical view, the value contributed by the lives in Z does not diminish with their number. Let Z^{++} be a world like Z^+, but with a trillion times more lives. Because the value contributed by such lives does not diminish, the value difference between Z^{++} and Z is *at least* a million times greater than the value difference between Z^+ and Z. (Indeed, the first value difference should be about a trillion times greater than the second.) Therefore the value difference between Z^{++} and Z is unambiguously greater than the value difference between A and Z. So Z^{++} is better than A, and the imprecise lexical view is false.

There are certainly ways to resist this argument, although I think it is harder than it may seem. Arguments involving very small probabilities, as this one does, often seem suspicious (see e.g. Monton, 2019). But the fact that value is vague or in some other sense imprecise is no objection, as far as I can tell. I did not say anything that presupposes precision. For example, the claim that one value difference is more than a million times greater than another does not presuppose that the first value difference is some precise number of times greater than the second.[17]

---

[17] I am grateful to Hilary Greaves, Ralf Bader, Miriam Schoenfield, Jimmy Goodrich, and Elliott Thornley for discussing aspects of this chapter. I am also grateful to the organizers and the audience at

References

Arrhenius, G. (2000). *Future Generations: A Challenge for Moral Theory*. Uppsala University Printers.

Bacon, A. (2018). *Vagueness and Thought*. Oxford University Press.

Barnes, E. (2014). Fundamental indeterminacy. *Analytic Philosophy*, 55:339–62.

Barnes, E. and Williams, J. R. G. (2011). A theory of metaphysical indeterminacy. In Bennett, K. and Zimmerman, D. W., editors, *Oxford Studies in Metaphysics*, volume 6, pages 103–48. Oxford University Press.

Broome, J. (1997). Is incommensurability vagueness? In Chang, R., editor, *Incommensurability, Incomparability and Practical Reason*. Harvard University Press.

Broome, J. (2013). *Rationality through Reasoning*. Wiley-Blackwell.

Bueno, O. and Colyvan, M. (2012). Just what is vagueness? *Ratio*, 25(1):19–33.

Carlson, E. (2007). Higher values and non-archimedean additivity. *Theoria*, 73(1):3–27.

Chang, R. (2002). The possibility of parity. *Ethics*, 112:659–88.

Chang, R. (2016). Parity, imprecise comparability and the repugnant conclusion. *Theoria*, 82(2):182–214.

Chen, E. K. and Rubio, D. (2020). Surreal decisions. *Philosophy and Phenomenological Research*, 100(1):54–74.

Edgington, D. (1996). Vagueness by degrees. In Keefe, R. and Smith, P., editors, *Vagueness: A Reader*. MIT Press.

Fine, K. (1975). Vagueness, truth and logic. *Synthese*, 30(3/4):265–300.

Gustafsson, J. E. (2020). Population axiology and the possibility of a fourth category of absolute value. *Economics and Philosophy*, 36(1):81–110.

Hájek, A, Rabinowicz, W. (2021). Degrees of commensurability and the repugnant conclusion. *Noûs*, 1–23. https://doi.org/10.1111/nous.12388.

Hausner, M. (1954). Multidimensional utilities. In *Decision Processes*. John Wiley.

Keefe, R. (2000). *Theories of Vagueness*. Cambridge University Press.

McCarthy, D., Mikkola, K., and Thomas, T. (2019). Aggregation for potentially infinite populations without continuity or completeness. arXiv:1911.00872.

Monton, B. (2019). How to avoid maximizing expected utility. *Philosophers' Imprint*, 19.

---

the 2018 conference in honour of Parfit at which a version of this chapter was presented. Parfit emailed me in the summer of 2016, sending me a copy of his paper that I discuss here, and graciously asking after some work about similar views that I had written for my thesis. The objection to the imprecisionist lexical view that I raise in the conclusion, as well as some of the material about scales of value, was originally written as comments for him, and I am very sorry I never heard what he made of it.

Parfit, D. (2016). Can we avoid the repugnant conclusion? *Theoria*, 82(2):110–27.

Peterson, M. (2006). Indeterminate preferences. *Philosophical Studies*, 130(2):297–320.

Pivato, M. (2014). Additive representation of separable preferences over infinite products. *Theory and Decision*, 77(1):31–83.

Rabinowicz, W. (2012). Value relations revisited. *Economics and Philosophy*, 28(2):133–64.

Schoenfield, M. (2015). Moral vagueness is ontic vagueness. *Ethics*, 126(2):257–82.

Sud, R. (2019). Moral vagueness as semantic vagueness. *Ethics*, 129(4):684–705.

Thomas, T. (2018). Some possibilities in population axiology. *Mind*, 127(507):807–32.

Thomas, T. (2021). Are spectrum arguments defused by vagueness? *Australasian Journal of Philosophy*, DOI: 10.1080/00048402.2021.1920622.

Thomas, T. (2022). Separability in population ethics. In Arrhenius, G., Bykvist, K., Campbell, T., and Finneron-Burns, E., editors, *The Oxford Handbook of Population Ethics*. Oxford University Press. Forthcoming.

Wasserman, R. (2017). Vagueness and the laws of metaphysics. *Philosophy and Phenomenological Research*, 95(1):66–89.

Wedgwood, R. (2001). Conceptual role semantics for moral terms. *Philosophical Review*, 110(1):1–30.

Williams, J. R. G. (2014). Decision-making under indeterminacy. *Philosophers' Imprint*, 14(4):1–34.

Wilson, J. (2016). Are there indeterminate states of affairs? Yes. In Barnes, E., editor, *Current Controversies in Metaphysics*. Taylor and Francis.

18
Sorites on What Matters

Theron Pummer

18.1 The Sorites Analogy

Ethics in the tradition of Derek Parfit's *Reasons and Persons* is riddled with sorites-like arguments, which lead us by what seem innocent steps to seemingly false conclusions.[1] One such argument goes as follows.[2]

Compared with the existence of ten billion people who all have a very high quality of life, there is some larger number of people whose existence would be better, even though these people all have a slightly lower quality of life. Better yet would be the existence of an even larger number of people, at a still lower—though again only slightly lower—quality of life. We can continue in this fashion. Assuming that at each step there is a sufficient gain in number and a merely slight drop in quality, each step seems one for the better. For some fixed precisification of 'slightly lower quality of life', there is a finite number of such steps that will lead us to a vast number of people, who all have lives that are barely worth living. Since each step is one for the better, all of them are. Therefore, compared with the existence of ten billion people who all have a very high quality of life, there is some larger number of people whose existence would be better, even though these people all have lives that are barely worth living. This seemingly false conclusion is what Parfit calls the *Repugnant Conclusion*.

This argument involves tradeoffs between quality of life and number of people. Not everyone believes that the existence of a larger number of people at a positive quality of life would be in one way better. Those who do not would reject every

---

[1] Many thanks to Farbod Akhlaghi-Ghaffarokh, Ralf Bader, Joe Bowen, David Brink, Tim Campbell, Ruth Chang, Matt Clark, Aaron Cotnoir, Roger Crisp, Tom Dougherty, Luke Elson, Johann Frick, Hilary Greaves, Katherine Hawley, Joe Horton, Hud Hudson, Tyler John, Kacper Kowalczyk, Andreas Mogensen, Jake Nebel, Julia Nefsky, Mike Otsuka, Ketan Ramakrishnan, Kevin Scharp, Larry Temkin, Teru Thomas, Ryan Wasserman, and audiences at the University of Oxford, the University of St Andrews, and the Institute for Futures Studies in Stockholm for tremendously helpful comments and discussions. I am extremely fortunate to have been mentored by Derek Parfit during the early stages of my career, and will always look back on our many hours of correspondence with profound happiness and gratitude. Derek passed away before I could talk with him about the main ideas presented in this chapter.

[2] See Parfit 1984, 1986, and 2016.

step of the above argument.³ But other structurally similar arguments involve tradeoffs between different evaluatively relevant dimensions, for example, intensity and duration of pain, severity and number of harms, pleasure and rational activity, and so on. Most of what I argue here applies to all these structurally similar arguments, which we can call *spectrum arguments*.⁴

Spectrum arguments are puzzling. Many of us find that, considered independently, their premises seem true and yet their conclusions seem false. Similarly, *sorites arguments* puzzlingly lead us by many small and seemingly innocent steps to seemingly false conclusions.⁵ One goes as follows.

A collection of ten billion grains of sand is a heap. For any number of grains n, if a collection of n grains is a heap, then a collection of n-1 grains is a heap. Since a collection of 10,000,000,000 grains is a heap, a collection of 9,999,999,999 grains is a heap. Then, since a collection of 9,999,999,999 grains is a heap, a collection of 9,999,999,998 grains is a heap. Continuing in this fashion, we eventually reach the seemingly false conclusion that a collection of one grain is a heap.

This argument involves the property of being a heap. Other structurally similar arguments involve other properties, such as being hirsute, or being rich. In all cases, we begin with a finite series of items in which each differs only slightly from the previous along a single dimension (number of grains, number of hairs, or number of pennies) relevant to the instantiation of the property in question (being a heap, being hirsute, or being rich). Next we offer an 'initiation premise', that the first item in the series instantiates the property in question. We then offer a 'tolerance premise', that if any item in the series instantiates the property in question, then so does the next item. Finally, we reason as before from these premises to the conclusion that the last item in the series instantiates the property in question (for example, that a collection of only one grain is a heap, that a head with only one hair on it is hirsute, or that a person possessing only a penny is rich). Arguments with this structure are sorites arguments.

Given the respects in which sorites arguments appear structurally similar to spectrum arguments, we may suspect that any particular spectrum argument is 'just another sorites'. Several authors accept what I call the *sorites analogy*, according to which, since spectrum arguments are relevantly structurally analogous to sorites arguments, the correct response to spectrum arguments is

---

³ Of course, several of Parfit's arguments for the Repugnant Conclusion do not presuppose that the existence of a larger number of people at a positive quality of life would be in one way better. See Parfit 1984 (chapter 19), 1986, and 2016.
⁴ See, for example: Temkin 1996 and 2012; Norcross 1997; Rachels 1998 and 2004; Carlson 2000; Arrhenius and Rabinowicz 2005; Pummer 2017.
⁵ See Hyde and Raffman 2018.

structurally analogous to the correct response to sorites arguments.[6] We may combine the sorites analogy with a particular view of the correct response to sorites arguments (for example, that there is a cutoff somewhere along the sorites series, so that a collection of n grains is a heap but a collection of n-1 grains is not). Or we may remain silent on how to solve the sorites, and claim that *whatever* the correct response to sorites arguments is, the correct response to spectrum arguments is structurally analogous.

The sorites analogy may inspire hope of resolving important debates in ethics at relatively low theoretical cost. For example, if the correct response to the sorites is one in which we reject one of its premises whilst explaining away its intuitive appeal, then, according to the sorites analogy, the correct response to spectrum arguments would be similarly sanguine. So perhaps, contrary to what Parfit and others sometimes suggest, it is not the case that, because there are no plausible solutions to the puzzles presented by spectrum arguments, the best we can do is to identify which solutions are the *least implausible*.[7]

In this chapter, I argue against the sorites analogy. I first consider some potential structural disanalogies between spectrum arguments and sorites arguments (section 18.2). Even if none of these provides an adequate response to the sorites analogy, there is another type of response. There are *content-based* disanalogies between spectrum arguments and sorites arguments. Even if these arguments are relevantly structurally analogous, they differ in their content in ways that show the sorites analogy to be implausible. I explore two content-based disanalogies—one is inspired by Parfit's work on reductionism (section 18.3), and the other involves what I call hypersensitivity (section 18.4). I conclude with a summary and a broader methodological lesson (section 18.5).

18.2 Structural Disanalogies

Parfit offers a brief response to the sorites analogy. He writes:

> It may be objected that my [spectrum] argument is like what are called *Sorites Arguments*, which are known to lead to false conclusions. Suppose we assume that removing any single grain of sand cannot turn a heap of sand into something that is not a heap. It can then be argued that, even if we remove every single grain, we must still have a heap... If my argument was like this, it could be referred to those who work on what is wrong with Sorites Arguments. But my argument is

---

[6] See, for example: Griffin 1986 (86–7); Qizilbash 2005; Voorhoeve and Binmore 2006; Knapp 2007; Katz 2015; Thomas 2016, 2018, and Chapter 17, this volume; Handfield and Rabinowicz 2018; Nebel 2018 and Chapter 8, this volume; Brink 2020; Wasserman ms; and Hare ms. Not all these authors accept the sorites analogy as I have stated it.

[7] See, for instance: Parfit 1984 and 2016; Temkin 2012; Kagan 2015; and Arrhenius ms.

not like this. A Sorites Argument appeals to a series of steps, each of which is assumed to *make no difference*. My argument would be like this if it claimed that [B] is *not worse* than [A], [C] is not worse than [B], [D] is not worse than [C], and so on. But the argument claims that [B] is *better* than [A], [C] is better than [B], [D] is better than [C], and so on. The objections to Sorites Arguments are therefore irrelevant.[8]

Parfit is here claiming that there is a structural disanalogy between spectrum arguments and sorites arguments. In the sorites argument, each step is claimed to make no difference in that if a given collection of grains of sand is a heap, then that collection minus a single grain is also a heap. In the spectrum argument for the Repugnant Conclusion, each step—which involves both a slight drop in the quality of life and a large gain in the number of people who exist—is claimed to make a difference in that each population in the series is claimed to be better than its immediate predecessor. But the fact that each step of the spectrum argument is claimed to make such a difference is not enough to show that it is not *relevantly* structurally analogous to a sorites argument.

There are various structural disanalogies between spectrum arguments and sorites arguments. The standard sorites argument involves a single dimension (number of grains) relevant to whether some item x (collection of grains) is an F (heap). Other arguments that appeal to a series of steps involve multiple dimensions (number of grains and distribution of grains) relevant to whether x is an F, or to whether x is F-er (heapier) than y. Spectrum arguments involve variation along multiple dimensions at each step, and they concern the instantiation of relations rather than monadic properties. These disanalogies notwithstanding, defenders of the sorites analogy might hold that spectrum arguments are relevantly structurally analogous to sorites arguments in that both make essential appeal to slight differences (along some dimension) between adjacent items x and x+1 in support of a tolerance premise. A tolerance premise can be formulated in terms of monadic properties: if x is an F, then x+1 is an F. But it can also be formulated in terms of relations: if x is F-er than y, then x+1 is F-er than y. Parfit's disanalogy, underpinned by the fact that in a spectrum argument x+1 is F-er (better) than x, may then be neither here nor there.

But these matters are somewhat delicate. The spectrum argument for the Repugnant Conclusion does not *itself* include a tolerance premise according to which if x is better than y, then x+1 is better than y. The argument, more precisely, is as follows.

---

[8] Parfit 1986 (footnote 12). Also see Rachels 1998 (74). Tenenbaum and Raffman 2012 (footnote 3) suggest a similar disanalogy between the sorites and Quinn's 1990 puzzle of the self-torturer. See Elson 2016 for a reply.

Finite Spectrum: There is a finite series of well-being levels (or levels of quality of life) $L_1, \ldots, L_k$ such that L_1 is a 'very high' positive well-being level, L_k is a 'very low' positive well-being level, and the difference between any two adjacent levels in the series is slight (for some fixed precisification of 'slight').[9]

Tradeoffs: For any positive well-being level L_i, and slightly lower positive level L_{i+1}, and any number of people n, there is some number of people n+ such that a population of n+ people at level L_{i+1} is better than a population of n people at level L_i (the difference between L_i and L_{i+1} is given by the fixed precisification of 'slight' in Finite Spectrum).[10]

Transitivity: The relation of being better than is transitive. (For any relation R, R is transitive if and only if for all x, y, and z, if xRy and yRz, then xRz.)

Therefore:

Conclusion: For any positive well-being level L_i, and any number of people n, there is some number of people n+ such that a population of n+ people at very low positive level L_k is better than a population of n people at level L_i. So, there is some number of people n+ such that a population of n+ people at very low positive level L_k is better than a population of ten billion people at very high positive level L_1. This is the Repugnant Conclusion.

We might thus claim that the fact that sorites arguments include a tolerance premise, whereas spectrum arguments do not, marks a crucial structural disanalogy between them.[11] But this may not constitute an adequate response to the sorites analogy. If we accept all the premises of the spectrum argument for the Repugnant Conclusion—Finite Spectrum, Tradeoffs, and Transitivity—then it is absurd not also to accept all the premises of the following 'transitivityless' spectrum argument.

Finite Spectrum: There is a finite series of well-being levels (or levels of quality of life) $L_1, \ldots, L_k$ such that L_1 is a 'very high' positive well-being level, L_k is a 'very low' positive well-being level, and the difference between any two adjacent levels in the series is slight (for some fixed precisification of 'slight').

---

[9] Some authors reject this claim (for example, see Nebel in Chapter 8, this volume, and Thomas 2018, who refers to what I call Finite Spectrum as 'Small Steps'). I believe, but will not show here, that the relevant spectrum arguments can replace Finite Spectrum with an analogous claim formulated in terms of slight natural (non-evaluative) differences, such as slight differences in pleasure intensity and/or duration. The content-based disanalogies between spectrum arguments and sorites arguments developed below in sections 18.3 and 18.4 would remain as effective against the sorites analogy.

[10] To appreciate the importance of using the same fixed precisification of 'slight' here as in Finite Spectrum, see Binmore and Voorhoeve 2003.

[11] See Temkin 1996 (section 5) and 2012 (chapter 9).

Initiation: There is some number of people n such that n people at very high positive level L_1 is better than X, a population of ten billion people at very high positive level L_1.

Tolerance: For any positive well-being level L_i, and slightly lower positive level L_{i+1}, and any number of people n, if a population of n people at level L_i is better than population X, then there is some number of people n+ such that a population of n+ people at level L_{i+1} is better than population X (the difference between L_i and L_{i+1} is given by the fixed precisification of 'slight' in Finite Spectrum).

Therefore:

Conclusion: There is some number of people n such that a population of n people at very low positive level L_k is better than X, a population of ten billion people at very high positive level L_1. This, again, is the Repugnant Conclusion.

Finite Spectrum is the same premise in both arguments. It is absurd to accept Tradeoffs but not Initiation. And Tradeoffs and Transitivity together entail Tolerance. According to Tradeoffs, for any positive well-being level L_i, and slightly lower positive level L_{i+1}, and any number of people n, there is some number of people n+ such that a population of n+ people at level L_{i+1} is better than a population of n people at level L_i. So, according to Transitivity, (for any positive well-being level L_i, and slightly lower positive level L_{i+1}, and any number of people n) if a population of n people at level L_i is better than population X, then a population of n+ people at level L_{i+1} is better than population X. This is Tolerance.

Defenders of the sorites analogy might then hold that, since the transitivityless spectrum argument is relevantly structurally analogous to a sorites argument in that both make essential appeal to a tolerance premise, if the correct response to a sorites argument is to reject its tolerance premise, then the correct response to the transitivityless spectrum argument is to reject Tolerance. This would in turn entail that the correct response to the original spectrum argument is to reject the conjunction of Tradeoffs and Transitivity. To those of us who cannot part with Transitivity, this would mean the correct response to the original spectrum argument is to reject Tradeoffs.[12]

We might appeal to a different structural disanalogy. According to a standard sorites argument, a collection of ten billion grains of sand is a heap, and, since for any number of grains n, if a collection of n grains is a heap, a collection of n-1 grains is a heap, it follows that one grain is a heap. We begin with an item that is intuitively a heap and end up with an item that is intuitively not a heap. We are also making things intuitively *less heapy* at each step (or at least at some of the

---

[12] Even setting aside any allegiance to Transitivity, it might seem plausible that if we ought to reject Tolerance, then we ought to reject Tradeoffs too. See Pummer 2018.

steps). Viewed purely from the relational perspective of being more or less heapy, then, there is no puzzle. Viewing things from the relational perspective of being better or worse clearly does nothing to take the puzzle out of spectrum arguments, as they come prepackaged in such relational terms—the first item is intuitively better than the last one even though each step is intuitively one for the better.

But even if this marks a crucial structural disanalogy between *standard* sorites arguments and spectrum arguments, there remain the multidimensional sorites arguments alluded to earlier. One such multidimensional sorites argument goes as follows.

Finite Spectrum*: There is a finite series of sand distribution patterns $D_1, \ldots, D_k$ such that D_1 is a perfectly heapy cone-shaped distribution, D_k is a perfectly flat and thin distribution, and the difference in flatness between any two adjacent distributions in the series is slight (for some fixed precisification of 'slight').

Initiation*: There is some number of grains n such that n grains with distribution D_1 is heapier than X, a collection of ten billion grains with perfectly heapy cone-shaped distribution D_1.

Tolerance*: For any sand distribution pattern D_i, and slightly flatter distribution D_{i+1}, and any number of grains n, if a collection of n grains with distribution D_i is heapier than collection X, then there is some number of grains n+ such that a collection of n+ grains with distribution D_{i+1} is heapier than collection X (the difference between D_i and D_{i+1} is given by the fixed precisification of 'slight' in Finite Spectrum*).

Therefore:

Conclusion*: There is some number of grains n such that a collection of n grains with perfectly flat and thin distribution D_k is heapier than X, a collection of ten billion grains with perfectly heapy cone-shaped distribution D_1.

Truth be told, I am not sure Tolerance* is very compelling (it strikes me as far less intuitive than Tolerance or Tradeoffs). But, assuming that Tolerance* is compelling, we restore the analogy with the spectrum argument. That is, taking up the relational perspective of being more or less heapy fails to remove the puzzle, as the first item is intuitively heapier than the last one even if each step is intuitively one for the heapier.[13]

---

[13] There is a further potential structural disanalogy. In the multidimensional sorites argument, we begin with an item that is intuitively a heap, take a number of steps each claimed to be for the heapier, and end up with an item that is intuitively not a heap. In the spectrum argument, we begin with an item that is intuitively good, take a number of steps each claimed to be for the better, and end up with an item that is still intuitively good (at least, assuming the quality of life of those in the last population is not too low). But this difference seems an artefact of the particular examples chosen. It is plausible that,

In this section, I considered some potential structural disanalogies between spectrum arguments and sorites arguments. Even if there is a crucial structural disanalogy between standard (one-dimensional) sorites arguments and spectrum arguments, arguably spectrum arguments are relevantly structurally analogous to multidimensional sorites arguments. Moreover, even though the original spectrum argument does not itself contain a tolerance premise, the transitivityless spectrum argument does. Defenders of the sorites analogy might argue that, if the correct response to a sorites argument is to reject its tolerance premise, then the correct response to the transitivityless spectrum argument is to reject Tolerance, and thus the correct response to the original spectrum argument is to reject the conjunction of Tradeoffs and Transitivity.

18.3 Indeterminacy

In this section, I highlight a relatively sanguine response available for many sorites arguments that is unavailable for spectrum arguments. As this disanalogy holds even if sorites arguments and spectrum arguments are relevantly structurally analogous, it is a content-based disanalogy. This disanalogy draws inspiration from Parfit's work on reductionism, and the response to sorites arguments it suggests.

Parfit famously defends what he calls *reductionism* about personal identity, according to which the fact that person X at time t_1 is one and the same person as person Y at time t_2 just consists in the fact that X stands in some other, 'impersonal' relation or relations to Y, such as that X is sufficiently psychologically or physically connected to or continuous with Y.[14] This view is controversial. But it is relatively uncontroversial that the fact that country X at time t_1 is one and the same country as country Y at time t_2 just consists in the fact that X stands in some other relation to Y, involving membership, territory, culture, or government. It is also relatively uncontroversial that the fact that country X at time t is a country just consists in the fact that X has some other property or properties, involving membership, territory, culture, or government. Most of us are, in Parfit's sense of the term, reductionists both about being a country and about being one and the same country.

---

in some spectrum arguments, we begin with an item that is intuitively good, take a number of steps each claimed to be for the better, and end up with an item that is intuitively bad (see Nebel 2018). And it is plausible that, in some multidimensional sorites arguments, we begin with an item that is intuitively a heap, take a number of steps each claimed to be for the heapier, and end up with an item that is still intuitively a heap (though intuitively less heapy than the first item). For two recent relevant discussions of comparatives and vagueness, see: Constantinescu 2016 and Silk 2019.

[14] Parfit 1984 (210–11).

The following soritical story illustrates one way in which Parfitian reductionism about personal identity is controversial:

Derek walks into an operating room at 9:12am, and a person Y walks out at 9:13am. During this minute, a scientist can slide her finger in a way that rapidly flips any number of one hundred (or one billion...) different switches. Each additional switch she flips would further slightly decrease the degree to which the relevant psychological and physical relations hold between Derek and Y. In the case in which one switch is flipped, Derek is one and the same person as Y. In the case in which all hundred (or billion...) switches are flipped, Derek is not one and the same person as Y—instead, Y is Greta.[15]

What happens in the cases in between? According to reductionism about personal identity, Derek and Y are one and the same person only if the relevant psychological or physical relations hold between Derek and Y to a *sufficient degree*. If we cannot say precisely what counts as sufficient, the view implies there is some n such that there is not a 'Yes or No' answer to the question 'Is Derek one and the same person as Y if n switches are flipped?'.[16] But according to Parfitian reductionists this would not present a deep puzzle. On their view, when n switches are flipped, there is in reality only *one* possible outcome: the relevant psychological and physical relations hold between Derek and Y to the precise degree that corresponds to n switches being flipped. Thus, 'Derek is Y' and 'Derek is not Y' are merely two ways of describing a single outcome. Alternatively, *if* we were 'tidy-minded' reductionists and precisified 'sufficient degree' in some arbitrary way, we would then find it relatively unpuzzling that there is some n for which Derek and Y are one and the same person, though for n + 1 Derek and Y are not one and the same person (that is, we would find it relatively unproblematic to reject the relevant tolerance premise).[17] Of course, many of us find both of these alternatives puzzling, even absurd. We could then view the choice between it being indeterminate what degree is sufficient and it being determinate what degree is sufficient as a fatal dilemma for Parfitian reductionism.

A lesson for sorites arguments is that, when it *is* true that whether x is an F relevantly just consists in whether x has gradable property P to a sufficient degree, it can be indeterminate whether x is an F, but in a relatively unpuzzling way.[18]

---

[15] This is a retelling of the *Combined Spectrum*, found in Parfit 1984 (section 86).
[16] See Parfit 1984 (206) on the antecedent of this conditional.
[17] Parfit 1984 (241) writes, 'By drawing our line, we have chosen to *give* an answer to this question. But, since our choice was arbitrary, it cannot justify any claim about what matters. If this is how we answer the question about my identity, we have made it true that, in this range of cases, personal identity is *not* what matters.' Also see Sider 2002 (63) on artificially sharpened boundaries.
[18] By 'relevantly just consists in', I intend to highlight the specific meaning that Parfit gives to the words 'just consists in'. As he notes in Parfit 1995 (33), his brand of constitutive reductionism is 'partly conceptual'. Also see Parfit 1999.

For instance, it is plausible that, when other things (like the sand distribution pattern) are equal, whether a collection of grains of sand is a heap can just consist in whether this collection has a sufficient number of grains. Clearly ten billion is a sufficient number of grains, and one is not. For some number n, it is plausible that there is not a 'Yes or No' answer to the question, 'Is a collection of n grains of sand a heap?'. But we would not be deeply puzzled by our inability to say whether a collection of n grains of sand is a heap. 'Heap' and 'Not Heap' are merely two ways of describing a single outcome. Correlatively, if we precisified 'sufficient number' in some arbitrary way, it would then be relatively unpuzzling that there is some number n such that n grains make a heap but n-1 do not (that is, we would find it relatively unproblematic to reject the relevant tolerance premise).

I am sympathetic to Parfit's view that this relatively sanguine response is available for many sorites arguments.[19] In addition to the case of being a heap, it also seems available in the case of being hirsute, and in the case of being rich. When other things (like the hair distribution pattern) are equal, whether a head is hirsute can just consist in whether this head has a sufficient number of hairs. And, when other things are equal, whether one is rich can just consist in whether one has a sufficient number of pennies. There will be points along the relevant sorites series at which we cannot say whether an item has the property of being hirsute, or the property of being rich (there is not a 'Yes or No' answer to these questions). But we will not be deeply puzzled by our inability to say. Again, what we will have are merely different ways of describing a single outcome.

But as the case of being one and the same person suggests, the sanguine response may not be available for all sorites arguments.[20] For another example, consider the property of being conscious in the sense of there being *something it is like* to be an individual at a given time. It seems that, for any putative sorites series in which an individual is conscious at the beginning and non-conscious at the end, there will nonetheless be a 'Yes or No' answer to the question 'Is this individual conscious?' at each step along the way. Suppose, for example, that this individual is very gradually anesthetized. It may be hard to say where the individual goes from being conscious to being non-conscious, but intuitively there is at each step either *something* it is like to be this individual, or there is not.[21] Here we do not have a single outcome, and two ways of describing it. We have two different possible

---

[19] The word 'relatively' is important. I do not intend to claim that Parfit's response resolves *all* that is puzzling about the sorites arguments to which it applies. It may remain an independently implausible solution, even if it is the least implausible solution of those available.

[20] Parfit 1984 (232) writes: 'When it is applied to other subjects, such as phenomenal colour, the Sorites Argument cannot be so easily dismissed. Nor does this dismissal seem plausible when the argument is applied to personal identity. Most of us believe that our own continued existence is, in several ways, unlike the continued existence of a heap of sand.' Also see Alter and Rachels 2004.

[21] See, for example: Unger 1988; Antony 2006; and Simon 2017.

outcomes. Similar remarks may be true of sorites series concerning when collections of objects compose further objects.[22]

It would appear, then, that even if sorites arguments involving being a heap, being hirsute, being rich, being a person, being one and the same person, being conscious, and being a composite object are all relevantly structurally analogous, there is a content-based disanalogy between them. Whereas it seems the relatively sanguine Parfitian response is available in the cases of being a heap, being hirsute, and being rich, it is significantly more controversial that such a response is available in the case of being a person, being one and the same person, being conscious, and being a composite object. This is already enough to cast doubt on the underlying logic of the sorites analogy, that if two arguments are relevantly structurally analogous, the correct response to one is structurally analogous to the correct response to the other.

Just as there can be content-based disanalogies between structurally analogous one-dimensional sorites arguments, so too can there be such disanalogies between structurally analogous multidimensional sorites arguments. Earlier I presented a multidimensional sorites argument concerning the relation of being heapier than. I noted that a defender of the sorites analogy might argue that, if the correct response to this multidimensional sorites argument is to reject Tolerance*, then the correct response to the transitivityless spectrum argument is to reject Tolerance (and thus the correct response to the original spectrum argument is to reject the conjunction of Tradeoffs and Transitivity). Even if these arguments are relevantly structurally analogous, the relatively sanguine Parfitian response is available in the case of the multidimensional sorites argument but not in the case of the transitivityless spectrum argument. Or so I argue.

Recall that the sorites series of the multidimensional sorites argument begins with X, a collection of ten billion grains with perfectly heapy cone-shaped distribution D_1, and ends with a collection of a (much) larger number of grains with perfectly flat and thin distribution D_k. At each step along the series, the distribution of grains gets slightly flatter (and some arbitrarily large number of grains gets added). At each step, we ask, 'Is there some number of grains n with sand distribution pattern D_i such that this collection is heapier than collection X?'. For the step featuring distribution D_2, it seems the answer is Yes. For the step featuring distribution D_k, it seems the answer is No.

For the answer to be Yes, the difference between D_i and D_1 must be sufficiently small. Crucially, it is also plausible that when other things are equal, whether there is a number of grains n such that n grains with distribution D_i that is heapier than

---

[22] See, for example: Sider 2001; Barnes 2007; and Korman 2010. Sider 2001 (125) and others argue that the argument from vagueness for universalism about composition is not 'just another sorites', even though it has the structure of a sorites argument. That is, they hold that there is a content-based disanalogy between Sider's sorites argument and the more familiar ones involving being a heap or being hirsute.

collection X can relevantly *just consist in* whether the difference between D_i and D_1 is sufficiently small. For some step featuring D_j, it is plausible that there is not a 'Yes or No' answer to our question. But we would not be deeply puzzled by this indeterminacy. 'Heapier than X' and 'Not Heapier than X' are merely two ways of describing a single outcome. Correlatively, if we precisified 'sufficiently small' in some arbitrary way, it would then be relatively unpuzzling that there is a number of grains n such that n grains with distribution D_i is heapier than collection X, but no number of grains with slightly flatter distribution D_{i+1} that is heapier than collection X (that is, we would find it relatively unproblematic to reject Tolerance*).

Next recall that the sorites series of the transitivityless spectrum argument begins with X, a population of ten billion people at very high positive level L_1, and ends with a population of a (much) larger number of people at very low positive level L_k. At each step along the series, the quality of life drops slightly (and some arbitrarily large number of people gets added). At each step, we ask, 'Is there some number of people n at well-being level L_i such that this population is better than population X?'. For the step featuring well-being level L_2, it seems the answer is Yes. For the step featuring well-being level L_k, it seems the answer is No.

For the answer to be Yes, the difference between L_i and L_1 must be sufficiently small. Crucially, it is also plausible that, whether there is a number of people n such that n people at well-being level L_i is better than population X *cannot* just consist in whether the difference between L_i and L_1 is sufficiently small.[23] For each step featuring L_j, it is plausible that there *is* a 'Yes or No' answer to our question. 'Better than X' and 'Not Better than X' are *not* merely two ways of describing a single outcome. Instead, what we have here are two different possible ways for things to be ('Not Better than X' covers a range of more specific possibilities, such as 'Worse than X', 'As Good as X', 'On a Par with X', 'Imprecisely as Good as X', or 'Incomparable with X').[24] Correlatively, if we precisified 'sufficiently small' in some arbitrary way, it would *remain* puzzling that there is a number of people n such that n people at well-being level L_i is better than population X, but no number of people at slightly lower well-being level L_{i+1} that is better than population X (that is, we would continue to find it difficult to reject Tolerance).

It is important to recognize that the content-based disanalogy I have just drawn between the multidimensional sorites argument and the transitivityless spectrum argument is not that we can appeal to indeterminacy in response to the former

---

[23] Note that this claim does not imply that such evaluative properties are irreducible to *any* other properties. Some hold that, while certain evaluative properties are reducible to other evaluative properties, evaluative properties are irreducible to non-evaluative properties. This is Parfit's view (see Parfit 2011, chapters 25 through 27). Others, such as naturalists, hold that evaluative properties are reducible to non-evaluative properties.

[24] Several of these 'more specific possibilities' I have parenthetically listed here are discussed by others in this volume, including Nebel (Chapter 8); Chang (Chapter 14); Rabinowicz (Chapter 15); Arrhenius (Chapter 16); and Thomas (Chapter 17).

only. It is that, while sometimes there is no 'Yes or No' answer to the question 'Is there some number of grains n with sand distribution pattern D_i such that this collection is heapier than collection X?', there is always a 'Yes or No' answer to the question, 'Is there some number of people n at well-being level L_i such that this population is better than population X?'. It is compatible with the claim that there is a 'Yes or No' answer to a question that it is indeterminate whether the answer is Yes or is instead No (it can be determinate that [either there will be a sea battle tomorrow, or there will not] even if it is indeterminate whether [there will be a sea battle tomorrow]). Yes and No correspond to *two* different possible ways for things to be, even if it is unsettled which way things actually are.[25] When there is no 'Yes or No' answer to the question 'Is there some number of grains n with sand distribution pattern D_i such that this collection is heapier than collection X?', this is because, while there is only *one* way for things to be, there are different (equally good) ways to describe it. This sort of indeterminacy is far less puzzling.[26]

18.4 Hypersensitivity

Recall that defenders of the sorites analogy might hold that, since the transitivity-less spectrum argument is relevantly structurally analogous to a sorites argument in that both make essential appeal to a tolerance premise, if the correct response to a sorites argument is to reject its tolerance premise, then the correct response to the transitivityless spectrum argument is to reject Tolerance. This would in turn entail that the correct response to the original spectrum argument is to reject the conjunction of Tradeoffs and Transitivity. To those of us who cannot part with Transitivity, this would mean the correct response to the original spectrum argument is to reject Tradeoffs.

In this section, I respond to this variant of the sorites analogy by offering another content-based disanalogy between sorites arguments and spectrum arguments. In particular, I argue that, while rejecting Tradeoffs of the spectrum argument yields what I call hypersensitivity, rejecting the structurally analogous premise of a structurally analogous multidimensional sorites argument does not.

I will say there is *hypersensitivity* when a slight difference in one sort of property makes a radical difference in another sort of property.[27] Equivalently, A-properties

---

[25] For discussion of this sort of metaphysical indeterminacy, see: Williams 2008; Barnes and Cameron 2009; Barnes and Williams 2011a and 2011b; and Eklund 2011.

[26] According to a further content-based disanalogy, the conclusions of sorites arguments are *more implausible* than the conclusions of structurally analogous spectrum arguments. For instance, we might argue that accepting the claim that a very flat collection of sand with enough grains is heapier than a paradigmatically very heapy collection of sand involves a conceptual mistake, whereas accepting the Repugnant Conclusion does not. For discussion of this kind of content-based disanalogy, see Campbell ms.

[27] I explore hypersensitivity and its significance for ethics in Pummer ms.

are hypersensitive to B-properties when a slight difference in B-properties makes a radical difference in A-properties. I assume for now that we have a decent enough intuitive grasp of 'slight' and 'radical' to understand what hypersensitivity is, but at the end of this section I offer a more precise definition of hypersensitivity, which does not appeal to the notions of 'slight' or 'radical' differences. One intuitive example would be deserving hell rather than heaven merely in virtue of uttering one additional mild obscenity.[28] Here a slight difference in one's conduct makes a radical difference to what one deserves. Another example of hypersensitivity would be that one life is radically better than an otherwise exactly similar life, merely in virtue of containing one fewer stubbed toe.[29] Such hypersensitivity is deeply puzzling, and views that entail that it exists bear a significant theoretical cost.

The hypersensitivity of A-properties to B-properties entails the existence of a cutoff somewhere along a relatively smooth spectrum of B-properties. But it is not the existence of a cutoff per se that makes hypersensitivity so puzzling. There are plenty of cutoffs and threshold phenomena that have nothing to do with hypersensitivity.

Some properties come with built in cutoffs. Consider the property of having at least a hundred grains. Clearly, a collection of ninety-nine grains does not have this property. There is no hypersensitivity here, as the difference between having this property and not can just consist in the slight difference of one grain. Next consider three lines on a Euclidean plane. Lines q and r are parallel, and line s is perpendicular to them. If the interior angle formed between q and s were not 90-degrees, but 89-degrees, q and r would no longer be parallel. That is, q and r would eventually intersect. Does the slight difference of a single degree make the large difference of q and r intersecting rather than running parallel? In some sense it does. But this is not the sort of difference-making involved in hypersensitivity. This is not a case of one difference that makes some further difference. Whether q and r are parallel *just consists in* whether q and r form 90-degree angles with s. If the difference between q and r intersecting rather than running parallel is large, so too is the difference between q forming a 90-degree angle with s rather than q forming an 89-degree angle with s.

Other properties are such that we can build cutoffs into them. For instance, the law often draws cutoffs in somewhat arbitrary ways, to avoid issues with borderline cases.[30] In some countries, only those who are at least 18 years old are legally permitted to vote. Someone a day younger does not have this legal property. It may thus seem that a slight difference in one's age makes a large difference in the legal properties one has. But a slight difference in age is not enough. What makes the large difference in one's legal properties is the non-slight difference between

---

[28] Sider 2002.   [29] Pummer 2017.   [30] See Glover's 1977 (166) discussion of speed limits.

[being under 18 *and* it being the law that those who are under 18 cannot vote] and [being at least 18 *and* it being the law that those who are at least 18 can vote].³¹

Some cutoffs involve slight differences in B-properties that make big differences in A-properties *by* causally triggering other, larger differences in B-properties. Take the case of placing a feather on one side of a perfectly balanced scale, which then knocks over the first in a series of dominos, or flips on a Rube Goldberg machine. Or the case of releasing a drop of water at the top of a snowy hill. Or the butterfly effect. Slight differences in B-properties can cause countless other differences in B-properties, often progressively larger ones, and often very rapidly (at the subatomic level very complex causal sequences can unfold seemingly instantaneously).³² There is no hypersensitivity here. In each of these examples, we do not have a slight difference in B-properties that is *itself* making a large difference in A-properties. Instead, we have a slight difference in B-properties that is causing other differences in B-properties which are together making a large difference in A-properties.

Consider a further illustration of this last distinction. Suppose that, were I to carefully remove a single topmost brick from a brick building, this would leave all the other bricks unperturbed. However, were I to remove a middle brick, this would cause adjacent bricks to wobble, leading the whole building to shake and topple over. The removal of a brick is itself a slight difference in B-properties, but if it is a middle brick, its removal triggers many other differences in B-properties, which together make a large difference to the A-property of being a building. It is more puzzling that I could make a large difference to the A-property of being a building merely by removing a single topmost brick.

The case of repeatedly removing topmost brick after topmost brick is another version of the original sorites case.³³ Suppose that in response to the sorites argument we reject its tolerance premise, and draw a cutoff for being a heap (or building) at some precise number of grains (or bricks). Suppose reductionism about being a heap is correct, so that when other things (like the sand distribution pattern) are equal, whether a collection of grains of sand is a heap can just consist in whether this collection has a sufficient number of grains. Then the difference between being a heap and not can be slight. But suppose instead that whether a collection of grains of sand is a heap does not just consist in whether this collection has a sufficient number of grains—that is, suppose that the former

---

³¹ Similar remarks apply to the creation of cutoffs with desires and promises. Suppose I desire at least a hundred grains of sand. It may seem that the slight difference of a single grain could then make a large difference in desire satisfaction. But a slight difference in grains is not enough. What makes the large difference in desire satisfaction is the non-slight difference between [having ninety-nine grains *and* not desiring them] and [having a hundred grains *and* desiring them].

³² Other examples include Sorensen 1988 (251–2) on the drop of rocket fuel needed to achieve escape velocity and Chang 2002 (136–7) on the straw that broke the camel's back.

³³ In the case of heaps of sand, the relevant structure is not as differentially affected by taking individual grains from the middle rather than from the top.

difference is some further difference, distinct from the latter one. This would at least pave the way for the view that the cutoff between being a heap and not being a heap entails the existence of hypersensitivity. But it is not clear that the slight difference in grain-properties would here be making a *radical* difference in heap-properties. Arguably the difference in heapiness between a collection of n grains that is not a heap and a collection of n+1 grains that is a heap is much less than the difference in heapiness between a collection of just one grain and a collection of n+10,000,000,000 grains. (At any rate, I say more below about how we could precisify 'radical'.)

Before returning to spectrum arguments, we need to observe a further point about what hypersensitivity can consist in. Large differences in properties include large differences in relations as well as in monadic properties. An item x can be *somewhat* A-er than another item y, or it can be *much* A-er than y. Hypersensitivity can accordingly be formulated in terms of relations: it occurs when a slight difference in B-properties between items x and y makes it the case that, while x is radically A-er than z, y is not A-er than z.

Now recall the spectrum argument for the Repugnant Conclusion, which involves tradeoffs between quality of life and number of people. The rejection of Tradeoffs in this argument entails that there is hypersensitivity, if the following two claims hold: (1) for any positive well-being level L_i, and slightly lower positive level L_{i+1}, and any number of people n, the difference between a population of n people at level L_i and a population of n people at level L_{i+1} is slight; (2) a radically larger number of people at the same positive quality of life is radically better. It is controversial that either (1) or (2) holds. Below I consider an objection to (1). Parfit defends (2) by arguing that, unless we accept it, we face what he calls the *Absurd Conclusion*.[34] Not everyone is convinced. Not everyone believes that the existence of a larger number of people at the same positive quality of life would be better, let alone that the existence of a radically larger number of such people would be radically better. Those who doubt (2) might wish to instead consider the 'negative' analogue of the spectrum argument, the conclusion of which is the *Negative Repugnant Conclusion* (that there is some number of people n, such that n people at a barely negative well-being level is worse than ten billion people at a vastly lower level).[35] It seems hard to deny that the existence of a radically larger number of people at the same *negative* quality of life would be radically worse. For simplicity, I assume that (2) holds.

Given (1) and (2), the rejection of Tradeoffs entails that there is hypersensitivity. If we reject Tradeoffs, we claim that there is some well-being level L_i and some number of people n, such that there is *no* number of people at slightly lower level

---

[34] Parfit 1984 (chapter 18). Also see Parfit 2016 (112).
[35] See Broome 2004 (213). Mulgan 2002 and others refer to this conclusion as the 'Reverse Repugnant Conclusion'.

L_{i+1} that is better than n people at level L_i. From (2), if n+ is radically larger than n, then n+ people at level L_i [population X] is radically better than n people at level L_i [population Z]. From the rejection of Tradeoffs, n+ people at level L_{i+1} [population Y] is not better than n people at level L_i [population Z]. From (1), the difference between n+ people at level L_i [population X] and n+ people at level L_{i+1} [population Y] is slight. Thus, we have a slight difference in B-properties (well-being levels) between population X and population Y that makes it the case that, while population X is radically A-er (better) than population Z, population Y is not A-er (better) than population Z. This is hypersensitivity.

While rejecting Tradeoffs of the spectrum argument yields hypersensitivity, rejecting the structurally analogous premise of a structurally analogous multidimensional sorites argument does not. I call the latter the 'toleranceless' sorites argument. It goes as follows.[36]

> *Finite Spectrum**: There is a finite series of sand distribution patterns $D_1, \ldots, D_k$ such that D_1 is a perfectly heapy cone-shaped distribution, D_k is a perfectly flat and thin distribution, and the difference in flatness between any two adjacent distributions in the series is slight (for some fixed precisification of 'slight').
>
> *Tradeoffs**: For any sand distribution pattern D_i, and slightly flatter distribution D_{i+1}, and any number of grains n, there is some number of grains n+ such that a collection of n+ grains with distribution D_{i+1} is heapier than a collection of n grains with distribution D_i (the difference between D_i and D_{i+1} is given by the fixed precisification of 'slight' in Finite Spectrum*).
>
> *Transitivity**: The relation of being heapier than is transitive.

Therefore:

> *Conclusion**: There is some number of grains n such that a collection of n grains with perfectly flat and thin distribution D_k is heapier than X, a collection of ten billion grains with perfectly heapy cone-shaped distribution D_1.

It is not plausible that rejecting Tradeoffs* yields hypersensitivity. The analogue of claim (2) is claim (2*): a radically larger number of grains with the same sand distribution pattern is radically heapier. While (2) is controversial, it is defensible. But (2*) is very implausible. First, if we have a perfectly cone-shaped distribution D_1, it is plausible enough that a radically larger number of grains with distribution D_1 is heapier, but it is not clear that it is *radically* heapier. Second, (2*) seems even less plausible for flatter distributions. When considering nearly flat distributions, (2*) seems absurd. Relative to such distributions, radically more grains may not

---

[36] From Wasserman ms and Temkin 2012 (chapter 9).

even make things heapier at all. If we reject Tradeoffs*, we claim that there is some sand distribution pattern D_i and some number of grains n, such that there is no number of grains with slightly flatter distribution D_{i+1} that is heapier than n grains with distribution D_i. But if n+ grains with D_i is not significantly heapier than n grains with D_i—let alone radically so—we do not get hypersensitivity of the form in question (in which a slight difference in B-properties between items x and y makes it the case that, while x is radically A-er than item z, y is not A-er than z). So, there is a content-based disanalogy between the spectrum argument and the toleranceless sorites argument.[37]

Let us now consider three objections to the above argument for this content-based disanalogy. The first objection is that the derivation of hypersensitivity from the rejection of Tradeoffs assumes that, if we reject Tradeoffs, we claim that there is some *determinate* well-being level L_i, and some number of people n, such that there is no number of people at slightly lower level L_{i+1} that is better than n people at level L_i. But this assumption is unwarranted. We can instead reject Tradeoffs by claiming that it is indeterminate which well-being level L_i is such that for some number of people n there is no number of people at slightly lower level L_{i+1} that is better than n people at level L_i.

Response to the first objection: The derivation of hypersensitivity from the rejection of Tradeoffs does not make the assumption in question. I *do* assume that there is always a 'Yes or No' answer to the question, 'For each well-being level L_i and each number n, is there some number of people n+ such that n+ people at slightly lower level L_{i+1} is better than n people at level L_i?' And hypersensitivity can be derived if for *some* level L_i the answer is No, even if it is indeterminate which particular L_i this is. Incorporating such indeterminacy does not block the derivation of hypersensitivity, though it can make it indeterminate *where* the hypersensitivity is located. And while incorporating such indeterminacy about the location of hypersensitivity can remove the arbitrariness of hypersensitivity being determinately located at one well-being level rather than another, it does nothing to mitigate the implausibility of hypersensitivity itself. Take a comparison with supervenience failures. The A-properties are said to supervene on the B-properties when there cannot be a difference in A-properties unless there is a difference in B-properties.[38] Many hold, for instance, that mental properties supervene on physical properties, and that evaluative properties supervene on natural properties. Suppose we have a hundred possible worlds that are exactly

---

[37] I take it this disanalogy is not restricted to the subject matter of grains and heaps of sand. For example, it is also implausible that for any hair distribution pattern D_i, a radically larger number of hairs with distribution D_i is radically more hirsute. Rejecting the analogue of Tradeoffs* in such relevantly analogous toleranceless sorites arguments would not yield hypersensitivity.

[38] Hypersensitivity does not yield supervenience failure. However, it does yield a failure of what Kim 1987 (324–5) calls 'similarity-based' supervenience, according to which there cannot be a large difference in A-properties unless there is a large difference in B-properties (also see Constantinescu 2014 (182)). Hypersensitivity yields a failure of similarity-based supervenience, but not vice versa.

similar with respect to their natural properties. If ninety-nine of them are very good, and one of them is not good at all, we have one kind of supervenience failure. Claiming that it is indeterminate which of these worlds is not good allows us to avoid the arbitrariness of the supervenience failure being determinately located at one of these worlds rather than another, but it does nothing to mitigate the implausibility of the supervenience failure itself.

The second objection is an objection to claim (1). (According to claim (1), for any well-being level L_i, and slightly lower level L_{i+1}, and any number of people n, the difference between a population of n people at level L_i and a population of n people at level L_{i+1} is slight.) The objection is that the sum of many individually slight differences might not itself be a slight difference. As Parfit writes, 'The greatest mass of milk might be found in a heap of bottles each containing only a single drop'.[39] Even if the mass of each drop tended to zero, we could arguably retain the same great total mass of milk with a supply of bottles that tended to infinity.[40]

Response to the second objection: It is indeed plausible that we should reject (1). But while (1), (2), and the rejection of Tradeoffs are together sufficient for hypersensitivity, (1) is not necessary. We can instead appeal to (3): for any well-being level L_i, and slightly lower level L_{i+1}, and any number of people n, if the only difference between two populations is that one contains n people at level L_i and the other contains n-1 people at level L_i & one person at level L_{i+1}, then the difference between them is slight. Claim (3) avoids the controversial implication that many individually slight differences collectively constitute a slight difference. Instead, (3) very modestly says that *one* individual slight difference between two populations constitutes a slight difference between them.

The conjunction of (2), (3), Transitivity, and the rejection of Tradeoffs, entails that there is hypersensitivity. To see this, consider the following sub-spectrum argument for Tradeoffs. At each succeeding step of this argument, there is only ever *one fewer* person who is at the slightly higher well-being level:

For any well-being level L_i, and slightly lower level L_{i+1}, and any number of people n, there is some number m such that n-1 people at L_i & one person at L_{i+1} & another m people at L_{i+1} is better than n people all at L_i. And, for any m, there is some m+ such that n-2 people at L_i & two people at L_{i+1} & another m+ people at L_{i+1} is better than n-1 people at L_i & one person at L_{i+1} & another m people at L_{i+1}.... and so on... And, for any m+...+, there is some m+...++ such that n-n people (0 people) at L_i & n people at L_{i+1} & another m+...++ people at L_{i+1} is better than n-(n-1) people (1 person) at L_i & n-1 people at L_{i+1} & another m+... + people at L_{i+1}.

---

[39] Parfit 1984 (388).
[40] For relevant discussion, see: Arntzenius and Hawthorne 2005; Russell 2008; and Chen 2020.

The claims of this sub-spectrum argument together with Transitivity entail that, for any well-being level L_i, and slightly lower level L_{i+1}, and any number of people n, there is some number m such that m people all at L_{i+1} is better than n people all at L_i. But this just is Tradeoffs. So, Transitivity together with the rejection of Tradeoffs entails the rejection of at least one of the claims of this sub-spectrum argument.

But, given (2) and (3), the rejection of any of the claims of this sub-spectrum argument entails that there is hypersensitivity. If we reject any of the claims of the sub-spectrum argument, we claim that there is some well-being level L_i some number of people n, and some number of people m, such that there is no number of people at slightly lower level L_{i+1}, together with n-1 people at level L_i, that is better than n people at level L_i & m people at level L_{i+1}. From (2), if m+ is radically larger than m, then n people at level L_i & m+ people at level L_{i+1} [population X*] is radically better than n people at level L_i & m people at level L_{i+1} [population Z*]. From the rejection of any of the claims of the sub-spectrum argument, n-1 people at level L_i & one person at L_{i+1} & m+ people at level L_{i+1} [population Y*] is not better than n people at level L_i & m people at level L_{i+1} [population Z*]. From (3), the difference between n people at level L_i & m+ people at level L_{i+1} [population X*] and n-1 people at level L_i & one person at L_{i+1} & m+ people at level L_{i+1} [population Y*] is slight. Thus, we have a slight difference in B-properties (well-being levels) between population X* and population Y* that makes it the case that, while population X* is radically A-er (better) than population Z*, population Y* is not A-er (better) than population Z*. This is hypersensitivity.[41]

The third objection is that the vagueness of terms like 'slight' and 'radical' make it impossible to tell whether and when hypersensitivity occurs. Relatedly, what will seem a slight or radical difference in one context may not seem so in another. The difference between stubbing one's toe and not, for instance, might seem a slight difference in the context of one's whole life, but a radical one in the context of a single moment.

Response to the third objection: There is a definition of hypersensitivity which avoids the non-comparative notions of 'slight' and 'radical' differences, and which holds that hypersensitivity is a matter of degree. Here it is.

Take two types of difference in B-properties, a 'B_1-difference' and a 'B_2-difference'. There is *some* degree of hypersensitivity of A-properties to B-properties when, while a B_1-difference is no greater than a B_2-difference, just *one* token B_1-difference makes an A-difference that is at least as large as the A-difference that *any* number of token B_2-differences could collectively make. This degree of

---

[41] I believe, but will not show here, that this argument can be reformulated so that the relevant differences in B-properties are strictly natural (non-evaluative) differences, such as slight differences in pleasure intensity and/or duration.

hypersensitivity is *greater*, the smaller a B_1-difference is relative to a B_2-difference, and the larger the A-difference that any number of token B_2-differences could collectively make.

Consider the sub-spectrum argument. Let a B_1-difference be the difference between someone being at positive well-being level L_i and someone being at adjacent lower positive level L_{i+1}. Let a B_2-difference be the difference of there being an additional person at positive level L_{i+1}. In the sub-spectrum argument, population X* differs from population Z* by some number of token B_2-differences—that is, X* contains some number of additional people at level L_{i+1}. The larger this number, the larger the degree to which population X* is better than population Z*. But, no matter how much larger this number is, population Y* is not better than population Z*, even though population Y* differs from population X* by one token B_1-difference. That is, the difference in betterness that one token B_1-difference makes is at least as large as the difference in betterness (the A-difference) that any number of token B_2-differences could collectively make. We have some degree of hypersensitivity here, if a B_1-difference is no greater than a B_2-difference. Token B_2-differences are smaller, the lower the level L_{i+1} is. So, to ensure that a B_1-difference is never any greater than a B_2-difference, we can set up Finite Spectrum with a precisification of 'slight' so that the difference between someone being at level L_i and someone being at slightly lower level L_{i+1} is no greater than the difference of there being an additional person at even the very lowest positive level in the series, level L_k.[42] Indeed, we can set up Finite Spectrum with a precisification of 'slight' so that our B_1-difference is as tiny a fraction of our B_2-difference as we like. Depending on the precisification of 'slight' we use in setting up Finite Spectrum, the rejection of any of the claims of the sub-spectrum argument will yield hypersensitivity to various degrees. So, given Transitivity, the rejection of Tradeoffs will likewise yield various degrees of hypersensitivity. But any degree of hypersensitivity seems deeply puzzling.[43]

---

[42] One might object that, since B_1-differences involve only quality of life whereas B_2-differences involve number of people as well, we cannot meaningfully compare the size of one difference with that of another. While there are difficult questions concerning the comparison of difference-size when a difference is larger along one dimension and smaller along another, B_1-differences are smaller than B_2-differences *both* in quality of life and in number of people (B_1-differences involve no difference in number of people).

[43] It is plausible that the difference in betterness (the A-difference) that any number of token B_2-differences could collectively make is greater, the higher level L_{i+1} is. For example, consider a pair of populations in which everyone in each is at a very low positive level, and consider another pair of populations in which everyone in each is at a very high positive level. The difference in betterness that any difference in population size between the second pair of populations could make seems greater than the difference in betterness that any difference in population size between the first pair of populations could make. There may accordingly be more or less hypersensitivity depending on where along the spectrum the rejection of Tradeoffs occurs.

18.5 Conclusion

Ethics in the tradition of Derek Parfit's *Reasons and Persons* is riddled with spectrum arguments. These arguments, such as the spectrum argument for the Repugnant Conclusion that I focused on here, have important theoretical and practical implications. According to the *sorites analogy*, since spectrum arguments are relevantly structurally analogous to sorites arguments, the correct response to spectrum arguments is structurally analogous to the correct response to sorites arguments.

I first considered some potential *structural disanalogies* between spectrum arguments and sorites arguments, including one according to which, while sorites arguments appeal to a tolerance premise, spectrum arguments do not. I showed how a transitivityless spectrum argument is structurally analogous to a multidimensional sorites argument—among other things, both appeal to a tolerance premise. This structural analogy invites defenders of the sorites analogy to argue that, if the correct response to the multidimensional argument is to reject Tolerance*, then the correct response to the transitivityless spectrum argument is to reject Tolerance. And, if we ought to reject Tolerance, then we also ought to reject the conjunction of Tradeoffs and Transitivity (of the original spectrum argument).

I then turned to two *content-based* disanalogies between spectrum arguments and sorites arguments. According to these disanalogies, even if these arguments are relevantly structurally analogous, they differ in their content in ways that show the sorites analogy to be implausible. I argued that, while we can offer a relatively *sanguine response* to the multidimensional sorites argument featuring the relation of being heapier than, we cannot offer such a response to the transitivityless spectrum argument. And I argued that, while rejecting Tradeoffs of the original spectrum argument yields *hypersensitivity*, rejecting Tradeoffs* of a relevantly structurally analogous sorites argument does not. Despite their structural similarities, it can be deeply distorting to think of a spectrum argument as 'just another sorites'.

There is a broader methodological lesson here. The logic underlying the sorites analogy is flawed. That is, it is dubious that if two arguments are relevantly structurally analogous, the correct response to one is structurally analogous to the correct response to the other. We should expect to see content-based disanalogies not just between spectrum arguments and sorites arguments, but also within the class of sorites arguments, and within the class of spectrum arguments.[44] While I have focused here on spectrum arguments involving tradeoffs

---

[44] In section 18.3, I highlighted a content-based disanalogy within the class of sorites arguments, and in section 18.4, I suggested a potential content-based disanalogy between the spectrum argument for the Repugnant Conclusion and the spectrum argument for the Negative Repugnant Conclusion.

between quality of life and number of people, others involve tradeoffs between different evaluatively relevant dimensions, for example, intensity and duration of pain, severity and number of harms, pleasure and rational activity, and so on. We should not ignore structural similarities between these arguments, but equally we should not ignore dissimilarities in their content.

The most puzzling spectrum arguments do not admit of sanguine solutions. They leave us with the humbler task of identifying which solutions are the least implausible. Solutions that avoid the repugnant conclusions of these spectrum arguments are far more implausible than most of us would like to believe.

References

Alter, T., and Rachels, S., 'Epistemicism and the combined spectrum', in *Ratio* 17/3 (2004): 241–55.

Antony, M., 'Vagueness and the metaphysics of consciousness', in *Philosophical Studies* 128 (2006): 515–38.

Arntzenius, F., and Hawthorne, J., 'Gunk and continuous variation', in *The Monist* 88/4 (2005): 441–65.

Arrhenius, G., *Population Ethics* (Oxford University Press, ms).

Arrhenius, G., and Rabinowicz, W., 'Millian superiorities', in *Utilitas* 17/2 (2005): 127–46.

Barnes, E., 'Vagueness and arbitrariness: Merricks on composition', in *Mind* 116/461 (2007): 105–13.

Barnes, E., 'Ontic vagueness: A guide for the perplexed', in *Noûs* 44/4 (2010): 601–627.

Barnes, E., and Cameron, R., 'The open future: bivalence, determinism and ontology', in *Philosophical Studies* 146/2 (2009): 291–309.

Barnes, E., and Williams, J. R. G., 'A theory of metaphysical indeterminacy', in K. Bennett and D. W. Zimmerman (eds.), *Oxford Studies in Metaphysics*, Volume 6 (Oxford University Press, 2011a), 103–48.

Barnes, E., and Williams, J. R. G., 'Response to Eklund', in K. Bennett and D. W. Zimmerman (eds.), *Oxford Studies in Metaphysics*, Volume 6 (Oxford University Press, 2011b), 173–82.

Binmore, K., and Voorhoeve, A., 'Defending transitivity against Zeno's paradox', in *Philosophy and Public Affairs* 31/3 (2003): 272–79.

Brink, D., 'Consequentialism, the separateness of persons, and aggregation', in D. Portmore (ed.), *The Oxford Handbook of Consequentialism* (Oxford University Press, 2020), 378–400.

Broome, J., *Weighing Lives* (Oxford University Press, 2004).

Campbell, T. 'Repugnance, extreme priority, and sadistic elitism', ms.

Carlson, E., 'Aggregating harms—Should we kill to avoid headaches?', in *Theoria* 66/3 (2000): 246–55.

Chang, R., *Making Comparisons Count* (Routledge, 2002).

Chen, L., 'Infinitesimal gunk', in *Journal of Philosophical Logic* (2020). https://doi.org/10.1007/s10992-020-09544-x.

Constantinescu, C., 'Moral vagueness: A dilemma for non-naturalism', in R. Shafer-Landau (ed.), *Oxford Studies in Metaethics*, Volume 9 (Oxford University Press, 2014), 152–85.

Constantinescu, C., 'Vague comparisons', in *Ratio* 29 (2016), 357–77.

Eklund, M., 'Being metaphysically unsettled: Barnes and Williams on metaphysical indeterminacy and vagueness', in K. Bennett and D. W. Zimmerman (eds.), *Oxford Studies in Metaphysics*, Volume 6 (Oxford University Press, 2011), 149–72.

Elson, L., 'Tenenbaum and Raffman on vague projects, the self-torturer, and the sorites', in *Ethics* 126/2 (2016): 474–88.

Glover, J., *Causing Death and Saving Lives* (Penguin, 1977).

Griffin, J. *Well-Being: Its Meaning, Measurement and Moral Importance* (Oxford University Press, 1986).

Handfield, T., and Rabinowicz, W., 'Incommensurability and vagueness in spectrum arguments: Options for saving transitivity of betterness', in *Philosophical Studies* 175/9 (2018): 2373–87.

Hare, C., 'The great spectrum paradox' (ms).

Hyde, D., and Raffman, D., 'Sorites paradox', in *The Stanford Encyclopedia of Philosophy* (2018), E. N. Zalta (ed.). https://plato.stanford.edu/archives/sum2018/entries/sorites-paradox/.

Kagan, S., 'The costs of transitivity: Thoughts on Larry Temkin's rethinking the good', in *Journal of Moral Philosophy* 12/4 (2015): 462–78.

Katz, L., 'On Larry Temkin's rethinking the good', in *Journal of Moral Philosophy* 12/4 (2015): 414–27.

Kim, J., '"Strong" and "global" supervenience revisited', in *Philosophy and Phenomenological Research* 48 (1987): 315–26.

Knapp, C., 'Trading quality for quantity', in *Journal of Philosophical Research* 32 (2007): 211–33.

Korman, D., 'The argument from vagueness', in *Philosophy Compass* 5/10 (2010): 891–901.

Mulgan, T., 'The reverse repugnant conclusion', in *Utilitas* 14/3 (2003): 360–64.

Nebel, J., 'The good, the bad, and the transitivity of better than', in *Noûs* 52/4 (2018): 874–99.

Norcross, A., 'Comparing harms: Headaches and human lives', in *Philosophy and Public Affairs* 26/2 (1997): 135–67.

Parfit, D., *Reasons and Persons* (Oxford University Press, 1984).

Parfit, D., 'Overpopulation and the quality of life', in P. Singer (ed.), *Applied Ethics* (Oxford University Press, 1986), 145–64.

Parfit, D., 'The unimportance of identity', in H. Harris (ed.), *Identity* (Oxford University Press, 1995), 13–45.

Parfit, D., 'Experiences, subjects, and conceptual schemes', in *Philosophical Topics* 26/1–2 (1999): 217–70.

Parfit, D., *On What Matters* (Oxford University Press, 2011).

Parfit, D., 'Can we avoid the repugnant conclusion?', in *Theoria* 82/2 (2016): 110–27.

Pummer, T., 'Lopsided lives', in M. Timmons (ed.), *Oxford Studies in Normative Ethics*, Volume 7 (Oxford University Press, 2017), 275–96.

Pummer, T., 'Spectrum arguments and hypersensitivity', in *Philosophical Studies* 175/7 (2018): 1729–44.

Pummer, T., *Hypersensitive Ethics: Much Ado about Nearly Nothing* (Oxford University Press, ms).

Qizilbash, M., 'Transitivity and vagueness', in *Economics and Philosophy* 21/1 (2005): 109–31.

Quinn, W., 'The puzzle of the self-torturer', in *Philosophical Studies* 59/1 (1990): 79–90.

Rachels, S., 'Counterexamples to the transitivity of better than', in *Australasian Journal of Philosophy* 76/1 (1998): 71–83.

Rachels, S., 'Repugnance or intransitivity: A repugnant but forced choice', in J. Ryberg and T. Tännsjö (eds.), *The Repugnant Conclusion: Essays on Population Ethics* (Kluwer Academic Publishers, 2004), 163–86.

Russell, J., 'The structure of gunk: Adventures in the ontology of space', in D. Zimmerman (ed.), *Oxford Studies in Metaphysics*, Volume 4 (Oxford University Press, 2008), 248–74.

Sider, T., *Four Dimensionalism: An Ontology of Persistence and Time* (Oxford University Press, 2001).

Sider, T., 'Hell and vagueness', *Faith and Philosophy* 19/1 (2002): 58–68.

Silk, A., 'Evaluational adjectives', *Philosophy and Phenomenological Research* (2019): 1–35. https://doi.org/10.1111/phpr.12635.

Simon, J., 'Vagueness and zombies: Why "phenomenally conscious" has no borderline cases', in *Philosophical Studies* 174 (2017): 2105–23.

Sorensen, R., *Blindspots* (Oxford University Press, 1988).

Temkin, L., 'A continuum argument for intransitivity', in *Philosophy and Public Affairs* 25/3 (1996): 175–210.

Temkin, L., *Rethinking the Good: Moral Ideals and the Nature of Practical Reasoning* (Oxford University Press, 2012).

Tenenbaum, S., and Raffman, D., 'Vague projects and the puzzle of the self-torturer', in *Ethics* 123/1 (2012): 86–112.

Thomas, T., *Topics in Population Ethics* (D. Phil. Thesis, University of Oxford, 2016).

Thomas, T., 'Some possibilities in population axiology', in *Mind* 127/507 (2018): 807–32.

Unger, P., 'Conscious beings in a gradual world', in *Midwest Studies in Philosophy* 12/1 (1988): 287–333.

Voorhoeve, A., and Binmore, K., 'Transitivity, the sorites paradox, and similarity-based decision-making', in *Erkenntnis* 64/1 (2006): 101–14.

Wasserman, R., 'Paradoxes of transitivity', ms.

Williams, J. R. G., 'Ontic vagueness and metaphysical indeterminacy', in *Philosophy Compass* 3/4 (2008): 763–88.

PART IV
PRIORITARIANISM IN POPULATION ETHICS

19
Prioritarianism, Population Ethics, and Competing Claims

Michael Otsuka

19.1 Introduction

These are Derek Parfit's last published words on his view that we should give priority to the well-being of the worse off:

> the Prioritarian Principles that I have considered cannot be applied to cases in which, in the different possible outcomes, different people would exist. When we consider these cases, we need other principles.[1]

Through reflection on these remarks and their underlying justification, it is possible to deepen our understanding, both of Parfit's conceptualization and defence of prioritarianism, and of the place and force of prioritarian principles in distributive ethics. That is what I shall try to do in this chapter.

I shall eventually reach the conclusion that Parfit stakes out an unstable position, both for himself and more generally. There is not a plausible rationale for a prioritarianism that is restricted only to outcomes in which the same people exist, which is consistent with the key features of Parfit's elaboration and defence of this view and his other commitments. The principles that might be appealed to, in an attempt to justify such a restriction of prioritarianism to what Parfit calls 'Same People Cases', give rise to a different view—one that is sensitive to the presence or absence of the competing claims of different individuals, where both

---

Earlier versions of this chapter were presented as the 2018 Mala Kamm Memorial Lecture at NYU and at Rutgers, the LSE, the Institute for Futures Studies, the Hebrew University of Jerusalem, and the Universities of Copenhagen and Oxford. I would like to thank Frances Kamm, Larry Temkin, Matthew Adler, and the other members of the audiences and participants for their comments. I also thank Simon Beard, Tomi Frances, Nils Holtug, Todd Karhu, Simon Knutsson, Jeff McMahan, Jacob Nebel, Theron Pummer, Wlodek Rabinowicz, Shlomi Segal, Peter Vallentyne, and Alex Voorhoeve for their written comments.

[1] 'Another Defence of the Priority View', p. 440. Nebel also endorses such a restriction of the scope of prioritarianism, in 'Priority, Not Equality', section IV. See also Crisp, who maintains—in 'Ethics and International Environmental Law', p. 482—that 'prioritarianism is best understood' as a view which is restricted in this manner.

the existence and the magnitude of these claims are determined by gains and losses to individuals in a manner that is not fully captured by Parfit's prioritarian weighting.

In what follows, I shall assume that prioritarianism is a view regarding the moral value or goodness of outcomes. I shall also assume that the magnitude of this value tracks the strength of the reasons a morally motivated agent has to bring about one or another outcome involving individuals to whom he is impartial. I shall therefore assume that moral goodness tracks what has been called (moral) 'choiceworthiness'. Here I draw my inspiration from Parfit's account of the nature of consequentialist goodness, and value more generally, in *On What Matters*, which he himself applies to prioritarianism in the piece from which my opening quotation is drawn. It is not merely fidelity to Parfit's approach which explains my choice of assumptions. I also find it hard to get a grip on what is meant by moral value or goodness except in terms of the strength of the reasons one would have to choose, if one could, to bring about one outcome rather than another, when one takes an impartial point of view.[2]

A consideration of a simple version of prioritarianism will form a useful starting point for this discussion. I shall call this version:

Priority-weighted total utilitarianism: Moral goodness is simply a function of the sum total of morally weighted utility.

To unpack this principle a bit: Given what I have just said, 'moral goodness' is to be understood as 'choiceworthiness'. 'Utility' should be understood here and elsewhere in this chapter as a synonym for 'well-being'—that is, how well an individual's life is really going (or would go) for him or her. The prioritarian weighting of utility is representable as a strictly increasing concave function of the utility of an individual, as illustrated by Figure 19.1.[3]

For classical utilitarianism, by contrast, there is no variable moral weighting of the different levels of utility an individual might enjoy. To paraphrase Bentham, every unit of utility to count for one, and none for more than one. What Bentham actually said, according to John Stuart Mill, was '*everybody* to count for one, nobody for more than one' (emphasis added).[4] It is worth noting that this famous dictum does not tell in favour of utilitarianism over prioritarianism, since neither view gives greater or lesser moral weight to different individuals per se. Bentham

---

[2] I define anonymous goodness in terms of choiceworthiness in 'How it Makes a Moral Difference', p. 194. Compare Broome: 'I cannot see what use we can have for the notion of quantities of good except when we weigh differences in good in comparing alternatives. So it is in weighing up differences that we can expect the notion to get its meaning' (*Weighing Goods*, p. 215).

[3] Parfit left open whether this should be the lifetime utility of an individual or the utility of an individual at a time, while noting that he had claimed, in section 117 of *Reasons and Persons*, 'that, on what I take to be the truth about personal identity, there is an argument for taking these units to be people at particular times' (*Equality or Priority?*, p. 41).

[4] Mill, *Utilitarianism*, p. 60.

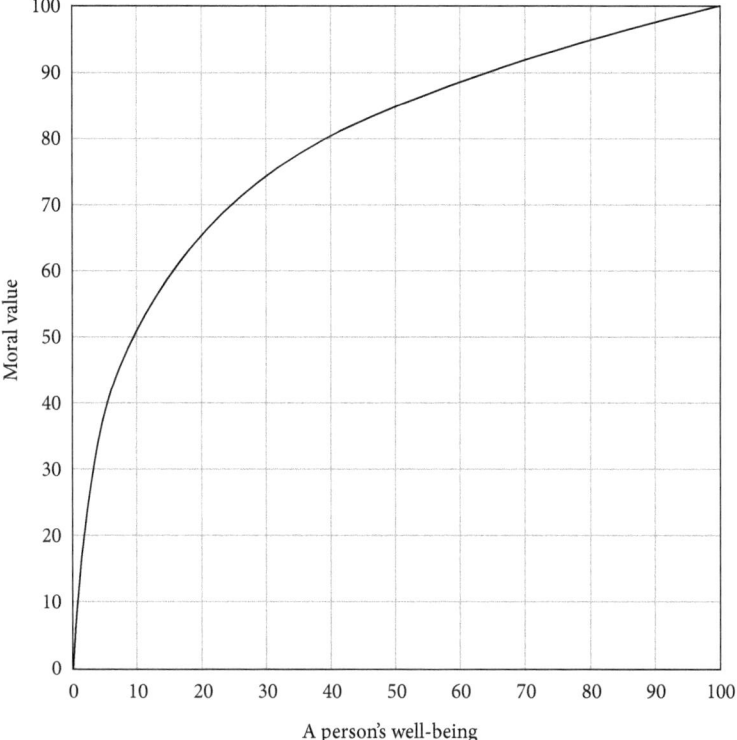

Figure 19.1 Prioritarian moral value of a person's well-being.

Notes: Here the curve in question is analogous to the sort of curve that is often used to represent the diminishing marginal utility of money. Parfit draws such an analogy in *Equality or Priority?*: 'Just as resources have diminishing marginal utility, so utility has diminishing marginal moral importance' (p. 24). If the x-axis in Figure 19.1 is a measure of units of money and the y-axis of units of utility, then the concave curve will represent the diminishing marginal utility of money.

makes clear in many passages, however, that he did not weight units of utility in prioritarian fashion. He writes, for instance, that:

> given any assemblage of men, any independent superior being who is benevolent enough to interest himself in their condition... will naturally find an equal pleasure in contributing to the happiness of any one among them as well as another. The happiness of any of them has no more value in his eyes than the equal happiness of any other. Nevertheless, any greater happiness obtained by any one among them has more value, in proportion to its quantity, than a lesser happiness obtained by another.[5]

---

[5] This is a translation—by and in Mack, *Jeremy Bentham*, p. 449—of a passage from Bentham's 'Essai sur la représentation'.

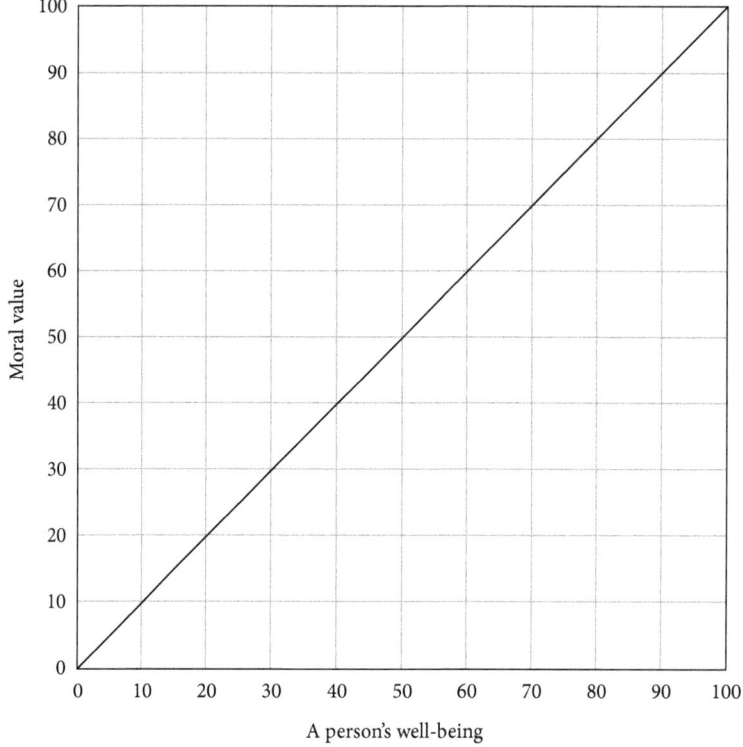

Figure 19.2 Utilitarian moral value of a person's well-being.

When, in classical utilitarian fashion, we accord the same weight to every unit of utility, Figure 19.2 provides a graph of the moral value or goodness of utility.

An understanding of prioritarianism as a weighted form of utilitarianism is perhaps suggested by a remark of Parfit's in his first publication on prioritarianism—his *Lindley Lecture*—when he invokes a moral 'law of diminishing moral goodness'.[6] As I shall explain in what follows, however, the form of prioritarian weighting that Parfit defends is more restricted in its scope than priority-weighted total utilitarianism.

19.2 Different Number Cases

Utilitarianism is generally understood as a moral theory which applies universally: not just to a particular society but more globally, not merely to populations consisting of the same people, but also to those consisting of different people,

---

[6] Parfit, *Equality or Priority?*, p. 24.

not merely to human but to all sentient beings, not merely to sentient beings that are actually alive today but to future sentient beings as well, and not merely to same-sized populations, but also to different-sized populations.

As Parfit made famous, there is, however, a notorious problem, involving what he dubbed the 'Repugnant Conclusion', with applying total utilitarianism to different-sized populations, which Parfit calls a 'Different Number Case'. According to the Repugnant Conclusion: 'Compared with the existence of many people who would all have some very high quality of life, there is some much larger number of people whose existence would be better, even though these people would all have lives that were barely worth living'.[7] If prioritarianism is understood as a morally weighted form of total utilitarianism that is meant to apply as universally as utilitarianism is meant to apply, the view will inherit and accentuate this problem with utilitarianism.

Recall, however, that, as my opening quotation indicates, Parfit maintains that prioritarian principles do not apply to cases in which different people would exist in the different possible outcomes. Parfit does not elaborate, either in the piece from which I quoted or elsewhere, on why he believed that these principles 'cannot be applied' to such cases. It is, however, reasonable to assume that a highly counterintuitive implication related to the Repugnant Conclusion was among his reasons for refusing to apply prioritarianism to Different Number Cases, while retaining confidence in its application to some other cases. Evidence that this was among his reasons can be found in Parfit's brief 'Postscript' to a book on *The Repugnant Conclusion*. There Parfit writes that the 'reasoning in this anthology shows how hard it is to form acceptable theories in cases that involve different numbers of people'. He maintains that this 'gives us ground for worry about our appeal to particular theories in the other two kinds of case: those which involve the same numbers, in the different outcomes, though these are not all the same people, and those which do involve all and only the same people'. Parfit suggests, however, that 'there may be some hope of "quarantining" the impossibility [of forming acceptable theories], and the resulting scepticism, to Different Number Choices'. He offers the following analogy: 'It's very difficult to formulate acceptable welfarist theories that could apply to cases that involve infinite quantities of such things as suffering and happiness. That's a worry, but it doesn't undermine our confidence in the theories that can handle cases with only finite quantities'.[8]

If we apply this analogy to prioritarianism, the repugnant or otherwise unacceptable implications of prioritarianism in Different Number Cases should not undermine our confidence that prioritarianism appropriately applies to one or both of the following different types of cases: (1) 'Same Number Cases', in which

---

[7] Parfit, 'Can We Avoid the Repugnant Conclusion?', p. 110.   [8] 'Postscript', p. 257.

there are different people in each of the different possible outcomes, but there are the same number of people in each outcome, and (2) 'Same People Cases', in which not only are there the same number of people in each possible outcomes, but these are also the same people.[9]

In his posthumously published piece on population ethics, Parfit suggests that the following principle, which he affirmed, might help avert the slide to the Repugnant Conclusion in Different Number Cases:

> (R) when two outcomes would give people the same total sum of benefits, it would be in one way better if these benefits were shared equally between fewer people.[10]

(R) reflects our preference for a small population of people, each of whose members leads an equally high quality life, to a much larger population of people, each of whose member's life is equally bad and barely worth living, even when the sum total of utility is the same in each population. (R) implies, for example, that, when the sum total of utility consists of 1000 units, it would be in one way better for 100 units of well-being to go to each of 10 people than for one unit of well-being to go to each of 1000 people.

Total utilitarianism is indifferent between these two populations, since, by stipulation, they each contain the same total sum of benefits. Hence, at least in this case, utilitarianism doesn't imply the Repugnant Conclusion that one would have stronger moral reason to bring about the very large population in which each person's life is barely worth living. If, however, we assume that prioritarianism is to be understood as a form of priority-weighted total utilitarianism, which applies to Different Number as well as Same Number and Same People Cases, here prioritarianism will decisively favour the larger population of 1000 individuals, each of whose life is barely worth living at level 1, to the smaller population of 10, each of whom enjoys 100 units of well-being. This is because, when the 1000 units are thinly spread among the larger population, there are many more units of utility clustered to the left of the x-axis at the origin of our graph (see Figure 19.1), which receive the most moral weight, and no units that extend very far to the right of the x-axis, where they receive little moral weight. Prioritarianism understood as weighted total utilitarianism therefore embraces the Repugnant Conclusion in a case in which classical utilitarianism at least has the decency to remain indifferent.

---

[9] Here I follow Parfit's terminology in 'Future People', p. 119. In what Parfit calls a 'Pure Same Number Case', entirely different people would exist in each of the different possible outcomes. In what he calls a 'Mixed Same Number Case', some but not all, of the same people would exist in the different possible outcomes. I shall return to this distinction later. Any unmodified reference in this chapter to a 'Same Number Case' is to a pure one in which entirely different people would exist in the different possible outcomes.

[10] 'Future People', p. 151.

A classical utilitarian deems a larger population better than a smaller population in which everyone's utility is higher, only when the sum total of utility of people in the larger population is greater. A priority-weighted utilitarian, by contrast, might deem a larger population better than a smaller population in which everyone's utility is higher, even if the sum total of utility of the people in the larger population is *less than* that of the smaller population. Nils Holtug has dubbed this the 'super-repugnant conclusion'.[11] To this, I would add the following observations. There is at least *something* to be said for a classical utilitarian's endorsement of the larger population in which everyone's life is barely worth living: namely, that the sum total of utility is greater. By contrast, it is hard to find *anything* to be said in favour of a prioritarian's claim that the higher sum total of priority-weighted utility renders a larger population better than a smaller population even when *both* the sum total of well-being and the level of each individual's well-being in the larger population is lower than that of the smaller population.

It is instructive, at this point, to draw an analogy to the levelling down objection to egalitarianism. Some egalitarian principles imply that it is in one way better if the sighted all go blind in a population in which half are sighted and half blind. This is claimed to be in one way better, because more equal, even if nobody benefits from this transformation and there is nothing but levelling down. According to the levelling down objection, there is *no* respect in which the greater equality achieved by such levelling down makes things better.[12] Something similar may be said of the prioritarian's super-repugnant conclusion that it would be better to bring about a population in which both the level of utility that each person enjoys and the sum total of utility is less great than in another population. Even though prioritarianism says that this is better because the sum total of *priority-weighted* utility increases, it is hard to discern *any* respect in which the greater sum of priority-weighted utility makes things better when this is achieved via sacrifice of both the individual level and the sum total of utility.

As I noted above, this contrasts with the Repugnant Conclusion the classical total utilitarian endorses. At least here we can discern a morally significant respect, to which classical utilitarianism is sensitive, in which the huge population with people whose lives are barely worth living is better than the smaller population consisting only of people leading wonderful lives: a greater sum total of happiness or well-being is enjoyed by people. Intuitively, this fact appears to make things better, at least in one respect. By contrast, the prioritarian's claim that the greater sum of priority-weighted utility makes things better is less plausible than even the

---

[11] *Persons, Interests, and Justice*, p. 246. Holtug (ibid., pp. 257–8) makes the nice point that prioritarianism is less repugnant than total utilitarianism when we consider different-sized populations all in which *nobody* has a life worth living, and therefore each person's lifetime utility is represented by a negative integer. Throughout this chapter, I consider only populations in which everyone's life is worth living, and hence each person's lifetime utility is represented by a positive integer.

[12] See Parfit's discussion of this objection in *Equality or Priority?*, pp. 17–18 and passim.

claim that a levelling down increase in equality makes things better. At least in levelling down cases, we can make intuitive sense of the claim that bringing about equality makes things better: it eliminates the unfairness of some being worse off than others through no fault or choice of theirs.[13] By contrast, it is difficult to make intuitive sense of how the increase in the quantity of priority-weighted utility makes things better in the case of a population with a lower sum total, as well as lower individual levels, of utility.

I grant the following respect in which the larger population may be regarded as better than the smaller population: more people would receive the non-comparative existential benefit of being brought into existence with a life worth living. This advantage would not, however, be *explained* by the fact that there is more priority weighted utility. It would not be explained by this fact because this advantage might obtain even if the larger population contained less utility, priority-weighted or otherwise, than the smaller one. It might obtain, for example, if the level of everyone's utility in a slightly larger population is *so much lower* than the level of everyone's utility in the smaller population that both the unweighted and the priority-weighted sum total of utility is lower in the larger population, as compared with the smaller population.

There is the following distinct but related respect in which the super-repugnant conclusion is more of an embarrassment for prioritarianism than the Repugnant Conclusion is for classical utilitarianism. Each adjacent step to the Repugnant Conclusion that a classical utilitarian takes is a step in which intuitively things are all things considered better than the previous step. It is only when we have travelled several steps towards the Repugnant Conclusion that it becomes clear that the population is all things considered worse than the one from which we started. By contrast, my objection to prioritarianism holds that, even for any given adjacent step along the way from a smaller population to a larger population that a prioritarian is committed to taking, it is hard to see how a larger population in which everyone is worse off *and* the sum total of utility is lower could be all things considered better than the smaller population. It is hard to see how this could be all things considered better even if we acknowledge the aforementioned respect in which each step is better than the last: namely, that there are more people with lives worth living. Prioritarianism therefore generates counterintuitive results even when comparing adjacent steps and not merely when comparing steps that are far apart.

As I have noted above, increases in the sum total of utility appear to be morally significant, even in different number cases. I believe that this is why Parfit did not apply his aforementioned 'quarantining' strategy to a principle of total utility.

---

[13] See Temkin, 'Equality, Priority, and Levelling Down', pp. 154–5.

Rather, in his posthumously published 'Future People', Parfit maintained that the following principle applies even to Different Number Cases:

The Wide Collective Principle: One of two outcomes would be in one way better if this outcome would together benefit people more, by giving people a greater total sum of benefits.[14]

Instead of quarantining Different Number Cases from this principle, he supplemented it with other principles, which he hoped would together block the Repugnant Conclusion when applied to Different Number Cases. One such principle is the aforementioned (R), which is implied by the following more general principle, which Parfit also endorsed:

The Wide Individual Principle: One of two outcomes would be in one way better if this outcome would benefit each person more.[15]

Along the lines of the claim that principles of average and total utility deliver the same verdicts when the size of the population is held constant, Parfit noted that:

When we compare outcomes in which the same number of people would exist, and there would be no inequality between people, these two ways of *benefiting people more* always coincide. If one of two outcomes would together give people a greater total sum of benefits, and each person would get an equal share of this greater sum, each person would get an equal benefit. In such cases, we need not distinguish between these two ways of benefiting people more.

When we consider Different Number Cases, however, we have reasons to draw this distinction.[16]

As the Repugnant Conclusion vividly illustrates, in a Different Number Case, the two principles do not coincide. Rather they pull in opposite directions, with the

---

[14] 'Future People', p. 153. Parfit notes, ibid., that he had earlier mistakenly rejected the application of this Wide Collective Principle to Different Number Cases.

[15] 'Future People', p. 153.

[16] 'Future People', p. 153. Note that the quoted claim, as well as (R), are restricted to populations all of whose members are equally well off. These claims are implied by principles of total and average utility. But they do not imply these principles of utility, since the latter are indifferent to whether the utility is distributed equally or unequally among members of the population. By contrast, Parfit's Collective Principle is not restricted in its application to cases involving equality. It amounts to a principle of total utility which is restricted in its application to benefits to people. But his Individual Principle is narrower than a principle of average utility which is restricted to people, since it maintains that an outcome is better when each person is better off and not merely when the average level of people's well-being is higher.

Collective Principle favouring the large population of people all leading lives barely worth living and the Individual Principle favouring the small population of people all leading wonderful lives. If we can find a way of prioritizing the Individual Principle when the two pull in opposite directions, that may provide a means of blocking the Repugnant Conclusion.[17]

As my earlier discussion brings out, however, prioritarianism might favour a larger population as all things considered better than a smaller population, even when neither the Collective Principle nor the Individual Principle tells in favour of the larger population. Moreover, even though we can identify something to be said in favour of the larger population—namely that more people enjoy the benefit of a life worth living—the fact that the sum total of priority weighted utility is greater does not appear to tell at all in favour of the larger population. We therefore have grounds for refusal to apply prioritarian principles to Different Number Cases—grounds, in other words, to quarantine such cases from them.

I shall draw this section to a close with a few thoughts on when it is and is not appropriate to quarantine cases from moral principles. Suppose one tried to neutralize the levelling down objection to egalitarianism by declaring a quarantine of cases in which equality is achieved only by making better off people worse off, so that the principle of equality applies only to cases in which greater equality is better for some. The problem with this move is that levelled-down outcomes share the same good-making feature of greater fairness that outcomes possess in which the worse off are made better off as well as the well off being made worse off. What is the justification for limiting the scope of a principle of equality to just some but not other ways of making things fairer in Same People Cases? Such a move seems ad hoc: done simply for the sake of trying to block unwelcome counterexamples to one's principles. By contrast, it is not on the face of it ad hoc to quarantine an entire class of Different Number Cases so that they are isolated from prioritarian principles. This is because such a quarantine cuts things at a conspicuous joint which we have independent reason to recognize as morally significant. We would be quarantining an entire area of discrete moral space. Recall Parfit's analogy to finite as opposed to infinite utility, which also cuts things at a conspicuous and apparently morally significant joint. We also have independent evidence, from non-identity cases, mere addition paradoxes, and the like, that different normative principles are in operation in Different Number Cases.[18]

---

[17] Parfit indicates on the last page of 'Future People' that we may also need to appeal to perfectionistic considerations, in tandem with the Individual Principle, in order to block the Repugnant Conclusion. See his discussion of perfectionism in 'Can We Avoid the Repugnant Conclusion?'.

[18] See, for example, Parfit's claim in section 144 of *Reasons and Persons*, and especially on p. 425, that when inequality comes about as a result of the 'mere addition' of extra people, it lacks the bad-making feature it has when it comes about in certain other ways.

19.3 Same Number and Same People Cases

Recall that, in Parfit's terminology, a Same Number Case is one in which there are the same number of people in each outcome, but different people in the different outcomes. In other words, nobody who exists in any one outcome exists in any other outcome. As I noted at the outset, Parfit said that prioritarian principles fail to apply, not only to Different Number Cases, but also to Same Number Cases. What explains this failure of application of prioritarianism to Same Number as well as Different Number Cases?

In answering this question, I begin by noting that we would not need to extend the quarantine of Different Number Cases from prioritarian principles to Same Number Cases as well, in order to block a version of the Repugnant Conclusion from breaking out in the latter cases. Recall Parfit's formulation of the Repugnant Conclusion: 'Compared with the existence of many people who would all have some very high quality of life, there is *some much larger number* of people whose existence would be better, even though these people would all have lives that were barely worth living' (emphasis added). The conclusion is regarded as repugnant, even though the population of people leading lives barely worth living is much larger than the population of people leading very high quality lives. Imagine, however, that the population of people leading lives barely worth living were *the same size as* the population of people leading very high quality lives. I shall dub the following a *Same Number Repugnant Conclusion*: rather than a population in which everyone leads a very high quality life, it would be better for there to be an equal-sized population in which everyone's life is barely worth living. This would be an extraordinarily repugnant conclusion, since here we could not even appeal to the fact that there would be more people enjoying the benefit of a life worth living, or else that the sum total of well-being would be larger, to try to justify the claim that we should prefer an outcome in which everyone leads a life barely worth living to one in which each has a very high quality life.

It could not, however, be in any way better, according to prioritarian principles, for everyone to lead a less good life in a Same Number Case. I acknowledge that a prioritarian will regard an outcome in which all lead lives barely worth living as better than a utilitarian will regard such an outcome, since utilities at that lower level will receive extra prioritarian weight, relative to the moral value a utilitarian assigns them. This is not, however, to maintain that it is in any way better to lower everyone's level in a Same Number Case. Imagine that one could either bring into existence some number of people with level of utility n, or the same number of people with level of utility $n + 1$. Those whose utility would be $n+1$ would receive the same prioritarian weighting for n of their $n+1$ units of their utility as the people whose utility would be n. Moreover, the further ($+1$) unit of utility would have additional positive value. So it is in no respect better, for a prioritarian, to bring people into existence with level of utility n than to bring the same number of people into existence with level of utility n+1.[19] Hence there is no need to quarantine Same Number Cases from prioritarian principles in order to block a Same Number Repugnant Conclusion.

How then, can we explain why Parfit maintains that prioritarian principles fail to apply to Same Number Cases as well as Different Number Cases—and apply only to Same People Cases? My hypothesis, which I shall defend in the remainder of this section, is that Parfit restricted prioritarianism to Same People Cases because he believed that prioritarian weighting applies only to gains and losses to people which render them better off or worse off than they would have been otherwise. Moreover, such gains and losses are possible only in Same People Cases and never in Same Number or Different Number Cases.[20]

In 'Another Defence of the Priority View', Parfit offers the following canonical formulation of prioritarianism:

> *Priority View*, we have stronger reasons to benefit people the worse off these people are.[21]

This is similar to his earlier canonical formulation in his *Lindley Lecture*, where Parfit introduces and names:

> *The Priority View*:   Benefitting people matters more the worse off these people are.[22]

In his *Lindley Lecture*, Parfit does not explicitly maintain that the view applies only to Same People Cases. But he considers only such cases and frames his discussion as follows: he writes that he will be concerned with a 'subject we can call *the ethics of distribution*', which, he maintains, 'is, in a way, simple', since:

> It is enough to consider different possible states of affairs, or outcomes, each involving the same set of people. We imagine that we know how well off, in these outcomes, these people would be. We then ask whether either outcome would be better, or would be the outcome that we ought to bring about.[23]

Parfit's above canonical formulations of prioritarianism are implied by, but do not imply, the 'weighted total utilitarian' view discussed at the outset of this chapter that moral goodness is simply a function of the sum total of morally weighted

---

[19] Here I reject Ingmar Persson's argument, in 'Why Levelling Down', that this lower level is in one way better for a prioritarian, because the average of the weighted moral value increases. I agree with Thomas Porter's critique of Persson in 'Prioritarianism and the Levelling Down Objection'.

[20] In saying that Parfit maintains that prioritarianism applies only to Same People Cases, I am oversimplifying things by treating the three categories of Different Number, Same Number, and Same People Cases as exhaustive. As I flagged in note 9 above, there is, however, a further category, called Mixed Same Number Cases, to which prioritarianism partially applies. I discuss this matter below.

[21] P. 401.   [22] *Equality or Priority?*, p. 19.   [23] *Equality or Priority?*, pp. 1–2.

utility. Parfit's prioritarianism is the view that moral goodness is a function of the sum total of utility, adjusted by priority weighted gains and losses to individuals across the different possible outcomes. Prioritarian weighting applies *only* to gains and losses that render people better or worse off than they would otherwise be.[24]

Prioritarian weighting does not apply to the benefit, if there is such a thing, of being brought into existence. Parfit is explicit that prioritarianism is inapplicable to the question of whether to bring a child into existence. He writes:

> It is sometimes claimed... that we have prioritarian reasons to have children, since we would thereby benefit some of the possible people who would otherwise be badly off, by never existing... But when we apply these distributive principles, we should not include, among the people who are badly off, possible people who never exist.[25]

In 'Future People', Parfit refers to being brought into existence as an existential but not an essentially comparative benefit, the latter of which is to be understood as a person's being made better off than he would otherwise be.[26] On my interpretation of his view, Parfit excludes such existential benefits from prioritarian weighting because he applies such weighting only to those benefits that make people better off than they would otherwise be.

In saying that 'the Prioritarian Principles that I have considered cannot be applied to cases in which, in the different possible outcomes, different people would exist', Parfit is not making the claim that these principles do not apply to any choice among outcomes in which not all the same people exist. That would have the implausible consequence that, if there were but a single person who would exist in one, but not the other, of two possible outcomes involving a large population, yet everyone else would experience gains or losses across these different outcomes, then nobody's gains or losses would receive prioritarian weighting. More plausibly, Parfit's view is that prioritarian principles apply to all gains and losses that render people better or worse off than they would otherwise be.[27] As noted above, Parfit draws a distinction in 'Future People' between 'Pure Same Number Cases' and 'Mixed Same

---

[24] It is noteworthy that, while Parfit sometimes referred to prioritarianism as 'weighted beneficence' (not in the published version of his 1991 *Lindley Lecture* but in, for example, a 1989 draft of that lecture entitled 'On Giving Priority to the Worse Off'), he never referred to the view as 'weighted utilitarianism'.

[25] 'Another Defence of the Priority View', p. 440.   [26] See pp. 130, 132, and 150.

[27] On this 'plausible' reading of Parfit's prioritarianism, the view respects a principle of separability. This is because, on this interpretation, in order to determine whether benefits to a person should be given prioritarian weighting, all we need to know is whether this person would exist and fare better or worse in different outcomes. We do not need to know anything about how other people will fare. This contrasts with the 'implausible' reading of Parfit, which implies a violation of separability for the following reason. Whether benefits to a given person who would exist in all outcomes, and fare better or worse in different outcomes, should be given prioritarian weighting will depend, on this reading, on how other people will fare in the following respect: it will depend on whether or not everyone else will exist in all outcomes. If but one of them will not, then nobody's benefits receive prioritarian weighting.

Number Cases'. In the latter category, 'though no one would exist in all of the outcomes that we are considering, some people would exist in more than one of these outcomes'.[28] Prioritarian weight would be applied to all and only gains and losses to people who would exist in more than one outcome in such mixed cases.[29] In the discussion that follows, I shall limit myself to Pure Same People and Pure Same Number Cases. I shall not consider Mixed Same Number Cases.[30]

The following pair of cases provides a simple illustration, on which I shall build my discussion, of the manner in which Parfit limits his prioritarianism to gains and losses that track the fates of the same (that is, numerically identical) individuals in different outcomes. The first of the pair is Case 1 in Figure 19.3. Here we assume that Amy and Bob will live contemporaneous lives in the near future. Amy's lifetime level of utility will be 100 if you choose D1 and 80 if you choose D2. Bob's will be 10 if you choose D1 and 30 if you choose D2. This is a Same People Case.

Case 1	D1	D2
Amy	100	80
Bob	10	30

Figure 19.3 Case 1.

Now consider Case 1* in Figure 19.4. This is a Same Number Case in which all morally relevant factors are the same as in Case 1, except that different people would exist in the different outcomes. If you choose D1, Amy and Bob will enjoy the same lifetime utilities as they would if you were to choose D1 in Case 1. But if you choose D2, Amy and Bob will never exist. Rather, Cathy and Dan will exist and enjoy the same levels of utility as Amy and Bob would enjoy under D2 in Case 1.

Case 1*	D1	D2
Amy	100	—
Bob	10	—
Cathy	—	80
Dan	—	30

Figure 19.4 Case 1*.

---

[28] 'Future People', p. 149.

[29] Some such Mixed Same Number Cases involve possible people who stand a chance of existing and whom you could make better or worse off than they would otherwise be in the event that they exist. As I would interpret Parfit's approach, one would assign prioritarian weighting to their gains and losses in the event that they exist. See my relevant discussion of *'The case of one actual but two possible persons'* in section VI of 'Prioritarianism and the Separateness of Persons'.

[30] I shall also not consider a different category, which might be labelled 'Mixed *Different* Number Cases'. In such cases, although the size of the population differs across different possible outcomes, some of the same people exist in more than one outcome. On the 'plausible' reading of Parfit, prioritarian weighting would apply to gains and losses to individuals who exist in more than one outcome, even when these outcomes involve populations that vary in size.

For a prioritarian who, unlike Parfit, conceives her prioritarianism as simply the view that one should maximize the sum total of weighted utility, one has reason to choose D2 over D1 in both cases. Moreover, one's reason to choose D2 over D1 is just as strong in Case 1* as it is in Case 1. This in spite of the fact that nobody is benefitted by the choice of D2 over D1 in Case 1*. All we need to know is the absolute level of people's utility to be able to compute the moral value of one outcome in comparison with that of another. It doesn't matter whether the people in the different outcomes are entirely non-overlapping. Gains and losses to particular individuals are of no intrinsic moral importance, when prioritarianism is understood as a weighted total utilitarianism.

On Parfit's version of prioritarianism, by contrast, one has reason to choose D2 over D1 only in Case 1, since only in that case does prioritarian weighting to benefits and losses apply, in a manner that accords greater weight to Bob's gain of 20 units of utility (from 10 to 30) than to Amy's equal-sized loss of 20 units (from 100 to 80). Parfit's prioritarian weighting simply fails to apply to the choice between D1 and D2 in Case 1*. I believe that Parfit would instead apply the classical principle of (unweighted) total utilitarianism to such a choice, the upshot of which is that one has equally strong reason to choose either D1 or D2 in Case 1*.[31]

The following is a striking implication of Parfit's limitation of his application of prioritarianism to gains and losses that track the fates of particular persons: such limitation gives rise to an inconsistency with his 'No Difference View', according to which, other things equal, it makes no moral difference whether our different choices all involve the same people or merely the same number of people.[32] It follows from the No Difference View that one has just as strong reason to choose D2 over D1 in Case 1* as in Case 1. We have seen, however, that Parfit's prioritarianism provides reason to choose D2 over D1 in Case 1, but not in Case 1*, and all other moral factors are equal in the two cases. It therefore makes a difference, after all, to Parfit, even when all else is held equal, that some are better or worse off than they would be otherwise. I would maintain that its inconsistency with Parfit's No Difference View is a virtue of his prioritarianism, rather than a drawback, since I have argued elsewhere that the No Difference View should be rejected.[33]

---

[31] Parfit doesn't explicitly commit himself to such application of classical utilitarianism. But this is implied by his embrace of consequentialism for Same Number Cases (which traces back to his discussion of the non-identity problem in *Reasons and Persons*) together with his clarification, on p. 440 of 'Another Defence of the Priority View', that he assigns prioritarian weights to benefits only when people are better off than they otherwise would have been. Considerations of egalitarian fairness would favour D2 over D1 in both Case 1 and Case 1*. But Parfit was famously sceptical of egalitarianism.

[32] Here is Parfit's own, somewhat opaque, formulation of the 'No Difference View': 'it makes no [moral] difference whether, because... future lives would be lived by the same people,... acts would be worse for these people' (*On What Matters*, vol. 2, p. 219).

[33] See 'How it Makes a Moral Difference'.

In 'Another Defence of the Priority View', Parfit says that prioritarian principles are 'Like the Principles of Personal Good, or Pareto Principles' in applying only to Same People Cases. According to:

The Principle of Personal Good, one of two acts would make the outcome better if this act would be better for one or more people and would not be worse for anyone else.[34]

The Principle of Personal Good is a *person-tracking principle*: it tracks the fates of the same (that is, numerically identical) individuals across different outcomes, where this is a matter of their gains or losses (better for some, worse for none).[35] It tracks the fates of individuals in this manner because the outcome of an act would be better or worse for a person than the outcome of another act only if the same person would exist in each outcome and would be at a higher or lower level of utility in the one outcome than in the other. Parfit has the following good reason to maintain that prioritarianism is 'Like the Principles of Personal Good, or Pareto Principles': his version of prioritarianism is also a person-tracking principle. It tracks and weights the gains and losses of particular individuals across different outcomes.

So long as we reject the No Difference View—and in the light of the reasons we have to reject that view—a restriction of prioritarianism to a weighting of gains and losses is defensible and principled rather than ad hoc. The principled reason is that it makes a moral difference whether one is better or worse off than one could have been.[36] Such restriction also provides a rationale for limiting prioritarian weighting to Same People Cases.[37]

In the light of the preceding discussion, it should now be clearer why we should not apply prioritarian weighting to Different Number Cases, where different possible outcomes contain entirely different people as well as different numbers of people. Assume a Different Number Case in which one can bring as many extra people into the world as one likes, subject to the following constraints: (i) everyone one brings into existence will experience the same level of lifetime utility, and (ii) the sum total of everyone's utility will be the same fixed amount, however many one chooses to bring into the world. It follows from (ii) that the more people one chooses to bring into the world, the lower the lifetime utility of each. It would,

---

[34] P. 404. Unlike Pareto Principles, the Principle of Personal Good does not involve any reference to a status quo benchmark against which an improvement is measured.

[35] What I call a 'person-tracking principle' is typically referred to in the literature as a 'person-affecting principle'. I avoid the term 'person-affecting', both because that term has recently come to be conceptualized differently by Parfit in 'Future People' and because I think 'person-tracking' provides a more accurate description of the content of such a principle.

[36] See Otsuka, 'How it Makes a Moral Difference'.

[37] As I have noted above, prioritarianism also applies to 'mixed' cases. But to simplify the discussion, I have set such cases to one side.

however, be a mistake to regard it as better to spread this fixed sum total of utility among more people whose lives would go less well—rather than among fewer different people whose lives would go better—on grounds that one thereby ensures that more utility will be clustered around the left-hand side of the *x*-axis in Figure 19.1. Units of utility farther to the left of the *x*-axis should not be accorded greater prioritarian moral weight when they are the result of such a choice to bring more people into the world. Rather, such utility matters more only when it corresponds to gains or losses to people, in a manner that tracks their fates across different outcomes. It is only in such cases where one must choose who will gain and who will lose that one should apply greater prioritarian weight to a person's benefits or burdens that are farther to the left of the *x*-axis.

19.4 Three Challenges for Parfit's Prioritarianism

There are, however, three sets of difficulties, which I shall explore in this final section, with Parfit's application of prioritarianism to a weighting of benefits and burdens, where such weighting is a function of nothing more than the absolute level of a person's utility from which that utility either rises or falls. All three of these difficulties can be traced to a common problem with prioritarianism: namely its failure to register the significance of the presence or absence and magnitude of competing claims. On account of these difficulties, Parfit's version of prioritarianism fails to exhibit both of the following virtues that he claims for it as an account of the ethics of distribution: (i) that it is a 'distinctive view'—one that provides a genuine and attractive alternative to egalitarian and other views that are essentially comparative in nature,[38] and (ii) that, unlike egalitarianism, prioritarianism can provide a 'complete moral view', which need not pluralistically be combined with other values but instead 'can be regarded as the only principle we need'.[39]

19.4.1 Disproportionately Large Losses

Although he applies extra moral weighting to nothing other than gains and losses to particular individuals, Parfit denies that the mere size of gains or losses to individuals is morally significant. He denies the:

---

[38] *Equality or Priority?*, pp. 22–4.
[39] *Equality or Priority?*, p. 22. By contrast, according to Parfit (ibid., p. 22 and passim), 'equality cannot plausibly be our only value', since then we would be indifferent between an outcome in which everyone is equally badly off and one in which everyone is equally well off. We need to appeal to some further value, such as a principle of utility, in order to explain why we should prefer the latter outcome.

Disproportional View: The moral importance of lesser benefits and burdens is *less* than proportional to their size.[40]

Parfit rejects that view, in favour of the following, which weights gains and losses in a manner that gives priority to the worse off:

> Though a great burden to one person should often be given disproportionately greater weight, that is true, I believe, only when and because this burden would make this person much worse off than other people. When this person would *not* be worse off, the Disproportional View is mistaken.[41]

The following escalator case, inspired by a case of Parfit's, provides an example of a Same People Case in which the Disproportional View delivers a different verdict from prioritarianism.[42] Imagine a 100-step escalator with equally small increments between each step. Each step will be occupied by a different individual. The height of each step above the ground represents that person's absolute level of lifetime well-being. Suppose that there are only two possible outcomes, and one must choose which of them to bring about: D1 in which Persons 1–100 occupy steps 1–100 respectively, and D2 in which each person in D1 occupies one step lower, except Person 1, who occupies the very top step.[43]

A principle of anonymity rates D1 and D2—and, for that matter, any other combination of 100 people on the different steps—equally good, where such a principle states that 'if the pattern of well-being levels in x is a permutation of the pattern in y, the two outcomes are equally good'.[44] Moreover, so long as we restrict ourselves to Same People Cases, Parfit's prioritarianism will always conform to a principle of anonymity.[45] Such conformity is, however, in conflict with an approach such as the Disproportional View, which also attributes moral significance to the mere size of gains and losses. Though D1 is anonymously equivalent to D2, a person-tracking approach such as the Disproportional View, which is sensitive to large losses, will not be indifferent between the two outcomes. Rather

---

[40] *On What Matters*, vol. 2, p. 206.   [41] *On What Matters*, vol. 2, p. 207.
[42] All references in this section will be to Parfit's version of prioritarianism.
[43] Save for the replacement of his metaphor of musical chairs with that of an escalator, this case is essentially the same as one that Parfit presents in *On What Matters*, vol. 2, p. 208.
[44] Adler and Holtug, 'Prioritarianism', p. 103. Note that this notion of anonymity can be applied to Same Number as well as Same People Cases. Different patterns of levels of well-being involving the same number of people can be permutations of one another, even if these different patterns involve different people. Counterparts to each individual across each outcome might be specified by definite descriptions: for example, the person born earliest in the year, the person born second earliest in the year, and so forth.
[45] As the discussion of Case 1 and Case 1* in section 19.3 above revealed, prioritarianism can give rise to a violation of anonymity when we compare the distributions of a Same People Case with those of a Same Number Case. Prioritarianism provides reason to prefer D2 to D1 in Case 1, but not in Case 1*, even though the D1 distributions across the two cases are anonymously equivalent, as are the D2 distributions.

D2 will be preferred to D1, since one person (Person 1) stands to lose an enormous amount in D1 relative to D2, whereas nobody loses much at all in D2 in comparison with D1. Everyone else either gains a little in D1 relative to D2, or loses the same small amount in D2 in comparison with D1.

I would maintain that the Disproportional View delivers the right verdict here. Rather than burdening Person 1 with a massive loss, relative to the alternative, intuitively one should burden several others with small losses, relative to the alternative. Note that there would be no case for choosing D2 over D1 if there were entirely different people in the different outcomes—that is, in a Same Number variant of this Same People Case. In a Same Number version of this case, one should be indifferent between the two distributions, since they are anonymously equivalent and there are no gains and losses to people which might morally differentiate the different outcomes.

Of the Same People version of this case, Parfit writes:

> On the Disproportional View, we ought to choose [D2]. If greater gains and losses had an importance that was more than proportional to their size, the single great gain to Person One of being ninety nine levels higher would clearly morally outweigh the ninety nine small losses of the other people. That is not plausible. Person One has no claim to be at the top.[46]

These are unsatisfactory grounds on which to object to the Disproportional View. Rejection of the outcome in which Person 1 is at the bottom of the escalator does not imply that he has a claim to be best off instead. Rather, we can justify a preference for D2 by means of an appeal to a principle that is insensitive to whether a particular person is best off but is merely sensitive to the relative size of different people's gains and losses. The principle might gain support from the claim that relatively small gains or losses are not 'relevant to' great gains or losses, irrespective of the level from which one gains or loses.[47] One might maintain, for example, that one should spare someone from paralysis in both legs even at the cost of not being able to spare a large number of other people from paralysis of the little finger on one hand. This might hold irrespective of how well off these people who would lose use of their little finger are. Even, for example, if they were all already paralysed in both legs, one might spare one further person from suffering this fate, even at the expense of not being able to prevent loss of use of the little finger in all of these others.[48]

---

[46] *On What Matters*, vol. 2, p. 208.
[47] See Kamm, *Morality, Mortality*, chaps. 8–10, and Voorhoeve, 'How Should We Aggregate Competing Claims?'.
[48] Temkin makes a similar argument against prioritarianism in *Rethinking the Good*, pp. 70–6.

Parfit cannot appeal to the mere fact that the different outcomes in the escalator case are anonymously equivalent as grounds for rejecting the Disproportional View. This is because I have earlier shown that Parfit's prioritarianism denies that anonymously equivalent profiles of distribution are always morally equivalent, since it denies the No Difference View. Moreover, though these outcomes are anonymously equivalent on the conception of anonymity introduced earlier, the one distribution can be shown to be superior to the other by a wider measure of anonymous equivalence, which takes account of gains and losses to individuals across different outcomes as well as the levels or patterns of the well-being of individuals within a given outcome. On this wider version of anonymity, D1 and D2 will not be anonymously equivalent.[49]

Even if one maintains that Parfit has good grounds for claiming that all we should care about is the sum total of priority weighted gains and losses in the Escalator Case, I do not think it will be possible to credibly maintain that this is all we should care about in two further cases to which I shall now turn in the next two sub-sections.

19.4.2 Rank-Switching versus Non-Rank-Switching Outcomes that Are More Equal

Recall the possible distributions of utility in Case 1 in Figure 19.3, which first appeared in section 19.3 and is reproduced here. Recall that Amy and Bob will live contemporaneous lives at some point in the near future. Amy's lifetime level of utility will be 100 if you choose D1 and 80 if you choose D2. Bob's will be 10 if you choose D1 and 30 if you choose D2.

Case 1	D1	D2
Amy	100	80
Bob	10	30

Figure 19.3 Case 1.

Now consider Case 1′ in Figure 19.5, which is a variation on Case 1. D1 in Case 1′ is identical to D1 in Case 1. D2 in Case 1′ is anonymously equivalent to D2 in Case 1, since these outcomes are permutations of one another.

---

[49] In 'Anonymity and Moral Equality', Campbell Brown has defended such a wider version of anonymity and notes that it captures the underlying idea of the moral equality of persons just as well as does the narrower version of anonymity that I introduced earlier. All subsequent references to anonymity in this chapter will be to the narrower version.

Case 1'	D1	D2
Amy	100	30
Bob	10	80

Figure 19.5 Case 1'.

As I noted earlier, even though in Case 1 the sum total of utility is the same in D1 as it is in D2, Parfit's prioritarianism favours D2 over D1 here, since prioritarian weighting will assign a greater moral weight to Bob's gain than to Amy's loss in D2 relative to D1 even though the latter is just as large as Bob's gain when measured in units of utility. I would now like to draw attention to the fact that prioritarianism favours D2 over D1 *to the same extent* in Case 1' as in Case 1. In other words, it provides equally strong reason to choose D2 over D1 in Case 1' as in Case 1. It does so for the following reason. In Case 1', Amy would suffer a greater priority-weighted loss in D2 relative to D1, as compared with Case 1. But Amy's greater loss in Case 1' is precisely cancelled out by Bob's greater priority-weighted gain in that case. The greater loss and gain traverse the same segment of the y-axis of Figure 19.1, but in opposite directions.

There is, however, intuitively *stronger* reason to choose D2 over D1 in Case 1 than there is in Case 1'. This stronger reason is grounded, at least among other things, in the fact that the choice of one outcome over the other is *non-rank-switching* in Case 1, whereas it is rank-switching in Case 1', where a *rank-switching* choice is one that makes a difference to who is better off than whom. Other things equal, it is harder for the person who would be better off in D1 to object to a non-rank-switching alternative of D2 than a rank-switching alternative of D2.

Something along the lines of a Pigou-Dalton principle captures this moral distinction, because it favours D2 over D1 in Case 1 but is silent regarding the choice between D2 and D1 in Case 1':

Pigou-Dalton: Other things being equal, an outcome D2 is morally better than an alternative outcome D1 if D2 can be represented as a non-leaky, non-rank-switching transfer of well-being from someone who would be better off in D1, to someone who would be worse off in D1.[50]

Pigou-Dalton is silent regarding the choice between D1 and D2 in Case 1', since there the choice between outcomes is rank-switching. In favouring D2 over D1

---

[50] This is a modified version of Adler's and Holtug's formulation of the principle in 'Prioritarianism', p. 104. A non-leaky transfer is one that does not decrease (and nor does it increase) the sum total of utility. In Adler's and Holtug's and many other formulations of Pigou-Dalton, it is assumed that the less equal distribution D1 is the status quo. In my formulation, this is not assumed. Hence, I speak of being able to 'represent' D2 as a transfer from D1. D2 needn't, however, involve an actual transfer from a D1 status quo.

only in Case 1, Pigou-Dalton violates anonymity, since the D2 outcomes in Case 1 and Case 1′ are anonymously equivalent (and the D1 outcomes are identical).

There is a more redistributive extension of Pigou-Dalton which favours D2 over D1 in Case 1′ as well as Case 1. This version applies to transfers that switch the ranks of individuals as well as those that don't:

> *Pigou-Dalton′*: Other things equal, an outcome D2 is morally better than an alternative outcome D1 if D2 can be represented as a non-leaky transfer of well-being from someone who would be better off in D1, to someone who would be worse off in D1, where this transfer decreases the difference in well-being between the two.

Pigou-Dalton′ endorses one outcome over another whenever the former can be represented as a non-leaky transfer from the latter which reduces the gap between the two parties, even if their ranks are switched. The fact that Pigou-Dalton is less controversial than this more redistributive extension Pigou-Dalton′ indicates the moral relevance of person-tracking features that distinguish anonymously equivalent outcomes. Other things equal, an outcome which can be represented as a non-leaky transfer from another outcome that doesn't also switch the ranks of individuals is easier to justify than one which switches ranks. But whether people switch ranks depends on how particular individuals are ranked in one outcome in comparison with another outcome: that is, it depends on person-tracking considerations.

Here's why a non-leaky transfer that doesn't switch ranks is easier to justify than one that does: in the non-rank-switching (but not the rank-switching) case, the worse off individual who stands to gain from this transfer can press the following complaint against the better off person who objects to the transfer. Taking Case 1 as an illustration, Bob could object as follows to Amy's insistence on D1 over D2: How can you justify D1 over D2 when you would remain better off than me in D2, while D1 would make you better off still, relative to D2, and at my expense? Compare the following argument of Rawls's for the difference principle: 'to regard persons as means is to be prepared to impose on those already less favored still lower prospects of life for the sake of the higher expectations of others.'[51] A comparable complaint against D1 is unavailable in Case 1′, since Amy would not remain better off than Bob in his preferred outcome D2. Rather, there would be a switch in their ranking, and Amy would be considerably worse off than Bob in D2. The presence or absence of the above complaint is a matter of how individuals fare relative to one another. In a manner that is contrary to Parfit's conceptualization and justification of prioritarianism, it matters how the worse off fare in comparison with others who are better off.[52]

---

[51] Rawls, *Theory of Justice*, rev. ed., p. 157.
[52] For further discussion of this point, including an explanation of the manner in which this sort of complaint involves an appeal to interpersonally comparative considerations that Parfit eschews, see Otsuka and Voorhoeve, 'Why it Matters', esp. pp. 183–4.

19.4.3 Saving the Greater Number Cases

Prioritarianism is also embarrassed when applied to cases involving saving the greater rather than the lesser number of lives, of the sort Elizabeth Anscombe and John Taurek have made famous.[53] It is insensitive to the moral difference between Case 2 and Case 2* in Figures 19.6 and 19.7 respectively, in each case of which one must choose between saving a greater or lesser number of people from death (where death = 0 and life = 100).

Case 2	D1	D2
Amy	100	100
Bob	0	100
Cathy	0	0

Figure 19.6 Case 2.

Case 2*	D1	D2
Amy	100	0
Bob	0	100
Cathy	0	100

Figure 19.7 Case 2*.

In both of these cases, if one does nothing, everyone will die. At no cost to oneself, one can, however, save either one person by choosing D1, or two people by choosing D2. The fact that one would save two lives rather than one provides strong reason to choose D2 in both cases. In Case 2*, however, people's claims to be saved are in competition with one another. In Case 2, they are not, since here saving two is not at anyone's expense. In Case 2, the Principle of Personal Good therefore provides additional reason to choose D2 which is lacking in Case 2*. Recall that this principle favours an outcome in which at least one person gains and nobody loses, relative to another outcome. In Case 2 alone, D2 is better for at least one person and worse for none than D1. The Principle of Personal Good therefore grounds the intuition that one has stronger reason to choose D2 over D1 in Case 2 than in Case 2*.[54] But, since D2 in Case 2 is anonymously equivalent to D2 in Case 2*, prioritarianism fails to register the stronger reason one has to

---

[53] See Anscombe, 'Who Is Wronged?', and Taurek, 'Should the Numbers Count?'.
[54] See section II of Otsuka, 'Skepticism about Saving the Greater Number', for further relevant discussion of the moral difference between Case 2 and Case 2*.

choose D2 in Case 2. It is insensitive to the virtue of nobody losing out, with at least one person gaining, relative to an alternative. More generally, prioritarianism is insensitive to the presence or absence of competing claims.[55]

In this section, I have presented a number of Same People Cases, which reveal that the moral significance of gains and losses to individuals is not exhausted by the sum total of priority weighted gains and losses. Prioritarianism therefore fails to live up to Parfit's ambition to provide a complete account of distributive ethics. It fails to provide such an account even within the limited domain of Same People Cases, outside of any quarantine that might apply to Same Number and Different Number Cases. In order to complete such an account, one must acknowledge the moral significance of the competing claims and complaints of individuals, in a manner that takes us farther from consequentialism than Parfit was willing to venture.[56] It turns out that we are not all climbing the very same mountain.[57]

References

Adler, M., and Holtug, N., 'Prioritarianism: A Response to Critics', in *Politics, Philosophy and Economics* 18/2 (2019): 101–44.

Anscombe, G. E. M., 'Who Is Wronged? Philippa Foot on Double Effect', in *The Oxford Review* no. 5 (1967): 16–17.

Bentham, J., 'Essai sur la représentation', in E. Halévy, *La formation du radicalisme philosophique*, vol. 1, *La jeunesse de Bentham* (Félix Alcan, 1901 [1789]).

Broome, J., *Weighing Goods* (Blackwell, 2004).

Brown, C., 'Anonymity and Moral Equality', unpublished (2018). http://personal.lse.ac.uk/browncf/anonymity.pdf

Crisp, R., 'Ethics and International Environmental Law', in S. Besson and J. Tasioulas (eds.), *The Philosophy of International Law* (Oxford University Press, 2010), 473–90.

---

[55] See Otsuka, 'Prioritarianism and the Separateness of Persons'.

[56] In this chapter, I have discussed only cases in which one is certain of the outcomes of one's choices. In various articles in which we discuss cases of choice under risk, Alex Voorhoeve and I have developed a line of criticism of Parfit's prioritarianism which is of a piece with the critique I have been pressing here. In that work, we argue that prioritarian weighting of gains and losses is not justified in Same People Cases involving perfectly correlated risks but neither competing claims nor inequality. In such cases—where one must choose between benefitting everyone if they turn out equally badly off and benefitting everyone if they turn out equally well off—there is no reason to give extra weight to benefitting people should they turn out badly off. Here one ought to maximize expected utility rather than priority weighted utility. I spell out the case for maximizing expected utility in 'Prioritarianism and the Measure of Utility'. See also Otsuka and Voorhoeve, 'Why it Matters', Otsuka, 'Prioritarianism and the Separateness of Persons', and Otsuka and Voorhoeve, 'Equality versus Priority'.

[57] Here I allude to some remarks of Parfit's in the concluding paragraphs of the first volume of *On What Matters*:

> [Moral] disagreements are deepest when we are considering, not the wrongness of particular acts, but the nature of morality and moral reasoning, and what is implied by different views about these questions... It has been widely believed that there are such deep disagreements between Kantians, Contractualists, and Consequentialists. That, I have argued, is not true. These people are climbing the same mountain on different sides. (*On What Matters*, vol. 1, pp. 418–19)

Holtug, N., *Persons, Interests, and Justice* (Oxford University Press, 2010).

Kamm, F., *Morality, Mortality: Death, and Whom to Save from It*, vol. 1 (Oxford University Press, 1993).

Mack, M., *Jeremy Bentham: An Odyssey of Ideas 1748–1792* (Heinemann, 1962).

Mill, J. S., *Utilitarianism* (Hackett, 1979 [1861]).

Nebel, J., 'Priority, Not Equality, for Possible People', in *Ethics* 127/4 (2017): 896–911.

Otsuka, M., 'Skepticism about Saving the Greater Number', in *Philosophy and Public Affairs* 32/4 (2004): 413–26.

Otsuka, M., 'Prioritarianism and the Separateness of Persons', in *Utilitas* 24/3 (2012): 365–80.

Otsuka, M., 'Prioritarianism and the Measure of Utility', in *Journal of Political Philosophy* 23/1 (2015): 1–22.

Otsuka, M., 'How it Makes a Moral Difference that One Is Worse Off than One Could Have Been', in *Politics, Philosophy and Economics* 17/2 (2018): 192–215.

Otsuka, M., and Voorhoeve, A., 'Why it Matters that Some Are Worse Off than Others: An Argument against the Priority View', in *Philosophy and Public Affairs* 37/2 (2009): 171–99.

Otsuka, M., and Voorhoeve, A., 'Equality versus Priority', in Serena Olsaretti (ed.), *Oxford Handbook of Distributive Justice* (Oxford University Press, 2018), 65–85.

Parfit, D., *Reasons and Persons* (Oxford University Press, 1986).

Parfit, D., *Equality or Priority? The Lindley Lecture* (University of Kansas, 1991).

Parfit, D., 'Postscript', in J. Ryberg and T. Tännsjö (eds.), *The Repugnant Conclusion: Essays on Population Ethics* (Kluwer, 2004), 257.

Parfit, D., *On What Matters*, 2 vols. (Oxford University Press, 2011).

Parfit, D., 'Another Defence of the Priority View', in *Utilitas* 24/3 (2012): 399–440.

Parfit, D., 'Can We Avoid the Repugnant Conclusion?', in *Theoria* 82/2 (2016): 110–27.

Parfit, D., 'Future People, the Non-Identity Problem, and Person-Affecting Principles', in *Philosophy and Public Affairs* 45/2 (2017): 118–57.

Persson, I., 'Why Levelling Down Could Be Worse for Prioritarianism than for Egalitarianism', in *Ethical Theory and Moral Practice* 11/3 (2008): 295–303.

Porter, T., 'Prioritarianism and the Levelling Down Objection', in *Ethical Theory and Moral Practice* 14/2: (2011): 197–206.

Rawls, J., *A Theory of Justice*, rev. ed. (Harvard University Press, 1999).

Taurek, J., 'Should the Numbers Count?', *Philosophy and Public Affairs* 6/4 (1977): 293–316.

Temkin, L., 'Equality, Priority, and the Levelling Down Objection', in M. Clayton and A. Williams (eds.), *The Ideal of Equality* (Palgrave, 2002), 126–61.

Temkin, L., *Rethinking the Good* (Oxford University Press, 2012).

Voorhoeve, A., 'How Should We Aggregate Competing Claims?', in *Ethics* 125/1 (2014): 64–87.

20
Quarantined Prioritarianism

Shlomi Segall

It has long been noted that the priority view generates counterintuitive recommendations when applied to future generations.[1] In this, it is hardly unique among distributive views. Prioritarians have sought several strategies for avoiding some of these difficulties, but here I am going to focus on one, the strategy known as *quarantining*. Derek Parfit's very last published words on prioritarianism (his 2012 *Utilitas* article) read: 'the prioritarian principles that I have considered cannot be applied to cases in which, in the different possible outcomes, different people would exist. When we consider these cases, we need other principles'.[2]

My task in this chapter is to answer the following question: how ought we to understand the phrase '*different people*' in this quotation from Parfit. I don't mean this question or the chapter as a whole to be an exegesis of Parfit's intention (although I will say something about that as well in the course of my discussion). Rather, it is to investigate what it is that prioritarians ought to believe about future generations, that will inevitably involve Mixed Populations. By 'Mixed Populations' I mean two or more alternative populations where at least some of the people are of different identity, whether or not these populations are of the same size. My conclusion could be summarized as a *conditional, limited* quarantined prioritarianism. More specifically, I will try to defend the following four related claims:

1. It is far from obvious that prioritarianism ought to be quarantined *in the first place*
2. *If* prioritarianism is (for whatever reason) to be quarantined, then that ought to take place *only* with regard to Different Number Choices

I am grateful to Matt Adler, Gustaf Arrhenius, Iwao Hirose, Nils Holtug, Gerald Lang, Jeff McMahan, and Mike Otsuka for extensive written comments on a draft of this chapter.

[1] Gustaf Arrhenius, 'Egalitarianism and Population Change', in Axel Gosseries and Lukas Meyer (eds.) *Intergenerational Justice* (Oxford: Oxford University Press, 2009), p. 337; Nils Holtug, *Persons, Interests, and Justice* (Oxford: Oxford University Press, 2010), p. 246; Matthew Adler, 'Future Generations: A Prioritarian View', *George Washington Law Review* 77 (2009), p. 1508; Michael Otsuka, 'Prioritarianism, Population Ethics, and Competing Claims', Chapter 19, this volume, p. 8; Ingmar Persson, 'Prioritarianism and Welfare Reductions', *Journal of Applied Philosophy* 29 (2012), esp. p. 298.

[2] Derek Parfit, 'Another Defence of the Priority View', *Utilitas* 24 (2012), p. 440.

3. Doing so:
   a. does *not* entail a person-tracking version of prioritarianism, that is, a version that respects the 'Separateness of Persons' (SOP), and
   b. is in line with other tenets of Parfit's population ethics that we have good reasons to endorse (The No Difference View, and Non-Existence as No Welfare rather than Zero Welfare)
4. But, to avoid some problematic implications in Mixed Population cases, prioritarianism does require a minor yet important revision to the way we standardly understand it

It would be useful first to fix some concepts, starting with the priority view itself. I understand *the priority view*, roughly (the sections below discuss the merits of several more formal definitions), as the view that benefitting someone matters more the worse off that person is. *Axiological prioritarianism*, in turn, is the view that the value of a population is an aggregate of the value of each person's wellbeing, where that value is represented by an increasing but concave function of how well off, absolutely speaking, she is. By *Same People Choices* I refer to two or more populations where all and only those who exist in one exist also in the other(s). In other words, in comparing two or more alternative scenarios, all the populations consist of the same people. *Non-Fixed populations*, in turn, are two or more populations where some people that exist in one do not exist in the other, whether these are populations of same number of individuals, or not. *Different Numbers Choices* refers to comparing populations that have different numbers of individuals, some of whom may exist in more than one population. *Same Number Choices* refers to populations that have the same number of members, where some or all the members comprising them are different. By *Quarantined Prioritarianism* I shall mean the view that at least in some cases of non-fixed population prioritarianism gives way to some other principle(s).

My argument unfolds as follows. I first explore why it is generally assumed, including by Parfit, that prioritarianism does not handle Non-Fixed Populations very well. This is illustrated by what is known as the Super Repugnant Conclusion to prioritarianism. Before we fall under the spell of that objection, I maintain, it would be useful to observe that the quarantining approach comes at a certain cost. In particular, it may involve a rather painful concession on the part of Parfitian prioritarianism, namely sacrificing its alleged 'completeness' (section 20.1). More generally, I show that the case for quarantining prioritarianism is not decisive (section 20.2). However, in so far as we do, for some reason, opt to quarantine prioritarianism we would do well to restrict it from, and *only* from, Different Number Choices and not also from Same Number Choices (section 20.3). An explicit statement by Parfit about our lack of prioritarian reasons to have children is *no* reason (contra Michael Otsuka) to quarantine prioritarianism also from Same Number Choices (section 20.4). But prioritarianism as standardly defined, does face another serious problem in Same Number Choices stemming from the way it is standardly defined (for example, by leading prioritarian Nils Holtug). Fortunately, that problem can be avoided by a minor yet important revision to the way we standardly understand prioritarianism (section 20.5).

20.1 Quarantining and Its Costs

The priority view says that benefiting individuals matters more, the worse off, in absolute terms, these individuals are. It has been noted that this view encounters difficulties when applied to future generations, especially of variable sizes. To see this, consider the familiar example in Figure 20.1.

Suppose that A and Z contain the same aggregate utility. Utilitarianism, of course, would be indifferent between the two, which results in the notorious Repugnant Conclusion. Yet, it has been noted that prioritarianism does even worse here. According to prioritarianism Z might be the preferable option even when A contains *more* aggregate utility.[3] And that is, of course, because the utility in Z occurs at a lower absolute level. Thus the aggregate *weighted* utility in Z could well be greater than that in A. Prioritarianism, therefore, appears to do *worse* than utilitarianism with respect to future generations, and in particular in cases involving populations of variable sizes.

Given this *Super* Repugnant Conclusion that is assumed to be implied by prioritarianism it is not surprising that, towards the end of his life, Parfit was drawn to the conclusion that the priority view ought to be restricted (henceforth 'quarantined') from applying to such cases. I begin my inquiry by showing, in this section, that whatever the circumstances and shape of quarantining, for prioritarians to embark on this strategy comes at a certain cost. This cost, in my view, is *not* a decisive reason against quarantining. Nevertheless, it should be enough to give prioritarians at least some pause. I will then consider two objections.

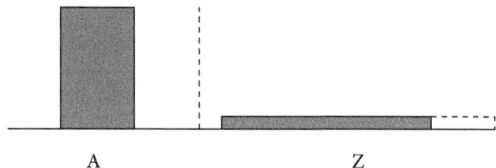

Figure 20.1 The Repugnant Conclusion.

---

[3] Ingmar Persson, 'Equality, Priority, and Person-Affecting Value', *Ethical Theory & Moral Practice* 4 (2001), pp. 33–4; 'Prioritarianism and Welfare Reductions', esp. p. 298; Arrhenius, 'Egalitarianism and Population Change', p. 337; Holtug, *Persons, Interests, and Justice*, p. 246; Adler, 'Future Generations, p. 1508; Otsuka, Chapter 19, this volume, p. 533.

In his 'Equality and Priority' paper Parfit has made the following point about the two rival views to prioritarianism, namely egalitarianism and utilitarianism. He observed that in their *pure* form, both these views are rather implausible. Utilitarianism would, famously, be indifferent between an additional utile to a worse off individual (say, a homeless person) and the same utility-sized benefit to an extremely wealthy individual (say, Donald Trump). Many people find this implausible, to say the least. To avoid such embarrassing implications utilitarians might want to consider endorsing value pluralism, and perhaps incorporate, minimally, a certain concern for equality, say in the shape of a Pigou-Dalton condition. (Pigou-Dalton is the condition that says that fixed transfers, that is, without waste, between fixed individuals, from a better off to a worse off person, always make an outcome better.) Utilitarianism would thus greatly benefit from value pluralism. The same applies for 'pure egalitarianism'. Pure egalitarianism is the view that 'it is in itself bad if some people are worse off than others'.[4] Understood this way, the view would be indifferent between perfect equality at some level of welfare (for example, 200, 200) and an equality that occurs at a lower level of welfare (for example, 100, 100). To avert that embarrassing conclusion, most egalitarians, Parfit speculated, would endorse a pluralist version of egalitarianism, whereby one would care about both equality *and* utility. Furthermore, when the choices are just equality and utility, it would be correct to go for a pluralist view combining the two.[5] So far so good.

In contrast to its two rivals, the priority view, Parfit said, was 'complete'. It need not be coupled with any other:

> How does this view differ from an egalitarian view? One difference is purely structural. As we have seen, equality cannot plausibly be our only value. If we are egalitarians, we must hold some more complicated view. [...] The Priority View in contrast, can be held as a *complete moral view*. [...] Unlike the Principle of Equality, which might be combined with the Principle of Utility, the Priority View can replace that principle. It can be regarded as the only principle we need.[6]

That was then. But if to take the quotation at the top of this chapter seriously, it now appears that later in his life Parfit no longer thought that that was the case. 'We need other principles' is an admission that just like its two main rivals, prioritarianism must resort to some pluralism of value. Some putative axiological 'completeness' can no longer be counted as a reason to prefer prioritarianism to its traditional rivals. Whichever way exactly Parfit is quarantining

---

[4] Derek Parfit, 'Equality and Priority', *Ratio* 10 (1997), p. 204.
[5] Parfit, 'Equality and Priority', p. 205.
[6] Derek Parfit, 'Equality and Priority?' *The Lindley Lecture* (Lawrence, Kansas: University of Kansas, 1991), p. 22. See also Otsuka's brief discussion of a similar point (Chapter 19, this volume, p. 543).

prioritarianism, this late-day move of his comes at a price of relinquishing an important advantage it was thought to have held over egalitarianism (and utilitarianism).

Let me consider two objections to what I have just said. It could be argued that a more careful reading of Parfit's comment would reveal that his later position is still consistent with prioritarianism being complete. And that could be so for at least two reasons. First, it could be suggested that the phrase 'the prioritarian principles that I have considered' does not in fact refer to the standard priority view. If so, it may follow that the quarantine strategy does not, to begin with, affect standard prioritarianism. Second, it could be that when Parfit says 'we need *other principles*', he in fact means other *prioritarian* principles. Either of the points, if true, would imply that prioritarianism's alleged completeness is uncompromised, after all.

The first objection centers on the phrase 'the prioritarian principles that I have considered'. In some Non-Fixed Population cases, Parfit seems to be saying, we need to quarantine prioritarianism and appeal to other principles. But what is it exactly that ought to be quarantined in the first place? My working assumption has been that it is the very standard priority view itself. Parfit's exact words, however, may reveal a certain complexity here. The quotation concerns 'the prioritarian principles that I have considered'. Presumably, since this is the sentence that closes a forty-odd page paper, the reference is to the prioritarian principles he has been considering *in that paper*. Some have inferred from this that Parfit meant to quarantine only *probabilistic* views about prioritarianism since the main preoccupation of that paper was how the priority view behaves under circumstances of uncertainty.[7] If this is correct, then we shouldn't take Parfit to mean that the priority view, pure and simple, ought to be quarantined. Again, it would follow that the priority view is complete after all.

Let me say three things in reply. First, it is true that the most interesting and revisionary bits of that *Utilitas* paper concern the way in which prioritarianism behaves under uncertainty, and Parfit's response to that challenge in the shape of his endorsement of what came to be known as *hybrid prioritarianism*. At the same time, less subsequent attention has been accorded (and probably rightly so) to the first part of the paper that deals with the levelling down objection and how prioritarianism and egalitarianism compare with regard to it. Indeed, the first time prioritarianism is mentioned in that paper it is introduced as the standard priority view, with no reference to or dependence on uncertainty.[8] So while it is true that the majority of that paper concerns prioritarianism under uncertainty, the paper is not structured (nor titled) as one about *probabilistic* prioritarianism exclusively. Second, notice that Parfit uses the plural so presumably the reference

---

[7] Gustaf Arrhenius, private communication, 28 July 2019.   [8] Parfit, 'Another Defence', p. 401.

is to the standard version of the priority view ('we have reason to benefit people more the worse off they are') *and* the revised version that is meant to improve on it ('we have reasons to benefit people more the more *expectedly* worse off they are'). If anything, then, I would take Parfit to be referring here, at the very least, *also* to the standard, *factualist* version of prioritarianism. (Factualist prioritarianism would be a formulation of the priority view that assigns value only to outcomes that are certain).[9] Third, would it make any difference to the question of quarantining if Parfit did refer exclusively to probabilistic principles? The answer is not at all, I think. And that is so for the simple reason that as we have already glimpsed most, if not all, of the challenging cases in this debate do not necessitate a measure of uncertainty. Just think of the Repugnant Conclusion; nothing in that example hinges on uncertainty. We can therefore safely assume that when speaking of the need to quarantine prioritarianism Parfit was not making any special assumptions about probabilistic as opposed to factualist principles (or in Parfit's terminology, evidence-relative prioritarianism as opposed to fact-relative prioritarianism).

On the second objection, Parfit intends quarantining to imply 'other *prioritarian* principles', thereby not sacrificing prioritarianism's completeness. Assessing the strength of this objection is complicated by the difficulty in speculating as to what Parfit may have meant by 'other principles'. We might do well to look beyond Parfit for a clue here. Gustaf Arrhenius, for example, has also (and even earlier than Parfit) made a case for quarantining prioritarianism. Arrhenius writes that 'it seems that the priority view is an idea mainly about how to distribute welfare among a fixed number of people'. Interestingly, Arrhenius adds 'the main work in different number cases will be done by the *aggregation* method, not by the Priority view'.[10] This version of quarantining (assuming for a moment it counts as quarantining), then, transforms the standard priority principle into *another* version of prioritarianism by attaching to it a different aggregation mechanism.[11] Prioritarians can still handle Different Number Choices, simply by adjusting the aggregation method they use. Prioritarianism is complete, after all.

In reply I want to first quickly concede that, on the face of it, this is a plausible interpretation of Parfit. Indeed, there is some evidence to suggest that Parfit does indeed mean 'other *prioritarian* principles' (more on which in the next section). So *if* it is indeed the case that 'other principles' means 'other *prioritarian* principles' then I am happy to withdraw the claim made earlier in this section. That is,

---

[9] More on factualist prioritarianism, see Nils Holtug, 'Prioritarianism: Ex Ante, Ex Post, or Factualist Criterion of Rightness?' *Journal of Political Philosophy* 27 (2019), 207–28.
[10] Arrhenius, 'Egalitarianism and Population Change', p. 339, emphasis added.
[11] This in fact ties in nicely with another claim made by Arrhenius about Parfit's prioritarianism. Namely, he observes that unlike other definitions of prioritarianism that conceive of it exclusively as a *total aggregate* view (for example, Nils Holtug's, more on which in the final section), Parfit himself never commits to total prioritarianism. Instead, he (Parfit) always phrased the priority view as having to do with 'reasons to benefit', or 'the weight of a single benefit'. He thereby never committed to one method of aggregation over another.

I concede, quarantining would not thereby amount to prioritarianism being 'incomplete' (the way egalitarianism and utilitarianism are). However, that is, indeed, a big 'if', and I now want to explain why.

Accepting Arrhenius's interpretation (that Non-Fixed Populations call for other *prioritarian* principles) would necessitate inquiry into the nature of these 'other prioritarian principles'. In particular, we would need to know how, on the one hand, they differ from the standard view (so that they would deliver it from the Super Repugnant Conclusion, for example), and what, on the other hand, still qualifies them as versions of the Priority view. This might be trickier than Arrhenius's brief comment betrays. Indeed, Parfit never commits himself to a particular method of aggregation, one that could deliver prioritarianism from the problems brought on by Non-Fixed Populations. And with good reason, I now want to quickly suggest. Total aggregated prioritarianism, we said, would be vulnerable to the Super Repugnant Conclusion. But *average* prioritarianism would be hardly an improvement, as Arrhenius himself would be the first to admit, I think. Average prioritarianism is the view that the value of a population is a function, increasing but concave, of the wellbeing of the average person. Now consider Figure 20.2.

Notice that this is a Different Number Choice. And here Average Prioritarianism may well prefer Y to X. The average utility in Y, we may suppose, is higher than that in X. And consequently the prioritarian value (of that average utility) is higher in Y than in X. If so, it follows that Quarantined Average Prioritarianism can escape the Super Repugnant Conclusion only by means of encountering a Sadistic Conclusion, which is hardly an improvement (indeed, as I hope to show in the next section, it is much worse). (A Sadistic Conclusion, briefly, is the preference for adding to a population a sub-population of individuals

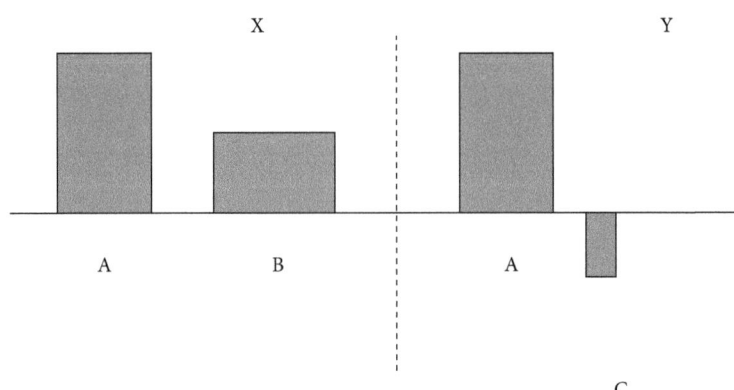

Figure 20.2 The Sadistic Conclusion.

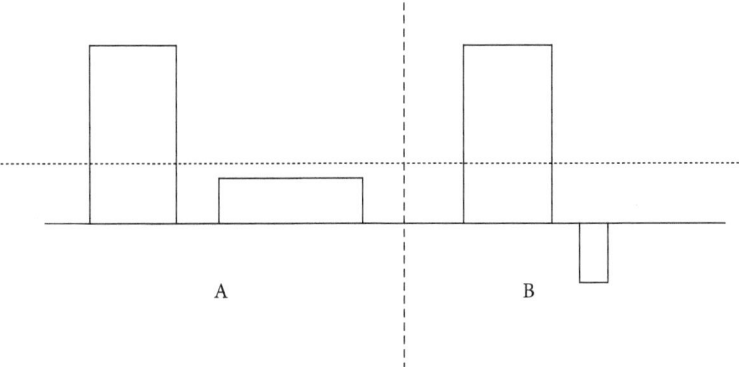

Figure 20.3 Critical Level Prioritarianism.

with lives that are worth not living, over adding a sub-population of individuals all of whom have lives that are worth living).[12]

As others have already observed,[13] introducing Critical-Level Prioritarianism would also not help (Figure 20.3).

If the below-critical-level subpopulation in A is large enough, Critical Level Prioritarianism may well deem B as better than A, and thus again yield a Sadistic Conclusion.

Summing, averaging, or limiting to Critical-Level, all would not deliver prioritarianism from difficulties encountered in Mixed Population cases. This does not mean that there isn't yet some method of aggregation that could save prioritarianism. But as Arrhenius's own work has shown, it is not obvious that such a method could be found.[14] In sum, I do not deny that quarantined prioritarianism could yet be standard prioritarianism fixed with a bayonet of some interesting aggregation method. But I do hope to have shown that there is still a large question mark over what 'other *prioritarian* principles' could do the trick.

20.2 Ought Prioritarianism Be Quarantined?

For prioritarians, quarantining comes with a price tag. For in so doing prioritarians would have to relinquish one of its characteristics (its alleged completeness) flagged by Parfit himself as one of the key advantages over its two rivals. Sacrificing completeness, I want to stress, is not a decisive reason against adopting it. In this section, I want to look more closely at weightier reasons for and against

---

[12] On the Sadistic Conclusion, see Gustaf Arrhenius, 'An Impossibility Theorem for Welfarist Axiologies', *Economics & Philosophy* 16 (2000), 247–66.
[13] For just one example, see Hillary Greaves, 'Population Axiology', *Philosophical Compass* (2017), 7.
[14] Arrhenius, 'An Impossibility Theorem for Welfarist Axiologies'.

quarantining. Ultimately I want to say that, despite the opening passage from Parfit, it is far from obvious that prioritarianism ought to be quarantined in the first place.

I want to begin by noting that there *is* a case for quarantining, and that it goes beyond the Super Repugnant Conclusion that we have already encountered. Consider the following example.[15] Suppose that level 100 represents a fantastic life, say the kind of life led by Bob Dylan (tons of creative accomplishment, and no material worries or health-related concerns). And suppose that level 1 is a life worth living, but only just. It is the kind of life led by Ukranian farm-wives in the 1950's, let us suppose. Life at level 0 is neither good nor bad. Now consider Figure 20.4.

In A one person exists at 100 and 99 individuals exist at level 0. In B a hundred individuals exist at level 1. A and B therefore contain the same number of individuals and the same aggregate utility. Because the two outcomes contain the same aggregate utility, and given that in B this utility is more evenly spread, standard (non-quarantined) prioritarianism favours B over A. That strikes many as the correct result.

But now compare with Figure 20.5, where in A one person exists at level 100, and in B 100 individuals exist at level 1.

Here many people (including Parfit) have the opposite intuition to Figure 20.4. That is, they think that here A is better than B. But standard, non-quarantined prioritarianism ought to favour B over A. That is because both outcomes contain the same amount of aggregate utility, but in B that utility occurs at lower absolute levels. But if prioritarianism does not apply to Different Number Choices, this allegedly unpalatable conclusion is avoided. Quarantining, arguably, makes sense.

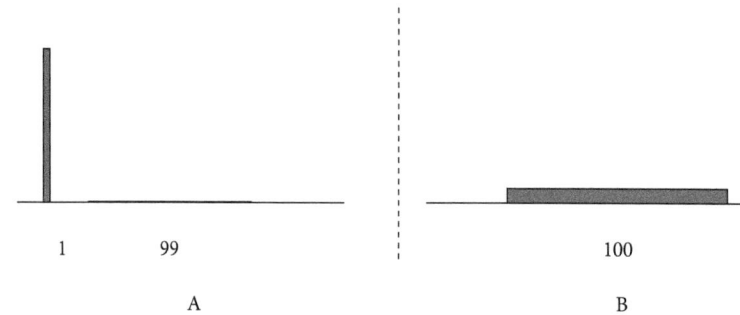

Figure 20.4 Welfare dispersal (fixed numbers).

---

[15] Adapted from Persson, 'Prioritarianism and Welfare Reductions', pp. 292–3.

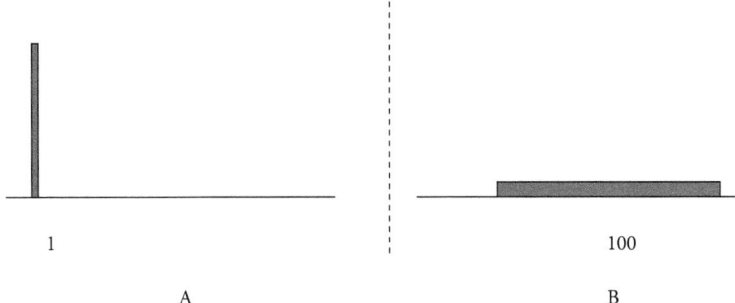

Figure 20.5 Welfare dispersal (non-fixed population).

The difference between Figures 20.4 and 20.5 illustrates what many people take to be the allure of quarantining. Standard prioritarianism delivers correct results in Fixed Number Choices, but not in Non-Fixed Number Choices.

Quarantining it in its application to Non-Fixed Populations cases helps prioritarianism avoid unpalatable implications. This simple example not only helps strengthen the case for quarantining, but it also helps us see that if, like Parfit, you found Figure 20.5 to be problematic for prioritarianism, quarantining it in its application to *Non-Fixed Populations* cases makes sense. It may be useful to say a little bit more about *why* that is. Now, one reason why you might think that 'dispersing welfare' (for example, a preference for B over A) is attractive in Figure 20.4 but repugnant in Figure 20.5 is due to a concern for equality. Equality gives us a reason to favour B in Figure 20.4 but is indifferent in Figure 20.5. But of course we can set this reason aside, as this is not the sort of consideration that prioritarians like Parfit can (or wish to) appeal to. Another reason for a shift in verdicts between Figures 20.4 and 20.5 is an anti-utilitarian reasoning about an asymmetry between actual and possible persons. We ought to care about improving the wellbeing of already existing people, not about creating new people. This again would yield the favoured result that B is better than A in Figure 20.4 but not in Figure 20.5. However, that reasoning, also, cannot be true for Parfit, as he is explicitly committed to *The No Difference View*. The No Difference View says that if some people are less well off, it makes no difference whether they are less well off than *they* themselves could have been, or less well off than *different people* might have been, if they had existed instead. An important implication for prioritarianism is that, according to the No Difference View, we should benefit the many rather than the few (given a fixed amount of utility), and the fact that the former are people who would otherwise never have existed makes no difference.[16] A preference for benefitting existing, rather than possible, people

---

[16] See for example, Derek Parfit, 'Future People, the Non-Identity Problem, and Person-Affecting Principles', *Philosophy & Public Affairs* 45 (2017), p. 123; *On What Matters* (Vol. 2) (Oxford: Oxford University Press, 2011), p. 219.

cannot therefore be the reasoning behind quarantining prioritarianism from applying to Different Numbers cases. A third reason that might come to mind (why quarantining is necessary in Figure 20.5 but not in Figure 20.4) is this. We have an intuition that it is important to improve the lives of existing people, but that we should not bring people into existence whose lives are going to be at the neutral (0) level. That would explain our preference for B in Figure 20.4, and our preference for A in Figure 20.5. Unlike the previous two replies, this intuition does seem like one that Parfit would endorse. However, here the problem is that it does not explain why such a preference (or a shift in our intuition) attaches to prioritarianism of all things. The intuition explains why we prefer dispersing welfare in fixed numbers cases, and against dispersing it in Non-Fixed Numbers cases. But it does not explain what all this has to do with prioritarianism, of all things.

All three of these reasons, then, cannot explain Parfit's opting to apply prioritarianism in Figure 20.4 but not in Figure 20.5. Instead, what seems to motivate prioritarians like Parfit in quarantining their view from Different Number Choices is something else, I think. Namely, I speculate that all Parfit wanted was to prevent prioritarianism from giving us *additional* reasons to have children.[17] That is why prioritarianism applies in Figure 20.4 but not in Figure 20.5. Now, you might ask, why should anyone think, to begin with, that prioritarianism might give us reasons to cause anyone to exist? After all, prioritarianism is, just like its rival egalitarianism, a view about the value of distributions. It was never meant to provide reasons to cause people to exist.[18] To answer this is to enter into a speculative discussion about the inception of prioritarianism. But for what it is worth, recall that Parfit thought of the priority view not only as an alternative to egalitarianism, but also as an alternative (be it a rival view, or a supplement) to *utilitarianism*. Utilitarianism, to state the obvious, is a view about the value of distributions, but one that also gives us reasons to cause people to exist. If it hadn't, we (Parfit included of course) would not have had to contend with the Repugnant Conclusion. Although the case is not as well known, some have suggested that the same is true also for egalitarianism. That is, some egalitarians have recently suggested that a certain (otherwise attractive) understanding of egalitarianism also gives us reasons to cause people to exist (say, when you can generate many more relations of equality by causing more people to exist).[19] I don't happen to find this version of egalitarianism to be attractive, but that

---

[17] Simon Beard advances a similar claim in his 'Parfit's Theory X and the Evaluation of Global Challenges', Unpublished.
[18] I am grateful to Jeff McMahan for pressing me on this.
[19] Gustaf Arrhenius, 'Egalitarian Concerns and Population Change', in Nir Eyal, Samia A Hurst, Ole F. Norheim, and Daniel Wikler (eds.), *Inequalities in Health: Concepts, Measures, and Ethics* (Oxford: Oxford University Press, 2013); cf. Shlomi Segall, 'Why We Should Be Negative about Positive Egalitarianism', *Utilitas* 31 (2019), 414–30.

is not the issue. The point is that all three distributional views—utility, priority, equality—may (*prima facie*) also entail reasons to cause people to exist.

I therefore speculate that Parfit endorsed the quarantine approach because and only because he wanted to prevent prioritarianism from giving us additional reasons to cause people to exist. We may suspend judgement on that speculation for now, but if I am right, here is a catchy way of capturing that sentiment. We might draw a parallel with Narveson's famous quip about what makes the Repugnant Conclusion (and utilitarianism in general) repugnant. 'We have reasons to make people happy, not to make happy people'.[20] If I am right, we could paraphrase Parfit as holding a somewhat similar sentiment: *On the priority view we have stronger reasons to benefit people the worse off they are; we do not have reasons to benefit people by merely giving them the benefit of existence.*

Up to now I canvassed the case for quarantining prioritarianism from Non-Fixed Populations (at least Different Number Choices), and speculated about the motivation behind it. One lesson that follows is that *if* prioritarianism is to be quarantined then, *at the very least*, this should be with regard to Different Number Choices. (As the cases discussed just now illustrate.) In the rest of this section, I want to explain why that statement is phrased as a conditional. In other words, I want to make the case for scepticism about the whole quarantining strategy. Here are two points to that effect.

First, with respect to the Repugnant Conclusion it is far from obvious that prioritarianism does *worse* than utilitarianism (with regard to Non-Fixed Populations).[21] In fact, as Nils Holtug has shown, prioritarianism might actually do better. Consider what is known as the Negative Repugnant Conclusion (Figure 20.6).[22]

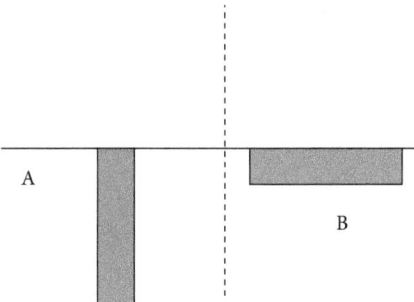

Figure 20.6 The Negative Repugnant Conclusion.

---

[20] Jan Narveson, 'Moral Problems of Population', *Monist* 57 (1973), p. 80. See also his 'Utilitarianism and New Generations', *Mind* 76 (1967), 62–72.

[21] Note that even the repugnant conclusion to utilitarianism is no longer considered unassailable. For a couple of examples, see Michael Huemer, 'In Defence of Repugnance', *Mind* 117 (2008), 899–933; Torbjorn Tannsjo, 'Why We Ought to Accept the Repugnant Conclusion', *Utilitas* 14 (2002), 339–59.

[22] Holtug, *Persons, Interests, and Justice*, pp. 256–7.

Suppose that A and B contain the same aggregate utility. Utilitarians would be of course indifferent here. But in this case it is plausible (although not necessary, I concede) to think that B is actually the less bad outcome. Prioritarianism (standard, un-quarantined) captures this, in that it favours B.[23] While the aggregate utility is the same, in B at occurs at a much higher level, so the prioritarian value of the distribution is higher. Indeed, it would take adding many more additional people with lives that are barely not worth living, in order to make B the worse outcome, on prioritarianism (whereas on utilitarianism the addition of just one more life barely not worth living would make B the worse outcome). Prioritarianism does better than utilitarianism. It is, in short, not settled that, overall, prioritarianism does worse than utilitarianism when it comes to Non-Fixed Populations. And if so, it is not obvious that prioritarianism should be quarantined in such cases, especially when quarantining implies resorting to an alternative which does not perform better (total utilitarianism). Of course, those who wish to quarantine prioritarianism are not compelled to endorse total utilitarianism in its stead, and the search for Theory X could still be on. But the point remains that our haste to abandon standard prioritarianism due to Different Number Choices ought to be tempered so long as there is no clear alternative that performs better. Different Numbers cases are difficult, but they are difficult for everyone.[24]

Here is my second point about why it is not obvious that prioritarianism ought to be quarantined in the first place. And it alludes to something Parfit himself has written. There is a suggestion in one of Parfit's unpublished papers that prioritarianism may after all yield the correct results in Different Number Choices. I offer this second point with a grain of salt as it relies on an unpublished draft by Parfit. I refer to a 2016 predecessor to what in all likelihood became his posthumous 2017 *Philosophy & Public Affairs* paper. The published version contains no reference to the Priority view, but it seems that the drafts leading to it did. There the following discussion appears:

Suppose instead that the possible outcomes are these:

A: Tom's total will be 100   Dick's total will be minus 100

C: Tom and Dick will never exist

[...] Most of us would believe that A would be worse than C. [...] In defending our belief that A would be worse than C, we could not appeal to the simplest version of the Priority View. We could not claim that C would give a benefit to Dick who would otherwise be very badly off. C could not benefit someone who

---

[23] Holtug, *Persons, Interests, and Justice*, pp. 256–7.

[24] One is reminded of Abraham Lincoln's response to one of his generals, very early in the Civil War, who complained that his soldiers are not ready to fight yet. 'You are green it is true. But they are also green. You are all green alike'.

will never exist. [...] We could appeal, however, to another version of the Priority View. We could claim that

(J) the badness of someone's being existentially harmed is greater than the goodness of someone's receiving an equally great existential benefit.[25]

Whatever you might think of the application of 'the simplest version of the Priority view' (more on which in section 20.5), Parfit here seems to affirm three important lessons for us. He holds that: (J) *is* a version of the priority view; it is one that *can* be applied to Different Number Choices (such as the comparison of A with C); and it yields a result that strikes us as the correct one (favouring C). This is indication that *after* the 2012 Utilitas paper Parfit held that a certain version of the priority view *could* apply successfully to Different Number Choices. It is not beyond doubt, I conclude, that prioritarianism needs to be quarantined in the first place. Notice, finally, that here the main work of delivering the desirable result is carried out not by some mysterious aggregation method, but by a certain 'version of the priority view' itself,[26] contra to Arrhenius' suggestion earlier.

All of this is important if only for stressing that our lesson up to now is very much a conditional one. *In so far* as you thought that prioritarianism faces trouble with respect to non-fixed populations, it would make sense to quarantine it away from Different Number Choices. Whether it should be quarantined also from Same Number Choices is a different question, and one to which I now turn.

20.3 Same Number Choices

It is not clear that prioritarians should endorse quarantining. But if they do, then, at minimum quarantined prioritarianism implies that prioritarian weights do not apply in Different Number Choices. What about Same Number Choices?

In Chapter 19 of this volume, Michael Otsuka puts forward the view that Parfit and his followers are committed to quarantining prioritarianism *also* from

---

[25] Derek Parfit, 'The Non-Identity Problem', 8 September, unpublished, pp. 5–6, full draft available upon request.

[26] Admittedly, one need not be a prioritarian in order to endorse (J). For example, a very similar view is defended by Jeff McMahan, but one that he does not couch as a form of prioritarianism. (See Jeff McMahan, 'Causing People to Exist and Saving People's Lives', *The Journal of Ethics* 17 (2013), 5–35.) I take it however that Parfit's explicit phrasing of (J) as 'another version of the priority view' is aimed at the intuition justifying (J). And that intuition seems to be the one according to which lowering a person's wellbeing by a fixed amount of utility is worse than raising another person's wellbeing by that fixed amount, *when the former takes place at a lower absolute level*. The italicized bit is crucial for otherwise the view would imply that lowering Tom from 100 to 90 is worse than raising Dick from 50 to 60, which is clearly not something Parfit believed. And it is the italicized bit that makes this a distinctly prioritarian view. (More accurately, it makes it distinct from utilitarianism. The view is made distinct from egalitarianism only once another feature is added, namely Parfit's refrain that inequalities as such do not matter.)

applying to Same Number Choices. Otsuka provides textual evidence for interpreting Parfit in this way, and goes on to explore some damning implications of quarantining prioritarianism in this way. In this section and the next, I will try to show that this reading is unwarranted.

Before I do that, it would be instructive to note that Otsuka has a horse in this race, potentially. Let me explain, as this will provide some useful context. One of Otsuka's objectives in his contribution is to show that this particular revision on Parfit's behalf entails that he came to endorse a version of prioritarianism that is more aligned with a Person-affecting principle. He (Parfit) has come to endorse a view according to which 'prioritarian weighting applies only to gains and losses to people which renders them better off or worse off than *they* would have been otherwise.'[27] If Otsuka is right about this, just to put things in perspective, this would entail that towards the end of his life Parfit came around to conceding at least some of the criticism leveled against his prioritarianism, and specifically objections put forward by Otsuka himself. Famously, in a series of articles, Otsuka (along with Alex Voorhoeve, and the latter along with Marc Fleurbaey) has levelled what is known as the Separateness of Persons (SOP) objection to Parfit's prioritarianism.[28] Very briefly, the suggestion is that prioritarianism violates the SOP, and in two distinct ways: it does not respect 'the unity of the person', in the shape of individuals' prudential interests, and it does not recognize the 'competing claims' that different individuals have against each other. I cannot go into this here, but it is my opinion[29] that if it now turns out that Parfit aligns his prioritarianism with a person-affecting principle then that represents an admission that prioritarianism ought to move towards a more SOP-friendly version. That is, prioritarianism ought to be adjusted in a way that would register a shift between inter-personal tradeoffs (where applying prioritarian weights is correct), and intra-personal tradeoffs, where something else, say maximizing expected utility, is endorsed instead. In restricting prioritarian weights only to benefits that make people better or worse off than they themselves would have been, Parfit's revised view would be more aligned with the unity of the person, and as such more respectful of the SOP. We can see, then, that quite a bit hinges for Otsuka on his claim as to how to interpret Parfit regarding the correct scope of quarantined prioritarianism.

But is all this true? Do prioritarians of the Parfitian ilk have reasons to *not* apply prioritarian weights in Same Number Choices? Let us start, in this section, with

---

[27] Otsuka, Chapter 19, this volume, p. 13 (emphasis added).

[28] See for example Michael Otsuka and Alex Voorhoeve, 'Why it Matters that Some are Worse Off than Others: An Argument against the Priority View', *Philosophy & Public Affairs* 37 (2009), 171–99; Michael Otsuka, 'How it Makes a Moral Difference that One is Worse Off than One Could Have Been', *Politics, Philosophy, & Economics* 17 (2017), 192–215; Alex Voorhoeve and Marc Fleurbaey, 'Priority or Equality for Possible People?' *Ethics* 126 (2016), 929–54.

[29] I should say that this interpretation is not shared by Otsuka. Personal correspondence, 7 September 2020.

Parfit's own stance, and then move, in the next section, to consider the more principled question.

I want to start by acknowledging that there may be some textual basis to the suggestion that Parfit's quarantined prioritarianism applies also to Same Number Choices. After all, the quote from the 2012 *Utilitas* paper does refer to 'different people'. That would seem to include also Same Number Choices. Moreover, in a postscript to an edited volume on the repugnant conclusion Parfit wrote:

> The reasoning in this anthology shows how hard it is to form acceptable theories in cases that involve different numbers of people. That's highly important. And it gives us ground for worry about our appeal to particular theories in the other two kinds of case: those which involve the same numbers, in the different outcomes, though these are not all the same people, and those which do involve all and only the same people.[30]

This passage, and indeed the book from which it is taken, do not focus on prioritarianism. Indeed, it is plausible to think that in that postscript Parfit was thinking of principles of population ethics, and that he never saw the priority view as that kind of principle. Instead, some have suggested that Parfit thought of the priority view as a principle to govern the distribution of gains and losses, in distinction from the way he thought of principles to govern population ethics.[31] Still I could see why someone might resist accepting this supposition (that Parfit never intended the priority view to be a principle of population ethics). And if so, there is more than a hint here that Parfit thought that as part of 'our appeal to particular theories' prioritarianism ought not apply (also) in Same Number Choices.

Now, incredibly, we can see, Parfit has also added that it may even be the case that whatever axiological principle one held (for example, prioritarianism) should not apply even in Same People Choices ('those which do involve all and only the same people'). I say incredibly, because the implication of this last bit, of course, is that it would *never* be right to apply prioritarianism. Parfit here seems to be suggesting that it might be the case that prioritarianism should not apply to Different Number, Same Number, and Same People Choices, which leaves no logical space in which it *does* apply. This remarkable implication, I think, should make us doubt whether this often-quoted postscript can be interpreted as encompassing prioritarianism as well. And even if it is, this incredible implication should give us pause about Parfit's overall resigned tone in that short postscript. There is,

---

[30] Derek Parfit, 'Postscript', in Jesper Ryberg and Torbjorn Tannsjo (eds.), *The Repugnant Conclusion: Essays on Population Ethics* (Dordrecht: Springer, 2004), p. 257.
[31] Jeff McMahan, personal correspondence, 15 August 2020.

then, a good reason to doubt whether Parfit did indeed mean the further extension of the quarantine approach beyond Different Numbers.

Moreover, after stating (in that Postscript) that the repugnant conclusion raises doubts also about the application of any axiological theory (presumably including prioritarianism) to Same Number Choices, Parfit goes on to say: 'But there is still a clear distinction between these three kinds of case. And there may be some hope of "quarantining" the impossibility, and the resulting scepticism, to Different Number Choices'.[32] So while Parfit thought, for some reason (more on which in the next section), that Same Number Choices might present some difficulty, his bottom-line position is nevertheless to restrict prioritarianism so that it lacks application only to Different Number Choices. Parfit's own pronouncements on the matter, we can see, are equivocal. We must dig deeper to find out what it is that prioritarians ought to think about Same Number Choices.

20.4 Prioritarianism and Our Reasons to Have Children

Is there a reason, beyond Parfit's mixed bag of pronouncements on the matter, why a prioritarian of Parfit's ilk should quarantine prioritarianism so that it does not apply to Same Number Choices?

Here is one such alleged reason. In the 2012 *Utilitas* paper Parfit writes that the benefits that prioritarians are concerned with do not apply to the benefit of bringing new people into existence. It is worth looking at the text that leads up to the last couple of sentences that have been occupying us:

> It is sometimes claimed, for example, that we have prioritarian reasons to have children, since we would thereby benefit some of the possible people who would otherwise be badly off, by never existing. [...] But when we apply these distributive principles, we should not include, among the people who are badly off, possible people who never exist. [...] the Prioritarian Principles that I have considered cannot be applied to cases in which, in the different possible outcomes, different people would exist. When we consider these cases, we need other principles.[33]

The discussion of alleged prioritarian reasons to have children, we see, is the prelude to the conclusion we have been discussing here (Quarantined Prioritarianism). Here lies one of the key pieces of evidence, for Otsuka, that Parfit has been moving towards a version of prioritarianism that respects the Separateness of Persons (maintaining a shift between inter- and intra-personal

---

[32] Parfit, 'Postscript', p. 257. [33] Parfit, 'Another Defence', p. 440.

tradeoffs). For Otsuka, if I understand him correctly, takes Parfit's claim about not having prioritarian reasons to have children as evidence that Parfit restricted prioritarianism to Same People Choices. Prioritarianism, then, applies only to gains and losses to people who will exist in *all* the outcomes that are being compared.[34] Reflecting on that passage from Parfit, Otsuka concludes:

> More Plausibly, Parfit's view is that prioritarian principles apply to all gains and losses that render people better or worse off *than they would otherwise be.* [...] Prioritarian weight would be applied to all and only gains and losses to people who would exist in more than one outcome in such mixed cases.[35]

Otsuka deduces—from Parfit's admission that people who do not exist do not count as the worse off for prioritarian purposes—that at the end of his life Parfit endorsed a narrow person-affecting version of prioritarianism.

Just to put things in perspective, if Otsuka is right about this, the implications would be far-reaching for prioritarianism. Consider the following simple example:[36]

A (9, 1, *, *)   B (*, *, 5, 5)

The sign * denotes a possible person who could have existed but does not exist. Suppose Otsuka is right that prioritarianism does *not* apply to Same Number Choices. In that case, prioritarian weights would not apply here. If so, prioritarianism *cannot* judge B to be better than A. Now, it is worth pausing to understand the radical implications for prioritarianism of such a restriction. Consider that the difference between A and B could be something extremely mundane, such as the difference between two sets of parents conceiving each a child today rather than tomorrow (when it would be a different sperm and ovum and so a different person). In other words, the example above, fancy as it may seem on paper, is the stuff of everyday life. I speculate that one would be hard pressed to find any prioritarian who would be happy to bite such a bullet, and be willing to be indifferent, just like utilitarians are, between A and B.[37] There is therefore an obvious challenge for prioritarians to show that Otsuka's interpretation of Parfit is wrong, and that prioritarianism does apply in Same Number Choices. But I think Otsuka's conclusion is unwarranted. Let me try and explain why.

---

[34] Notice, these need not be only actual people, but can also be possible people, as long as they would exist in all future outcomes that are being compared. (Michael Otsuka, private communication, 28 August 2019, and again 7 September 2020.)

[35] Otsuka, Chapter 19, this volume, pp. 539–40.

[36] Holtug, 'Prioritarianism and Population Ethics', p. 6.

[37] Campbell Brown makes a similar observation in 'Prioritarianism for Variable Populations', *The Philosophical Quarterly* 134 (2007), p. 325.

The crucial bit in the Parfit quotation is the claim that 'we should not include, among the people who are badly off, possible people who never exist'. Prioritarianism is obviously concerned with benefitting individuals the worse off they in fact are, and Parfit here explicitly says that possible people are not among those worse off. That is, people who do not currently exist are not to count as worse off *merely by virtue* of not existing. This, I think, makes a lot of sense. For one thing, this claim ties in with another long-held view of Parfit's. I refer to the position he took on the vexing question of the value of existence. Unlike some other prioritarians (Holtug and Adler) Parfit was of the opinion that it is better to think of merely possible people as having *no* welfare rather than *zero* welfare.[38] I think he was absolutely right about this (but am not going to argue for that in this chapter). Importantly, whatever one's opinion about the value of existence, one can now see how nicely this dovetails with the position Parfit takes in the quotation above. If merely possible, non-existing, people had zero welfare then that would make them (in most normal, non-infernal, circumstances) among the worst off people around. But if they have *no* welfare then they do not count as the worse off or badly off.

Parfit's claim about possible people, then, is in line with his long held views on the value of existence, and does not at all constitute a break from his traditional axiology. It is also in line with the suggestion I offered in section 20.1 regarding his overall motivation in quarantining prioritarianism. There, recall, I speculated that Parfit's motivation in quarantining prioritarianism away from Different Number Choices was his belief that prioritarianism does not give us *additional* reasons to have children. Counting not-yet-existing people as among the worst off would naturally conflict with that. But to say that non-existing people do not count as among the worse off people is *not* to say that they do not count. Parfit's assertion is that 'we should not include, *among the people who are badly off*, possible people who never exist' (my emphasis). But that does not mean that we should not include them, tout court. We just should not include them among the worse off people. It is therefore not the case that possible people do not count according to prioritarianism. Quite the contrary—bringing people into existence cannot *but* matter according to prioritarianism. And that is so for the obvious reason that like utilitarianism, prioritarianism (when un-quarantined, that is) is a view concerned with *aggregating (weighted) utility*. Other things equal, the more positive utility, the better the outcome.[39] (Recall that we have earlier set aside the quite

---

[38] Derek Parfit, *Reasons and Persons* (Oxford: Oxford University Press, 1984), p. 488.

[39] See also Holtug, 'Prioritarianism and Population Ethics', p. 3. Otsuka rejects the reading of prioritarianism as total weighted utility (Chapter 19, this volume, section 19.1). But the reasons he provides for this rejection are the very problems that non-fixed populations present to prioritarianism (namely, the Super Repugnant Conclusion). *That* reasoning, in my view, belongs to the debate about what ought to happen to prioritarianism in these cases of Non-Fixed populations (namely, if and how it ought to be quarantined). But to use this reasoning to reject the definition of *standard*, non-

implausible average version of prioritarianism, primarily because of the Sadistic Conclusion, to which it, along with Critical Level prioritarianism, is vulnerable). To sum up the point so far, other things being equal, prioritarians cannot *but* favour generating evermore lives worth living. This is a feature that the prioritarian shares with the utilitarian—though total, not average. Parfit was therefore correct in thinking that while prioritarians *do* have reasons to have children, they (compared to utilitarians) do not have *additional* reasons to have children.

The upshot of this discussion is this. Prioritarians have reasons to bring people into existence but these are reasons they share with the utilitarian; what prioritarians lack, on my reading of Parfit's quarantined prioritarianism, is a reason to bring people into existence *given a fixed aggregate sum of utility*. This would have been a uniquely prioritarian reason to have children, and it is this reason that we ought to block, according to Parfit. My interpretation of Parfit, if correct, implies quarantining prioritarianism from Different Number Choices, but not from Same Number Choices.

There is more evidence that this is the correct interpretation in Parfit's 2017 discussion of the question of the benefit of coming into existence. Parfit says there that a person *does* benefit from coming into existence. But he adds that this benefit is what he calls 'intrinsically good' rather than one that is 'essentially comparative'.[40] As mentioned, Parfit dropped all mention of prioritarianism contained in drafts leading up to that 2017 paper, but this claim of his dovetails perfectly with his quarantined prioritarianism. Coming into being is not an essentially comparative benefit because non-existing people have no welfare. It nevertheless *is* a benefit, an intrinsically good one, which is why a prioritarian cannot but favour bringing new people into existence, provided their lives would be good and holding everything else constant.

I conclude that Parfit's statement that possible people are not to count among the worse off is of a piece with other long-held tenets of his axiology. It does *not* represent a departure from his standard view of prioritarianism or population ethics, nor does it imply that a prioritarian could be indifferent about bringing about lives worth living (other things being equal).

20.5 The Puzzle Restated

Let us take stock. *If* prioritarian weights ought *not* to apply in Same Number Choices (or, of course, in Different Number Choices) then that cannot be due to

---

quarantined prioritarianism strikes me as double accounting. The Super Repugnant Conclusion is a reason for quarantining prioritarianism (though hardly a decisive one, as we saw); it is not a reason for rejecting standard definitions of prioritarianism in its original, un-quarantined, format.

[40] Parfit, 'Future People', 131–2. See also Krister Bykvist, 'The Benefits of Coming into Existence', *Philosophical Studies* 135 (2007), 335–62.

the puzzle over whether or not non-existing people should count among the worse off. Prioritarians may well take the potential welfare of such individuals into account with*out* counting them as among the worse off. But this merely removes one reason for endorsing strict quarantining. There is indeed another, perhaps more challenging reason to think prioritarians face a problem in applying their weights also in Same Number Choices. To see it consider the following standard formulation of prioritarianism from Holtug:

> *The Priority View*: An outcome is non-instrumentally better, the larger the sum of weighted individual benefits it contains, where benefits are weighted such that they gain a greater value, the worse off the individual is to whom they accrue.[41]

Now recall Parfit's assertion that non-existent individuals do not count among the worse off, because they have no welfare. Such an understanding would generate a problem, I want to say, when the above definition of prioritarianism is adopted. That is because there is then no independent absolute level of welfare against which we could measure the improvement that the definition depends on ('the worse off the individual to whom they accrue') when applied to non-existing people. And if we cannot do that, then we cannot know what weight to attach to the welfare of such individuals, when they are brought into existence. Notice that this is a different problem from the one discussed in the previous section. It is not just that possible people cannot count among the worse off; it is that they cannot count *at all*. Now, if this is true, standard prioritarianism could be in a lot of trouble, as we saw earlier:

A (9, 1, *, *)   B (*, *, 5, 5)

On the definition provided by Holtug we cannot judge B to be better than A because there is no benchmark against which to measure the 'individual benefit' that that definition calls for.

Prioritarians Nils Holtug and Matt Adler's preferred solution to this problem is to reverse Parfit, and to understand non-existence as comprising of zero welfare.[42] Doing so bypasses the impediment to applying prioritarian weights to the welfare of possible people in Same Number Choices. Compare the example above with:

A' (9, 1, 0, 0)   B' (0, 0, 5, 5)

---

[41] Holtug, 'Prioritarianism and Population Ethics', p. 2.

[42] Holtug is less explicit on this than Adler. The closest he gets to saying so explicitly is the following. 'Yet, on the basis of the metaphysical and value-theoretical assumptions I made above, we can in fact assign zero value to non-existence.' *Persons, Interests, and Justice*, p. 142.

Assigning possible people with zero welfare allows prioritarians to attach weights to *all* individuals in a set, actual as well as possible. This allows them to generate the attractive and straightforward verdict that B′ is better than A′.

The result is no doubt the desired one but the move generating it is, I think, both controversial and unnecessary. I think it may well be possible to think of possible persons as having no welfare (consistent with Parfit's view, which strikes me as the correct view) while generating the more attractive judgement in the case just given. If we are able to pull that off we could thereby free prioritarianism from the embarrassing inability to judge B as better than A, *while* not relying on controversial premises such as assigning zero welfare to non-existent persons. I think we could do so, and with little effort. To see this, take Holtug's definition that we employed so far, but consider the following slight amendment to it (the italicized bit):

> *The Priority View*: An outcome is non-instrumentally better, the larger the sum of weighted individual benefits it contains, where benefits are weighted such that they gain a greater value, *the lower the absolute level at which they accrue*.

Holtug's definition refers to how badly off *individuals* are, whereas my definition speaks of the absolute level at which benefits accrue.[43] The definition just laid out tells us that (*, *, 5, 5) *is* better than (9, 1, *, *). The two outcomes, to state the obvious, have the same aggregate amount of benefits, but in B more of these benefits accrue at lower absolute levels. It is not that they accrue to *worse off individuals*, but rather, at lower absolute levels.

If I am right about this, then prioritarians *can* apply their weights in Same Number Choices *without* the controversial mechanism of assigning non-existence as zero welfare, and without resorting to a person-tracking variant of prioritarianism. If so, this constitutes a minor (yet still significant) amendment to canonical statements of prioritarianism. Prioritarianism is not about priority to worse off *individuals*; it is about priority to the worse off *condition*.[44]

---

[43] Persson floats a similar idea, I think, in 'Prioritarianism and Welfare Reductions', pp. 297–8. He offers the idea that instead of 'benefiting individuals', prioritarians should aim at producing 'the outcome in which individuals have the greatest sum of priority-weighted benefits'. I am happy to sign up to this.

[44] Cf. Jacob Nebel, 'Priority, Not Equality, for Possible People', *Ethics* 127 (2017), p. 911. Such an understanding of prioritarianism has, as I have argued elsewhere, other happy implications, such as endorsing the temporal view known as Time-Slice Prioritarianism, which itself has quite attractive implications. See my *Why Inequality Matters* (Cambridge: Cambridge University Press, 2016), ch. 7.

20.6 Conclusion

There is far from a decisive reason, I argued, for prioritarians to embark on quarantining their weights in Non-Fixed Populations. But if they do, for some reason, feel compelled to quarantine prioritarianism so that it does not apply to Different Number Choices, they certainly should avoid doing so in Same Number Choices. Parfit's ambiguous sporadic statements about quarantining prioritarianism so that it *also* does not apply to Same Number Choices, I showed, ought to be dismissed. Furthermore, I tried to show that this narrow interpretation of quarantined prioritarianism still makes for a tenable and robust prioritarian view. Consequently, it is *not* the case that prioritarians who opt to endorse restricted quarantining (in Different Number Choices only) must thereby endorse some person-affecting version of prioritarianism. Moreover, understanding prioritarianism as the urgency of alleviating the worse off condition (rather than a person) allows prioritarians to pass attractive judgements in mixed population cases.

References

Adler, Matthew (2009). 'Future Generations: A Prioritarian View', *George Washington Law Review* 77 (2009), 1478–520.

Arrhenius, Gustaf (2000). 'An Impossibility Theorem for Welfarist Axiologies', *Economics & Philosophy* 16, 247–66.

Arrhenius, Gustaf (2009). 'Egalitarianism and Population Change', in Axel Gosseries and Lukas Meyer (eds.) *Intergenerational Justice* (Oxford: Oxford University Press, 2009), 325–48.

Arrhenius, Gustaf (2013). 'Egalitarian Concerns and Population Change', in Nir Eyal, Samia A Hurst, Ole F. Norheim, and Daniel Wikler (eds.), *Inequalities in Health: Concepts, Measures, and Ethics.* Oxford: Oxford University Press.

Beard, Simon (2019). 'Parfit's Theory X and the Evaluation of Global Challenges', Unpublished.

Brown, Campbell (2007). 'Prioritarianism for Variable Populations', *The Philosophical Quarterly* 134, 325–61.

Bykvist, Krister (2007). 'The Benefits of Coming into Existence', *Philosophical Studies* 135, 335–62.

Greaves, Hillary (2017). 'Population Axiology', *Philosophical Compass* (2017), 7.

Holtug, Nils (2010). *Persons, Interests, and Justice.* Oxford: Oxford University Press.

Holtug, Nils (forthcoming). 'Prioritarianism and Population Ethics', in G. Arrhenius et al., *The Oxford Handbook of Population Ethics.* Oxford: Oxford University Press.

Huemer, Michael (2008). 'In Defence of Repugnance', *Mind* 117, 899–933.

McMahan, Jeff. (2013). 'Causing People to Exist and Saving People's Lives', *The Journal of Ethics* 17, 5–35.

Narveson, Jan (1967). 'Utilitarianism and New Generations', *Mind* 76, 62–72.

Narveson, Jan (1973). 'Moral Problems of Population', *Monist* 57, 62–86.

Nebel, Jacob (2017). 'Priority, Not Equality, for Possible People', *Ethics* 127, 896–911.

Otsuka, Michael (2017). 'How it Makes a Moral Difference that One is Worse Off than One Could Have Been', *Politics, Philosophy, & Economics* 17, 192–215.

Otsuka, Michael and Voorhoeve, Alex (2009). 'Why it Matters that Some are Worse Off than Others: An Argument against the Priority View', *Philosophy & Public Affairs* 37, 171–99.

Parfit, Derek (1984). *Reasons and Persons*. Oxford: Oxford University Press.

Parfit, Derek (1991). 'Equality and Priority?' *The Lindley Lecture*. Lawrence, Kansas: University of Kansas.

Parfit, Derek (1997). 'Equality and Priority', *Ratio* 10, 202–21.

Parfit, Derek (2004). 'Postscript', in Jesper Ryberg and Torbjorn Tannsjo (eds.), *The Repugnant Conclusion: Essays on Population Ethics*. Dordrecht: Springer, p. 257.

Parfit, Derek (2011). *On What Matters* (Vol. 2) (Oxford: Oxford University Press).

Parfit, Derek (2012). 'Another Defence of the Priority View', *Utilitas* 24, 399–440.

Parfit, Derek (2016). 'The Non-Identity Problem', 8 September, unpublished.

Parfit, Derek (2017). 'Future People, the Non-Identity Problem, and Person-Affecting Principles', *Philosophy & Public Affairs* 45, 118–57.

Persson, Ingmar, 'Equality, Priority, and Person-Affecting Value', *Ethical Theory & Moral Practice* 4 (2001), pp. 33–4.

Persson, Ingmar (2012). 'Prioritarianism and Welfare Reductions', *Journal of Applied Philosophy* 29, 289–301.

Segall, Shlomi (2016). *Why Inequality Matters*. Cambridge: Cambridge University Press

Segall, Shlomi (2019). 'Why We Should Be Negative About Positive Egalitarianism', *Utilitas* 31, 414–30.

Tannsjo, Torbjorn (2002). 'Why We Ought to Accept the Repugnant Conclusion', *Utilitas* 14, 339–59.

Voorhoeve, Alex, and Fleurbaey, Marc (2016). 'Priority or Equality for Possible People?' *Ethics* 126, 929–54.

Index

abortion 112–128, 136–138, 144–145
Absurd Conclusion 73, 89, 191–199, 292, 358–361, 442
actualism
  metaphysical 68, 78
  moral 39, 71–78
Adams, R.M. 149
Adler, Matthew 544, 547, 570, 572–573
aggregation 32–34, 62–63, 162–163, 175, 199, 202, 208–209, 212, 220, 226, 259–260, 269, 286, 305, 311–313, 316–318, 361–362, 394, 553–554, 557–560, 564–565, 570–573
Andreou, Chrisoula 449
anti-natalism 45
Arrhenius, Gustaf 71, 75, 85, 88, 164, 206, 218, 225, 286, 365–366, 392, 433, 441, 484, 557–559, 565. *See also* Sadistic Conclusion
Asymmetry, the (Procreation) 15–37, 39, 170, 176, 191–197, 234, 266, 276–309
autonomy 144, 148–153, 171, 174, 194

benefit 19, 30–31, 36, 42, 95, 115–119, 132, 139, 144, 150, 195, 204, 214, 224, 264–309, 311, 318, 326, 348, 350, 352, 362, 364–366, 373, 377–378, 381–383, 479, 527–550, 552–574. *See also* harm
  comparative/non-comparative 19, 36, 132, 319, 364–366, 534, 539, 543
  existential 95, 139, 364–366, 382–383, 534, 539, 565
Beisner, Lynn 136–153
betterness 17–24, 34, 41–56, 61–90, 232–258, 392, 395–396, 402, 408, 412–425, 434–458, 487–493
Boonin, David 153, 394
Bostrom, Nick 334, 340, 344–346
Broome, John 44, 65–66, 84, 96, 110–111, 168, 234–235, 314–315, 378, 479. *See also* neutrality intuition
Bykvist, Krister 81, 85–87

capabilities 38, 167, 208
Chang, Ruth 430–431, 446, 465, 479
Chipman, John S. 206

collective action problems 40, 94
comparison-dependence 232–262
complaint 94–95, 97, 102, 108–111, 144, 245, 256–262, 267, 275, 304–309, 548–550
completeness 210–221, 399, 441, 453, 553, 555–559
conception 54, 96, 120, 123, 127, 135, 137, 140–152
confirmation bias 343–346
consent 132, 139–140, 144–145, 148–149, 220, 267, 305–306
context-dependence 232–262
continuum argument 389–426, 430–456. *See also* spectrum argument
critical level 286–289, 559, 571
Cureton, Adam 322–324

Diamond, Peter 319
Dickert, Stephan 322–323
Different Number Choices 33–36, 116, 268, 276–282, 286, 303, 365–366, 463–464. *See also* Same Number Choices
Different People Choices 131–133, 139–145, 152–153, 266–274, 531, 552–554, 559–565
Doolabh, Keyur 144

Ebersbach, Mirjam 316
egalitarianism 62–63, 236, 245, 286, 301, 370, 382, 469–473, 533, 536, 541, 543, 555–559, 562–565. *See also* equality
elitism 363, 382, 411, 466, 470, 473–475
equality 62–63, 167, 171, 174–176, 187, 194, 237, 240–248, 254–255, 259, 271–273, 278, 301, 347, 390, 401, 404–409, 413, 420–421, 430–432, 437, 447, 465, 469–474, 484, 487, 529–530, 533–550, 555, 561–574. *See also* egalitarianism
essentially comparative view 240–242, 392, 435–436, 539, 543
existence. *See* non-existence
experience machine 214
exploitation 245–246, 250–254
extinction 291, 333–334, 341–343, 350–352, 372–375, 380–382

fairness 20, 38, 272, 534, 536, 541
Fetherstonhaugh, David 322
Fine, Kit 78
Fleurbaey, Marc 68, 566
Frick, Johann 273, 290–291, 284–295, 303–304

Goodall, David 147–148
Goodrich, James 45, 431
Greaves, Hilary 296, 299
Greene, Joshua 318, 321
Griffin, James 201–202, 207, 209, 219, 433

Handfield, Toby 398, 400, 410, 419–421, 437, 444, 446
harm 35–36, 93–111, 112–128, 132–133, 139, 141–152, 220, 267, 305–306, 364, 381, 499, 520, 565. *See also* benefit
  comparative/non-comparative 35–36, 132, 139, 364
  existential 95, 139, 152, 364, 382–383, 565
  overdetermined 94, 100, 107–110
Harman, Elizabeth 305
hedonism 80–81, 162, 167, 208, 220, 462
Hitler, Adolf 135, 337
Holtug, Nils 88, 533–534, 547, 563–564, 570–574
Hsee, Christopher 313
Huemer, Michael 221–222, 315–318

imprecision 212, 324–325, 359, 365–371, 373, 378–384, 391, 394, 405–426, 430–432, 437–438, 447, 461–475, 478–495, 509. *See also* incommensurability, incomparability, indeterminacy, vagueness
incest 142–143, 150–151
incommensurability 211, 218–221, 223, 367, 397–400, 406–411, 413, 430–458, 485–486. *See also* imprecision, incomparability, indeterminacy, vagueness
incomparability 61, 71, 379, 391–392, 398–405, 412–426, 431, 447–448, 475, 479, 509. *See also* imprecision, incommensurability, indeterminacy, vagueness
incompleteness. *See* completeness
independence of irrelevant alternative 242–247, 255
indeterminacy 379, 391–392, 396, 401–411, 414–425, 445, 483, 486–489, 505–510, 515–518. *See also* imprecision, incommensurability, incomparability, vagueness
inequality. *See* equality

infinity 21–24, 179–180, 185–186, 205–206, 348, 377, 408, 434, 442, 454–455, 480–482, 516, 531, 536
injustice. *See* justice
internal aspects view 47, 240–242, 254, 436
intransitivity. *See* transitivity

Jackson, Frank 222
James, Daniel 134–135, 147–148
Jensen, Karsten Klint 433–434, 438, 454–455
justice 20, 30, 51, 167, 171, 174–176, 187, 194–195, 202, 245, 248–262, 381, 390, 394, 416

Kagan, Shelly 135
Kahneman, Daniel 319–322
Kavka, Gregory 51–52
Kitcher, Philip 205–207
Kling, Catherine L. 320
Knetsch, Jack 321
Kogut, Tehila 325–326

Lazar, Seth 377–380
Lee-Stronach, Chad 377–380
lexical superiority 200–226, 359, 366–383, 391, 405–425, 433, 440, 470, 478–483, 493–496
levelling down 62, 271, 533–538, 556
Levy, Neil 146
Lewis, David 67
love 119, 136–141, 161, 166, 203, 292–293, 368, 465

McMahan, Jeff 134–135, 139, 166, 176, 184, 364
McTaggart, J.M.E. 203–205, 209
Mere Addition. *See also* Repugnant Conclusion
  paradox 232–262, 284–296, 308, 359–360, 366–384, 536
  principle 45–46, 62–63, 469
Mill, John Stuart 175, 202–206, 528–530
money pumps 39, 243, 256–258, 298
moral progress 348–350, 375
moral status 112–128

Narveson, Jan 17, 38, 168, 170, 563
neutrality intuition 15–17, 30, 44, 168–171, 176–187, 234–254, 315
No Difference View 101–111, 363–366, 541–543, 546, 561–565
non-existence 15–37, 61–90, 132, 139, 277–278, 572–573
non-identity problem 93–111, 112–128, 130–153, 259, 305, 358–359, 364–366, 536. *See also* personal identity
Nozick, Robert 214

objective list theory 80, 162, 167, 196, 462
Ord, Toby 350, 352–353
Otsuka, Michael 110–111, 553–554, 565–571
overdetermination 95, 99–101, 107–110

pareto principle 44–46, 50–57, 63, 69–72, 192, 267, 283–309, 382–383, 415, 542
parity 44–45, 389–426, 431, 447–458, 479–481, 484–491, 494
perfectionism 167, 208, 221, 362–363, 367–371, 382–384, 413, 418, 454–455, 536
person-affecting
   approaches, principles, theories, or views 15–37, 39, 61–71, 94–96, 241, 261, 272, 359, 364–366, 371–372, 384, 390, 566, 569, 574
   narrow version 272, 364, 569
   wide version 359, 365–366, 371–372, 383
   wrong 131, 139, 141–142, 146, 151–152
personal identity 220, 438, 505–507, 528. *See also* non-identity problem
preference satisfaction theory 80–81, 162, 167
prioritarianism 236, 245, 259, 269, 382–383, 527–550, 552–574
prospect theory 322–323
Pummer, Theron 312, 395, 401

Qizilbash, Mozaffar 412, 421, 447–449
Quinn, Warren 223, 391–392, 410, 501

Rabinowicz, Wlodek 71, 75, 81, 85, 88, 205, 209, 218, 408–410, 420–421, 425, 467, 494
rape 134, 138, 142–143, 146, 150–151
reasons
   agent-relative 264, 282, 293, 309
   conditional 260, 303–304
reductionism 505–506, 512
regret 130–153, 166, 245–246, 255, 274, 299
Repugnant Conclusion 62–63, 159–199, 200–226, 232–258, 266, 311–327, 358–384, 389–426, 430–458, 461–475, 479, 483–495, 498–520, 531–538, 552–574. *See also* Mere Addition
Ridiculous Conclusion 305, 382
rights 20, 32, 114, 132, 139–142, 152
risk 32, 34, 50–51, 54, 107, 110, 132–134, 145, 150–151, 213, 221–225, 305, 317, 322–323, 333–354, 371, 375–380, 495, 550
Risky Policy Case 51, 132, 376
Ritov, Ilana 321, 325–326
Roberts, M.A. 88, 96, 122–123

Sadistic Conclusion 164–165, 225, 558–559, 571
Sagan, Carl 333

Same Number Choices 31, 33–34, 116, 152, 169–171, 196, 266–204, 466, 565–574. *See also* Different Number Choices
Same People Choices 45, 50–52, 96, 131–133, 141–145, 266–276, 284–289, 303–304, 531, 541–543, 550, 553–555, 567–573
Sandel, Michael 123
Scanlon, T.M. 252
Scheffler, Samuel 184, 293, 299–300, 390
Schoenfield, Miriam 488–493
self-torturer 223, 392, 410, 501
Sen, Amartya 206
separability of lives 204, 210–221, 539
Slovic, Paul 316–317
Smith, Michael 222
sorites paradox 219, 221, 445, 485–487, 494, 498–520
spectrum argument 233–239, 389, 446, 483–495, 499–520. *See also* continuum argument
Stefánsson, Orri 225
Sud, Rohan 488, 490, 492

Temkin, Larry 44, 47. *See also* internal aspects view; essentially comparative view.
Theory X 358–384
Thomson, J.J. 122–123
totalism 62, 200–226, 233–237, 528, 531–543
Trammell, Philip 336, 348, 350
transitivity 62, 210–214, 217–219, 232–262, 267, 286, 293–298, 380, 389–396, 411–412, 418–419, 431–458, 463–471, 488, 502–520

utilitarianism 46, 62, 162–165, 168, 187, 192, 196, 233, 286–287, 300–301, 461–462, 466, 528–550, 554

vagueness 195, 217–221, 402, 405, 417, 478–479, 483–495, 505, 508, 517. *See also* imprecision, incommensurability, incomparability, indeterminacy
Vastfjall, Daniel 325
Voorhoeve, Alex 68, 278, 550, 566

Wedgwood, Ralph 491–493
Wilkening, Friedrich 316
Williamson, Timothy 67, 75
wrongdoing 50–53, 58, 152, 250–254, 259

Yudkowsky, Eliezer 334, 344–346

Zhang, Jiao 321